THE COMPLETE BOOK OF

GARDEN MAGIC

THE COMPLETE BOOK OF
GARDEN MAGIC

ROY E. BILES

There is magic in the garden. I cannot create a daffodil in all its color and grace. No man can. I do not know how a daffodil is created. Yet each spring thousands and thousands of them are seen dancing in our gardens. There is law in the garden. It is the law of creation. If we follow that law we deal in magic. We cannot see the stuff of which the daffodil is made,—we need not care by what process it comes into being. If we take the dark brown bulb, plant it according to that law at the right time—we achieve a miracle.

J. G. FERGUSON, *Publisher*
Chicago

AUTHOR'S PREFACE

If there be merit in this book, it lies chiefly in the manner of presentation and secondly in its contribution of some labor-saving methods evolved by the writer in his twenty-five years as an amateur gardener.

He has probably made about every mistake that the poorest gardener can make or conceive, and therefore knows just how it feels. There is considerable repetition in the book because he knows just how irritating it is to be referred back to some particular chapter when he is in a hurry and wants specific directions.

It was once stated in "Flower Grower" magazine that: "It is a fact that the authorities are often not the best ones for beginners, or even average gardeners, to go to for advice. Their information is, indeed, liable to be too brief. They take too much for granted, and cannot get the common scrub's viewpoint. Then, too, they just don't know the answers to many questions such as come to you. The reason is simple. The man who does his work perfectly makes no mistakes, therefore, he does not know how to advise those who do. But the duffer who has blundered and found a way out, can tell others how to correct or avoid those same mistakes. That is why great men's children so often fail to amount to anything, while those who would be classed as failures raise their children to be geniuses."

This book is designed to help the amateur gardener avoid common mistakes (as above referred to) and get the most from the money and effort expended on his or her garden. To attain these results, it is necessary for the reader to consider the book as a whole. To seize some information piecemeal concerning a single feature or phase of gardening is to invite disappointment. As the poet has said: "A little learning is a dangerous thing."

A thorough reading of Chapters 1, 2, 3, 17, 18 and 25 is essential to a full understanding of, and complete success with, the other chapters. Suggestions made in those just indicated may not be possible of fulfillment at once, but any steps taken should be taken with a definite, general program in mind. Make generous use of plant, nursery, and seed catalogues in checking up plant descriptions, cultural recommendations, and the new plant materials and gardening aids that are constantly being made available.

The poems heading or following certain chapters are quoted from memory and may be somewhat inaccurate, but wherever the authors could be identified, credit has been given.

I wish to acknowledge my indebtedness to the American Home Magazine Corporation for permission to use the color chart on Page 170; to the Davey Tree Expert Company for the use of the method of filling in around a tree; to the bulletins of The Ohio State University at Columbus, Ohio, and their authors; to the O. M. Scott Company, Marysville, Ohio, for the quotations from their magazine "Lawn Care"; to the Agricultural Experiment Station at Wooster, Ohio, and its director, C. G. Williams; and last, but not least, to my friend—Jos. E. Ebertz, and other artists who drew the pictures and without whose painstaking work and patience this book could never have been published.

ROY E. BILES

EDITOR'S FOREWORD

I never met Roy E. Biles. I had never read, but had only heard about, The Book of Garden Magic when I was invited to go over the proofs of a new, revised and amplified edition. After doing so, I felt almost as though I knew him and had added another to my many valued gardener friends.

I happen to have had some experience in the compiling of horticultural books, so I can realize and appreciate the long hours, the hard work and the unremitting care that have gone into the making of this one. But in addition, this book tells unmistakably of the author's personal, first hand familiarity with the plants and practices about which he has written; and of the keen interest and deep affection he feels for all the beautiful and useful things that Nature has given us with which to make our gardens.

I do not say that I agree with his every view and recommendation; or that I might not do certain things differently than he has done them. But that is the joyful privilege of all gardeners: To have their own, pet methods of working toward a common goal, and to defend them valiantly in friendly discussion and debate.

The important and significant thing is that we gardeners all have that common goal—greater beauty and happiness for mankind and the world through the cultivation of plants in gardens. And it is not only a common goal. It is also a bond of interest and sympathy for which we can be everlastingly grateful.

E. L. D. SEYMOUR
Horticultural Editor, The American Home

HEMPSTEAD, N. Y.
FEBRUARY, 1941

EDITOR'S FOREWORD TO THIS
NEW REVISED EDITION

Having been privileged to work on "The Complete Book of Garden Magic" when it was first published and also when the first revised edition was prepared, I am deeply gratified that it has been so warmly received that this second revised edition has been found necessary. I am glad, too, that, after much thought and discussion, it was decided to leave the original text almost as Mr. Biles wrote it and to bring to the reader's attention significant changes, developments, and trends that have occurred by adding a final, supplementary chapter, starting on page 439. This chapter bears the title, "Garden Magic Marches On," which, I think, is apt. For while many basic operations and principles of gardening remain the same as they have been for many years, there has been a remarkable, even phenomenal, advance in many directions and details.

The supplement has been planned to follow in general the arrangement of subject matter as found in the book proper and set forth in the Table of Contents. But it has not been possible to stick to this order exactly, since some discoveries, inventions, or improvements concern several different subjects. Also, it has been possible to call attention to only some of the many new techniques, materials, and appliances that have appeared in the field. Further, detailed information and directions about things mentioned herein and others that are not can be obtained from manufacturers, from bulletins and other publications of horticultural institutions for teaching and research, and from current periodicals and books that deal with specialized activities and branches of gardening. I call attention again to the advice offered in Mr. Biles' Preface—to "Make generous use of plant, nursery, and seed catalogues in checking up plant descriptions, cultural recommendations, and the new plant materials and gardening aids that are constantly being made available."

In addition to paying tribute to the memory of Mr. Biles for the fine work he did in conceiving and executing the task represented by "The Complete Book of Garden Magic," I want to thank two friends—Mrs. Margaret Boardman, for invaluable cooperation and assistance in carrying out this revision, and Mr. Laurence Blair (who contributed to the first revised edition) for the new illustrations incorporated in this one.

E. L. D. SEYMOUR
Horticultural Editor,
The American Home

HUNTINGTON, N. Y.
SEPTEMBER, 1955

ix

TABLE OF CONTENTS

COLORED ILLUSTRATIONS

CHAPTER I

PLANNING

*"The kiss of the sun for pardon,
The song of the birds for mirth.
I am closer God's heart in a garden
Than anywhere else on earth."*

A landscape gardener of wide experience said to me, "Folks are interested in plants, but not in planting." The reason so many people become discouraged in trying to plan their gardens is that the instructions are often very confusing. One authority will say that shrubbery borders, perennial beds, etc., should be in straight lines upon a small lot. Others will say that the curved line lends beauty and informality. These so-called authorities will then set forth ideal garden plans, and as the amateur studies them he will find many things in the plans to be at variance with experience he may have had in the past.

For instance, some plans which we study have shrubbery borders and perennial beds located in dense shade, lily pools are located under trees, etc., until the amateur becomes so confused that he abandons all pretense of planning or attempts to make the plan according to his past experience. The result is that he clutters up his garden with many things which do not belong there, and it becomes a number of disconnected features and plants rather than a harmonious plan.

When we select our homes we decide what we would like to have in the way of space and conveniences. We say we want hardwood floors in these rooms, this kind of tile in the bath, this kind of mantel in the living room, the walls shall be built of such and such a material, etc. In other words, we assemble our desires either on paper or otherwise, making a list of the things in our home which will add to our pleasure or convenience. If our pocketbook holds out we get all these features into our house. However, if we find that we have not sufficient funds to

What careful planning can do. Here we have a vista from the house, a pool which does not cut up the plan and shrubbery and flowers which grow in proper locations. Rhododendrons flourish in specially prepared, acid soil close to the house and recreation space is provided within easy reach.

build all of the features into the house, we select the ones which we desire the most and place this information in the hands of the architect, who does the best he can for us with the funds at hand.

Now it would be a fine thing if we all could afford the services of a competent landscape gardener to plan our lot. This is no doubt money well spent and will add to the permanent satisfaction and value of a home. However, if the owner is unable or unwilling to make this original outlay and wishes to do the planning himself, he should take the attitude of the architect about to design a house. He should decide what features are to go into the garden, what are the needs of each feature, and then try to fit them together in a plan according to a few simple rules here set forth so that each feature will so far as possible get the proper location.

Here is a list of the things which the amateur gardener is most likely to want in his garden design:

Plant Interest

Open Lawn	Water Garden
Foundation	Vines
Planting	Flowering
Perennials	Shrubbery
Annuals	Trees
Dahlias	(a) Fruit
Iris	(b) Shade
Bulbs	(c) Grove
Rose Garden	(d) Specimen
Climbing Roses	(e) Flowering
Rock Garden	

Utility Features

Arbor or Garden	Outdoor Living
House	Room
Play Yard	Propagating Bed
Drying Yard	Vegetable
Terraces, Patios	Garden
Service Plot	Cold Frame
Greenhouse	Drive, Parking

Ornamental

Fences	Sun Dials
Trellises	Globes
Gates	Bird Baths
Seats	Fountains
Walks, Paths	Miniature
Steps	Garden
Vases	Mirror Pool
Statuary	Bird Houses

These features are all so desirable and the cultivation of each plant is so alluring that many gardeners, who start out to make a picturesque combination, end by cluttering up the plan with too much variety. This is the most frequent and flagrant sin of the amateur.

I was riding on a street car conversing with the conductor. Passing an attractive stone and stucco house of about fourteen rooms he said, "I'm going to build in a few months and want that house in six rooms. I want stone and stucco and a sloping roof just like that." Now it happened that I had designed the house and knew that the change of size must completely change the lines and design, and while my conductor friend could get a charming, six-room stone and stucco house, he could not get that house in miniature.

So it is with our garden; we must fit the features to the lot and the planting comprising several acres cannot successfully be reproduced, in miniature, in a fifty-foot back yard. If you intend to cover all your area with flowers, shrubs, etc., the need of planning is minimized. But we must always bear in mind that the ideal garden represents a pleasing aspect from all points.

Let us now consider the advantages of each feature and what is necessary for its successful growth. *Bear in mind that the information now given is for location in the plan and that cultural directions will appear elsewhere.*

Open lawn: It has been said that the lawn is the canvas upon which you paint your garden picture. Nothing sets off the beauty of the features of your garden like a stretch of well-kept weedless lawn. Keep it open in the center, and use it as a setting for the various other things of which your garden is composed. Except in extremely small plans, the lawn should dominate all other features. It should be at least two or three times the width of the borders surrounding it.

Foundation Planting: Planting around the foundation of the house is primarily for the purpose of adding to or correcting house proportions. Many small homes are two stories high and the fact that they cover a very small ground area makes it hard for the architect to get the correct proportions between height and other dimensions of the house. Then, too, the contractor, because he can save on the cellar excavation, sets the house higher than is necessary. We, therefore, plant about the foundations of the house to make it look lower and wider, "tie it to the ground," soften its lines, or add a touch of decoration.

Because foundation planting is an all year around feature, we use mostly evergreens and such shrubbery as will harmonize with them in summer, yet at the same time give the decoration of their bark or berries in winter.

Perennials and Annuals: While some of these flowers will grow in semishade, the most generally successful location is open sunlight. On the small plan they are usually planted as a border along the property lines. The bed should be at least five feet wide (eight feet is better if you have room) and at least twice or three times as long as wide.

Dahlias: Almost every gardener wants a few dahlias. However, these plants require quite a bit of room and the tall stalks upon which the blossoms are borne are usually not very decorative. Many people handle them in a separate area devoted to them, like vegetables. Sometimes this can be located in back of some low growing shrubbery or other plants, so that the tops of the dahlias bearing the blossoms can be seen although the stalks are hidden.

Iris: Iris are of so many kinds that it is very difficult to speak of placing them under one heading. However, the most easily grown and generally used varieties are adaptable in either semishade or in the open. Of course, better results are had in the open. They may be used as fill-ins between beds or borders, as edgings for a drive or walk or as a temporary planting between young shrubbery while waiting for it to obtain its proper growth. By using various kinds of iris, the blooming period may be extended over several months. Many varieties have the advantage that their foliage stays green and sightly until severe frost.

Bulbs: There are so many kinds of bulbs, each requiring a somewhat different position and flowering at a different time, that we advise the planner to read Chapter XII on Bulbs before locating them in the garden scheme.

Rose Garden: The best site for a rose garden is said to be an open space on a southerly slope sheltered to the north and east by higher ground, walls or hedges. The bed must not be too close to the wall or hedge and must have sunlight for at least half the day and air all around it. Confined rose gardens are invitations to all the pests to which roses are heir. Roses need a well-drained soil. The beds must not be too wide or it will be necessary to tramp upon them to cut the blooms or attend to them, thus undoing the effects of cultivation. They will grow in any soil that is not wet or soggy and where they have the sunlight for more than half of the day.

Climbing Roses: An area of at least three square feet of ground should be assigned to each climbing rose. The same ground conditions apply as in the rose garden. For successful growth they should have the sunlight upon them for at least two-thirds of the day.

Rock Gardens: If you have on your grounds a small natural slope, fairly well exposed to the light and sun, this is the place to locate your rock garden. A few stones placed as outcroppings will make it look like a natural formation. However, if this is not available, construct it at the edge or boundary of the lot, backing up on the fence or shrubbery. It is seldom that a rock garden can be artistically located in the shape of a

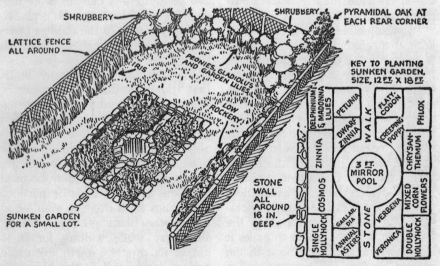

A rather crowded, semiformal garden, designed to minimize the lack of space. The interesting central feature avoids dwarfing by being sunken 12 to 24 inches (according to the area covered), below the lawn surface. Borders are narrow and balance each other.

mound in the center of the yard.

Water Garden: Water plants are easily grown and very adaptable. All they need is sunlight and food. Unless you wish to confine your efforts to very small blooms or to the plants which are rampant growers, it must be in the all-day sunlight. A little shade on the north may be had for background, but any shading directly over the pool will interfere with the number, size and health of the lilies themselves. Do not be misled by the many plans which you see published showing the pools in semishade. This is not the place for a water garden. Informal pools may be used in connection with almost any feature but formal pools must be located very carefully so that they are in complete balance with the rest of the plan.

Vines: Vines may be grown almost anywhere. Many creepers will grow in the densest of shade. Ground carpeting plants will grow where no other plants thrive. Therefore, if you want to blot out any certain view or to cover any object, you only have to select the kind of vine which will grow in this location.

Flowering Shrubbery: Flowering shrubbery is best planted as a border on the edge of the garden. Beds should be six to eight feet deep and at least twice or three times as long. Flowering shrubbery can be selected to grow in either shade or sunlight. The most popular varieties, however, grow best when they have sunlight at least half the time.

TREES

Fruit Trees of the larger size, of course, require a considerable area. However, dwarf fruit trees of various kinds can be included at the edge of the vegetable garden or in the borders. They have the advantage of the blossoms in the spring and, given proper care, they will yield a fair amount of full-sized fruit.

Shade Trees are of many uses to the planner of the small garden. They may be used to shade the front yard, to frame the house or for the outdoor living room. In planting shade trees, always remember that in five or six years they will make considerable growth and try to imagine what your yard will look like when they are full-sized. A very nice way of handling shade in a small garden is to plant a group of trees in a *Wild Grove*. The planting of half a dozen trees, from six to eight feet apart, gives quicker and better results than planting one tree and waiting for it to grow to maturity. Let the trees grow together and force each other up. Trim them where they rub together and injure each other and you will find the results are very satisfactory. Of course, trim off the lower branches so they are considerably above your head. If you wish, you may cut out the weaker trees as they mature, leaving only the stronger ones for permanent effect. For even distribution of foliage and quick shade, this is to be highly recommended. Select the easiest growing, healthiest trees for your locality. It is best to use one variety. The writer has had success with Elm, Maple, Linden, etc. An interesting variation is to plant a white blossoming tree such as Wild Cherry, Wild Plum, White-flowering (Japanese) Peach, Pear, Apple, etc., with a Redbud

(Judas tree). These, planted on the edge of the group facing the lawn, will bloom together in spring, giving a beautiful effect.

If the grove is in the corner of the lot, a screen or hedge of Regel Privet, Forsythia or such plants as grow in shade, should be used to insure privacy.

Specimen Trees are used in detached positions about the plan for particular emphasis. For instance, on either side of the walk at the entrance or in some other detached position on the plan. However, they should never be set out in the middle of the lawn to spoil the effect.

UTILITY FEATURES

Garden Houses or Arbors: This is one of the features which make the garden a real part of the home, make it livable instead of just something to look at. What could be nicer than a little house about eight feet square or larger in which could be placed a few benches or chairs for rest or the entertainment of friends. This house may be rustic if at a distance, but should match the architecture of the home if close by. Covered with vines or equipped with awnings, it will be a popular place with both children and grownups. It should be located some distance from the house and may be the objective of the garden path. In planning, leave space for planting of vines or shrubs so that it may look as though it grew up as part of the garden.

The Outdoor Living Room is becoming increasingly popular. It used to be that the house was the home and everything outside of the house was the out of doors. This is the idea we got as children and it is sometimes very hard to break away from it. The first requisite of the outdoor living room is privacy. It should be completely screened by shrubbery from the entrance walk or drive. It may be located under the wild grove or under trees, arbor or pergola. It should contain a hammock and easy-chairs. A water-proof box seat may be used to contain cushions or the hammock when not in use. If it is located in shade where grass will not

grow, pave it or cover the ground with stone chips or pea gravel (sometimes called torpedo sand).

A Play Yard for Children will save a lot of wear and tear on the rest of the garden area. A sandbox, and room enough to play store and other games so dear to childhood may be provided. Screen this off with a little shrubbery and have it within calling distance of the house.

Drying Yard: The plans of many homes where hand laundry is done frequently feature a drying yard. However, a collapsible clothesrack or revolving device located on a post in an inconspicuous part of the lot serves this purpose very well. Then there are the removable metal clothes posts which drop into sockets in the lawn to make this space temporarily adaptable for drying purposes.

Terraces: A terrace or patio is usually adjacent to the house, whence it is reached by a door opening from the dining room or living room. It is often slightly raised to overlook the garden and may be paved with stone or brick and equipped with furniture like that of an outdoor living room.

A Garden Service Plot: We describe in Chapter XVIII, Equipment, a garden laboratory or kitchen which contains the things useful for easy gardening. It contains a vegetable garden, tool house, manure pit, cold frame, propagating bed and other features. Of course some parts of it may be combined, or the features may be worked in separately.

A Propagating Bed for growing a variety of plants will be found very helpful and economical. In the spring it may be used for the raising of an-

nuals which are to be transplanted to other locations, after which summer planting of perennials is comparatively simple. (See Chapter XIX.)

Vegetable Garden: Many folks omit the vegetable garden because they think it is not worth while or is too much trouble. Even though small, it can be a very handy thing and a considerable convenience to the cook. In it may be raised some of the vegetables which quickly lose their flavor after being picked; tomatoes, onions, radishes, lettuce, etc. And do not forget beets and carrots which are of such easy culture as to almost grow themselves. The vegetable garden should, of course, be a thing to itself. Place it in a corner, or at the end of the lot behind some low-growing shrubbery. Although it is not a part of the garden scene, it need not be unsightly. It may be developed along a formal or semiformal plan, with beds of vegetables surrounded by grass walks or separated by flower borders. Or it may be kept strictly utilitarian and made on the straight row system as described in Chapter XV.

ORNAMENTAL ACCESSORIES

It is not necessary to describe the list of ornamental accessories previously given. However, a few rules for their use should be carefully considered before lugging them into the picture. They should not compete for attention with plants or planting. Remember they are not the main part of the garden. They are the accessories. They accentuate the beauty of the garden much as jewelry should be used to add to personal appearance. Overdressing in the garden is

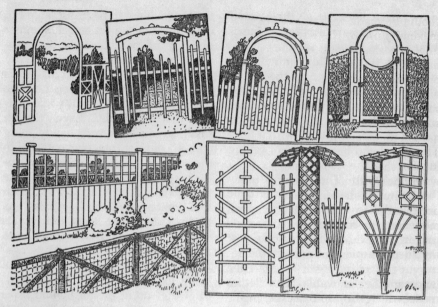

bad taste, too. They should represent something connected with the garden. The iron stag and the hunting dog, as lawn ornaments, went out of fashion with the gingerbread ornamentations of the American home so much in vogue shortly after our Civil War.

Walks and Steps should lead somewhere. A gate should be an entrance or egress. If we place a seat somewhere, there should be some reason for wanting to sit on it. It should overlook some garden feature or be a place where the gardener can take a short rest from his labors. If of the more permanent or comfortable variety, it should be located in the shade, and be inviting. A *trellis* should be for the display of vines. *Statuary* must be used sparingly and be appropriate to the woodland or the garden. *Sun Dials, Reflecting Globes, Bird Baths, Fountains, etc.,* may be located by themselves as distinct accents. They are usually placed upon pedestals, and care should be taken to place them substantially and usefully. A *Sun Dial* should be readily accessible as we must get very close to it in order to tell the time. It must be placed in relation to compass directions, and the angle of the projection that casts the shadow on the dial must be regulated according to the latitude in which the garden is located. Therefore a dial secured in and adapted to a distant city may not show accurate time in your garden.

Fountains are used largely in connection with mirror pools or water gardens, but in case a fountain has a pedestal or is part of a bird bath or similar bowl, the rule for locating the sun dials, globes and bird baths will apply to it. *Bird Houses* are more for the purpose of attracting our feathered friends than ornamentation. Any location of them in the plan should be made with a view to their maximum use by the birds. A *Mirror Pool* is a small pool usually located flush with the surface of the garden or lawn. As a rule it has few or no water plants growing in it, but is supposed to reflect the sky and the surrounding foliage. It acts in the garden much as the reflecting globe. This type, of course, may be located in the shade or semishade, where waterlilies will not grow well.

Miniature Gardens are a suitable outlet for the person who is fond of modeling. In almost every garden contest where a prize is to be awarded for excellence in gardening, the judges are besieged by amateur landscapers who construct intricate models of lighthouses, castles, wind-mills, etc., and place them as features of a water garden or rockery. Some of these I have seen are so excellent as to call forth sincere admiration for the imagination and care shown in their construction. However, it is rather grotesque to see an admirably executed model of a castle, complete in every detail with drawbridge and towers, directly by the side of a lovely example of a water lily which is about half as large as the castle itself. All of these things are fine separately but they do not belong to-gether. An interesting garden feature can be made by constructing a castle in a little plot by itself and surround-ing it with miniature plants which in comparative scale will be suitable for trees and other things usually found

around a castle. Moss will do nicely for grass and the imagination of the constructing genius will soon find other things to make an interesting feature.

MAKING THE PLAN

Now let us carry farther into our garden planning the idea of an architect about to build a house. The architect knows that it is too expensive to move around walls and schemes until the house assumes the shape which he has conceived in his mind. Therefore, he sits down to his drawing board and proceeds to draw plans to scale. This means that for every foot in the length of a room, he will use one-quarter of an inch or one-eighth of an inch. This may sound intricate to the novice, but if you are sporty enough to try it, you will find that the awkwardness you feel when you first use the common ruler for this purpose will soon wear away.

In applying this rule to your garden plans, if your back yard is fifty by sixty feet and you wish to draw it to one-eighth inch scale, you will draw a rectangle 6¼ inches wide by 7½ inches long. You will find that this will go nicely on a sheet of ordinary letter paper. If you do not have a square to make the corners, you may use the corner of another sheet of letter paper. Having gotten the canvas upon which you are going to paint your picture, you next take a few pieces of cardboard and out of these cut the various beds and borders which we are about to use.

If you have decided that your shrubbery borders will be five by ten feet, you will cut it out of cardboard, making it ⅝ of an inch wide by 1¼

inches long. By shading it a little bit with the pencil, it will appear darker than the outline of your yard which you have just drawn. Proceed to do the same with your perennial beds, water gardens, rock garden and other features, then move them around on the plan until you have them fitted.

Make it seem as though you were a great giant working out the actual garden itself. Try to imagine what these features will look like when placed side by side. Try to remember differences in the height of the plants, where the sun will be in certain portions of the day and what plants will be shaded by other plants or existing trees.

If you have trouble in understanding this method, ask some of your friends to help you. Most men understand drawing to scale and a great many of them have fitted furniture in their stores, offices or homes, by cutting out little cardboard pieces the right size and shape and moving them around on the plan until they fit. Many five and ten cent stores and all stationery and school supply stores sell cross section paper. This paper is ruled into tiny squares each representing one square foot. By counting off the number of feet in width and length of your garden and marking its outlines you can then draw in the various features without the use of a ruler.

THE DESIGN

Now for some simple principles of design:

1. Do not attempt too many features. The plan should fit the lot it is made for.

2. If your lot is long and narrow,

cut off the rear for special features and use narrow borders.

3. If your lot is short and wide, use wide borders and a shallow border along the rear of the property. A single row of shrubs is never as good as a broad belt or a "staggered" row.

4. Borders with straight or slightly curved edges will give an appearance of length and greater scale. Sharp curves will dwarf the beds and lawn. A graceful curve is a broad one, but it is impossible to adopt the plan of the park or estate in miniature for home grounds. Peninsulas or out-juttings of shrubs are used in large scale to break up long tiresome lines; they only cut up the small plan. Keep the curves simple and easy.

5. The human eye has been trained to demand balance. A certain amount of bulk along one border or in one corner calls for a corresponding planting or bulk opposite. Even the most informal planting must have balance. Draw an imaginary line (called an axis) down the center of your planting. Lawn on one side should approximately balance the area of lawn on the other side and so we should weigh, as nearly as possible, shrubbery border against perennial border, feature against feature.

Do not make curved borders on either side correspond. Stick to irregularity but get balance.

If you are not satisfied when the planting is finished, introduce a large shrub, a Lombardy or Bolleana Poplar, Cut Leaf Maple, or Pyramidal Oak in the proper place. Be careful of the Lombardy, however, as poplars are surface rooting trees; planted near perennials or roses, they will rob them of their nourishment.

6. Choose between the formal and informal plan, or if you use both, be sure to separate them into distinct features. An informal general plan with a formal intimate garden such as a cutting garden, rose garden, etc., goes very well.

The generally informal plan requires much less upkeep, less strict attention to detail of design. However, the plantings must be good as the interest centers on them rather than the design.

With the formal or semiformal plan the emphasis is on the design and mass effect of the plantings rather than on individual specimens.

Where growing conditions are good the informal or semiformal style usually gives the most satisfaction.

7. Plant groupings must harmonize in color and texture of foliage. In the border tall plants should be in the rear, medium in the center and the dwarf material in front.

8. In using shade trees, place them where you may look into the shade, as well as out from the shade. A restful, inviting patch of shade, equipped with comfortable seats is as desirable a feature as any planting. Trees, flower beds, or other large features placed in the middle of your lawn dwarf its size and spoil the vista. Unless you are building your plan around them, as in the case of existing trees, use them only as separate features, for accent or to frame a vista.

9. The screening of your grounds depends entirely upon their size. If the lot is ample, the shrubbery borders, etc., may act as a screen, but if

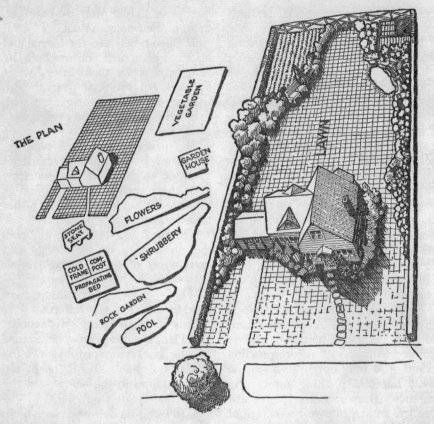

THE PLAN

VEGETABLE GARDEN

GARDEN HOUSE

LAWN

FLOWERS

STONE SEAT

SHRUBBERY

COLD FRAME | COM-POST

PROPAGATING BED

ROCK GARDEN

POOL

it is narrow, such as a fifty foot lot, it may be too small to use many trees or much shrubbery. Walls many times are too expensive and wooden fences may not be suitable enclosures. In this case a wire fence may be constructed to keep out the neighborhood pets and a hedge grown inside of it. Except for trimming, a hedge need not involve much labor or expense for upkeep. Trees may be worked into the hedge either for accent or to blot out objectionable neighboring scenery. In the informal plan where the hedge is used because of lot narrowness, plant a tree of compact habit in one corner and round out the other corners with flowering shrubbery.

10. In selecting plants remember height, color of bloom and fragrance. Try to put colors together that harmonize if they bloom at the same time. You may as well have fragrance, it goes with the picture without cost. Succession of bloom is a very important matter. Study your planting lists well.

In considering the height of taller plants, try to remember where shade will fall and select planting material accordingly. Try to imagine what plants will look like at maturity.

11. Do not make walks or drives

more extensive than necessary. Utility is the yardstick by which you measure. Bright glaring walks cut up and dwarf the plan. Steppingstones or walks with grass between the stones are the least conspicuous. Dull slate or dull colored pre-cast concrete slabs will not detract from the plantings.

12. A plan must conform to the grade or slope of the lot, existing trees and any other permanent features.

DISAPPOINTMENT SAVERS

1. I feel like starting each heading under planting instructions with the caution, "Don't crowd and don't attempt too much."

2. If you will get yourself some experience with the cheaper, easier-to-grow plants, you may as you become more expert, go in for rare specimens. The reason our more common, let us say, more popular, types of garden plants are so much used and produced is because they grow well in many places and are comparatively free from insect pests. Growers have no hesitancy in recommending them and, as they grow them in large quantities, they are cheap in price. This does not necessarily make them cheap in quality or merit.

Do not think I advocate bargain-counter plants. Far from it. Plants cost so little for the length of time we have them with us that it pays to buy them from reliable dealers and pay a fair price. Cheap plants give cheap results. Quality pays. A few well-grown plants are better than a quantity of poor ones.

3. When you visit a distant state and see beautiful plants which you would like to transplant to your own garden, remember that soil and other conditions may be distinctly different in your locality and that it is better to buy the plants grown close to your home where they are inured to your own climate and soil.

Consult local growers. Inquire as to hardiness. Unless you have plenty of time, money and patience, don't experiment. Go to growers or dealers when plants are in bloom as much as possible. You can select most of your smaller plants that way and know exactly what you are getting. There will be but little difference in cost between good hardy clumps and small sickly ones.

4. In locating shrubs in a border, try to remember that they will grow to considerable size in a few years. They may come to you as small plants, but plant them where you want them to grow at the proper distance apart and fill in between with temporary plantings. When necessary, remove the temporary plantings as the permanent plants reach maturity.

5. There is nothing so essential to most plants as the sunlight. If you try to impose a set pattern upon your plan without regard to shade and sun, you are in for a lot of disappointment with sickly plants. Use your densely shaded area for games or recreational purposes and your semishade for the plants which enjoy that environment. Select these plants from the list given later.

6. Drainage is an important matter in your garden. Few plants like wet feet. Full instructions for drainage are given in Chapter II.

7. Don't try to transplant large

trees or shrubs unless you know how, and take at least a year to do it. A small healthy tree or shrub properly planted, watered and fed will give better results in shorter time than the large one. A large tree or shrub may stop growing for years after being transplanted and in that case will be more likely to be attacked by enemies and disease.

8. If you love birds, don't forget some berries or small fruit to attract them; Weeping Mulberry, small Cherry or Wild Cherry usually fit into the plan somewhere. Also keep water easily accessible for them to drink and bathe.

ASSEMBLING THE PLAN

Having first carefully selected the features which we want in the garden from the list previously given and having carefully studied the ideas of design, we will now try to assemble the various features into a harmonious whole. It has been said that the way to make a gentleman is to start with his grandfather. We might paraphrase this to say that the way to make a perfect plan is first to carefully select the site.

Those who are about to build a new home or to design the grounds around a new one, are fortunate. Most of us are trying to better the grounds which we already have and to overcome previous mistakes in design and planting. We will, therefore, first consider the business of improving the plan which we have and afterwards take up the business of the completely new plan.

Americans have, for years, referred to the front and the back of the house. The English have a better idea. They speak of the garden side of the house. Folks who used to like to sit on their front porch and watch their neighbors go by are coming more and more to the idea of making their garden a private affair and sitting in the back yard or on the garden side of the house.

The Front Yard: Planting the front yard depends to a large extent upon the contour of the ground and the particular type of architecture used in the house. If the architecture of the house is good, it is a shame to screen it from the street with too much shrubbery. However, if the house has been selected because the inside of it is comfortable, we sometimes put up with the outside because it would cost too much to remodel it. In this case tree planting may be used to screen it. A few quick growing trees, like poplars, will soften the features of the house which are objectionable until permanent trees can be grown.

Our planting in the front yard is primarily for two or three purposes: First to mark the boundaries of the lot, second to frame the house and third to correct architectural weaknesses or emphasize outstanding features.

If all the houses along the street are enclosed by hedges or fences, of course we will want a hedge. If, however, this is not the rule, putting a hedge around our front yard will dwarf it and certainly not improve it. If the front yard is a part of a vista of unbroken lawn along the street, we do not want to clutter it up with shrubbery. If we do plant shrubbery it should be of the low growing sort.

Shrubbery for the front yard should be selected more for foliage effects than flowers. Conspicuous flowers are much better avoided. Trees are used to frame the house, that is, so that the house will be seen between them. A tree set directly in front of the house spoils the view and may throw the plan off balance. In planting either trees or shrubbery try to get an equal amount of bulk, height, or width on either side of the imaginary line (axis) which we have drawn down the middle of the garden.

Foundation Planting: A certain amount of planting is usually necessary around the foundation and this is said to tie the house to the ground and make it look as if it belonged there. Your house will always appear to better advantage if it seems to nestle upon the ground.

Almost all old houses are set too high and too much of their foundation is exposed. If your house has this fault perhaps a terrace of earth thrown against it will somewhat remedy the defect. This terrace need not be over four feet wide at the top in order to sustain your foundation planting but it should be made of good soil. It will certainly make your home look lower.

Planting at the corners of the house will give it width and, if it is a small one, this is necessary. Do not plant the same number of shrubs on either side of your door; also the planting need not be continuous. A little foundation showing through it will do no harm. You must remember that this planting will be seen in winter as well as summer and if you use shrubs, select those with decora-

NEITHER THE GROUND PLAN NOR THE VERTICAL SECTION GIVES A TRUE PICTURE...

—BUT ARRANGE SMALL BLOCKS AND OTHER OBJECTS ON A SCALED PLOT AND YOU CAN WORK OUT "SPATIAL DESIGN"

AND ACHIEVE MAXIMUM RESULTS.

tive bark or berries and try to imagine what they will look like when the leaves are gone. You may also select shrubs whose foliage remains all winter, such as yews, etc. Of course, evergreens are always useful in foundation planting if of the slow-growing type. And don't forget to put in a few broad leafed evergreens if they are known to do well in your locality.

Avoid monotony. Don't use too many of any one variety of plants and use different heights to add interest. A tall pyramidal evergreen sticking up above the planting, outlined against the color of the house, adds to artistic interest. But a row of these planted in front of the house has little or no value. If you are interested in the location of walks, entrances, etc., these are discussed under "New Properties" below.

The Garden Side: Having been obliged to surrender the front yard to semipublic use and to ornamental planting, the gardener naturally turns to the rear for outdoor comfort, privacy and the satisfaction of his own artistic desire for color and design. If he really wants privacy one thing is essential, that the service entrance to the house (the kitchen door) be screened somewhat from his garden and that another entrance, either from the living room or the dining room, be constructed for entrance into his own private garden. If the garden is to be a real intimate thing, we do not wish to drag our friends around from the front of the house, nor yet to take them through the kitchen, therefore another entrance besides the kitchen door is essential.

French doors are very popular for this purpose. The opening being wider than the usual door, makes the room lighter and adds to the ventilation during warm weather. If a terrace is constructed just outside these French doors and overlooking the garden, it can constitute an outdoor living room, convenient to the telephone and kitchen, a modern development of yesterday's porch. The terrace forms a sort of transition from the interior to the exterior. It may be paved with solid concrete, flagstones, brick or pre-cast concrete.

Next comes the question, what type of garden? If your yard is a small city lot, it has almost been cut out for you as a formal or semiformal garden. However, if it is an irregular lot or one having more than one level, it will lend itself very well to development along informal or "naturalistic" lines. Before deciding what type to adopt, it would be well to study some of the many excellent books that deal especially with garden planning and that you can consult at your local library or garden center, if there is one in your community. Whatever design you select remember there should be a vista from the house and don't forget the imaginary line (axis) by which you balance your planting. The vista may be down this line. However, be careful to have some object of interest or accent just off the end of it not exactly in the center. The object of interest may be a pool, a bench or some garden ornament. Do not construct your garden house or tea house on the axis at the rear of your lawn, but put it over at one side and balance it with some feature or planting on the other side of the axis. Broad steps from your terrace to the lawn with steppingstones leading to the object of interest at the end of the vista, lend a constant invitation to wander out through the beauties of the garden, regardless of the conditions of the ground due to summer showers.

Even though you are not going to completely redesign your garden, it will pay you to read all of this chapter as it may be easy to rearrange some of your service facilities so that you will have more room for planting.

NEW PROPERTIES

Selecting the Lot: In constructing a home, people will plan for years the kind of house which they wish and then, with very little consideration, select a lot and attempt to make the house fit it.

A few years ago everyone wanted a level lot. Today we are coming more and more to the idea that the greatest charm is possible in a slopping lot. Unless it is very small, in which case, level ground or a slight slope is the most desirable. If it has a gentle slope to the rear it will aid in entering the garage which should be attached to or in the basement of the house.

A lot that is not too precipitous will lend itself to a plan which calls for a series of levels, each level having possibilities of becoming an intimate garden in itself. If you wish a few flowers easily obtained nothing can compare with a gently sloping lot. If you wish an interesting development, something original or different, a little irregularity of slope has more possibilities.

Architecture Must Fit the Plan: The type of architecture which you have selected for your house also has a great deal to do with the lot selection. If you are fond of gardening, be a little generous with the size of your lot. It is better to pay a little more, than to put an entire investment into the building and provide no fit setting. Many people will buy a small lot which is hard to develop because it has a view. Views, while inspiring at first, may soon lose their effect upon the occupants of the house. It is much more important to pay attention to conveniences such as transportation, schools, churches, sunlight and air than to a flashy environment. A European cottage style home would not be in keeping with a stiff, formal garden. An informal or semiformal arrangement would fit this type of home best. Informal or semiformal does not mean a hodgepodge of planting. If you have carefully studied what has gone before you will make it a balanced informality. A Colonial home fits very well with a somewhat formal plan. We should remember however that a formal plan once inaugurated is hard to change, whereas a plan which is not so stiff may be altered more easily.

Setting the House on the Lot: Now as to my authority for what I am about to say, let me state that the writer has been a subdivider and developer of residential tracts as well as a home builder for the major portion of his life. From this experience it is his opinion that the greatest sin in landscaping lies in the setting of the house upon the lot. Small houses are very difficult to design because they do not cover enough ground area to make the other dimensions correspond to the height. They are usually two stories high and only by using sweeping roof lines and various other tricks of the architectural trade are we able to make them appear of the proportions which we have been taught to desire by looking at the more elaborate homes.

The first and most important thing in setting the house is to try to reduce as far as possible the apparent height. Each day you pass homes exposing so much of their foundation that they seem ready to uproot themselves and walk away. People have an idea that cellar windows must be above ground to light the basement. This is not true as a small areaway or light-well around them will permit them to be below-grade. If the light-well is made of tile, brick or concrete it can be painted white and give excellent light. This feature may mean considerable in the outward appearance of the home.

Watch your building contractor. The farther a house sets into the ground the greater the cost of excavation and moving of material. A saving on this item is a profit to him. Many shortsighted builders, with little artistic ability, will commit this particular offense. If you must have the foundation exposed in order to get headroom for your garage, grade your lot in such a manner that the ground will slope away from it in all directions. This slope will carry the eye to the foundation gradually and its height will not be such a shock. A bank around the front or side of the home, five or six feet wide and sloping more or less abruptly to the level of the lawn, is a very good way to overcome this defect. Also careful foundation planting is important. Both of these matters have been discussed.

Walks and Drives, Etc.: Next in importance to the setting of the house upon the lot is the planning of the entrances to the home. The driveway, the walk, kitchen service entrance, coal chute, etc., should be placed as nearly as possible on one side of the house. Do not jam the entrances against the wall but leave a little space well out from under the eaves for planting. Some evergreens and other plants will do well here; but Euonymus vegetus especially will hold its leaves the major portion of the winter and has bright berries

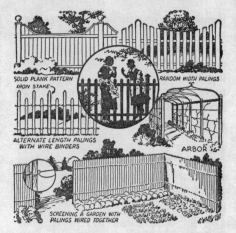

which are always an additional attraction.

Do not make a drive wider than is necessary, but remember that automobiles need more room than carriages used to; also the safety factor must be considered. The walks may be quite narrow and if you wish to curve them, make this curve very slight. Remember broad curves are graceful and give the effect of sweep and size, whereas short curves give a wiggly appearance and may dwarf the entire plan.

Try to arrange your kitchen entrance on the side of the house and screen it from your back garden. This leaves the garden side of your house free for planting and privacy.

THE PROBLEM OF A DETACHED GARAGE

The problem of the detached garage is not hopeless. The same principle which goes to make up any good plan may be used to a large extent after the garage and driveway are screened out. This, of course, makes the garden smaller but permits proper balance of its elements just as in the unobstructed lot.

The first thing to do in renovating any property is to draw a plan changing all the scattered plants or features to fit it. In the one illustrated here, we use quadrille (cross-ruled) paper as it enables us to figure dis-

tances at a glance. It is made for a sixty foot lot and each square represents an area two feet each way.

In this case we arrange to "plant out" the garage and driveway to exclude it from the plan. The balance of the area is then divided down the

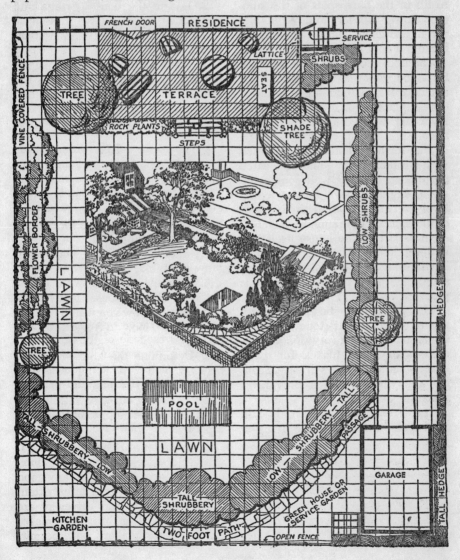

center by an imaginary line called the "axis." A central panel of lawn dominates the plan and on either side of the axis at a suitable distance are placed the various enclosing plantings.

The useful little service plots supply cut flowers for the house or plants to fill in the bare spots of the summer flower border, and vegetables for the kitchen. Here, too, may be located a cold frame or green house.

The pool should be flush with the turf and fancy edging should be avoided. It must be more of a mirror than a planting or it will cut up the lawn and dwarf the general appearance.

The terrace should be provided with a rolling awning and be located on a small bank of well compacted earth, slightly above the lawn and level or nearly level with the floor of the house. In the summer it should seem a part of the house itself and nothing defeats this as thoroughly as having to step down to it. Its center should be as near the axis as it is practical to have it.

The floor may be paved with gravel, brick, or flat stone but nothing is so useful as a very smooth concrete slab. This makes for good drainage after showers or easy cleaning and when waxed it provides a space for dancing.

The French doors not only add light and ventilation to the living or dining room but make the terrace more a part of the house.

SUMMARY

Here are the things to do to get started on making your plans:

1. Draw a sketch of your yard in scale.

2. Locate the house, garage and permanent features. Give these matters in detail showing measurement in scale.

3. Trees should be marked showing the approximate spread of the foliage, the approximate area and course of the shade thrown by them.

4. Locate the walks, drives, fences, etc.

5. Decide what views in the neighborhood you wish to screen out, and plan for that planting.

6. Try to arrange for an easy entrance to your rear garden from your house and a handy place for storage of tools and equipment.

7. Mark where shady plants will grow and sun-loving plants will grow.

8. Take some pictures of the different sides of your house. Study them and visualize how you would like the planting to look in regard to the house.

9. Determine the kind of garden features you are going to have, whether formal or informal planting.

Then, having cut your various features to scale, attempt to fit them into a plan.

CHAPTER II

SOIL FERTILITY AND HOW TO MAINTAIN IT

In the spring when seeds are sprouting,
  Stir the land.
In the summer, nothing doubting,
  Stir the land.
Stirring helps each little seed,
Stirring kills each little weed,
Stirring—let this be your creed:
  Stir the land.

—M. G. KAINS.

No one can expect much success until he has learned something about what makes plants grow; what makes them healthy in certain locations and sickly in others. Once started along this line, an enthusiastic amateur will become fascinated by the study and will have a greater appreciation of plant life and his garden.

It is impossible to give a complete discourse on this subject in so small a book, but we will attempt to make the reader understand why he must follow certain rules, which he will find later.

A great many people think that fertility means merely placing in the soil chemical elements which are part of and necessary to plants. This is but a very small part of it.

Water: A certain great desert of our country was visited by a number of rainstorms just a few years ago. To the knowledge of the oldest inhabitant, no vegetation had ever grown there. However, after a short period of rain, new plants and wild flowers began to spring up all over the desert.

Other sections of our western country, desert lands, have been reclaimed by irrigation. Water is brought to the gardens by little trenches and thus, in areas where there is little rainfall, abundant crops are produced. These soils have been found to be very fertile, but water is needed to release their fertility.

The lesson that we learn from this is that the first necessity in growing plants is water. Someone has said, "Plants live on soup, and mighty weak soup at that."

Plants use about 300 pounds of water to produce 1 pound of solid matter. That is to say, for every pound of lumber from the forest, hay or hemp from the field, it took 300 pounds of water to sustain the plant while it was manufacturing this pound of solid matter. Plants do not eat, they only drink. The food must be in very weak solution, in order for the tiny fiber roots to take it up into the chemical laboratory of the plant. The leaves evaporate the excess moisture, taking from it the things which they need to sustain life. Even after the fiber roots (food absorbing part of the plant) take up the solution it must still be in liquid form to be able to circulate.

It stands to reason that, as plants themselves are made up for the most part of water (69 to 90%), this water must need frequent renewing. In the desert and the irrigated land, all the elements of fertility were present, but the country was arid. As soon as water is supplied vegetation springs into life.

On the other hand, we have marshes where there is plenty of water; temperature and climate are ideal and yet very little vegetation is grown because of the lack of other essentials.

Bacteria: Suppose, for instance, that we have achieved the ideal combination of all elements of fertility. What then goes on in the soil to transform this into stalk, leaves and blossoms of the plant?

I have in mind one instance of a gardener, who grew beautiful delphiniums. In an adjoining garden,

the owner had poor results from similar plants. One day he secured a large clump of especially fine delphinium from his neighbor and with it a small basket of soil. He planted the clump in the bed with the other delphiniums and quite by accident scattered the soil over the surface of the bed and, in cultivating, worked the soil from his neighbor's garden in with his own. Within a few months his plants improved and soon his delphiniums were as good as those of his neighbor. I have had people question this story several times but it is true, nevertheless. The answer to this seeming riddle is that the unproductive garden was inoculated with beneficial bacteria from the successful garden.

In your garden there are countless workers—working for you day and night enriching the earth and making possible all plant life. These minute organisms are visible only under a powerful microscope and are so sim-

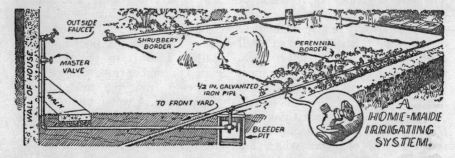

Above is shown an irrigation system which makes watering of the garden easy. The pipe is laid on top of the ground in the rear of the border out of sight, and the short remnants of hose are left out all summer. They can be coiled up in the shade when not in use. A few low-priced automatic sprinklers will make it possible to cover the entire garden area without the fuss of unscrewing hose and moving it from place to place. The system should drain to one central spot, if possible, and if all the faucets are left open in winter it will not freeze. The sprinklers can be allowed to run during the evening, being turned off at bed time by the use of the master valve without going through the wet shrubbery or grass to operate individual lines. Second-hand pipe may be used to try out this idea replacing it in a few years with galvanized pipe or the new plastic kind.

ple in structure that for years scientists were in doubt as to whether they were animals or plants; even now there is disagreement except that they are known to be a very low form of life.

Bacteria are everywhere; we find more and more precautions against unfriendly bacteria in our hospitals and food factories. The introduction of bacteria into the human body, by vaccination, turns smallpox from a scourge to a little feared disease and so with typhoid and many other diseases dreaded in days gone by.

Bacteria swarm in the bodies of animals. We read more and more of the friendly bacteria in the human body.

As it is in the body, so it is in the soil. Bacteria are continually living and dying. This process may be completed within half an hour. Under favorable circumstances, the number of these bacteria may increase with amazing rapidity. Without these tiny organisms, it would be impossible to extract from humus (the decomposed bodies of plants and animals) such elements as calcium, hydrogen, nitrogen and sulphur for plant food. These bacteria are for the major part living in the humus in the soil. If there is little humus there are few bacteria. The increase ceases when there is only 2 or 3% moisture and is most notable when there is 25 to 40%. Warmth, too, is necessary

HOW PLANTS USE WATER

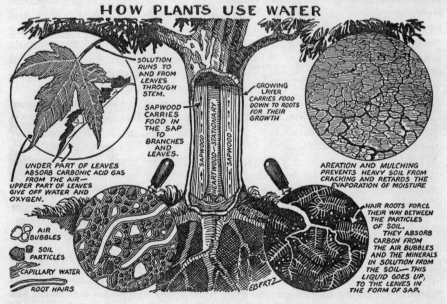

A great deal of the water used by plants is in the form of a thin film adhering to the surface of the soil particles and is called capillary water. Between the soil particles surrounded by this film of water are air bubbles which absorb the food elements released from the decaying humus. This being transferred to the capillary water is carried up in solution as shown above to be manufactured into plant food in the marvelous chemical laboratory of the plant.

and they have been found to increase enormously after a warm summer rain.

This friendly army has a means of preserving itself under adverse conditions by producing spores. These spores may be called seed. In other words, it is a young plant having surrounded itself with a sort of armor, hard cell or wall so that it may retain life amid uncongenial surroundings for years. When conditions again become suitable this shell breaks open and the bacteria multiply in the usual manner.

So it is that these spores lying frozen all winter in our garden are only waiting for the sun and rain of the springtime to awaken them to activity. How important then, is the character of our soil. If it is sand, little water is retained in it and the air is circulated rather freely. Under these conditions it is almost impossible to keep bacteria alive, because of evaporation and the easy passage of water to the lower level of the soil. Again there is the fine grain soil (clay), so compact that there is practically no space for circulation of air, and bacterial life is smothered.

It is, therefore, necessary to condition our soil, that is, to make it possible for the water to enter the soil in such a manner that some of it is retained for a long period of time. Too much water is just as bad as not enough, and so it must be allowed to run through the soil, and away from the plant. This is called drainage; it is discussed in detail farther on. By taking the two opposite kinds of soil, sand and clay, and mixing them together, using one to remedy the defects of the other, we may arrive at a happy solution of our drainage problem. Then if we work into this mixture a proper amount of vegetable matter, we will have the ideal soil for most plants.

Your garden should consist of good garden loam, which should be made up of about 60% minerals and 40% decaying vegetable matter, known as humus. This humus may be placed in your soil as manure, peat moss, leaf mold or homemade compost. If your soil is clay and sticky and has the tendency to bake and crack, it needs sand for drainage and humus for conditioning. If the water runs from it too freely, it needs the addition of humus and clay to keep the water in the soil ready for the plant. A good garden loam is about 40% clay, 40% humus and 20% sand.

SOIL DRAINAGE

As we have seen, water is essential to plant life, but it must be present in the soil in such form that the plants can take it up. To be available it must be stored in the tiny spaces between the soil particles; that is, it practically forms a thin film around each particle. But too much moisture is, for most plants, as undesirable as too little. Some plants, of course, live in water but they are especially designed to do so. On land, an excess of water drives and keeps out the air that plant roots must obtain; it prevents the growth and activity of bacteria; and it may dissolve and wash away valuable plant food. For these reasons, surplus moisture must be removed by drainage.

Probably no land improvement has as much interesting recorded data as drainage. Almost every country has stories of how thousands of acres of land have been reclaimed for agriculture by drainage.

It is remarkable how many problems of infertility can be traced to excess water in the soil. In a farm book recently issued the writer read this injunction: "First see that your land is thoroughly drained before wasting time on any other reasons for lack of success." But drainage is more than the run-off of surface water. Many gardeners think that sloping land is a guarantee of effectiveness and thus enjoy a false sense of security. For excess water will remain in the soil unless it is removed by percolation or evaporation of some sort.

Water which enters the soil during rains seeps either downward, or horizontally, through porous soil toward lower levels. When it reaches a layer of rock, hardpan, shale, or clay which is impervious or only slightly porous, the passage of water is stopped or slowed up. The point at which this happens is called the water table.

The depth of the growing soil above this table determines, to a large extent, what plants will grow on the land and how well they will grow.

We must therefore give attention both to surface runoff so that excess water will not stand on top of the soil, and to sub-drainage so that it will seep out of the growing layer. We must also avoid confusing the water table with subterranean water which flows in veins far beneath the surface and appears in the form of artesian wells or springs. This type of ground water sometimes complicates a drainage problem by forming a hidden spring in a hillside which flows near the surface to soil below and causes wet areas. The cure for this is shown in one of our illustrations.

Drainage does many things but the first and most important reason for it is the fact that plant roots will not enter saturated soil. Almost all cultivated plants must have air in the soil to complete root growth and feeding processes. Soil is made of particles of eroded rock mixed with decaying vegetable matter. If the larger spaces between soil particles are filled with water no air can penetrate and without air the crops will die.

In land where the water table is close to the top of the ground, the growing layer is too shallow to allow the deep rooting necessary for healthy plant growth. Also in heavy soil with a fairly deep growing area in summer, the water does not percolate fast enough during spring rains and

Some of the water coming from above is absorbed by the soil particles. The balance should drain through to the water table. Some of it is again soaked up through capillary action to the upper soil during dry weather. The method of installing tile is discussed herewith.

as a consequence the water table is temporarily raised.

In either of these cases, the shallow root systems that plants are able to develop in spring are unable to reach water during the summer dry spells. Such land is given a constant and desirably lower water table if drained with farm tile.

The tile quickly lowers the water table after a rain and holds it at the proper level. The plants root deeply in the spring and are able to withstand drought in summer. No fear should be felt that it will dry out the soil too much, for it only drains to the depth at which it is placed and leaves available plenty of moisture where the roots can get it.

When Drainage Is Needed: Let us consider what type of soils are most likely to need drainage. First, there are marsh lands to be reclaimed for agriculture by removing excess water. Second, there are the lands which are inundated by streams at flood time. These often are very valuable agriculturally, but need to be drained so they will dry out quickly after being overflowed, and warm up for planting. Third, we have lowlands adjacent to higher ground which are too flat to quickly get rid of the water which flows down upon them. In this class comes the seepage from hillside springs, above mentioned. Fourth, and perhaps more important to the home gardener is the type of land which is underlain by a retentive subsoil which prevents the escape of water from growing layer above it.

Some signs which indicate a need of drainage are often apparent upon the surface. Inspection should be made at the wettest season of the year. When water stands upon the surface after rains or if a saturated soil fails to dry out promptly during subsequent favorable weather, it can be taken as a definite sign that something is wrong.

The type of vegetation which grows upon the ground naturally is also a good indication. The absence of normal grasses coupled with the presence of coarse wire grass, rushes, mint, willows or spruce is a sign of too much moisture. Frequent winter-killing of fruit trees, shrubbery, etc., is an indication of shallow rooting. Often these show rank growth in the spring when the water is high in the ground and a yellowing of their overgrown foliage during the summer when it recedes.

A sure indication of excess water

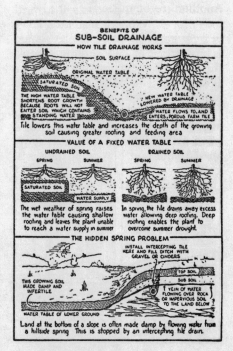

BENEFITS OF
SUB-SOIL DRAINAGE
HOW TILE DRAINAGE WORKS

Tile lowers this water table and increases the depth of the growing soil causing greater rooting and feeding area

VALUE OF A FIXED WATER TABLE

The wet weather of spring raises the water table causing shallow rooting and leaves the plant unable to reach a water supply in summer

In spring, the tile drains away excess water allowing deep rooting. Deep rooting enables the plant to overcome summer drought.

THE HIDDEN SPRING PROBLEM

Land at the bottom of a slope is often made damp by flowing water from a hillside spring. This is stopped by an intercepting tile drain.

is the presence of crawfish (properly crayfish) also known as crawdads, land crabs, lobster crabs, etc. They abound in warm regions of the United States and feed on roots doing a vast damage to corn and cotton crops. Their burrows run straight down to water. They mold the soil into pellets with which they form chimney-like turrets about their holes to keep out surface water and protect them from their natural enemies, snakes and kingfishers. These chimneys do much damage to mowing machinery.

If left alone crayfish multiply fast, often running 8,000 to 12,000 to the acre. The United States Agricultural bulletins recommend eradication by an application of a spoonful of carbon bisulphide to each hole which is then closed with the foot. Another recommendation suggests the use of the cyanide materials, sold in seed stores for moles. The writer has disposed of crayfish in small quantities with many remedies but the one which is perhaps the cheapest and easiest is corrosive sublimate (bichloride of mercury) applied in solution. As there is no means of estimating the amount of water in the hole, it is best to use it in fairly concentrated form—two ounces to 10 gallons of water. It must be remembered that this material is deadly poison and care must be taken to avoid contact with the skin at this strength. Avoid splashing and leaking containers.

To be sure of the character of the soil, it is customary to take samples at various depths with a ground auger or a post-hole digger. This will show the depth of the top soil and many times reveal the cause of the difficulty. Before proceeding with the actual work of draining, be sure that there is no water trapped upon the top of the ground by uneven grading of the slope. Also remove any near-by causes by intercepting and tiling hillside springs in the manner already illustrated. Such springs can be traced by surface vegetation or a series of borings starting at the edge of the wet spot.

Directions for laying tile depend on slope of land and character of soil. Unless the lines are very long or the land is very wet, four-inch tile is large enough. It is best to keep the lines as straight as possible, and abrupt corners or right angles should always be avoided as they interfere with the free flow of the water.

Lateral joints with a main sewer are often called "Y branches" or

PLANNING FOR A DRAINAGE SYSTEM

Test holes to determine need for drainage or the depth of tile may be made with a post-hole digger or a ground auger.

Tile lines should follow natural slopes. They usually take herring-bone or gridiron shapes or sometimes combine the two.

If the outlet is to be on open ground prepare a hinged grill or cage to keep rodents from nesting in them and stopping up drains.

CRAWFISH A WET SOIL PEST

Land crabs or Crawfish cause considerable damage to plants on or near wet soil.

The turrets which they build of moulded pellets to protect the holes are unsightly and damage mowing machinery.

They are eradicated by pouring carbon bisulphide or corrosive sublimate solution into the holes and tramping them down.

"slants," because they come in at an angle of about 30 degrees to the line of flow. Where lines of tile connect, wrap heavy paper strips about the joints and cover with concrete after tile is in trench. It is not necessary to have concrete or paper on the bottom of the joints.

To avoid excessive digging through hills, tile should go around them, following the natural slopes of the land. For this reason a system takes many forms over a large area. All lines must have adequate slope or fall. The greater the fall the faster the tile works. Six inches of fall to 100 feet of tile may be used if the line is carefully and firmly laid to maintain an even slope. One foot of fall to 100 feet of tile is safer.

Any great amount of tiling should be laid out with a leveling instru-ment, but small operations can be done with a line. The illustration shows a way to keep the fall even and save labor. Batterboards which straddle the trench are placed at in-tervals of 25 to 50 feet. From the highest of these is stretched a level line.

The desired fall is measured down from this line and the next batter-board driven into that depth. An overhead working line may now be stretched from one batterboard to the other to get the right slope. A gauge or measuring stick is cut to fit between this and the top of the first tile laid. If each tile is laid the same depth from the working line, the finished line of tile will slope evenly and avoid trapping water.

In hand digging much labor will be saved if only a short section of tile is laid at a time. About six to eight feet of trench is opened and the tile is placed in it. When the next length of trench is dug, it is easy to dig off the top soil and toss it forward into the first strip on top of the tile. As the best soil should be about the tile to make them work better this is a sure way to handle this situation. The soil in the bottom can then be thrown into the trench being filled, to complete it, saving the labor of throwing it to the surface and han-dling it again.

How deep to place the tile de-pends upon the kind of soil and the kind of plants to be grown upon it. Grass grows well with a water table two feet from the surface, grain, clover, etc., require three feet, al-falfa will die out in a few years with less than four feet, trees and shrub-bery need four feet or more, etc. For

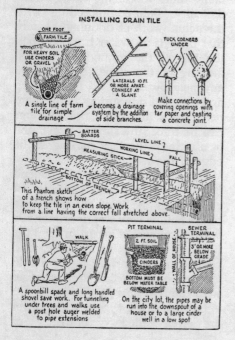

INSTALLING DRAIN TILE

ONE FOOT
FARM TILE

FOR HEAVY SOIL USE CINDERS OR GRAVEL

TUCK CORNERS UNDER

LATERALS 10 FT. OR MORE APART. CONNECT AT A SLANT.

A single line of farm tile for simple drainage

becomes a drainage system by the addition of side branches.

Make connections by covering openings with tar paper and casting a concrete joint.

BATTER BOARDS
LEVEL LINE
MEASURING STICK
WORKING LINE
FALL
BOTTOM OF TRENCH

This Phantom sketch of a trench shows how to keep the tile in an even slope. Work from a line having the correct fall stretched above.

WALK

A spoonbill spade and long handled shovel save work. For tunneling under trees and walks use a post hole auger welded to pipe extensions

PIT TERMINAL
SEWER TERMINAL

2 FT. SOIL

WALL OF HOUSE

3' OR MORE BELOW GRADE

CINDERS

BOTTOM MUST BE BELOW WATER TABLE

On the city lot, the pipes may be run into the downspout of a house or to a large cinder well in a low spot

general garden use a good depth is about four feet in ordinary soil.

The deeper the tile is laid the farther apart the tile lines may be placed. The distance varies with the density of the soil. In sandy or open soil, lay the lines deeper and farther apart. In clay soil, lay them more shallow and closer together. In sandy or very porous soil, the lines will attain maximum efficiency at once, but in heavier soil, they increase each year as the finer particles are washed out and the soil becomes more open.

Start at the outlet and lay the tile upgrade. Screen any exposed outlets to prevent rodents from entering, building nests and clogging them. Two ways to do this are shown (page 27). Place tile ends closely together to avoid stoppage by entrance of dirt—⅛-inch is the proper distance. Place in a straight line and secure them on either side with earth so that they will not roll out of place when filling is done. All broken or cracked tile should be discarded.

If you have a problem of water-bearing soil or land that is so heavy that it makes gardening difficult, a line of tile, four feet or more deep, down the middle of a lot will be sure to help. Well-placed tile will in time improve almost any land for 50 feet on either side of it. Its presence will be noticed by the brighter and more intense green of the vegetation above it which spreads from year to year as its efficiency increases.

Soil Texture and Structure: Through the courtesy of O. M. Scott & Company, seedsmen of Marysville, Ohio, we quote the following from their magazine "Lawn Care":

"All soils are composed of particles of varying sizes. In one gram of very fine sand there will be approximately two million particles while in the same amount of clay there would be about forty-five million particles— more than twenty times as many. The size of particles in a soil determines what is called its texture. These particles have a certain arrangement. In some soils each particle acts as a separate unit whereas in other cases various minute particles become grouped together so that groups act as single units. The arrangement of soil particles is called its structure.

"These mechanical characteristics are of great importance in determining the moisture movement in soils. The best turf soils are those having a 'crumb' structure. Where many small particles are grouped together to act as a single large unit such a crumb structure permits easy and rapid movement of air and water, at the same time presents a condition where the optimum moisture supply is retained.

"Soil 'puddling' occurs in the heavier soil when small soil particles are forced or floated in between larger particles. Thus the soil becomes more compact and at the same time plastic. The potter works clay to break down crumb structure so he can mold it into any desired shape.

"Heavy soils become compact and tight because of excessive moisture or of having been worked when wet to a heavy, gummy mass. Sooner or later, this soil will dry very fast with the advent of warm weather. As the soil loses so much water its volume shrinks greatly, making large cracks in the lawn. These in turn cause a great loss of moisture from the subsoil by evaporation. So the condition is continually aggravated.

"One of the principal factors involved in improvement of compact soils is provision for adequate surface and underground drainage. The former can be taken care of by surface grading while the installation of tile drainage is about the only means of improving underground drainage.

"At the same time a friable, loamy topsoil should be installed, if possible. Extremely sandy or clay soils will never support good turf. Heavy soils should be broken up with coarse sand and a liberal supply of organic matter. This furnishes a home for the needed friendly bacteria, and retains moisture and plant food. A sandy soil may be made more compact by adding soil of heavier texture and also incorporating enormous quantities of organic materials."

Chemical Elements: It is essential that the soil contain all the elements found in the plant itself, and that it retain them long enough for the plant to absorb them during its life. The chemical elements most used and most liable to rapid exhaustion are nitrogen, phosphoric acid (phosphorus), and potash (potassium). There are, of course, other chemical elements but they are used in such small quantities that they are exhausted from the soil only in exceptional cases. These elements are used only by the plant in solution.

NITROGEN:
Makes leaf and stem
Promotes quick growth—weight and bulk
Gives good color to foliage

PHOSPHORUS:
Promotes fruits and flowers
Makes strong roots
Insures crop maturity

POTASSIUM:
Promotes general health of plant and of flowers
Strengthens stems or stalks
Increases size and flavor of fruits

Acidity and alkalinity also affect fertility but these matters are treated as a separate subject in Chapter VII.

Location: Certain plants desire shade, others exposure. Such plants as roses prefer shelter from wind and weather. Chemical and physical soil fertility is, therefore, worthless if we try to grow a sun-loving plant in deep shade, or vice versa.

Fertilizer: Plant foods or prepared chemical fertilizers come in salt form, readily available, easily soluble in water. They are balanced to contain all the elements necessary for the plant. There are different fertilizers offered for various types of plants. For instance a general purpose lawn fertilizer is not as suitable for dahlias and other bulb or root plants and so on.

Use chemical fertilizers sparingly. Far more material is likely to be wasted than can be taken up by the plant. It is readily dissolved in water and is therefore soon washed into the lower soil where plant roots cannot absorb it.

Organic fertilizers are those which come from plant and animal materials. Bone meal is in two forms: steamed ground bone which is slow acting compared with chemical fertilizers, and raw ground bone which is still slower. It has been called the safe fertilizer because it does not burn leaves or stems and can be applied to almost any plant without injuring it. Use it on bulbs, dahlias, roses, etc. It is rich in phosphoric acid.

Dried blood is good for rhododendrons and water plants for it contains much nitrogen and lasts longer than chemical mixtures.

Cottonseed meal is good for acid loving plants; tankage, a slaughterhouse by-product, is a variable material and less used than it formerly was.

Animal manures are not as rich in plant food as is generally supposed, but are excellent ground conditioners. Fresh manures may be applied to fallow ground in fall or winter to be worked in later, or may be used as a mulch around trees, shrubbery, etc., if kept from touching their stems, roots or other parts. Care must be taken to have them thoroughly decomposed when they are mixed with soil around plants.

In the use of any fertilizer we must know what we are doing. If we apply nitrogenous material in proper quantities to a bed of lettuce, it will give fine results, for nitrogen makes leaves. If, however, we apply it in excess to beets or root crops, they will all "go to tops" and give the opposite of the desired results. Roots are formed from phosphates and potash.

Overstimulation is weakening to any plant. Young plants especially must be fertilized with care and only

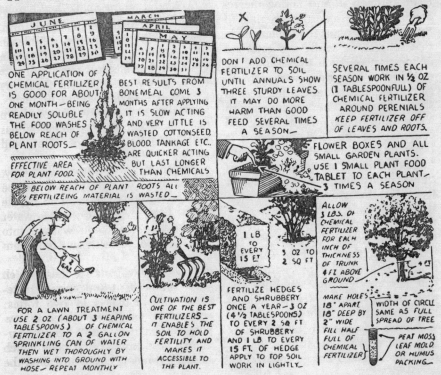

ONE APPLICATION OF CHEMICAL FERTILIZER IS GOOD FOR ABOUT ONE MONTH – BEING READILY SOLUBLE THE FOOD WASHES BELOW REACH OF PLANT ROOTS –

EFFECTIVE AREA FOR PLANT FOOD.

BELOW REACH OF PLANT ROOTS ALL FERTILIZEING MATERIAL IS WASTED –

BEST RESULTS FROM BONEMEAL COME 3 MONTHS AFTER APPLYING IT IS SLOW ACTING AND VERY LITTLE IS WASTED COTTONSEED, BLOOD, TANKAGE ETC.. ARE QUICKER ACTING BUT LAST LONGER THAN CHEMICALS

DON I ADD CHEMICAL FERTILIZER TO SOIL UNTIL ANNUALS SHOW THREE STURDY LEAVES IT MAY DO MORE HARM THAN GOOD FEED SEVERAL TIMES A SEASON –

SEVERAL TIMES EACH SEASON WORK IN ⅓ OZ (1 TABLESPOONFULL) OF CHEMICAL FERTILIZER AROUND PERENIALS KEEP FERTILIZER OFF OF LEAVES AND ROOTS.

FLOWER BOXES AND ALL SMALL GARDEN PLANTS. USE 1 SMALL PLANT FOOD TABLET TO EACH PLANT – 3 TIMES A SEASON

1 LB TO EVERY 15 FT

3 OZ TO 2 SQ FT

ALLOW 3 LBS. OF CHEMICAL FERTILIZER FOR EACH INCH OF THICKNESS OF TRUNK 4 FT ABOVE GROUND

FOR A LAWN TREATMENT USE 2 OZ (ABOUT 3 HEAPING TABLESPOONS) OF CHEMICAL FERTILIZER TO A 2 GALLON SPRINKLING CAN OF WATER THEN WET THOROUGHLY BY WASHING INTO GROUND WITH HOSE – REPEAT MONTHLY

CULTIVATION IS ONE OF THE BEST FERTILIZERS – IT ENABLES THE SOIL TO HOLD FERTILITY AND MAKES IT ACCESSIBLE TO THE PLANT.

FERTILIZE HEDGES AND SHRUBBERY ONCE A YEAR – 3 OZ (4½ TABLESPOONS) TO EVERY 2 SQ FT OF SHRUBBERY AND 1 LB TO EVERY 15 FT. OF HEDGE APPLY TO TOP SOIL WORK IN LIGHTLY –

MAKE HOLES 18" APART 18" DEEP BY 2" WIDE FILL HALF FULL OF CHEMICAL FERTILIZER

WIDTH OF CIRCLE SAME AS FULL SPREAD OF TREE

PEAT MOSS LEAF MOLD OR HUMUS PACKING.

after they are making healthy growth as a result of watering and cultivation.

Practical Fertility: How then are we to combine all the elements necessary to successful plant growth? *First,* by proper selection of location. *Second,* by addition of enough vegetable matter or humus, and *Third,* by the addition of any necessary chemicals. Having added the water-holding, soil-conditioning humus, our chemical elements are held in solution for a longer time. Also the humus itself, having a quantity of slowly available chemical elements, helps to provide a balanced ration for the plant.

Soil Testing: It is possible, by applying certain chemicals to a small amount of soil, or to water allowed to leach through it, and noting the reaction, to determine the amounts of the important plant food elements in that soil. To be really accurate and of most value, such tests should be made in a laboratory with complicated apparatus, and the results should be studied in connection with a careful examination of the physical condition of the land, the crops it bears, its management. State agricultural experiment stations and sometimes county agents will make such tests. But for gardeners who want to try their hand at simple soil testing there are inexpensive outfits with detailed instructions.

However, the testing of soils for acidity is a simpler procedure and can be done by almost any one. It is discussed in Chapter VII which deals with Acid-loving Plants.

Humus: If time can be taken for it, a fine way to condition soil is to plow under green forage crops, such

as clover, rye, vetch, etc.; but this is a long process and most of us want immediate results.

Other sources of humus are leaf-mold (decomposed leaves) such as accumulates on the floor of a forest or wood lot; commercial humus products dug from former swamps, ground and dried; and the compost heap, which should be a feature of every garden. Located where it is handy but not obtrusive, it is made of layers of vegetable refuse from garden and kitchen alternating with layers of soil, old sods and manure, if obtainable; dust occasionally with ground limestone, superphosphate, a complete fertilizer, or some special "activator" to hasten decomposition. See sketches on pages 46 and 280.

Animal manures make fine humus and fertilizers when properly decayed. Before they can be safely incorporated in the soil around a plant, they should be rotted for at least a year by composting. The danger from manures lies in the weed seeds they may contain as well as the heat in fresh horse manure which will burn off plant roots when they come in contact with it.

Peats: A good source of humus for small gardens is peat, which is divided into three classes: Swamp or Wood Peat, Bog or Sphagnum Peat, and Marsh or Sedge Peat.

Wood Peat is made largely of decomposed forest litter, tree branches, etc. Of swamp origin, it is highly acid. It is sometimes sold in seed stores, but as it may contain a percentage of soil it is likely to be expensive.

Bog Peat is largely derived from sphagnum moss. This is low in nitro-

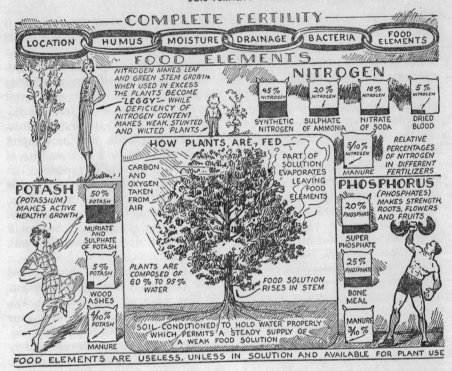

COMPLETE FERTILITY

LOCATION | HUMUS | MOISTURE | DRAINAGE | BACTERIA | FOOD ELEMENTS

FOOD ELEMENTS

NITROGEN MAKES LEAF AND GREEN STEM GROWTH. WHEN USED IN EXCESS THE PLANTS BECOME "LEGGY" — WHILE A DEFICIENCY OF NITROGEN CONTENT MAKES WEAK, STUNTED AND WILTED PLANTS.

NITROGEN

45% NITROGEN — SYNTHETIC NITROGEN
20% NITROGEN — SULPHATE OF AMMONIA
16% NITROGEN — NITRATE OF SODA
5% NITROGEN — DRIED BLOOD

5/10% NITROGEN — MANURE

RELATIVE PERCENTAGES OF NITROGEN IN DIFFERENT FERTILIZERS

HOW PLANTS ARE FED

CARBON AND OXYGEN TAKEN FROM AIR

PART OF SOLUTION EVAPORATES LEAVING FOOD ELEMENTS

POTASH (POTASSIUM) MAKES ACTIVE HEALTHY GROWTH

50% POTASH — MURIATE AND SULPHATE OF POTASH
5% POTASH — WOOD ASHES
4/10% POTASH — MANURE

PLANTS ARE COMPOSED OF 60% TO 95% WATER

FOOD SOLUTION RISES IN STEM

PHOSPHORUS (PHOSPHATES) MAKES STRENGTH, ROOTS, FLOWERS AND FRUITS

20% PHOSPHATE — SUPER PHOSPHATE
25% PHOSPHATE — BONE MEAL
3/10% — MANURE

SOIL CONDITIONED TO HOLD WATER PROPERLY WHICH PERMITS A STEADY SUPPLY OF A WEAK FOOD SOLUTION

FOOD ELEMENTS ARE USELESS, UNLESS IN SOLUTION AND AVAILABLE FOR PLANT USE

gen and highly acid. It is usually sold in bales imported chiefly from Canada, Germany, Holland and Sweden. It has not the readily available mechanical condition of domestic peat. It is suitable for acid loving plants such as Rhododendrons, Azaleas, etc., and has many other uses.

Sedge Peat is a marsh peat, made by the laying down of thousands of generations of grasses, sedges and reeds under water. Being only partly decomposed, it contains most of the elements of the plants in their original state.

In buying domestic peat moss, get sedge peat and see that it is not full of soil. The quantity of organic material determines how much dirt it contains.

If it is 95% organic it means 95% humus and 5% soil; but some wood peat runs as low as 50 or 60% organic and is expensive at any price. Ask for an analysis of any domestic peat before you purchase it.

SOIL PREPARATION

Careful tilling of the soil is one of the first essentials of making a flower bed or in fact of any kind of gardening. There are three types of ground preparation, as follows:

Digging: Turning the ground or ordinary digging is done with a spade or garden fork. Ground is turned one spit deep (a spit means the depth of soil that can be conveniently moved in one spadeful). In this operation, any ground conditioner such as humus or fertilizer should be first spread over the ground and then worked through the soil. If the ground is to lie through cold weather, the clods should not be broken up but left rough. All roots, woody weeds and large stones should be gathered up and removed. A small wooden scraper is convenient for cleaning wet soil off the spade.

Ridging: Vacant beds of heavy soil may be ridged for winter freezing by throwing the ground into little hills from six to twelve inches high so that the frost may penetrate more of the ground. Freezing breaks up soil into fine particles, leaving it more porous. It also kills the eggs of many insects by exposing them to the sun, wind, and birds which will help thin the ranks of next season's pests.

Double Digging: This is a lot more trouble, but is well worth while in making a garden. A line is stretched across the plot to be dug two feet from the end. A trench one spit deep and two feet wide is then dug, the dirt being wheeled to the opposite end of the area. On the bottom of the open trench may be thrown a quantity of sand or coal ashes, cinders or similar rubbish, together with leaves, straw, manure or other conditioning material, and this is spaded into the second spit of ground or subsoil. If this soil is hard clay use plenty of sand or cinders to make it light so that it will drain well and warm up more quickly. If it is sandy use more humus, leafmold, peat moss, etc. The garden line is then moved two feet more and the topsoil, mixed with suitable conditioning materials as in simple digging, is used to fill the first trench as a new one is dug.

The process is then repeated until the soil first removed is used to fill the last trench at the end of the garden.

Trenching or Triple Digging: This is a similar operation to double digging. Mark off with line, remove the topsoil two feet wide and the subsoil one foot wide. Dig up the soil beneath the second spit and move forward as previously explained.

The effects of trenching and double digging last for years, but of course, the surface soil is cultivated often. In respading, keep working in vegetable matter to further improve the surface soil.

Mulching: Frequent cultivation not only breaks up the particles of soil so that water is held in the spaces between more particles, but also keeps it from drying out by forming a dust blanket or mulch on the surface. This soil loosening also makes it easier for plants to send out roots thereby increasing their capacity to feed and grow.

Mulching is also done by covering the earth about plants with leaves, straw or manure. Sometimes this is done to keep moisture in the soil, to lower the soil temperature in summer, or to prevent root breakage from alternate freezing and thawing in winter. This feature is covered in several places later in this book.

SOME FERTILIZERS

Cow Manure: This is a "cold" manure but rich in plant food elements. Being wet and heavy, it is therefore a first-class manure for light to medium loams.

Horse Manure: A hot, dry manure which warms up the land and is excellent for heavy, cold, clayey soils: there is, as a rule, a fairly large percentage of litter in it, and this also adds to its warming effects. It is best where straw or peat is used for bedding. If wood shavings have been used the manure is of less value in the garden for the shavings when incorporated with the soil rot very slowly and may produce fungous growth. Such manure is, however, good for liquid manure or surface mulching.

Pig Manure: This is not unlike cow manure generally; a rich, strong manure, but rather cold. It is smelly stuff to work with unless well rotted. Most useful on light land.

Sheep, Poultry and Pigeon Manures: These, when free of litter, are more like a bulky guano than manure

in the ordinary sense of the term, they should be stored under cover and kept dry, and, if to be stored for any length of time, they will benefit considerably if each day's accumulation is very lightly dusted with superphosphate. Use ½ to ¾ lb. per square yard and hoe it in lightly, applying at cropping time or as a top-dressing to plants. When mixed with an equal quantity of fine soil it forms a good top-dressing.

Decayed farmyard manure should be dug in the ground in spring, fresh manure in autumn.

Green Manure: No scientific gardener will allow his land to stand long vacant, but immediately sows it down to seed of a quick-growing and leafy plant; this is then allowed to grow and is dug in when partly

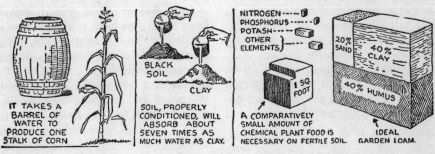

IT TAKES A BARREL OF WATER TO PRODUCE ONE STALK OF CORN

BLACK SOIL / CLAY

SOIL, PROPERLY CONDITIONED, WILL ABSORB ABOUT SEVEN TIMES AS MUCH WATER AS CLAY.

NITROGEN / PHOSPHORUS / POTASH / OTHER ELEMENTS / 1 SQ. FOOT

A COMPARATIVELY SMALL AMOUNT OF CHEMICAL PLANT FOOD IS NECESSARY ON FERTILE SOIL.

20% SAND / 40% CLAY / 40% HUMUS

IDEAL GARDEN LOAM.

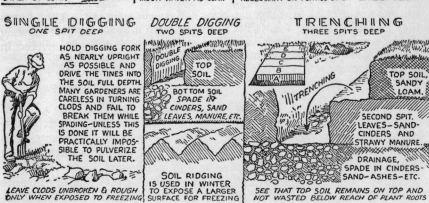

SINGLE DIGGING ONE SPIT DEEP

HOLD DIGGING FORK AS NEARLY UPRIGHT AS POSSIBLE AND DRIVE THE TINES INTO THE SOIL FULL DEPTH. MANY GARDENERS ARE CARELESS IN TURNING CLODS AND FAIL TO BREAK THEM WHILE SPADING—UNLESS THIS IS DONE IT WILL BE PRACTICALLY IMPOSSIBLE TO PULVERIZE THE SOIL LATER.

LEAVE CLODS UNBROKEN & ROUGH ONLY WHEN EXPOSED TO FREEZING

DOUBLE DIGGING TWO SPITS DEEP

DOUBLE DIGGING / TOP SOIL / BOTTOM SOIL SPADE IN CINDERS, SAND LEAVES, MANURE, ETC.

SOIL RIDGING IS USED IN WINTER TO EXPOSE A LARGER SURFACE FOR FREEZING

TRENCHING THREE SPITS DEEP

TRENCHING

TOP SOIL, SANDY LOAM.

SECOND SPIT. LEAVES—SAND—CINDERS AND STRAWY MANURE.

DRAINAGE, SPADE IN CINDERS—SAND—ASHES—ETC.

SEE THAT TOP SOIL REMAINS ON TOP AND NOT WASTED BELOW REACH OF PLANT ROOTS

grown. Italian Rye Grass, Buckwheat, Vetch, Rye, Soy Beans, Rape and Turnip make excellent green manure.

Bone Dust and Bone Meal: These are excellent fertilizers for general use, and have more lasting effect than many; the finer they are ground, the more quickly they act. They contain much phosphate and some nitrogen.

Nitrate of Soda: Rich in nitrogen, it is concentrated and quickly available. It is powerful material and will kill many plants if used in quantity or applied directly on their tissues. Dissolve a tablespoonful in a little hot water and dilute to two gallons.

Sulphate of Ammonia: One of the most powerful of all nitrogenous manures, slightly acid and valuable when fast growth is desired. It is not as apt to be washed away by rain as the nitrates. Beware of letting this fertilizer come into contact with vegetation as it is caustic.

Sulphate of Potash and Muriate of Potash: The two forms of potash most commonly in use. They are obtained as a white powder and should be applied to the ground a week or two before the growing season or even as a top-dressing to crops which have already started their growth.

Superphosphate: This material, sometimes called acid phosphate, supplies phosphoric acid more quickly available than does bone meal and is therefore used on root plants such as dahlias, peonies, gladiolus to stimulate growth. It is always well to add an equal amount of the more slowly available bone meal to provide for later fertility.

Wood Ashes: The ashes left after vegetable matter of any kind is burnt help to loosen and "sweeten" soil, and the fine dust has a percentage of potash in a most useful form. Use at cropping time or later, as a top-dressing around established plantings.

Coal Ashes: Fine, sifted ashes from small size hard coal sometimes obtainable from steam plants, etc., provide little if any food for plants, but are excellent for lightening the texture of a heavy soil. They should be spread and plowed or dug in the same as sand or peat moss, etc.

EDITOR'S NOTE: Much attention has been, and is constantly being, given to soil fertility problems. Among the results of this research are new recommendations as to soil management methods as well as endorsement of some old ones; new cultural machinery; and various measures for freeing soils of plant enemy organisms and improving soil texture. For more on these subjects see "GARDEN MAGIC MARCHES ON," page 439.—E.L.D.S.

CHAPTER III

LAWNS AND GRADING

*A child said, "What is the grass?" fetching
it to me with full hands;
How could I answer that child? I do not
know what it is any more than he.*

⁕ ⁕ ⁕ ⁕ ⁕

*I guess it is the handkerchief of the Lord,
A scented gift and remembrancer, design-
edly dropped,
Bearing the owner's name somewhere in
the corners, that we may see and re-
mark and say,
Whose?*

—WALT WHITMAN.

The first requisite of a lawn is adequate drainage. The ground must
have sufficient slope to carry off the
surface water, or be sufficiently open
and porous to absorb it; otherwise, it
must be drained with agricultural
tile as directed in Chapter II. A
good lawn can never be obtained
upon water-logged soil.

Secondly, a good lawn requires a
suitable topography, not too steep
nor broken with irregularities or
changes of level, partly for appearance sake, but largely to make the
maintenance of good sod easier. If
your house sits high above the street,
the lawn surface should slope down
so that it may be seen from the street.
Remember that a gradual leading of
the eye from house to lowest point
lessens the apparent height of the
building. A rise of one foot in four
is about the limit for a successful

lawn. If this does not take care of the
elevation it may be necessary to use
one or more terraces, but in this case
special attention must be given to
conditioning the soil as described
farther on.

It is hard to keep grass growing on
steep grades, especially if the surface
is convex or rounded upward (as
many terraces are). Most all of us
have observed that grass "burns"
first on steep banks and that at the
end of each winter much repairing
has to be done in such places, both
because of this injury and because
of soil washing. Consequently terrace
soil should be rich and deep, and in
seeding, grasses that are naturally
adapted to withstand drying out
should be used. Proper watering also
is indicated.

Sometimes, where conditions are
unusually bad, and when extensive
regrading is impracticable, it becomes
necessary to replace grass with
ground cover plants such as English
Ivy, Periwinkle, Japanese Spurge or
Evergreen-bittersweet (*Euonymus
radicans*), all of which are also useful
for covering bare spots beneath trees
and in other shady places where it
is hard to grow grass of any kind.
However, in most cases, especially
where the grounds are being laid out
and developed around a new house,

it is practical and most successful to take care of lawn and other garden problems by means of grading, carefully planned and carried out.

Grading: Thoroughness pays almost anywhere but especially in grading. The character of soil in your garden may be to a large extent determined by it. It is not a great deal of trouble for your contractor to scrape off the topsoil when making your cellar excavation. Also he can arrange to protect the topsoil around the house or to remove it so that the excavated material may go on the bottom, and the topsoil be respread in its proper place. If it is mixed up with the excavated material it is usually lost and considerable time and money must be spent to bring it to a point where it will successfully support vegetation.

The real way to grade, of course, as in all other things, is first to do it on paper. This means making what is called a topographic survey and usually requires the services of a civil engineer. If the plan is comparatively simple you may grade it with an ordinary chalk line or heavy cord. Fasten the string at the highest point in your grade and continue it to the lowest point. If there are humps in the grade, which do not permit this, a trench a few inches wide may be dug so that the line is stretched straight and tight. This line will enable you to see how much you will have to remove or fill. Stakes should then be driven into the ground in the bottom of the trench, leaving them exposed about six inches.

If you have an ordinary laborer doing your grading this will enable you to explain to him that the grade is to be six inches (6″) below the top of these stakes. By repeating this sort of check every five to ten feet, your laborer cannot go wrong with the grade no matter how uneven it may be. This is especially good when the lawn does not slope evenly to the street or other boundary of your lot. When this occurs the grade must be warped, so to speak, to fit the sidewalks along the street or the shifting grade of your neighbor's lawn. The grade along your foundation planting should be level if possible and all grades should start from this point.

By the above method, as you will change your grade every five or ten feet, your stakes will be set correctly at every point along the line. It is only necessary to have two fixed points—the top and bottom of the grade.

If you do not want an even grade, and would prefer a rolling one, it is always safe to use what is known as the OG curve. An OG curve is simply a compensated curve, that is, if your grade curves several inches or feet above your line at the starting point, it should be hollowed out an equal number of inches or feet below your line at the bottom of the grade. Both of these curves should be approximately the same length. Do not have a long mound and then have a little short curve at the bottom. This may look all right, but the balanced curve is always safe.

HOW TO MAKE A LAWN

Time: For over one hundred years, experts have been advising fall sowing but the fact remains that much grass seed is still sold in the spring, and the late spring at that. Nature sows her seed in the fall, but man seems to think it more convenient to do his lawn work in the spring. Every hour of intelligent effort expended during September is worth several hours in the spring.

Weeds disturbed in the fall must go through the hardship of winter in a weakened condition with little chance for survival. But fall-sown grass has the benefit of the fall rains and mild weather (cool, damp nights and warm days) in which to ger-

SOME PRINCIPLES OF GRADING

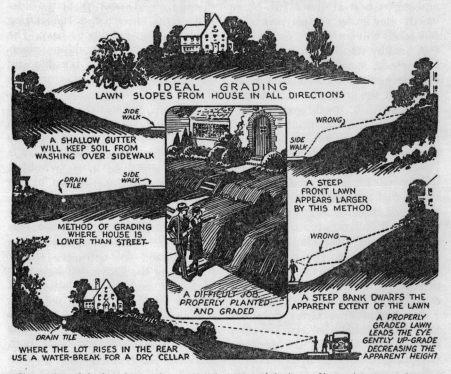

The grading of the front lawn makes or ruins the setting of the house. Sloping lots are coming more and more to be appreciated for their possibilities in adding interest to the landscape plan. The opportunities for original planning and a unique setting of the house are so much greater than in a level plot that their value outweighs the obstacles to be overcome.

A steep bank leads the eye abruptly from the street and as the flat surface above it is not visible, the house appears to be built directly above the sidewalk. When the lawn is so sloped as to be readily visible from the street the travel of vision is prolonged and the distance from the street appears greater. The more gently these exposed surfaces are presented to the eye the greater this distance appears. For instance, if a sharp rise is necessary it should be offset by a gentle slope. This will minimize the effect of the abrupt rise, causing a break or pause in the travel of vision.

In the rear of the house this same principle applies to the construction of the garden. If it is to be viewed from the house it must be so sloped that the flat surfaces do not present their edge to the observer nor appear to be standing on end.

minate and become established before winter.

Late August or early September is the ideal time but even a planting in October is better than waiting until spring. The warm days of the fall are sufficient for the grass but not hot enough to sprout weed seeds. Grass grows at a temperature of 45° and grows best at about 70°. Some weeds may grow at this point but few seeds will sprout.

A healthy stand of grass will combat weeds successfully. Once the seed is germinated and established in the fall, the grass seems to toughen and develop a sturdy root system; thus it is ready in the spring to spread into a good thick turf and hold its own against the weeds.

The most important fact to be remembered in grass seed germination is that the seeding must be kept moist for three or four weeks. Seed requires from ten to fourteen days to germinate and once allowed to dry the process stops. The difficulty of holding moisture in the late spring or summer is one of the obstacles to any great success at those times.

The Foundation: Grass does not grow well on either hard packed clay, incapable of allowing the penetration of air or water, or in a thin sandy soil so porous that no water will remain in it. Most lawns receive too much water in the spring and fall and this causes them to pack. Unless the drainage is good the grass may be killed by the standing water, no matter how much other care has been bestowed upon it.

Examine your soil by digging down through it. If it has two to three inches of good friable loam on top and four to six inches of good drainage soil below, you can turn it from a poor or below average lawn into a fine one as follows:

Remove all weeds in an intelligent manner. This includes crab grass and all coarse textured grasses. See special instructions for this under their headings. Level up any resulting depressions and seed them and the rest of the lawn, using a good mixture. Stir or shake it constantly to keep the smaller seeds from going to the bottom. Sow the seed on a still dry day, or in the evening.

Roll lightly and when the new grass is up, fertilize the entire lawn using five pounds of a good lawn food to 1000 sq. ft., washing it well into the grass roots to avoid burning. Apply it dissolved in water with a sprinkling can, if you wish.

A still better treatment is to apply a top-dressing of fine compost, made of one part sand to two parts domestic peat humus, before applying the fertilizer. This will work into the soil during the heaving and thawing of winter and provide better conditions for the following season. It will also keep the fertilizer available for a longer period, and repeated over a period of years will work wonders in building up a good turf. A full sized bale of peat moss will cover from 200 to 500 sq. ft. of lawn.

Making a New Lawn: Many lawns started on earth removed from cellar excavations have little chance to be anything but a nuisance to their owners. If the grass is patchy and the soil hard packed and bare of water-holding humus, it is best to remake it. This is a considerable undertaking, both as to labor and expense, and should not be taken lightly. However, it is more economical in the long run to get a good foundation than to spend money year after year without getting results.

If the expense is too great, it is a good plan to rebuild a part each year simply removing weeds and freshening up the remainder as directed above. Thus over a period of years the entire lawn may be rebuilt without severe expenditure at any one time.

The making of a new lawn is not intricate when once we understand the reasons for it. First, stake out the area and, beginning at one edge, use a spade to remove a strip of topsoil

four feet wide and four inches deep, piling it on old sacks or carpets outside the staked area. This exposes the bottom ground or subsoil. If this is hard clay, we spread over it one inch of sand or two inches of fine ashes, cinders, etc., together with an inch or two of old manure, leafmold, peat moss, compost, etc. Scraps of old sod, lawn clippings, leaves, etc., may also be incorporated in reasonable amounts.

The use of lime in the topsoil of a lawn is to be discouraged unless a soil analysis has definitely revealed an excess of acidity. It encourages weeds in ordinary growing soil and is generally unbeneficial. However, it is of great use in break-

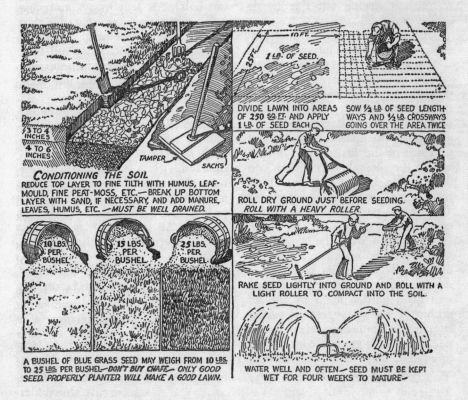

CONDITIONING THE SOIL
REDUCE TOP LAYER TO FINE TILTH WITH HUMUS, LEAF-MOULD, FINE PEAT-MOSS, ETC.—BREAK UP BOTTOM LAYER WITH SAND, IF NECESSARY, AND ADD MANURE, LEAVES, HUMUS, ETC.—MUST BE WELL DRAINED.

DIVIDE LAWN INTO AREAS OF 250 SQ. FT. AND APPLY 1 LB. OF SEED EACH. SOW ½ LB. OF SEED LENGTH-WAYS AND ½ LB. CROSSWAYS GOING OVER THE AREA TWICE.

ROLL DRY GROUND JUST BEFORE SEEDING. ROLL WITH A HEAVY ROLLER.

10 LBS. PER BUSHEL — 15 LBS. PER BUSHEL — 25 LBS. PER BUSHEL

RAKE SEED LIGHTLY INTO GROUND AND ROLL WITH A LIGHT ROLLER TO COMPACT INTO THE SOIL.

A BUSHEL OF BLUE GRASS SEED MAY WEIGH FROM 10 LBS. TO 25 LBS. PER BUSHEL.—DON'T BUY CHAFE.—ONLY GOOD SEED, PROPERLY PLANTED, WILL MAKE A GOOD LAWN.

WATER WELL AND OFTEN.—SEED MUST BE KEPT WET FOR FOUR WEEKS TO MATURE.—

ing up hard packed clay and if your subsoil is composed of this, use it generously. Use ground limestone or hydrated lime distributing it upon the ashes and sand until they are well covered. Do not be afraid of using too much.

Work these materials into the bottom soil, breaking it up finely. This is most easily done with a spading fork. It is essential that this layer not only drain well and quickly but that some moisture be retained in it at all times.

If the subsoil is sandy or loose, the sand and cinders will not be needed, but a larger quantity of water holding material (old manure, peat moss, leafmold or humus) will be required to prevent drying out due to the easier drainage.

The bottom soil of the first strip is now firmed back into place with a tamper and the topsoil of the second strip is removed. Instead of piling it upon the sacks, we sift it through a coarse wire screen or otherwise remove all roots and lumps, and deposit it upon the packed bottom soil of the first strip. The subsoil of the second strip is then conditioned as before stated and the process repeated over the entire area. The topsoil on the sacks is used to cover the last strip.

The topsoil over the entire area should then be mixed to a fine condition. All grass roots must be removed and the entire top area made into good garden loam by the addition of rotted vegetable matter, commercial humus, leafmold, fine peat, etc. Good garden loam is made up of 40% clay, 40% vegetable matter and 20% sand. If the soil is heavy,

sand should be added; if sandy, more humus is needed.

Cottonseed meal, sewage sludge, tankage and bone meal may be thoroughly worked into this soil at the rate of 25 lbs. to 1000 sq. ft. If this is done, water well and do not seed for several days. If chemical plant food is used, it is best applied in weak solution after the grass is sprouted. Seeds do not need fertilizer to germinate—they need moisture and warmth.

After the soil is prepared, rake it smooth and roll firm with a light roller while it is still dry. Roll it twice, the second time at right angles to the first. Now sow the seed using one pound to each 250 sq. ft. sowing one-half of it lengthways and one-half across, thus covering the area twice. Rake in the seed lightly or better still cover with sifted soil, then roll with a light roller to firm the seed in the soil, sprinkle lightly but well, and keep it wet.

The covering of the thoroughly moist seed bed with a single thickness of burlap or muslin will help keep it wet until the seed has germinated, when the cloth can be raised ten inches high, by stakes, for a day or two to allow the young grass to harden before its full exposure to the sun. All watering may be done during germination, through the cloth.

The young grass should be allowed to grow three inches high before the first cutting.

SEED FOR THE LAWN

Use the best of seed and see that it is guaranteed weed free. Heavy grass seed is usually free from chaff and is the most economical in the long run while light cheap seed gives poor germination.

It is important that the same kind of grass seed be used consistently over the whole lawn. Changing from one seed mixture to another is bound to make the lawn patchy. For even texture or a velvety appearance, plant together only the kind of seeds which will grow in the same kind of soil.

Beware of ready mixed seed unless it comes from or over the name of a highly reliable firm. Know what you are getting in grass seed.

In the northern section of the United States the following grasses are recommended:

Kentucky Blue Grass: In buying it do not let yourself become confused into taking Canada Blue Grass or Orchard Grass which are very inferior. While Kentucky Blue Grass is considered the best lawn grass, it has the drawback that it needs a resting period in midsummer; it also may stain light clothes and shoes. It has the advantage of forming a thick turf which will grow in either alkaline or slightly acid soil. It starts slowly but once established puts up a good fight against weeds.

Red Top: Second in importance is Red Top, which goes well with Kentucky Blue because they make up for each other's deficiencies. Red Top is a good beginner, will grow most anywhere and has its resting period in the fall after the Blue Grass has recovered. It does not stain and is often used for grass walks and play spots.

Fescues: Chewings Fescue is the only fine textured grass which has been successful in shade. Red Fescue and Various-leaved Fescue are sometimes used in lawn mixtures of Blue Grass and Red Top. They mature late in the season and are drought resisting, making a good summer and fall lawn. They grow well in acid soil which is *not* a congenial home for weeds, and will survive some shade as well as dry conditions.

Mixtures: If you prefer to buy ready mixed seed, get it only from a thoroughly reliable dealer. Try to analyze your conditions and plant accordingly. Four parts of Kentucky Blue Grass to one part Red Top is a good base mixture. To this you may add the other grasses suited for your conditions. If you are starting a new lawn in spring, add one part of Italian Rye Grass and a small amount of Timothy. These are quick growing annuals which will help start the first year's crop and "nurse" it.

Perennial Rye Grass: This is a tough, quick-growing grass which is added to starting mixtures. It helps keep out weeds until the lawn is established. It is tough, can stand much traffic, and for this reason is used on playfields and exhibition grounds. It is hard to cut, but will yield to the other grasses in a few years.

Shade Mixtures: For shade, add to the base mixture some Chewings Fescue, which is fine textured; *Poa trivialis* (Rough Stalked Meadow Grass), or *Poa nemoralis* (Wood Meadow Grass). The denser the shade, the larger the proportion of shade enduring types used.

Many shady seedings fail because of the use of cheap seed. Seedsmen don't sell cheap seed because they like to, but because you demand price. Good shade seed costs money; it is hard to raise and harvest.

White Clover: Many owners insist upon clover in the mixture—why has never been satisfactorily disclosed. Where a lawn is to be left to shift for itself, it may have some uses, but in a well-kept lawn, it has many drawbacks and few advantages. It leaves a bare spot to carry through the winter and its texture and many white flower heads spoil the velvety appearance of any lawn. It thrives only in alkaline soil which favors weeds. A luxuriant crop of clover usually means plenty of lawn pests. Its only advantage is that it may, in conjunction with Blue Grass, survive sandy alkaline conditions where Red Top burns out.

Bent Grass: This is a very particular plant, susceptible to drought and pests, and most successful only on the northern Pacific coast, New York and New England states. Unless you live in these areas or are willing to give a large amount of intelligent care, including almost daily watering, don't attempt its cultivation. If you are intrigued by its velvety appearance, ask the manager of a golf course concerning the cost of construction and care of Bent Grass putting greens.

CARE OF THE LAWN

Water: To do a lawn any good, water should penetrate four inches. Light sprinklings do injury—not good; they are about the worst treatment you can give your lawn. The idea that watering should not be done in sunlight is wrong. If enough water is applied, it can be done at any time.

Data compiled in golf course irrigation studies show that grass on ordinary clay soil requires at least one inch of water weekly. Rainfall in the north central states is rated at about 3½ inches per month. Were these rains nicely spaced, little watering would be necessary but it is usually a flood or a drought. Constant vigilance is required to carry over dry spells.

It is best to water only once a week on clay soil but it should be applied so that the water is quickly absorbed into the soil. Standing water is harmful. We should also bear in mind that sandy soils dry out more quickly and lighter and more frequent waterings are necessary.

How much water to put on a lawn is always a problem. We show here a simple method of measuring. Cut off the bottom three inches of three tomato cans and fasten them upon a light board so that they are under the sprinkler at equal distances. The amount of water in each can will show how much the area has received. We use three because lawn sprinklers do not all distribute evenly.

Left out in a rain this device will

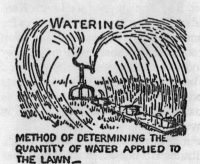

METHOD OF DETERMINING THE QUANTITY OF WATER APPLIED TO THE LAWN—

measure the precipitation and enable you to judge how much supplementary watering is necessary.

Rolling: A lawn should be rolled just once or at the most twice each year, at the time when the frost is coming out of the ground. The idea is not to smooth out the lawn—this is done by filling and grading. Rolling is for the purpose of pushing the grass roots back into contact with the soil, after the heaving due to frosts. If it is gone over twice, roll at right angles. If you roll when it is wet enough to puddle the ground, you smother the grass roots by ejecting all the air necessary to the growth of beneficial bacteria. There is no reason for or point in rolling in dry weather.

As elsewhere explained, high cutting in warm weather shades the grass roots and helps the cooling of the soil to the state most favorable for the action of nitrifying bacteria. Many people become discouraged by the burning out or browning of grass each summer. This is due to two causes—lack of moisture, and the resting period of the grasses of which the lawn is made. As previously explained, Blue Grass matures and rests (thins out—turns brown) in midsummer. But it recuperates early in the fall. Red Top stays green all summer but rests in the fall. By a proper combination of grasses, we can have green lawns all season if we maintain food and moisture conditions.

Importance of Moisture: Grass and other leaf crops require large quantities of nitrogen. This, to be of any use to the grass, must be in the form of nitrates, and also in solution. Nitrates do not form at all at over 115 degrees and form best at 85 degrees. Under a summer sun the soil often goes over this latter temperature for long periods. Water is the greatest temperature regulator known. So it must not only be applied but also be held in the soil to be of use.

Water is only held in the soil by decayed vegetable matter. If this is placed in the soil when the lawn is made, all is well; but even so, it is still good practice to apply a yearly dressing of compost. This may be made of a mixture of domestic sedge peat humus or if this is not obtainable, shredded peat moss. Mix with one-third sand, if your soil is clay, or one-third finely pulverized clay, if it is sandy. Apply the mulch half an inch thick in fall, finely pulverized so it will wash into the roots. Any bulk left on the grass will smother and kill it. The heaving due to thawing and freezing in winter, tears the grass roots loose from the soil. The compost then washes into these spaces and when compacted by rolling in the spring, remains part of the turf. The mulch also holds in suspension for plant use any other fertilizer applied. The peat (either moss or humus) is slightly acid. Most grasses grow well in a lawn slightly acid, while weeds love lime or alkaline soil. In applying peat mulches, we discourage weeds without harming the grass. Most city water contains some lime and if applied to the soil in watering encourages weeds. Peat helps to counteract this condition. You may also mulch with rotted leafmold or home-made compost, filling out any deficiency of supply with the above mentioned materials.

Mowing: Mowing must be done

with intelligence. Grass allowed to go to seed does not spread and causes a spotty lawn. The little seed gained by this process is more than offset by the lack of root increase and unsightly appearance. Grass should be cut quite short until the middle of May. Fertilize it well and try to get a complete ground cover. After this is accomplished, keep it cut as long as possible. Lower the wooden roller on your mower, or better still, alter your mower or secure one that will cut three inches high.

Plenty of leaf growth will shade the grass roots in hot weather and,

best of all, provides a simple, laborless way of preventing weeds and crab grass from seeding. Weeds will not grow in a thick, shady stand of grass and crab grass will not germinate even in semishade. Mow frequently and let the clippings work down to the roots. Short grass clippings are the easiest way to return vegetable matter to the soil.

Long grass, however, must be removed, as must leaves, and no compost should be added in hot weather. Grass is easily smothered during this period. All grasses should go into the winter not less than one inch long.

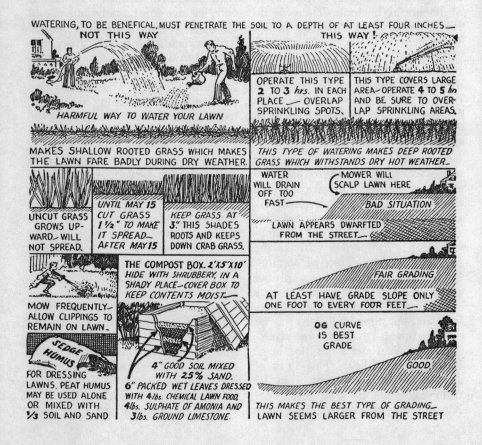

WATERING, TO BE BENEFICAL, MUST PENETRATE THE SOIL TO A DEPTH OF AT LEAST FOUR INCHES —

NOT THIS WAY

HARMFUL WAY TO WATER YOUR LAWN

MAKES SHALLOW ROOTED GRASS WHICH MAKES THE LAWN FARE BADLY DURING DRY WEATHER.

THIS WAY!

OPERATE THIS TYPE 2 TO 3 *hrs.* IN EACH PLACE — OVERLAP SPRINKLING SPOTS.

THIS TYPE COVERS LARGE AREA— OPERATE 4 TO 5 *hrs* AND BE SURE TO OVERLAP SPRINKLING AREAS.

THIS TYPE OF WATERING MAKES DEEP ROOTED GRASS WHICH WITHSTANDS DRY HOT WEATHER.

UNCUT GRASS GROWS UPWARD— WILL NOT SPREAD.

UNTIL MAY 15 CUT GRASS 1½" TO MAKE IT SPREAD— AFTER MAY 15

KEEP GRASS AT 3." THIS SHADES ROOTS AND KEEPS DOWN CRAB GRASS.

WATER WILL DRAIN OFF TOO FAST

MOWER WILL SCALP LAWN HERE

BAD SITUATION

LAWN APPEARS DWARFTED FROM THE STREET

MOW FREQUENTLY— ALLOW CLIPPINGS TO REMAIN ON LAWN.

THE COMPOST BOX. 2'X5'X10' HIDE WITH SHRUBBERY, IN A SHADY PLACE— COVER BOX TO KEEP CONTENTS MOIST—

FAIR GRADING

AT LEAST HAVE GRADE SLOPE ONLY ONE FOOT TO EVERY FOUR FEET—

SEDGE HUMUS

FOR DRESSING LAWNS, PEAT HUMUS MAY BE USED ALONE OR MIXED WITH ⅓ SOIL AND SAND.

4" GOOD SOIL MIXED WITH 25% SAND. 6" PACKED WET LEAVES DRESSED WITH 4 *lbs.* CHEMICAL LAWN FOOD, 4 *lbs.* SULPHATE OF AMONIA AND 3 *lbs.* GROUND LIMESTONE.

OG CURVE IS BEST GRADE

GOOD

THIS MAKES THE BEST TYPE OF GRADING— LAWN SEEMS LARGER FROM THE STREET

Fertilizers: Chemical fertilizers offered for lawn foods are usually salts, easily dissolved, and therefore readily available for plant use. They should contain mostly nitrogen, such as 10 per cent nitrogen to 4 each of phosphate and potash (10-4-4). This when properly applied lasts about four to six weeks and an even distribution is necessary and essential. If distributed dry by hand, divide the quantity in two and scatter it both ways across the area, following the directions given for sowing grass seed. The use of a mechanical distributor or spreader (which can also be used for seeding) is to be recommended. Distribution in solution is always good, but in any case be sure to wash any fertilizer off the leaves to avoid burning them.

We illustrate a water siphon which will distribute chemical fertilizer without the risk of burning the grass leaves. The pipe fittings are readily obtainable and the spout is made to spray the water in a fan shape. Cut

WATER SIPHON FOR APPLYING CHEMICAL PLANT FOOD TO THE SOIL, SAFELY AND EVENLY

the pipe with a hack saw and hammer it into the shape shown.

Dissolve as great a quantity of chemical lawn food as your bucket of water will take up and apply the proper amount to the area which you have measured off. Five pounds to 1,000 sq. ft. every four to six weeks is the usual method of application.

The same applies to sulphate of ammonia which is also to be recommended. It is high in nitrogen, has a slight acid reaction and when used on alkaline or neutral soils, discourages weeds.

Organic fertilizers such as bone meal, sewage sludge, blood, tankage, and the like, while usually more expensive, work excellently in compost. They are not so quickly exhausted as the chemical foods. Sludge and bone meal are also valuable because of their ground conditioning effect.

Bone meal applied in the fall is recommended for established lawns. A good fall (September) application is 3 parts bone meal, 3 parts wood ashes and one part sulphate of ammonia, applied at the rate of 7 lbs. to 1,000 sq. ft. and washed into the roots. Cottonseed meal is sometimes low enough in price to be used. Mix it with the compost. A growing season application of cottonseed meal, 3 parts, and sulphate of ammonia, 1 part, is very good. Sewage sludge and sulphate of ammonia in the same proportions is excellent. These materials or mixtures are applied 25 lbs. to 1,000 sq. ft. Their chief advantage over chemical foods is that they last longer, being slowly available and not being washed quickly below the reach of the grass roots. The use of manure in the topsoil or as a dressing is to be discouraged as it is a source of weed seed, no matter how well rotted. It is also liable to smother patches of grass and leave bare spots. Only finely shredded material should be used upon grasses, as they smother easily. Mushroom soil and spent hot-bed manure make good compost and the weed danger is somewhat less.

Grass Under Trees: The denser the shade, the harder it is to grow grass. For shade sow 5, 6, or 7 lbs. to 1,000 sq. ft. Few people are willing to put forth the effort necessary to keep grass under trees. First, it requires good cultivation and conditioning as

CRAB GRASS ERADICATION—
SUMMER AND FALL TREATMENT—

PULL UPRIGHT WITH RAKE

MOW AS SHORT AS POSSIBLE

DIG OUT WITH STRAIGHT KNIFE

RESEED AREAS. *KEEP WET FOR TWO WEEKS*

SPRING CARE

TO MAY 15 *th*.: TO INCREASE SIDE-WARD GROWTH, CUT GRASS SHORT.

FROM MAY 15 *th*. TO SEPT 15 *th* KEEP GRASS THREE INCHES LONG—THIS PROVIDES SHADE UNDER THE GRASS—
CRAB GRASS WILL NOT GERMINATE IN, EVEN, PARTIAL SHADE

deep as the surface roots of the tree permit, and then the planting of a shady grass seed mixture. With these factors properly cared for and the right seed used, the balance is a matter of watering and feeding.

The fine tree roots come to the surface in search of food and water and are in constant competition with the grass for nourishment. The tree, being the stronger, usually wins.

Grass can usually be maintained by a good soaking once a week. Double the amount needed for open lawns is necessary, and remember that you are also supplying water to a tree which transpires it quickly and that much of the lighter rainfall does not penetrate to the grass beneath the tree at all. Frequent applications of fertilizer allow the grass to get its share before the hungry tree roots snatch it up. Application of a solution of one pound of chemical lawn food to each 200 sq. ft. twice a month will insure a luxuriant growth; use one pound to 100 sq. ft. if applied monthly.

In summary, if your grass dies under the trees, it is either starved or parched. Many carpeting or ground cover plants will grow where grass will not. See Chapter IX, "VINES."

CONTROLLING SOME LAWN ENEMIES

Crab Grass: (When Mr. Biles wrote this book, he reflected the general opinion in saying, "There are no cures; once this pest has infested your lawn, it is there until frost." Although that is no longer true, as noted in "GARDEN MAGIC MARCHES ON," page 439, his advice is still sound.—EDITOR)

Prevention is comparatively simple. Bear in mind that the plant is an annual. It originates only from seed during June. Its roots are killed by frost each fall and offer no further danger. It will not grow in even partial shade and is seldom if ever seen where the shadow of a tree or building passes.

After it has sprouted it is a rampant grower. The shoots spread out like the fingers of a hand, rooting at every joint to repeat the process of sending out more. In this way it is able to cover large areas, smothering the other grasses and leaving bare spots when it is killed by frost.

Keep down the spread of the pest during the summer by pulling it upright with a rake and cutting it short with the mower. Be careful to catch and burn all the seeding stalks. Its vitality is so great that the smallest stalk allowed to lie will take root, flower and produce seed. In September, if feasible, dig it out completely two inches deep, fill the cleared spots with new soil and seed with perennial grasses. Be careful to keep these spots moist so as to obtain a good stand of grass before frost.

In the spring, until May 15th, the grass should be cut short to develop a strong root system and to encourage it to spread sideward into a thick turf. From May 15th until September 15th it should be kept cut three inches high. No crab grass will grow in this shade and in addition, this shading will keep the grass from burning during hot weather. It may be necessary to make alterations to your mower to cut three inches high, but it is the only sure way.

One very effective way of killing crab grass is by shading with tar paper pegged down tightly with long heavy wire staples. Ten days usually finishes it in hot weather. The Blue Grass will be browned and perhaps killed but will start again from the roots. In either case (weeding or covering) start on the plants early in July, while they are small and easy to kill, and you will not have to discolor the lawn by causing large bare spots. Be sure to cover enough ground to get the entire patch of crab grass.

Other Weeds:

*Now 'tis spring, and weeds are shallow
   rooted;*
*Suffer them now, and they'll o'er grow the
   garden*
And choke the herbs for want of husbandry.
                                    —SHAKESPEARE.

You may remove the plantain and buckhorn from the lawn by the use of a weed knife or long-handled weed spud. One cutting will usually be sufficient as the plants are shallow rooted. The yarrow is easily controlled by mowing or cutting early in the season.

Cutting the tops off the dandelion is very foolish practice, unless you expect to repeat every two weeks. This will weaken the plant and kill it, but unless a cutting is followed up, it will do more harm than good. The root of a dandelion is sometimes 18 inches long and stores up enough food to send out several new shoots after each cutting. If the cutting is repeated often enough this food supply will eventually be exhausted and the plant will die. If not repeated sufficiently, it will cause several plants to grow in the place of the one.

Stab the single dandelion with a rod dipped in acid (Sulphuric 1800 gravity, or Nitric). Hang a glass jar or bottle on wires and use a long rod to avoid stooping. Do not let the acid come in contact with skin or clothing as it is very corrosive.

If the lawn is so infested as to make this treatment too laborious, spray with iron sulphate, mixed 1½ lbs. to the gallon of water, spraying one gallon to 300 sq. ft. Apply as a fine mist until leaves are thoroughly wet, first bruising them slightly with the back of a rake. This must be repeated about three times, ten days apart, and should not be done in hot, dry weather as it may injure the grass. It will kill plantain and other broad-leaved weeds but will also kill clover and will make rust stains on concrete walks and foundations.

Speedwell is that tough-rooted weed, which lies close to the earth, rooting at nearly every joint and spreading out over the edge of your walk. Pull it out and you have several plants instead of one. Its leaves are about a quarter of an inch broad and it propagates from seed as well as by rooting at the joint.

Chickweed comes to us in two varieties. The common chickweed which is an annual and propagates from seed, blooms throughout the year and may be found in gardens and cultivated fields as well as the lawn. Its leaves are somewhat oval and it has small white flowers, which bloom all summer and at every warm period during the winter. Mouse-ear chickweed is a perennial and also propagates from seed. The whole plant is covered with tiny hair, a sort of dirty gray.

These three plants with the common ground ivy, which has a small purple bloom and would be somewhat decorative if it were not a pest in our lawns, constitute the most prevalent creeping weeds.

The common chickweed may be controlled by hand pulling in small quantities, but it is foolish to attempt large scale control in that manner. One ounce of sodium chlorate in a gallon of water will cover 100 square feet (10 x 10) of these pests. Sodium chlorate may be obtained at most drug stores in small quantities, and almost any creeping weed can be controlled by spraying with it. But it

KILLING WEEDS—

DANDELIONS: IN LARGE AREAS THEY CAN BE KILLED BY SPRAYING WITH IRON SULPHATE—FIRST BRUISE LEAVES WITH BACK OF RAKE—

ALL CREEPING WEEDS: CHICKWEED, GROUND IVY, ETC., CAN. BE EASILY ERADICATED WITH A SODIUM CHLORATE SPRAY

KILL SCATTERED DANDELIONS WITH ACID APPLICATION.

PLANTAINS AND OTHER WEEDS YIELD READILY TO THE WEED SPUD.

is dangerous, because it is an extreme fire hazard; it is not inflammable by itself, but spilled upon a floor, clothing or anything burnable, it may take fire as it becomes dry. Keep it out of doors in tight glass containers. Shoes and clothing worn while spraying should be kept away from the building or washed thoroughly. Use metal containers, wear rubber boots that can be easily washed, or old shoes that can be discarded. Don't light matches or smoke near it. Keep tightly corked and destroy papers, etc., used in making up a solution and mix the spray out of doors. Two or more sprayings are necessary; use the spray as soon as the plant begins to reproduce and reseed at once.

If you do not care to try the sodium method, wet the plant and apply ammonium sulphate direct to the leaves. This, repeated, will kill them and allow the grass to come through as the ammonium sulphate will also fertilize the soil.

There are many recommendations for killing weeds with gasoline. But this writer has never found them particularly efficient. If you wish to try this material and have only a few weeds to kill, you can use the following method:

Solder a large nail to the end of an ordinary large squirt oil can. Jab the nail into the heart of the weed and squirt the gasoline. One application should kill common broad-leaf weeds except dandelions which will need several. Some success can be obtained by merely applying the gasoline with a squirt can without the nail. Many people are enthusiastic users of this method.

Moss: Moss is not truly a weed nor is it a sign that your ground is sour or acid. Moss grows on the alkali fields of the west. It is, however, a sure sign that the soil is poor. Supply food and moisture and the grass will come in thicker and the moss disappear.

Pests: Most grass is usually free from insect attack. *Grubs and earthworms* may be destroyed by the application of 5 lbs. of Arsenate of Lead mixed with a bushel of slightly damp (but not wet) sand, and applied to 1,000 sq. ft. when the grass is thoroughly dry. It may be necessary to repeat yearly for several years. *Sod Web Worms* are the caterpillars (½ to ¾ inches long) of a small moth or miller. They hatch from eggs in the grass and cut it off at or below the surface. They are indicated by small brown patches of grass which gradually become larger. They may be found hidden in their webs among the grass roots. Apply Arsenate of Lead 7 or 8 lbs. to 1,000 sq. ft. either with sand, as above described, or very lightly with a dust gun. Distribute evenly, dust in with a broom and wash into the soil with a hose, nozzle removed.

Ants may be killed by squirting Carbon Bisulphide into the holes with an oil can. Use it only out of doors and away from fire and cover treated hills with wet newspapers. Another method is to soak hills with kerosene or gasoline, and set them afire; this, however, will destroy the grass.

Moles can be killed with a trap sold for that purpose or by fumes from an automobile exhaust conveyed into the holes by use of a garden hose. Allow motor to run twenty minutes or more and retard spark if possible. Calcium cyanide powder is sold to be placed in the runs at five-foot intervals. It gives off a strong poisonous gas and must be handled carefully if at all. Close all openings to the runways before fumigating. Pepper inserted in the burrows liberally is said to drive moles away if repeated once or twice. About ¼ lb. per application is necessary for a small burrow. Poisoning by opening the shells of several peanuts and inserting a crystal of Strychnine in each has been recommended, as has shelled corn soaked in Arsenic.

Sometimes moles may be drowned by flooding their runways with a hose. They usually work in these burrows between 7 and 8 o'clock in the morning. By watching at that time, armed with a pitchfork, they can be killed as they are seen moving the earth in going through the runways.

CARE OF THE LAWN MOWER

A little regular care of your lawn mower will make a lot less labor. If you wish to clean it and make it run easier, remove the gear wheels with a screw driver or wrench (Fig. 1) then flush out the interior with gasoline or kerosene and clean each individual tooth or gear with a stiff brush. Remove the pinion housing and slip off the pinion gear (Fig. 2). Figure 3 shows the ratchet arrangement which allows the mower to run freely backward, but propels the revolving blades when pushed forward. If this is removed, care should be taken to get it back exactly as it was taken out. All these parts should be carefully washed and repacked with cup grease. The gears should be then lubricated with a good grade of lubricating oil.

Figure 4 shows method of raising

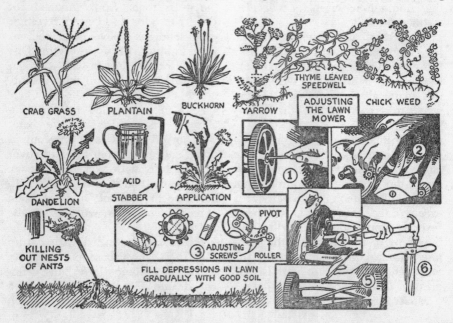

CRAB GRASS PLANTAIN BUCKHORN YARROW THYME LEAVED SPEEDWELL CHICK WEED

ADJUSTING THE LAWN MOWER

DANDELION ACID STABBER APPLICATION

KILLING OUT NESTS OF ANTS

PIVOT

3 ADJUSTING SCREWS ROLLER

FILL DEPRESSIONS IN LAWN GRADUALLY WITH GOOD SOIL

the lower blade by lowering the wooden roller; the illustrated method of tightening the handle (Fig. 6) is obvious. Paint the mower with a good grade of metallic paint (Fig. 5); it will help keep it in good condition.

When the mower leaves ridges in the lawn, it may be dull or there may be play in the bearings of the revolving blade assembly. There is usually some means provided for tightening these. Sometimes it is necessary to have the sharpening done by machinery in the hands of a professional, but often it can be done with one of the sharpeners sold for this purpose. Try clipping a piece of newspaper at different places on the lower blade. This will give you an idea of the proper scissors-like contact necessary between the fixed lower and the revolving ones.

Most people make the mistake of using cheap household machine oil or cylinder oil on the mower. Use only a high-grade light machine oil and see the difference it makes in operation.

EDITOR'S NOTE: There have been many important developments in the lawn management field which make it easier for home owners to establish and maintain attractive lawns. They include the discovery of new types and strains of grass; the perfection of weed-killers of the selective type (which destroy certain plants without harming others); the improvement of power mowers, especially of the rotating blade type, soil aerators, and other machines; methods for chemically modifying or stabilizing soil structure, etc. Progress along these lines is summarized in "GARDEN MAGIC MARCHES ON," page 439.—E.L.D.S.

A PRAYER

> Now I shall make my garden
> As true men build a shrine,
> An humble thing where yet shall spring
> The seeds that are divine,
> Since each a prayer I sow them there
> In reverential line.
> —THEODOSIA GARRISON.

CHAPTER IV

TREES AND SHRUBS

"Jock, when ye hae naething else to do, ye may be aye sticking in a tree; it will be growing, Jock, when ye're sleeping."
—WALTER SCOTT.

The difference between trees and shrubs is not very clearly marked. A tree has been described as having but one stem or trunk while a shrub has several. This is a rather weak distinction, but as many cultural directions are similar we may study them together with some profit.

Men cannot get along without trees. Apart from their practical value, they make for better manhood and womanhood by inspiring cleaner thoughts and higher ideals. The spiritual value of loving them and being with them is beyond estimate.

When we look at a tree we can recognize in its make-up three principal parts. They are the roots, the stem, and the crown. The roots comprise that part of a tree that is usually found below the ground. Our common trees have two general types of root systems, namely, shallow-rooted and taprooted. Such trees as the spruces, the hemlocks, and the pines have roots that tend to spread and lie close to the ground. These shallow-rooted trees are, as a rule, not windfirm. Other trees, such as the hickories, the oaks and the walnuts develop a long taproot. These firmly anchored trees are rarely uprooted.

Roots have three main functions. They anchor the trees to the ground, absorb water and dissolved food from the soil, and transport these to the stem and thence to branches, twigs, leaves, and other parts of the crown. The principal work of the big roots near the stem is to help the trees stand up, while the fine root hairs at the end of the rootlets are the ones that absorb the water from the soil.

The stem of a tree, also called trunk or bole, is the main axis extending from the roots to the crown, or to the tip in case of an unbranched stem. Tree stems show a wide range in form. They range from long to short, straight to crooked, and from erect to prostrate. An examination of a cross-section of a stem will show three principal parts—bark, wood and pith. In the central part of the stem is the pith which in an old tree trunk, may not be noticeable. About it is the wood, which in many trees can be divided into the darker heartwood and the lighter sapwood. Between the wood and the bark is a very thin layer of growing cells known as the cambium. This is the most vital part of a tree, for it is here that all new wood and bark are made. When a tree is girdled, the ring of cambium is severed and this helps to kill the tree.

The most valuable part of a forest tree is the stem, for it produces the wood that is used so extensively by man. The principal functions of the stem are (1) support of the tree crown; (2) transportation of food and water; and (3) storage of food. During the winter months considerable food is stored in the stem for use early in spring when growth starts.

We know that trees grow. They get bigger from year to year. In order that they can grow they must feed. The raw material out of which trees make their food comes from two sources—the soil and the air. The rootlets with their many small roothairs absorb water and with it the food substances that are held in solution. During the growing season there is a continuous flow of sap from the roots through the stems to the leaves, where it is converted into nutritious tree food. When the sunlight plays upon the granules of leaf green, tree food is manufactured. To make the food, water is brought from the stem through the leafstalks into the leaves. Then a complex chemical process takes place. This is the reason why leaves have been called the laboratory of the trees. The principal product derived from this process, known by the technical name of photosynthesis, is starch. As rapidly as the food is manufactured in the leaves, it makes its way down through the cells of the twigs, branches, and the stem. A continuous stream of nutritious sap is moving downward. The thin layer of cambium cells which encircle the tree then draws upon this food supply to build up new wood, bark, and other tree tissue. When there is an excess of food material it is stored in the roots, stems, branches, and twigs for later use.

It is interesting to know that in making the starch, oxygen is a by-product. This explains why it is healthy to have green growing plants about us in daytime. Leaves prepare food only in daytime, and their output is the greatest in full sunlight, and is almost negligible during dark nights. This is the reason why we find the most luxuriant tree growth in moist, sunny, and warm regions. It is also worth knowing that during the period of the year when the leaves are not manufacturing food, the trees live upon a food supply stored up during the long and light days of summer time.

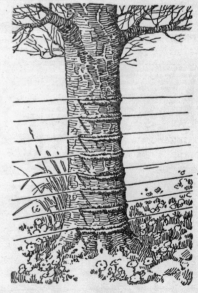

Don't nail a fence to a tree! This picture shows the result of a tree's efforts to overcome such mistreatment. The growing bark of the tree (cambium) protects it from insects and disease. Anything driven into it wounds this membrane and is an invitation to trouble.

Trees have many enemies. They are fighting for their lives all the time. There are 200,000 known kinds of insects that attack trees. It is estimated that caterpillars, beetles, borers, and other insects cause a loss of one hundred million dollars every year. Birds help us a lot in holding the insects in check. But they cannot wage war unaided.

When we think of tree enemies we must not overlook tree diseases, such as blights, rusts and rots. They, too, are a serious menace.

Most people believe that trees grow from early spring when the leaves begin to come out until the first frost when they start to show their autumn color. That this widespread belief is not correct is now known. For instance, in the latitude of southern Pennsylvania, the native forest trees make 90 per cent of their height growth in 40 days of spring and early summer.

That trees breathe is a firmly established scientific fact. Year after year, during night and day, in sum-

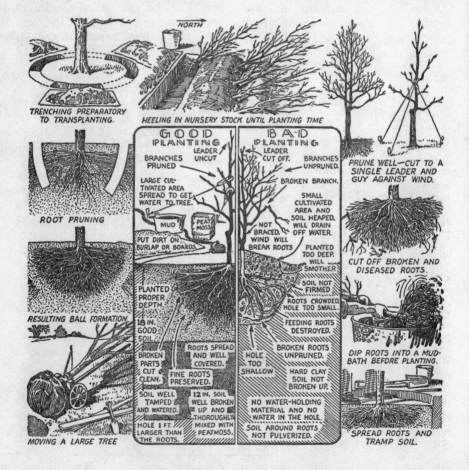

TRENCHING PREPARATORY TO TRANSPLANTING.

HEELING IN NURSERY STOCK UNTIL PLANTING TIME

ROOT PRUNING

RESULTING BALL FORMATION

MOVING A LARGE TREE

GOOD PLANTING
BRANCHES PRUNED
LEADER UNCUT
LARGE CULTIVATED AREA SPREAD TO GET WATER TO TREE.
MUD
PEAT MOSS
PUT DIRT ON BURLAP OR BOARDS.
PLANTED PROPER DEPTH.
18 IN. GOOD SOIL
BROKEN PARTS CUT CLEAN.
ROOTS SPREAD AND WELL COVERED.
FINE ROOTS PRESERVED.
SOIL WELL TAMPED AND WATERED.
12 IN. SOIL WELL BROKEN UP AND THOROUGHLY MIXED WITH PEATMOSS.
HOLE 1 FT. LARGER THAN THE ROOTS.

BAD PLANTING
LEADER CUT OFF.
BRANCHES UNPRUNED.
BROKEN BRANCH.
SMALL CULTIVATED AREA AND SOIL HEAPED. WILL DRAIN OFF WATER.
NOT BRACED, WIND WILL BREAK ROOTS
PLANTED TOO DEEP. WILL SMOTHER.
SOIL NOT FIRMED.
ROOTS CROWDED HOLE TOO SMALL.
FEEDING ROOTS DESTROYED.
BROKEN ROOTS UNPRUNED.
HOLE TOO SHALLOW
HARD CLAY SOIL NOT BROKEN UP.
NO WATER-HOLDING MATERIAL AND NO WATER IN THE HOLE. SOIL AROUND ROOTS NOT PULVERIZED.

PRUNE WELL—CUT TO A SINGLE LEADER AND GUY AGAINST WIND.

CUT OFF BROKEN AND DISEASED ROOTS.

DIP ROOTS INTO A MUD-BATH BEFORE PLANTING.

SPREAD ROOTS AND TRAMP SOIL.

mer and in winter, trees breathe from the time they are seeds until they have completed their full growth and die.

Trees also transpire, that is, give off water. We may call it perspiring or "sweating." When an excess amount of water is delivered to the leaves it is given off through small stomata, the same openings through which the trees breathe. This excess of water is given off as an invisible vapor. Scientists have estimated that a big oak may transpire as much as 150 gallons of water during a single day in summer.

Some trees reach a great size and become very old, while others remain small and die young. A definite age limit cannot be set for each kind of tree, but for general use our common trees may be said to be long-lived or short-lived. Of our native trees, the White Oak, Buttonwood, White Pine and Hemlock are long-lived trees, and the Poplars, Willows, Birches, Sassafras, and Locust are short-lived.

By counting the growth rings, it has been found that trees are probably the oldest living things on earth. The famous "great tree of Tule," a Cypress near Oaxaca, Mexico, is apparently close to its reputed age of 4,000 years. A Sequoia gigantea in King's Forest, California, was found by John Muir to be over 4,000 years, and in 1947 a fallen Redwood (S. sempervirens) was found to be 2,200 years old.

If a little forethought is exercised in their planting, trees well repay all the care that may be given them. It is obviously not enough merely to set a tree in the ground and expect it to grow into a perfectly healthy and stately old specimen without assistance.

All trees are not lawn trees but some are most attractive because of graceful habit, pleasing foliage or showy bloom. Some of the finest small lawn trees belong to the ornamental flowering fruits which are discussed on the next page.

Of our native trees the Redbud or Judas tree, producing lavender rose flowers before the leaves appear, and the Flowering Dogwood (see "Acid Plants") are both popular. The various sorts of Hawthorns usually have more or less horizontal branches so that they have a distinctive appearance in a planting.

Of the larger trees for lawns, the Elms and Maples have few rivals. The Elm is admired for its sheltering branches and the Maples (the Norway, and Sugar and the Red) for their ability to grow into well-formed trees.

More Lindens or Basswoods should be planted as they are symmetrical and handsome in flower and foliage.

The Pin Oak may be used for its graceful drooping habit, and bright red fall leaves; the Bolleana and Lombardy Poplars for pyramids of growth to screen unsightly places and to improve the skyline; the Pussy Willow (of which the sort known as the Goat Willow, *Salix caprea,* is the best) for its display of large "pussies" which are such a joy to cut and force in water in late winter; the Sycamore for its white bark; the Birches for their truly feminine characteristics; the Purple Beech for its color needed in many plantings; the Ginkgo for its curious leaves and upright habit when young.

FLOWERING FRUIT TREES

Probably no group of trees has so much to offer to lovers of flowers with as little care as the flowering fruits. They have been developed for flowering qualities and their fruit is ornamental or negligible. They usually take the form of a shrub or dwarf tree which does not take up so much room and is appropriate for the small place.

Among the most popular of this group are the stone fruits called Prunus which belong to the rose family. They include the orchard fruits as well as the decorative kinds of plum, cherry, almond, apricot, and peach, and no genus of trees adds more to the beauty of spring. Planted preferably in the fall against a background of evergreens they are set out to the greatest advantage.

Ease of growth and free flowering make them very popular. As the blossoms appear on the stems before the leaves in the early spring, they are doubly welcome to the winter-worn flower lover, but this places them in jeopardy from frost. Therefore, it is better to plant them on the north side of the house where development is retarded until the spring frosts are likely to be over.

This position must not deprive them of a number of hours of sunlight each day. Shelter from prevailing winds in the form of taller shrubbery is also helpful as an exceptionally severe winter may kill the flower buds just as it freezes those of fruit trees.

The first and best known is the Flowering Almond, a hardy bush usually growing up to four feet. It is

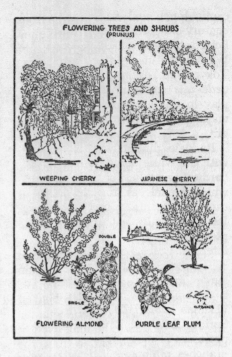

FLOWERING TREES AND SHRUBS
(PRUNUS)

WEEPING CHERRY

JAPANESE CHERRY

FLOWERING ALMOND

PURPLE LEAF PLUM

offered in single and double varieties. When grafted on plum stock it must be watched for suckers. The apricot is usually sold as Japanese Flowering Plum and comes in white and double pink flowers—very decorative.

Flowering Peach is a small showy tree with double pink and white flowered forms coming into flower after the almond. Plum comes in a number of flowering forms. Japanese plum is a larger tree cultivated in several varieties. But favorite among the decorative plums is the Purple Leafed Plum, a free growing and highly ornamental subject. It presents double pink flowers with reddish or bronze-purple foliage which makes it different as well as ornamental when the flowers are gone.

The Flowering Cherry lends an

exotic touch and flavor suggesting century-old gardens. It is much publicized because of the planting at Washington of a gift of trees from Tokyo. The Yoshina Cherry (*Prunus yedoensis*) makes up the greatest display in this group as these were a major part of the original Japanese gift.

Its pale pink flowers harmonize with the white Sargent Cherry (the hardiest and tallest of the Orientals) which blooms at almost the same time. The Yoshina is more spreading. Its size usually makes it unfit for planting in a small space, but it is interesting otherwise.

The most widely planted by home gardeners, because it flowers freely, is the single-flowered Higan Cherry (*Prunus subhirtella*), which is the Spring Cherry of Japan and bears a profusion of pink flowers so that the branches often are literally hidden from sight. It is of bushy growth and has the advantage of usually staying small, a desirable quality in a city garden.

There is a variety of the Higan Cherry that blooms again in lesser degree in the fall. The Weeping Cherry is a form of the Higan and varieties differ slightly in color of flowers, but the kind usually sold is the Japanese Weeping Rose Cherry. It has been used in this country for 50 years, which is a tribute to its beauty, popularity, and hardiness.

Flowering crab apples are useful and lovely. (Though now classed by botanists as species and varieties of the genus Pyrus, we are retaining the old name, Malus, still used in many nursery catalogues.)

Of the flowering apples, Bechtels crab (*Malus ioensis*) is a variety of our native prairie crab apple, also sometimes known as Iowa Crab.

Flowering in May and June, it is often so densely covered with the delicate pink blossoms that it suggests the appearance of a huge bouquet. Its flowers are doubles or semidoubles, reminding one of a small exquisite rose. It grows 15 to 20 feet high when fully developed and has fruit of a waxy green color.

Next in popularity is the Japanese Crab (*Malus floribunda*), a well-shaped bush which will grow up to 20 feet. The buds are a warm red, turning to light pink as they open into full bloom. It is a free bloomer and has yellow fruit about as big as a pea.

The Scheidecker Crab (*Malus scheideckeri*) is thought by many to

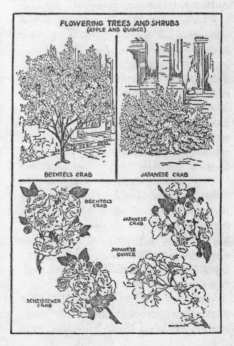

FLOWERING TREES AND SHRUBS
(APPLE AND QUINCE)

BECHTELS CRAB

JAPANESE CRAB

BECHTELS CRAB

JAPANESE CRAB

JAPANESE QUINCE

SCHEIDECKER CRAB

be the best of the crab apples. A compactly formed tree or shapely bush, similar in foliage to Japanese, it has large double flowers of a light rose color, which have a sweet fragrance and last a long time. It has round, waxy, green fruit less than an inch in diameter.

Aside from these most popular kinds, there are many other varieties. The Redvein Crab (*Malus neidzwetkyana*) is a looser-growing variety than the floribunda, having pink flowers fading into white and dark red fruit. Sargent Crab (*Malus sargenti*) is a spiny shrub six feet high with clustered white flowers and red fruit. Paul's Double Scarlet Thorn (*Malus crataegus*), often called the Tree-of-Fire is loaded during May and June with rich, glossy foliage which assumes brilliant colors in autumn. Its scarlet fruits are very attractive. The Purple Crab (*Malus purpurea*) has purplish-red or rosy-crimson flowers and purple fruits.

Next comes the Flowering Quince, well known as Japanese Quince, and often called "Firebush," because in May it is covered with clusters of bright scarlet flowers. Its foliage develops soon after flowering, forming a fine background for foliage. Its fruit is used for flavoring jellies and preserves. Flowering from February to June, it reaches a height of four to nine feet. Grown against a wall with Southern exposure, it blooms often as early as January and running as late as June. Cydonia (or *Chaenomeles*) *japonica* is the usually planted variety described above. *C. maulei* is a dwarf about three feet high. Other varieties are offered, differing mainly in the shade of their blossoms from pink-tinted white to deep crimson. *C. sargenti* is a prostrate variety.

All flowering fruits flourish under the care given other fruits. They are best planted in fall after a good ground freeze, but they may be planted any time until late February.

Choose sunny positions with a little shelter from prevailing winds. Dig deep, large holes (two feet deep), put old manure or peat in the bottom and refill with good soil. Mix in lime generously, for they love an alkaline condition. If the soil is acid, relime yearly. A yearly mulch of manure is good. The smaller-size stock will take more time to mature, but is better and cheaper to plant.

Prune out the oldest wood to stimulate production and open up the plant to the sunlight. Members of the Prunus genus especially flower on shoots of the previous year, so young wood coming along means a vigorous plant. Prune, if possible, in November. The Prunus varieties bleed in the spring and should be coated with tar or a tree paint whenever pruned. But then, that is a good plan in all pruning.

A dormant spray (either spraying oil or lime sulphur compound) applied just before the buds open is a safeguard against a host of ills. It is the easiest way of all to prevent pest injury on these plants for these and all shrubs and evergreens. Spray with arsenate of lead for leaf chewers. Almost any seed store will furnish a spray chart for apple, cherry, and plum put out by the manufacturers of spray materials in case special treatment is needed.

Last and very important be sure to leave space for them to spread when planting. The space between can be filled with temporary plants until these reach maturity.

HANDLING TREES AND SHRUBS

Selection of Material: The first thing a gardener must decide is whether he will plant nursery-grown or collected stock. Most amateurs have been disappointed at some time or another with the results from a tree which they had attempted to transplant from field or woodland.

Plants in their natural state have great sprawling root systems, and when we attempt to transplant them we must cut off the major portion of the roots. This shock usually results in unsuccessful transplanting.

Nursery stock, on the other hand, if purchased from a reliable grower, has already had its root system restricted several times by root pruning. When trees or shrubs are propagated they are purposely moved several times in order that the roots will not spread too much. The top growth is also pruned to strengthen the roots so that the plant reaches you ready to go to work in the small place usually prepared for it.

Material taken from natural growing conditions should first be root pruned, and in case of larger plants this takes at least two years. We illustrate this root pruning or trenching on page 56. A part of the circle is completed one spring and the balance of the trench is dug out the following spring. This causes the tree to make a fine growth close to the trunk and when it is finally moved the ball is filled with fine roots. The tree is then pulled over and the bottom roots cut, and in this way the root shock is divided into three parts. The moving of large trees is a job for experts or someone with patience and equipment and requires the preparation of a hole of great size and depth.

In addition there are a number of trees which can only be transplanted successfully when very young. These are the ones with a "tap" root, that is, the strong center root which grows straight down. This type usually receives special root treatment in the nursery, and includes such nut-bearing trees as Hickories, Walnuts, and Chestnuts; also the Oaks.

It is better for an amateur to buy small stock and to use the balance of the money in preparing the ground. Someone has said that it is better to plant a fifteen-cent tree in a fifty-cent hole than a fifty-cent tree in a fifteen-cent hole.

Properly planted, even "switches" or "whips," as the nurserymen call them, will outgrow a larger tree for which proper preparation has not been made.

It is remarkable the growth that will be made by small trees if the soil is enriched and water plentifully supplied during the growing season. The usual period for establishing small high class nursery stock in its new location is one to two years, whereas the usual period for establishing collected stock even though carefully transplanted may range from three to six years.

In addition to the above, we must consider the suitability of the plant for the purpose for which we are to use it. First it must fit our soil and then be adapted to our location. For this we will have to consider spread, height, sun, shade, texture of foliage, etc. If your soil is alkaline, it will fit most plants, but it is well to consult the list of acid plants given in Chapter VII before making your selections.

The quickness of growth should also enter into the selection. Quick growing trees, such as Silver Maples, Willows and Poplars, should be considered as temporary and used only until the slower growing permanent trees have matured. These trees are usually dirty, will litter up a lawn throughout the season and break off during a windstorm. Poplars and Willows also are a nuisance, clogging up drains because, in their search for moisture, they often send their roots out to the nearest drain or sewer line, sometimes completely filling them up. Silver Maples are much more useful, but they too, should be supplemented by more permanent planting.

Time of Planting: The time of planting is determined somewhat by the selection of material. Almost all woody deciduous plants are easily transplanted from the beginning of the dormant period in the fall until the time of sap activity in the spring, providing temperature conditions are favorable.

Because the spring is crowded with other tasks and the weather uncertain during the winter freezing, the best time is considered to be just after the first thorough ground freeze in the fall. The outstanding exceptions to this rule are the Magnolia, Birch, Tuliptree and Poplar.

If the planting is done in spring it is best to wait until the soil warms up a little. Light soil permits planting earlier than heavy clay soil and, of course, no planting should be done when the ground is lumpy or frozen.

Planting: Care in handling and planting of the material is real economy and the least expensive way in the long run of obtaining good results. To paraphrase a well-known maxim, "You may plant with poor preparation and fool yourself and your neighbors, but you can't fool the plants."

First, in purchasing stock, you should insist that it be properly packed to keep the roots from drying out. Second, you should see that it is heeled into a vacant flower bed as soon as you receive it where it may be kept as long as it is dormant or until you are ready to plant it.

When taking a tree from the soil it is best to dip it into a bath of mud, which is called "puddling." This protects the roots from exposure to the air before planting, and also from any air pockets which may exist after planting. It enables it to get into quicker and closer contact with the planting soil.

We have already spoken of the importance of the size of the planting hole. The hole should be excavated two feet deep and should be at least one foot wider each way than the full spread of the roots. Any increase in these dimensions will be repaid by quicker growth and plant health. The bottom of the hole should be broken up with a fork and thoroughly mixed with water holding material, such as peat, leafmold, thoroughly rotted manure, etc. If the ground is inclined to be hard, work in some sand or fine gravel, cinders, etc. The hole must drain readily.

The excavated soil should be placed upon a piece of burlap cloth or boards with the best soil separated from the subsoil. If the plant is one which grows in alkaline soil, work in a generous quantity of coarse raw bone and place the best soil in the bottom of the hole.

Manure should be used with care. Unless thoroughly rotted, it will burn new, growing roots. Always avoid manure in which wood shavings have been used for bedding. The wood may produce fungous growths as it decays.

Remember you have but one chance to cultivate under the plant and that is when you plant it. You may cultivate around it, but you cannot thereafter dig it up and put nourishment under it.

The balance of the soil should be well mixed with peat moss, humus, etc., and if it is hard, work in some sand to make it friable. Sometimes it is well to abandon the soil altogether and bring in some good garden loam for the planting. Having filled the hole to the depth required by the roots of the plant, flood it with water to settle the bottom soil, and when this has drained away, place the tree in the position in which it is to grow and work the soil about it. Be sure that there are no air pockets; use a stick or shovel handle, as well as your hands and feet, to work the soil under and around all roots. But use care in doing this to see that they are not injured. The roots are important,

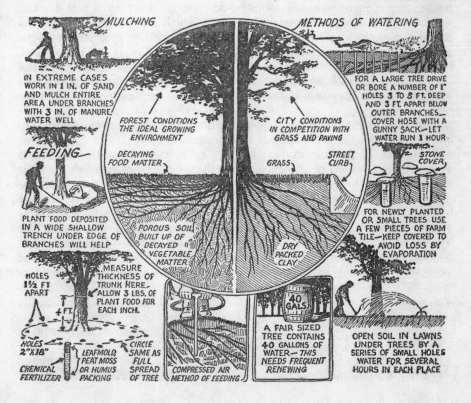

as the fine fiber-like ones are feeders for the plant. If any of them are broken or diseased, they should be cut off clean.

Plant the tree at approximately the same depth as it grew in the nursery. You can gauge this by the ring of dirt on the trunk. Lay the roots out naturally. When the hole is two-thirds filled tramp it firmly with the feet and again flood it with water to compact the soil and destroy air pockets. Now place the balance of the soil loosely in position. Do not tramp or firm it, but grade it so that any water will drain toward the trunk of the tree. The crown of the tree should now be cut back considerably, perhaps at least one-third. If it has only one leader or principal stem, this should *not* be topped. (See Chapter V for pruning directions.)

If the tree has any size it should be braced with guy wires run through pieces of old rubber hose where they touch the tree so as not to injure the bark.

The larger the cultivated area around the tree, the more quickly it will recover. If possible mulch the area with two inches of strawy manure.

Cultivation and Care: On younger trees it is good practice to apply this mulch each fall, cultivating it into the soil in the spring. If the planting is done in the spring, a mulch of straw or leaves will hold the moisture in the ground. Strawy manure is good, but the odor may be objectionable.

It is essential that young trees and shrubs obtain a ready supply of moisture, and excellent results can be obtained from placing a piece of tile upright in the planting hole. A hose may be placed in this and the subsoil supplied with water by allowing it to run for ten or fifteen minutes slowly. Or, better still, put a "Y" in your hose and supply several trees at the same time. Chemical fertilizer can also be supplied by pouring it in solution into this hole.

Sometimes, waste water from the kitchen sink can be used as shown below. (But be sure washing powders used will not injure plants.) The pipe which conveys it to the ground may be of iron, pierced with holes, or 4-inch sewer tile. If the tile is used, the joints should be cemented except over the lengths of farm tile which are placed vertically under the pipe line and act as a reservoir. This joint is uncemented so that the water may run out.

The only objection to this system is that the roots of rampant growing trees will clog it up and for this reason a clean-out should be constructed at either end so it may be rodded every two or three years. Also the open joint should be covered with three or four inches of cinders (not ashes) and it is well to fill the farm

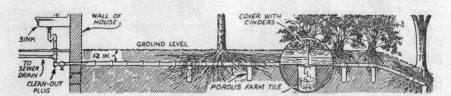

tile full of cinders. The farm tile will drain better if the hole in which it is placed is back-filled with cinders instead of soil.

The supply pipe should be laid almost level to give each opening an equal chance. It will be noted that the sink waste is arranged so that any excess will flow into the sewer.

Few people realize the spread of the roots of a tree. Fifty feet is not unusual for a root to travel to reach water and nourishment. Many feeding roots, however, are just under the edge of the branches where the drip of the water falls upon them. Nature has arranged the tree to conserve for its own use almost all moisture which falls upon its surface. Part of the rainfall is siphoned down the stem of the leaf upon the branch, and then down the trunk. If the ground is properly graded, this water flows deep into the soil where it is held for the use of the taproot during dry weather. The water which drips off the edge of the leaves falls directly upon the feeding roots where it can be used by the tree at once.

Most people know that the tree breathes through its leaves, but few people realize the necessity for air around its feeding roots. In the forest, trees are fed under natural conditions by a decaying litter of leaves returning to the soil food and water-holding material previously taken from it.

Under city conditions, trees are brought into competition with grass from which all leaves are carefully raked. They are often planted in ground from which all semblance of topsoil has been graded in the building of a house. In this case they must be fed by artificial means and if they show signs of distress, the soil should be loosened under their branches to prevent the smothering of the feeding roots by tight, heavy clay. In dry weather the lawn should be kept well watered and, if the soil is heavy, sand should be worked in with a mulch of compost. If the trees appear to be dying in the top during the summer, if the foliage is pale and thin, or if the leaves have a slightly wilted appearance in the morning, the distress signals are flying. The first and most probable reason is that they are dying of hunger and thirst. The second is that they have received some wound. The third is that they have been attacked by some insect or disease.

For the first we apply restorative measures to the soil. We water well, cultivate the area beneath the branches and work in some fertilizer. A fertilizer made of four parts raw bone, five parts wood ashes, and one part dried blood or tankage, is a good long-life fertilizer, but a balanced chemical fertilizer will do the work if we remember that it is usually exhausted in sixty days and needs frequent applications. We illustrate (on page 63) methods of application.

A method of restoring to the ground some of the natural growing conditions is to mulch the area with finely pulverized peat moss, sedge humus or leafmold, and work in plenty of sand. Leaves should never be burned. Compost them as illustrated elsewhere and use this compost mixed with sand to return the vegetable matter to the soil. Don't expect your trees to continue to grow in a four-foot space between curb and sidewalk unless you feed and care for them and also prepare a space beyond the sidewalk where they may feed. In almost all cities there is a process available by which the ground can be broken up and fertilizer injected by compressed air.

If your tree has suffered the loss of a part of its root system by the installation of gas, sewer or water, or by the paving of a street or walk, feed it well until it has time to form new roots. If they have enough stored vitality they will send their roots 200 feet under walks and paving in search of food, but unless they find it they simply dry up.

Insects and Disease: If the leaves of your trees are full of small holes, or are eaten away, you need a poison spray of arsenate of lead applied as soon as this is discovered. The chewing insect eats this stomach poison with the leaves. If tiny insects (scale) form along the trunk and branches they are best eradicated by spraying with an oil emulsion in winter or with lime sulphur in the spring before the buds start to open. Prune off or wipe out with rags moistened with kerosene.

Borers sometimes attack the trunk and branches, leaving holes and many times sawdust where they enter. Puncture the borer by running a wire into the hole; or, if the tree is young (five to fifteen years old), dig it out carefully, disinfect the wound with creosote oil and seal with tar or grafting wax.

Never cut a branch if it can be avoided. Do not let butchers mutilate your trees. Do not cut them back to make them thicker. Coat all wounds with a good tree paint, liquid asphaltum, a good grade shellac, or even a good lead house paint. Do not coat the entire trunk.

If borers are very bad it may be advisable to kill as many as possible by thrusting a flexible wire into the tunnels. Or jelly-like chemicals sold by seed stores can be squeezed into the openings which are then plugged with putty, chewing gum, etc. The vapors destroy the borers within.

Some of the best friends that the tree has are insectivorous birds. For this reason they should be encouraged to stay in the garden. We should have water available for them to bathe and drink, houses for them to live in and include in our planting small fruits, such as berries, cherries, etc.

Cats should be kept out of the trees. This can easily be done by fastening a strip of sheet metal 18 inches long loosely about the tree four or five feet from the ground; it will prevent the use of its upper branches by any kind of animals except birds. The cat climbs the tree by sinking its claws into the bark. It cannot sink its claws into the sheet metal. The metal can be painted to make it inconspicuous.

Repair Work: The profession of tree surgery or repair work is a much-abused one. Many tree surgeons are university men who have made a lifetime study of trees. However, many so-called tree men are merely butchers who have taken up this line with no preparation.

Any considerable amount of work calls for expert attention, but there are many small things which the amateur can do for his own trees.

"The best and safest and most economical means of preventing extensive decay, disfigurement or death of a tree is to attend to each injury as soon as it occurs. This kind of work is simple and comparatively inexpensive. If the injury is allowed to remain untreated for some years (as commonly happens), decay-producing organisms almost invariably enter the wound and produce a rotted area in the wood beneath, often of such an extent that a violent wind may break the tree at the decayed and weakened spot. Uninjured bark or an injured area promptly and properly treated usually prevents the entrance of decay organisms." The foregoing quotation from a bulletin of the United States Department of Agriculture sums up the tree surgery idea perfectly. We quote further: "In repair work a few fundamental principles must be observed in order to secure permanently good results. These may be summarized briefly as follows:

"(1) Remove all dead, decayed, diseased, or injured wood or bark. When on a limb this can often be done best by removing the entire limb; on a large limb or on the trunk it may mean at times digging out the decayed matter so that a cavity is formed.

"(2) Sterilize all cut surfaces.

"(3) Waterproof all cut surfaces.

"(4) Leave the work in the most favorable condition for rapid healing; this may sometimes necessitate filling or covering deep cavities.

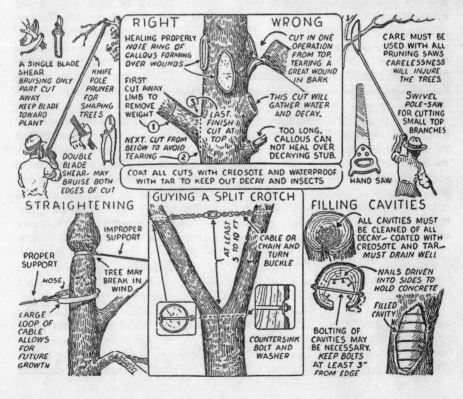

"(5) Watch the work from year to year for defects, and if any appear, attend to them immediately.

"The careless use of a long pruning hook or other implement to break off small dead twigs should be avoided, as every bruise may become the point of entrance of disease or decay. Climbing spurs produce wounds that are very easily and frequently infected. Spurs should never be used except on a tree that is to be removed or destroyed. A man who insists on using climbing spurs in tree surgery work should never be allowed to work on trees. Nails and leather soles and heels on shoes often cause injury. Rubber-soled tennis shoes, or 'sneaks,' or some similar soft-soled shoes that will not slip should be used in tree-surgery work."

If the amateur will learn some simple rules he will be able to solve many a tree problem for himself. As previously stated several times, the bark keeps out insects and disease, therefore, we wish to keep the bark-growing tissue (the cambium) as healthy as possible. The removal of branches must be done so that new growth, called a callus, may completely heal over the wound before decay sets in.

It is important that all wounds drain, hence any cut upon a tree should be perpendicular, and as close to the bark as possible without injuring it. Large branches should be cut off in two sections. The first cut is to get rid of the weight, the second is to prevent any tearing below the branch to be removed, and the third is to finish the cut.

As previously stated, trees should not be allowed to grow with two leaders. If you have a tree in this shape you may prevent it from splitting by guying it with a chain or cable and a turn buckle as illustrated. Do not be deceived by the fact that the split is healed over each year. Disease and germs enter while it is open, and it is much better to close it permanently.

The filling of cavities is a job to be handled with great care. All diseased tissue must be removed, and a certain amount of apparently healthy tissue must also be taken to insure a complete removal of the diseased parts. This is done with a gouge chisel or knife after which all exposed sapwood is given a coat of good shellac. If the cavity is to be left unfilled, the surface can be given a protective coat of liquid asphaltum, *not* creosote or any strong corrosive material. White lead or paint is not satisfactory here.

Most people think that filling the cavities with cement is for the protection of the tree. It is usually done

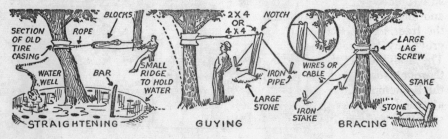

STRAIGHTENING · GUYING · BRACING

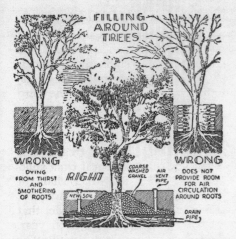

FILLING AROUND TREES

WRONG
DYING FROM THIRST AND SMOTHERING OF ROOTS

RIGHT
NEW SOIL
COARSE WASHED GRAVEL
AIR VENT PIPE
DRAIN PIPE

WRONG
DOES NOT PROVIDE ROOM FOR AIR CIRCULATION AROUND ROOTS

for appearance sake. A cavity if well waterproofed and drained may be left open for inspection at any time. If cement is used it should be remembered that the tree is not a rigid object. The cement should be placed in horizontal layers, each covered with tarpaper and allowed to harden slightly before the next layer is set.

If the trunk or branch is weakened by the rotting of its interior, the walls should be braced together by bolting which should be kept at least three inches from the edge of the cavity. Bark around a wound should be cut to a point at the top and bottom to facilitate callusing and so that the entire cavity will drain to the lowest point.

Crooked or distorted trees may be straightened with a block and tackle and guyed to keep them in shape. If the tree is erect it will usually outgrow any irregularity of its trunk. The straightening should be done by thorough soaking of the ground and the tightening of the rope daily over a period of weeks. A good time to start is in early spring and the tightening process should be continued throughout the summer.

Be sure to protect the bark of the tree with some heavy material such as an old tire casing and see that there is a large loop allowed for the future growth of the tree.

By courtesy of the Davey Tree Expert Company we are able to illustrate the proper method of filling around trees. But this should never be done unless absolutely necessary.

Filling around a tree is an expensive operation and the gravel should be extended well out beyond the spread of the branches. A drain pipe running to lower ground should be placed one foot below the original soil, and should run from the trunk of the tree in two directions.

SHRUBS

Like trees, shrubs need to be carefully selected and should be purchased, freshly dug, from reliable firms. One advantage of fall planting is that the nursery stock is likely to be fresher.

Most large nurseries dig their trees and shrubs in the fall, placing them in dormant storage. As the earth is entirely removed from the roots, this constitutes a set-back. These plants will recover and become perfectly hardy, but as previously explained, any drying out of the roots is detrimental and freshly dug plants are the best.

Select only those plants which grow well in your locality. Buy the best of them and be sure that they are hardy.

You may be able to replant your shrubbery border by dividing the old
[continued on p. 72]

PLANTING LIST OF TREES, SHRUBS, EVERGREENS, AND VINES FOR HOME BEAUTIFICATION

All plant names are taken from "Standardized Plant Names," by the American Joint Committee on Horticultural Nomenclature

Scientific name	Common name	Planting distance, feet	Height in feet	Spread in feet	Exposure	Growth	Flowers Season	Flowers Color	Fruit Seas.	Fruit Color	Size to Order
Acer ginnala	Amur Maple	4-6	8-15	5-10	SA	M	April	White	H-C	Red	3-4'
Acanthopanax pentaphylla	Five-leafed Aralia	4	4-5	3-5	SSh	M					3-4'
Berberis thunbergi	Japanese Barberry	3-4	3-5	5-6	SSh	M					18-24"
Buddleia davidi (magnifica)	Butterfly bush	4-5	3-5	4-5	S	F	July	Lilac			2 yr.
Calycanthus floridus	Sweetshrub	4-5	6-10	4-5	S†	M	May	Red			3-4'
Caragana arborescens	Siberian pea-tree	5†	15-25	Tree	S*	R	May	Yellow			3-4'
Cercis canadensis	Redbud		5-15	Tree	S*	R	May	Dk. Pink		Seedpod	3-4'
Chionanthus virginica	White Fringetree	6-8‡	4-5	Tree	S*	R	June	White			3-4'
Cotoneaster divaricata	Cotoneaster	4	4-5	4-5	A	M	May	Yellow	C	Red	3-4'
Cornus alba	Red twig Dogwood	5	8-20	5-7	A	F	May	White	E	White	3-4'
Cornus florida	Flowering Dogwood	10	8-20	Tree	A	R	May	White	E	Red	5-6'
Cornus paniculata	Gray Dogwood	5	5-6	5-7	S	M	May	White	E	Twigs Yel.	3-4'
Cornus stolonifera flaviramea	Goldentwig Dogwood	5	5	4-5	S	R	May	White			3-4'
Deutzia formosa magnifica	Double White Deutzia	5	5-8	3-4	S	M	May	White			3-4'
Deutzia gracilis (tender)	Slender Deutzia	2-3	2	2	S	M	May	White			12-18"
Deutzia lemoinei	Lemoine Deutzia	3-4	3-4	3	S	M	May	White			18-24"
Euonymus alatus	Winged Euonymus	5-6	5-6	4-5	S	M	May	Cream	E-H	Red-Orng.	2-3'
Euonymus europaeus	European Burningbush	5-6	6-10	Tree	S	M	May	Cream	H	Red-Orng.	3-4'
Eleagnus angustifolia	Russian Olive	5-6	15-20	8-20	S	R	May	Yellow		Silver	3-4'
Forsythia intermedia spectabilis	Showy Border Forsythia	5	6-8	6-8	A	F	April	Yellow			3-4'
Forsythia suspensa	Weeping Forsythia	5	6-8	6-10	A	M	April	Yellow			3-4'
Hibiscus syriacus	Shrub-Althea	4-5	6-8	3-4	S	M	August	Various			2-3'
Hydrangea paniculata grand	Peegee Hydrangea	4	4-6	3-4	A	M	Sept.	Wh.-pink			2-3'
Hydrangea arborescens sterile	Snowhill Hydrangea	3-4	4	3-4	A	M	July	White	E		2-3'
Hypericum aureum (tender)	Golden St. Johnswort	3	3-4	3-4	A	M		Yellow			2-3'
Kerria japonica	Kerria	3	3-4	3-4	A	M	May	Yellow			18-24"
Koelreuteria paniculata	Goldenrain Tree	10	10-20	Tree	S	R		Yellow	E-H	Br'n Pods	5-6'
Ligustrum ibolium	Ibolium Privet	4	6-8	4-5	SSh	M	May	Cream	E-C	Blue-Blacks	3-4'
Ligustrum ibota	Ibota Privet	5	3-4	4-5	SSh	F	May	Cream	E-C	Blue-Blacks	2-3'
Ligustrum regelianum	Regel Privet, dwarf form	5	3-4	4-5	SSh	F	May	Cream	E-C	Black	3-4'
Ligustrum vulgare	European Privet	5	6-8	4-6	SSh*	F	April	Cream			3-4'
Lonicera fragrantissima	Winter Honeysuckle	5-8	6	6-10	SSh	FF	May	Cream	E	Red	3-4'
Lonicera morrowi	Morrow Honeysuckle	5-8	8-15	5-8	SSh	FF	May	Cream	E	Red	3-4'
Lonicera tatarica	Tatarian Honeysuckle, Pink	5-8	10-15	5-8	SSh	FF	May	Pink	H-C	Red	3-4'
Lonicera maacki	Amur Honeysuckle	5-6	8-15	4-7	A	F	May	Pink			3-4'
Philadelphus coronarius	Sweet Mockorange	3	3-5	3	A	M	May	White			18-24"
Philadelphus lemoinei	Lemoine Mockorange	3	6-8	6-8	A	M	May	White			3-4'
Philadelphus virginal	Virginal Mockorange	5-8	8-15	6-8	S	M	April	White			18-24"
Physocarpus opulifolius aurea	Goldleaf Ninebark	3	6-10	3-4	S	R	May	Cream	E	Red-Green	3-4'
Prunus othello or pissardi	Purpleleaf Plum	3	8-15	4-5	A†	M	May	White	E	Purple	18-24"
Prunus glandulosa (Amygdalus)	Flowering Almond	3	3-4	2-3	S	M	April	Pink-Wh.			2-3'
Rhodotypos kerrioides	Jetbead	3	4-5	4-5	SSh	M	May	White	E-C	Black	2-3'
Rhus canadensis	Fragrant Sumac	3	3-5	5-8	S	M	April	Yellowish	E-H	Red	3-4'
Rhus glabra	Smooth Sumac	5	8-15	5-10	S	M	July	Greenish	E-H	Scarlet	3-4'
Rhus typhina laciniata	Cutleaf Sumac	5	6-12	5-7	S	M	July	Greenish	E-H	Crimson	2-3'
Ribes alpinum	Alpine Currant	3	4	4-5	S	F	May	Greenish			3-4'
Ribes odoratum (aureum)	Golden Flowering Currant	3	4-5	5-7	SSh	M	May	Yellow	E	Black	3-4'
Rosa hugonis	Hugonis Rose	4	4-5	4-5	S	F	June	Yellow			2-3'
Rosa wichuriana	Wichuriana Rose	4	1-2	10	S	F	Jun.-Jul.	White			2-3'
Sorbaria aitchesoni (Spirea)	Kashmir False-spirea	4	5-6	4-6	S	MF	July	Cream			3-4'
Spiraea anthony waterer	Anthony Waterer Spirea		2-3		S						3-4', 9"

Plant	No.	Ht.	Dist.	Exp.	Growth	Bloom	Flower Color	Fr. Exp.	Fruit Color	Specimen
Spiraea froebeli .... Procel Spirea	4			S	M		White			18-24"
Spiraea thunbergi .... Thunberg Spirea	5	3-4	3-4	A	F	April	White			3-4'
Spiraea vanhouttei ...... Van Houtte Spirea	3	5-6	5-6	S	M	May	White			2-3'
Stephanandra flexuosa (tender) .... Cutleaf Stephanandra	3-4	3	3	SSh	M	June	Plksh-wh.			2-3'
Symphoricarpus racemosus ..... Snowberry	3	3	3	SSh	M		White	E-H	White	18-24"
Symphoricarpus (rothom'gn's) ..... Coralberry	5	6-10	6-8	S	M	May	Lilac	E-C	Red	3-4'
Syringa chinensis ..... Chinese Lilac (use French hyb.)	5	6-12	6-8	S	M	June	Various			3-4'
Syringa vulgaris ..... Com. Lilac (use French hyb.)	5	8-10	6-10	S	MF	July	Lilac			2-3'
Syringa villosa ..... Late Lilac	5	6-10	6-8	S	M	June	Pink			2-3'
Tamarix pentandra (hisp. aest.) ..... Tamarix	3-4	3-5	3-4	SSh	M	May	White			3-4'
Viburnum cassinoides ..... Witche-rod	5	5-8	3-5	SSh†	MF	May	White	H	Blue-Black	3-4'
Viburnum dentatum ..... Arrowwood	5	6-10	5-6	A†	M	May	White	E	Red-Black	3-4'
Viburnum lantana ..... Wayfaring Tree	5-6	6-10	5-6	A†	MF	May	White	E-H	Blue-Black	3-4'
Viburnum lentago ..... Nannyberry	4	10-15	6-8	A	M	June	White	E-C	Red	2-3'
Viburnum opulus ..... European Cranberrybush	5	6-8	5-6	A	M	June	White	E	Red-Black	2-3'
Viburnum tomentosum ..... Japanese Snowball	4	6-8	4-5	S	M	June	Red			2-3'
Viburnum tomentosum plicatum ..... Doublefile Viburnum	5	6-8	5-6	S	M	June	Pink-wh.			2-3'
Weigela eva rathke ..... Eva Rathke Weigela										
Weigela rosea ..... Pink Weigela										
TREES										
Acer saccharum ..... Sugar Maple	50	50	35	SSh	M					2"
Acer platanoides ..... Norway Maple	40	40	35	S	R	May	White			2-4"
Aesculus hippocastanum ..... Horsechestnut	50	50	35	S	M					1"
Celtis occidentalis ..... Hackberry	50	50	35	SSh	M					1-2"
Liriodendron tulipifera ..... Tuliptree	50	50	35	S	F	May	Yellow			8-10'
Populus bolleana ..... Bolleana Poplar	6-15	40	35	S	F					1-2"
Quercus palustris ..... Pin Oak	50	50	35	SSh	M					1-2"
Quercus rubra ..... Red Oak	50	50	20	S	R					2-4"
Salix pentandra ..... Laurel Willow	25	30	20	SSh	M					
Ulmus americana ..... American Elm	50-75	75	50	S	M					
EVERGREENS										
Euonymus radicans ..... Wintercreeper	4	Vine		SSh	R					
Juniperus chinensis pfitzeriana ..... Pfitzer Juniper‡	6-10	3-6	6-10	S	M					2 yr.
Juniperus virginiana cannarti ..... Cannart Juniper	5	15		SSh	R					
Mahonia aquifolia ..... Oregon Grape	3	3-4	2-3	A	R					
Picea excelsa ..... Norway Spruce‡††	10-20	50	20-30	S	R					
Pinus nigra ..... Austrian Pine††	10-20	30	20-30	S	R				H	
Pseudotsuga douglasi ..... Douglas Fir‡	10-20	50	10-20	S	R					
Taxus cuspidata ..... Japanese Yew‡	3-5	3-5	5-10	SSh	R					
Thuja occidentale ..... Arborvitae‡	20	50	15-30	S	R					12-18"
Tsuga canadensis ..... Hemlock‡	6-20	50	15-30	SSh	R					
VINES										
Ampelopsis quinquefolia ..... Virginia Creeper	10	15-35	Vigor.	SSh	F		Wings	E-H	Black	2 yr.
Ampelopsis tricuspidata (veitchi) ..... Japanese Creeper (Boston)	10	10-50	Good	A	M					3 yr.
Aristolochia sipho ..... Dutchmans-pipe	15	35	Vigor.	S	M					2 yr.
Bignonia radicans ..... Trumpetcreeper	20	50	Vigor.	A	F	June	Brown	E-H	Br'n Pods	2 yr.
Clematis paniculata ..... Japanese Clematis	6	15	Fair	S	R	May	Orange			2 yr.
Celastrus scandens ..... Bittersweet	10	25	Good	SSh	M	August	White	H-C	Orng-Red	2 yr.
Hedera helix ..... English Ivy	6	25	Fair	A	R				Evergreen	2 yr.
Lonicera halliana ..... Hall Japanese Honeysuckle	6	25	Vigor.	A	F	June	Cream			2 yr.
Polygonum auberti ..... China Fleecevine, Silverlacev.	10	25		S	M	Summer	White			2 yr.
Wisteria sinensis ..... Chinese Wisteria (grafted)	20	50	Vigor.	S	F	May	Lavender			2 yr.
Yucca filamentosa ..... Common Yucca	2									
Vinca minor ..... Periwinkle (myrtle)	1									
Pachysandra terminalis ..... Japanese Pachysandra	1									

SYMBOLS USED — Growth: F—Fast; M—Medium; R—Slow } Preferred exposure: S—Sun; Sh—Shade; A—Partial shade; SSh—Sun or shade. Season of fruit: E—Summer; H—Fall; C—Winter. * For wet ground. † For dry ground. ‡ Specimen plant. †† Windbreak.

(From Ohio State Bulletin 73—by Victor H. Ries.)

bushes which have outgrown their location. Their crowns may be split with a hatchet and the divisions pruned both as to roots and top. The oldest wood should be removed as should all broken or bruised roots.

New stock, meaning young, vigorous plants, is always better than decrepit old plants. However, the older stock can be renewed by cutting back and dividing into sections as above described.

Shrubs should be selected carefully as to height. A shrub which normally grows six feet high is very hard to keep pruned back to three feet. Care must be taken to give them a reasonable amount of space. They usually appear best in groups and are rarely good in single rows or as specimens. Where space is available a border is best—on small properties it is better to fill the corners.

Shrubs are more or less of a permanent planting and not like smaller plants which are easily moved. Therefore, they require more planning and more careful selection.

Planting: The same planting instructions apply to shrubs as to trees except that more of them are safely planted in spring.

All shrubs are greedy feeders and the soil must be prepared carefully. For best results it should be trenched, as shown in the illustration and description on pages 34 and 35, and conditioned with leafmold or other humus.

Mulch the plants with manure, as previously instructed, and use about a pint of wood ashes and another of coarse raw bone meal to each heaping wheelbarrow of planting soil. See that the ground is firm about the roots to avoid air pockets, and settle the ground by watering.

Arrangement: Avoid straight lines both as to the shape of the border and the planting. Do not get too many of one variety in a group. Three or four are sufficient for the ordinary border. The taller plants should be in the rear, the medium in the middle, and the smaller at the front.

Straight top lines should also be avoided by keeping in mind the ultimate height of the various plants. Alternate the rows by high and low plantings. Where the border is deep, that is, from front to back, tall plants may be used in the background; but where the border becomes shallow, lower plants should be used. This gives an appearance of greater depth. Variety may be obtained by the introduction of groups of bulbs. However, during the first few years of the planting these groups should be carefully marked to avoid injury in cultivation. After the border is well established this is not so particular. If the ground is properly trenched cultivation will not be necessary except for the first year or two. Mulching with manure, as above described, is a good way of fertilizing and the use of some ground covers is recommended.

After the plants are once established, cultivation or refertilization is necessary only once in three or four years or whenever the plants seem to need it.

Pruning: Do not prune early flowering shrubs each spring or you will cut away the flowering branches. Pruning of flowering shrubbery is divided into two classes, dormant pruning and summer pruning. The majority of flowering shrubs bloom on the new wood produced during the growing season of the year previous. Prune within a few weeks after the flowers fall to give new wood a chance to ripen for next year's bloom. Here is a list of such plants for July pruning:

Fringe-tree (Chionanthus)	Shorten stray shoots
Dogwood	Remove old wood
Japanese-quince	Trim to preserve form
Deutzia	Trim sparingly
Pearlbush	Trim sparingly
Forsythia or Golden Bell	Trim severely— 1st to 10th of July
Kerria	Remove dead wood
Ibota Privet	As desired
Fragrant Honeysuckle	Prune lightly in spring and fall
Standish Honeysuckle	Prune lightly in spring and fall
Magnolia	As little as possible
Flowering Crab	Cut back when young
Tree Peony	
Mockorange	Remove dead wood
Flowering Plum	Cut budded plants severely
Flowering Peach	Cut budded plants severely
European Bird Cherry	Cut budded plants severely
Jetbead	Remove dead wood
Slender Golden Currant	Remove dead wood
Billiardi Spirea	Remove old wood
Bridalwreath	Remove old wood

LARGE SHRUBS IN REAR

MEDIUM IN CENTER

DWARF IN FRONT

LARGE SHRUBS WHICH GROW IN CLUMPS CAN BE DIVIDED WITH A HATCHET

USE ZIG-ZAG ARRANGEMENT. NOT STRAIGHT LINES.

2 FT. EXCAVATED PREPARED SOIL

BOTTOM SPIT BROKEN UP—BUT NOT REMOVED. SAND, CINDERS, ETC.—FOR DRAINAGE.

2 FT.

1 FT.

(See instructions for trenching on pages 34 and 35)

Van Houtte Spirea ⎫
Common Lilac ⎬ Remove oldest wood only
Persian Lilac ⎭

Viburnum (Flowering varieties)	Prune to keep in form
Weigela or Diervilla	Trim sparingly
Tamarix (Early flowering)	Prune severely

The following plants should be pruned in March:

Indigo Bush	Cut to ground
Butterfly Bush	Cut to ground
Shrub Althea	Cut back severely
Hydrangeas	Cut back severely
Regel Privet	Trim sparingly
Honeysuckles (Fruited varieties)	Trim sparingly
Sweetbrier	Remove old wood
Spirea Ant. Waterer	Cut ½ last year's growth
Snowberry	Remove old wood
Coralberry	Remove old wood

The general rule is, trim early flowering shrubs just after they bloom. Trim late (summer or fall) flowering or berry-bearing shrubs in March.

Temper your shears with brains; do not just lop off a few outer branches. The neglected shrub may seem to be a hopeless mass of branches, but proceed gradually. Reach into the bush and remove first all dead wood. This may be done at any season. Second, cut off some of the oldest branches right down to the base. Always keep some of the old wood and yet have new shoots coming from the bottom, not only on the outside of the plant, but in the center. This means that your trimming must admit light and air to the center to support this growth. Remember, shrubbery does not have to be pruned every year. It is more a process of thinning out than of trimming back, and, instead of being a seasonal flurry, it can be spread over the year or several years with benefit to the gardener as well as to the plant.

Overgrown screen and massed shrubs can be cut to the ground as a last resort, but if this would leave an ugly gap, the renovating, as described above, can be extended over several seasons. Shrubs with arching branches such as *Buddleia alternifolia,* Forsythia, Kolkwitzia and *Spirea vanhouttei* present a difficult problem if allowed to get out of hand, for they should not have their sweeping grace marred by the ugly stubs and laterals left by top cutting. They require thinning from the ground and careful heading in of the tops when removing the branches with their faded flowers.

Shrubs for Various Purposes

Low and Medium Shrubs for Foundation Planting:

Cotoneaster ....In Variety
Deutzia .... D. lemoinei carnea
Hydrangea quercifolia
               Oakleaf Hydrangea
Mahonia aquifolium
               Oregon Holly-grape

Philadelphus virginalis
                Double Mockorange
Ribes alpinum . . . . . . Alpine Currant
Spiraea bumalda var. Anthony Wa-
    terer . . . . Anthony Waterer Spirea
Spiraea prunifolia . . . Bridalwreath
Symphoricarpos chenaulti
                Chenault Coralberry
Viburnum burkwoodi
                Fragrant Viburnum
Viburnum opulus nanus
                Dwarf Cranberry Bush

*Medium and Tall Screen
and Border Shrubs:*

Caragana arborescens
                Siberian Pea Tree
Cornus paniculata . . Gray Dogwood
Ligustrum vulgare . European Privet
Lonicera fragrantissima
                Winter Honeysuckle
Lonicera maacki
                Amur Honeysuckle
Lonicera morrowi
                Morrow Honeysuckle
Lonicera tartarica
                Tartarian Honeysuckle
Philadelphus coronarius
                Sweet Mockorange
Syringa chinensis . . . . Chinese Lilac
Syringa vulgaris . . . . Common Lilac
Viburnum trilobum
                American Cranberry Bush
Viburnum cassinoides . . Withe-Rod
Viburnum dentatum . . . Arrowwood
Viburnum tomentosum
                Doublefile Viburnum
Viburnum tomentosum plicatum
                Japanese Snowball

*Trees for Tall Screen and
Accent Planting with Shrubs:*

Acer ginnala . . . . Amur Maple
Cercis canadensis . . . . Redbud

Cornus florida
                White Flowering Dogwood
Crataegus cordata
                Washington Hawthorn
Eleagnus angustifolia . Russian Olive
Euonymus europaeus
                European Burning Bush
Hibiscus . . . . Shrub Althea
Malus in variety . . . . Chinese Crabs
Populus bolleana . . Bolleana Poplar
Prunus blireana . . . Purpleleaf Plum
Prunus Newport
                Minnesota Purpleleaf Plum
Tilia pyramidalis . Pyramidal Linden

*Excellent Foliage for Background
and Border Plantings:*

Aronia melanocarpa elata
                Glossy Chokeberry
Chionanthus virginica
                White Fringetree
Euonymus alatus
                Winged Euonymus
Euonymus alatus compactus
                Dwarf Winged Euonymus
Ligustrum in variety . . . . Privet
Lonicera fragrantissima
                Winter Honeysuckle
Lonicera korolkowi
                Broad Blueleaf Honeysuckle
Lonicera maacki . Amur Honeysuckle
Rhus cotinus . . . . Purple Fringetree
Viburnum lantana . . . . . Arrowwood
Viburnum rufidulum
                Southern Black Haw
Viburnum tomentosum
                Doublefile Viburnum

*Background Shrubs for
Flower Borders:*

Buddleia in variety
                Charming, Dubonnet, Fortune
Hibiscus . . . . Tree and Bush Forms

Kolkwitzia amabilis ... Beauty Bush
Philadelphus virginalis
                   Double Mockorange
Philadelphus virginalis var. Boquet
   Blanc .... Mockorange
Prunus glandulosa sinensis
                Flowering Almond
Prunus tomentosa . Nanking Cherry
Prunus triloba plena
            Double Flowering Plum
Syringa vulgaris hybrids
                 Named Varieties
Viburnum burkwoodi
                 Fragrant Viburnum
Viburnum carlesi
            Mayflowering Viburnum
Vitex agnus-castus .... Chaste Tree

*Spreading Shrubs for Banks
and Rough Places:*

Berberis thunbergi
                Japanese Barberry
Cornus stolonifera var. flaviramea
             Goldentwig Dogwood
Forsythia suspensa
                Weeping Forsythia
Lonicera maacki . Amur Honeysuckle
Prunus pumila .... Sand Cherry
Rosa Max Graf ..... Max Graf Rose
Rosa wichuraiana .. Memorial Rose
Rhus in variety .... Sumac
Spiraea tomentosa ...... Hardhack
Symphoricarpos chenaulti
              Chenault Coralberry
Symphoricarpos racemosus (albus)
                     Snowberry
Symphoricarpos vulgaris . Coralberry

Shrubs that Endure Shade:

Aronia melanocarpa elata
              Glossy Chokeberry
Cornus florida . Flowering Dogwood

Cornus racemosa ... Gray Dogwood
Cornus sanguinea
                 Bloodtwig Dogwood
Euonymus alatus
                 Winged Euonymus
Euonymus europaeus
            European Burning Bush
Forsythia suspensa
                Weeping Forsythia
Hamamelis in variety.. Witch Hazel
Hydrangea arborescens grandiflora
              Snowhill Hydrangea
Ilex verticillata
              Common Winterberry
Ligustrum in variety .... Privet
Lonicera in variety ... Honeysuckle
Magnolia virginiana .... Sweet Bay
Rhamnus frangula ..... Buckthorn
Rhodotypos kerrioides .... Jetbead
Rhus canadensis .. Fragrant Sumac
Ribes alpinum .. Mountain Currant
Ribes odoratum.. Flowering Currant
Symphoricarpos in variety
           Snow- and Coralberries
Syringa vulgaris alba
            Common White Lilac
Viburnum in variety

Shrubs for Winter Twig Effects:

Cornus stolonifera var. flaviramea
            Goldentwig Dogwood
Cornus alba siberica
             Redtwig Dogwood
Cornus sanguinea viridissima
            Greentwig Dogwood
Forsythia intermedia spectabilis
       Showy Forsythia (Yellow)
Kerria japonica .... Kerria (Green)
Rosa virginiana
            Virginia Rose (Red)
Rosa rubrifolia
           Redleaf Rose (Purplish)
Salix purpurea .... Purple Osier

Specimen and Accent Trees and Shrubs:

Acer palmatum .... Japanese Maple
Hibiscus syriacus ... Rose of Sharon
Betula alba laciniata
           Cutleaf Weeping Birch
Buddleia alternifolia
           Chinese Butterfly Bush
Ginkgo biloba .... Maidenhair Tree
Halesia tetraptera . Great Silverbell
Koelreuteria paniculata
                Goldenrain Tree
Laburnum vulgare ... Goldenchain
Malus floribunda
           Japanese Crab—Standards
Prunus subhirtella pendula
           Japanese Weeping Cherry
Syringa vulgaris hybrida
           Hybrid Lilacs—Standards
Wistaria sinensis
           Chinese Wisteria, Tree Form

Red Berries

Aronia arbutifolia . Red Chokeberry
Berberis thunbergi
                Japanese Barberry
Cornus florida . Flowering Dogwood
Cotoneaster dielsiana
                Diels Cotoneaster
Cotoneaster divaricata
           Spreading Cotoneaster
Cotoneaster horizontalis
                Rock Cotoneaster
Cotoneaster racemiflora songarica
           Songarica Cotoneaster
Crataegus coccinea
                Thicket Hawthorn
Crataegus cordata
           Washington Hawthorn
Crataegus crusgalli
           Cockspur Hawthorn
Euonymus bungeanus
           Winterberry Euonymus

Euonymous europaeus
           European Burning-bush
Euonymus atropurpureus
                Native Wahoo
Ilex opaca .... American Holly
Ilex verticillata .... Winterberry
Lonicera maacki . Amur Honeysuckle
Lonicera morrowi
           Morrow Honeysuckle
Photinia villosa . Redberried Photinia

Rose Species

Sorbus americana
           American Mountain-ash
Sorbus aucuparia
           European Mountain-ash
Crataegus pyracantha lalandi
                Laland Firethorn
Viburnum americanum
           American Cranberry Bush
Viburnum opulus
           European Cranberry Bush
Viburnum dilatatum
                Linden Viburnum

White Berries

Symphoricarpos racemosus
                Snowberry
Cornus racemosa . Panicle Dogwood
Cornus alba ... Tartarian Dogwood
Cornus stolonifera
           Red-Osier Dogwood

Black Berries

Aronia melanocarpa
                Black Chokeberry
Ligustrum regelianum . Regels Privet
Ligustrum vulgare . European Privet
Rhamus caroliniana .. Indian-cherry
Viburnum lantana . Wayfaring Tree
Viburnum prunifolium .. Black haw
Viburnum sieboldi
                Siebold Viburnum

Deep Blue-Black Berries

Mahonia aquifolium
        Oregon Holly Grape
Viburnum cassinoides .. Withe-Rod
Viburnum dentatum ... Arrowwood
Viburnum lentago .... Nannyberry
Viburnum molle
        Kentucky Viburnum

Blue Berries

Ampelopsis brevipedunculata
        Porcelain Ampelopsis
Callicarpa purpurea
        Chinese Beauty Berry
Cornus amomum ... Silky Dogwood
Symplocos paniculata ... Sweetleaf

Bloom throughout the Year

January) Chinese and Winter
February) Witchhazel.

March—Cornelian-cherry, Winter
    Honeysuckle.

April—Goldenbell, Star Magnolia, Nanking Cherry, American Red-bud, Flowering-quince, Saucer Magnolia, Oriental Cherry, Wilson Pearlbush, Chinese Lilac, Fragrant and Burkwood Viburnum, Purple-leaf Plum, Double Flowering Almond.

May—Flowering Dogwood, Garland-flower, Deutzia, Chinese Crabs, Hybrid Lilacs, Doublefile Viburnum, White Fringe-tree, Beauty Bush, Hawthorn, Bridalwreath, Vanhoutte Spirea.

June—Philadelphus coronarius and virginalis, Froebel Spirea, Japanese Tree Lilac, Chinese Butterfly Bush, Ecae Rose, Hugonis Rose.

July) Smoketree, Rose of
August } Sharon, Butterfly Bush,
September) Sweetbay, Chaste Tree, Tamarisk.

October—Common Witchhazel.

THE PRAYER OF THE TREE

(A notice found nailed to a tree in one of the parks of Seville, Spain. Copied from the book "Spanish Sunshine," by Elinor Elsner.)

> *"To the Wayfarer—*
> *Ye who pass by and would raise your hand against me*
> *Harken ere you harm me!*
> *I am the heat of your hearth on the cold winter nights,*
> *The friendly shade screening you from the summer sun.*
> *My fruits are refreshing draughts,*
> *Quenching your thirst as you journey on,*
> *I am the beam that holds your house,*
> *The board of your table,*
> *The bed on which you lie,*
> *And the timber that builds your boat,*
> *I am the handle of your hoe,*
> *The door of your homestead,*
> *The wood of your cradle,*
> *And the shell of your coffin.*
> *I am the bread of kindness, and the flower of beauty.*
> *Ye who pass by, listen to my prayer; harm me not."*

CHAPTER V

PLANTING, TRANSPLANTING AND PRUNING

"He who plants a tree,
Plants a hope."

PLANTING

Planting, or rather transplanting, is a violent shock to any plant. Its food supply is curtailed by the cutting of some of its roots and for this reason we must cut down the demand on the remaining roots by pruning the top growth. These two processes constitute a severe operation and, as in the case of an operation on a person, should usually be performed when the plant is nearest asleep or when the chances of immediate recuperation are most favorable.

Someone has said, "If you love a plant you can transplant it and make it live any time." This means that if you are interested enough you will give the plant sufficient care before and after transplanting to watch it and help it overcome adverse circumstances.

For instance, small shrubbery may be moved in midsummer if the roots are cut six months to a year before transplanting. It will also be necessary to cut the tops back sharply, to "strip" off a large part of the leaves and to water and shade it until it recovers. Shrubs and small trees handle safely in all but extreme weather conditions if dug with a ball of earth. Allowing them to harden off out of reach of sun and wind will reduce the shock of transplanting and little pruning will be necessary. Specimen shrubs are also moved in this way, and their slight extra cost is more than justified. Also annuals or perennials may be moved any time without injury if they are grown in pots which confine the roots within a planting ball.

Thus season and condition are overcome but at added cost of time and labor. These instances should be the exception rather than the rule. Woody stemmed plants should be moved when they are nearest dormant. For perennials the general rule is to transplant them in spring or late summer when they are resting or farthest away from their blooming period.

General rules are always dangerous because there are usually many exceptions. Among the perennials, oriental poppies are best moved soon after blooming (when their foliage has withered) in order to avoid loss of bloom the following season; while windflowers, chrysanthemums and a few fall bloomers do not do well at all unless allowed to get a start before being moved the following spring.

November, just after the first good ground freeze, is considered best for deciduous trees and shrubs, yet Silver Maple and Poplars move better in the spring. Magnolias transplant best just before their blossom-buds begin to form, and Snowball, Butterfly Bush, Tamarix, Sumac, Strawberry Shrub and a few others do not seem to stand the winter's cold if weakened by fall transplanting. Coniferous evergreens transplant best in late summer—August or September.

Thus we see that time varies and that we must know our plant; also that we must write down the information so that we may use it again.

One of the most important things to know about a plant is how much room it will need when matured. The result of too close planting is an overcrowded condition which makes for unhealthy plants and the loss of flowers or fruit.

Most plants need air all around them as well as through the center. If we plant too close, the branches intertwine and, except in the case of hedges of specially selected plants, the result is not a beautiful thing. Many amateurs plant young stock too closely, expecting to thin it out at some future time but seldom do so when the time comes.

Shrubs usually mature and fill up the gaps in two to three years; trees in eight to ten years, while perennials take but two seasons. When we consider how many years they will grow if properly planted we should be willing to wait this length of time for the full effect.

There are several other things which we must consider in selecting planting material. We must visualize its appearance when fully grown: whether it will fill the space which we have selected for it; whether it will grow in shade or sun and fit itself to the soil in which we wish to plant it.

It is seldom that planting should be done in frozen ground. Sometimes big trees are moved when the ground is frozen in order to get a large solid ball to insure protection to the fine roots. In this case a supply of unfrozen soil is provided for filling around the ball in order to get rid of any air pockets.

It is better to do any transplanting on a dull moist day than a bright one. The drying out of roots is extremely bad for any plant. Winds are as injurious as sunlight, and it is always best to protect bare roots by a covering of wet sacking or other cloth.

Foliage is often more important than flowers. We may have a plant which has beautiful blooms for a few weeks and is an eye-sore the rest of the season.

In selecting a location remember that there is considerable difference in the shade cast by a building and that cast by a tree or shrub. The tree lets in air and some light.

Mulching: An important part of planting is "mulching." Mulching as previously explained is the covering of the soil about the plant to prevent alternate freezing and thawing in winter or to conserve moisture in summer. Mulching is not to keep the plants warm; it is to keep them cold. We repeat this several times in this book because it is so generally misunderstood.

The heaving of most soils during sudden weather changes breaks roots. A blanket of leaves is used to prevent this. If it is desired to fer-

The chief glory of the Dolgo Crab Apple is not blossoms, which are a modest white, but its deep crimson-purple fruit. These apples are not only larger than most ornamental crabs, but make fine jelly, rich in color and flavor.

One of the easiest flowers to grow from seed, and tolerant of many kinds of soils, climates and growing conditions, the Zinnia has many varieties. These blossoms are produced from a strain catalogued as "Persian Carpet."

tilize at the same time, new strawy manure will do it. The finer part is turned under in the spring.

Special mulches are indicated for the less hardy perennials and other plants in their respective chapters. These plants many times cannot stand a wet, packed down mulch.

In using straw do not make it too thick as it may form a nesting place for mice, which will feed upon the bark of shrubs and trees, often killing them. If you find indications of bark chewing, dust the mulch around the base of the plant with red pepper from a kitchen shaker and thin it out considerably.

Soil: The character of the soil has much to do with the time of transplanting in the spring. Light soils warm up more quickly than clay soils, and for this reason planting in them can be undertaken earlier.

Watering: Trees and shrubs need extra water for at least a year after planting. They may carry on with normal rainfall, but make little growth. A cultivated area about the trunk will catch surface water, and a weekly soaking with a hose, letting the water run slowly without a nozzle, will do wonders.

Summary: The successful moving of a tree, shrub or hardy flowering plant hinges first of all upon taking it up, transporting it and resetting it with the least possible disturbance of the original soil about those delicate fibrous rootlets which are its direct gatherers of the essential soil moisture and plant food. Upon the rapidity with which these rootlets resume their normal functioning in the new site depends the immediate,

and consequently the future, success of the subject.

Successful growth many times depends upon the cultivated area around the plant. It may seem foolish to cultivate a large area around a small plant and work in plant food, but this is common sense. Water the plant well to compact the soil and firm the earth around the roots. Cut back the top growth sharply to relieve the strain on the roots. No manure must touch the roots. If you use manure, be sure that it contains no wood shavings and is well rotted (two to three years old); even then keep it two to three inches away from the root ends.

Specific directions for moving different plants are given in their respective chapters.

PRUNING

Why We Prune: Pruning induces good habits in plants. There are a number of reasons for doing it, each one requiring its own particular method of procedure. Planting and pruning go hand in hand because it is necessary to maintain a balance between the plant top and its roots. The roots take up the moisture (and with it the food from the soil) and distribute it to the upper part. The leaves evaporate the excess moisture, leaving the food elements in the chemical laboratory of the plant where they are changed into cell building material. Part of this goes into the leaf enlargement, some into the stem and the rest returns to the building of the roots themselves.

Whenever the demand for moisture in the upper plant becomes greater than the supply available from the roots, the plant dies. When it becomes necessary to cut the roots to transplant, it also becomes necessary to curtail the top growth to relieve the demand from below. Therefore, we prune at planting time, especially in the spring when the general practice is one third reduction. But this does *not* apply to stock moved carefully with a ball of soil to protect the root system.

After the plant has grown we may prune it again to limit its height or secure some desired form. It is also pruned to remove diseased, injured or dead branches.

In the case of some roses and many shrubs and vines, the blossoms are borne upon new wood only. In this instance we remove the worn-out branches to stimulate the growth of the new ones.

Where exceptionally large specimen or exhibition flowers are desired, plants are sometimes cut back so that all their energy is thrown into the producing of the blossom. A modification of this is the removal of all but a few flower buds; this is called disbudding.

In the case of a sickly plant it is sometimes necessary to cut it back so that it may get a new start. Oftentimes a plant becomes so overgrown with old branches that it is cut back right to the ground.

In the case of hedges, evergreens or specimen plants we often prune

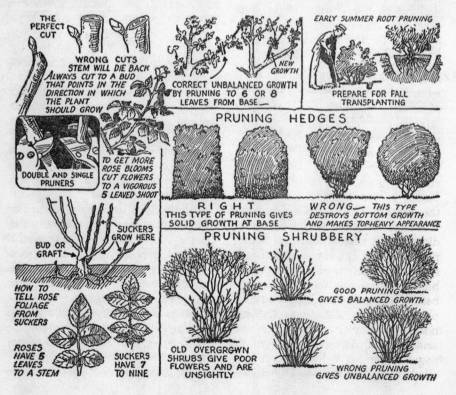

them or cut them with shears to some desired form or effect. This is usually known as shearing.

Special instructions for each of these operations are given in the cultural directions for the various plants themselves. These should be studied as pruning is not a job for an unskilled workman.

General Rules: The general rules are simple, yet no greater crimes are committed against our plants than in the name of pruning. Often the ignorant workman or the gardener becomes too enthusiastic. The use of the small knowledge necessary will save much grief.

Tools must be sharp and properly selected. A single-bladed shear is best. Cut with the blade toward the growing plant; this bruises only the part to be thrown away. Double-bladed pruners may bruise both parts. Use a saw on large branches and if it is double-edged use care to avoid damage to the rest of the plant. Use good sharp tools. Pay a fair price for them. It always pays to use good tools.

Cut near a vigorous bud. The new shoot developing will have a tendency to grow the way that bud points, so the plant can be shaped the way you wish.

A vigorous bud on a branch indicates that there is vitality at that point. If you cut close to and in a slanting direction down from the bud, the wound will soon callus over before withering or decay can take place. This idea should also be carried to the cutting of flowers for vase arrangement. (See illustrations on pages 82 and 177.) Proper cutting allows for future blooming on the

same joint. All cuts on larger branches should be coated with liquid asphaltum or any good wound dressing to keep out air and disease.

The cutting out of the heads or leading branches of many trees will cause them to become bunchy and ugly at that point besides making an opening where disease may enter.

It is generally best to do the pruning of trees in the winter, evergreens in the early spring and shrubbery in the spring or summer, according to the blooming period.

Root Pruning: Root pruning is good practice if you wish to transplant a large shrub or tree. In the spring, a trench is dug completely around the plant at a suitable distance from its base according to its size. This causes it to develop a compact ball of fine fiber-like feeding roots close to the plant and helps it to get started again after the transplanting.

Fill the trench with compost or earth rich in water holding material. Do not use manure which will burn the root ends. Soak the trench with weak chemical fertilizer solution (a tablespoonful to two gallons of water) several times during the growing season.

Small plants may be root pruned by driving a spade around the ball to be removed and fertilizing closely around the plant. At least six months of growing time should elapse between the root pruning and the transplanting.

Suckers: Many improved varieties of plants will not do well grown on their own roots. For this reason they are grafted on stronger plants, known as mother stock. For instance, lilacs may be grafted upon privet, and bedding roses upon brier stock. This mother (or root) stock often sends out shoots from below the graft or bud. These shoots, which are called suckers, can often be recognized by the character of their leaves in roses, lilacs, flowering almonds, etc. They should be cut off *below the ground* as soon as they are discovered so they will not compete with, or even dominate and take the place of, the improved variety. This frequently happens when the variety which has been grafted on is winter killed. If the gardener does not note where the sucker shoot originates and lets it grow, he will have a plant of the wild root stock, not of the named variety he bought and planted.

"Bleeding": Prune Maples and Elms in the fall or late summer, but not in early spring as they may "bleed." While this loss of sap does not injure the tree, it is not beneficial or necessary, and may be unsightly. If it is necessary to cut them back in spring, wait until they are out in full leaf.

EDITOR'S NOTE: Modern developments in planting technique make it possible to extend the planting season far beyond the traditional spring and fall periods. Protective coatings sprayed on plants reduce transpiration and the need for severe cutting back and reduce losses during planting and transplanting operations. These and related matters are discussed in GARDEN MAGIC MARCHES ON, page 439.

—E.L.D.S.

MUSKETAQUID

All my hurts
My garden spade can heal. A woodland walk
A quest of river-grapes, a mocking thrush,
A wild rose or rock-loving columbine,
Salve my worst wounds.

—EMERSON.

CHAPTER VI

CONIFEROUS EVERGREENS

It always here is freshest seen
'Tis ever here, an evergreen.
—CROWLEY.

The range of plants covered by the term coniferous is wide. They get their name from the cone which is the bloom of the plant and later its fruit. But in size they range from the little round Swiss Mountain Pine (*Pinus mugo*) in the yard to the giant Sequoia of our Pacific coast which was a large tree when the Pharaohs built the pyramids.

One of the conifers (or cone-bearers) is the Larch, which is not evergreen at all, but sheds its needle-like foliage in autumn the same as other deciduous plants. The cultural directions following apply also to them and they are to be recommended as graceful ornamental trees in their localities. The American Larch is the Tamarack, but a wider range of location is enjoyed by the Chinese Golden and the European Larches.

Often included in discussions of conifers because of their similar habits and uses, and because they are narrow-leaved evergreens, are the Yews and the Junipers or Red-cedars, even though they do not bear cones, but rather berry-like fruits. These are red and fleshy in the Yews and bluish-gray, small and firm in the case of the Junipers.

Moving Conifers: The two seasons when transplanting of evergreens may be most safely carried on are from the middle of August to the middle of September and from the time the frost is out of the ground in spring until the plants start to make new growth.

The advantage of late summer planting is that the roots get a chance to re-establish themselves before winter and are ready to make new growth promptly in the spring. The disadvantage is that the plants go into the rigors of winter in a weakened condition.

The advantage of spring planting is that the plant gets the benefit of the most favorable growing season while weakened by the transplanting operation. However, the subsequent hot dry days of summer may prove trying.

Larger trees may be handled more easily in February or March when a ball of frozen earth can be taken. The freezing of the soil to a solid mass makes possible the taking of the larger ball necessary to a tree of greater size.

It is the writer's opinion that early September planting is best except in the extreme northern part of the United States. The establishment of the roots before spring helps, and the need of less watering over the winter season, the chance to do a more leisurely job than in the short spring season, and the opportunity to get a fresh start before hot weather seem to outweigh all the other advantages.

I have seen an evergreen carelessly planted in the fall lose all its foliage over the winter only to come out again the following spring.

There is a type of evergreen adaptable to almost every need, locality and condition. Some varieties grow in swamps, at the water's edge, others upon rocky cliffs. However, the kinds used for ornament to which we now refer have for the most part two basic needs: good drainage and adequate moisture. It seems that even the kinds which grow wild in damp places require good drainage when planted under conditions of cultivation.

They are really never dormant and even in winter, when other plants are bare of leaves, constant transpiration is going on (in a lessened degree, of course) through their foliage. Therefore, water must be supplied during a prolonged dry spell even if the weather is moderately cold and especially in late fall after a dry summer.

They seem to grow best in soil underlaid with glacial drift and we must strive to imitate these conditions if we wish to quickly overcome the shock of root disturbance. Proper planting and care will enable the plant to maintain one-half its normal growth for the first two years after which it will probably have regained full vigor.

The most usual cause of failure of evergreens is lack of water. The foliage presents a large exposed surface for evaporation. If a plant loses water through its leaves faster than it can take in water through its roots, it dies. Water must get down at least three feet. Grade the surrounding soil and drive holes in the ground if necessary. All the roots should be constantly wet, but it should be a "drinking wetness," not a bath. Always cultivate an area one to two feet beyond the branch spread.

In transplanting, a few things are essential:

The trees should be transplanted with a ball of earth. The larger the ball the quicker the recovery. The method of procuring this ball is illustrated on page 88.

If the season is at all dry, first cultivate the area around the tree, then force a bar into the ground in a series of holes two or three feet deep around the tree. This circle should be of the size of the ball which you intend to take. Water this for several hours daily with a gentle stream, putting a gunny sack over the end of the hose. Grade the ground to turn the water into the holes. Repeat for about a week and allow to dry for several days.

Now prepare the planting hole in the new location. Dig it twice as large as the ball and half again as deep. If your soil is clay or is heavy, work deeply into the bottom a quantity of sand and gravel. Fill the hole with water and allow to drain away several times. If the soil removed is heavy, make it friable with sand and work in some thoroughly rotted manure or humus and bone meal.

Dig a trench around the tree to be moved, sloping one side to admit a wooden platform. Cover the ball tightly with burlap pinned together and held in place with nails. Work the earth from beneath, laying the ball against the platform, securing it with rope. Now cut the bottom roots cleanly with a knife or saw, trim all broken roots cleanly and secure burlap around the ball. These roots are very susceptible to injury and air. They should be kept covered and moist at all times.

The rope handle is used as a harness over the shoulders to facilitate lifting. The platform method allows moving a larger ball; if this is firmly secured in place, breakage and jar are minimized. Lower the ball into the new location and then untie. Remove burlap and proceed to plant, using care to firm all earth to avoid future settling and do not allow manure to come into contact with the roots. Firming the soil around evergreen roots is second in importance only to watering. Keep soil from drying out for several months.

Handling Bought Trees: If you are buying an evergreen and if the tree is large it will come to you with the branches tied to avoid injury to them. If you are unable to plant the tree at once and the weather is warm, it is well to untie the branches until you are ready to plant.

Also wet the ball and cover it with straw, sacks, or material to keep it from drying out. The foliage, too, must be protected from the sun and winds.

It is well to plant the tree as soon as possible, but do not plant it hastily. Better keep it a few days until you have time to do the job properly than to sacrifice good plant-

ing. When you are ready, place the tree with its branches tied at a convenient spot near the hole. You will notice upon the trunk a soil line which indicates the depth at which it was planted in the nursery. Your planting is to be one or two inches lower than the nursery planting. Be very careful to see that the tree is planted on a bed of well-firmed soil, so that it will not settle after it is wet. The preparation of the hole and the actual planting will be as already described. Some nurseries coat the roots with mud or clay by dipping them before shipment when they are not protected by a good ball. This coating should be softened by soaking before planting is done. Be sure that all broken or injured roots are cut off cleanly. Cracks or bad bruises may form a place for disease to enter and cause trouble later.

If the tree is of considerable size, it is important that its branches be kept tied in during the planting so the ends will not become bruised or broken. It is difficult to set the tree in its proper position without knowing something of its shape. We, therefore, recommend that the branches be loosened after the tree has been placed in the hole when it may be turned about before the burlap is removed, so that the best setting position may be obtained. Then tie them up again loosely to get them out of the way until the planting is finished.

The final loosening is after the arrangement of the earth has been made as above described. Any branches which do not conform to the desired shape may be taken off at this time, but it is better to wait until a little later.

If the planting location is exposed to strong winds it is well to support the tree by tying some soft material about its trunk and fastening it to a stake or post driven into the ground. Also, if the season is well advanced, it may be well to erect a windbreak of some kind on the windward side to prevent the drying out of the tender new foliage.

During the mild weather of spring it is quite beneficial to newly planted evergreens to keep the ground loosened beneath their branches until June 1. After June 1, mulch, by covering the space around them with about two inches of some loose, porous material which will help retain the moisture and keep their roots cool. The best material for this purpose is strawy manure. It may be fresh manure, if not found objectionable, or otherwise well-rotted manure.

Next we recommend homemade or granulated peat moss. These materials may be cultivated into the ground the following spring, but if they are not available straw, hay or even a loose mulch of leaves will help. Be sure that the mulch stays loose and that the air penetrates it easily. If possible use leaves of tough, durable texture that are less likely to mat, decay and cause heating.

Liquid manure during the growing season is the ideal stimulant for

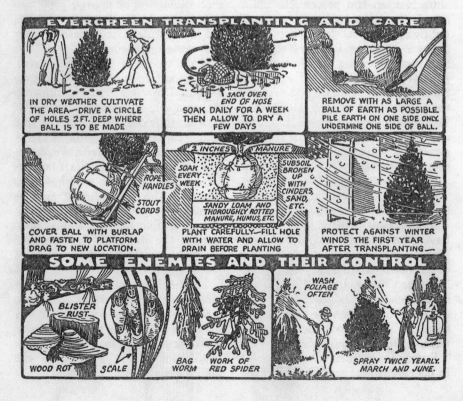

EVERGREEN TRANSPLANTING AND CARE

IN DRY WEATHER CULTIVATE THE AREA—DRIVE A CIRCLE OF HOLES 2 FT. DEEP WHERE BALL IS TO BE MADE

SACK OVER END OF HOSE
SOAK DAILY FOR A WEEK THEN ALLOW TO DRY A FEW DAYS

REMOVE WITH AS LARGE A BALL OF EARTH AS POSSIBLE. PILE EARTH ON ONE SIDE ONLY. UNDERMINE ONE SIDE OF BALL.

ROPE HANDLES
STOUT CORDS
COVER BALL WITH BURLAP AND FASTEN TO PLATFORM DRAG TO NEW LOCATION.

2 INCHES MANURE
SOAK EVERY WEEK
SUBSOIL BROKEN UP WITH CINDERS, SAND, ETC.
SANDY LOAM AND THOROUGHLY ROTTED MANURE, HUMUS, ETC.
PLANT CAREFULLY—FILL HOLE WITH WATER AND ALLOW TO DRAIN BEFORE PLANTING

PROTECT AGAINST WINTER WINDS THE FIRST YEAR AFTER TRANSPLANTING—

SOME ENEMIES AND THEIR CONTROL

BLISTER RUST
WOOD ROT
SCALE

BAG WORM
WORK OF RED SPIDER

WASH FOLIAGE OFTEN
SPRAY TWICE YEARLY. MARCH AND JUNE.

newly planted or ailing trees. Mulching with two inches of manure in the fall after a ground freeze and cultivating it lightly into the soil in the spring, have proved very stimulating. After spring transplanting, peat humus or moss may be used as a mulch to avoid odor.

Pruning: The balsam and concolor firs may be thickened by judicious shearing when young, but the concolor should be planted where it can develop naturally as its greatest charm is in the young growth as it fans out each spring.

The upright junipers respond to light shearing where a formal effect is desired. The Canaert red cedar makes a fine specimen and bears more berries when unsheared; for a tall hedge, it should be topped lightly as should the Keteleeri variety. Other upright forms are best allowed to follow their own habit of growth. All spreading varieties may need heading back to keep them under control in restricted places. The Pfitzer juniper makes a rapid growth and will give trouble if allowed to get out of hand. Take off the oldest branches by slipping the shears in under new shoots so the stubs will not show. The natural grace should be preserved.

The spruces can be thickened by having the center bud on each twig pinched off in early spring, or half of each new twig clipped off in June. They can be sheared when young, but, as with the firs, the leader must not be cut. Specimen trees must have room to develop without interference, especially the blue spruces.

Swiss mountain pines can be kept in compact shape by shearing, or by taking off one half of each soft leader in June.

The yews and arborvitaes respond readily to pruning if the shape of the plant is kept in mind, and shear readily into hedges when young. Taxus media hybrids can be trimmed into globes but the Hatfield variety should be left in its natural irregular form. Wire its upright stems together lightly with insulated electric wire to avoid snow damage, as is sometimes done with pyramidal arborvitaes. This also makes formal shearing easier. To get the desired outline, shear horizontally around the bottom for a foot or so, then work to the top with vertical cuts. To trim globes, trim a zone around the middle and work up and down to it.

Enemies: If evergreens are kept growing well, with all necessary food and water, they will be less susceptible to disease and pests than those with casual care. Nevertheless, they may be attacked by enemies from other plantings and therefore need constant watching. Cedar rust, bagworms and red spider are the most common sources of trouble.

The cedar-apple, or gall, is caused by the apple-rust fungus whose life cycle includes 4 to 5 months spent on the apple and 18 or more on the redcedar. Its presence on the latter causes a brownish gall to form on the tree which becomes active after the warm spring rains and throws off spores from its soft orange colored horns. These spores infect apple leaves and there develop new spores which are carried by the wind to the same or other cedars. Hawthorns, native crabs and their hybrids are also susceptible to this and other fungous pests, and in some sections cannot be used with success. The Chinese crabs seem to be resistant and are replacing the Bechtels in many places. Control consists in destroying badly infected cedars and replacing them with less susceptible varieties, though the best plan is not to grow the alternate host plants within a mile or two of one another. The galls can be reduced by handpicking throughout the year as they mature, and both cedars and apples should be sprayed in the spring with lime-sulfur.

Bagworms weave spindle-shaped bags on a foundation of the needles of the trees on which they live. In them the young are hatched in the spring to carry on in the same manner. They are found on many varieties of evergreens, but seem to prefer juniper, spruce, arborvitae and larch. Hand-picking the bags and destroying will take care of light infestations, but spraying all trees with arsenate of lead will kill the young worms. Morning is the best time, when they come out to feed. The pests seem to like thick plantings with shade and northern exposures. They will often defoliate parts of trees.

The red spider is really an 8-legged mite visible only under a magnifying glass. It weaves fine webs on the underside of branches, sucks the plant juices and can cause the death of the tree if not combated. Since the spider flourishes under hot, dry conditions, it can be discouraged by deep watering and by washing off the tree each week.

This is done best with a round or flaring rose nozzle, directing the stream of water up and under the branches. To avoid burning wait until the sun is low and the tree has cooled off after the heat of the day. Dusting with sulfur is a cure and should be a routine treatment.

In cities and suburbs, wash off frequently the soot and grime deposited from the air. Evergreen foliage is sticky and dirt and soot soon tend to smother it. An occasional shower is an excellent tonic and also helps keep down red spider.

Watering: Emphasis has been placed upon this in other parts of the text, but an additional word on watering in the fall is important. The ground should be soaked to below the frost line before it freezes over each fall, using a hose without a nozzle and a gentle stream of water. This enables the roots to supply moisture to replace that which the winter sun draws from the foliage and a tree will be much more likely to come through severe weather without weakening.

The writer has kept evergreens healthy and beautiful for many years by a simple system. In February or March give a dormant spray with miscible oil according to directions on the container. Procure it from your seedsman, it is good for your other trees and shrubbery, too. In June, spray with the oil as directed for summer use, mixing it with Arsenate of lead. (If you have sprayed with sulfur, do not use oil for several months. They do not mix.)

A fall mulch of manure, an occasional shot of liquid manure, an occasional watering, bathing, and that's all. Spray, water and feed and people will say of your trees, as nurserymen have sometimes said of mine, "The healthiest we have ever seen."

If your trees turn brown in winter, protect them against the drying out caused by excessive winds. This is advisable for all fall transplanted stock if in an exposed location.

Last, but not least, buy healthy stock from reliable local nurserymen. They will sell you trees which will

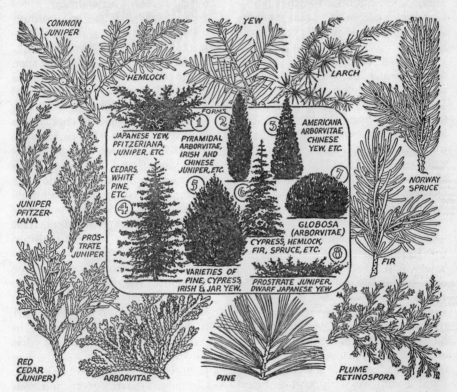

Above are shown the foliage structures of our most popular evergreens; also the eight general forms taken by coniferous trees, with the names of some running most true to these forms. Many plants do not run true to these forms, but are combinations of two or more of them. The forms taken by the foliage of various evergreens are very confusing as some plants of the juniper species have sharp-pointed needlelike foliage and others scalelike leaves which sometimes overlap. In the case of the redcedar both may appear on the same plant. The arborvitae is easily detected by its flat leaves which look as if they had been pressed in a book. The forms and sizes of this variety are numerous. Cypress for landscaping is usually known as retinospora. The branches resemble those of arborvitae, but are more plumelike. In our illustration the hemlock might be confused with the juniper beside it, but hemlocks are easily distinguished by their soft beauty and the nodding top and branch ends. Yews are slow-growing trees usually of dwarf habit and are distinguished by the extreme darkness of their foliage which comes in flat sprays. Spruce is the well-known Christmas tree of commerce—its foliage standing rigid and straight away from its branches, while the fir has a somewhat blunt end, flat, leaf arranged in two rows. These vary in different species. The larch (European) is not a true evergreen as it drops its foliage in the fall to take on soft bright green tufts of needlelike foliage in the spring. It is noted for the brightness of its foliage.

grow in your soil. Trees pushed out of their natural latitude are likely to fail. No matter how beautiful they may appear, the trees grown in the southern lowlands will not grow well under some conditions farther north. Cheap evergreens are usually expensive in the end as well as unsatisfactory.

More live Christmas trees (which may be any of various kinds of conifers) are being used each year and many times a family would like to keep and plant the tree after the holidays. This can be done, but the trees need special handling as they suffer severely from the hot, dry air of the average home; also sudden changes from outdoors to a living room for a fortnight or so and then out again, are hard on them.

If you wish your live Christmas tree to grow after the holidays, keep it in a pan where its burlaped roots may be kept moist. Keep it as far away from direct heat as possible. When indoor use is over, place it in the cool cellar, where its foliage may be washed off, its roots moistened and the plant hardened gradually to cold over a period of a week or two. Plant it outdoors with good drainage in mild weather, then water and mulch it well.

CONIFEROUS EVERGREENS IN GENERAL USE

ABIES balsamea (Balsam Fir). 60–70 ft. Narrow pyramidal growth; dark green fragrant needles. Use as specimen, windbreak, border planting.

A. concolor (White Fir). 90–100 ft. Symmetrical; grayish blue. Specimen, group, border.

JUNIPERUS chinensis (Chinese Juniper). 20 ft. Light green to blue; columnar cone. For accent, group, border.

J. chinensis japonica (Japanese). 8–12 inches. Spreading; blue-green, white lines on pointed leaves. Decorative.

J. chinensis pfitzeriana (Pfitzer). Broad, spreading, ironclad, endures shade. Foundation, bank, group plantings.

J. chinensis sargenti (Sargent). Low, creeping; blue-green, rugged.

J. excelsa stricta (Spiny Greek). 4–5 ft. Semi-dwarf, conical, glaucous blue; slow growth. For foundation, groups, formal accent.

J. horizontalis plumosa (Andorra). 15–18 inches. Low; silvery purple. For banks, steps, foundation, rock garden.

J. scopulorum (Rocky Mountain). 20–25 ft. Columnar cone; silver whipcord foliage. For accent, groups, formal effects.

J. squamata meyeri (Meyer). 3–4 ft. Irregular form; bright blue to pinkish. For specimen, accent, rock garden.

J. virginiana (Redcedar). 30–35 ft. Columnar; grayish green, purplish in winter. Hedge, background.

J. virginiana canaerti (canaert). 12–15 ft. Deep green whipcord foliage; blue berries. For accent, hedge, specimen.

J. virginiana glauca (Silver Redcedar). 15–18 ft. Pyramidal; white to blue. Against house; for color, accent.

LARIX (Larch). 90 ft. Deciduous conifer. Broad, conical; soft, tufted needles; soft spring color. Specimen.

PICEA abies (Norway Spruce). 80–

90 ft. Dark green; conical. Windbreak and woods.

P. glauca (White Spruce). 60–70 ft. Compact pyramidal; light green. Background, windbreak, screen, group.

P. glauca densata (Black Hills). 50–60 ft. Compact, widespreading; bluish green. Specimen, naturalistic plantings.

P. glauca conica (Dwarf Alberta). 4–6 ft. Dwarf compact cone; miniature needles; grass green. Formal decorative; for small areas.

P. pungens (Colorado Spruce). 80–150 ft. Green to blue. Specimen, windbreak, woods.

P. pungens kosteriana (Koster Blue). Silver-blue. Specimen, group.

PINUS mugo (Swiss Mountain Pine). 4 ft. Shrubby; dense growth; dark green. Foundations, groups, accent planting.

P. nigra (Austrian Pine). 60–70 ft. Pyramidal, spreading; deep green. City, seashore, forests.

P. strobus (White Pine). 75 ft. Pyramidal, spreading; soft, blue-green needles. Specimen, group, screen, forests.

P. sylvestris (Scotch Pine). Irregular, rapid growth; gray-green needles. Woods.

PSEUDOTSUGA taxifolia (Douglas-fir). 70–80 ft. Colorado-spruce type pyramidal; green to blue. Hardy, useful; endures shade; specimen, forest.

TAXUS (Yew). An increasingly popular material for ornamental use over much of the country. Especially adapted for foundation plantings, hedges, etc. Has deep green, waxy, flat foliage and scarlet berries. Does well in full sun or shade; thrives in various soils. Hardy and ordinarily free from disease. The various forms can be pruned into many forms from straight hedges to topiary figures.

T. cuspidata (Japanese Yew). 40 ft. Pyramidal, dense. Seedlings develop various forms; two of these follow:

T. cuspidata expansa (Spreading Japanese Yew). 10–12 ft. Broad, V-shaped bush form. Hedges, foundation, groups.

T. cuspidata nana (Dwarf Yew). 2–3 ft. Slow growing. Specimen, low hedge, in tubs.

T. media (Intermediate Yew). 40 ft. but usually lower. Hybrid of Japanese and English (T. baccata). Columnar to pyramidal; dense. Var. hatfieldi bushy, and var. hicksi more columnar.

THUJA (Arborvitae). Flattened, scaled foliage. Can endure little shade and like abundant moisture. For hedge, groups, foundation, accent.

T. occidentalis (American Arborvitae). To 60 ft. Foliage yellowish green beneath. Many varieties of different sizes and forms—pyramidal, conical, globular, etc.

TSUGA canadensis (Canada Hemlock). 75–90 ft. Conical, with drooping branches; soft green foliage. Likes shade and protection of other trees. Specimen, tall hedges, background, woods. Must have moisture good part of year.

T. carolina (Carolina Hemlock). 75 ft. Stands shearing and city conditions well.

CHAPTER VII

ACID-LOVING PLANTS

No more beautiful flowers grace our gardens than those of the acid-loving plants, those that tolerate or need acid soil conditions. The instructions for raising these plants sound more troublesome than the actual operation really is.

The best known of them are our broad-leaved evergreens, chief among which are the Mountain-laurel and the glorious Rhododendron which includes species ranging from six inches to fifty feet high and of practically every color except vivid blue. Also some deciduous shrubs such as Dogwood, the Heather tribe, Trailing-arbutus, etc.; certain well-known perennials, and the Azaleas which come in both evergreen and deciduous species. Many of these have the reputation of being temperamental, but if their soil needs are once understood and supplied, the rest of their culture is simple. They will grow in many localities if the kinds are properly selected and if the soil is not too alkaline. Most failures are due to careless, unintelligent planting and culture.

Instructions call for the removal of the clay or sandy loam in which most of our garden favorites thrive and the substitution of soil prepared and made acid for their use. Sometimes plants do well in this medium for about two years, and then, just as the owner becomes thoroughly enamored of their charms, they sicken and die. This often results from the fact that the surrounding soil, by the percolating of lime-carrying water, has been rendered alkaline. Earthworms are attracted to this soil and they, too, bring lime. City water, many times, contains lime and watering with it in summer tends to lessen acidity.

These plants simply will not tolerate lime in any form, and every effort must be used to maintain acidity by using soil-acidifiers, acid fertilizers and other chemical agents.

Too much trouble you say? Not at all; not if you consider the beauty of their bloom and foliage. Any plant must be properly set and very little more care in planting is needed for these than for others. Once established they need less care than almost any other plant. If you have a planting already established, aluminum sulphate is a safe, reliable method of adding acid to the soil. Spread over the planting about ¼ or ½ pound to the square yard. It is considered better than tannic acid for this purpose.

In starting any planting it is always well to remember that very few shrubs and trees brought from the wild are successfully planted in our gardens. Their root system is too poor. A nursery grown plant is first prepared by root pruning and a reliable nurseryman will know what species and kind will grow in your locality; how tall it will grow; how far apart to plant for future growth and the proper kinds for you.

Rhododendrons: Rhododendron maximum grows in the wooded uplands from Nova Scotia to the Carolinas, yet each year thousands are brought from our southern mountains and planted in the open and subjected to winds and sun where they become sickly growthless eyesores. This type, as with most common Rhododendrons, requires shade. Three or four hours of sun per day is all that it can stand. Some other hybrid Rhododendrons require less shade, but all are better for some of it. Do not expect them to grow in dense shade of trees and buildings. They require several hours of sun each day but not at noontime when it is hottest.

If properly selected and planted they do not need the coddling and winter protection which we see given to exotic varieties.

Shelter from high winds, especially north and west, may be provided by trees, buildings, a hill or a wall. Plant four or five feet away from walls because of the lime in the cement, stucco, etc., which will eventually wash into the soil. You may plant under partial shade of Oak, Birch, Cherry, Pine and other deep-rooted plants provided their branches are fifteen or twenty feet above the plants. If you trim the lower branches from such trees to provide a location,

do it over a period of years and when the tree is dormant. Maple, Poplar, Linden, Elm and Willow must be avoided because their surface roots will rob the plants of food and moisture.

Low, damp spots should be avoided. Late frosts damage the growth and frosts are most severe in such places.

The need of some shade is acute in winter as a protection against sudden changes in temperature due to warm days followed by cold nights. In summer, as in winter, transpiration is going on. Winter killing is usually caused by excessive evaporation of moisture during sudden warm days and the inability of the plant to take it up quickly enough from the still frozen soil. A good autumn drenching will help store the water in the plant. It is also necessary to conserve moisture in hot, dry weather to allow the root system to keep up with the upper plant.

Rhododendrons well established, fed and watered, have few enemies. If tips wilt or die in summer, cut away until you have clean wood with no brown spots or holes. Thus you easily control borers and blight which destroys large branches unless removed. Laceflies sometimes feed on the underside of the foliage, giving it a sickly brown appearance. Spray leaves with a hand or bath soap, one pound to 20 gallons of water and repeat until the pest is eliminated. Get the spray on the underside of the leaves.

Newly planted, the tendency is to overproduce, so cut away at least half of the large fat buds the first two winters, leaving the smaller buds

for new growth. After this prune only to keep in shape and size and do it in April and September. Excessive pruning will not hurt the plant but may spoil the flower effect the following season.

Overgrown plants may be renewed by cutting out one-half the branches, half-way back in the spring. New growth will come from these. The following spring the other half may be cut. Do not hesitate to cut through thick branches.

The best transplanting time is April and September, but if it is done in the fall plants must have time to get root growth started before frost. Flower buds should be thinned out in April for larger and better flowers.

Some Rhododendrons are easily propagated by layering. Cut a notch in a branch and peg down firmly. Stake the branch to keep it from swaying in the wind. It takes about twelve months for roots to form. Do not be in a hurry to sever from the parent plant.

Flowers removed from the plant in their early stage will open if placed in water for a few days.

Azaleas: Most of the foregoing instructions for Rhododendrons fit Azaleas also. They are smaller and will stand more sunlight; in fact, most of them will grow in full sun. Otherwise the planting requirements for soil and protection are much the same. Transplant them in the spring. Their demand for water is heaviest then, when new shoots are developing. They must receive it to bloom freely.

Planting: Our illustration shows the construction of three kinds of pits for isolating the acid soil from the alkaline surrounding it. The cinders and sand in the bottom permit the ready passage of surface water and prevent the entrance of earthworms. No water will enter from the bottom unless the soil is a water-bearing stratum in which case these plants will not grow until it is tiled for drainage.

This writer can see little advantage in the brick and cement types, although they are recommended. The only real advantage is that they readily turn back water and exclude the roots of some trees and shrubs. Poplars and Willows will enter anywhere. The materials from which these pits are made contain lime and this is poison to acid plants. If used, they must be soaked with a strong solution of aluminum sulphate several times before filling and, in treating the plants with this chemical as later described, care should be used to soak the soil nearest them to overcome the alkalinity which they will send out.

The wooden pit has no such drawbacks and backed with cinders, well tamped, will turn ground water and last for many years. Make it as tight as possible and do not use cedar or resinous pine, as such woods are injurious. Two-inch plank is best and use no wood preservatives upon it.

Acid-loving plants are surface feeders and fine rooted. They are much easier planted and will seldom lose their flowering season if they come with a large burlaped ball which should be soaked in water before planting. Plant by slitting the burlap in numerous places after it is set in the hole. It may then be loosened, unwrapped and left to rot.

Set the plants as deep as they grew and do not tamp the soil. They need air in the soil for the development of bacteria upon which their health depends. Settle the soil by thorough watering.

The surface should be shaped to run the water to the plants during the summer and the mulch (described later) should drain it away from them in winter. Plant them close enough so they will shade each other slightly when mature, but allow for future growth.

Soil: They prefer porous, open textured soil. If your ground is heavy, add about 20% to 30% clean washed sand. White sand is also good; silicate sand is said to be best. Sandy soils, however, need special attention. Some heavier soil should be added. Wood soil, if black with leaf mold, needs no addition of sand. Soil from beneath Oak, Hickory, Birch and White Pine trees is best. Rotten bark (except from cedar and resinous pine) or any rotted wood can be mixed with the soil, and aged sawdust is recommended.

Where we find White Oak, Birch, Larch and White Pine trees growing, we may be sure of success, for they flourish in slightly acid soil. Soil from beneath these trees is the best to use in the compost. Rotting leaves from other trees quickly lose their acid in the process.

It is best to prepare a compost in the fall, allowing it to mix and mellow during winter for use in planting in April. First spread a layer of finely pulverized imported peat moss or wood peat such as is used upon golf courses. This should be six inches deep, about four feet wide, and as long as is necessary. Over this spread a layer of six inches of cow manure or well-rotted horse manure and on top of this one foot of good soil. Turn several times during the winter, allowing the lumps to freeze and crumble.

Be sure to prepare enough of it. Any left over is useful in many other garden activities.

In the spring, when planting mix with each barrow load of compost one quart of cottonseed meal and one pint of aluminum sulphate.

Mulching and Care: When we consider that the plants are moisture-loving and surface-rooting and are constantly sending their feeding roots toward the surface in search of food and moisture, it becomes apparent that they will stand no cultivation. Never stir the earth. Any cleaning up of the bed must be done with a rake and weeds should be pulled out. Do not allow other plants to crowd.

It is also apparent that a mulch will save much watering and prevent ground drafts, keeping the ground cool in summer and protecting against sudden change in winter. This mulch should consist of about two and one-half inches of a mixture of equal parts peat moss and cow manure applied in May. It may be renewed each year as the lower portion decomposes.

Fertilization: The fertilizers for acid plants are in a separate class from the usual run. Bone meal, wood ashes and lime are poison. One compound used for years is as follows:

1 lb. Ammonium Sulphate
3½ lbs. High Grade Acid Phosphate
2 lbs. High Grade Sulphate of Potash

3 lbs. Cottonseed meal
1 lb. Aluminum Sulphate

This makes an acid reaction mixture of 4% nitrogen, 6% phosphoric acid and 8% potash.

Another recommended by the U. S. Dept. of Agriculture is:

5 lbs. Cottonseed meal
2 lbs. Acid Phosphate
1 lb. Sulphate Potash
1 lb. Aluminum Sulphate

These materials, thoroughly mixed, are applied to the bed, a generous one-fourth pound to the square yard. Mix lightly with the mulch and water so it will soak into the soil. Keep the fertilizer a few inches away from the stems and carry it out well beyond the tips of the branches. The aluminum sulphate is not a fertilizer but is added to these mixtures to renew acidity in the soil. Tannic acid is also used for this purpose.

The use of liquid manure just before the blooming season is to be recommended as it is with most other plants. Cow manure is especially good.

Water: The only remaining requirement is water. Watering is essential to these moisture lovers. If they wilt, spray the leaves and soak the soil in summer. Next season's blooms are formed in summer and autumn and depend on summer care. They, as other evergreens, must not go into winter without a thorough soaking or they will winter kill.

Special: Be sure to remove all seed pods after flowering. Never, never allow the plants to seed if you want maximum flowers next year.

Other Plants: Other plants which prefer acid conditions are listed on page 101. They do not need such complete isolation as the Rhododendrons and Azaleas. Try raising them separately in a bed of soil full of leafmold or peat moss. Weak applications of aluminum sulphate solution (ranging from one ounce to the gallon upward) should prove beneficial.

Be careful not to interfere with the soil conditions of surrounding plants which may be killed by acid. You may plant in an old tub as illustrated at the bottom of page 121.

Soil Testing: The use of simple soil-testing apparatus as pictured and described on page 100, is a sure way of keeping tabs on the soil. Your seedsman can get it for you.

Litmus paper, for an even simpler test, is procurable at druggists. It will give a rough indication, but does not tell if the soil is acid enough.

A frequent error of the home gardener is to assume that his soil is acid or "sour." The presence of moss or the absence of grass in shady spots is seldom due to acidity, but more often to bad physical soil condition or lack of plant food, and water. The application of lime to these spots is more likely to do harm than good.

Leafmold, peats, manure, and other sources of humus are acid while in a state of decomposition. Therefore, peat bogs or peaty soils usually hold organic acid. In woodlands, too, acidity is developed by decomposing leaves, but in sections where the soil is naturally alkaline, the acidity in the decomposing leaves is rapidly overcome.

Alkaline soils usually predominate. In limestone regions the clay soil is so alkaline that it is hard to keep it acid for such plants as require it. Lime is frequently exhausted from the soil in the process of farming by being washed away and by being used up by the crops. It is necessary to corn, wheat, and oats, but more especially to clover.

In the home garden, however, it should be used with care. Do not apply it unless you are sure that it is needed to correct acidity or unless you do so under specific instructions for lime-loving plants.

Ground limestone is best for general use. The finer it is ground, the quicker the action. Hydrated lime acts more quickly but does not last as long. If the soil is acid, anywhere from one to six pounds per square yard may be needed to change it.

Limestone may be applied at any time without injury to plants, but several light applications are better than a single heavy one.

There are four methods often used to test soil for acidity. The addition of dilute hydrochloric acid to a little dry soil will cause an effervescence if lime is present. The ammonia test is more often recommended for soil made dark by leafmold or peat. Simply shake up a tablespoon of soil in one-half pint of water, then add one tablespoon of strong ammonia. After standing for a few hours the liquid will be brown if organic acid is present and clear if there is sufficient lime to offset it.

To merely determine acidity or alkalinity, procure some litmus paper (red and blue) from your druggist; shake up some soil with a little water and allow to stand for a short time. Now, holding the litmus paper with a pair of tweezers, drop some of this water upon it. The blue litmus will turn red if the soil is acid and the red litmus will turn blue if it is alkaline. Use rainwater or distilled water; city or well waters may have lime in them and spoil the test. Also avoid touching the paper with the hands, which give off a slight acid through perspiration.

These tests will tell whether soil is acid or alkaline, but not how strongly they run in either direction. The degree of variation can be determined by the theory of concentration of hydrogen ions. These are some big words for a simple process.

The symbol of measurement of this soil reaction is pH. Most plants do well in soil running from slightly alkaline (pH7.5) to slightly acid (pH6.0), but greater extremes are required for many of our popular acid or lime-loving plants.

We show in our illustration one of a number of these soil-testing sets, together with a table showing the meaning of symbols of degrees. The testing process with one of these sets is called colorimetric determination (measurement by color) and is simplicity itself.

A bottle of testing solution is furnished, together with a small porcelain dish; soil is placed in a depression in the dish and wet with the testing solution. The solution then runs into a smaller depression where its color is compared with a chart.

The various colors determine the degree of acidity. A list of plants showing their preference also comes with most of these sets, together with the instructions for obtaining proper condition.

Consider the acid requirements of a few well-known plants, remembering that pH7.0 is neutral and all below is acid: Vernal Iris 4.0 to 5.0, Rhododendron 5.0 to 6.0, White Ageratum 5.0 to 6.0, Magnolia (except M.

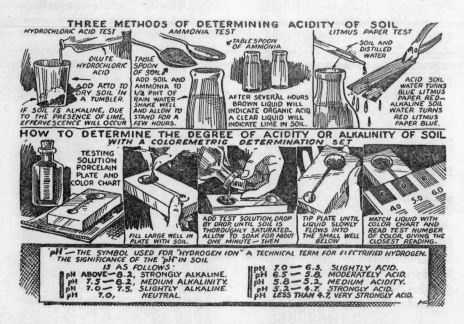

THREE METHODS OF DETERMINING ACIDITY OF SOIL

HYDROCHLORIC ACID TEST — AMMONIA TEST — LITMUS PAPER TEST

DILUTE HYDROCHLORIC ACID
ADD ACID TO DRY SOIL IN A TUMBLER.
IF SOIL IS ALKALINE, DUE TO THE PRESENCE OF LIME, EFFERVESCENCE WILL OCCUR

TABLE SPOON OF SOIL
ADD SOIL AND AMMONIA TO 1/2 PINT OF RAIN WATER SHAKE WELL AND ALLOW TO STAND FOR A FEW HOURS.

TABLESPOON OF AMMONIA
AFTER SEVERAL HOURS BROWN LIQUID WILL INDICATE ORGANIC ACID. A CLEAR LIQUID WILL INDICATE LIME IN SOIL.

SOIL AND DISTILLED WATER
ACID SOIL WATER TURNS BLUE LITMUS PAPER RED. ALKALINE SOIL WATER TURNS RED LITMUS PAPER BLUE.

HOW TO DETERMINE THE DEGREE OF ACIDITY OR ALKALINITY OF SOIL
WITH A COLOREMETRIC DETERMINATION SET

TESTING SOLUTION PORCELAIN PLATE AND COLOR CHART

FILL LARGE WELL IN PLATE WITH SOIL.

ADD TEST SOLUTION, DROP BY DROP, UNTIL SOIL IS THOROUGHLY SATURATED. ALLOW TO SOAK FOR ABOUT ONE MINUTE — THEN

TIP PLATE UNTIL LIQUID SLOWLY FLOWS INTO THE SMALL WELL BELOW

MATCH LIQUID WITH COLOR CHART AND READ TEST NUMBER OF COLOR, GIVING THE CLOSEST READING.

pH — THE SYMBOL USED FOR "HYDROGEN ION" A TECHNICAL TERM FOR ELECTRIFIED HYDROGEN. THE SIGNIFICANCE OF THE 'pH' IN SOIL IS AS FOLLOWS:

pH ABOVE 8.2, STRONGLY ALKALINE.	pH 7.0 — 6.5, SLIGHTLY ACID.
pH 7.5 — 8.2, MEDIUM ALKALINITY.	pH 6.5 — 5.8, MODERATELY ACID.
pH 7.0 — 7.5, SLIGHTLY ALKALINE.	pH 5.8 — 5.2, MEDIUM ACIDITY.
pH 7.0, NEUTRAL.	pH 5.2 — 4.7, STRONGLY ACID.
	pH LESS THAN 4.7, VERY STRONGLY ACID.

glauca) 5.0 to 6.9, Flowering Dogwood 6.0 to 7.0, and Garden Lilies 5.0 to 6.0.

With testing equipment the gardener needs to do no guessing. It enables the grouping of plants with like preferences, which adds much to their success and health.

ACID SOIL PLANTS
Broad-Leaf Evergreens

Andromeda
(Pieris
japonica)
(Pieris
floribunda)
Galax (Galax
aphylla)
Leucothoe
(Leucothoe
catesbaei)
Sand Myrtle
(Leiophyllum)

Mountain Holly
(Nemopanthus
mucronata)
American Holly
(Ilex opaca)
Oconee-bells
(Shortia)
Rhododendron
Azaleas
Mountain Laurel
(Kalmia
latifolia)

Deciduous Shrubs

Azaleas
Birch (Betula
glandulosa)
Dogwood,
Flowering
(Cornus
florida)
Blueberry
(Vaccinium)
Fringetree
(Chionanthus)
Heather
(Calluna,
Erica)
Huckleberry
(Gaylussacia)
Rhodora
(Rhodora
canadensis)

White Elder
Summer Sweet
Sweet Pepper
Bush
(Clethra)
Trailing-arbutus
(Epigaea)
Withe-Rod
(Viburnum
cassinoides)
Smooth Withe-
Rod (Viburnum
nudum)
Hobblebush
(Viburnum
alnifolium)

Trees

Chestnut
(Castanea
dentata)
Scrub Oak
(Quercus
ilicifolia)
Sweet Birch
(Betula lenta)
Fir (Abies)
Carolina
Hemlock
(Tsuga
carolinana)
Striped Maple
(Acer
pennsyl-
vanicum)

Mountain Maple
(Acer
spicatum)
Blackjack Oak
(Quercus
marilandica)
Willow Oak
(Quercus
phellos)
Post Oak
(Quercus
stellata)
Pine (Pinus)
Spruce (Picea)

Perennials

Bogbean
(Menyanthes
trifoliata)
Bluebells
(Mertensia
virginica)
Buttercup
(Ranunculus)
Bleeding Heart,
Fringed
(Dicentra
eximia)
Columbine,
Rocky Moun-
tain (Aquilegia
caerulea)
Coreopsis, Rose
(Coreopsis
rosea)
Coreopsis,
Threadleaf
(Coreopsis
verticillata)

American
Turkscap Lily
(L. superbum)
Marsh-marigold
(Caltha
palustris)
Primrose
(Primula)
Phlox amoena
Phlox, Mountain
(Phlox ovata)
Phlox,
Creeping
(Phlox
stolonifera)
Polemonium,
Creeping
(Polemonium
reptans)
Snakeroot or
Bugbane
(Cimicifuga
racemosa)

Gayfeather
(Liatris)

Blazing Star
(Liatris
graminifolia)

Gentian
(Gentiana)

Globeflower
(Trollius)

Iris, Cubeseed
(Iris
prismatica)

Pink Turtlehead
(Chelone
lyoni)

Painted Trillium
(Trillium
undulatum)

Valerian
(Valeriana
officinalis)

Wild-indigo
(Baptisia
tinctoria)

Iris, Vernal
(Iris verna)

Ladyslipper
(Cypripedium)

Lily-of-the-valley
(Convallaria)

Carolina Lily
(L. caroli-
nianum)

Orangecup Lily
(L. philadel-
phicum)

Wolfsbane
(Aconitum)

Monkshood
(Aconitum)

Woodsorrel
(Oxalis
acetosella)

Man, thought to be God's finest work,
Must give way to the flowers,
That pray for little but water
As they thrive in alluring bowers.
—MAURICE F. LYONS.

CHAPTER VIII

HEDGES

Row upon row
The hedges are robing in green.
Behold,
How plainly the lilacs are seen
To quiver and thrill.
— GRIFFITH.

Hedges or living fences, as they are sometimes called, combine utility with beauty. Aside from protecting our property from trespass by careless neighbors, canvassers, or solicitors, they lend an air of formal dignity, which cannot be given by a fence, no matter how ornamental.

They are used as screens to promote privacy or hide the objectionable, while permitting the passage of air; also for windbreaks in exposed situations, and as a background for landscape features.

When the average home gardener thinks of a hedge, he usually refers to privet or barberry, which are much used for hedges because of their easy adaptability. The term does not necessarily mean rigidly pruned or restrained growth. Many flowering shrubs planted in a row will form a casual hedge of the more free-and-easy type. Some of these may be pruned or sheared to a fairly regular form.

Evergreens make fine hedges because they retain their appearance in winter, but for simple purposes tall growing annuals or even ornamental grasses may be used.

It is well to consider how you want the hedge to look in winter as well as in summer before you make your selection. Also the cost enters into the question.

Although deciduous (leaf losing) material should not be planted until late October or November, when the plants are dormant, cuttings may be propagated in summer for planting in spring, making the hedge cost very little. Although these plants will take several years to grow from cuttings to hedge size the cost of the operation aside from the labor will be quite trifling.

If evergreens are used the best time to plant them is about September 1. When this is done the roots will become established during the cool fall months which are to follow and will be prepared for the winter by the plentiful fall rains. In the spring the evergreens make new growth and there is a great advantage in having had several months of growing weather in the fall to first establish the plant underground. Spring planted evergreens face the hot trying conditions of summer while in a weakened state because of the demands of new growth and the root shock due to transplanting.

In planting hedges, as in any other type of garden material, it pays to be careful. If your soil is very good it may be all right to excavate holes big enough to receive the individual plants, but if you want quick sturdy sure growth the best way is to excavate a trench and fill it with good soil, breaking up the subsoil to insure drainage and possibly adding some sand or cinders to the bottom in especially bad situations.

After the plants are placed the ground should be shaped so that water runs toward the plant when applied to it. After the growing season, however, the water should run away from the plant and the ground should be shaped accordingly.

There are some materials which will serve for hedges and grow in damp places, but the majority of them need drainage. If this is the case, in damp spots, it is well to dig a trench or a wide drain, as we illustrate, using the excavated material to form a ridge upon which the planting may be done.

This same method also may be well used on a steep hillside to act as a waterbreak to prevent washing away of the soil about the plant roots and also to hold some of the water for deep penetration. Be sure to plant deep enough.

In most instances a single row of plants will be sufficient, but where a very heavy screen is desired it may be necessary to use a double row. In this case, the plants should be staggered in two straight lines a suitable distance apart according to the material used. In all cases, a line should be used to get a straight row.

Most types of privet and many kinds of flowering shrubbery are propagated from cuttings. In the early summer this may be done from softwood cuttings by merely setting them

in a saucer depression, where the ground has been well worked up and mixed with sand to insure thorough drainage.

The depression enables easy watering as the soil must be kept moist (but not wet) at all times. The cuttings are taken from the plant about 8 inches long and containing three or more joints or nodes with a node at the top of each. Insert them into the soil, heavy end down, two inches deep. Seed stores offer newly discovered preparations which will cause them to root faster and more freely.

As several months are required to establish this root growth before cold weather, the cuttings must be placed in boxes if taken late in the summer so that a glass frame can be used to cover them on cold nights to prolong the season well into freezing weather. After this the plants can be

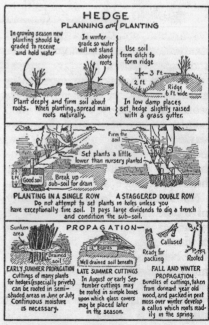

protected by covering with leaves.

Hardwood cuttings may be taken in the same manner after the plants become dormant. The wood should be one year old, firm and strong, and should have two or more nodes. They are then packed in peat moss and kept in a temperature of forty-five degrees. Here they will form a callus on the end, from which, when planted outdoors in the spring, will develop husky new roots.

It must be remembered that raising plants from cuttings is a long process, and that it may take several years for them to develop into plants ready for use.

If an immediate effect is desired it is much better to purchase two or three year old stock from a reliable nursery. In addition to improved appearance this will minimize the necessity for replacement.

PRUNING AND SHEARING

Whether your hedge is newly planted or an overgrown old one, it can be made a thing of beauty. Perhaps the most important thing in achieving and maintaining this beauty is correct pruning.

First, we must learn the difference between pruning and trimming or shearing. We prune mostly to keep the plants vigorous. We shear to give them appearance.

No shrubbery can remain beautiful unless new growth is constantly replacing the old wornout branches. In deciduous hedges or flowering shrubbery the first step in promoting this new growth is to cut off the oldest branches systematically at the ground to stimulate new shoots. If this process is carried on a little each

year the shape or appearance of the plant need not be marred by drastic measures made necessary by accumulated neglect.

The best time to do the pruning varies according to the type of plant. For shrubs which are grown for their foliage only, the best time is after the leaves are dropped in the fall or before they appear in the spring. While this is the ideal time do not hesitate to prune moderately while they are in leaf. Take out a stick or two here and there, then wait for vacant spots to grow together and go at it again.

In the case of flowering shrubbery the time of cutting must vary according to the time of bloom. To trim a shrub before it blooms means loss of the flower buds. The majority of flowering shrubbery blooms on the new wood produced during the growing season of the previous year. It is wise to prune within a few weeks after flowers fade to give this new wood a chance to ripen for next year's flowering.

The general rule is to prune spring-flowering shrubbery before July and the summer-flowering kinds any time after bloom but before March of the following spring.

It is this writer's experience that the best way to handle newly planted hedges is to keep them short until they branch freely at the ground. Allow the plant to increase in height as it shows increasing vigor.

The length of life or success of a formal hedge may be determined, to a large extent, by the way it is sheared. We must remember that each leaf and branch demands its share of light, air, and rain. Rain not only moistens the soil but washes off the surface of the leaves, allowing them to perform their part in maintaining growth.

Shearing tools should be sharp, well oiled, and clean. A pair of scissors-type shears is sufficient to care for the small planting but for large jobs mechanical types are available which save much time.

In addition to correct renewal and shearing, hedges need a regular system of watering and feeding. Cultivation about the base of the plants makes plant food more readily available and helps conserve moisture. Be careful how you do it, however, for incorrect cultivation can do more harm than good.

Cultivate the area under the branches but do not hill the soil around the stem. Shape the ground so that the water will run toward the stem—not away from it. Never work with the soil when it is wet or you may have a hard time getting it to crumble again.

If the plants show signs of failing, give them a feeding of balanced plant food. Scatter a large handful under the branches of each large shrub or one pound to each 15 feet of hedge. Water it down well and repeat monthly. Discontinue all feeding or heavy shearing by August, or you may stimulate new growth which will not have time to harden before frost. This kind of soft growth may winterkill and cause other wood to die with it.

Starting with the largest first, we find hedges of trees such as Lombardy Poplar. These make beautiful screens, if planted five or six feet apart where no other plants conflict and where they do not have to compete with paving. They are gross feeders, fast growers and will send their roots forty feet to find an opening in a drain which they proceed to fill and clog up. Near a flower bed, their surface feeding roots will rob it of every vestige of food and moisture. If the roots are cut yearly to avoid this, the trees will suffer and soon dry up. So if you want to make a hedge of poplars give them a well cultivated space of fifteen to twenty feet on either side and feed well. Grass grows fairly well with them.

The Bolleana Poplar is a tougher, not so shapely, and much slower growing tree. It has a silver underside to its leaf and birch-like bark. It is pyramidal in shape. The Pyramidal English Oak (*Quercus robur fastigiata*) is well fitted for hedge making and is well worth waiting for.

To protect the larger grounds from intrusion another rampant grower is used. Osage-orange is really a tree but, if properly pruned, becomes a thick tangled thorny hedge, which makes passage impossible. It is hardy except in the North and can be allowed to grow to tree size later. It has the drawback of unkept appearance and its rampant feeding roots throttle all shrubbery near it. It should be carefully watched as it may become a host to several pests. Honeylocust is used much the same way.

Some prefer to plant rooted switches about one foot apart and cut back until hardy growth is assured; others advise planting two feet apart and cutting to the ground after the trees become one inch thick, promoting a rank thick growth.

Most types of flowering shrubbery make good hedges, but occupy considerable space and require careful pruning.

Japanese Barberry is perhaps the best low-growing hedge for semiformal effect, growing to four feet high in a great variety of soils and standing some shade. It is hardy almost anywhere and, if clipped, makes a dense wall. It has bright berries in winter. Plants to be sheared are set eighteen inches apart or for natural growth, twenty-four to thirty inches.

Privet of various kinds comes next in usefulness. It is the most used in the United States because of its quick growth. Carefully planted and fertilized it will give excellent results. Plants should be set rather deep and cut back to 6 in. as soon as planted to stimulate the growth of side branches. When the new shoots are a foot tall,

cut them back half way; repeat as growth is made so as to develop a thick, bushy base. After the desired height is reached shear once in June and again in late July if necessary to keep hedge in form. Plants can be set from 8 to 10 or 12 in. apart depending on the size of the hedge desired. For an extra thick tight one, set 1 ft. apart in two rows about 10 in. apart "staggering" the plants in the rows.

Prune it as shown so that the lower branches get plenty of light as well as the upper ones and are not shaded by them.

When privet dies at the bottom from bad pruning or lack of other care, it is best to cut it to the ground and thin it out. It will grow back surprisingly fast if given water and food. Before doing this try watering, fertilizing and spraying.

Apply chemical fertilizer in spring and again in July, one pound to every fifteen feet of hedge. Do not fertilize later than midsummer and stop pruning as soon as possible. Pruning and fertilizer stimulate new soft growth which, if it does not have enough warm weather to harden, may winterkill.

Many varieties of privet are offered but for taller hedges in sun or shade, none of them (in this writer's experience) equals Regel Privet. It will grow seven feet or more tall, is of compact habit and if not pruned will develop a profusion of white bloom. In a year when practically all privet hedges were injured in the vicinity of the writer's home, most of them having to be cut down to the ground, it came through with little or no damage to main stalks.

There are several admirable hedge

TRIMMING DECIDUOUS HEDGES

Flowering shrubbery hedges need a yearly removal of some older wood after blooming to stimulate new growth from the base

New hedges should not be allowed to grow too tall until they have become bushy at the bottom.

SHAPING

TRIMMING SMALLER AT TOP SO THAT EACH BRANCH MAY GET LIGHT AND RAIN PREVENTS THIS

WHICH EVENTUALLY DEVELOPS INTO THIS

Shearing and cultivation, to a large extent, determine success with hedges.

Scissors type shears are sufficient for small hedge areas and are necessary for heavier trimming.

For clipping new growth over large areas, a mechanical shear (hand-driven or electric) saves much labor.

plants among the evergreens. They serve the same purpose in winter as in summer and always present a uniform appearance.

Norway spruce comes in several varieties which vary in height, shape, and color. All make good hedges if well clipped or rather pruned. If they are allowed to grow too high they get a coarse appearance. Plant four or five feet apart and in a fairly short time the branches will intertwine.

Arborvitae, in the larger spreading variety, is a good shearing evergreen which makes a dense, close hedge. Its chief enemy is red spider. Spray it with oil in March and spray again in May. Glue solution is also effective until washed off by the rain. Plant four to six feet apart, according to effect desired.

Junipers are beautiful and reliable. The family is large and well known (ask your nurseryman). Get the type which fits the hedge height that you need.

Japanese Yew (*Taxus cuspidata*) is hardy in most of the United States whereas the English Yew is not, and makes an excellent broad, dark green hedge in various heights, according to variety. It is good for city use as it will stand much smoke and dust and can be used clipped formally or trimmed to bushiness at natural height.

The plant is ordinarily grown as a low bush to fifteen feet across but it has been developed into upright, low, dense, shrubby forms. There are some excellent hybrids, the result of crossing *T. cuspidata* and *T. baccata*, the English Yew; *T. media hicksi* and *hatfieldi* are two of them.

Properly planted, two feet high and two and one-half feet apart, they will touch in two years and grow about six inches per year thereafter.

They hold their shapes and require so much less pruning than privet that when this is added to the factor of year around foliage, their larger first cost is really economy. Dwarf Japanese Yew (*T. cuspidata nana*) makes a good dwarf hedge but grows more slowly. (See chapters on Evergreens, Sprays, and Pruning.)

Euonymus radicans vegetus, Hardy Evergreen Azalea, Bush English Ivy (see chapter on vines) and in some locations American Holly (see Acid Plants) make good evergreen low-growing border or barrier plants. If supported by a fence or wires the Euonymus will grow bushy and eight feet high.

For background an excellent evergreen hedge effect, in little space, is obtained by training climbing vines on a wire net fence (see "Vines").

Low Hedges—Sheared

Berberis thunbergi plurifolia erecta
        Truehedge Columnberry
Buxus microphylla koreana
        Korean Box
Euonymus radicans carrieri
        Glossy Wintercreeper
Euonymus radicans coloratus
        Red-leaved Wintercreeper
Euonymus radicans vegetus
        Bigleaf Wintercreeper
Salix purpurea nana
        Dwarf Purple Osier

Low Hedges—Unsheared

Berberis thunbergi nana
        Thunbergs Barberry, Dwarf Type

Spirea Anthony Waterer
Viburnum opulus nanum
          Dwarf Cranberrybush

Low Hedges—Evergreen

Taxus cuspidata nana
          Dwarf Japanese Yew
Taxus media hicksi......Hicks Yew
Thuya occidentalis globosa
          Globe Arborvitae
Thuya occidentalis pyramidalis
          Pyramidal Arborvitae

Medium to Tall Hedges—Sheared

Berberis mentoriensis
          Mentor Barberry
Berberis thunbergi plurifolia erecta
          Truehedge Columnberry
Berberis thunbergi
          Japanese Barberry
Berberis thunbergi atropurpurea
          Red-leaf Barberry
Cotoneaster lucida.....Cotoneaster
Forsythia intermedia spectabilis
          Showy Border Forsythia
Hibiscus syriacus....Shrub Althea
Ligustrum amurense...Amur Privet
Ligustrum ibolium...Ibolium Privet
Ligustrum ibota regelianum
          Regel Privet
Lonicera fragrantissima
          Winter Honeysuckle
Lonicera bella albida
          White Belle Honeysuckle
Rhamnus frangula. Glossy Buckthorn
Ribes alpinum......Alpine Currant
Ulmus pumila..........Asiatic Elm

Medium to Tall Hedges—Unsheared

Caragana arborescens
          Siberian Pea Tree
Cotoneaster acutifolia
          Peking Cotoneaster
Crataegus crusgalli. Cockspur Thorn

Crataegus cordata
          Washington Hawthorn
Forsythia suspensa
          Weeping Forsythia
Hibiscus syriacus.....Shrub Althea
Lonicera fragrantissima
          Winter Honeysuckle
Lonicera bella rosea
          Pink Belle Honeysuckle
Malus sargenti........Sargent Crab
Prunus tomentosa...Nanking Cherry
Spirea van houttei
          Van Houtte Spirea
Syringa chinensis.....Chinese Lilac
Syringa vulgaris hybrids
          French Lilacs
Viburnum dentatum....Arrowwood
Viburnum rufidulum
          Southern Black Haw

Medium to Tall Hedges—Evergreen

Juniperus virginiana canaerti
          Canaert Redcedar
Juniperus virginiana glauca
          Silver Redcedar
Juniper virginiana Platte River
          Platte River Redcedar
Taxus cuspidata densa
          Spreading Japanese Yew
Taxus cuspidata
          Upright Japanese Yew
Taxus media hicksi......Hicks Yew
Thuya occidentalis
          American Arborvitae
Tsuga canadensis..Canada Hemlock
Tsuga caroliniana.Carolina Hemlock
Picea excelsa.......Norway Spruce
Pinus strobus..........White Pine
Pseudotsuga douglasi...Douglas-fir

Hedges with Colored Foliage

Berberis mentoriensis
          Mentor Barberry
Berberis thunbergi
          Japanese Barberry

Berberis thunbergi atropurpurea
          Red-leaf Barberry
Berberis thunbergi plurifolia erecta
    Truehedge Columnberry
Cotoneaster lucida..... Cotoneaster
Euonymus alatus
          Winged Euonymus
Euonymus alatus compactus
      Dwarf Winged Euonymus
Euonymus europaeus
     European Burning Bush
Euonymus radicans coloratus
     Red-leaved Wintercreeper

Juniperus virginiana glauca
            Silver Juniper
Salix purpurea........Purple Osier

Hedges with Colored Fruits

Barberry in variety
Buckthorn
Cotoneaster
European Burning Bush
Hawthorns
Privet in variety
Viburnums

See list of berried shrubs in Chapter IV—Trees and Shrubs.

EDITOR'S NOTE: In recent years much attention has been given to *Rosa multiflora,* a Japanese species, from which the popular Ramblers are descended. Hardy, vigorous, bearing abundant small white flowers and red fruits, it makes a dense, thorny, almost impenetrable hedge or hedgerow that may exceed eight feet in height and breadth. It is therefore an excellent barrier where there is plenty of room, but not (as has been asserted) for small suburban house lots. Its use along heavily traveled highways has been urged because an established planting can bring an automobile running off the road to a stop quickly, smoothly, and with remarkably little damage to car, occupants or hedge.—E.L.D.S.

CHAPTER IX

VINES

Ordered vines in equal ranks appear,
With all the united labours of the year;
Some to unload the fertile branches run,
Some dry the blackening clusters in the
sun.

—HOMER.

Vines have a place in garden decoration that cannot be taken by any other plant. They have the ability to produce a large quantity of flowers in the minimum of space and to hide or soften ugly materials or outlines.

They should be selected for the purpose for which they are adapted. Certain groups work well on masonry, others make good ground cover, while some must have artificial support or help in their climbing.

They are divided into two general classes: herbaceous (annual and perennial), and woody or hardy. The annual vines as well as some of the smaller hardy types grow very well in well-drained soil which has received ordinary digging. The larger hardy varieties, however, are often expected to remain in a single spot for many years and so merit about one cubic yard of good soil.

The hole for a vigorous vine should be at least two feet square and two feet deep, or better, three feet each way. The ground in the bottom should be broken up and made to drain if the soil is hard. The excavation should then be filled with good soil, well supplied with rotten manure and coarse raw bone. Each plant should have a space three to six feet square in which it will not have to compete for food and moisture with other strong-growing plants.

No vine should be planted where water drips on it every time it rains. This is bad for the foliage but worse still for the plant in winter. Much winterkilling is caused by the drip of water on warm days which coats the plant with ice at sundown. The ice coated vine swaying in the wind suffers many cracks and wounds which offer means for the ready entrance of pests and the loss of stem juices in the spring.

Large plants should be dormant if possible when planted. Spread the roots to the fullest extent, cutting off all broken or injured ones and take care to see that wooden supports are made of substantial, long-lasting material.

Plants grown against a sunny wall should receive special watering. They get the heat not only from the sun but also that reflected from the wall. Also at night the wall will reflect the heat long after sundown.

Use vines for screening, for correcting or softening architectural lines, for flowering beauty; but do not cover and blot out good architectural detail.

Hardy vines are divided into two or three overlapping classes: those raised for foliage, for fruit, and for flowers.

Here are listed some of the best known vines and cultural directions for them:

IVIES, REAL AND SO-CALLED

Virginia Creeper, sometimes called Woodbine or American Ivy, is that plant which we see twining around trees and covering the ground in our woodlands. It has five distinct dark green leaves in a group, which enables us to distinguish it from the three-leaved poison ivy. For covering banks, fences or buildings it is excellent, but may become heavy and need thinning out. Botanically, it is Parthenocissus quinquefolia.

It grows well in shade, but being a native of woodland, does best in a moist, loose soil. The Engelmann Creeper is a variety of Woodbine having a different foliage.

Boston Ivy (*P. tricuspidata*) is fine for growing, without fastening, over masonry walls. It also grows well on frame structures, doing no harm, public opinion to the contrary. It does not do well on south walls in the country farther north. It kills easily by late frosts after it has started to bud; therefore keep it dormant with a mulch if necessary.

Geranium Ivy (a form of the variety vitacea) has smaller, more deeply cut leaves, and gives a delicate tracery on limited surfaces where pattern, not coverage is wanted.

English Ivy (*Hedera helix*), one of our most useful vines, is slower of growth and does not grow well on wooden walls but is too strong a plant to train on trees. In northern sections it must be sheltered from direct winter sun and does best on north exposures. It can be easily propagated as a vine by layering or by selecting cuttings from creeping branches and inserting them in sandy loam.

English Ivy becomes a low-growing shrub, used for hedges without support when cuttings are taken from the flowering portion of the plant. It then becomes Bush English Ivy (*Hedera helix arborescens*).

If you deprive the shrub ivy of support it will grow about six feet high, but if you wish a good evergreen hedge-effect background, using little space, train the vine variety over a wire netting, being careful to clip the trailing sprays at the ground to keep them from rooting.

Its usefulness as a house plant is discussed elsewhere in this book, Chapter XXII.

It will grow under trees if the soil is broken up with sand, supplied with humus and supported by water and plant food.

Baltic Ivy (*Hedera helix baltica*) has much smaller foliage, is hardier and makes a satisfactory bank and ground cover.

All ivies are benefited by water, good soil and a mulch of rotted manure or leafmold. They thrive in rich, moist soil.

EUONYMUS

Euonymus radicans or **fortunei** (Wintercreeper), is a vine or trailing shrub that comes in several excellent varieties. Some make good

One of the most popular of all flowering perennial vines, and justly so, is the Clematis, of which this one of most spectacular of hybrid forms, the variety Nelly Moser. The requirements easy, the rewards handsome.

One of the great delights of the true wildflower enthusiast is to grow the Fringed Gentian well. This tiny but beautiful native to sunny pastures blooms in autumn. The clear color varies from intense blue to violet.

ground cover as well as wall plants, rarely growing over ten feet high. It thrives well on north sides of buildings as well as in exposed location, will grow readily in semishade, and reasonably well in dense shade.

The variety **Euonymus radicans vegetus** (Scarlet fruited Big leaf Wintercreeper), is an excellent variety, half shrub, half vine. For low-growing hedges or rounding out corners in the foundation planting it has the advantage of growing under broad eaves clinging closely to the building but having the appearance of an evergreen shrub. Its glossy rich green foliage attracts much attention as do its red berries. Once established for a year or so it grows and spreads rapidly but is easily confined to the space desired. Give it good soil and it is an economical evergreen in your planting. Pinching out the tops during the first year will produce healthy bottom growth in both ivy and euonymous.

CARPETING PLANTS

For steep banks, shady places under trees, **Japanese Spurge** (Pachysandra terminalis), has turned many an eyesore into a thing of beauty. It is six inches tall, about the easiest grown evergreen, enduring shade and drought, and does equally well in sunshine. It has succeeded where other plants fail. Its cuttings root easily and planted in ground properly manured it spreads quickly if the tops are pinched back occasionally. Used as a border for walks, it is easily kept within bounds. Try it where everything else has failed.

Periwinkle, also called running myrtle (Vinca minor) is another evergreen making excellent ground cover. Grows in shade, is vigorous in habit and has lilac-blue flowers in

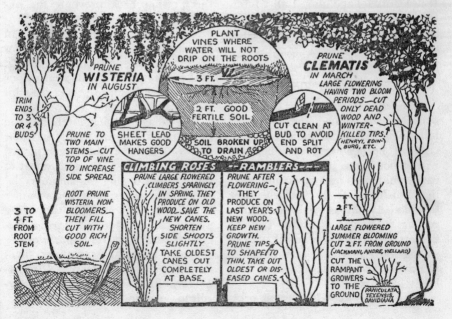

PLANT VINES WHERE WATER WILL NOT DRIP ON THE ROOTS

3 FT.

2 FT. GOOD FERTILE SOIL

SOIL BROKEN UP TO DRAIN

PRUNE **WISTERIA** IN AUGUST

TRIM ENDS TO 3 OR 4 BUDS

PRUNE TO TWO MAIN STEMS—CUT TOP OF VINE TO INCREASE SIDE SPREAD.

SHEET LEAD MAKES GOOD HANGERS

ROOT PRUNE WISTERIA NON-BLOOMERS—THEN FILL CUT WITH GOOD RICH SOIL.

3 TO 4 FT. FROM ROOT STEM

PRUNE **CLEMATIS** IN MARCH LARGE FLOWERING HAVING TWO BLOOM PERIODS—CUT ONLY DEAD WOOD AND WINTER-KILLED TIPS. (HENRYI, EDIN-BURG, ETC.)

CUT CLEAN AT BUD TO AVOID END SPLIT AND ROT

CLIMBING ROSES

PRUNE LARGE FLOWERED CLIMBERS SPARINGLY IN SPRING. THEY PRODUCE ON OLD WOOD. SAVE THE NEW CANES. SHORTEN SIDE SHOOTS SLIGHTLY TAKE OLDEST CANES OUT COMPLETELY AT BASE.

RAMBLERS

PRUNE AFTER FLOWERING—THEY PRODUCE ON LAST YEAR'S NEW WOOD. KEEP NEW GROWTH. PRUNE TIPS TO SHAPE TO THIN. TAKE OUT OLDEST OR DISEASED CANES.

2 FT.

LARGE FLOWERED SUMMER BLOOMING CUT 2 FT. FROM GROUND (JACKMAN, ANDRE, VIELLARD)

CUT THE RAMPANT GROWERS TO THE GROUND PANICULATA, TEXENSIS, DAVIDIANA

early summer. The new Bowles variety is superior to the type, with stronger foliage and more profuse flowers of deeper blue. There are also white flowering varieties.

An annual vine, **Kenilworth Ivy** (Cymbalaria muralis), is a good climber and ground cover for shady places. It roots freely at the joints.

Matrimony Vine (Lycium) is often recommended, but this writer has found it a rampant nuisance. Once planted it is almost impossible to exterminate. Weeded out, it comes back among the better plants. It grows two to three feet tall and is not particularly pleasing. On steep banks, it will, when established, prevent soil-washing. Best grow it for this purpose only.

Hall's Evergreen Honeysuckle (mentioned later), makes excellent ground cover on banks. Sheared each spring it lies flat and will not bloom. It holds its foliage almost all winter. If not controlled it becomes a nuisance, growing over and strangling shrubs and trees.

FLOWERING VINES

American Bittersweet (Celastrus scandens) is valued for its heavy foliage as well as for the orange and crimson berries used so much for winter bouquets. It is comparatively easily cultivated and especially good in semishade. It is scarcely ever troubled by disease and sometimes reaches a height of thirty feet. If flowers are desired, prune it well in spring and give it, as near as possible, wood-soil conditions—moisture and fairly loose ground.

False-bittersweet (Celastrus orbi-culatus), while lacking the profuse berries of the above, has a better habit and foliage, and the growth is more vigorous.

Clematis has many diversified varieties, but their requirements are quite simple: rich, well-drained soil with plenty of lime. Bone meal in generous quantities is needed as is a thick layer of rotted manure or leaf compost. They thrive in peaty soil if it is thoroughly limed; peat alone is too acid. They need shaded roots and partial shade is also all right for the vine. Protect roots from winter winds and summer sun by a thick mulch. Cultivation, if at all, must be shallow.

Plant on trellises, fences, walls, etc., and support them early. When planting, cut the top of vine back to the lowest large eye and cover entire plant with four inches of soil. As the wood is brittle and easily cracked, this cutting back prevents the entrance of disease into any wood injured in moving or planting. In pruning or rearranging the vine after growth, be careful to avoid splitting. Make clean pruning cuts near eye or leaf bud with sharp shears. See instructions in Chapter V, Pruning.

The foliage is thick and handsome but plants are grown mostly for their flowers which, on the larger plants, come in June and July and repeat to some extent during the summer, depending on water, food, and weather conditions. The smaller flowering plants bloom later but have a fragrance lacking in the larger types.

Probably the most popular small flowering type is known as **Virgins-Bower,** either the Japanese **C. paniculata,** or the less used native C.

virginiana. This plant with bright cheerful foliage and fine clusters of cream-white, hawthorn-scented flowers grows rampantly and blooms from August to October. It forms a good foliage vine all summer and flowers are followed by attractive feathery seed pods.

Above ground it should be treated as a perennial and cut back to the ground each spring, unless great masses of foliage are desired, then prune to keep in shape and cut back every three years to strengthen. It requires practically no other care.

Blue-flowered **Clematis davidiana** (a variety) requires the same pruning but **Texas Clematis** (Clematis texensis) which has scarlet flowers, dies to the ground each year.

Anemone Clematis (Clematis montana) is a hardy, strong-growing, disease-proof plant. It has pinkish white flowers like a Windflower, one to two inches in diameter. Frequently opens about May first and continues well through May. It should be pruned lightly in February or March. There are varieties almost identical with the above, but with rose and blue flowers.

The most popular large flowering types are: **Henryi,** white; **Jackmani,** blue or purple; **Madame Edouard Andre,** red; **Ramona,** lavender; **Duchess of Edinburgh,** double white; and **Madame Baron Veillard,** mauve. The purple Jackmani is perhaps the best known of these. When training it, remember that healthy shoots often grow ten feet a year, five before flowering and five later.

Henryi and Duchess of Edinburgh start flowering early in spring and have a fall display also, the spring bloom being an old wood and the fall flowers on wood of the current season. To preserve both blooming seasons, little pruning must be done. A part of the vines winterkill and early in spring we remove these together with any dead wood.

Jackmani, Andre, and Veillard bloom first in July and continue to some degree until frost. We therefore cut them to within two feet of the ground in March to stimulate new growth.

Dutchman's Pipe (Aristolochia durior) is an excellent quick-growing foliage plant with an odd pipe-shaped greenish brown flower.

The best of the old-fashioned honeysuckles is **Hall's Evergreen** (Lonicera japonica halliana) with its exquisitely perfumed white flowers which turn yellow before they fade. It holds its foliage almost all winter and is good alike for banks, arbor or trellis. Another excellent type is **Trumpet Honeysuckle** (L. sempervirens) of heavier and more rampant growth. Also good for covering and climbing. It has no odor, but bright orange-red flowers; it is evergreen in the South.

Both grow well in good loamy soil in either sun or partial shade and are easily propagated by layering and cuttings.

Goldflame Honeysuckle (Lonicera heckrotti) is a recent introduction combining flame and gold, heavily fragrant clusters of flowers with dark, glossy, semi-evergreen foliage. It is a continuous bloomer with a restrained habit of growth.

China Fleece Vine (Polygonum auberti) is a rapid grower, covered with a foam of white flowers in the fall. It is easily trained around downspouts which adds to its value.

Perennial Sweet Pea (Lathyrus latifolius) grows six to eight feet tall with pink-white blossoms.

The **Trumpet Creeper** (Bignonia or Campsis radicans) is useful for covering stumps, fences, etc. It grows ten feet high with bright orange-red flowers.

A variety of this vine, Madame Galen, with wide-open orange flowers, is a fairly recent introduction highly recommended.

Lack of bloom in **Wisteria** is always a problem. The solution is, correct pruning and planting. When it blooms well it is one of America's best vines, having clusters of scented (white to purple) blossoms in May. It is unequaled for trellis or pergola.

It has exceptionally heavy growth and must have stout support. Its branches must not entwine as they will choke one another.

It requires little care if properly planted. Full sunlight, plenty of manure (rotted, of course), plenty of moisture and some bone meal.

Seedlings may not bloom at all, so buy grafted plants from reliable nurseries; they often bloom the second year.

Prune to two main stems or not over three or four and administer hard top pruning after the first year, monthly in June, July and August. On young plants remove one-third of the top to develop side growth. Cut back the side growth monthly on young plants to two or three buds.

Prune older plants in August by cutting back all growth to within four feet of last year's wood to encourage blooming and to make a dense plant. If after proper planting and pruning, it does not bloom or stops flowering, it is time to root prune to keep it from going to stem and leaves.

Dig a narrow trench one spade length deep completely around the plant. Loosen the soil in the bottom and drive a spade down full length, cutting all roots in the circle. The trench may then be filled with good composted soil. On young plants the circle should be about three feet from the stem; from that it ranges up to six feet for very large ones.

Roses are treated separately in Chapter XI. The conditions applying to the bush type also apply to some extent to climbers. Planting in shade under the drip of trees will result in mildew. They must have drainage, and raising their planting ground above the surrounding level sometimes avoids loss. Follow instructions on page 177 for planting bush roses.

There are two distinct types of climbers whose pruning needs are often misunderstood. The rambler type bears its best blooms on new canes which spring from the base of the plant. Therefore we remove all old canes, which we do not need, as soon as the flowering is over. This usually reduces the plant close to its supporting trellis and has the advantage of removing old wood and preventing disease spread. Train the new branches to replace the old. The idea is to renew the plant above ground each year.

Any pruning, of course, should be tempered to fit the needs of the plant. If a large cover or tall plant is desired cut back side growth, in the spring, close to the main stems to stimulate, removing a part of the oldest canes each summer.

For the many larger flowered roses, which bloom abundantly on old canes, only light pruning is necessary and that in spring. We prune to remove dead or diseased canes and to thin rank growth. The rest of the vine is pruned only to shape it.

ANNUAL VINES

The following is based upon a list from Ohio State University Bulletin 101 (Victor H. Ries), with additions and omissions.

BALLOONVINE (*Cardiospermum halicacabum*)

Height 8–10′. Plant 12″ apart.
Small white flowers, balloon-like seed pods. Prefers a warm situation. Excellent to cover fences.

BALSAM-APPLE (*Momordica balsamina*)

Height 15–20′. Plant 12″ apart.
A handsome vine with good foliage and warty, apple-shaped fruits which expose a brilliant carmine interior when ripe.

BALSAM-PEAR (*Momordica charantia*)

Height 10′. Plant 12″ apart.
Resembles the balsam-apple, but has pear-shaped fruit.

CANARY-BIRD FLOWER (*Tropaeolum peregrinum*)

Height 15′. Plant 8–12″ apart.
A dainty vine with finely cut leaves and sprays of small yellow flowers. Resembles its relative, the common garden Nasturtium, except that it is much daintier.

CARDINAL CLIMBER (*Quamoclit coccinea*)

Height 10–20′. Plant 12″ apart.
A striking vine with bright red flowers, resembling miniature morning glories. It will blossom all season.

CUP AND SAUCER VINE (*Cobaea scandens*)

Height 30′. Plant 5′ apart.
One of the most rapid growing vines, which is a perennial farther south. Large bell-shaped violet or greenish-purple flowers, plum-shaped fruits. Seeds germinate best if planted edgewise rather than flat. Start seeds early indoors.

CYPRESSVINE (*Quamoclit pennata*)

Height 15–20′. Plant 12″ apart.
A delightful, charming vine, very finely cut leaves and a large number of small starry flowers, either scarlet or white. Prefers sunny location. May be used for small trellis, posts, or other places where a small vine is desired.

GOURD (*Cucurbita*)

Height 8–20′. Plant 24″ apart.
The gourds are grown more for their curiously shaped fruits, which may be dried, than for any beauty they possess.

Perhaps no other vegetable family serves so many purposes as the gourd family, which includes plants bearing fruits of various types, sizes, shapes, and colors. The family also includes pumpkins and melons. Primitively many of the fruits were used as kitchen utensils. Now they are used principally as decorations. Their decorative and artistic value seems to be endless. A few of the ideas illustrated have been called to my attention recently, the most novel of them being the shadow box, on page 118. We have seen some gourds which have produced beautiful effects when treated with varnish and stains.

If you have had any trouble in raising gourds in the past, perhaps the difficulty was with the soil, as deep cultivation is necessary as well as plenty of humus. Each gourd vine should have a space four feet each way. Each vine must have a bushel of manure dug well into the soil so that it will be on its way toward being converted into humus at planting time, which should be after danger of frost is past in the spring. To get a little start on the season and to help the fruit mature before winter, some gardeners start their gourds inside. The best way is to sow the seed in small pots which can be transferred to a well-dug bed without disturbing the roots and checking the growth.

Gourds, when properly grown, are free from the usual plant diseases. Sometimes they do have a powdery mildew which appears as a white coating, but this yields readily to any dust containing a large proportion of sulphur. Also it must be remembered that since the gourd vine is a large plant it needs great quantities of food and evaporates large quantities of water. So it must be watched during dry spells, as it cannot be expected to put forth its best when suffering from lack of water.

There is a New England Gourd Society which supplies information to members. Its headquarters are Horticultural Hall, Boston, Mass.

HYACINTH-BEAN (*Dolichos lablab*)
Height 15′. Plant 12″ apart.
A rapid growing vine with good foliage and profusion of flowers, white in variety Daylight, purple in variety Darkness. Good for cut flowers. Train on strings.

MORNING GLORY (*Ipomoea*)
Height 15–25′. Plant 12″ apart. Avoid the related bind weed (*Convolvulus*) since it soon seeds and becomes a pest. The "Japanese Morning Glory" prefers a warm, sheltered location. The "Mexican Morning Glory," with its evening blooms of white and pink, and the true Moonflower (*Calonyction aculeatum*) gives evening charm in the garden, having fragrant six-inch white flowers, opening late in the day and remaining open until the sun strikes them in the morning. For best results get plants from florist. Also grows well from seeds. Plant with it the species leari (Blue Dawn Flower) which has violet-blue flowers and requires the same culture. The east or west side of a building makes the best location.

GOURDS

For a vigorous vine, cultivate a space four feet each way containing about a bushel of manure.

USED AS AN ORNAMENTAL CHARM STRING

USED AS A HANGING BRACKET FOR IVY.

GOURD POTTERY

AS A CALABASH

A HALVED GOURD FITTED WITH A PICTURE FRAME MAKES A SATISFACTORY SHADOW BOX.

A.R.BAKER.

The variety of size, shape, and color makes possible an endless list of interesting novelties.

Finest of all is the "Heavenly Blue" Morning Glory, with its huge, pale blue flowers. Scarlett O'Hara, a soft velvety scarlet, and Cornell, carnelian red and white, are fine new colors, effective with Heavenly Blue, but not so vigorous in growth.

Soak all seed several days, or better still, notch it with a file or chip the end off with a knife.

NASTURTIUM (*Tropaeolum majus* in many varieties)

Height 8–15′. Plant 12″ apart. The climbing forms, although gaudy, are useful, easily grown, and popular for sunny locations. Aphides, which often infest plants, can be controlled by contact sprays.

SCARLET RUNNER BEAN (*Phaseolus coccineus*)

Height 8–15′. Plant 12″ apart. A mass of brilliant scarlet flowers. Showy, attractive, easily grown. Blooms all summer.

BLACK-EYED SUSAN (*Thunbergia alata*)

Height 3–5′. Plant 12″ apart. A really charming little vine for rock gardens, porch boxes or hanging baskets. Covered with numerous creamy white flowers with purple throats, it never fails to attract attention. Best to sow seed early in the cold frame or indoors.

WILD-CUCUMBERS (*Echinocystis lobata*)

Height 10–25′. Plant 24″ apart. A rank-growing weed which soon becomes a pest. It is of doubtful value for gardens. Once it goes to seed it will come up for years. Use only in waste places.

CHAPTER X

THE FLOWER GARDEN

In all places, and all seasons,
  Flowers expand their light and soul-like
    wings,
Teaching us, by most persuasive reasons
How akin they are to human things.
                    —LONGFELLOW.

Although we have already discussed several of the essential factors in successful garden making, such as planning its layout, preparing the soil that is to support it, making the lawn to serve as a background, etc., we now come to the most important single division of all—the flower garden. Indeed, this is, in many cases, the picture that first comes to the minds of many people when the word garden is mentioned—an arrangement of brilliantly colorful flowers, varying in types, textures, sizes and habits of growth, but so placed and cared for as to give maximum pleasure to all the senses that a garden delights. As we have seen, flower effects can be created in many ways, that is in formal and informal gardens; with the help of flowering shrubs, trees and vines; over large areas separated and isolated from the house, or in small, intimate nooks and corners just outside the dwelling where they become a part of what is almost another room of the house itself.

But in all these cases, the basic principles of growing the flowers,

and the kinds that can be used, are pretty much the same. So the flower garden as a unit can well be thought of as a fully developed flower bed or flower border, even though that latter term has come to be restricted largely to a strip of planting, considerably longer than wide and used to skirt a building or wall, outline a lawn, or flank a path. Consequently, while throughout this chapter, we frequently speak of border or bed, you should remember that what we are talking about is, after all, the flower garden as a whole.

It is very hard to give a set of rules for planning a flower border. Each garden is a problem unto itself governed by its limits of size, exposure, shade, soil, etc. We set forth here some general ideas leaving the detailed working to the taste and initiative of the individual.

Planning on paper saves much labor and disappointment. If drawn to a large scale notes may be made directly on the plan. The border should be at least six or eight feet deep and the individual plant groups should be shallow from front to back and wide rather than round. This gives a better chance for display.

Site: The ideal site is close to the house; preferably it should face south or southwest, but this is not of great consequence if it has sun and is well away from the robbing roots of trees or shrubbery. No border can be successful if the plants are constantly robbed of food and moisture.

We show a method of keeping less rampant roots away from the bed. A wall, one brick wide and two feet deep, is placed in the ground between the plants and the flower border. This, of course, is best laid in mortar but loose brick will do if no crevices or openings are left. A wall of tight boards will also last for many years. If boards are used, fill the excavation with cinders to prevent rotting and help keep away roots.

These barricades will do no good against poplars and willows, which have no place in the small garden. Their robber roots will run twenty to fifty feet to stop a drain or desiccate a flower bed. Even with the separating wall, keep the border two to three feet at least away from any hedge.

A good background always adds to the picture. It may be a rough-textured wall, a view of distant trees or shrubbery, or a low fence covered with climbing roses. Above all there should be surrounding relief and nothing sets off the border better than a stretch of lawn. It is better to have a smaller border than to deprive it of the grass setting.

The old star and diamond shaped beds, edged with bricks on end and set in midlawn do not fit into garden planning today. Isolated beds are not only hard to fit into the plan but break up the appearance of space. If such beds are used, plant the high growing plants in the center, then the medium sized ones and the edging plants on the outer circle.

Arrangement: In the border as in

the bed we should try to avoid stiffness caused by too regular an arrangement. Do not place the plant groups in regular lines, like rows of cabbages, but in clumps which are wider than deep. This gives each group a chance to be seen to good advantage from the front of the border.

Of course taller plants (tie them to stakes early) should be at the rear, then medium height and the dwarfs in the front. This does not mean that some of the taller plants should not come out into middle ground or the medium toward the front. For the charm of irregularity, we must break up height lines as well as planting lines. We are striving to imitate the irregular way in which nature grows her plants and still place them in order for display, within the limits of our space. Also we must strive for proportion; if the border is very narrow, tall plants should be avoided except for occasional accent. The border will appear top heavy if it is too tall and narrow. Groups should be of sufficient size for display but large masses of single plants in a border are seldom successful. Borders which are more than eight feet wide should have a two-foot grass service path behind them.

We hear a great deal about the gardens of our ancestors, which outlasted the stones of the doorstep. This is purely a myth. With few exceptions perennials must be divided every three or four years. The plant starts from the original clump and grows in all directions. After a while the center exhausts the food within reach and dies, leaving a ring of live growth with a dead center. The best portions of this ring must be lifted and divided, cutting away all dead roots and stalk, starting a number of new plants. Make the holes wide enough to spread out the roots. If your bed has been properly prepared they need not be deep. In case of deep-rooted varieties, such as lupin, the holes must be as deep as the root, which should be dug without breaking.

The border must also be done over to correct the encroachments of rampant-growing plants which try to smother their less hardy neighbors, and to replace the wayward seedlings which have a habit of growing in the wrong place. The seedlings can usually be turned to good account in regrouping but it is best to discard seedling phlox as it never runs true to original color and invariably disappoints.

Time: Some authorities recommend spring as the time to make over the border. Many things seem in favor of autumn. First there is the weather which is more stable in the fall, and then the fact that any desired changes are fresher in the mind, just at the close of the season. When we add to these the freedom from the rush of spring tasks, the more easy identification of plant groups and their limits, and the chance that winter freezing has to pulverize the newly turned soil, it seems that the weight is largely in favor of September or October. This time allows the plants to get a new root start before becoming dormant at freezing time. Be sure to give them water.

Of course some perennials transplant better in the spring. Plants such as chrysanthemums do not divide well so soon after their blooming period. We should move these with as large a clump of earth and as little root disturbance as possible. If division is desired this may be done in the spring when they are more nearly dormant.

The general rule is to try to get well away from their blooming period. Divide spring and early summer perennials in the fall, and late summer bloomers in the spring. Remember this is a general rule and general rules must be used carefully. Phlox and Oriental Poppies, for instance, must be transplanted shortly after their flowering period to avoid loss of bloom the following season.

Directions for raising plants from seed are given elsewhere in this volume. Some perennial seeds are planted in spring and bloom the first year. Some are planted in fall just before frost in a sheltered spot under shrubbery, convenient for winter inspection. They seem to need freezing to germinate. The majority, however, do best sown in summer. Be sure to get good fresh seed.

Division of perennials or propagation by cuttings are the sure method of having plants come true to color and shade.

Preparation of the Bed: The digging and preparation of a bed is very important. There are few border perennials which are not better for drainage and friable soil. We usually get some sort of condition in our surface soil but few amateur gardens have properly prepared subsoil. The bottom soil need not be as well tilled as the top but once prepared it will last for many years, making it necessary to renew only the fertility of the topsoil from time to time.

If the bottom soil is heavy, incorporate in it some sand, cinders or a large quantity of ashes to break it up. Lime is one of the best soil looseners and strange as it may seem it will also compact sandy soil. Use it generously in the bottom spit. Work in here also a lot of partially decayed leaves, grass clippings, manure, peat moss or humus. If the soil is sandy you may add clay or a large amount of vegetable matter. Do not firm it down but let it settle naturally.

Topsoil, if heavy, can be made into good loam by the addition of sand and well-rotted manure, humus, peat moss or finely sifted leafmold. Bone meal is very useful and should be used generously. Keep plant roots away from immediate contact with manure, for it is likely to burn them no matter how well rotted it appears. Wood ashes in the spring are excellent. Lime may be used in the topsoil for loosening. Most perennials grow well in limed soil. Lilies and acid plants, however, will need special ground treatment to overcome alkalinity. See Chapter VII for lists of acid plants.

After a bed has been double dug (see page 34) it will be higher than before but will soon settle. In planting, take care to firm the earth around the roots. Air pockets in the soil adjoining the roots may cause loss of plants.

It is a good plan to divide the bed into three or four sections, doing over one section each year. In this way the entire job is done over completely every three or four years without so much effort at any one time. We show on page 121 a method of separation of plant groups in the border by single strands of heavy galvanized wire.

This, at first glance, may seem crude and unnecessary. During the spring rush, weeding must sometimes be entrusted to unskilled labor. The use of these divisions makes it possible to point out plant and weed vegetation in any one area and in the summer, too, it spots quickly the encroachments of more rapid growers.

The pegs, which should be light and about fifteen inches long, should be driven twelve to thirteen inches in the ground. The wire should be stretched loosely along the ground so that it will not pull upon the pegs if trampled. It will soon weather into invisibility until wanted.

Selection of Plants: Selection of plants for the flower border is a weighty problem. All amateurs must expect to learn by experience the trial and error method. This means planting and testing after carefully studying your plant lists, looking up the description of such plants as are not familiar, in several good catalogues. Use reference books such as Bailey's "Standard Cyclopedia of Horticulture" and "Hortus II"; the "Wise Garden Encyclopedia," and others to be found in garden center, horticultural society, and some public libraries. Also write to the Office of Information of the U. S. Department of Agriculture, Washington, D.C. and of your State Agricultural Experiment Station for free lists of bulletins on gardening matters.

One old book, E. C. Volz' "Home Flower Growing," lists the following points to be kept in mind in making an effective selection of plant material.

"1. Length of life of the plant. Is it annual, biennial or perennial?

2. Height under different soil and moisture conditions.

3. Lateral spread or breadth.

4. Growing habit: prostrate, erect or climbing.

5. Time and length of flowering period.

6. Color of flowers.

7. Color of foliage.

8. Persistence of foliage and decorative effect.

9. Moisture requirements.

10. Soil and plant food requirements.

11. Sun or shade loving?

12. Hardiness in a given region.

13. Does the plant spread freely?

14. Best methods of propagation."

We cannot hope to get this knowledge without observation, study and trial over several seasons. We must know how long plants last, when and how long they bloom, the color, height, and texture of their foliage, and their freedom of growth before we can include and place them in our plans. Get this information for the plants listed farther on.

Then we must add to this a knowledge of their soil and location requirements, their insect and disease enemies, and their hardiness under our weather conditions, in order to know how to care for them.

Many questions are asked concerning the disappearance of various plants and their reverting to other colors. Of course plants die for various reasons, but many times the amateur confuses a biennial (a plant lasting only two years) with a perennial which, under proper conditions, remains indefinitely. Many annuals are also confusing because they are self-sowing and come up each spring from seed.

Apparent change of color is due to the fact that the parent plant has perished from disease, or lack of division or other attention, and its place has been taken by seedlings which do not run true.

Knowledge of height and freedom

PLANT SUPPORT SUGGESTIONS

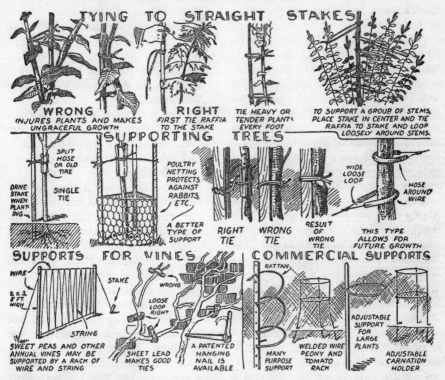

Use raffia for the smaller plants and binder twine for the heavier ones. Never use close woven cord no matter how strong. It will cut the plant and cause it to break off or become diseased. Use stakes to suit the plant. Bamboo canes are best for the smaller plants, but dahlias and heavier ones require wooden stakes from one to two inches square. Painting these stakes green before use improves their appearance.

Never tie to, or pass the tie around, the plant stem. As the plant enlarges, this chokes the growing layer at this point, preventing proper growth above and causing much other damage. Knot firmly to the stake and if the knot is on the side away from the plant it allows for greater freedom. Loop the other ends of the tie loosely about the stalk. Do not hug it closely to the support or it will chafe as it sways in the wind. Use several stakes if necessary upon bushy plants. Always try to conceal the stakes as much as possible.

Annual climbers do better if trained upon a support, as shown, rather than against a wall where light and ventilation are restricted to one side. It is considered the best practice to run them east and west if possible.

of growth is necessary for display in the border. Dwarf plants behind tall ones or hidden by the more spreading ones do us no good. We must remember that spread and height will be governed by the soil, water and food which we supply, also by the extent to which the area is shaded, and the chemical condition of our soil.

Color: We see so many lists of flowers for the blue garden, flowers for the white garden, etc. Few amateurs have space for such distinct features. The charm of the perennial border is change and we should strive for succession of bloom rather than everblooming flowers.

Color combination is much easier in the border planting than in a bouquet or in matching the colors of a costume. The amateur must not strive for too much close harmony. Even the best of colorists fail sometimes and to plan too cleverly is to open the door to disappointment.

Do not be afraid to mix colors. They are usually separated by green foliage. White or shades of cream or gray are always safe separators. They are the canvas on which we paint our color picture. Of course too much white will give an impression of coldness. Such dominating strong-colored plants as Oriental Poppy, etc., should be separated from their more delicate shaded neighbors by a space of white blooming selections or plants of good foliage, which bloom at other times. Some of our favorites of strong color spoil pastel beauty if too near. Omit massing such plants as bright red salvia—they clash with most everything. Plant them separately or among greens. Red is the hardest

color in the border. Softer colors are safer and need no great effort to keep them separate.

The following are a few color combinations which mix well:

Blue (pale) with rose pink

Blue with other shades of pink must shade together

Blue (deep) with pastel yellow (avoid deep yellow)

Blue with orange—if red is kept away

Orange with bronze

Yellow with orange

Yellow with purple

Yellow with blue (equal shades)

Yellow with pink (equal pastel shades) except lavender pink

Blue clashes with red, crimson or scarlet

Red clashes with almost everything but white, which is likely to enhance it and make it more dominant. Dark green foliage softens red

Yellow clashes with red, crimson or scarlet

First in selection should be our accent plants, and those which are to be the backbone of planting. Iris, peony, larkspur, columbine, veronica, Canterbury bells, chrysanthemum, hollyhock, phlox, asters, pinks, lupin, lily, anemone, etc. The red foliage of Japanese Maple forms a pleasing foliage contrast and pyramidal evergreens are used as occasional accent or to break up height lines. Any border which is dependent upon too large a massing of one species is liable to become uninteresting as the season advances and the blooming period of these varieties expires. Change from week to week adds interest and there is also the safety of numbers. The failure of one planting does not spoil the season. Continuous bloom—an uninterrupted show of colors, from spring to fall—is feasible by selection. The garden need not go dead in August.

Annuals: Annuals are the answer to the vacant space problem. The little effort needed to raise them coupled with their low cost and easy maintenance make them very popular.

They make the finest of cut flowers and used in a border of their own or among the dominating perennials they have many points of value. In rented property or for a short season at a summer home they have no equal.

Sown with bulbs they cover the space before or after the bulbs bloom and make it unnecessary to lift them before they ripen. Also they easily cover the bare spots left by early maturing perennials or those that fail.

A secluded bed from which annuals and such showy plants as gladiolus may be borrowed do much to fill out the summer deficiencies of the border. Many annuals may be easily transplanted, when small, to pots to mature until needed in the border. Gladiolus are planted directly in good-sized pots from which

they are easily set into the vacant spaces to be filled.

The chief requisite for success with annuals is good soil, proper location and first class seeds.

Seeds purchased from reliable companies are grown by experts in soil selected for their needs. Home-grown seed is usually unreliable and mixed seeds rarely give satisfaction. See Chapter XIX for propagation by seeds.

Novelties in both annuals and perennials had best be tried out in a secluded place rather than risk failure and disfiguration of the border.

Care of the Border: Both annuals and perennials may be stimulated with chemical plant food but care must be used to avoid an excess of nitrogen or the plant will go to leaves at the expense of bloom. Plant tablets used one to the plant once a month is a good form of balanced ration. Remember chemical fertilizers add nothing to the soil. They are a short time stimulant.

Just prior to and during the blooming season, liquid manure will give wonderful results in increasing size and quality of bloom.

Get ahead of insects and disease. Spray with Bordeaux mixture the crowns of such plants as are subject to mildew (peonies, phlox, delphini-

WINTER PROTECTION

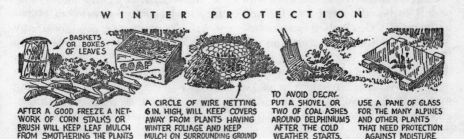

AFTER A GOOD FREEZE A NET-WORK OF CORN STALKS OR BRUSH WILL KEEP LEAF MULCH FROM SMOTHERING THE PLANTS

A CIRCLE OF WIRE NETTING 6 IN. HIGH, WILL KEEP COVERS AWAY FROM PLANTS HAVING WINTER FOLIAGE AND KEEP MULCH ON SURROUNDING GROUND

TO AVOID DECAY- PUT A SHOVEL OR TWO OF COAL ASHES AROUND DELPHINIUMS AFTER THE COLD WEATHER STARTS.

USE A PANE OF GLASS FOR THE MANY ALPINES AND OTHER PLANTS THAT NEED PROTECTION AGAINST MOISTURE

ums, hollyhocks) and spray often, dusting the soil with sulphur. Use arsenate of lead for insects that eat holes in leaves and nicotine sulphate or pyrethrum for plant lice. When hollyhocks, peonies, etc., wilt or break off easily look for stem borer. Pierce the holes with a wire or cut open the stem and kill.

Cut and remove hollyhock, foxglove, phlox and delphinium stalks as fast as they fade. Burn them to keep down mildew and black spot.

Plants subject to ground pests, such as asters, should have powdered tobacco mixed generously with the immediate topsoil when planted and again just before blooming time. Sulphur and tobacco are usually safe things to mix in the soil around the plant.

Especially remember, each fall, to remove and burn all dead stalks, leaves and branches of dormant perennials, or dead annuals. This is destroying just so many spores or eggs against next year's crop of insects and fungus. Mulching material will do double work if five per cent tobacco dust is incorporated in it.

Cultivate often until July first and then, if you wish to avoid labor and watering, try mulching with an inch of peat humus or peat moss, keeping this material slightly away from the stem. This can be raked off in the fall or left to be cultivated into the soil in the spring. Cultivation is necessary for the entrance of moisture and air. Bacteria cannot exist without air in the soil and plants cannot grow without bacteria. Break up the ground as soon as it dries sufficiently in spring and repeat after each rain until July first.

Pinch back tops to produce compact plants. In dry spells water thoroughly rather than often. Stake such tall plants as delphinium at once. Tie a raffia strip to the stake first and then to the plant. Remove all blossoms as soon as they fade to induce a prolonged flowering season. A second flowering can be secured from such plants as Canterbury bells by this method. Cut delphinium stalks to the ground after flowering to get new bloom stalks. Pansies bloom continuously if not allowed to seed.

Winter Protection: Winter protection is something that is generally misunderstood. We do not use a mulch to keep plants warm but to keep them cold. Sudden changes in temperature cause the ground to heave and break tiny roots. Warm days followed by cold nights do much damage and most winterkilling is from this cause rather than from extreme cold.

We, therefore, as one writer puts it, use the mulch as a parasol, not a blanket. If we place a layer of hardwood leaves, which take a long time to decay, over the bed, it lies loose during the whole season if lightly held in place with brush or wire. It must be light and airy and stay dry. If we use ordinary leaves they soon pack into a heavy wet mass, which excludes air, smothers the plants, and induces decay. In the spring this type of leaf ferments and produces heat which helps the dormant plants to awaken too soon and defeats the very purpose for which it was placed over them.

One solution is to place an open layer of cornstalks or other rough material which acts as the handle of the parasol and holds the leaves away from the soil. Brush or wire should be placed upon the leaves to hold them in place.

All protection should be applied only when the ground is well frozen. Remember it is to keep it cold. Do not cover too early. Let the mice find a winter home first. If they nest in your mulch they may feed upon your roots and bulbs.

Do not cover the plants which carry leaves over the winter. Use a row of stakes to keep mulch away or the poultry netting method shown at the bottom of page 127.

Sometimes it is necessary to further protect plants which come to us from warmer climates (tritomas, etc.). Use boxes of leaves or baskets loosely filled with leaves and protected from moisture by roughly formed sheet metal roofs. Fuzzy leaf alpines and rock plants often winter better if protected from moisture by panes of glass.

How necessary then it seems that we must study plant needs to avoid disappointment. If we start our borders with simple plants, hardy in our localities they will need no coddling. We may then add to them, one by one, those plants whose needs we master from time to time.

THE PERENNIAL BORDER

When we think of a garden, our visual image is fairly certain to center around an English flower border, laid out in great drifts of glowing color, relieved by masses of white lilies and accented with towering spires of blue. Even though we know that, in America, this ideal can seldom be approached except in the moist climate of the Pacific Northwest, it is good to keep this picture in our minds. It expresses the beauty of form and color that every real lover of flowers tries to create to the best of his ability and resources. He may have only a few dozen plants, but if they are well-grown and cared-for, he has created a measure of beauty.

If we can learn to restrict our plantings of all types to material that will do well for us and that we can care for easily, we will have taken an important step forward. Proper maintenance is the great need of American gardens.

A few years ago, the possibility of continuous bloom under average conditions was considered remote. However, the progress made in creating new varieties and keeping them free from disease, and our increasing opportunities for horticultural education, have changed the whole garden picture.

The first step in planning the material for an all-season, mixed perennial border, is to select key plants for line, mass, color and dependability. Four of the families discussed in this chapter—hemerocallis, delphinium, phlox and chrysanthemums—are in this class, and with iris, peonies, lilies, and a few edging, filler and background plants, will set us far on our way.

Three forms of iris are useful, dwarf, bearded and Siberian. Use the dwarf for accent in the edging strip, spacing the clumps two to three feet apart to allow groups of perennial edging plants between them. Arabis, candytuft, creeping phlox, the sedums, plumbago, and dwarf asters are suitable. Plants of dwarf ageratum, petunias, blue cup-flower and sweet alyssum can be worked in behind them for late color, and crocus, grape-hyacinths and other small bulbs will heighten the effect. To

avoid a spotted effect use only a few varieties.

The second band may carry dwarf anchusa, sweet william, blue phlox, coral bells, Elder daisies, sea-laven-

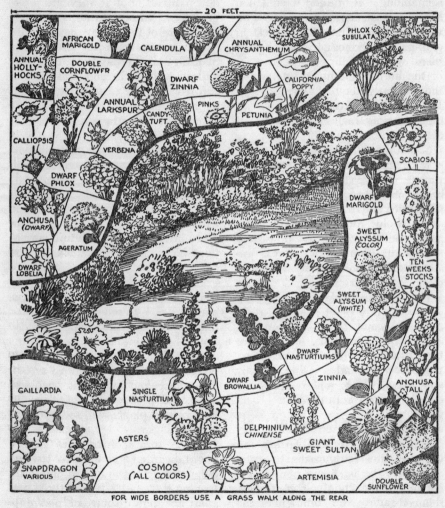

FOR WIDE BORDERS USE A GRASS WALK ALONG THE REAR

Here are plans for two colorful borders which will bloom the first year from seed. See descriptions and cultural directions on pages 152 to 169. These easy culture plants are arranged, as to height and color contrast, to fit into corners. If some of them are transplanted into pots (paper or otherwise) when small they will serve for transplanting to fill out the bare spots in the mixed flower borders which occur later in the summer when early blooming perennials become dormant.

der and cushion chrysanthemums, worked in groups or overlapping bands between clumps of tulips. Plants of scabiosa, dwarf snapdragons, periwinkle, tall ageratum or other annuals of neat growth, can be set among the tulips when their bloom is past. Plant the early perennials with the tulips, the latter with clumps of intermediate iris that will blend with the tulips. Near the ends of the border, group the blue false-indigo, early daylily and daffodils. For later bloom try Peruvian daffodils, tall pink snapdragons and blue salvia. Use bulbs and salvia in clumps, the others in singles.

So far we have used no large masses except false-indigo, but we are now ready for the peonies to be distributed, five to six feet apart. Only choice varieties, selected for beauty of foliage as well as flowers, should be considered. Plant tall, bearded iris between and to the front of the peonies, and set them off with generous amounts of phlox, veronica, shasta daisies in singles and doubles, and Canterbury bells.

Behind the peonies, allowing for their future growth, prepare a special place for a band of lilies—regale, speciosum, pink and white, and candidum and auratum if they will grow well for you. Behind them double gypsophila to soften delphiniums, foxgloves, daylily Hyperion and tall pink and rose poppies.

Reserve the tiger and henryi lilies for nearer the ends and plant with them meadow rue, bronze Korean chrysanthemums and blue globe thistles. This is a good spot for the deep red oriental poppies, with artemisia Silver King behind them.

Both like a well-drained spot and the stems of the Silver King will hide the bare ground when the poppies go dormant.

At this point in a twelve foot border, you can begin to put in butterfly bush, chaste tree, flowering almond, or Prunus triloba. Work tall hardy asters in with them, new choice kinds; various meadow rues, hollyhocks with discretion, and the taller types of Siberian iris. At the ends of the border, tree form wisterias kept well headed in, and tree lilacs give a charming effect.

This is suggestive for a ten to twelve foot border, long in proportion, and one which could be built up through several seasons. To do this, leave out all edging perennials except the iris, substitute annual plants, not more than two kinds, or make sowings of candytuft, mixed colors or dwarf phlox art shades. The number of bulbs can be cut down and the second strip varieties reduced to columbines, pyrethrum, sweet william and cushion mums combined with lilliput zinnia, Spun Gold or Pastel Mixed.

The candidum, henryi and auratum lilies can be dispensed with and cosmos and larkspur seeds sown to pad out the background. Plant only the best stock obtainable, and grow as many things as you can yourself. It is thrifty as well as being good sport.

For a border five to seven feet wide, use peonies only at the ends; move tulips and iris back with the lilies and delphiniums and use gypsophila and gas plant for accents. Use no plants with heavy foliage if it can be avoided, and thin background types such as liatris and salvia should replace hollyhocks and meadow rues. Also narrow down the edging strips.

A border under five feet should have all except essential or key plants reduced, no bulky annuals planted and all clumps kept well divided. In estimating the number of plants needed, even the old rule of allowing an average of one and one-half square feet per plant will break down. Peonies need from four to nine square feet according to size. Figure as nearly as you can, locate your key plants and work from them. For planting, care, color, height, consult the lists included in this chapter. Their study, seasoned with a reasonable amount of experience and imagination should bring you enjoyment and success.

EDGING THE FLOWER BORDER

All gardeners have at some time or other tried something to beautify the margins of beds between the lawn and the cultivated area—a barrier so that neither the grass nor the plants will encroach upon the other.

Stone and brick edgings are effective, but it is difficult for a mower to get close enough to do a good job. The grass will grow tall and scraggly against them and must be trimmed with shears. A sickle or other cutting tool will not stand up under such service very long, since it is almost impossible to keep from striking it against the stone.

Stratified rock, however, can be used to advantage, where the ground is sloping and a level bed is desired. The rock can be laid up as a low wall, and sedums planted at the base.

There has recently been put on the market a rust-resisting metal strip

ARTISTIC EDGING OF FLOWER GARDENS

LOW EVERGREEN HEDGE

SWEET ALYSSUM

BRICK

RUST RESISTANT METAL

STONE

STRATIFIED ROCK

furnished with spikes to fasten it to the ground. It can be bent to fit curves and placed less than an inch above the ground so that it will permit the mower to pass without interference.

Concerning the use of small plants for edgings, be sure they are compact and full as to foliage and have a long season of bloom. The dwarf compact petunia, Nierembergia or blue cupflower, dwarf ageratum, and the old standby sweet alyssum, can all be kept under control and give good service.

Hardy candytuft is the ideal perennial border in sections where it will not burn in the winter sun. It has white flowers in masses and evergreen foliage. Vinca minor, Bowles variety, creeping euonymus, and the hardier evergreens are always in order. Behind them can be used a secondary line of flowering dwarf perennials, selected for succession of bloom: Arabis alpina, Alyssum saxatile, dwarf asters, Campanula Carpatica, dianthus, Nepeta mussini, pulmonaria, sweet william, Veronica incana. These, planted in bands which overlap slightly, and interplanted with small bulbs, will give a good effect, and form a charming transition from the low edge to the higher plants in the beds.

For heavy plant material woody plants may be used, such as the evergreen dwarf boxwood, Korean box and dwarf Japanese yew, and the dwarf cranberry bush which is deciduous.

NOTES ON IMPORTANT GARDEN FLOWERS

CHRYSANTHEMUMS

There has always been an interest in hardy chrysanthemums, and a persistent effort to develop types that were not only hardy, but that would bloom before frost. The introduction of the Korean hybrids several years ago and their subsequent improvement has made a new sensation in flower history. Not only are the Koreans early, often blooming in July, and hardy; but they come in luscious colors in a wide range, in singles and doubles, and can be flowered the same year from seed sown in the greenhouse in January.

In addition, all the other types have been improved. The Azaleamums, which started with the pink Amelia as sole representative, now boast a color range of white, red and bronze. The globular-shaped pompons are called "Buttons" when only one-half inch across, and Pompons when larger. The smaller are the hardier of the two.

Chrysanthemums are sun-loving plants, and for this reason should be planted where they have the sun the majority of the day. The south side of a wall or building is ideal to hold the heat and protect from frost. The single Koreans are especially adapted to use on sunny terraces and in courtyards, as the heat of stones or brick forces their growth. They like a circulation of air as well as sunlight and well-drained ground, and respond to manure, superphosphate, or a good commercial.

Old plants should be divided in the spring as soon as growth starts; the divisions should consist of only one or two sprouts taken from the outside of the clump. They should be spaced fifteen to eighteen inches apart and dusted regularly; some kinds should be pinched back. As a rule, the single Koreans do not need this and it would retard their bloom. The following are a few of the noteworthy introductions:

Singles—Clara Curtis, pink; Agnes Selkirk Clark, apricot salmon; Saturn, bronze

Red—The Moor and Burgundy, doubles

Yellow—Acacia, King Midas, Pale Moon

Bronze—Romany, Goblin

Blends—Symphony, pink; Roberta Copeland, salmon bronze; Mandarin, coral to bronze

Lavender—Lavender Lady

Pink Spoon

GARDEN CHRYSANTHEMUMS

W.P.BAKER

MANY VARIATIONS OF SHAPE, SIZE AND TEXTURE

shades of blue and purple, but hybrids have been developed in a range of colors including crystalline white, and pink. As to sizes and shapes, the development has also been wide. The improved belladonna types have been generally grown for some time, and the hybrids do not surpass their usefulness as cut flowers. Their graceful spikes are produced in profusion in June and September.

The English hybrids were the first of a race of giants with which we have been familiar for a decade or so. These were followed by the originations of our growers who found the Pacific northwest favorable to delphinium culture. While these types gave us a vision of size and color which we had never dreamed possible, the strain that will persist a reasonable length of time in various parts of the country still seems to be a dream of the future.

It is the opinion of many growers of experience that the best way to avoid disappointment is to keep young plants growing on to replace those that are lost. One year plants, of the fine strains now being offered, make a good showing in the flower border in August when planted in among the older clumps.

Growing plants from seed need not be difficult, and is an absorbing occupation. It is wise to start with good seed, fresh, hand-pollinated if possible; at least the best obtainable from originators' stocks. The investment may seem high, but it is low compared to the cost of plants. Sow as soon as seed is obtainable; August is good, but July is better. Put a pinch of Semesan in the packet and shake it about.

DELPHINIUMS

Almost every home which has a garden has a few plants of delphiniums, which speaks eloquently for the value and popularity of the flower. Native of Siberia, it originated in

If you have an empty coldframe, sowing is reduced to a minimum of trouble. If not, a bed should be made in a cool corner shaded for part of the day, and equipped with simple means of shading the young plants from direct sunshine.

No more care of the soil is necessary than should be given any other seed bed. Cultivate deeply, add sand if the soil is heavy, and work enough leafmold or peat in the top 2 or 4 inches to make it handle easily. When finished, water it down and let stand for a day or two to settle and drain. The level should be slightly above the surrounding ground.

Seed sowing in rows is recommended to allow for loosening the soil between the plants and for applying a winter mulch. A light board four inches wide and three feet long will serve to mark the rows and firm in the seeds. A frame of boards about the bed will support a lath or slat screen after the seeds germinate. This can be made in sections for ease in handling.

After sowing, cover the bed with wet burlap to hold moisture and hasten germination. Water through this until the seedlings show, using a French type watering can or gentle spray from a round or flaring type hose nozzle. Lift the burlap every day to check progress, and when the seedlings show (in about fifteen days), spread it over the lath screen for extra protection. The first days are critical for the young plants, for drip from can or hose is often fatal and watering too late in the day may cause damping-off. But once started well they go merrily along. They are

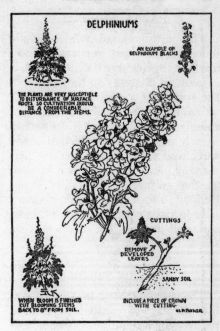

DELPHINIUMS

AN EXAMPLE OF DELPHINIUM BLACKS

THE PLANTS ARE VERY SUSCEPTIBLE TO DISTURBANCE OF SURFACE ROOTS SO CULTIVATION SHOULD BE A CONSIDERABLE DISTANCE FROM THE STEMS.

CUTTINGS

REMOVE DEVELOPED LEAVES

SANDY SOIL

WHEN BLOOM IS FINISHED CUT BLOOMING STEMS BACK TO 8" FROM SOIL.

INCLUDE A PIECE OF CROWN WITH CUTTING

H.R.BAKER

best left in the bed over winter, with a half inch layer of sand or peat as a mulch. In the spring the plants can be lined out or put in their permanent places; putting some in both places is advisable.

The care of the delphinium follows variation in climate and soils so closely that few general rules can be laid down. In heavy soil it resents loose dirt washing over the crown, especially when young. Hilling up will often cause loss of a plant in a day, and any type of cultivation is dangerous for small plants. Dusting is universally needed to control several ills and pests. One grower suggests if you cannot grow hybrids, revel in the belladonnas, and he might add the Chinese which are lovely and should be treated as annuals.

HARDY ANNUALS

The hardy annuals, which include many of the most important kinds, are best sown where they are to grow as soon as the soil can be worked in the spring. If a greenhouse, hotbed, or coldframe is available, many of these sorts may be started in flats in March and April, like the half-hardy sorts, and transplanted to their permanent place in the garden as soon as the ground is workable. Types difficult to transplant should be sown only in their permanent place. Some sorts self-sow readily; others may be sown in the fall.

HARDY PHLOX

The glory of the summer garden is the display of brilliantly colored phlox which continues throughout the season—a flow of pink, white, red purple, blue and violet. Over the last two decades, the types have been greatly improved not only as to color and size of bloom, but also as to hardiness and resistance to disease. Neglect and the lack of its simple requirements are the most frequent causes of failure, as gardens full of dried-up magenta phlox will attest. The reason for this apparent reversion is that phlox reseeds easily, and only a small percent of the seedlings will come true, as is the case with seeds of most hybrids. For this reason seedlings must be treated as weeds to keep them from stealing the show and crowding out the old plant, which does not revert but may disappear.

We have also learned that phlox requires more water than the average perennial, not only for sustenance, but to control red spider to which it is susceptible. Therefore we should water, weed out all seedlings, clear the borders of all the old plants that have no good reason to remain, and select and plant new varieties for color and succession of bloom. A good cultural program can then be carried out starting with bone meal and a winter mulch in the fall. The second step is to spray the crowns and the ground with Bordeaux mixture early in the spring, and dust weekly with a dust of sulphur, arsenate of lead and tobacco colored green. This may also be used instead of the spray. Water twice a week during the flowering season; weed out all volunteers; label the parent plant to avoid confusion and divide and replant every three years, discarding the woody center of the clump.

SUCCESSFUL CULTURE OF GARDEN PHLOX

DUSTING AND SPRAYING

Most important of all, spray the plants as the crowns come through the ground with Bordeaux Mixture

Dust weekly with a good general purpose dust throughout season to prevent dried or shriveled leaves.

AT FLOWERING TIME

Shaking or picking off flowers as they fade will cause new ones to form and make the blooms last much longer

Remove stalks as blooms fade to avoid scattering seeds.

PROPAGATING

JOINT OR NODE

FROM SLIPS IN SPRING

FROM ROOTS IN FALL

For best results start new vigorous plants each year.

A great deal can be done to keep bloom continuous. Water will encourage new flower stalks from the bottom, and the faded flowers can be removed. The method will vary with the type of plants; in some, the very tip of the head can be pinched out to encourage the growth of the laterals. On more compact varieties, the buds will develop in the tops beside the fading flowers which should be removed. Unless wanted for cut flowers the whole stalk should not be cut down if it can be avoided. One plant, if cared for, will produce a show of bloom for two months or more. Slight shade is an aid to this and some kinds bloom longer.

The following is a suggested selection of varieties: Light pink—Painted Lady, Special French and Columbia; Salmon—E. I. Farrington, Daily Sketch, George Stipp; White—Mrs. Jenkins, Von Lassburg, Marie Louise; Red—Leo Schlaegeter, Feuerbrand; Blues and purples—Ethel Prichard, Caroline Vandenberg. Miss Lingard (white) and Border Queen (salmon) are early varieties.

HEMEROCALLIS—DAYLILY

One of the horticultural triumphs of recent years has been the development of a class of hemerocallis hybrids from the "lemon lilies" of our grandmothers' gardens. These were species and included *flava*, with fragrant yellow lilylike flowers in May or June; *dumortieri*, a clear orange which bloomed at about the same time; *fulva*, now the tawny lily of our roadsides, and *thunbergi* the late yellow daylily of July.

From these have sprung a world

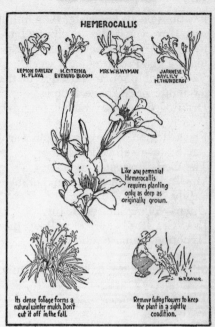

HEMEROCALLIS

LEMON DAYLILY H. FLAVA | H. CITRINA EVENING BLOOM | MRS. W. H. WYMAN | JAPANESE DAYLILY H. THUNBERGI

Like any perennial Hemerocallis requires planting only as deep as originally grown.

Its dense foliage forms a natural winter mulch. Don't cut it off in the fall.

Remove fading flowers to keep the plant in a sightly condition.

of beauty and satisfaction. More than two hundred hybrids are listed in variations of apricot, yellow, orange and buff, with shadings of brown, red and pink. Besides having charm of color, foliage and habit of growth, this is a plant without a pest, possessed of the ability to protect itself from enemies and requiring little fussing over, no staking, and a minimum of care.

There are few cultural directions for the plant. Like any other perennial, it profits by, and produces better results from, soil supplied with plenty of humus. Blood meal is recommended for quick results in growth and fine color of flowers and foliage. The removal of faded flowers adds to neatness. The daylily supplies its own winter mulch, so leave the dead tops for protection. It grows very well in part shade and in such locations needs less water than in full sun. However it should always have the full requirement of all perennials, a good soaking each week.

A list of popular varieties in the moderate price range follows:

Dr. Regel—orange yellow, fragrant, early

Flava—lemon yellow, fragrant, early

Bay State—deep yellow, June

The Gem—apricot, June

Mrs. A. H. Austin—lemon and orange, July

Ophir—yellow and gold, July

J. A. Crawford—apricot yellow, July

Hyperion—canary yellow, July, August

Mikado—orange, red splotch, July, August

Thunbergi—lemon yellow, July, August

Mrs. W. H. Wyman—lemon yellow, August

Sunny West—yellow, August

PAPAVER ORIENTALE—ORIENTAL POPPY

This plant was introduced from Persia and eastward. It has been developed in its present state of variety by hybridizing sports and seedlings. The original colors were orange and scarlet and the first color break was discovered in England in 1780 by Amos Perry, an apprentice in the Ware nurseries. Today we find the name of Perry running through the best lists of poppies. Dr. J. H. Neely, B. H. Farr and many others have carried on the work in this country until today we have more than 250 named varieties.

Poppy stems attain heights of up to four feet, which lift the flowers far above their surroundings. Colors range from white through many shades of pink, rose, red to lavender, with great variation in height and in size of bloom. There are doubles which vary from fifteen to more than a hundred petals, and a bicolor which may be the beginning of a new series.

Oriental poppies thrive in any garden soil, their sole essential requirement being good drainage. They will not grow well in damp situations and for that reason, seem to do best in a sandy, gritty loam. They also prefer exposure to the full sun, but will stand a small amount of shade. They require ample room for development of their roots.

Transplanting is most successfully done when the plant is dormant, in August or September. Unless such a course is followed, there may be a

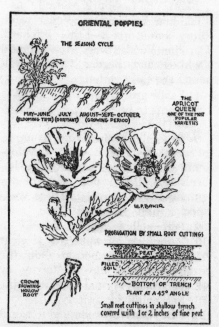

ORIENTAL POPPIES

THE SEASONS CYCLE

MAY—JUNE (BLOOMING TIME) JULY (DORMANT) AUGUST—SEPT—OCTOBER (GROWING PERIOD)

THE APRICOT QUEEN ONE OF THE MOST POPULAR VARIETIES

W. P. BAKER

PROPAGATION BY SMALL ROOT CUTTINGS

PEAT
FILLED SOIL
BOTTOM OF TRENCH
PLANT AT A 45° ANGLE

CROWN SHOWING HOLLOW ROOT

Small root cuttings in shallow trench covered with 1 or 2 inches of fine peat

loss of bloom for an entire season. The plants can be raised from seed, but seedlings seldom come true to color, so root propagation is necessary. This is very easy, as a two-inch root cutting as thick as a lead pencil will, if properly planted, grow into a blooming plant. Cuttings should be taken from mature plants about two or three years old. Root growth starts in about three weeks, so keep the planting well-watered and shaded after growth starts.

Care must be exercised to avoid disturbing the plant or its roots by cultivation, especially during the period when no foliage is showing. Too deep planting is often the cause of lack of bloom, as the crowns seldom bloom well if set more than two or three inches deep. They also resent transplanting, preferring to remain in one place.

A recommended list for selection includes: Purity and Fairy, soft pinks; Mrs. Ballego, Mrs. Perry and Princess Victoria Louise, salmon; Wunderkind, carmine rose; Joyce, cherry red; Lulu Neely and Beauty of Livermore, reds; Henry Cayeux, lavender and Perry's White and Silver Queen, whites.

DIRECTORY TO 39 LISTS OF PLANTS FOR THE FLOWER GARDEN

1. Some perennials whose leaves should not be covered.
2. Plants which winterkill easily.
3. Seeds which should be sown in the fall.
4. Easily grown hardy perennials.
5. Plants to be handled as biennials (renew every other year).
6. Perennials enduring shady conditions.
7. Perennials enduring semishady conditions.
8. Perennials requiring well-drained situations.
9. Perennials for dry sandy soils.
10. Perennials for wet situations.
11. Perennials for borders of ponds and streams.
12. Perennials for naturalizing.
13. Perennials for ground cover.
14. Perennials for banks and terraces.
15. Perennials for edging.
16. Perennials for background.
17. Perennials for cut flowers.
18. Perennials for fragrance.
19. Bloom calendar. March to October.
20. Tender annuals.
21. Half hardy annuals.
22. Annuals difficult to transplant.
23. Annuals which often self sow.
24. Annuals that may be sown in the fall.
25. Annuals useful for succession of bloom.
26. Edging annuals.
27. Rock Garden annuals.
28. Annuals for shady locations.
29. Annuals for porch boxes.
30. Annuals for poor soil.
31. Annuals for hot dry places.
32. Fragrant annuals.

33. Annuals suitable for cut flowers.
34. Types for foliage effects.
35. Types for winter bouquets.
36. Tall annuals for the background.
37. Interesting groupings of annuals.
38. List and description of some annual flowers.
39. Plants that bloom the first year from seed.

Many of the above recommendations are taken from Ohio Experiment Station Bulletin No. 525 by Alex Laurie, Victor H. Ries, L. C. Chadwick and G. H. Poesch; also from "Annual Flowers" by Victor H. Ries. The table on pages 170 and 171 is reprinted by special permission of The American Home Magazine.

No. 1. Some Perennials Whose Leaves and Roots Should Not Be Covered

Alyssum (perennial)
Candytuft (Iberis sempervirens)
Campanula medium
Coral Bells
Coreopsis
Delphinium
English Daisy
Flax (perennial)
Forget-me-not
Foxgloves
Germander
Grass Pink (Dianthus plumarius)
Hollyhocks
Hardy Bulbs
Iris (Bearded Dutch, etc.)
Madonna Lily
Pansy
Perennial Poppy (Oriental, etc.)
Sedums (various)
Sweet William
Violas

No. 2. Plants which Winterkill Easily

Campanula medium (Canterbury Bells)
Digitalis purpurea (Foxglove)
Early flowered Chrysanthemums
Salvia patens (Gentian Sage)
Shasta Daisy

If you have been disappointed with these plants, try removing them to the coldframe for the winter. Heavy outside mulching results in crown rot. Cover with leaves (consult list number one and cover roots only), straw or evergreen boughs. Keep dry by covering frame with boards.

No. 3. Seeds which Should Be Sown in the Fall

Actaea (Baneberry)
†Aconitum (Monkshood)
†Adonis (Adonis)
Anthericum (St. Bernard Lily)
*†Baptisia (Wild Indigo)
Belamcanda (Blackberry Lily)
Bellis (English Daisy)
Bocconia (Plume Poppy)
Cassia (Senna)
Catananche (Everlasting)
Cimicifuga (Bugbane)
*Clematis
*Delphinium (Larkspur)
Dicentra (Bleeding Heart)
*†Dictamnus (Gasplant)
Echinops (Globe Thistle)
*Funkia (Plantain Lily)
Gunnera (Prickly Rhubarb)
†Helleborus (Christmas Rose)
Hypericum (St. John's Wort)
Liatris (Gayfeather)
Lobelia
Oenothera (Evening Primrose)
†Phlox decussata (Hardy Phlox)
†Primula polyantha (Cluster Primrose)
Romneya coulteri (California Tree Poppy)
Sidalcea (Prairie Mallow)
Silene (Catch Fly)
†Spiraea
†Trollius (Globe Flower)

† Do not bloom for several years after germination.

* Seeds lose their vitality quickly and must be sown as soon as they ripen.

[continued on page 142]

No. 4. Easily Grown, Hardy Perennials

The Varieties Marked R Are Particularly Suited for the Rock Garden

	Color	Blooming Season	Height	Location
Achillea (Milfoil) Boule de Neige	White	July-Oct.	2 Ft.	Dry, sunny
Achillea Perry's White	White	July-Oct.	1–2 Ft.	Dry, sunny
Acorus calamus (Sweet Flag)	Yellow	June-Aug.	2 Ft.	Marshy
Agrostemma coronaria (Rose Campion)	Deep crimson	July-Aug.	2½ Ft.	Dry, sunny
R Alyssum saxatile compactum (Gold Dust)	Yellow	April-May	6 Ins.	Dry, sunny
R Aquilegia (Columbine) alpina	Blue	May-June	1–2 Ft.	Sunny or semi-shade
R Aquilegia coerulea	Blue and white	May-June	1½–2½ Ft.	
Aquilegia chrysantha alba	White	May-June	2–3 Ft.	
Aquilegia Pink Shades	Pink	May-June	2–3 Ft.	Moist loam soil
Aquilegia nivea grandiflora	White	May-July	2–3 Ft.	
R Armeria formosa (Sea Pink)	Pink	May-Aug.	12 Ins.	Sandy
R Armeria formosa alba	White	May-Aug.	12 Ins.	Sandy
R Armeria Laucheana	Bright rose	May-July	3–6 Ins.	Sunny
Aster Belgian Queen	Bluish lilac	Sept.-Oct.	3–4 Ft.	Average garden soil, sunny
Aster Emilie Thoury	Light blue	Sept.-Oct.	3–4 Ft.	partial shade
R Aster Mauve Cushion	Light mauve	Oct.-Nov.	9 Ins.	
Baptisia australis (False Indigo)	Dark blue	May-July	2–3 Ft.	Sunny, rich soil
Centaurea montana	Blue	June-Sept.	15 Ins.	Sunny border
R Cerastium tomentosum	White	May-July	6 Ins.	Sunny border
Chelone Lyoni (Shell Flower)	Rosy purple	July-Sept.	3–4 Ft.	Sunny or shade
R Dianthus deltoides (Maiden Pink)	Pink	June-July	9 Ins.	Sunny, dry
R Dianthus plumarius (Cyclop)	White and crimson	May	6–8 Ins.	Sunny, dry
Euphorbia corollata (Spurge)	White	June-Aug.	18 Ins.	Sunny, dry
Heliopsis pitcheriana (Hardy Zinnia)	Orange	July-Sept.	3 Ft.	Sunny
Heliopsis scabra zinniaeflora	Yellow	July-Aug.	2–3 Ft.	
Hemerocallis aurantiaca (Daylily)	Orange-yellow	June-Sept.	3 Ft.	
Hemerocallis minor (Dwarf Daylily)	Bright yellow	June	1 Ft.	Moist, semishade
Hesperis matronalis (Sweet Rocket)	Purple	June-July	2–3 Ft.	Moist, sunny
Hesperis matronalis alba	White	June-July	2–3 Ft.	

	COLOR	BLOOMING SEASON	HEIGHT	LOCATION
R Linum perenne (Blue Perennial Flax)	Blue	June-Aug.	2 Ft.	Sunny
R Linum perenne (White)	White	June-Aug.	2 Ft.	Sunny
Lobelia cardinalis (Cardinal Flower)	Rich red	Aug.-Oct.	2-2½ Ft.	Moist, rich soil
Lobelia syphilitica (Great Blue Lobelia)	Blue and white	July-Sept.	2½-3 Ft.	Moist, rich soil
R Monarda, Cambridge Scarlet (Bergamot)	Scarlet	June-July	3 Ft.	Sun or semishade
R Myosotis palustris semperflorens	Blue	June-Oct.	1 Ft.	Moist, shady
Pentstemon barbatus torreyi	Scarlet	June-Sept.	2-3½ Ft.	Rich, sunny
R Phlox amoena	Rose-pink	April-June	6 Ins.	Sunny and dry
Physalis franchetti (Chinese Lantern)	Scarlet seed pods	Sept.-Oct.	2 Ft.	Sun or semishade
Polemonium coeruleum (Jacob's Ladder)	Sky-blue	April-Sept.	1-1½ Ft.	Semishade, well drained
Polemonium album	White	April-Sept.	1-1½ Ft.	Semishade, well drained
R Potentilla formosa (Cinquefoil)	Cherry-rose	June-Sept.	2 Ft.	Sunny, bright soil
R Potentilla rupestris	White	June	1 Ft.	Sunny, bright soil
Ranunculus acris fl. pl. (Buttercup)	Yellow	April-Aug.	2 Ft.	Moist, sunny
R Ranunculus repens fl. pl.	Golden yellow	May-June	3-4 Ins.	Moist, sunny
Rudbeckia newmani (Cone Flower)	Gold, black center	Aug.-Sept.	2-3 Ft.	Sun or shade
R Ruta patavina (Paduan Rue)	Yellow	June	1 Ft.	Shady
Salvia azurea	Light blue	June-Aug.	2-3 Ft.	Sunny border
R Sedum acre (Wall Pepper)	Yellow	June-Aug.	3 Ins.	Sunny, dry, or semishade
R Sedum album	White	June-July	3 Ins.	Sunny, dry, or semishade
R Sedum ibericum (Spurium)	Pink	August	6 Ins.	Sunny, dry, or semishade
R Sedum kamtschaticum (Evergreen)	Yellow	June-July	6 Ins.	Sunny, dry, or semishade
R Sedum spectabile, Brilliant	Deep red	Aug.-Sept.	16 Ins.	Sun or shade
R Spirea ulmaria fl. pl. (Meadow Sweet)	Creamy white	July-Aug.	5 Ft.	Sun or shade
R Veronica amethystina (Speedwell)	Deep blue	May-July	2 Ft.	Good garden soil
R Viola Blue Perfection	Deep blue	May-Oct.		Semishade or sun, rich soil
R Viola G. Wermig	Violet-blue	May-Oct.		Semishade or sun, rich soil
R Viola G. Wermig alba	White	May-Oct.	6 Ins.	Semishade or sun, rich soil
R Viola lutea splendens	Golden-yellow	April-Sept.		Semishade or sun, rich soil
R Voila papilio (Butterfly Violet)	Violet and dark blue	April-Sept.		Semishade or sun, rich soil

CREDIT. The above and many other lists were compiled by the writer during his long experience in amateur gardening. Victor H. Ries of Ohio State University, is the author of the list and descriptions of "Annual Flowers" on pages 155 to 168 inclusive which has now been supplemented with the latest developments, and other authorities are mentioned upon page 140.

No. 5. Plants to Be Handled as Biennials (Renew Every Other Year)

Althaea rosea (Hollyhock)
Anchusa azurea (Alkanet)
Campanula medium (Canterbury Bells)
Campanula pryramidalis (Chimney Bell-flower)
Dianthus barbatus (Sweet William)
Digitalis purpurea (Foxglove)
Hesperis matronalis (Sweet Rocket)
Lunaria biennis (Honesty, Money plant)

No. 6. Perennials Enduring Shady Conditions

Aconitum fischeri (Azure Monkshood)
Ajuga genevensis (Geneva Bugle)
Amsonia tabernaemontana (Willow Amsonia)
Anemonella thalictroides (Rue Anemone)
Convallaria majalis (Lily-of-the-valley)
Cornus canadensis (Bunchberry)
Dicentra eximia (Fringed Bleeding-heart)
Dodecatheon meadia (Shooting Star)
Helleborus niger (Christmas Rose)
Hosta caerulea (Blue Plantain Lily)
Hosta plantaginea grandiflora (Big Plantain Lily)
Lobelia cardinalis (Cardinal Flower)
Mertensia virginica (Virginia Blue Bells)
Myosotis palustris semperflorens (Dwarf Perpetual Forget-me-not)
Polygonatum biflorum (Small Solomon Seal)
Thalictrum adiantifolium (Low Meadowrue)
Trillium grandiflorum (Snow Trillium)

No. 7. Perennials Enduring Semishady Conditions

Anchusa italica (Dropmore Bugloss)
Anemone japonica (Japanese Anemone)
Aquilegia hybrids (Columbine)
Asperula odorata (Woodruff)
Belamcanda chinensis (Blackberry Lily)
Campanula rotunifolia (Hare Bell)

Chelone lyoni (Pink Turtlehead)
Cimicifuga racemosa (Cohosh Bugbane)
Digitalis purpurea (Common Foxglove)
Doronicum plantagineum (Leopard-bane)
Heracleum villosum (Cow Parsnip)
Heuchera sanguinea (Coral Bells)
Monarda didyma (Bee Balm)
Primula veris (Cowslip Primrose)
Pulmonaria saccharata (Bethlehem Lungwort)
Silene pennsylvanica (Peat Pink)
Trollius europaeus (Globe Flower)

No. 8. Perennials Requiring Well-Drained Situations

Arabis alpina (Alpine Rock-cress)
Asclepias tuberosa (Butterflyweed)
Aubrietia deltoidea (Purple Rock-cress)
Coreopsis grandiflora (Tickseed)
Delphinium hybrids (Delphinium)
Dianthus barbatus (Sweet William)
Digitalis purpurea (Common Foxglove)
Echinops ritro (Steel Globe Thistle)
Eryngium maritimum (Seaholly)
Gaillardia aristata (Blanket Flower)
Globularia trichosantha (Globe Daisy)
Helianthus maximiliana (Maximilian Sunflower)
Iris germanica (German Iris)
Liatris pycnostachya (Cattail Gay-feather)
Papaver nudicaule (Iceland Poppy)

No. 9. Perennials for Dry, Sandy Soils

Achillea ptarmica (Sneezewort)
Ajuga reptans (Geneva Bugle)
Anthemis tinctoria (Yellow Camomile)
Asclepias tuberosa (Butterflyweed)
Aster novae-angliae (New England Aster)
Callirhoe involucrata (Poppymallow)
Cassia marilandica (Wild Senna)
Coreopsis grandiflora (Tickseed)
Dianthus plumarius (Grass Pink)
Echinops ritro (Steel Globe Thistle)
Euphorbia corollata (Flowering Spurge)
Helianthus (various) (Sunflower)

Limonium (Statice) latifolium (Bigleaf Statice)
Lychnis chalcedonica (Maltese Cross)
Papaver nudicaule (Iceland Poppy)
Rudbeckia laciniata (Goldenglow)
Yucca filamentosa (Common Yucca)

No. 10. Perennials for Wet Situations

Arundo donax* (Giant Reed)
Asclepias incarnata (Swamp Milkweed)
Boltonia asteroides (White Boltonia)
Caltha palustris* (Marsh Marigold)
Eupatorium purpureum (Joe-pye-weed)
Helenium autumnale (Sneezeweed)
Hibiscus moscheutos (Rosemallow)
Iris pseudacorus* (Yellow Flag)
Iris veriscolor* (Blue Flag)
Lobelia cardinalis (Cardinalflower)
Lysimachia clethroides (Clethra Loosestrife)
Lythrum salicaria (Loosestrife)
Miscanthus sinensis (Eulalia)
Monarda didyma (Bee Balm)
Myosotis palustris (True Forget-me-not)
Onoclea sensibilis (Sensitive Fern)
Osmunda cinnamonea (Cinnamon Fern)
Osmunda regalis* (Royal Fern)
Sarracenia purpurea (Pitcherplant)

No. 11. Perennials for Borders of Ponds and Streams

(*Well-drained soil*)

SUNNY LOCATIONS

Anchusa myosotidiflora (Siberian Bugloss)
Chrysanthemum uliginosum (Giant Daisy)
Cimicifuga racemosa (Cohosh Bugbane)
Grasses (Ornamental grasses)
Hemerocallis (various) (Daylily)
Iris (various) (Iris)
Lythrum salicaria (Loosestrife)
Myosotis palustris semperflorens (Dwarf Perpetual Forget-me-not)
Tradescantia virginiana (Spiderwort)

May be grown in water.

Trollius europaeus (Globe Flower)

SEMISHADY LOCATIONS

Anemone japonica (Japanese Anemone)
Cimicifuga racemosa (Cohosh Bugbane)
Epimedium macranthum (Longspur Epimedium)
Eupatorium purpureum (Joe-pye-weed)
Ferns (Ferns)
Iris cristata (Crested Iris)
Lythrum salicaria (Loosestrife)
Tradescantia virginiana (Spiderwort)

No. 12. Perennials for Naturalizing

Asclepias tuberosa (Butterflyweed)
Aster (various) (Aster)
Cimicifuga racemosa (Cohosh Bugbane)
Convallaria majalis (Lily-of-the-valley)
Coreopsis grandiflora (Tickseed)
Geranium maculatum (Spotted Geranium)
Helianthus (various) (Sunflower)
Hemerocallis (various) (Roundlobe Hepatica)
Lythrum salicaria (Loosestrife)
Mertensia virginica (Virginia Bluebells)
Monarda didyma (Bee Balm)
Physostegia virginica (False Dragonhead)
Polemonium reptans (Creeping Polemonium)
Rudbeckia subtomentose (Sweet Coneflower)
Sanguinaria canadensis (Bloodroot)
Smilacina racemosa (False Solomonseal)
Solidago canadensis (Canada Goldenrod)

No. 13. Perennials for Ground Cover

SUNNY LOCATIONS

Cerastium tomentosum (Snow-in-summer)
Ceratostigma plumbaginoides (Larpente Plumbago)
Coronilla varia (Crownvetch)
Dianthus plumarius (Grass Pink)

There is no more dependable sign of spring than the myriad golden florets of the Forsythia. There are numerous shapes and sizes of this graceful shrub. One of the best varieties, in form and color, is called Spring Glory.

A few packets of seed make this effective border of annual flowers.

Roses and Delphiniums, king and queen of early summer.

Helianthemum mutabile (Fickle Sun-rose)
Iberis sempervirens (Evergreen Candy-tuft)
Nepeta mussini (Mussini Mint)
Phlox subulata (Moss Phlox)
Sedum Sarmentosum (Stringy Stone-crop)
Sedum spurium (Running Stonecrop)
Thymus serphyllum (Mother-of-thyme)
Veronica teucrium (rupestris) (Rock Speedwell)
Vinca minor (Periwinkle)

SHADY LOCATIONS

Aegopodium podograria (Goutweed)
Ajuga reptans (Geneva Bugle)
Asperula odorata (Woodruff)
Convallaria majalis (Lily-of-the-valley)
Hedera helix (English Ivy)
Mitchella repens (Partridgeberry)
Nepeta mussini (Mussini Mint)
Pachysandra terminalis (Japanese Pachysandra)
Sedum ternatum (Mountain Stonecrop)
Vinca minor (Periwinkle)

No. 14. Perennials for Covering Banks and Terraces

Ajuga reptans (Geneva Bugle)
Alyssum saxatile (Goldentuft)
Arabis Alpina (Alpine Rock-cress)
Cerastium tomentosum (Snow-in-summer)
Coronilla varia (Crownvetch)
Dianthus deltoides (Maiden Pink)
Hedera helix (English Ivy)
Nepeta mussini (Mussini Mint)
Pachysandra terminalis (shade) (Japanese Pachysandra)
Phlox subulata (Moss Phlox)
Saponaria ocymoides (Rock Soapwort)
Sedum sarmentosum (Stringy Stone-crop)
Veronica teucrium (rupestris) (Rock Speedwell)
Vinca minor (Periwinkle)

No. 15. Perennials for Edging

Aegopodium podograria (Goutweed)

Ajuga reptans (Geneva Bugle)
Alyssum saxatile compactum (Dwarf Goldentuft)
Arabis alpina (Alpine Rock-cress)
Bellis perennis (English Daisy)
Campanula carpatica (Carpathian Bell-flower)
Cerastium tomentosum (Snow-in-summer)
Ceratostigma plumbaginoides (Larpente Plumbago)
Dianthus plumarius (Grass Pink)
Festuca glauca (Blue Fescue)
Heuchera sanguinea (Coralbells)
Iberis sempervirens (Evergreen Candy-tuft)
Papaver nudicaule (Iceland Poppy)
Primula veris (Cowslip Primrose)
Sedum album (White Stonecrop)
Sedum reflexum (Jenny Stonecrop)
Statice armeria (Thrift)
Tunica saxifraga (Tunicflower)
Veronica teucrium (rupestris) (Rock Speedwell)
Viola cornuta (Tufted Pansy)

No. 16. Perennials for Background Planting

Althea rosea (Hollyhock)
Aster novae-angliae (New England Aster)
Aster tataricus (Tartarian Aster)
Bocconia cordata (Plume Poppy)
Boltonia asteroides (White Boltonia)
Campanula pyramidalis (Chimney Bell-flower)
Cimicifuga racemosa (Cohosh Bugbane)
Delphinium hybrids (Delphinium)
Helenium autumnale (Sneezeweed)
Helianthus maximiliani (Maximilian Sunflower)
Hibiscus grandiflorus (Great Rose-mallow)
Rudbeckia laciniata (Goldenglow)
Solidago altissima (Tall Goldenrod)
Valeriana officinalis (Common Valerian)
Yucca filamentosa (Common Yucca)

No. 17. Perennials Suitable for Cut Flowers

Achillea millea millefolium rosea (Pink Yarrow)
Anemone japonica (Japanese Anemone)
Aster (various) (Aster)
Chrysanthemum maximum (Shasta Daisy)
Coreopsis grandiflora (Tickseed)
Delphinium hybrids (Delphinium)
Dianthus barbatus (Sweet William)
Gaillardia aristata (Blanket Flower)
Gypsophila paniculata flore pleno (Babysbreath)
Helenium autumnale (Sneezeweed)
Iris (various) (Iris)
Paenia (various) (Peony)
Pyrethrum roseum (Painted Lady)
Rudbeckia (various) (Coneflower)
Salvia azurea grandiflora (Azure Sage)
Veronica longifolia subsessilis (Clump Speedwell)

No. 18. Fragrant Perennials

Centranthus ruber (Jupiter's Beard)
Convallaria majalis (Lily-of-the-valley)
Dianthus plumarius (Grass Pink)
Hemerocallis flava (Lemon Daylily)
Hosta plantagineagrandiflora (Big Plantain Lily)
Lathyrus grandiflorus (Perennial Pea)
Valeriana officinalis (Common Valerian)
Viola cornuta (Tufted Pansy)

No. 19. Bloom Calendar

PERENNIALS FOR MARCH BLOOM

SCIENTIFIC NAME	COMMON NAME	HEIGHT, IN INCHES	COLOR
Helleborus niger	Christmas Rose	12	White
Iberis sempervirens	Evergreen Candytuft	12	White
Sanguinaria canadensis	Bloodroot	8	White
Galanthus nivalis	Common Snowdrop	6	White
Scilla siberica	Siberian Squill	6	Blue
Chionodoxa luciliae	Glory-of-the-snow	4	Blue
Claytonia virginica	Virginia Springbeauty	4	Pink
Crocus vernus	Common Crocus	4	Various
Eranthis hyemalis	Winter Aconite	3	Yellow

PERENNIALS FOR APRIL BLOOM

Cheiranthus cheiri	Common Wallflower	24	Yellow
Iberis gibraltarica	Gibraltar Candytuft	18	White
Aquilegia canadensis	American Columbine	18	Red-Yellow
Dodecatheon meadia	Common Shootingstar	15	Lilac
Saxifraga cordifolia	Heartleaf Saxifrage	12	Purple
Pulmonaria angustifolia	Cowslip Lungwort	12	Blue
Mitella diphylla	Common Bishop's cap	12	White
Arabis alpina	Alpine Rock-cress	12	White
Adonis amurensis	Amur Adonis	12	Yellow
Tulipa (early)	Tulip	12	Various

Scientific Name	Common Name	Height, in Inches	Color
Narcissus (various)	Narcissus	12	Yellow
Leucojum vernum	Spring Snowflake	12	White
Dicentra cucullaria	Dutchman's Breeches	10	White
Primula elatior	Oxlip Primula	9	Various
Primula veris	Cowslip	9	Yellow
Anemone pulsatilla	European Pasqueflower	9	Purple
Viola cornuta	Tufted Pansy	8	Various
Viola odorata	Sweet Violet	8	Violet
Muscari botryoides	Common Grape Hyacinth	8	Blue
Hyacinthus orientalis	Hyacinth	8	Various
Hepatica triloba	Roundleaf Hepatica	6	Blue
Aubrietia deltoidea	Common Aubrietia	6	Purple

Perennials for May Bloom

Scientific Name	Common Name	Height, in Inches	Color
Dicentra spectabilis	Bleedingheart	36	Pink
Iris germanica	Iris	18–36	Various
Thalictrum aquilegifolium	Columbine Meadowrue	36	Purple
Hemerocallis flava	Lemon Daylily	36	Yellow
Paeonia officinalis	Common Peony	30	Various
Aquilegia chrysantha	Golden Columbine	24	Yellow
Doronicum caucasicum	Caucasian Leopardbane	24	Yellow
Euphorbia epithymoides	Cushion Spurge	24	Yellow
Chrysanthemum coccineum	Painted Lady	24	Various
Trollius europaeus	Common Globe Flower	24	Yellow
Alyssum saxatile	Goldentuft	18	Yellow
Tulipa gesneriana	Darwin Tulip	18	Various
Gaillardia aristata	Common Peren. Gaillardia	15	Red-Orange
Anchusa myosotidiflora	Siberian Bugloss	12	Blue
Convallaria majalis	Lily-of-the-valley	12	White
Nepeta mussini	Mussini Mint	12	Blue
Phlox divaricata	Blue Phlox	12	Lavender
Asperula odorata	Sweet Woodruff	8	Yellow
Ajuga reptans	Carpet Bugle	6	Purple
Phlox subulata	Moss Phlox	6	Pink
Polemonium reptans	Creeping Polemonium	6	Blue
Ranunculus repens	Creeping Buttercup	6	Yellow
Silene alpestris	Alpine Catchfly	6	White

Scientific Name	Common Name	Height, in Inches	Color
Cerastium tomentosum	Snow-in-summer	6	White
Veronica teucrium (rupestris)	Rock Speedwell	4	Blue

Perennials for June Bloom

Scientific Name	Common Name	Height	Color
Althea rosea	Hollyhock	72	Various
Astilbe davidi	David Astilbe	60	Rose
Delphinium hybrids	Larkspur	24–60	Various
Digitalis purpurea	Common Foxglove	48	Purple
Lilium regale	Royal Lily	48	White
Anchusa italica	Italian Bugloss	36	Blue
Gypsophila Bristol Fairy	Babysbreath	36	White
Lupinus polyphyllus	Washington Lupinus	36	Various
Pentstemon barbatus torreyi	Torrey Pentstemon	36	Scarlet
Papaver orientale	Oriental Poppy	36	Red-Pink
Lilium candidum	Madonna Lily	36	White
Aconitum napellus	Aconite	24	Blue-White
Baptisia australis	Blue Wild-indigo	24	Blue
Campanula medium	Canterbury bells	24	Blue
Chrysanthemum maximum	Shasta Daisy	24	White
Platycodon grandiflorum	Balloonflower	24	Blue-Violet
Achillea ptarmica	Sneezewort	24	White
Lilium tenuifolium	Coral Lily	24	Red
Achillea millefolium rosea	Common Yarrow	18	Rose
Centranthus ruber	Jupiter's beard	18	Crimson
Dianthus barbatus	Sweet William	18	Various
Linum perenne	Perennial Flax	18	Blue
Oenothera fruticosa	Common Sundrops	18	Yellow
Dianthus plumarius	Grass Pink	12	Various
Lychnis viscaria	Clammy Campion	12	Purple
Papaver nudicaule	Iceland Poppy	12	Various
Thalictrum minus adiantifolium	Maidenhair Meadowrue	12	Yellow
Veronica spicata	Spike Speedwell	12	Purple
Astilbe japonica	Japanese Astilbe	12	White
Dianthus deltoides	Maiden Pink	9	Pink
Campanula carpatica	Carpathian Bellflower	8	Blue

Perennials for July Bloom

Scientific Name	Common Name	Height	Color
Bocconia cordata	Pink Plume Poppy	72–96	Cream
Lilium tigrinum	Tiger Lily	24–60	Orange
Cimicifuga racemosa	Cohosh Bugbane	48	White

Scientific Name	Common Name	Height, in Inches	Color
Hemerocallis thunbergi	Japanese Daylily	48	Yellow
Lythrum salicaria	Purple Loosestrife	48	Rose-Purple
Heliopsis pitcheriana	Pitcher Heliopsis	36	Orange
Physostegia virginiana	Virginia False-dragonhead	36	Pink
Monarda didyma	Oswego Beebalm	36	Scarlet
Echinops ritro	Steel Globe Thistle	36	Blue
Phlox paniculata	Garden Phlox	24	Various
Asclepias tuberosa	Butterflyweed	24	Orange
Lychnis chalcedonica	Maltese Cross	24	Scarlet
Eryngium amethystinum	Amethyst Eryngo	24	Amethyst
Lychnis haageana	Haage Campion	12	Orange-Scarlet
Heuchera sanguinea	Coralbells	18	Crimson
Veronica incana	Woolly Speedwell	12	Rosy purple
Tunica saxifraga	Tunicflower	8	White

Perennials for August Bloom

Scientific Name	Common Name	Height, in Inches	Color
Eupatorium purpureum	Joe-pye-weed	72	Purple
Campanula pyramidalis	Chimney Bellflower	72	Blue
Lilium henryi	Henry Lily	60–72	Orange
Artemisia vulgaris lactiflora	White Mugwort	48	White
Liatris pycnostachya	Cattail Gayfeather	48	Purple
Lilium speciosum	Speciosum Lily	24–48	Pink
Solidago canadensis	Canada Goldenrod	36	Yellow
Rudbeckia speciosa	Showy Coneflower	36	Golden
Lilium superbum	American Turk's cap Lily	24–36	Orange-Red
Veronica longifolia subsessilis	Clump Speedwell	24–36	Blue-Purple
Inula royleana	Blackbud Inula	24	Golden
Aster spectabilis	Seaside Aster	24	Purple
Liatris spicata	Spike Gayfeather	24	Purple
Stokesia laevis	Stokesia	12–24	Lavender-White
Limonium latifolium	Bigleaf Sea-lavender	20	Lavender
Coreopsis rosea	Rose Coreopsis	12	Pink-Rose
Hosta plantaginea	White Plantainlily	12–18	White
Colchicum autumnale	Common Autumn Crocus	3–4	Purple

Perennials for September and October

Scientific Name	Common Name	Height, in Inches	Color
Boltonia asteroides	White Boltonia	60–72	Creamy
Aster tataricus	Tatarian Aster	60–72	Violet-Blue
Boltonia latisquama	Violet Boltonia	48–72	Pink
Chrysanthemum uliginosum	Giant Daisy	60	White

Scientific Name	Common Name	Height, in Inches	Color
Aconitum wilsoni	Violet Monkshood	48–60	Blue
Aster novibelgi	New York Aster	36–60	Blue
Salvia azurea grandiflora	Great Azure Sage	48	Blue
Aster novae-angliae	New England Aster	36–48	Various
Helenium autumnale	Common Sneezeweed	36–48	Yellow
Kniphofia uvaria	Common torchfly	36	Orange
Echinacea purpurea	Purple Coneflower	36	Purple-Rose
Anemone japonica	Japanese Anemone	24–36	Various
Chelone lyoni	Pink Turtlehead	24–36	Pink
Aconitum fischeri	Azure Monkshood	24–36	Blue
Salvia patens	Gentian Sage	12–24	Blue
Sedum spectabile	Showy Stonecrop	18	Crimson
Eupatorium coelestinum	Mistflower	18	Blue
Anemone hupehensis		12	Rose
Chrysanthemum arcticum	Arctic Chrysanthemum	6	White
Ceratostigma plumbaginoides	Larpente Plumbago	6	Blue

No. 20. Tender Annuals

The tender annuals may be sown outdoors during May or earlier indoors.

Ageratum houstonianum (Floss Flower)
Callistephus chinensis (China-aster)
Celosia plumosa (Cockscomb)
Cobaea scandens (Purplebell Cobaea)
Emilia flammea (Tasselflower)
Lobelia erinus (Edging Lobelia)
Lunaria biennis (Honesty)
Mimulus luteus (Monkeyflower)
Nemophila maculata (Spotted Nemophila)
Phaseolus coccineus (Scarlet Runner Bean)
Reseda odorata (Mignonette)
Salpiglossis sinuata (Painted Tongue)
Schizanthus pinnatus (Poorman's Orchid)
Trachymene caerulea (Blue Laceflower)
Tropaeolum peregrinum (Nasturtium)

No. 21. Half-Hardy Annuals

Many of the half-hardy sorts require a long growing season for proper development and should be sown in March in a greenhouse, coldframe, or hotbed.

Antirrhinum majus (Snapdragon)
Arctotis grandis (Bushy Arctotis)
Centaurea cineraria (Dusty Miller)
Dianthus chinensis (Pink)
Dimorphotheca aurantiaca (Winter Cape-Marigold)
Gilia capitata (Globe Gilia)
Helichrysum bracteatum (Strawflower)
Limonium (Statice)
Lobelia erinus (Edging Lobelia)
Lupinus (Lupine)
Matthiola incana (Stocks)
Nemesia strumosa (Pouched Nemesia)
Nicotiana sylvestris (Flowering Tobacco)
Pentstemon gloxinioides (Gloxinia Pentstemon)

Petunia hybrida (Common Petunia)
Quamoclit coccinea (Starglory)
Ricinus communis (Castor-bean)
Salpiglossis sinuata (Painted Tongue)
Salvia farinacea (Mealycup Sage)
Salvia splendens (Scarlet Sage)
Scabiosa atropurpurea (Sweet Scabiosa)
Verbena hybrida (Garden Verbena)
Zinnia (Youth and Old Age)

No. 22. Annuals Difficult to Transplant

Argemone grandiflora (Showy Prickle-poppy)
Eschscholtzia californica (California Poppy)
Godetia grandiflora (Whitney Godetia)
Gypsophila elegans (Common Gypsophila)
Helianthus annuus (Sunflower)
Lathyrus odoratus (Sweet Pea)
Lavatera trimestris (Herb Treemallow)
Lupinus (Lupine)
Nigella damascena (Love-in-a-mist)
Oenothera drummondi (Evening Primrose)
Papaver (Poppy)
Phaseolus coccineus (Scarlet Runner)
Portulaca grandiflora (Rose Moss)
Trachymene caerulea (Blue Laceflower)
Tropaeolum (Nasturtium)

No. 23. Annuals which Often Self-Sow

Alyssum maritimum (Sweet Alyssum)
Browallia
Calendula officinalis (Pot-marigold)
Centaurea cyanus (Cornflower)
Cleome spinosa (Spiderflower)
Coreopsis tinctoria (Calliopsis)
Cosmos bipinnatus (Cosmos)
Delphinium ajacis (Rocket Larkspur)
Eschscholtzia californica (California Poppy)
Euphorbia marginata (Snow-on-the-mountain)
Gypsophila elegans (Common Gypsophila)
Ipomaea purpurea (Common Morning Glory)

Kochia trichophylla (Common Summer-cypress)
Mirabilis jalapa (Common Four-o'clock)
Nicotiana sylvestris (Flowering Tobacco)
Petunia hybrida (Common Petunia)
Portulaca grandiflora (Rose Moss)
Salvia farinacea (Mealycup Sage)

No. 24. Annuals that May Be Sown in the Fall

Alyssum maritimum (Sweet Alyssum)
Antirrhinum majus (Snapdragon)
Calendula officinalis (Pot-marigold)
Centaurea cyanus (Cornflower)
Clarkia elegans (Clarkia)
Coreopsis tinctoria (Calliopsis)
Cosmos bipinnatus (Cosmos)
Delphinium ajacis (Rocket Larkspur)
Dianthus chinensis (Chinese Pink)
Eschscholtzia californica (California Poppy)
Gypsophila elegans (Common gypsophila)
Iberis (Candytuft)
Lathyrus odoratus (Sweet Pea)
Lavatera trimestris (Herb Treemallow)
Nigella damascena (Love-in-a-mist)
Papaver (Poppy)
Saponaria vaccaria (Cow Soapwort)
Viola tricolor (Pansy)

No. 25. Annuals Useful for Succession of Bloom

Several sowings should be made of these annuals to obtain a succession of bloom.

Alyssum maritimum (Sweet Alyssum)
Centaurea cyanus (Cornflower)
Coreopsis tinctoria (Calliopsis)
Dimorphotheca aurantiaca (Winter Cape-marigold)
Gypsophila elegans (Common Gypsophila)
Iberis umbellata (Purple Candytuft)
Myosotis (Forget-me-not)
Nigella damascena (Love-in-a-mist)
Papaver (Poppy)
Phlox drummondi (Drummond Phlox)
Reseda odorata (Mignonette)
In planting annuals in vacant spaces

in rock gardens or perennial borders, a group of five or seven plants will present a more pleasing effect than will single plantings. All annuals should receive a liberal amount of water after they are transplanted.

The annual beds should be watched closely so that weeds do not overtake the young plants. Cultivation after each rain is recommended. Annual plants should never be allowed to remain dry.

No. 26. Edging Annuals

Edging plants should be short and compact and should continue to flower the entire season. The following are the best for this purpose:

Ageratum nanum compactum (Little Bluestar Ageratum)
Ageratum (Tom Thumb, Little Bluestar)
Alyssum maritimum (Sweet Alyssum)
Celosia lillipot (Fire Feather)
Centaurea cineraria (Dusty Miller)
Lobelia erinus Crystal Palace (Edging Lobelia)
Petunia hybrida (Common Petunia)
Phlox drummondi (Drummond Phlox)
Portulaca grandiflora (Common Portulaca)
Tagetes signata pumila (Striped Marigold)
Tropaeolum majus (Common Nasturtium)
Verbena hybrida (Garden Verbena)
Viola tricolor (Common Pansy)

No. 27. Rock Garden Annuals

Dwarf, compact, and not-too-spreading annuals are good rock garden plants. Among the best for this purpose are:

Abronia umbellata (Pink Sand Verbena)
Ageratum houstonianum (mexicanum) (Mexican Ageratum)
Alyssum maritimum (Sweet Alyssum)
Antirrhinum (dwarf) (Snapdragon)
Browallia speciosa major

Dianthus chinensis (Chinese Pink)
Dimorphotheca aurantiaca (Winter Cape-marigold)
Emilia flammea (Tasselflower)
Eschscholtzia californica (California Poppy)
Gazania longiscapa
Hunnemannia fumariaefolia (Goldencup)
Iberis umbellata (Purple Candytuft)
Lobelia erinus (Edging Lobelia)
Petunia hybrida (Petunia)
Phlox drummondi (Drummond Phlox)
Portulaca grandiflora (Rose Moss)
Sanvitalia procumbens (Common Sanvitalia)
Silene armeria (Sweet William Campion)
Tagetes signata pumila (Dwarf Marigold)
Verbena hybrida (Garden Verbena)
Verbena venosa (Tuber Verbena)
Viola tricolor (Common Pansy)

No. 28. Annuals for Shady Locations

Annuals are not lovers of shade, but a few succeed under partial shade. The following sorts may be recommended:

Alyssum maritimum (Sweet Alyssum)
Antirrhinum majus (Snapdragon)
Centaurea americana (Basketflower)
Centaurea imperialis (Royal Sweet Sultan)
Centaurea suaveolens (Sweet Sultan)
Clarkia elegans
Cynoglossum amabile (Chinese Forget-me-not)
Eschscholtzia californica (California Poppy)
Godetia amoena (Farewell-to-spring)
Lupinus hartwegi (Hartweg Lupine)
Myosotis palustris (True Forget-me-not)
Phlox drummondi (Drummond Phlox)
Viola tricolor (Common Pansy)

No. 29. Annuals for Window and Porch Boxes

Ageratum houstonianum (Mexican Ageratum)

Alyssum maritimum (Sweet Alyssum)
Browallia speciosa
Centaurea cineraria (Dusty Miller)
Lantana camera (Common Lantana)
Lobelia erinus (Edging Lobelia)
Maurandia barclaiana (Barclay Maurandia)
Petunia hybrida (Petunia)
Phlox drummondi (Drummond Phlox)
Portulaca grandiflora (Rose Moss)
Tagetes signata pumila (Dwarf Marigold)
Thunbergia alata (Black-eyed Clockvine)
Verbena hybrida (Garden Verbena)
Vinca rosea (Madagascar Periwinkle)

No. 30. Annuals that Will Grow in Poor Soil

Alyssum maritimum (Sweet Alyssum)
Amaranthus caudatus (Love-lies-bleeding)
Browallia speciosa
Calendula officinalis (Pot-marigold)
Celosia plumosa (Feather Cockscomb)
Centaurea moschata (Sweet Sultan)
Cleome spinosa (Spiderflower)
Coreopsis tinctoria (Calliopsis)
Eschscholtzia californica (California Poppy)
Gaillardia lovenziana (Gaillardia)
Godetia grandiflora (Whitney Godetia)
Impatiens balsamina (Garden Balsam)
Mentzelia aurea (Bartonia) (Blazing Star)
Mirabilis jalapa (Common Fouro'clock)
Papaver rhoeas (Corn Poppy)
Petunia hybrida (Petunia)
Portulaca grandiflora (Rose Moss)
Tropaeolum majus (Nasturtium)

No. 31. Annuals for Hot, Dry Places (Drought Resistant)

Argemone grandiflora (Showy Pricklepoppy)
Centaurea cyanus (Cornflower)
Convolvulus tricolor (Dwarf Convolvulus)
Coreopsis tinctoria (Calliopsis)

Delphinium ajacis (Rocket Larkspur)
Dimorphotheca aurantiaca (Winter Cape-marigold)
Euphorbia marginata (Snow-on-the-mountain)
Helianthus annuus (Common Sunflower)
Ipomoea purpurea (Morning Glory)
Kochia trichophylla (Common Summer-cypress)
Mesembryanthemum crystallinum (Ice Plant)
Mirabilis jalapa (Common Fouro'clock)
Perilla frutescens (Green Perilla)
Phlox drummondi (Drummond Phlox)
Portulaca grandiflora (Rose Moss)
Salvia splendens (Scarlet Sage)
Sanvitalia procumbens (Common Sanvitalia)
Zinnia elegans (Common Zinnia)

No. 32. Fragrant Annuals

Alyssum maritimum (Sweet Alyssum)
Antirrhinum majus (Snapdragon)
Centaurea moschata (Sweet Sultan)
Delphinium ajacis (Rocket Larkspur)
Dianthus chinensis (Chinese Pink)
Heliotropium peruvianum (Common Heliotrope)
Iberis umbellata (Purple Candytuft)
Lathyrus odoratus (Sweet Pea)
Lupinus luteus (European Yellow Lupine)
Matthiola incana (Common Stock)
Mimulus moschatus (Muskplant)
Nicotiana affinis (Jasmine Tobacco)
Phlox drummondi (Drummond Phlox)
Reseda odorata (Mignonette)
Scabiosa atropurpurea (Sweet Scabiosa)
Tropaeolum majus (Nasturtium)
Verbena hybrida (Garden Verbena)
Viola tricolor (Common Pansy)

No. 33. Annuals Suitable for Cut Flowers

Antirrhinum majus (Snapdragon)
Arctotis grandis (Bushy Arctotis)

Browallia speciosa
Calendula officinalis (Pot-marigold)
Callistephus chinensis (China Aster)
Centaurea cyanus (Cornflower) and imperialis (Sweet Sultan)
Chrysanthemum
Coreopsis tinctoria (Calliopsis)
Cosmos bipinnatus (Common Cosmos)
Delphinium ajacis (Rocket Larkspur)
Dianthus chinensis (Chinese Pink)
Dimorphotheca aurantiaca (Winter Cape-marigold)
Gaillardia lorenziana (Gaillardia)
Iberis umbellata (Purple Candytuft)
Lathyrus odoratus (Sweet Pea)
Limonium sinuatum (Notchleaf Sea-lavender)
Phlox drummondi (Drummond Phlox)
Reseda odorata (Mignonette)
Salpiglossis sinuata (Scalloped Salpiglossis)
Scabiosa atropurpurea (Sweet Scabiosa)
Schizanthus pinnatus (Wingleaf Butterflyflower)
Tagetes erecta (Aztec Marigold, African) and patula (French Marigold)
Tropaeolum majus (Nasturtium)
Verbena venosa (Tuber Verbena)
Viola tricolor (Common Pansy)
Zinnia elegans (Common Zinnia)

No. 34. Types for Foliage Effects

Amaranthus caudatus (Love-lies-bleeding)
Argemone grandiflora (Showy Prickle-poppy)
Briza maxima (Big Quaking Grass)
Cardiospermum halicacabum (Balloon-vine)
Coix lacryma (Job's Tears)
Coleus blumei (Common Coleus)
Euphorbia marginata (Snow-on-the-mountain)
Kochia trichophylla (Common Summer-cypress)
Lagurus ovatus (Rabbittail Grass)
Perilla frutescens (Green Perilla)
Ricinus communis (Castor-bean)

No. 35. Types for Winter Bouquets (Everlastings)

Ammobium alatum (Winged Everlasting)
Celosia cristata (Common Cockscomb)
Gomphrena globosa (Common Globe-amaranth)
Gypsophila elegans (Common Gypsophila)
Helichrysum bracteatum (Strawflower)
Helipterum manglesi (Mangles Everlasting)
Helipterum roseum (Rose Everlasting)
Lunaria biennis (Honesty)
Limonium sinuatum (Notchleaf Sea-Lavender)
Xeranthemum annuum (Common Immortelle)

No. 36. Tall Annuals for Background Effect

Amaranthus
Calliopsis, tall variety
Cosmos
Larkspur, tall
Marigold, tall African
Princesplume
Scarlet Sage
Spiderflower
Sunflower
Summer Fir
Tobacco
Zinnia

No. 37. Interesting Groupings of Annuals

Ageratum and Calendula
Tasselflower and Browallia
Spiderflower and Tobacco
Gaillardia, Petunia, and Verbena
Mexican Zinnia and Ageratum
Pricklepoppy, French Marigolds, and Cape Bugloss
Calendula and Mealycup Sage
Cape Bugloss and Striped Marigold
California Poppy, Cornflower, and French Marigolds
Nemesia, Stocks and Ageratum
Gypsophila, Cape-marigold, and Browallia
Snapdragon, Phlox, and Spiderflower

Cosmos, Spiderflower, and Giant Zinnia
Pricklepoppy, Perilla, and Tobacco
Clarkia, Browallia, and Mignonette
Perilla, Snow-on-the-mountain, and
　Summer-cypress
Tasselflower and Ageratum
Pinewoods Coneflower, Gaillardia, and
　Gypsophila
Gilia, Striped Marigold, and Chinese
　Forget-me-not
Chinese Forget-me-not and Calendula
Forget-me-nots and Gypsophila
Flax and Ageratum
Salpiglossis and French Marigolds
Thrift, Oriental Woodruff, and Cal-
　liopsis

No. 38. List of Annual Flowers

Accepted scientific name is in italics, unaccepted name in parentheses.

Symbols: H.—Height of plant. P.D.—Planting distance.

AGERATUM. *A. houstonianum (mexicanum)* H.—6 to 24″ P.D.—8 to 12″
A charming, constant bloomer, essential in every garden. The blue-violet color combines with practically any other garden color, but the white varieties are not as decorative. The dwarf and compact forms are generally preferred to the tall ones, which are useful for cutting. Blue Perfection is standard. Midget Blue, new, is the first dwarf to come true from seed, and while not as uniform as Riverside, from cuttings, is within the reach of everyone and valuable. All self-sow under certain conditions. For early bloom, start seed indoors.

AMARANTHUS. *Amaranthus.*
　　　　　H.—3 to 5′ P.D.—2′
A coarse group of plants, related to cockscomb and pigweed, some with colored foliage, others with long red spikes of flowers. They should be used sparingly, if at all, and then only with the coarser annuals and shrubs. They

will stand the hottest and driest locations.

ARCTOTIS. *Arctotis grandis*—Blue Eyed African Daisy. H.—24″ P.D.—8 to 12″
A day-time bloomer, closing at night, white flowers, lilac blue outside, effective gray-green foliage. Easily grown in the borders. Good for cutting. Giant hybrids.

BALSAM. *Impatiens balsamina.*
　　　　　H.—18″ P.D.—12″
An old-fashioned favorite now obtainable in double, camellia-flowered hybrids in separate colors. Effective for garden or cutting, the individual blooms can be floated, or the whole flower stalk used. Take off part of the leaves to show off the flowers.

BARTONIA. *Mentzelia aurea.* (Bartonia)
　　　　　H.—12″ P.D.—8 to 12″
An interesting but little grown plant with grayish foliage and gorgeous golden flowers. Sow the seed where it is to bloom.

BLISTERCRESS (Annual Wallflower). *Erysimum perofskianum.*
　　　　　H.—12 to 15″ P.D.—8″
A really delightful flower resembling an orange wallflower. Although blooming best in cool weather it is worthy of trial. It will often self-sow and even naturalize.

BROWALLIA. *Browallia.*
　　　　　H.—12″ P.D.—12″
Effective and free blooming, it makes an excellent filler among tulips, where if winter mulched it will often self-sow. The flowers are good for cutting as well as garden effect. Both *B. speciosa* and *B. demissa (alata)* should be grown. Potted up in fall they will bloom during winter.

BUTTERFLYFLOWER. *Schizanthus pinnatus.* H.—2 to 3′ P.D.—15 to 18″
Although commonly grown as a greenhouse plant, it is worthy of garden

culture. It will appreciate just a little shade from the intense sun and several pinchings back to make it more bushy. Foliage attractive, flowers interesting.

CAPE BUGLOSS. *Anchusa capensis.*
H.–12″ P.D.–6 to 8″
It is surprising that this gorgeous blue flower is not grown more extensively. A constant bloomer under all conditions, it supplies the clear blue given only by the forget-me-not and Chinese forget-me-not. It will often self-sow. Variety Blue Bird is dwarf and compact.

CALIFORNIA POPPY. *Eschscholtzia californica* H.–8″ P.D.–8 to 12″
This favorite hardly needs an introduction, with its colors of brilliant yellow, white, pink, and red, with the intricate pattern of its grayish-green foliage, and its constant bloom from June until frost. Difficult to transplant; should be sown in place. Hybrids come in singles, erect singles and doubles. Named varieties include many color variations of which Buff Pink, Carmine Queen, Golden Rod and Ramona are typical.

CALENDULA. *Calendula officinalis.*
H.–12″ P.D.–6 to 8″
No garden is complete without calendulas, hardy, free-blooming, decorative, making excellent combinations with blue and lavender flowers. They have been widely hybridized and many varied types are offered. Golden Ball, Lemon Queen, and Orange Ball are standard; Pale Moon a fine cut flower; and the miniatures should have a place in the garden for cutting. Some self-sow.

CALLIOPSIS. *Coreopsis.*
H.–16 to 36″ P.D.–8 to 12″
The calliopsis in its several forms is an asset to any garden. Its one handicap is its profuse blooming and abundance of seed; unless the old flowers are removed it will soon spend its energy and cease

blooming. This is especially true during hot weather.

Reds, crimsons, browns, rich yellows, are the colors found in the many varieties of annual coreopsis.

The dwarf forms are useful for borders and mass effects, whereas the taller forms are better for cutting as well as garden effect.

Goldenwave (*C. drummondi*) has large yellow flowers with mahogany around center. H.–18 to 24″

Crown Coreopsis (*C. coronata*) has pure yellow flowers. H.–24″
The several dwarf forms (including *C. radiata* or Quill Coreopsis) are delightful. H.–4 to 8″

CANDYTUFT. *Iberis.*
H.–6 to 12″ P.D.–8″
An old favorite, worthy of greater recognition today. *Iberis umbellata*, with its rather flat heads of flowers, comes in beautiful colors, but *I. amara*, the rocket and hyacinth flowered candytuft, with its long spikes of flowers, is more showy. They are all fragrant and profuse blooming. Several sowings should be made for continuous bloom.

CAPE-MARIGOLD. *Dimorphotheca aurantiaca.* H.–8 to 12″ P.D.–8″
Often listed as African Daisy. Although coming in colors from white to salmon, the orange is most interesting. Excellent for cutting and garden effects. Several sowings should be made.

CASTOR-BEAN. *Ricinus communis.*
H.–4 to 8′ P.D.–3 to 5′
This is the most vigorous of all annuals, giving a coarse, luxuriant, even rank growth, which soon crowds out all other flowers. It is best used as a shrub. Caution is necessary in regard to the seeds, since they contain a very active poison. Dropped in mole-runs they are an old-fashioned remedy for ridding the garden of these pests.

CHINA-ASTER. *Callistephus chinensis.*
H.—12 to 36″ P.D.—8 to 12″
At one time the china aster was one of our most important annual flowers. Today the aster yellows and the aster blight often make it difficult and sometimes impossible to grow it successfully.

The aster blight (wilt) is controlled by growing the plants on new soil and selecting seed from disease-resistant plants. The aster yellows may be controlled by regular applications of Bordeaux mixture to repel the leaf hopper which transfers the disease from perennial weeds. The tarnished-plant-bug and blister-beetle may be controlled by spraying with one of the pyrethrum extract sprays. All badly diseased plants should be burned.

Asters will do best in good rich soil, where they may be given liberal cultivation and plenty of space to grow. In many cases a partial shade may be beneficial.

Great progress has been made of late in producing wilt-resistant strains, and while they are not entirely fixed under some growing conditions, the gardener should not hesitate to try them. Among the types, Early Giant, Light Blue, Peach Blossom and Rosalie are a great advance, with long stems and loose, shaggy flowers. Royal, American Beauty, Ball's type and Heart of France are standard strains. Seeds should be sown under glass, and regular dusting with a green combination sulphur, arsenate of lead and nicotine dust is suggested for the amateur.

CHINESE FORGET-ME-NOT. *Cynoglossum amabile.* H.—2′ P.D.—15″
A glorified blue forget-me-not which should be in every garden. Keep the old flowers removed or production of seed will stop blooming. Even then the plants may be cut back and will produce a crop of flowers in September. Plants will self-seed although seeds are a nuisance on the plants, being of a stick-tight type.

CLARKIA. *Clarkia elegans* and
C. pulchella. H.—2′ P.D.—8″
An old-fashioned annual which is worthy of the attention it receives. The colors run from white through the pinks to deep rose, in single and double flowers. It is free blooming and makes an excellent cut flower. The seed may be sown in the fall or spring.

COCKSCOMB. *Celosia.*
A revival of appreciation for this old-time favorite extends from its use in the garden for effect and cutting, to all types of flower decoration. This coincides with color selection and the production of more refined varieties. The widest range of form and color is still found in the mixtures such as *Thompsonia magnifica.* Sow seed in rows in the open ground, and weed out colors not wanted when seedlings are small. The crested varieties come in dwarfs and separate colors of crimson and yellow; Chinese woolflower in crimson, pink and yellow. If the latter is allowed to self-sow interesting forms and colors are created. This type dries successfully.

COLLINSIA. *Collinsia.*
H.—6 to 8″ P.D.—6″
A native western plant, preferring cool weather and a well-drained soil. It will generally require special care to last through our hot, dry summers but it is charming when well grown.

CONEFLOWER. (Pinewoods Coneflower)
Rudbeckia bicolor. H.—2′ P.D.—12″
Resembling our wild Black-eyed Susan except that it often has mahogany in with the orange color; it is surprising that it is not grown more often. A constant bloomer, an excellent cut flower, and an interesting garden subject.

CORNFLOWER. *Centaurea cyanus.*
H.—18 to 24″ P.D.—6 to 8″
This flower is available in a variety of colors from white to lavender through to purple and blue and pink; the pink and the blue, however, usually are preferred.

Easily grown, absolutely hardy, always self-sowing, it produces a wealth of flowers which are enjoyed by ourselves as well as by the gold-finches. Use named varieties of the double strains. Jubilee Gem is a blue dwarf. If allowed to self-sow, pull out inferior plants as soon as they bloom. Always fall-sow a few for early bloom.

COSMOS. *Cosmos bipannatus.*
H.—4 to 6' P.D.—2'
Many disappointments with cosmos are due to the use of the late blooming type rather than the early types. Only the early blooming can be depended upon to give any amount of bloom before frost. In addition to the standard single form the double or crested type is worth growing. Cosmos prefers plenty of room to grow. It may be planted in among the shrubs or even in back of the lower ones. As a cut flower it is unexcelled. The early strains come in single, double-crested and mammoth-flowering (Sensation strain), and disbudding is suggested for still larger flowers. Orange varieties are available. Seed may be sown in the fall for earlier blooming. The new Orange Flare variety, though smaller growing and more delicate in appearance, supplies attractive flowers of a rich pleasing color.

COW SOAPWORT. *Saponaria vaccaria.*
Another short season bloomer used for cutting or general border planting. Sow at intervals for succession. It is used mainly as a filler.

CHRYSANTHEMUM. H.—2 to 3' P.D.—18"
The Crown Daisy (*Chrysanthemum coronarium*) and annual Chrysanthemum (*Chrysanthemum carinatum*) are surprisingly little grown when one considers their value. Interesting divided foliage, large daisy-like flowers, in yellow or white, often with darker rings in the center, they may be either used for cut flowers or for general garden effect.

Given a good soil and plenty of room they seldom fail to give results.

CUP-FLOWER. *Nierembergia rivularis.*
H.—6" P.D.—6"
A compact plant covered with a mass of lavender tinted white flowers. Useful as rock plant or in the front of borders. Variety coerulea (hippomanica) new, half-hardy, forms a dense mat of fern-like foliage with masses of lavender-blue, cup-like flowers borne profusely all summer. It is a perfect low border plant used alone or with dwarf pink or white petunias, or pansies; is easily controlled and of great beauty. As seed is sometimes hard to start, it is wise to buy plants. It likes abundant water.

DAHLIAS.
The small-flowered varieties may be classed as annuals since they may be flowered in July from seed sown in the greenhouse in winter. They come in mixtures such as Unwin's Dwarf Hybrids and Dobbie's Orchid flowered Hybrids, and have added a wealth of color and charm to our plantings. Their cut flower use is interesting and success is reported in wintering the tubers in peat moss.

DATURA. *Datura.* Angel's-Trumpet.
This is a large plant adapted to unrestricted areas, and grown for the fragrance and beauty of its large trumpet-shaped white flowers, which can be used in decoration. *D. metel* is the commonly grown annual kind. *D. arborea* is tree-form; tender.

EVENING PRIMROSE. *Oenothera.*
H.—12 to 36" P.D.—18"
Resembling some of our common weeds, it is doubtful if this group will ever be very popular. The plants are rather coarse, but their brilliant flowers of yellow, rose or white attract some. Difficult to transplant, they should be sown in place in the early spring. They are of little value as cut flowers.

EVERLASTING. *Helipterum.*

H.–12″ P.D.–6″

Although this name is often applied to any type of flower which may be dried, it is properly applied to Helipterum, which is usually catalogued under the name of *Acrolinium roseum* and *Rhodanthe manglesi.* Rather small, delicate plants, they are really grown more for their dried flowers than for their garden effect. The best place for them is in rows in the vegetable garden, where they may be cut when in bud and hung up to dry.

Many people consider it best to strip the leaves off all forms of everlastings and strawflowers before drying. Others prefer to leave them on for their decorative effect. See Strawflower, Winged everlasting, Thrift, Honesty, Immortelle and Cockscomb.

FEVERFEW-CAMOMILE. *Matricaria parthenoides (capensis).*

H.–2 to 3′ P.D.–18″

A sturdy, dependable plant bearing a profusion of white flowers. Not especially beautiful but always reliable. It will often live over in protected situations. There is also a dwarf form, with yellow or white flowers.

FLAX. *Linum grandiflorum coccineum.*

H.–12″ P.D.–6″

Although the commercial flax with its blue flowers, *Linum usitatissimum*, is sometimes grown, far superior is *L. grandiflorum coccineum*, the scarlet flax, with its brilliant red flowers. It blooms day after day throughout the summer. Several sowings may be made for late summer.

FORGET-ME-NOT. *Myosotis.*

H.–6″ P.D.–6″

The annual varieties are as fine as the perennial. If not allowed to seed, the plants will bloom all summer. Partial shade will help during hot, dry weather. Grow in masses. Forget-me-nots will often self-sow.

FOUR O'CLOCKS. *Mirabilis jalapa.*

H.–24″ P.D.–15″

Although most of us know the four o'clocks as annual hedge plants, they may be used in other ways. Not mixing well with flowers, due to their colors, they should be grown by themselves or as a group in front of the shrubs. The plants self-sow or the heavy roots may be dug in the fall and stored in the cellar over winter.

GAILLARDIA. *Gaillardia.*

H.–12 to 24″ P.D.–15″

One of the old standbys necessary to every garden. Easily grown, vigorous and free blooming, it is highly desirable for cutting or garden effect. *G. amblyodon* has single maroon flowers—interesting but not as showy as *G. pulchella,* with its globular heads of yellow, pink, and red.

GILIA. *Gilia.*

G. capitata with its dainty blue flowers is good for relieving the "heavy" effect of such plants as petunias, gaillardias.   H.–12″ P.D.–12″

G. coronopilfolia, a newcomer to most American gardens, gives sturdy accents of red, yellow and pink.

H.–36″ P.D.–12″

GODETIA. *Godetia grandiflora.*

H.–12″ P.D.–12″

A relative of the evening primrose; the commoner form, *G. grandiflora*, forms a dwarf, compact plant bearing a mass of large flowers. Adapted to poor and sandy soil. An all season bloomer. Sow early if possible.

GOLDENCUP. *Hunnemannia fumariaefolia.* H.–18 to 24″ P.D.–12″

A relative of the poppy, sometimes called Bush-eschscholtzia. It forms a mass of golden yellow blooms. The plants prefer full sun and will withstand drought. If flowers are cut in the bud they will keep very well.

GOMPHRENA. *Gomphrena globosa.*
H.—18″ P.D.—12″
Another of our everlastings of easy culture, with white, rose, purple and salmon flowers. It is decorative as a garden plant.

GYPSOPHILA. *Gypsophila elegans.*
H.—12″ P.D.—6″
The annual babysbreath is useful as a cut flower and temporary garden effect. Its short blooming period of three weeks necessitates resowing every three weeks, but it will bloom six weeks from sowing. *G. muralis* is daintier and blooms all summer.

HOLLYHOCK. *Althaea rosea.*
H.—5 to 6′ P.D.—2′
Similar to the well-known perennial form, this stately flower blooms the first year, during late summer. Combined with its perennial sister it will give us hollyhocks all summer long. Variety Indian Spring, new, has semi-double fringed flowers in shades of pink and will bloom in early summer from seed sown indoors. It rivals the choice doubles in size and beauty but is not entirely hardy. Seedlings give a variation in tints. It likes sunshine and ample water.

HONESTY. *Lunaria annua* (or *L. biennis*)
H.—2 to 3′ P.D.—15″
Although uninteresting as a garden subject, it is useful for its seed pods which may have the outer layer removed after they are dried, leaving a thin transparent disk for decorative use in winter bouquets. Plants, unless seed is started very early indoors, will not produce seed pods until the second year.

IMMORTELLE. *Xeranthemum annuum.*
H.—3′ P.D.—12″
A good garden plant and a source of flowers for winter bouquets. Foliage silver-gray, flowers in clusters, purple, lavender, pink and white. Sow seed in April.

LACEFLOWER. *Trachymene* (*Didiscus*)
H.—24″ P.D.—12″
An interesting cut flower, but usually difficult to grow. It is not particularly ornamental as a garden plant but excellent as a cut flower. Difficult to transplant. Sow in pots or where it is to bloom, in early spring.

LARKSPUR. *Delphinium.*
H.—24 to 36″ P.D.—12″
One of the most widely grown annuals. The Giant Imperial strain with wide color range, compact growth and long stems for cutting is supplanting all others for garden and cut flower use. Seed may be sown outdoors in the fall, under glass, or outside in early spring, or all three. Interplant with china asters or other late annuals.

LEPTOSYNE. *Coreopsis stillmani.*
H.—12″ P.D.—8″
Coreopsis maritima.
H.—2′ P.D.—12″
Interesting variations, with yellow flowers, closely resembling calliopsis.

LOBELIA. *Lobelia erinus.*
H.—6″ P.D.—6″
A low compact plant with brilliant blue flowers. Unfortunately it is often associated only with straight line flower bed edging, whereas it is really charming in mass plantings. The trailing varieties are fine for porch boxes or hanging baskets. Sow seed early.

LOVE-IN-A-MIST. *Nigella damascena.*
H.—8 to 12″ P.D.—8″
A delightful hardy annual flower with finely cut leaves and lacy blue and white flowers. It blooms when very small. May be fall or spring sown or even early summer sown. It is often used to add grace to the flower garden.

LUPINE. *Lupinus luteus, L. hirsutus, L. hartwegi.* H.—24 to 36″ P.D.—12″
Interesting as border plants, exquisite as cut flowers. Sow in pots or where they

are to bloom. Partial shade will give better results. There are several species, of different colors. Removal of old flowers will increase bloom.

MADAGASCAR PERIWINKLE. *Vinca rosea.*
H.—18″ P.D.—12″
One of the best annuals for blooming under all conditions. It forms bushy, compact plants, the seed of which must be sown very early indoors or the plants purchased from a florist. Its dark shiny foliage is a foil for the star-shaped flowers in light pink, blush, rose, white and white with red eye, and adds brilliancy to any planting. It is the satisfactory plant in general use, fine for cutting, for growing in the shade and in many types of soil, and has no enemies.

MARIGOLDS. *Tagetes.*
Marigolds in their common forms need no introduction. For tall plants use African Marigold (H.—3′; P.D.—18″), which has large, heavy flowers and is rather stiff and formal. More graceful are the French Marigolds (H.—12 to 18″; P.D.—15″), of compact, free-flowering habit. There are fine varieties of both groups in bewildering array, in some of which little odor of flower or foliage is apparent. In the tall plants, the peony-flowered strain of Supremes is standard, as is the Dwarf Harmony and its hybrids in the French type.

For a dainty plant, use the Mexican Marigolds, *Tagetes signata pumila* (H.—15″; P.D.—12″), with small, starry, orange flowers. Hardy, free blooming, easily grown, there are few other annuals so universally satisfying.

MIGNONETTE. *Reseda odorata.*
H.—12″ P.D.—8 to 12″
Everyone knows and enjoys the fragrance of this old-fashioned flower. Although blooming best during cool weather about May, sowings in partial shade will give mid-summer bloom. Dif-ficult to transplant, seed should be sown in pots or where it is to bloom. Liberal fertilization will increase size of flowers.

MONKEYFLOWER. *Mimulus luteus,*
M. moschatus. H.—12″ P.D.—12″
Brilliant, curiously shaped flowers preferring partial shade and plenty of moisture. Started indoors or in a coldframe they should be set out after weather warms up. Sometimes used for porch boxes or hanging baskets.

MORNING-GLORY, dwarf. *Ipomea.*
H.—12″ P.D.—12″
A very low, compact, free-blooming plant, inclined to trail a little. Prefers full sun. Does *not* transplant easily; should be sown in early spring, where it is to bloom.

NASTURTIUM, dwarf. *Tropaeolum.*
H.—12″ P.D.—12″
Nasturtiums may be sown where they are to bloom as early as ground can be worked. The plants are sometimes bothered with lice, which can be controlled by spraying or dusting. The Double Gleam hybrids have a wide range of color in both dwarf and vining types, and are now universally grown.

NEMESIA. *Nemesia strumosa,*
N. versicolor. H.—12″ P.D.—8″
A worthy plant, all too little known. The "saucy little faces" of the various colored flowers are borne in profusion from June until frost. Sow seed in April. The large flowered hybrids are most showy.

NEMOPHILA. *Nemophila.*
H.—8 to 12″ P.D.—6 to 8″
Small dainty flowers, preferring partial shade and fairly moist soil. Profuse bloomers throughout the summer. May be used in rock gardens or on shady side of house. Best adapted to cooler climates, and consequently need attention to produce results.

NICOTIANA. *Nicotiana.*

H.—2 to 4' P.D.—8 to 12"

The fragrant, evening blooming white flowered *Nicotiana affinis* is by far the commonest flowering tobacco, due possibly to its ability to self-sow. Even more decorative, however, is *N. sanderae* with pink, red, and lavender flowers. *N. sylvestris* is a day blooming, white flowered variety.

The nicotianas are desirable for use among the coarser flowers, such as zinnias or even cannas, to give a more airy effect.

OENOTHERA. Evening Primrose. (See also page 158.

Large flowered rather coarse plants, demanding full sun. They are showy in the garden but useless for cutting. Do not transplant easily, so seed should be sown early, in open ground.

O. drummondi (H.—1 to 2'; yellow to white), *O. mollissima* (H.—2½'; yellow), and *O. rosea* (H.—1 to 2'; rose-purple) are annuals or grown as such. But more useful are the biennial or perennial day-blooming Sundrops.

PAINTED SPURGE. (Mexican Fire Plant) *Euphorbia heterophylla.*

H.—24 to 36" P.D.—18"

An interesting foliage plant; the margins of leaves and sometimes the entire leaves turn scarlet, especially in September. It prefers heat and full sun but will stand rather poor soil. Sow after danger of frost is past.

PANSY. *Viola tricolor.* H.—6" P.D.—6"

Although everyone loves the pansy, few grow it successfully from seed. This is best sown in August and wintered with a light mulch of straw, in a shaded coldframe sash. Seed may also be sown in early spring for summer bloom. Buy only the very best fresh seed, even though it seems expensive; old pansy seed is unsatisfactory. Many of the best colors are slowest to germinate and de-

velop. Partial shade and sufficient moisture will give best results, especially for summer bloom. Many people prefer to buy their pansy plants each year rather than to grow their own.

PERILLA, PURPLE. *Perilla frutescens nankinensis.* H.—18" P.D.—12"

An old-fashioned plant with dark purple leaves resembling the coleus. Used only as a foliage plant, either with flowers such as pink balcony petunias or with gray foliage such as Dusty Miller. This annual usually self-sows, coming up year after year.

PETUNIA. *Petunia hybrida.*

H.—12 to 24" P.D.—8 to 12"

Another of our old faithful friends. Always satisfactory. Seed should be sown early indoors or in a coldframe. The smallest and slowest growing seedlings are often the best colors. The best seed, although costing considerably more, will give the finest flowers.

Small, single flowered forms are the hardiest and most vigorous, but larger flowers are usually preferred. Borders, banks, rock walls, porch boxes, and hanging baskets are some of the possible places to use petunias.

It has been called the national flower on account of its great popularity and use. It ranges through miniatures, compact dwarfs, dwarf giants, bedding, balcony, giants, giant doubles in plain, fringed or frilled types. Even a suggestive list would fall from its own weight. There are many varieties that are almost duplications and others that are obsolete. The dwarfs are an advance in control over the more vining types and some doubles should be grown for cutting at least.

PHACELIA. *Phacelia campanularis.*

H.—9" P.D.—6 to 8"

Another blue flower, giving a full season of bloom. It prefers full sunlight and a light soil. Pinch when small to produce bushy plants. Useful for border effects.

PHLOX. *Phlox drummondi.*
H.—6 to 12″ P.D.—8 to 12″
A continuous bloomer, producing a brilliant mosaic of color when planted in mixtures. Both the dwarf and tall forms are very fine for garden effects and cut flowers. Sow in coldframe, or in open ground in April.

If planted in full sun, and the seed pods removed, the annual phlox will seldom disappoint the gardener.

PINKS. *Dianthus chinensis.*
H.—8 to 12″ P.D.—6 to 8″
As desirable as its perennial sisters, the several forms of annual pinks come in single and double forms. Constant bloomers, they desire rich soil and sunlight. Plants will live over if mulched and give early bloom, but cannot always be depended upon the second year.

POPPY. *Papaver.*
Gorgeous flowers in a variety of colors and forms. The Shirley Poppy, *P. rhoeas* (H.—24 to 36″; P.D.—12″), with long, slender, hairy stems and single or double flowers, is more dainty and graceful than the Opium poppy, *P. somniferum* (H.—18 to 24″; P.D.—8″), with heavy leafy stems and larger flowers. Forms of this are known as the tulip, peony, and carnation flowered poppies.

The very fine seed of poppies should be sown where the plants are to bloom, either fall, spring, or summer. To keep up a supply of bloom do not allow seed pods to develop.

Poppies are excellent cut flowers if cut in the bud stage.

PORTULACA. *Portulaca grandiflora.*
H.—6″ P.D.—6″
Possessing an ability to grow in hot, dry, almost impossible places, we must respect this brilliant flower, even if we hesitate to grow it in our borders. Try the double varieties in hot, dry spots where nothing else will grow.

PRICKLEPOPPY. *Argemone mexicana.*
H.—3′ P.D.—18″
Interesting as a foliage plant, with its spiny white-veined leaves; also as a flowering plant. It is a vigorous, hardy plant with yellow flowers, often self-sowing. It is a good filler in any border. Difficult to transplant, it should be sown in its permanent bed.

PRINCESPLUME. *Polygonum orientale.*
H.—5 to 6′ P.D.—2′
Also called "kiss-me-over-the-garden-gate." A tall, graceful plant with pendulous terminal panicles of pink flowers. May be used as a background for other flowers or as spots of color in the shrub border. Sown early out of doors, it will bloom until frost.

ROSE-OF-HEAVEN. *Lychnis* (*Agrostemma*) *coelirosa.* H.—12″ P.D.—6″
A dainty flower which must have several sowings made for succession of bloom. Apt to seed too freely in some gardens.

SALPIGLOSSIS. *Salpiglossis sinuata.*
H.—2 to 3′ P.D.—12″
Highly decorative in the garden or as cut flower. Resembles a refined petunia but with more delicate effects, and more intricate color patterns. Sow seed early, preferably indoors. Pinch seedlings back to produce bushy plants. It will grow in the sun or in partial shade and prefers a sandy soil. Charming flower arrangements may be made with the cut flowers.

SALVIA. *Salvia.* H.—2 to 3′ P.D.—18″
Commonest of all is the scarlet sage, *Salvia splendens,* although unfortunately so often misused and overused in our yards and gardens. When grown it should be used with other foliage as a background and in relatively small masses. Sow seed early indoors or in coldframe and plant out after last frost.

Mealycup sage, S. *farinacea,* also usually listed as a perennial, is a free blooming, attractive plant worthy of wider use. Its blue flowers and gray stems make it useful as a cut flower or as garden subject. Often self-sows profusely and never fails to give satisfaction.

The perennial blue sage, *Salvia patens*, has brilliant blue flowers and is attractive and valuable. Not as showy as the Scarlet sage, it is far more suitable for garden use.

Blue Bedder and Royal Blue are improvements on the type—all are lovely threaded through the flower border. Salmon Queen is a delightful companion if used with restraint. Indian Purple is a novelty.

SANVITALIA. *Sanvitalia procumbens.*
H.—6″ P.D.—8 to 12″
A very satisfactory ground cover and edging plant, it is surprising that it is not grown more extensively. The golden yellow flowers with dark centers resemble small zinnias, and are borne in profusion until frost. Sow seed in early spring. Try a few in the rock garden.

SCABIOSA. *Scabiosa atropurpurea.*
H.—24″ P.D.—12″
One of our best annual cut flowers. The wide range of colors—white, pink, rose, scarlet, yellow, blue, and maroon —may either be grown as single colors or in mixture. Sow seed indoors or out, give sufficient room and fertilizer and they will bloom until frost if not allowed to go to seed. Imperial hybrids are offered in all colors and Imperial Giants Heavenly Blue and Blue Moon, are a new departure with a bee-hive shape and broad-wavy petals crowding out the old pincushion center.

SNAPDRAGON. *Antirrhinum majus.*
H.—12 to 36″ P.D. 8 to 12″
The variety of colors, the differences in height of dwarf, medium, and tall, and the long season of bloom, make these charming flowers beloved by all.

Use either as border plants, or in rows for cutting.

The very small seed is best sown early but may be sown outdoors in May for later bloom. Snapdragon rust may be a serious handicap in some sections. Destroy any snapdragon plants which have lived over winter and allow no old leaves or stems to remain. This sanitary precaution, together with a sulphur dust, will help to check the rust. Make this a routine protective measure before, not after, any trouble starts. Rust resistance has been developed in several strains: English bedding, with Guinea Gold, St. George and Royal Rose, as well in the outstanding Giants—Canary Bird, Loveliness, Rosalie and Shasta.

SENSITIVE PLANT. *Mimosa pudica.*
H.—8 to 12″ P.D.—12″
An odd plant, grown not for its beauty but for its sensitive leaves which slowly fold together when disturbed. Sow seed indoors and set out in hot, dry place after all danger of frost is past.

SNOW-ON-THE-MOUNTAIN. *Euphorbia marginata.* H.—3′ P.D.—12″
An old-fashioned flower which has escaped and become a pest in some gardens. The upper leaves, margined with white, make a showy effect. A few in the border give an interesting effect. May easily be naturalized and will hold its own. Milky juice poisons some people.

SPIDERFLOWER. *Cleome spinosa.*
H.—3 to 4′ P.D.—12″
A vigorous, rather coarse plant, well adapted to poor soil, and useful as an accent among the shrubs or a filler in an odd corner of the yard. Plants have a peculiar odor—objectionable near windows or porches.

Flowers are lavender, pink, or white. In a small garden a few plants will suffice. Sow seed in early spring. You may find it will self-sow.

STOCK. *Mathiola incana.*
                    H.—12 to 18" P.D.—12"

Although stocks prefer a cool, moist climate with a rich soil, they often do well in other gardens. Sow some seed early and some later for continuous garden effect.

Stocks come in several forms, dwarf and tall, and a variety of colors. Some strains seem to bloom better than others in our warm dry summers.

The sweet-scented stocks, *Mathiola bicornis,* are a more graceful, less showy, but highly desirable form.

STRAWFLOWERS. *Helichrysum*
    bracteatum.   H.—3' P.D.—12"

This name is properly applied only to the *Helichrysum,* although often loosely to any flower which may be successfully dried. The *Helichrysum* is the largest and most showy of the everlastings. Start the plants early indoors or in the coldframe if possible, and give them plenty of space to grow.

Remember to cut the flowers before they are open—since small buds will open when dried. Tie in bunches and hang up until dry.

SUMMER-CYPRESS. *Kochia scoparia.*
                 H.—24" P.D.—18 to 24"

Whether we like it or not, the summer-cypress demands admiration for its ability to grow under most trying conditions, produce its formal light green bushes, turn brilliant red in the fall and then self-sow most profusely. Once you grow it you will always have it.

SUMMER-FIR. *Artemesia sacrorum*
    viridis.   H.—3' P.D.—18 to 24"

An interesting foliage plant for background effects or temporary hedges. Leaves finely cut, delicate green. It will sometimes self-sow.

SUNFLOWER. *Helianthus.*
            H.—3 to 7' P.D.—2 to 3'

The annual sunflowers are an interesting group of plants giving a variety of flowers both in size, form, and color.

The red flowered forms seem to appeal to many gardeners.

The larger forms are rather coarse, but the lower-growing varieties with small flowers harmonize with zinnias and cosmos. Useful as a background for other annuals or as color accents among shrubs. If started early indoors many will go to seed and die before frost. The seed makes excellent bird food.

SWAN-RIVER-DAISY. *Brachycome*
    iberidifolia. H.—6 to 12" P.D.—6 to 8"

A dainty dwarf plant with blue, white, or mauve daisy-like flowers. Often used in rock gardens. It prefers full sun but unless liberally watered does better in partial shade during hot weather.

SWEET ALYSSUM. *Lobularia maritima.*
                       H.—8" P.D.—12"

Everyone knows and grows this sweet-scented flower, but all too many seem to feel it must be grown in straight rows along the edge of beds. It is really more effective in masses in informal beds. Really a perennial, it is usually grown as a hardy annual. Sown early it will bloom in six weeks from sowing. There are many varieties, some slightly colored, some compact, others trailing. They all bloom early from summer until they freeze up in October.

SWEET SULTAN. *Centaurea moschata.*
                       H.—2' P.D.—12"

Showy flowers and decorative plants preferring non-acid soil. Flowers will last well if cut when in bud. It will bloom from June till frost.

There is also the Royal Sweet Sultan, *Centaurea imperialis,* H.—2'; P.D.—12"; the flowers are sweet-scented, lasting well as cut flowers. It is an enlarged form of the Sweet Sultan, and preferred by many.

SWEET PEA. *Lathyrus odoratus.*
                   H.—5 to 8' P.D.—3'

The sweet pea is distinctly a cool season crop and to be grown well requires care and attention. Preferring a cool deep soil, the ground should be thoroughly prepared in the autumn by digging a trench two feet deep. Place several inches of manure in the bottom and fill in with the best soil or compost available. Mound it up well as it will settle during the winter.

Sowing seed: If soil is well drained, seed (especially of dark seeded varieties) can be sown in late November; otherwise sow in early spring. The old rule of Good Friday is not as far off as most of the old garden myths, for it insures early sowing.

It is not necessary to sow the seed in a trench and fill it in, as some people aver, as sweet peas need little attention, if the soil has been properly prepared.

Support: A support of string or wire (string is less likely to burn stem) should be ready for the seedlings as soon as they start to climb. It is neater than brush.

Summer blooming will be obtained in most sections only by liberal weekly watering, together with a mulch of straw, leaves or peat moss. Monthly applications of a complete chemical fertilizer (2 pounds to 100 square feet of soil) or other plant food are helpful.

Keep all old flowers picked. To control the red spider which so often ruins the vines, spray daily with a garden hose or dust with sulphur every two weeks.

TASSELFLOWER. *Emilia (Cacalia) sagittata.*

The tasselflower, although dainty and far from showy, always attracts attention. Its feathery tufts of orange or yellow give a charming and unique effect. Combined with ageratum or browallia it is stunning. It may be used in the rock garden, the border, or as a cut flower.

THRIFT. (Statice). *Limonium.*

Although always catalogued as Statice, this should be called Thrift; the scientific name is *Limonium,* instead of

Statice. It is considered by many as the choicest of the everlastings. *Limonium sinuatum* with its open airy sprays of flowers, comes in white, pink, and lavender. *L. bonduelli* resembles *sinuatum* except that the flowers are yellow. *L. suworowi* produces gorgeous pink spikes. All of these flowers are equally effective in the garden, as freshly cut flowers, or as dried winter bouquets.

Seed is best sown early, and if potgrown will start blooming surprisingly soon. Staking may be necessary unless the plants are protected from the wind. They prefer sandy soil.

TIDYTIPS. *Layia elegans.*
H.—18″ P.D.—12″

Resembling *Gaillardias,* these flowers are seldom seen although relatively easy to obtain. Grow in full sun and pinch when small to produce branching. They will amply reward us for their care.

TORCH-LILY. *Kniphofia.* (*Tritoma*).
H.—2′ P.D.—12″

Although we all enjoy the perennial Torch-lily, but few try the annual form; it is not as showy but is worth trying. Sow seed early indoors, even though they do not bloom until August.

TORENIA. *Torenia fournieri.*

A low, compact plant producing a constant mass of flowers until frost. The lavender flowers with intricate markings of white and yellow are interesting in themselves. It is suitable for use in the border or as a pot plant.

Sow seed indoors or in coldframe in March. Do not set plants out until weather is warm.

TREEMALLOW. *Lavatera trimestris.*
H.—2 to 3′ P.D.—12″

Resembling a hollyhock, these rather coarse annuals are effective. May be used for accent in the border, for color among the shrubs, or by themselves as bold masses of rose, red, or white blossoms.

Seed best sown where they are to bloom, but well thinned and spaced 18 inches to 24 inches apart. Abundant moisture and plenty of sun are their preference.

VERBENA. Verbena.

H.—8 to 12″ P.D.—12″

We all know and enjoy the common type of verbena with its brilliant flowers, especially in the newer, large-flowered types. These are fine for border effects or cutting.

The new Giant and Mammoth Flowering types include the Beauty of Oxford strain with variations from pink to rose red and scarlet; Royale, blue with yellow eye; Ellen Willmott, pink with white eye and many others with size and color heretofore unknown. Seed must be sown under glass, and sun and water will bring rich reward.

The moss verbena (V. laciniata) although not as showy, has lilac, cloverlike heads and fern-like leaves. Ideal for a ground cover.

The perennial V. venosa is coarser and more compact, but equally fine for foliage effect. Its lavender flowers add to its decorative value.

VIRGINIAN STOCK. Malcomia maritima.

H.—6 to 8″ P.D.—8″

Not as showy as the common stock, but more delicate in appearance. Often used for rock gardens as well as borders. Seed may be fall or spring sown. In fact, it will often self-sow.

WINGED EVERLASTING. Ammobium alatum. H.—18″ P.D.—8″

A satisfactory everlasting having white flowers with yellow centers. More interesting as a cut flower than as a garden subject. Prefers a sandy soil.

WOODRUFF. Asperula orientale.

H.—12″ P.D.—6″

Although many know the perennial sweet woodruff, few grow the oriental annual species named above. A splendid

airy effect is obtained with its blue flowers, which tend to relieve the heaviness of coarser flowers.

ZINNIA. (Youth and Old Age) Zinnia.

No one need be ashamed to confess to a liking for zinnias. They have long been popular, and in their many forms and colors provide one of the most inexpensive, easy to grow, and reliable of materials for the annual garden.

The present forms have been developed from the Mexican species, Z. elegans, an erect, hairy annual about 3′ tall with, mostly, lilac or purple flowers. The varieties now offered fall into three classes—Tall, to 30″ or more; Medium, averaging about 20″, and Dwarf, from 12″ to 15″. Another 12″ species, Z. linearis, with yellow flowers has lately become popular.

The number of types are bewildering, and as with petunias, it is impossible to list varieties. In the large flowering it is well to try a new one each year; Fancy Tints and the Super Crown of Gold are not widely grown and are very interesting. In the lilliputs, the pastel mixture excels all others and Spun Gold is a treasure. All the fantasy type are good for cutting. Z. linearis should be sown where it is to flower. Open ground sowing is to be preferred and not too early. Seed under glass often makes more foliage than flowers; commercial growers for bloom, sow seed in hills about the first of June. Buy only named kinds except for mixtures of note, and do not save seed for you will have reversion and your entire planting may be ruined. Do not buy cheap seed for it seldom is true to name and will not give satisfaction.

GRASSES

The various grasses tend to give an airiness, a lightness and daintiness to the garden. They tend to relieve the heaviness of the coarser annuals, besides serving as excellent material for winter bouquets. Sow all grass seed as early as possible in March or April.

BROME GRASS. *Bromus brizaeformis.*
H.—2′ P.D.—12″
Resembles quaking grass with its large drooping panicles.

CLOUD GRASS. *Agrostis nebulosa.*
H.—18″ P.D.—12″
A fine hairlike grass giving a misty effect.

FOUNTAIN GRASS. *Pennisetum.*
H.—3 to 5′ P.D.—18 to 24″
There are several species of fountain grass with various colored foliage and flowers, green and white, green and purple and bronze.

JOB'S TEARS. *Coix lachryma-jobi.*
H.—2 to 3′ P.D.—18″
A coarse grass with large pearly seeds often strung for children's necklaces. Not especially decorative in the garden.

QUAKING GRASS. *Briza maxima.*

RABBITTAIL GRASS. *Lagurus ovatus.*
H.—12 to 18″ P.D.—12″
White downy tufts. Fine for drying.

SQUIRRELTAIL GRASS. *Hordeum jubatum.* H.—2 to 3′ P.D.—12 to 18″
Short, feathery heads of bloom.

No. 39. Perennials that Will Bloom the First Year from Seed

Achillea (Yarrow)
Anthemis (Camomile)
Arabis (Rock-cress)
Bellis
Cerastium
Coreopsis
Gaillardia
Linum (Flax)
Lychnis (Champion)
Myosotis (Forget-me-not)
Pyrethrum
Tunica (Tunic-flower)

SOMETHING ABOUT THE NAMES OF PLANTS

EDITOR'S NOTE: This seems a good place to comment on the confusing (and somewhat confused) subject of plant names. Their purpose is, of course, to identify and distinguish individual plants from one another and also indicate the botanical relationship, if any, between them. The trouble is that most (but not all) plants have two kinds of names. One is a botanical or scientific name, always Latin in form (because that is the language of science the world over). The other is a "common," popular, or vernacular name that varies according to the language of which it is a part, and also according to the region where it originated and is used. That is, common names of plants, like nicknames of people, are largely a matter of usage or custom. Hence a plant may be called several things in different places—as cornflower, bachelor's-button, and bluebottle in this country, kaiser-blume (or emperor's flower) in Germany, etc., all these referring to the plant that botanists know as *Centaurea cyanus,* and nothing else.

If every plant had but one scientific and one common name, there would be no problem. But in addition to the way people and places mix up common names, scientists do not all agree as to where certain plants fit into the botanical picture and what names they should bear. Moreover, study of a plant may reveal reasons for shifting it from the group in which its discoverer placed it and giving it a different name from that he gave it! Thus some plants may be found under different botanical names in different books, lists, or catalogues. Nevertheless, the botanical name is the best identification because it is the same in all countries and, usually, does not change with the years. Common names may be picturesque, have sentimental or historical significance, and seem, at first, easier to use. But when you understand the form and meaning of botanical names, their usefulness becomes apparent; and it doesn't take long to get into the habit of using both kinds interchangeably. Indeed, you do just that when you speak of Chrysanthemum, Zinnia, Iris, Salvia and many other familiar garden flowers—for their botanical and common names are the same.

A botanical name tells a good deal about the plant it refers to, and singles it out from its relatives, just as your full name—Mary Robinson Jones, for example—singles you out from your brothers and sisters, and from members of the Smith, Brown, and Thompson families who may live on the same block. This is how and why it does so:

Ever since the early 1700's, when the great botanist, Linneaus, ended what had been hopeless confusion by devising a plant name system, every plant has been given at least two names which correspond, roughly, to our surnames and given names. The first, always spelt with a capital, indicates the plant group or *genus* the plant belongs to, as Rosa, Dahlia, Iris. The second indicates the *species,* or group within a genus, to which it and its close relatives belong, as Rosa *rugosa,* Iris *tingitana,* etc. Within a species there may be numerous *varieties* which differ in only a single character, as color, height, doubleness of flower, etc.; a variety name may be in botanical form (sometimes preceded by *var.*) or it may be merely a proper name like the many found in seed catalogues. To be especially accurate, horticultural writers often use a plant's common name followed by its botanical name, in italics, in parentheses.

As an example of all this, the name "Double peach-leaved bellflower (*Campanula persicifolia flore-pleno*)" simply says the same thing twice. *Campanula* (genus or generic name) comes from the Latin for "little bell"; *persicifolia* (species or specific name) is the combination of botanical Latin for leaf (folia) and the specific name for peach (persica); and the varietal label, *flore-pleno* is botanical Latin for "double-flowered." But whereas the English name would mean something only to one speaking that language, the botanical name would mean the same thing to all persons in all countries.

As noted, botanical and horticultural authorities do not all agree on all names, although international congresses are working on rules that would enable them to do so. Meanwhile, there are various reference books that you can use for checking names; and if you find conflicts or inconsistencies, you can always consult horticultural librarians or the horticultural department of the nearest agricultural college or experimental station as to the latest, approved or recommended name.

In writing this book, Mr. Biles apparently depended mainly on the volume called "Standardized Plant Names," published by a Committee on Horticultural Nomenclature in 1923 and again in 1942, in an endeavor to straighten out the confusion that had long existed in plant catalogues, garden writings, etc. Others have chosen to follow "Hortus II" by Dr. L. H. Bailey, published in 1941 as a revision of "Hortus I" published in 1930. Still others use both, and also turn to Dr. Bailey's monumental "Standard Cyclopedia of Horticulture."

Since any attempt completely to modernize and make uniform the plant names in this book would have involved much remaking and resetting of lists, pages, and tables, we have made only urgent corrections. Where changes have occurred, it will not be difficult to check them in the books mentioned above—E.L.D.S.

WHAT TO PLANT FOR GARDEN COLOR

The best in hardy perennials arranged by size and season

SEASON	WHITE AND SHADES	YELLOW—ORANGE	PINK	RED	BLUE—PURPLE
SPRING Bulbs in great variety are also valuable spring flowers. Most things in this group are best if planted in the fall.	DWARF Arabis Dianthus Hepatica Iberis Iris pumila Papaver nudicaule Phlox subulata Sedum Viola MEDIUM Aquilegia Campanula TALL Gypsophila Peony (tree)	DWARF Alyssum Caltha Erythronium Iris pumila Papaver nudicaule Primula Sedum MEDIUM Aquilegia Doronicum Hemerocallis Trollius TALL Hemerocallis Peony (tree)	DWARF Aubrietia Gypsophila Lychnis Papaver nudicaule Phlox subulata Primula Sedum Viola MEDIUM Aquilegia Campanula Dicentra Megasea TALL Peony (tree)	DWARF Lychnis Papaver nudicaule Phlox subulata MEDIUM Papaver orientale TALL Peony (tree)	DWARF Anemone pulsatilla Aster alpinus Aubrietia Gentiana Hepatica Iris pumila Nepeta Phlox divaricata Trillium Veronica Viola MEDIUM Anchusa Aquilegia Campanula
EARLY SUMMER In most gardens this is the height of the color display. Many in this season group are also found in the next two because of their continued blooming. Bulbs such as Lilies, Montbretias, Tigridias, Gladiolus and others add to the display during the summer months.	DWARF Achillea Arenaria Cerastium Dianthus Gypsophila Helianthemum Heuchera Saxifraga Sedum Silene Thymus Viola MEDIUM Achillea Aquilegia Astilbe Campanula Gypsophila Hesperis Iris Linum Lychnis Papaver orientale Phlox Platycodon Pyrethrum Scabiosa	DWARF Alyssum Helianthemum Potentilla Primula Sedum Thalictrum Viola MEDIUM Aquilegia Coreopsis Doronicum Gaillardia Geum Helenium Hemerocallis Iris Oenothera Potentilla Thalictrum Trollius TALL Althaea rosea Digitalis Iris Lupinus Thalictrum Thermopsis	DWARF Allium Dicentra Dodecatheon Erica Heuchera Potentilla Sedum Silene Thymus Viola MEDIUM Achillea Agrostemma Aquilegia Armeria Astilbe Dianthus Hesperis Incarvillea Iris Lychnis Papaver orientale Pyrethrum TALL Althaea rosea Digitalis	DWARF Armeria Erica Helianthemum Heuchera Primula Thymus MEDIUM Agrostemma Astilbe Dianthus Gaillardia Geum Lychnis Papaver orientale Phlox ovata Potentilla Pyrethrum TALL Althaea rosea Dictamnus Iris Monarda Peony	DWARF Campanula Myosotis Nepeta Veronica Viola MEDIUM Agapanthus Anchusa Aquilegia Campanula Delphinium Geranium Iris Linum Mertensia Phlox Platycodon Scabiosa Thalictrum TALL Aconitum Anchusa Campanula Delphinium Iris Liatris Lupinus

NOTE—These classifications as to color and height indicate in a general way the variations.

Check all varieties carefully in one or more comprehensive catalogs where many additional kinds will be found.

Color indications are approximate as so many varieties come in between the above groups.

	Column 1	Column 2	Column 3	Column 4	Column 5
EARLY SUMMER — Early summer is the time to plan and plant for fall color.	Thalictrum, Veronica; **TALL** Aconitum, Althaea rosea, Delphinium, Dictamnus, Digitalis, Iris, Lupinus, Monarda, Peony, Yucca		Iris, Lupinus, Monarda, Peony, Valeriana		
LATE SUMMER — This period is likely to be lacking in color unless special efforts are made both in planting and care. Annuals in masses should freely supplement the perennials. Shearing back and feeding help many varieties.	**DWARF** Arenaria, Dianthus, Sedum, Silene, Viola; **MEDIUM** Campanula, Erigeron, Gypsophila, Linum, Phlox, Physostegia, Scabiosa, Sidalcea, Stokesia; **TALL** Aster, Boltonia, Cimicifuga, Delphinium, Eupatorium, Hibiscus, Phlox, Romneya coulteri	**DWARF** Achillea, Alyssum, Dianthus, Hypericum, Sedum, Sempervivum, Viola; **MEDIUM** Centaurea, Coreopsis, Gaillardia, Geum, Oenothera, Potentilla; **TALL** Cassia, Helenium, Helianthus, Heliopsis, Rudbeckia, Senecio, Thalictrum, Tritoma, Verbascum	**DWARF** Dicentra, Sedum, Silene, Tunica, Viola; **MEDIUM** Achillea, Armeria, Centaurea, Erigeron, Lythrum, Phlox, Physostegia, Sedum, Sidalcea; **TALL** Aster, Boltonia, Hibiscus, Phlox	**DWARF** Sempervivum; **MEDIUM** Gaillardia, Geum, Pentstemon, Phlox, Potentilla; **TALL** Helenium, Hibiscus, Lobelia, Phlox, Senecio, Tritoma	**DWARF** Gentiana, Myosotis, Plumbago, Veronica, Viola; **MEDIUM** Campanula, Centaurea, Erigeron, Funkia, Lavandula, Linum, Phlox, Scabiosa, Statice, Stokesia, Veronica; **TALL** Aconitum, Anchusa, Aster, Campanula, Delphinium, Liatris, Lobelia, Senecio, Thalictrum
FALL — The right varieties supply color even after early frosts.	**DWARF** Viola; **MEDIUM** Anemone, Stokesia; **TALL** Aster, Chrysanthemum, Delphinium, Pyrethrum uliginosum	**DWARF** Sempervivum, Viola; **MEDIUM** Coreopsis, Gaillardia; **TALL** Chrysanthemum, Helenium, Helianthus, Senecio	**DWARF** Aster, Viola; **MEDIUM** Achillea, Anemone; **TALL** Aster, Chrysanthemum	**DWARF** Sempervivum; **MEDIUM** Gaillardia; **TALL** Chrysanthemum, Helenium	**DWARF** Viola; **MEDIUM** Delphinium, Stokesia; **TALL** Aconitum, Aster, Delphinium, Echinacea purpurea

The greatest degree of success with flowers is acquired by knowing the likes and dislikes, the natural habits

Red	Pink	Orange	Yellow	Blue	Purple	White	Height in Inches	May	June	July	August	September	October	Variety Name	Sun	Shade	Partial Shade	Cutting	Flower Boxes	Cemetery	Rock Gardens	Borders	Bedding
	X						6	X	X					Abronia umbellata—Sand Verbena	X				X		X		
X	X		X				36–48			X	X	X	X	Abutilon—Flowering Maple	X								X
	X					X	24			X	X			Acroclinium—Everlasting	X							X	
X							12	X	X	X	X			Adonis—Pheasant's Eye	X		X	X				X	
				X			24–36			X	X	X		Agathea—Blue Daisy	X								X
			X			X	6–18			X	X	X	X	Ageratum—Floss Flower	X			X	X	X	X		X
X							18–20			X	X	X		Agrostis nebulosa—Cloud Grass	X			X				X	
X							15–18			X	X	X	X	Alonsoa—Maskflower	X			X			X		
					X	X	2–6			X	X	X	X	Alyssum—Sweet Alyssum	X	X	X		X	X	X		X
X		X		X	X		6–8			X	X	X	X	Anagallis grandiflora	X				X		X		
				X			18–24			X	X	X	X	Anchusa, Annual	X		X	X			X		
X	X	X	X			X	X	8–24			X	X	X	X	Antirrhinum—Snapdragon	X		X	X		X		X	X
				X		X	24			X	X	X	X	Arctotis—Lavender Daisy	X		X				X	X	
	X		X			X	24–36			X	X	X	X	Argemone—Prickly Poppy	X						X	X	
X	X	X	X	X	X	X	12–18			X	X	X	X	Asters—China Asters	X		X	X				X	X
X	X	X			X	X	18–24				X	X		Balsam—Lady's Slipper	X		X					X	
	X					X	12–24			X	X	X		Bartonia—Blazing Star	X							X	
				X			9–12			X	X	X		Brachycome—Swan River Daisy	X				X		X	X	
				X		X	12–18	X	X	X	X	X	X	Browallia	X				X		X	X	
X		X					18	X	X	X	X	X		Cacalia—Devil's Paint Brush	X			X			X		
X	X						6–18			X	X	X		Calandrinia	X						X		
		X	X				12–18			X	X	X	X	Calendula—Pot Marigold	X		X					X	X
X	X	X	X			X	12–18			X	X	X	X	Calliopsis—Annual Coreopsis	X		X					X	
X						X	6–15	X	X	X	X	X	X	Candytuft—Iberis	X		X	X	X	X	X		
X	X	X	X			X		24–30			X	X	X		Celosia—Various	X							X	
X	X				X		18–24			X	X	X		Centaurea cyanus—Bachelor's Button	X		X	X				X	X
X	X		X		X	X	18–24			X	X	X		Centaurea—Sweet Sultans	X		X	X				X	
X	X		X			X	24–36			X	X	X		Chrysanthemums—Annual Painted Daisy	X		X					X	X
X	X	X					24			X	X	X	X	Clarkia	X		X	X	X			X	
	X						24–48			X	X			Cleome—Spiderflower	X							X	
X							9–12			X	X	X		Collomia coccinea	X						X		
				X			12			X	X	X		Convolvulus mauritanica	X				X		X	X	X
			X				24			X	X	X		Cosmidium burridgeanum	X							X	
X	X		X			X	48–72			X	X	X	X	Cosmos—Mexican Aster	X		X					X	
			X				12–24	X	X	X				Cynoglossum—Summer Forget-Me-Not	X		X			X		X	
	X				X	X	24–36			X	X	X	X	Datura—Horn of Plenty	X							X	
X	X	X			X	X	9–12			X	X	X	X	Dianthus—Carnations and Pinks	X			X		X	X		
	X						12			X	X	X		Diascia—Twinspur	X			X			X		
			X				12–24			X	X	X	X	Didiscus—Queen Anne's Blue Lace Flower	X		X	X				X	X
	X						8–12			X	X	X		Dimorphotheca—African Daisy	X			X			X	X	
	X						18–24				X	X	X	Erysimum—Fairy Wallflower	X					X	X	X	
		X					9–12	X	X	X				Eschscholtzia—California Poppy	X		X				X	X	X
X	X		X			X	24–30			X	X	X		Four O'Clocks—Marvel of Peru	X							X	
X			X				18	X	X	X	X	X	X	Gaillardia—Blanket Flower	X		X				X	X	X
	X	X					8–10			X	X	X		Gamolepis tagetes	X						X	X	
X	X	X	X		X	X	24			X	X	X		Gerbera—Transvaal Daisy	X		X					X	
	X			X	X	12–24			X	X	X		Gilia—Thimble Flower	X			X				X	X
X		X			X	X	12–18			X	X	X		Globe Amaranth—Gomphrena	X							X	X
X	X	X				X	9–15	X	X	X	X	X	X	Godetia—Satin Flower	X		X	X				X	
X	X					X	12–24			X	X	X		Gypsophila—Annual Baby's Breath	X		X	X			X	X	
X	X	X	X		X	X	24–36				X	X		Helichrysum—Strawflower	X							X	
				X	X	24			X	X	X		Heliotrope	X			X	X				X
			X				24					X	X	Hunnemannia—Golden Buttercup Poppy	X			X		X	X	X	

FLOWER CHART

and the best treatment of each individual variety. We hope this chart will help you to this knowledge.

Color							Height in Inches	Blooming Season						Variety Name	Other Details								
Red	Pink	Orange	Yellow	Blue	Purple	White		May	June	July	August	September	October		Sun	Shade	Partial Shade	Cutting	Flower Boxes	Cemetery	Rock Gardens	Borders	Bedding
X	X						18			X	X	X		Impatiens—Garden Balsam			X					X	
				X		X	3–4			X	X	X		Ionopsidium acaule—Diamondflower			X				X		
		X	X	X		X	10–12			X	X	X	X	Lantana	X								X
X	X	X	X	X	X	X	24–30			X	X	X		Larkspur, Annual	X		X					X	
X	X					X	24–30			X	X	X		Lavatera—Annual Mallow	X		X					X	
		X	X	X	X	X	10			X	X	X		Leptosiphon	X						X		
			X				18			X	X	X		Leptosyne stillmani—Stillman Coreopsis	X		X					X	
			X			X	6	X	X	X				Limnanthes douglasi—Marshflower			X					X	
X	X	X		X			12–18			X	X			Linaria, Annual	X		X				X	X	
X							12–18	X	X	X	X	X	X	Linum—Flowering Flax	X		X				X	X	X
				X			6–9			X	X	X	X	Lobelia, Annual			X		X		X	X	
	X			X		X	18–24			X	X			Lupines, Annual			X	X				X	X
X	X					X	24–30			X	X	X		Malope—Mallow Wort	X							X	
		X					6–18			X	X	X	X	Marigold—Tagetes	X			X					X
		X				X	9–36			X	X	X	X	Matricaria—Double Feverfew	X						X	X	X
					X		15–18		X	X	X	X	X	Matthiola—Evening Scented Stocks	X							X	
X					X	X	6			X	X	X		Mesembryanthemum—Ice Plant	X				X		X		
X	X	X	X				12			X	X	X	X	Mignonette—Reseda			X	X	X	X			X
X	X	X	X				6–12	X	X	X	X	X	X	Nasturtium	X			X					X
X	X	X		X			9–12			X	X			Nemesia	X							X	X
				X		X	12			X	X	X		Nemophila—Baby Blue Eyes		X	X					X	
X	X				X		24–36	X	X	X	X	X	X	Nicotiana—Flowering Tobacco	X		X					X	
				X		X	15–18			X	X	X		Nigella—Love-in-a-Mist	X							X	
				X			6			X	X	X		Nolana	X				X		X		
		X					18–24			X	X	X		Oenothera—Evening Primrose	X		X					X	
X	X	X	X	X	X	X	4–6	X	X	X	X	X		Pansy—Heartsease	X		X	X					X
X	X				X	X	9–18			X	X	X	X	Petunia	X		X		X	X		X	X
				X			9–12			X	X	X		Phacelia—Harebell Phacelia	X						X	X	
X	X	X	X			X	6–18			X	X	X		Phlox, Annual	X			X	X	X	X	X	X
X	X	X	X			X	18–24			X	X			Poppy, Annual	X							X	X
X	X	X	X			X	2–6			X	X	X	X	Portulaca—Rose Moss—Sun Plant	X				X	X	X		
			X				24–30				X	X	X	Rudbeckia—Coneflower	X		X					X	
X	X	X	X	X	X	X	24–30			X	X	X		Salpiglossis—Velvet Flower	X		X	X				X	
X							24–36				X	X	X	Salvia—Scarlet Sage	X							X	X
			X				6	X	X	X	X	X	X	Sanvitalia	X			X	X	X	X	X	
	X						8–24			X	X	X		Saponaria—Bouncing Bet	X		X				X	X	
X	X	X	X		X	X	24–30			X	X	X	X	Scabiosa—Mourning Bride—Pincushion Flower	X		X					X	
		X	X		X	X	12–18			X	X	X		Schizanthus—Butterfly Flower			X	X				X	
					X		6–8				X	X		Sedum—Annual Stonecrop	X						X		
X					X	X	18			X	X	X		Senecio elegans—Ragwort	X	X						X	
	X				X		18–24			X	X			Statice—Limonium	X			X				X	X
						X	24			X	X	X		Stevia serrata	X			X				X	
X			X				42–84				X	X	X	Sunflower—Helianthus	X							X	
X	X	X	X	X	X	X	12–30				X	X	X	Stocks—Gilliflower	X			X				X	X
X	X	X	X	X	X	X	12–48	X	X	X	X			Sweet Peas	X			X	X			X	X
		X			X		12	X	X	X	X	X		Ursinia anethoides	X		X					X	
	X						24–36			X	X			Venidium fastuosum	X							X	
X	X			X	X	X	6–12			X	X	X	X	Verbena	X			X	X	X	X	X	X
	X					X	18–24			X	X	X	X	Vinca—Periwinkle	X							X	
	X					X	8–12			X	X	X		Virginian Stocks—Malcomia	X						X	X	
X			X				12–18			X	X			Wallflower, Annual	X		X						X
					X		9			X	X			Zaluzianskya capensis—Night Phlox	X						X		
X	X	X	X			X	12–24			X	X	X	X	Zinnia	X					X		X	X

Flower Chart by Permission of the Templin-Bradley Company, Cleveland, Ohio.

CHAPTER XI

ROSES

Who loves not roses, knows not Beauty's
smile;
Romance hath spurned him—
Poetry passed him by

   ʘ   ʘ   ʘ   ʘ   ʘ

Roses, all roses, bloom for the soul's delight.
                    —ROCKWELL.

In 1867 the firm of Guillot Fils introduced the La France Rose, the first Hybrid Tea variety. It resulted from crossing a Hybrid Perpetual variety with one of the Tea Roses which originated in China. Since then we have been given all sorts of rules for raising roses. The prospective rose gardener hears so much about heavy soil, sunny positions and deep trenches that he is sometimes discouraged before he starts. Actually, roses are not difficult to grow, and no flower is more adapted to as many uses. If you will follow the following rules you can confidently look forward to success.

1. Buy good bushes.
2. Select a location where you have sun at least half of the day and then protect them from foraging roots of other plants.
3. Plant them properly.
4. Prune them early in the spring.
5. Start weekly cultivation and dusting early in the spring.
6. Protect them in the winter.

Most improved varieties of bush roses do not possess adequate vigor and are therefore grafted on to what is known as a root stock, which is usually a hardy wild form. It is rarely advisable for the amateur to attempt to propagate his own bedding roses from cuttings. A good field-grown budded rose will endure for years. If you are inclined to doubt this, buy a cheap rose plant (which may have been discarded after having been forced for flower production in a greenhouse) and put it among those bought at a fair price from a reliable nursery; the difference in health and production will convince you.

The best site for a rose garden is conceded by most authorities to be an open space on a southerly slope, sheltered to the north and west by higher ground, walls or hedges. The beds should not be too close to the walls or hedge and should have some sunlight and plenty of air all around them. Confined gardens are productive of disease. We cannot always select the site, and if you must place them close to a hedge or wall, use care to see that they have direct sunlight a little better than half the day. We must see, however, that they are kept free from the roots of trees or other shrubbery. If the site must be close to these other plants, cut down into the ground near the bed, the full length of a spade, several times each year, to see that the roots do not grow into the bed itself. Poplars and willows of all kinds are extremely dangerous to rose beds. Roses should not have to compete with tree roots for food moisture. Do not make the beds too high or too wide. If the beds are more than four feet wide, it will be necessary to walk on them in pruning, picking the flowers, etc., and thus undo the effect of cultivation.

A medium heavy soil, well supplied with humus and well drained, is all that is necessary. Every kind of soil capably handled will support roses. The secret is deep cultivation. The top four to six inches is not so important; but the next twelve inches of soil in the bed, should contain the plant food. Generous quantities of humus, well-decayed manure if you have it, and plenty of bone meal should be added. Do not force the plants too fast with chemical fertilizer, and above all do not fertilize late in the season. Chemical fertilizer applied at this time will stimulate new growth during warm days and the plant may not winter well.

The best time to plant is in October. This will allow the roots to obtain a good start and the plants will bloom sooner the following year. No hesitation, however, should be felt in planting in the spring, but do it as early as you are able to dig in the ground.

Take the tree from the package upon receipt from the grower. If it is in leaf, free it from all buds and most of the foliage. Shorten the long shoots that offer resistance to the wind so it will not sway and disturb the roots while they are getting established. Cut off damaged or broken roots and cut the thick ones back six inches from their starting point. Preserve as much as possible the tiny fibrous roots, as these are the ones which feed the plant. Heavy roots may take up a little water, but the fibrous roots are the important ones. If a root has a crack in it, cut it off clean as it will breed disease. If the bark is shriveled when the plants are received, bury them under six inches of moist soil for a few days. If there are signs of mildew, dip in a solution of one ounce of Liver of Sulphur (potassium sulphide) in one gallon of soft water. Spread the roots to the fullest extent laterally in an amply large hole, and do not plant too deeply. Combine your headwork with footwork. Make the soil firm as the hole is filled. Use your hands and doubled fists. As soon as there is sufficient earth around the roots to prevent damage, step on it and rock backward and forward to make the soil very firm. It is well to mound the soil 4 to 6 inches up around the plants to prevent excessive evaporation after planting. In spring, lift off in two or three weeks and mulch with peat moss.

It used to be the firm rule that plants should be set two to two and one-half feet apart, but most gardeners get excellent results and a better looking bed at twelve to fifteen inches for Hybrid Teas and Floribundas. Hybrid Perpetuals and shrub roses of course need more room.

A well-known authority states that we should regard rose plants merely as machines for the production of blooms. For this reason pruning is very essential. The purpose of pruning is to produce strong roots and shoots. New shoots must come from the base to take the place of old woody branches. Pruning opens the plant to the sun and air by taking away the dense middle growth. It cuts away diseased and exhausted wood, prevents legginess and restricts the plant to the proper dimensions. The number of shoots must be limited, in order to encourage blooms. In general, it is best to prune the weaker plant severely and to allow the stronger plant more freedom. In March and even up to mid-April, prune just above a bud that points outward from the plant so that the branch from that bud will grow away from the center, leaving it open to the sun and the air. Leave from three to five buds on each stem. Cut in a slanting direction so that the moisture from the plant and the water will drain off the wound.

If you wish perfection, dress cut ends with pine tar, which can be obtained in cans at most drug stores. Remember, no new growths—no blooms.

One of the most important steps in the summer care of roses is disease protection and prevention. A homemade dust can be made of nine parts of dusting sulphur by bulk mixed with one part of arsenate of lead, to which tobacco dust may be added for aphis. This formula, called Massey Dust, can be bought under trade names either plain or colored green to make it less noticeable on foliage. All-purpose sprays are also available and highly recommended by rose growers. They combine a fungicide and insecticides effective against chewing and sucking insects.

The dust should be applied not only to the top of the leaves but to the underside as well. A thorough dusting requires the use of a dust gun but the cost of this article soon pays for itself. Dusting should be done once a week, as should cultivation.

A light working of the topsoil helps to make plant food available besides conserving the moisture. In watering soak the ground, never sprinkle, and to avoid black spot, water in the morning and do not wet the foliage if it can be avoided. Many rose growers prefer to mulch their plants about the first of July with peat moss or some other humus. It is a good practice to mix with this mulch about 10% of tobacco dust or stem-meal. Cultivation must be stopped in September, to discourage late growth, but the plants must be soaked with water late into October before hilling up for the winter.

Hybrid Teas and Perpetuals need no coddling, just shelter from the coldest winds. Also hill up the soil until it covers the six lowest buds to prevent winter drying of the canes.

If you wish to mulch with leaves, use only hardwood leaves and surround the bed with stakes closely set or wire netting to hold them in place.

Most people do not understand the reason for a mulch. Its chief purpose is to keep the plants from drying out, not to keep them warm. It protects them from the sun and wind and sudden changes in temperature, but the air should circulate freely through it at all times. A little brush may be laid upon the top but do not pack down the leaves—a damp mulch that

Blaze, one of the most luxuriant and dependable climbing red Roses.

One of the few members of the Holly tribe, the Winterberry makes up for the fact that it loses its leaves every fall by producing, on fertile plants, brilliant berries which are much loved by wild birds.

HOW TO PLANT AND PRUNE

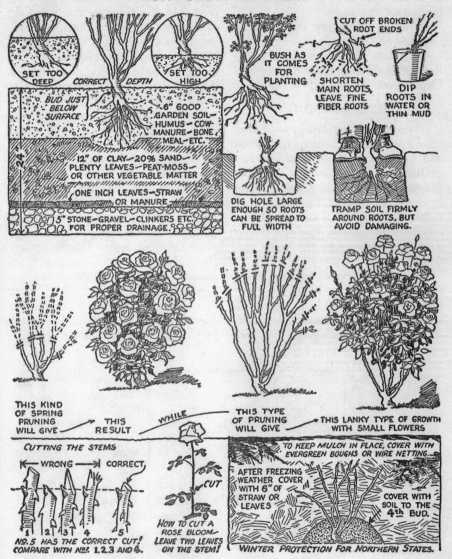

SET TOO DEEP · CORRECT DEPTH · SET TOO HIGH

BUD JUST BELOW SURFACE

6" GOOD GARDEN SOIL — HUMUS — COW-MANURE — BONE MEAL — ETC.

12" OF CLAY — 20% SAND — PLENTY LEAVES — PEAT-MOSS OR OTHER VEGETABLE MATTER

ONE INCH LEAVES — STRAW OR MANURE

5" STONE — GRAVEL — CLINKERS ETC. FOR PROPER DRAINAGE.

BUSH AS IT COMES FOR PLANTING

CUT OFF BROKEN ROOT ENDS

SHORTEN MAIN ROOTS, LEAVE FINE FIBER ROOTS

DIP ROOTS IN WATER OR THIN MUD

DIG HOLE LARGE ENOUGH SO ROOTS CAN BE SPREAD TO FULL WIDTH

TRAMP SOIL FIRMLY AROUND ROOTS, BUT AVOID DAMAGING.

THIS KIND OF SPRING PRUNING WILL GIVE → THIS RESULT

WHILE

THIS TYPE OF PRUNING WILL GIVE → THIS LANKY TYPE OF GROWTH WITH SMALL FLOWERS

CUTTING THE STEMS

← WRONG — → CORRECT

1 2 3 4 5

NO. 5 HAS THE CORRECT CUT! COMPARE WITH NOS. 1, 2, 3 AND 4.

CUT

HOW TO CUT A ROSE BLOOM — LEAVE TWO LEAVES ON THE STEM!

TO KEEP MULCH IN PLACE, COVER WITH EVERGREEN BOUGHS OR WIRE NETTING.

AFTER FREEZING WEATHER COVER WITH 6" OF STRAW OR LEAVES

COVER WITH SOIL TO THE 4TH BUD.

WINTER PROTECTION FOR NORTHERN STATES.

freezes solid in winter is injurious. In the spring, remove the mulch a little at a time so that the plants will harden off gradually.

Climbing roses are discussed in Chapter IX, "Vines."

We quote the following propagation methods from Ohio Agricultural Experiment Station Bulletin 525:

PROPAGATION

Roses are propagated by seed, root sprouts, suckers, layers, hardwood and softwood cuttings, budding and grafting. The production of rose plants by seed, budding, and grafting is done extensively by commercial growers, but the skill and equipment required for success preclude this as a general practice by the home gardener.

Root Sprouts and Layers: Many species, such as *Rosa blanda, R. carolina, R. lucida, R. nitida, R. rugosa, R. setigera, R. spinosissima,* and *R. wichuraiana,* are propagated by root sprouts or layers. Sprouts may be separated and planted either in the spring or fall. The process of layering is simple and involves the notching of the stem on the underside, bending it to the ground, and covering with soil early in the summer. By fall or the following spring, these buried sections will have rooted and may be severed and transplanted.

Hardwood Cuttings: Climbing roses, hardy species or shrub roses, and Hybrid Perpetuals are often propagated by hardwood cuttings. These are taken in the fall of the year from well ripened wood and cut in sections of 6 to 8 inches in length. The best guide to the time of taking is the dropping of the foliage after the first frost. These cuttings should be tied in bundles, a label attached, and the bundles buried in sand in a cold cellar or out of doors deeply enough to avoid freezing. The recommendation often made relative to placing of the butts up and tips

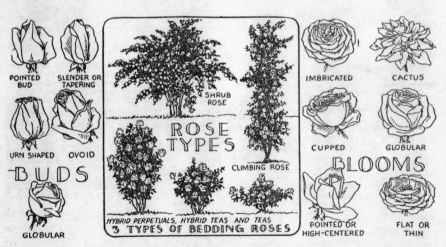

Here are illustrated, in the center, five basic types or classes of rose plants, and beside them typical forms taken by buds and open flowers.

down when burying is not essential. They may be buried horizontally with equally desirable results.

In the spring of the year these cuttings should be planted 4 to 6 inches apart and deep enough so that only an inch of the cutting with a single bud shows above the ground.

Softwood Cuttings: These cuttings may be made in late June and July from wood of the current year's growth. They should contain three buds. The leaves should be taken off the two lower ones and partially trimmed off the upper one. They should be inserted in sand in a hotbed and kept close and moist to hasten rooting. Shade to reduce evaporation, moisture to prevent wilting, and bottom heat to hasten rooting are the essentials for success. After rooting, the cuttings should be potted and kept shaded and close until proper root action has taken place.

If a hotbed or coldframe is not available, a box of sufficient size to hold 3 to 4 inches of sand and leave an air space of 6 to 8 inches between the rooting medium and a sheet of glass used to cover the box and maintain the humid condition essential for the rooting of cuttings may be used.

SOME RECOMMENDED ROSES

In compiling the following list of suggested rose varieties, attention has been given to beauty of flower, consistent performance, simple cultural requirements, and adaptability to various parts of the country. Recent years have seen the introduction of fine foreign roses and the development of splendid ones by American originators. Progress has been stim-

ulated by the Plant Patent Act and the establishment of the All-America Rose Selections (both discussed in "Garden Magic Marches On," page 439); by the perfection of improved methods of culture, handling, and packing of plants, and by a steady growth of popular interest in the flower. But the story of the rose in America is not yet written, though interesting and exciting chapters are constantly being added.

In the case of the Hybrid Teas, Floribundas, and Climbers, the varieties suggested are those with the highest scores in the American Rose Society's "1955 Guide for Buying Roses." On this basis, a rating of 10 means a "perfect" rose; 9 to 10, outstanding; 8 to 8.9, excellent; 7 to 7.9, good. We have arbitrarily included only those scoring above the figure noted for each type. In the other classes, the recommendations are Mr. Biles'; while they may not include the newer sorts, those named are still worthy varieties.

Trailing Roses

Rosa wichuraiana (species)...white
Rose Max Graf (hybrid)......pink

Climbers (8 and above)

Pauls Scarlet Climber (9.1)....red
Chevy Chase (8.9)............red
New Dawn (8.8).............pink
Dr. W. Van Fleet (8.7)........pink
City of York (8.6)...........white
Climbing Santa Anita (8.5)....pink
Cl. Crimson Glory (8.3).......red
Climbing Picture (8.4).......pink
Pauls Lemon Pillar (8.2)....yellow
Cl. Christopher Stone (8.2)....red
Climbing Goldilocks (8.1)...yellow

Blaze (8.1) ....red
Glenn Dale (8.0)...........white
Silver Moon (8.0)...........white
Gardenia* ....yellow
Jacotte* ....copper-yellow
Mary Wallace* ....pink

Harisons Yellow...........yellow
Mabelle Stearns.....pink (double)
Pink Grootendorst ....pink
Pink Profusion ....pink
Rosa hugonis ....yellow
Rosa rubifolia.... pink (red leaves)

Floribundas (8 or above)

Frensham (9.0) ....red
Betty Prior (9.0).............pink
Fashion (8.9).............blend
Red Pinocchio (8.8)..........red
The Fairy (8.6).............pink
Vogue (8.5) ....blend
Donald Prior (8.3)...........red
Floradora (8.2) ....red
Pink Bountiful (8.2).........pink
Rosenelfe (8.2) ....pink
Dagmar Spath (8.2).........white
World's Fair (8.0)............red
Goldilocks (7.3) ....yellow
Carillon* ....coral flame
Mrs. R. M. Finch*...........pink
Pink Gruss an Aachen*.....salmon

Hybrid Teas (8 or above)

Peace (9.6) ....blend
Crimson Glory (9.1)..........red
Charlotte Armstrong (9.0).....red
Chrysler Imperial (8.7).......red
Tallyho (8.4) ....red
Dainty Bess (8.4)....pink (single)
Good News (8.4)...........blend
Mme. Henri Guillot (8.4)....blend
Rubaiyat (8.2).............red
Christopher Stone (8.1).......red
Etoile de Hollande (8.1)......red
Grande Duchesse Charlotte (8.1)

                                red
Nocturne (8.1)...............red
Eclipse (8.1) ....yellow
Saturnia (8.1) ....blend
Sutters Gold (8.1)..........blend
Tip Toes (8.1).............blend
First Love (8.0).............pink
Picture (8.0) ....pink
New Yorker (8.0) ....red
Condesa de Sastago*...copper-pink
Dame Edith Helen*.........pink
Kaiserin Augusta Viktoria*...white
McGredys Yellow*.........yellow
Mme. Jules Bouche*.........white
Mrs. P. S. duPont*.........yellow
Mrs. Sam McGredy*
              copper-orange scarlet
Pink Dawn*...............pink
President Herbert Hoover*
               maroon-orange
Radiance* ....cameo-pink
Red Radiance*...............red

Polyanthas*

Cameo ....salmon
Cecil Brunner ....pink
Chatillon Rose........bright pink
Ellen Poulsen.........soft pink
Triomphe Orleanais........crimson

Hybrid Perpetuals*

Frau Karl Druschki..........white
J. B. Clark.................red
Mrs. John Laing........clear pink
Paul Neyron.................rose

Shrub (Species) Roses*

Agnes (Hybrid Rugosa).....yellow
H. J. Grootendorst...........red

*Mr. Biles' selection.

CHAPTER XII

BULBS, CORMS AND TUBERS

The little brown bulbs went to sleep in the
*   ground,*
In their little brown nighties they slept very
*   sound,*
And Winter he raged and he roared over-
*   head,*
But never a bulb turned over in bed.

But when Spring came tip-toeing over the
*   lea,*
Her finger on lip, just as still as could be,
The little brown bulbs at the very first tread
All split up their nighties and jumped out
*   of bed.*

—(AUTHOR UNKNOWN.)

No type of garden flower gives so much for so little care and effort as the group of plants known, to the amateur, as bulbs. With them, it is easily possible to have a complete succession of bloom all the year around. Starting with the Snowdrops and similar small plants, which seem to come with the melting snow, we go down the list: daffodils, tulips, iris, gladiolus, lilies, tuberous begonias, cannas, etc., until dahlias end the season in a burst of glory. The winter months also may be filled with bloom by anyone who has a dark closet and a sunny window. It is no wonder that these plants are finding more and more favor in all gardens.

Some confusion results from the various classes which are called "bulbs." A true bulb is really a bud containing in it the flower in miniature. It needs only warmth, moisture and the means of absorbing the moisture (roots), to grow and flower. The true bulb is composed of layers of overlapping scales and increases chiefly by division. The scales divide from the parent plant and these form new bulbs, actually parts of the old plant.

Among them we have the lily, made up of loose scales, each one of which may become a new plant, and the tight-scaled variety which appear to be solid, such as the onion, hyacinth, tulip, etc.

The corm, the best known example of which is the gladiolus, is solid flesh. It blooms for a single season and an entirely new corm grows above it to take its place. In addition to this it forms cormels or bulblets

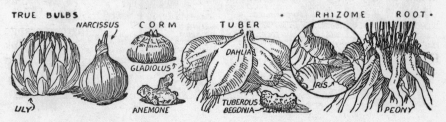

TRUE BULBS   NARCISSUS   CORM   TUBER   RHIZOME   ROOT
GLADIOLUS   DAHLIA
LILY   ANEMONE   TUBEROUS BEGONIA   IRIS   PEONY

around its base which are also new growths.

An example of the true tuber is the potato; it has buds or "eyes" scattered over its surface from which new sprouts start, while the dahlia, which is really a tuberous root, sprouts only from its crown or the neck of the root. Each of these plants forms a new bulbous growth every year, but the thickened root of the tuberous begonia lasts from season to season.

The three bulbous types are alike in one respect. They all need deep cultivation and thorough drainage. Cold stiff clay soil may rot them. Moisture may be held for them by a liberal supply of peat; all types like it. Where alkalinity is required a slight degree of acidity is easily over-come by the application of lime.

Spring Flowering Bulbs: Because for many years the entire supply of this type of bulb was imported from Holland, they are sometimes called "Dutch Bulbs." This is now somewhat of a misnomer as they are produced extensively in some parts of our country.

The growing of narcissus bulbs on a large scale was stimulated by a quarantine on imported bulbs which was in effect for a number of years. The world war also induced further efforts to develop domestic cultures. Fortunately, the soil and climate of Long Island, Michigan, and the Pacific Northwest favor these bulbs and production in such places is increasing.

They are the easiest grown of all bulb type plants, and are almost free from pests. Someone has said: "All you do is plant them, cover them, and forget them until they remind you by blooming in the spring." No hoeing, no weeding, no pruning.

Cultivation of tubers and corms may contain some element of chance, but only gross carelessness can cause failure in fall planted bulbs.

Spring flowering bulbs bloom so early in the season that they do not have time to develop a root structure if planted that same season. The quick top growth must have immediate response from below or failure will result. We therefore plant the different varieties from late September until November so that roots will have time to develop before winter. Narcissus, crocus, bulbous iris, snowdrops, snowflakes and winter aconite should be planted in September—tulips, hyacinths, scillas may go in later.

If you wish to plant in beds do so by excavating the whole area to the proper planting depth and laying out the bulbs as you wish them to grow. They may then be covered with soil and this uniform depth of planting will cause them to bloom at the same time in the spring. If it is desired to have clumps bloom at the same time, planting with a trowel must be done carefully, using a notched stick to get uniform depth.

It is best to start at the outer edge of the bed setting the bulbs in even rows which may be broken up as the center is approached. Avoid the beds of complicated shapes such as were popular a generation ago and stick to simple design.

It is not necessary to plant in beds, however, as the flowers of all the spring bulbs appear well against the dark green foliage of the evergreens or in groups in the flower border. The tall Breeder tulips go well in the background; medium varieties, with the tall narcissus in the middle, and dwarf narcissus, bluebells, etc., in the front.

Planting in the border or among the evergreens has an advantage over planting in beds in that the plants can be left to ripen and not lifted too soon. If planted deep enough they will not interfere with cultivation of other plants.

Give particular attention to planting with perennials which mature later. Make a plan before purchasing bulbs to avoid having too many of one kind and too few of another.

Many bulbs, such as daffodils and narcissus can be naturalized among shrubbery or trees, but care should be taken to see that the foliage fully matures if you want the bloom repeated next year.

As previously mentioned the bulb is a complete plant when you cover it with soil, therefore it pays to plant only top quality, number one bulbs

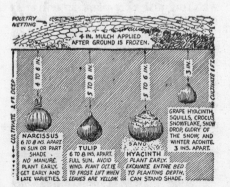

HOW TO PLANT BULBS

bought from reliable dealers. We should not, however, go to extremes in seeking the largest bulbs. Exhibition sizes are for indoor forcing, and they do not always give as satisfactory results in the garden as firm, fair sized, healthy stock of choice outdoor varieties.

In the case of corms and tubers, the flower depends largely upon the cultivation given; with the bulb it depends upon what is in it when planted. It would seem that this being the case, we need pay little attention to soil. If we want one crop of blooms from our bulbs this would be all right but if they are to bloom from year to year they must be given food and water.

The soil must be reduced to good physical condition about two feet deep, the bottom foot being made to drain freely; in the case of water-bearing soil or damp locations, a three-inch layer of cinders must be placed in the very bottom. The bulbs will rot if not freely drained. The topsoil should be mixed with peat moss and lightly dusted with lime (remember that no lime should ever be used for lilies).

There are more failures because of the use of fresh manure than from any other cause. It is an excellent material if properly rotted and composted, but the touch of fresh manure means death to many bulbs. Mix it with the soil in spring, fork it over several times during the summer, and then sift it through a coarse screen in the fall. This is the ideal planting material.

The idea is to make the top foot of soil a rich sandy loam, free of stagnant water but moisture-holding. Use one large handful of coarse raw bone meal, one of steamed bone and two of wood ashes to each square yard of planting surface. Mix deeply and thoroughly with soil. The potash in wood ashes develops firm new bulbs.

Firm the soil beneath the bulbs, and press the bulbs firmly upon it. Air pockets underneath may cause the bulb to die before its roots reach the moist soil. It is important to plant with a trowel when naturalizing under trees or in the grass, to be sure that the bulb (no matter how small) sits firmly on the soil.

In naturalizing put a thin layer of sand under the bulb and dust the bottom well with bone meal.

Much failure is due to too shallow planting. Rather too deep than too shallow, but best of all is the right depth. This varies with soil condition; in sandy soil plant deeper. The general rule is to cover the top of the bulb with soil, to three times its greatest diameter. Specific planting directions for various bulbs will be given later.

Plant all bulbs in each clump at the same depth regardless of size or they will bloom unevenly. A thorough watering just after planting will start root growth at once.

After the ground has frozen, cover the plants with four to six inches of leaves (hardwood, if possible) and surround these with stakes to keep the wind from blowing them away. Wire netting is also good for this purpose. Remember not to mulch until the ground is frozen and field mice have gone into winter quarters. Hardwood leaves, wheat straw, excelsior are good materials, and glass wool and cranberry tops are worth a trial.

In the spring examine the mulch to see that it is light and dry, but leave it in place until danger of late frost is over. This will keep the bulbs from premature growth and injury by late frost. Take the mulch off carefully to avoid injury to any young sprouts that may have started through it.

After bulbs have bloomed the top growth must mature three to five weeks in order for the bulbs to develop for the following season. If it is necessary to lift them at once do it with as little root disturbance as possible and heel them in somewhere in semishade. Never lift them if it is possible to wait.

It is not natural for bulbs to remain out of the soil. When for some reason it becomes necessary to take them out, we must try to imitate nature as much as possible. Keep them in boxes of dry sand, sawdust or peat until needed.

If bulbs are lifted, do this as soon as the tops dry. Some bulbs begin to develop roots soon after wilting and if moved after development starts, the new roots may be injured. When necessary to move them after root growth starts, lift them with a clump of earth and, above all, do not let it or the roots dry out.

Discard any soft small bulbs, replacing them with good ones. It is almost impossible to dig them without injuring some and yearly replenishment should replace any doubtful ones.

Hyacinths, tulips and other fall

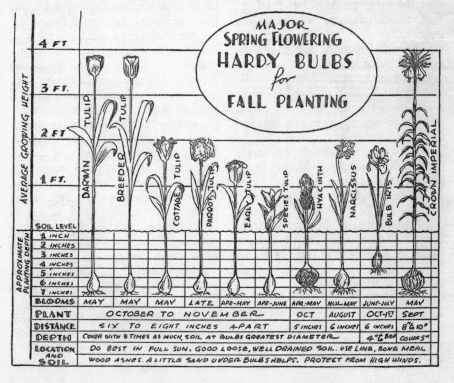

MAJOR SPRING FLOWERING HARDY BULBS for FALL PLANTING

	DARWIN TULIP	BREEDER TULIP	COTTAGE TULIP	PARROT TULIP	EARLY TULIP	SPECIES TULIP	HYACINTH	NARCISSUS	BULB IRIS	CROWN IMPERIAL
BLOOMS	MAY	MAY	MAY	LATE	APR-MAY	APR-JUNE	APR-MAY	MCH-MAY	JUNE-JULY	MAY
PLANT	OCTOBER TO NOVEMBER						OCT	AUGUST	OCT-1ST	SEPT
DISTANCE	SIX TO EIGHT INCHES APART						5 INCHES	6 INCHES	6 INCHES	8"&10"
DEPTH	COVER WITH 3 TIMES AS MUCH SOIL AT BULBS GREATEST DIAMETER							4"&5"	COVER 5"	
LOCATION AND SOIL	DO BEST IN FULL SUN. GOOD LOOSE, WELL DRAINED SOIL. USE LIME, BONE MEAL WOOD ASHES. A LITTLE SAND UNDER BULBS HELPS. PROTECT FROM HIGH WINDS.									

planted bulbs may be kept in well-ventilated trays or bags (never air tight). Moisture will cause premature sprouting. When buying new ones, it is best to plant them as soon as received.

Liquid manure (two weak dressings) just as the buds are forming will increase flower size. The number of blooms is determined by your bulbs. Nitrate of soda, or chemical plant food, as a substitute for liquid manure, may be given in weak solution—one tablespoon to a gallon of water. Wet the ground well, and then wash the fertilizer into the soil by a good watering. This is more successful on tulips than others.

The varieties of spring flowering types are so well known and well described in good plant catalogs, that no descriptions will be given here.

Cultural directions for the more popular bulbs follow.

Crocus: A good reliable bulb. Cover three inches deep—two to three inches apart for mass effect. Subject to fungus, so use no manure, leaf mold or humus, discard all injured or diseased bulbs. Best in sandy or well-drained soil; avoid very damp situations. Use bone meal and leave for several years. Plant in sun or partial shade in September or as soon as received. Naturalize in grass or shrubbery. Will disappear if top is mowed too soon. Excellent in rockery—renovate or renew every two years. Multiplies rapidly with care.

Glory of the Snow: Plant in sun or light shade. Cover three inches deep, three inches apart in September or October. Good for naturalizing in groups. Likes moist but not wet soil while growing. Leave undisturbed. Blooms with Scilla siberica.

Snowdrops: About the first to bloom in early March. Plant in mass by dozens or hundreds. Cover two to three inches and space same distance apart. Like moist semishade. Will increase and last in sandy soils. In beds, mulch with manure in fall. Naturalized, apply bone meal. Dislike being disturbed.

Spring Snowflakes: White, three to four inches high. Plant in groups; cover three inches deep. Moist rich soil, in shaded corner or semishaded rock garden. Blooms early. Summer Snowflake blooms April, May, or early June, same culture.

Grape Hyacinths: Prefer rich, sandy or gritty soil, not particular. Cover two or three inches deep; set three inches apart. Will thrive if left undisturbed and leaves are allowed to fully ripen.

Squills (Scillas): Wood hyacinths thrive in any good garden loam if an occasional top dressing of manure is applied in fall. No culture required. Cover two inches deep—three inches apart—in September or October. Makes dense mat of foliage, thrives for years, will stand some shade.

Scilla siberica: Blue flower to combine with Snowdrops for early spring bloom. Naturalizing and in lower rock garden. Sandy soil, top dress manure. Raise from seedlings. Will grow under evergreens.

Scilla hispanica: Spanish Squill, best of Scillas. Blooms May and June. Goes with some Darwin tulips. Edging beds or in borders. Several colors. Cover three inches and four inches apart. Fine for naturalizing under trees.

Scilla bifolia: Earliest Squill. Blue, three to six inches high. Rock garden or indoors.

Winter Aconite: Buttercup family, not showy, but early, yellow, March or April, three to eight inches high. Cover two to three inches, in semishady location moist while growing. Plant as early as possible. Good among trees or shrubbery.

Star of Bethlehem: Avoid it. It is not very showy and soon becomes a weed pest.

Narcissus (Daffodil, Jonquil): All Narcissi are not Jonquils, but the name Daffodil is commonly applied to all Narcissi with large trumpet flowers.

In the open garden all varieties except the Polyanthus type are hardy, and reproduce tremendously. There are small varieties for the rock garden.

It is desirable when purchasing to get both early and late varieties to prolong the bloom from early spring to the Iris season. Also in purchasing pay attention to the crown division. Bulbs which are double-nosed, are about to divide and may not bloom effectively the first season. A small number of them may be satisfactory.

They are great feeders and fast growers, and soon crowd each other, exhausting the food. They must then be separated or they cease to bloom. Roots may go down fourteen inches or more so double spading is advisable for any great success. Unless the ground is naturally rich, trowel planting is not highly profitable. They are the most intolerant of manure of all the bulbs. Never use it unless composted, thoroughly decayed, with soil as previously described. When planting apply a mixture of raw bone as before instructed. A yearly top dressing of bone one pound to each twenty square feet is excellent. Work in carefully. A 4:12:4 chemical fertilizer may be applied in April or May—three pounds to one hundred square feet. They delight in moist soil and drainage. Will stand some shade.

Plant the new bulbs as early as possible. They are best left undisturbed for several years, but when the clumps get to be twenty to thirty bulbs they should be dug and replanted. Reset six to ten inches apart according to size. Depth of planting depends upon size; cover about five or six inches.

Keep the sun from drying the bulbs while out of the ground and get them back as soon as possible. They start to make roots almost as soon as the foliage wilts and the best time to divide is short. Blooming success the following season depends much upon transplanting as soon as the foliage withers.

Water thoroughly as soon as planted.

Tulip: Tulips, favorite flowers for centuries, are the last planted of all fall bulbs. From October 15 until the ground freezes is the best time; they are likely to send up top growth if planted too early.

In formal bedding new bulbs must be used each year to maintain uniform height and size of flower. After blooming, lift and heel in in a trench until foliage ripens, then dig, clean and store in dry place in flats and replant in borders in the fall. In perennial borders, deep planting, 10 to 12 inches in medium soil retards splitting up into many of small bulbs; it also prevents injury in cultivation. When cutting flowers for indoors, leave foliage untouched; otherwise, flower stalks can be cut off as soon as the petals fall, and a third of the leaf area reduced. When all foliage is limp and yellow, it can be cut to the ground.

Avoid planting in open windswept places where the heavy blooms may be blown about.

Tulips need especially good drainage, adequate moisture and a sunny location, although Parrot types will stand some shade.

The procession of bloom starts in April with Single and Double Early (six to fifteen inches high), then Cottage (sixteen to thirty inches high), Parrot (twenty-two to thirty-six inches high), and in late May, Darwins (twenty-four to thirty-six inches high), Breeders (twenty-four to thirty-two inches high), and Mendel, each class having a wide range of colors.

Hyacinth: These plants prefer very light sandy soils which drain easily and are more easily warmed in spring. They root deeply and the bed should be cultivated and fertilized two feet deep. Clay must be broken up with wood ashes or sand. Well-rotted cow manure is permitted. Apply bone meal and other fertilizers together with humus materials as previously directed, using more lime than for the other bulbs.

Plant six inches apart and four to six inches deep (three times their greatest diameter) in a sunny location and protect them from strong winds which will blight their blooms and make them lopsided.

Best results are obtained from early planting. September or early October produces good roots. Plant at a uniform depth to have them bloom at the same time. It is not necessary to buy the largest bulbs. Good two to two and a quarter inch bulbs are satisfactory. Place a little sand under and around them if planted in clay soil.

For larger flowers use liquid manure upon them as buds begin to form, or 4:12:4 fertilizer, three pounds to one hundred square feet. Wet down well or apply in solution. Remove flowers as they fade.

It is best to lift them each year after foliage ripens and store them in a cool dry place until ready to plant again. Replace all soft or small bulbs.

SUMMER FLOWERING BULBS

Anemone: St. Brigid and Japanese or Poppy-flowered are the hardiest. Plant in October or as early as possible in spring, three inches deep and eight to ten inches apart, placing the bulbs on edge. They need partial shade and plenty of water during the blooming season and dry weather. Will winter in well-drained soil or in the rock garden if well mulched.

May be planted in early spring and lifted for the winter if sufficient mulching material is not available.

Autumn Crocus or Meadow Saffron (Colchicum): These plants are not particularly adapted to garden use, but are so interesting as to merit cultivation. Planted in early fall two inches deep the leaves appear in the spring to die and be followed in the fall by white to lavender flowers rising directly from the ground. Planted in late summer they will bloom in fall. Leaves will follow in spring. Plant in gardens close to the house where flowers will be protected from the hot sun. In the house the plant is a novelty. Placed in sun in mid-winter it will bloom without water or soil, having lavender flowers. Away from direct light its bloom is almost white.

Halls-amaryllis (Lycoris squamigera): An interesting plant blooming like the Autumn Crocus. The bulbs planted in early fall are perfectly hardy and should be set four inches deep and six to eight apart, in groups of three or more.

Plant in perennial border or in very slight shade. The foliage dies down in early summer and is followed by fragrant rose-lilac flowers, two feet high, in August, rising directly from the ground. It will multiply and must be divided after three or four years. For the true Amaryllis see "HOUSE PLANTS," Chapter XXII.

Calla: Yellow and white. These are best known as indoor bulbs; for culture see Chapter XXII. However, they can be handled like other tender kinds and planted outdoors in spring, dug in fall and wintered in a cool, dry place. Use rich heavy soil in a sunny spot with ample drainage. They bloom beautifully in August or September just when the garden slumps. Sometimes handled as semi-aquatics on margins of pools.

Canna: These plants require the same culture as Dahlias, thriving in any well drained soil, away from strong winds, where moisture is readily obtainable.

They are vigorous growers but sensitive to frost. Do not plant outdoors

until the weather becomes warm. Of easy culture they may be started indoors in pots or in the open in soil top dressed with well-rotted manure. Divide last year's roots into fairly large sections with several buds on each, and plant two inches below the surface and one to three feet apart. Wide planting for specimen plants; close for mass effect.

Given good soil they will bloom by midsummer. Liquid manure at blooming time increases bloom size. Lift after frost kills the tops and store in cool place in dry sand soil or peat moss to avoid shriveling.

They come in a wide range of color. Get the newer and better varieties. Seeds do not come true to color.

Dahlia: Strange to say, in spite of the great popularity of the Dahlia, its simple cultural requirements are many times misunderstood. Its chief needs are drainage and moisture rather than fertility. The ideal soil is one-half sand and one-half loam. A fair standard of fertility is required but excessive richness is to be avoided. An excess of nitrogen will make the plant run to stem and leaves at the expense of flowers. Heavy soil should be prepared in the fall with a good application of manure and bone meal. Superphosphate and manure may be used in spring on light or sandy soil.

To plant, dig a generous-sized hole, fourteen inches deep in heavy or clay soils; sixteen inches in sandy soil. Now condition the soil as previously instructed and replace eight inches or more of it in the bottom, firming it well. Drive stakes before planting in order that no damage be done to the tender new roots and so the young plant will have support during its early development.

Plant the tuber flat as illustrated on page 192 with sprout end nearest to stake, covering the crown two inches deep. As soon as growth has risen above the soil fill in around it, and repeat until the hole is level full. This method keeps the tuber deep in the ground where it is cool and moist during hot weather.

After the plant has reached one foot in growth use a good 2:10:6 fertilizer at the rate of two to three ounces to the plant. Stir into upper few inches only; it will wash in. Consult your seedsman about the many excellent fertilizers offered and use as directed.

The plants should be kept well and deeply cultivated until blooming commences. After that ordinary tillage is sufficient. This treatment is better than any amount of water, as it produces normal rather than sappy growth. Mulch in August with two inches of humus, peat or well-rotted manure to cool the ground, and conserve the moisture. Remember that careful culture produces not only good flowers but also good roots for next year.

Dahlias are commonly grown in masses by themselves rather than singly in garden beds of mixed flowers. There is no reason why they should not be grown as specimens in the border, except that they can be more easily handled in beds by themselves or in rows in the vegetable garden. They respond best to open culture with abundant air and sunlight and they should not be subjected to high winds, which break the brittle stems and beat the heavy blossoms about.

Large growing varieties need from four to five feet of space each way, smaller varieties about three feet, varying according to size, down to two feet. The smaller varieties are admirably suited to borders. All kinds need four to five hours sunshine and to be kept free from the foraging roots of trees, shrubbery, or other plants, which deprive them of food and moisture.

As soon as tops are killed by frost in the fall, they should be cut off to eight inches above the crown, and the roots dug from the ground. After a few hours drying in the air, they are stored in any of several materials in a cool cellar protected from freezing.

In spring do not be in too big a hurry to plant. Dahlias are very susceptible to injury from cold. Lift them from the box and divide as shown in illustration on page 192. Handle with care to avoid bruising, which will produce decay. Note the sprouting part or "neck" of the tuber which has no eyes as has the potato. If the neck or crown is broken the tuber is worthless.

The practice of disbudding varies somewhat. On the Dahlia shoot the top or terminal flower bud is the first to develop. If all the conditions of growth and weather are perfect it makes the finest flower. The other flowers are produced on side shoots from the axils of the leaves, which are paired. The illustration shows the customary way of disbudding in order to obtain a fair number of flowers of fine quality with long stems. Very good flowers can be raised when the three pairs of flower buds below each terminal bud are removed, but further disbudding will concentrate more strength in the terminal flower and give longer stems for cutting.

Elephant's-Ear (Caladium): Plant late in May two to three inches deep. Give well spaded soil plenty of water and 4:12:4 fertilizer and it will grow six feet high with immense leaves. Too large for the average garden. Lift after frost.

Gladiolus: The Gladiolus is deservedly popular for its wide variety of color and uses, its ease of culture and general adaptability. It will grow almost anywhere in the United States in any kind of soil that is well drained and sunny.

The preference of the plant seems to be for a sandy loam well pulverized, mellow and deeply cultivated. In clay soil sand should be added to make it drain well and in lighter soils an extra amount of decayed vegetable matter is necessary. Cultivating the soil 18 inches deep cannot be too highly recommended. If the soil is double spitted, well-decayed manure may be worked into the lower digging. Manure may be used if the bed is dug in the fall (good practice) and allowed to lie rough all winter, but it should not be used on beds about to be planted. The idea is to get the manure as deep as possible so that the roots may go deep into the ground in search of moisture and cool temperature. The gladiolus corm is planted four to six inches deep and its roots will go considerably farther to feed. The black sedge humus sold commercially is ideal for use if the bed is

made at planting time. It has the moisture holding qualities so necessary during hot dry weather and is a long-time investment. Use it generously (one-fifth humus to four-fifths soil in extreme conditions). Peat moss may be used, but keep it away from the corm.

Contrary to popular belief, gladiolus need not be planted in beds by themselves or in rows in the vegetable garden. Try them in groups between the peonies or in the open spots of the perennial border. They will give color, when many of the early plants have stopped blooming. A little thought along this line will open interesting possibilities of experiment.

Planting may be commenced in the spring as soon as the ground has warmed up. After experimenting to ascertain the best time, it is well to make a series of succession plantings ten days apart to give a long season of bloom.

The approved distance for planting is six inches apart, but the early corms may be planted twelve inches and then by successive plantings each two weeks brought to the proper distance. Varieties must also be taken into account in the spacing. Those of the primulinus type for instance, may be close while larger types need more space.

Many of the best growers mark their bulbs with the number of days in which they will bloom. By selecting different blooming dates it is possible to have a succession of bloom with only monthly planting. Late June is the last that planting can be done for bloom before frost.

Good bulbs pay. Large old bulbs

(usually flat and slightly hollowed on the bottom) are not as good as smaller high-crowned young bulbs. No. 2 size gives a good flower spike as it gives more support to the plant. Soak soil six inches deep when needed.

If the corms purchased are healthy and the site of planting is changed often, little disease will affect them. Disease is best checked by fumigating the corms before planting. Some prefer to place their corms in airtight bags with about two tablespoons of naphthalene flakes to 100 bulbs for three weeks. Another method is to immerse them peeled in a solution of bichloride of mercury (1 oz. to 3 gallons of water) for two hours at

70° temperature. Plant while wet. Keep the bichloride from all metal, including rings, wrist watches, etc. If there is danger of infestation by thrips, use a spray of one heaping tablespoon of Paris Green in three gallons of water and two pounds of brown sugar. Spray as early as plants come up and repeat every fortnight until flowering time.

For wire worms, sprinkle planting soil with a weak solution of permanganate of potash. Burn any rotted corms to prevent spread of disease.

First cultivations may be fairly deep (3 inches), but as plants advance it should be done with a rake. Merely keep the topsoil loosened to prevent weeds starting and to form

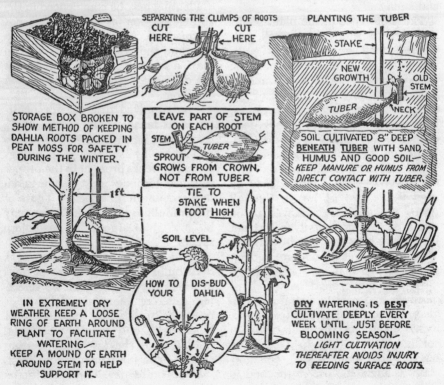

STORAGE BOX BROKEN TO SHOW METHOD OF KEEPING DAHLIA ROOTS PACKED IN PEAT MOSS FOR SAFETY DURING THE WINTER.

SEPARATING THE CLUMPS OF ROOTS
CUT HERE   CUT HERE

PLANTING THE TUBER

STAKE
NEW GROWTH
OLD STEM
TUBER
NECK

SOIL CULTIVATED 8" DEEP BENEATH TUBER WITH SAND, HUMUS AND GOOD SOIL— KEEP MANURE OR HUMUS FROM DIRECT CONTACT WITH TUBER.

LEAVE PART OF STEM ON EACH ROOT
STEM
TUBER
SPROUT GROWS FROM CROWN, NOT FROM TUBER

TIE TO STAKE WHEN 1 FOOT HIGH

SOIL LEVEL

1ft.

IN EXTREMELY DRY WEATHER KEEP A LOOSE RING OF EARTH AROUND PLANT TO FACILITATE WATERING. KEEP A MOUND OF EARTH AROUND STEM TO HELP SUPPORT IT.

HOW TO YOUR   DIS-BUD DAHLIA

DRY WATERING IS BEST CULTIVATE DEEPLY EVERY WEEK UNTIL JUST BEFORE BLOOMING SEASON. LIGHT CULTIVATION THEREAFTER AVOIDS INJURY TO FEEDING SURFACE ROOTS.

a dust mulch. If done often the rake is sufficient and will save the labor of breaking up the ground after it has packed.

Staking should be done only when necessary to keep plants from drooping or working loose at the roots. If you stake, first tie the cord or raffia to a small bamboo plant stake, then around the plant.

Cutting the spike as soon as the first flower opens allows the plant strength to go into the corm. Planting of favored corms as early in the season as possible allows more time for the formation of new bulbs and bulblets (properly called cormels).

Fine flowers come from fertilizing. Dress the plant with equal parts of fine steamed bone and dried blood (about one level teaspoon to each plant) when they are six to eight inches high and give liquid manure just as plants are ready to bloom.

Liquid manure is made by suspending a sack containing a bushel or more of cow manure in an ash can. Tie a cord to the sack and to a handle of the can. The lid can then be applied to prevent unpleasant odors. Dilute the liquid until it resembles weak tea and apply with watering can nozzle removed, first thoroughly wetting the ground.

Chemical fertilizer can be used to stimulate exhibition quality flowers. Plant tablets are a good way to make the chemical applications.

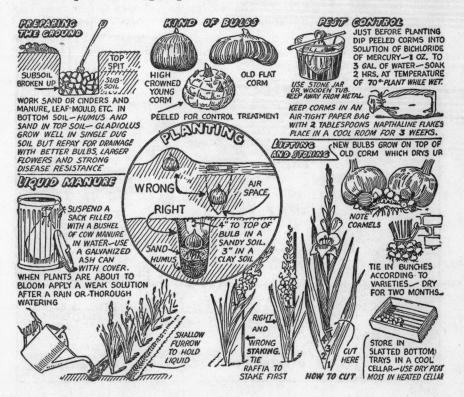

The best time to lift the corms is when the tips of the leaves begin to turn brown. Cormels adhere to them better; the bulbs, too, are then fully matured.

Store them in bunches for about eight weeks in open slatted trays in a cool cellar. Never remove stalks as long as any green shows—meaning that growth is still present. If they must be stored in a furnace-heated cellar, they may be placed in dry sand or dry peat moss. Avoid dampness.

Cormels or bulblets may be planted in shallow trenches in mellow soil either in the open or in cigar boxes or trays inside in early spring. They will grow into flowering bulbs in about two seasons. Store for the winter in slightly (very slightly) moistened peat moss.

Summer-hyacinth (Galtonia): This is a good plant for the back of the perennial border. It bears white, drooping, bell shaped flowers on slender 1 to 4 ft. stems in midsummer. Plant in early spring 6 inches deep and six inches apart in clumps of several bulbs. Best to lift in the fall and store until spring. For best results buy new bulbs each year.

Iris (Bearded): Of the several kinds of Iris, all of which are worth cultivating, tall bearded (so called German) varieties lead all the rest in well deserved popularity. For ease of culture, ability to stand neglect and for range of color and variety they are unsurpassed.

They need little attention but being strong growers they must be divided every two to five years (according to variety) if you wish good results as to bloom and health. Left longer than this they so fill the bed

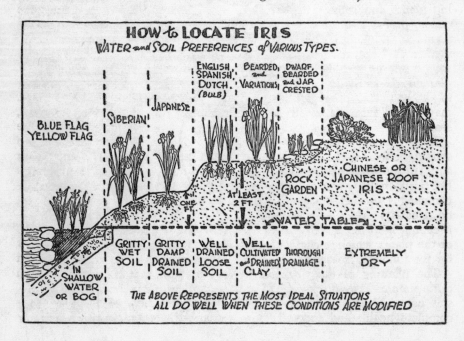

HOW to LOCATE IRIS
WATER and SOIL PREFERENCES of VARIOUS TYPES.

BLUE FLAG YELLOW FLAG — SIBERIAN — JAPANESE — ENGLISH, SPANISH, DUTCH (BULB) — BEARDED and VARIATIONS — DWARF, BEARDED and JAP. CRESTED

AT LEAST ONE FT. — AT LEAST 2 FT. — ROCK GARDEN — CHINESE OR JAPANESE ROOF IRIS — WATER TABLE

IN SHALLOW WATER OR BOG — GRITTY WET SOIL — GRITTY DAMP DRAINED SOIL — WELL DRAINED LOOSE SOIL — WELL CULTIVATED and DRAINED CLAY — THOROUGH DRAINAGE — EXTREMELY DRY

THE ABOVE REPRESENTS THE MOST IDEAL SITUATIONS ALL DO WELL WHEN THESE CONDITIONS ARE MODIFIED

that they choke themselves. The time to divide is soon after they have finished blooming in order that they may become established for results next spring.

The question of how to transplant without weakening the bloom of the whole border the following year puzzled the writer until he hit upon the scheme of transplanting a part each year. This allows for a succession of strong plants to bear sturdy bloom.

Another bugbear which he overcame in transplanting was that most instructions for dividing say to cut at the places marked "A" in the illustration on page 196. If a large number of new plants is desired, this is good practice but blooms the following season will be lessened. So division at points marked "B" is advised to give stronger, quicker acting plants and some practical gardeners prefer to leave three to five plants in a clump. The old roots marked "C" are of small value and should not be included in the new planting. If you wish to plant them in a bed for propagation, they may make fair plants in several seasons.

After transplanting, the leaves should be cut back to relieve the strain of the weakened root structure but this is the only case in which leaf trimming is justified. Many gardeners do it each year for appearance but it cannot help but affect the energy of the plants which is accumulating for the following season.

The planting of the rhizomes is quite simple. They do not need rich soil but drainage is necessary for complete health and success. They originally grew as hillside plants and thrive best in slightly raised beds or upon banks. Do not confuse them with flags which grow in the water or the Japanese Iris which like dampness. They will give reasonable results in semishade, but full sun is best.

They will grow well in clay soil if sand is added for drainage. It has been said that any soil which will grow corn will grow Iris. As they are very shallow rooted it is a waste to add fertilizer to any greater depth than five inches. In clay the soil below this depth should be about one-third sand thoroughly mixed, but no plant food need be added.

In first making the bed, work in deeply some well-rotted manure and lime; the former must be so well rotted as to have lost all its former appearance. If peat humus or leaf mold is used for this purpose, give it a generous dressing of hydrated lime or ground limestone. Lime in small quantities sometimes proves very beneficial to these plants.

Having prepared the soil, pulverize it and you are ready to plant. Rake off an inch or so of topsoil, press the rhizome down so that the roots are spread and then sweep back the removed soil. Do not plant too close—give them room to spread. Feeding roots do not mean much as they grow rapidly and will be replaced quickly if accidentally removed. No chemical fertilizer is to be recommended, but a dressing of three generous handfuls of wood ashes and one of bone meal to each square yard is recommended yearly. Work in lightly to three or four inches. Never mulch with manure or other materials as this is conducive to rot.

Bearded Iris have few enemies, the only prominent ones being root rot and the Iris borer. Root rot is indicated by an unpleasant odor and the roots become soft and watery. This has been ascribed to lack of lime in the soil but is more likely to be from lack of drainage. If the plants are in a low spot, transplant them, cut away the diseased parts and dust well with sulphur or wash with a formalin solution (4%).

The Iris borer is a night flying moth which lays its eggs in the leaves. These hatch after flowering time and the larva eats its way down through the leaf and when full grown enters the rhizome (root) near the flowering stem often destroying the lateral bud, which produces the bloom for the following year.

If you find a slimy trail of leaves eaten, remove them, mash the intruder and destroy the chewed leaves. The borer usually leaves behind a little patch of plant material resembling sawdust where it enters the root. If the borer has entered the rhizome destroy it with a sharp knife and you may save the roots. If not destroyed it will eat through the root and enter the soil for pupation and damage the succeeding year. Examine new purchases carefully for both rot and borer.

In a bad infestation, a reasonable

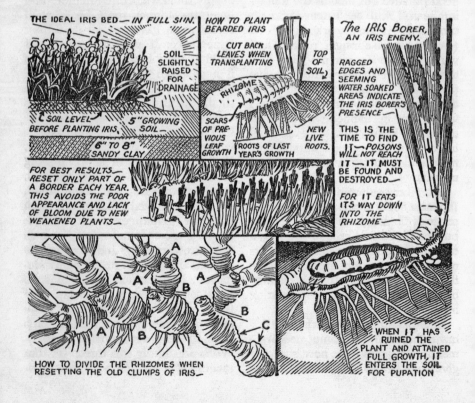

THE IDEAL IRIS BED — IN FULL SUN.

SOIL SLIGHTLY RAISED FOR DRAINAGE

SOIL LEVEL BEFORE PLANTING IRIS.
5" GROWING SOIL.
6" TO 8" SANDY CLAY

HOW TO PLANT BEARDED IRIS
CUT BACK LEAVES WHEN TRANSPLANTING
TOP OF SOIL
RHIZOME
SCARS OF PREVIOUS LEAF GROWTH
ROOTS OF LAST YEAR'S GROWTH
NEW LIVE ROOTS.

The IRIS BORER, AN IRIS ENEMY.
RAGGED EDGES AND SEEMING WATER SOAKED AREAS INDICATE THE IRIS BORER'S PRESENCE —
THIS IS THE TIME TO FIND IT — POISONS WILL NOT REACH IT — IT MUST BE FOUND AND DESTROYED —
FOR IT EATS ITS WAY DOWN INTO THE RHIZOME —

FOR BEST RESULTS — RESET ONLY PART OF A BORDER EACH YEAR. THIS AVOIDS THE POOR APPEARANCE AND LACK OF BLOOM DUE TO NEW WEAKENED PLANTS —

HOW TO DIVIDE THE RHIZOMES WHEN RESETTING THE OLD CLUMPS OF IRIS.

WHEN IT HAS RUINED THE PLANT AND ATTAINED FULL GROWTH, IT ENTERS THE SOIL FOR PUPATION

measure of control can be secured by digging all Iris in August or early September when the pupae are in the top soil around the base or in the center of the clumps. They are soft, pinkish brown bodies 1 to 1½ inches long, and the moths emerge in October to lay their eggs on the basal leaves for April hatching. Their flight range is great enough to infest nearby plantings as well as their own.

In digging the Iris, the soil should be examined with great care for the pupae, and prepared thoroughly; the best rhizomes divided and replanted, and a careful check made throughout the following season.

In spring the eggs are just below the dead leaves and may be easily destroyed by fire. Raise leaves with a rake and allow the sun to dry them thoroughly. When dry sprinkle lightly (as a laundress dampens for ironing) with gasoline. Have someone present to help to prevent spread of fire and then burn the leaves. This is best done on a windy day, when the leaves may be fanned into a quick hot blaze. Do not allow a prolonged fire to injure the roots.

Careful burning is good practice upon any type of Iris planting.

Iris, Fibrous-rooted: The Siberian, Japanese, and similar kinds do not properly belong in a chapter on bulbs. They are fibrous rooted and care must be taken to see that these roots are spread when planting, like those of any perennial. They are lime haters. The Siberian is the most hardy.

In regions of heavy clay soil they have the name of being temperamental. This need not be the case if given loose soil (Japanese espe-

cially), in which they delight. Mix sand with the clay and put in a large amount of rotted manure, peat, leaf mold, etc., until there is always a supply of moisture held for them. The ground should be very damp but not swampy. They are not water plants, and although they grow in wet sunny places, they are more likely to winter kill in damp spots.

They bloom in June and July abundantly but daintily. Some varieties of Siberian grow two to five feet high. The foliage is excellent and this type is much used on slightly raised banks about pools. Set them (always in the sun) among the perennials in especially prepared soil; keep free from weeds. Cultivate well, using a little bone meal from time to time and take care to avoid damage to the roots.

The common varieties are shades of blue but an attempt to describe the shades of the hybrids (red, yellow, lavenders, purples, orchids) would be futile.

The Siberian are the easiest of culture, the Japanese more exacting.

Plant late in August or September, in extra well-drained soil, placing crowns two inches below the soil, two inches apart for mass effect. Light shade seems to help. Mulch with leaf mold, peat or well-decayed manure. The first year's plantings of all beardless Iris should have a protective mulch during the winter.

Propagate from seed or by division. Seedlings will vary somewhat. The finest blooms come from extra feeding (liquid manure) at budding time.

Water Iris: This type is also fibrous rooted and consists for the main part of two sections; Iris versicolor, the common blue flag of the American prairies and Iris pseudacorus, the European yellow flag. Both are true water plants growing best in boggy situations where the water does not stand over their crowns.

The yellow flag will grow freely in both sun and shade in fairly dry moist locations, and is excellent for wild plantings. It comes in several color forms. If grown in the garden, remove the seeds or the plants may become weeds in a few years. The blue variety is not so rampant growing and is useful mostly for edges of ponds and bog situations.

Bulbous Iris: This type is not so common in most American gardens but some varieties have for years been popular florists' flowers for forcing. It is strictly a garden flower, not suitable for landscape purposes. If raised, put it in the perennial border where the foliage may ripen without becoming an eyesore.

They are large plants, mostly late and long bloomers, and quite tender.

Once established they are free and easy bloomers, needing sun for best development.

They like a gritty, deeply dug soil in a warm sunny place. In warmer climates they are planted from August to October, 8 to 10 inches apart, twice as deep as the height of the bulb and divided every three years.

In colder climates they often succeed if given heavy winter protection or they may be dug each year to be replanted in the spring. If lifted, transplant to a new location and reject all diseased or injured bulbs.

The Dutch Iris are most tender and usually least desirable. Spanish and English are more generally used. Spanish will grow in comparatively dry soil, but English require more moisture. The foliage takes an autumnal spurt and should be protected against injury by frost before ripening, also against heavy summer rains. Fertilize heavily with rotted manure and apply in liquid form as well. They do not multiply well and the

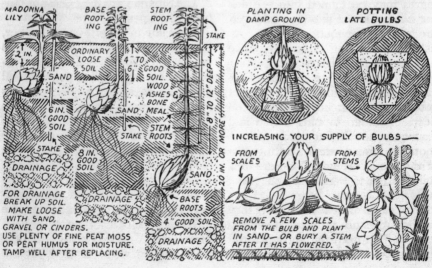

MADONNA LILY

2 IN.
ORDINARY LOOSE SOIL
SAND
6 IN. GOOD SOIL
STAKE
DRAINAGE

FOR DRAINAGE BREAK UP SOIL. MAKE LOOSE WITH SAND, GRAVEL OR CINDERS. USE PLENTY OF FINE PEAT MOSS OR PEAT HUMUS FOR MOISTURE. TAMP WELL AFTER REPLACING.

BASE ROOTING
STEM ROOTING
STAKE
4 TO 6"
GOOD SOIL, WOOD ASHES & BONE MEAL
SAND
STEM ROOTS
STAKE

8 IN. GOOD SOIL
DRAINAGE
8" TO 12" DEEP
20 IN. OR MORE
SAND
BASE ROOTS
4" GOOD SOIL
DRAINAGE

PLANTING IN DAMP GROUND

POTTING LATE BULBS

INCREASING YOUR SUPPLY OF BULBS—

FROM SCALES

FROM STEMS

REMOVE A FEW SCALES FROM THE BULB AND PLANT IN SAND— OR BURY A STEM AFTER IT HAS FLOWERED.

supply should be augmented by new purchases each year.

Lilies: The beauty of garden lilies and the ease with which some kinds can be raised from seed, should make them one of our most prized plants even though it is not always easy to keep a planting free of bulb diseases. Yet, sometimes, properly planted, a twenty-five cent bulb will bloom for five years without further attention, and give, not one bloom a year, but a dozen or more after full development has taken place.

The name lily, as applied to some of our garden plants, is very confusing. Lily-of-the-Valley, African-lily, Daylily, Arum-lily, Waterlilies, etc., are misnamed and are so called not because they belong to the lily family but because their flowers bear a resemblance to the true lilies.

Not all lilies are adaptable to garden use but a proper selection will give fragrant bloom from June to September. As a rule, a moderate sized bulb is best for outdoor planting. It may not give the best results for the first season but will give better results when permanently established.

Some of the reasons for lack of success are: 1. Planting too shallow; all lilies except the Madonna Lily and other base-rooting kinds need deep planting. 2. Lack of proper drainage; this is one thing all authorities agree upon. 3. Lack of food or the use of manure; it is better for the amateur to avoid manure in lily culture. 4. Planting certain varieties in lime or alkaline soil. 5. Failure to provide moisture in hot dry summer days. 6. Too frequent transplanting; they should be transplanted only

about every three to five years according to variety.

The lily family is divided into two main groups, stem-rooting and base-rooting, each demanding a different planting depth. A planting of eight to twelve inches (to base of bulb) is needed for stem-rooting varieties and four to six inches for bottom-rooting types.

Most of them should be planted three times as deep as the height of the bulb. That is, if a bulb is two inches high, its top should be four inches below the top of the soil. A slightly deeper planting for stem-rooting sorts is permissible.

The most popular stem-rooting species are: Auratum, regale, philadelphicum, speciosum, longiflorum, batemanniae, browni, croceum, dauricum, elegans, hansoni, henryi, japonicum, rubellum, sargentiae, tenuifolium, tigrinum, umbellatum, and wallacei.

Base-rooting species are: Candidum, superbum, canadense, chalcedonicum, giganteum, martagon, monadelphum, and testaceum.

Use care in planting. Remember, that if properly planted, they give results for years with no further attention. The following are general rules: First, select a proper site. As these plants are rarely planted in beds by themselves, it is necessary to dig holes separately for each group. These groups should consist of three to six bulbs. All but the Madonna Lily may be planted among perennials between peonies, shrubbery, evergreens, etc. They thrive in partial shade especially about their roots. A ground cover of Ferns, Ivy, Petunias, Sedums, low-growing

Veronica, etc., works very well.

Surface-rooted trees and shrubbery, such as Elms and Maples, etc., are not good for them and heavy feeding, deep-rooted perennials should be kept at a distance. They will grow in full sun but most of them do well shaded for a part of the day—do not plant in complete shade.

In case of strong prevailing winds, use a fence, building or planting of shrubs to act as a windbreak. Keep the lilies five to six feet away. Place low-growing varieties at the front of the border, taller ones in the rear. Group each species by itself for best arrangement. The time of planting must be governed by the end of the blooming season. The general rule is to lift the bulbs about four weeks after they have finished blooming. They are nearest dormant at this time. Of course, it is understood that once planted the bulbs should remain in place three to five years according to crowding. They do not thrive with more frequent division.

The trick of planting is to get the bulbs into their new location as soon as possible in the late summer or early fall. In this manner they have a chance to establish the root system before cold weather. In the case of newly purchased bulbs, those that may be obtained before frost should be planted as soon as possible. Preparations for planting those arriving later must be made in advance. Cover the ground with six inches of well tramped leaves or straw to keep it from freezing.

Another method advocated for bulbs arriving later than early October is to pot them in carefully prepared soil, using a pot six inches or larger. Plant the bulb (surrounded by sand) two inches below the surface, moisten the soil, allow to drain and keep from freezing in a cool, dark cellar. In April break out the bottom of the pot and plant it at the proper depth, without removing from the pot. This bulb may then be taken from the pot for replanting at the proper time next fall.

It has been reported that good results have been obtained in furnace-heated cellars with pots buried in a box of dry peat moss, placed in the coolest corner. Some authorities say it is best to pot all imported bulbs. This gives a chance for disinfection for two successive years to avoid spread of disease.

All bulbs should be replanted as soon as possible after being dug. They are really never dormant and exposure weakens them. If possible, have new site ready or keep them covered. Dust all bulbs thoroughly with sulphur before planting. Or better still, give all your bulbs a Semesan (procured at your seedsman) bath before planting. This mild disinfectant destroys mold and other disease organisms.

Drainage and proper depth are more important than fertility. One thing they cannot tolerate is an excess of water. The Meadow Lily (Canadense) and American Turk's-Cap Lily (Superbum) like marshes and wet places; all others need perfect drainage. No decomposing vegetable matter should be used in the soil. Manure should be avoided even if well rotted. For the base-rooting varieties, dig a hole at least sixteen inches deep and more than twelve inches square. If the ground is clay, fork into the bottom of this hole about four inches of sand, cinders or fine gravel, and one inch of thoroughly rotted leafmold or peat humus, working it thoroughly and deeply. If the soil is sandy, use more humus. Now tamp this down firmly and water to settle it. Next place in the hole enough good, rich soil (mixed with four handfuls of wood ashes and two of coarse raw bone) to fill it to within six inches of the surface when well tamped. It is important that this soil be thoroughly settled so that the bulb remains at proper depth.

The bulb is then planted in a layer of clean, sharp sand, thick enough to leave three-quarters of an inch of sand above and below the plant. Some authorities recommend a pad of finely shredded peat moss just below the bulb and the sand. This is to give the roots their first start. The soil above the sand need not be fertilized and should not be firmed but settled by watering.

For the stem-rooting varieties, dig the hole twenty inches deep, work in the gravel and peat humus and fill with soil prepared as above described to twelve inches from the surface. The bulb is then placed with some clean sand above and below it and the hole filled with soil and settled by watering. In this instance the topsoil should be fertilized the same as the bottom soil for base-rooting lilies.

Lilies do not do well in decaying vegetable matter such as manure, therefore the soil used should be black and mellow. It is better to buy a little of such soil or bring it in sacks from the woods (sifting out all leaves

and roots), than to risk loss of bloom. The cost will be found very small when divided over a period of five years. In damp soils some growers plant the bulbs upon inverted flower pots filled with sand (see illustration, page 198).

It is important that a stake (bamboo cane, thirty inches or more long) be set for each bulb as it is planted. This avoids root injury later. Also label substantially.

Just before or during the blooming season the application of a (1 oz. to a gallon) solution of 4:12:4 chemical fertilizer is sometimes beneficial. Weak liquid manure is also good at that time. Occasional thorough soaking should be carried on during dry weather and a summer mulch of one inch of peat during July and August is recommended.

If the foliage or buds show signs of blight (turn brownish) spray three or four times a week with Bordeaux mixture until it disappears. If the bulbs are properly planted in well-drained soil the danger of disease is reduced.

In cutting the blooms from the plant, be sure to cut reasonably near to the flower, leaving as much as possible of the long green stem. If this is cut off short the plant may die.

Lilies may be planted in spring but may not grow the first year. In this case, protect the spot from cultivation. They will probably come out, with renewed life the second season. In spring planting take care to avoid injury to sprouts upon the bulbs.

Many authorities maintain that certain varieties do not tolerate alkaline soil. Lilies have been known to grow well even in limed soil, but as a rule prefer a neutral or slightly acid condition. A good perennial bed should be slightly alkaline, therefore, it sometimes becomes necessary to treat the soil in which you plant lilies with aluminum sulphate, one-half ounce to the square foot. Do not treat a larger space than is necessary for the lilies themselves. If you are planting properly and not getting results, try this. The use of sifted leaf soil from beneath trees in woods usually gives sufficient acidity.

Regardless of hardiness, mulch lilies always. All wild plants are mulched naturally each year. We must try to imitate natural conditions. To fool the mice, wait until the ground is thoroughly frozen, then cover with one inch of straw or three inches of leaves, held loosely in place. Leave a small part of it in place in spring until all danger of frost is past. Early sprouts must be protected.

The Madonna Lily: The Candidum or Madonna Lily is the most popular of all lilies but differs in several ways from other base-rooting varieties. It thrives best when planted shallow and needs a sandy loam where other lilies require clay loam.

It should be planted in August if possible (about four to six weeks after blooming season is over) in order that it may become established and develop leaves before cold weather. It has, however, been successfully planted as late as October. The evergreen leaves are carried over the winter and must be protected along with the bulb by mulching after the ground is frozen with sev-

eral inches of straw or leaves held in place by boughs or wire netting. This mulch is left until all danger of freezing is past.

These leaves (especially the base leaves) should be protected from cultivation injury and no other plants should be allowed to interfere with them. Remove weeds carefully. The plant requires full sun and will tolerate a certain amount of lime in the soil, although it does better without it.

Propagation of Lilies: All lilies are increased by natural division, but propagation may be carried on from the outer scales of the bulbs and in the case of the Madonna by cutting off a stem immediately after blooming and burying it in a tray of sand at a temperature of not less than sixty degrees. This sand must be kept wet and about a dozen bulblets will form. These may be replanted in the ground where they will come to blooming size in a year or so. Cover the propagating bed with a mulch for winter protection whether bulbs show leaves or not.

The scale method may be applied to most lilies. It consists of removing four or five thick outside scales of the old bulb at replanting time. These are then planted in sand as described for stems above. Some growers merely plant the scales in a trench four inches deep surrounded by an inch of sand (above and below). This is mulched during the winter and the bulbs are transplanted the following year when they have formed at the base of the scale.

Tiger Lilies and several others may be increased by planting the tiny bulbs which form in the axils of the leaves. Plant as above described in a shallow trench.

Many gardeners prefer to raise lilies from seed, as the surest way to raise healthy bulbs. It has the disadvantage that all hybrids do not come true from seed and that it takes two to three years to produce blooming plants. To the person interested in propagation, it forms an interesting economical and simple way of obtaining a large number of plants, the seeds being inexpensive.

Plant in a cold frame or sheltered spot in the open. If planted in late August, they will germinate and get a start before cold weather. If planted late in the fall, they will not germinate until spring. Fall planting is best, but they can be raised by spring planting if protected by slat screens.

Plant about one inch apart and cover lightly with soil. Watch to see that it is replaced at once if washed off by the rain. Mulch during the winter as for other lilies.

Transplant them to nursery rows as soon as they become crowded. Do not plant too many of one variety.

List of the Most Popular Lilies

L. AURATUM (Golden banded Japan Lily). Stem-rooting. Ivory spotted and striped. 3 to 4 inches tall. Blooms July, August.

L. BATEMANNIAE (Turk's-cap Lily). Large pale orange, red or apricot. 3 to 4 feet tall. July and August.

L. CANADENSE (Canadian Lily). Medium sized, orange yellow flowers, spotted brown. June to August. 2 feet tall.

L. HENRYI (Yellow Show Lily). Apricot and yellow. Few spots, stem-rooting. 3 to 5 feet tall. Blooms August.

L. REGALE PLATYPHYLLUM (Regal Lily). Stem-rooting. White, yellow spots. 5 to 6 feet. Blooms July, August.

L. SPECIOSUM ALBUM (White Show Lily). Stem-rooting. White, greenish stripe. Blooms August and September.

L. SPECIOSUM RUBRUM (Show Lily). Stem-rooting. White tinted, rose pink, crimson spots. Blooms August and September.

L. SPECIOSUM MAGNIFICUM. Stem-rooting. Large flowers, rosy crimson. Blooms August and September.

L. TIGRINUM SPLENDIDUM (Tiger Lily). Stem-rooting. Bright orange, black spots. 4 to 5 feet high.

L. CANDIDUM (Madonna). Base-rooting. Fragrant white blooms. Blooms June and July. 3 to 4 feet tall. Plant in August if possible.

L. SUPERBUM (Swamp Lily). Base-rooting. Brilliant orange, scarlet spotted. 5 to 6 feet tall. Blooms July to September.

Mariposa-lily (Calochortus): Known as Globe-tulip, Star-tulip, Mariposa-tulip, etc., though it is neither lily nor tulip. White, red, yellow, pink, lilac, and purple. One to two feet high. Plant in well-drained soil in October or November and cover well in early December. Plant two to three inches deep in groups of 6 to 12 and two to three inches apart. May be dug and stored after blooming if bed is to be heavily watered.

Montbretia (Tritonia) and Tiger Flower (Tigridia): Both require well-drained soil, a protected location, and much the same culture as gladioli, although they may be wintered with a heavy mulching. They do best in colder locations if lifted and stored. Flower spikes two to four feet high —orange and yellow. Plant in early May when the trees are coming out in leaf, two to three inches deep and three to six inches apart in large clumps or masses.

Oxalis: A trailing plant sometimes used for borders, flowers beautifully in several colors, bulbs must be dug each season. Complete culture in Chapter XXII, "House Plants."

Peonies: Quoting from "The Diary of a Plain Dirt Gardener" by Harry R. O'Brien in a June issue of "Better Homes and Gardens." "Do you know, I really began next year's garden this

morning. I first began on the peony bed, using the two-pronged weeding hoe and digging deeply to cultivate well around the plants. The bloom next spring will depend upon what I do from now until September."

How many times have you heard the question, "Why don't my peonies bloom?" It seems I have always heard it. After blooming, peonies rest somewhat and perfect their foliage. This period is completed in August when a season of intense root activity commences. Energy and food are then stored in the roots to be used the following spring when the blossoms and leaves burst forth as if by magic. This mass of foliage and blossoms produced in so short a time is a great strain on the plant's resources.

SPRING CARE

HOOP AND STAKE SUPPORT

WELDED WIRE SUPPORT

PLANTS 3' TO 4' APART

—30"—

EACH SPRING GIVE SPROUTING PLANT A DRESSING OF 1 LARGE TROWEL OF SHEEP MANURE MIXED WITH 1 TABLE SPOON OF CHEMICAL FERTILIZER — WORK INTO CULTIVTED AREA KEEP AWAY FROM ROOTS, STEMS AND LEAVES. AVOID INJURING ROOTS — CULTIVATE 3" TO 4" EACH WEEK

PROPER SUPPORT

BAD

GOOD

PROPER SUP PORT MAKES SIGHTLY PLANTS AND TAKES LESS ROOM

DISBUDDING

CUT → MAIN BUD FOR LATE BLOOM

CUT SIDE BUDS FOR EARLY BLOOM

CUTTING OFF ALL BUT ONE BUD GIVES LARGER AND BETTER FLOWERS CUT OFF SIDE BUDS FOR EARLIER BLOOM AND THE TOP BUD IF LATER BLOOM IS DESIRED

WATERING

WATERING IS NECESSARY IN DRY WEATHER.— ESPECIALLY IN MAY, AUGUST AND SEPTEMBER — DO NOT GET WATER ON LEAVES OR FLOWERS. IF WATER DOES NOT RUN INTO SOIL QUICKLY, MAKE HOLES WITH IRON PIPE OR BAR — BE CAREFUL NOT TO INJURE ROOTS.

SUMMER CARE

WOOD ASHES

FINE STEAMED BONE

AFTER BLOOMING SEASON WORK IN 2 HANDFULS OF WOOD ASHES AND ONE OF FINE STEAMED BONE DUST TO EACH PLANT — CULTIVATE MONTHLY

SANITATION

REMOVE AND BURN ALL DISCOLORED FOLIAGE

FALL CARE

AVOID POSSIBLE SPREAD OF DISEASE BY CUTTING AWAY AND BURNING FOLIAGE AS SOON AS WILTED BY FROST.— DRESS CULTIVATED AREA WITH 1 HANDFULL OF STEAMED BONE AND 2 OF WOOD ASHES

If the foliage is completed successfully the root activity is helped and consequently the bloom for the following year. Fertilize as shown in the illustration and cultivate monthly. Do not over fertilize.

In working around the roots use care so as not to injure them. A light double-pointed weeding hoe is good. Careful observation and practice will teach you how.

Peonies are remarkably free from disease. Many growers have them for years without any disease being manifest. However, there are a few foliage and stem diseases, which may cause bud blight. Usually they respond to sprays of Bordeaux mixture, but Botrytis Blight sometimes needs a slightly different handling. This trouble does not always show on the foliage, unless in an advanced stage. Dark-colored areas at the base of stems and below the soil level are early indications. If it does not respond to Bordeaux Mixture, dust it with a Copper-lime mixture obtainable at seed stores.

Watering in dry weather, during early spring or in summer may be necessary. Care should be used to keep the water off the foliage and flowers. In extremely dry weather mulching with peat moss or humus is good but care must be used to keep it several inches away from the stems.

Peonies should be properly supported. If they are full grown it is difficult to provide support. But do the best you can, and remember to do it next spring when the plant is young and easily trained. Supports can be made of barrel hoops and stakes, but welded iron rod supports

are for sale very reasonably, and will last for years.

Disbudding before the blooming period is desirable under many conditions. Where a profusion of bloom is desired it is not necessary, but where fine flowers are wanted all buds but one should be removed from each stem. If any early bloom is desired remove all but the terminal bud. Removing all but one of the side buds will delay the bloom somewhat. Disbudded plants are less likely to have sagging blooms.

In the fall, plants should be treated with two handfuls of wood ashes and one of steamed bone meal worked into cultivated soil area. Use care to keep fertilizer away from roots. Cut off foliage as soon as frost kills it and burn to avoid spread of disease.

Peonies survive and bloom without all this care, but they do much better with it. Professional peony growers cultivate and fertilize much as a farmer cares for his crops. Care pays.

Reasons listed for lack of bloom in peonies are as follows:

1. Too deep planting: Look after this in September.

2. Excessive shade: Though they grow well in partial shade.

3. Poor drainage: They do not like wet feet.

4. Late freezing in spring: Protect temporarily with crates covered with carpet or straw, etc.

5. Root disease: This will be discussed later (see illus. page 207).

6. Too small a division in transplanting.

7. Lack of fertility.

8. Lack of moisture at flowering

time or at root building time in late August and September.

9. Loss of moisture by proximity to trees and shrubbery roots.

10. Delayed division and transplanting. Divide every four or five years.

The uses for peonies in landscape design are numerous. In beds or rows by themselves they do very well and they may be mixed with shrubbery or used as a background for the perennial border.

An odd corner may be brightened by using peonies four feet apart each way. The space between should be planted in the fall with early spring flowering bulbs (snowdrops, crocuses, scillas, chionodoxas, and early tulips). These are followed by gladiolus, hardy lilies, etc. If necessary a little cutting of the peony foliage will do no harm.

I wish I knew the identity of the witty writer who said, "The proper time to transplant peonies is nine A. M. September the 15th. I don't like to hurry with breakfast." This sums up the idea precisely.

Some do's and don'ts on peony planting will save much space and reading time.

Don'ts

Don't allow plants to go without transplanting over four or at most five years. They will stop blooming or bloom unsatisfactorily.

Don't try to divide roots in less than three years. At least four eyes to each new root are necessary for quick growth. A smaller number takes longer to develop and may not bloom for years.

Don't bruise or injure roots in transplanting. Don't buy old clumps. Get new, active roots. Don't plant in the same place twice if it can be conveniently avoided. New locations help prevent root diseases.

Don't leave earth on clumps to be planted. Wash clean and avoid possible root infection from old peony soil.

Don't plant in a small hole; use one thirty inches wide and two feet deep.

Don't use fresh manure and, better, use no manure, unless it is black and decomposed.

Don't let any fertilizer come in contact with roots in any appreciable quantity. Mix it with soil.

Don't transplant all your peonies at once. They are liable not to bloom the following year. Spread transplanting over several years.

Don't plant in soil too light or too stiff. Make clay friable with sand and humus and haul garden loam in too sandy locations. A rather heavy clay soil produces the best blooms.

Don't plant too close to trees or shrubbery where robber roots will take away moisture and food.

Don't leave parts of old roots in peony beds when transplanting, they may sprout and cause confusion as to variety, after new plants have been arranged.

Do's

Do remove seed pods and stems after blooming; this conserves the vitality of the plant. Do remember to look at field-grown peonies in a good nursery while in bloom next spring for selection of new plants. Best results are received from field selection as against selection from cut flower displays or catalogue.

Do remember that an expensive peony may not be a fine peony. It may be a new variety of questionable merit. Good old varieties may be cheap because of large production.

Do remember that a peony is an investment for years—buy carefully. Plant well. Handle carefully to protect from injury before planting. Peonies need a sunny location. They will bloom in medium soil but respond to well-prepared soil.

Prepare the holes in advance and if possible in a new location. The lower twelve inches of the hole should be filled with friable soil well mixed with perfectly rotted manure

and coarse ground raw bone. This slow-acting material is for the future growth of the plant when its new roots shall have reached into it.

Tamp this layer of soil well and *soak it several days before planting*.

Now prepare the top soil with several handfuls of wood ashes, one of fine ground steamed bone, a bucket or two of commercial humus and sprinkle well with hydrated lime or a few handfuls of ground limestone.

If possible two people should dig against each other in removing the old plant. Watch this operation in a nursery where trees and shrubbery are dug with a ball. Remove as large a ball of earth as possible. Stay away

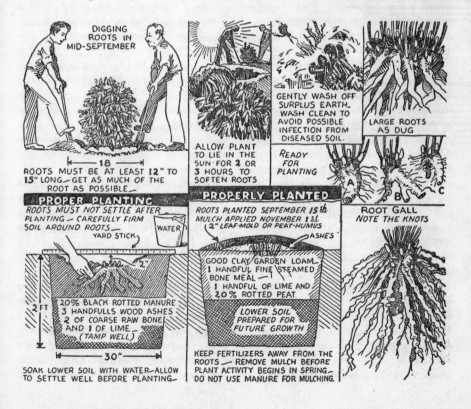

DIGGING ROOTS IN MID-SEPTEMBER

ROOTS MUST BE AT LEAST 12" TO 15" LONG—GET AS MUCH OF THE ROOT AS POSSIBLE.

ALLOW PLANT TO LIE IN THE SUN FOR 2 OR 3 HOURS TO SOFTEN ROOTS

GENTLY WASH OFF SURPLUS EARTH. WASH CLEAN TO AVOID POSSIBLE INFECTION FROM DISEASED SOIL.

READY FOR PLANTING

LARGE ROOTS AS DUG

PROPER PLANTING
ROOTS MUST NOT SETTLE AFTER PLANTING—CAREFULLY FIRM SOIL AROUND ROOTS—YARD STICK

WATER

20% BLACK ROTTED MANURE 3 HANDFULLS WOOD ASHES 2 OF COARSE RAW BONE AND 1 OF LIME (TAMP WELL)

SOAK LOWER SOIL WITH WATER—ALLOW TO SETTLE WELL BEFORE PLANTING—

PROPERLY PLANTED
ROOTS PLANTED SEPTEMBER 15th MULCH APPLIED NOVEMBER 1st. 2" LEAF-MOLD OR PEAT-HUMUS

ASHES

GOOD CLAY GARDEN LOAM— 1 HANDFUL FINE STEAMED BONE MEAL— 1 HANDFUL OF LIME AND 20% ROTTED PEAT

LOWER SOIL PREPARED FOR FUTURE GROWTH

KEEP FERTILIZERS AWAY FROM THE ROOTS— REMOVE MULCH BEFORE PLANT ACTIVITY BEGINS IN SPRING— DO NOT USE MANURE FOR MULCHING.

ROOT GALL NOTE THE KNOTS

from stem 15 to 18 inches. Use forks
—not spades. Go as deep as possible.

When dug, the roots will be brittle.
Allow the ball to be exposed to sun
and wind a few hours until tops wilt.
Roots will then be more pliable.

Wash off earth with a hose spray,
until thoroughly clean. Cut back tops
to two inches.

Examine roots for diseases; if they
have any, they will be knotted or
rotted. Disease is usually indicated
in advance by the sickly color of the
foliage—thin stalks and curled leaves.
In this case the smaller roots should
be removed to a large extent and the
plant carefully washed of all old soil.
Immerse in hot water (120 Fahren-
heit) for thirty minutes, then plant
in a new location. This trouble
is caused by a soil parasite. A
new location gives the plant a new
chance.

Bend the large clump carefully to
find weakest part and divide there.
Cut with a strong sharp knife. Then
subdivide each section into strong
roots having four or five eyes. Rub
cuts with powdered charcoal. Roots
without eyes are worthless.

As the crown of the plant must remain at exactly two inches from the
surface, it is most essential that all
soil be firmed with the fingers, fists
and trowel handle to avoid later
settling. Water as planting proceeds
to settle earth. Use a yardstick to
keep depth exact.

A root planted too deeply may not
bloom next year and one too shallow
may suffer winter injury. Plant the
more delicate colors in somewhat
shaded places; give the plants protection from the wind in exposed
spots. Also in selecting roots secure

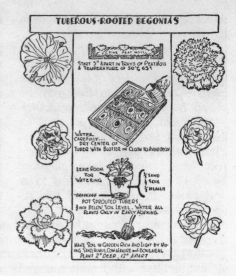

early and late blooming varieties to
prolong the blooming season.

**Peruvian Daffodil (Ismene or Hy-
menocallis calathina):** This is an old
garden favorite which has returned
to popularity. It is a member of the
amaryllis family and its large white
flowers suggest the relationship. The
broad strap foliage is valuable as a
garden accent after the flowers are
past. In clumps of six or a dozen it is
effective in front of dark shrubs and
evergreens.

Planted in May or June six inches
deep in any good garden soil, it
flowers quickly. The bulbs should be
dug before a hard frost and stored in
a cool dry place. The heavy roots
must not be injured or removed until
dry. It gives rich reward for the small
amount of care necessary in its handling and growth, multiplies rapidly
and is an effective cut flower.

Tritoma (Red Hot Poker): Strictly
not a bulbous plant, this is a half-
hardy subject, growing well in rather
light, sandy, well-drained soils. It can

Dwarf marigolds are effective "fillers" for both foliage and flowers.

Zinnias range in height from one to three feet and in color from white to yellow, orange and red. No garden annual is more striking in bold masses.

Among the most beautiful of all summer flowers are those from tuber-rooted begonias, shade-loving warm weather plants. The blossoms take the forms of roses, carnations and camellias, as well as frilled and ruffled types.

be planted out quite early in the spring in well-enriched soil, and will grow very vigorously and flower profusely, even after severe frost in the fall. When the flowers have been killed by frost tie up the long leaves over the center of the plant, as this tends to shelter the crown and keeps out any moisture, and cover the whole plant with leaves or strawy manure to the depth of ten or twelve inches; then place over the plant a box or barrel, which will further protect it. This may be removed early in the spring. Where the winters are very severe the plants may be taken up and planted in a box, to be stored in the cellar during the winter months.

Tuberous Begonia: A beautiful plant which deserves more recognition from the average gardener is the tuberous-rooted begonia. Few flowers are more easily grown and it has the added advantage of growing in partial shade where other blooming plants are not at their best.

The tuberous-rooted, which are quite different from other begonias, are divided into two general classes, single and double.

They come in such a wide range of form and color that they resemble and also rival in beauty Roses, Waterlilies, Camellias, Primulas, Carnations, Gardenias, Narcissus, and many others.

All members of the begonia family are natives of the jungle and, in varying degree, need its light soil rich in leaf mold and slightly acid. They are not swamp plants, so although the soil must be moist at all times, it should be well drained, never soggy. The conditions of the jungle as to light, sun, and air also apply. Total

shade will not do, but shade from direct noon sun (10 to 3 o'clock) is absolutely necessary. Ventilation is also essential, but protection from strong winds is required. The stems are tender, and must be staked in almost any exposed position.

They are profuse bloomers in anything even approximating their needs. The single varieties often have blooms up to six inches across and doubles up to five inches. Colors are variations in red, pink, crimson, yellow, orange, and white. It is rare to find two blooms of exactly the same shade. The foliage is rich velvety crinkled and prettier than that of any other begonia.

They may be grown from seed planted in a greenhouse in January or February, but for the amateur it is far better to purchase tubers. Considering that they last for years, these are quite cheap. They may be planted directly out of doors after all danger of frost is past, but a much longer blooming period can be obtained from a start indoors. Some gardeners plant them in trays of loose soil about a month before outdoor planting. Unless the tubers show signs of growth when received, the amateur may be confused as to which is the top. It is essential that they be planted with the concave top side up.

The best way to start is in trays of fine peat moss. First dampen the peat, then place the flat or bottom side of the tubers in little depressions in the peat, three inches apart. Firm them down so that only a little of the tuber remains out of the soil.

The concave top of the tuber will decay quickly if any water is allowed to remain in the depression. Water must be poured on the peat only. If any drops fall into the top of the tuber, they should be soaked out with cloth or blotting paper.

The tray should be placed in a warm spot (60 to 80 degrees). Light is not necessary until the little pink sprouts begin to show. Then the plants need a sunny window and a uniform temperature of 50 to 65 degrees. They may be left in the peat tray until they have made good top growth if they are to be planted directly outside, which is not practical in most localities until early June, as they are strictly warm weather plants. If they are to be planted directly outside from the sprouting tray, they should be started indoors about May 1.

The best way, however, is to transplant them into small pots when they have four leaves. Those that go outside can then be planted without root disturbance, and those for potting into slightly larger pots. Crowding of roots seems to make better top growth. If they are pot grown they may be started about April 1 and be well on their way to bloom before being planted out of doors in beds, window boxes, or hanging baskets. In transplanting from the tray, shake gently the ball of peat which clings to the roots, and plant with most of it still in place.

These plants will grow in open beds on the north side of the house, or under trees whose roots are not too greedy and whose branches are cut off for a considerable distance above the ground. They will be found very useful to fill out the semi-shaded end of the perennial border. Unlike most plants which profit from a frequent change of location, begonias seem to do best in the same bed year after year, if it is enriched each season with cow manure and bone meal. Plant them two inches deep and 10 to 12 inches apart.

After growth has been well established in outdoor beds a mulch of oak leaves, peat moss, garden humus or thoroughly exhausted hotbed manure will help. This is spaded in the following year. Soak them thoroughly about once a week in the morning only. They also profit indoors and out from a weekly application of weak liquid manure.

Upright growing kinds are used for beds but trailing kinds are obtainable to add variety to porch boxes and hanging baskets.

In the late season be careful to remove all dying stems or leaves, as these cause decay to spread to the tubers. Two weeks before frost is expected, take up the tubers with a little soil attached. When the tops have wilted remove them, also cleaning off the soil. Cool, dry storage in slat-bottomed trays at about 45 degrees until the following spring will insure years of productiveness. They are very susceptible to decay and dry storage is essential. Dusting with powdered charcoal is said to help.

Tuberose: Fragrant summer flowering bulb requiring little care. Plant outdoors about May 15th after danger of frost is past, setting bulb one inch deep; or bulbs may be started indoors in pots in April for early bloom. They need rich soil and plenty of moisture and warmth. Flowers are produced in profusion from July to September on two-foot spikes.

Dig after frost and store in cool

cellar. Some prefer to buy fresh stock each year—very inexpensive.

Only largest size bulbs will bloom and this but once. In digging numerous bulblets will be found which, if dried and planted in spring (six inches apart), will attain size enough to bloom the following year.

The variegated varieties can be kept from year to year as they are grown for leaf beauty and edging of the flower beds.

For vines growing from bulbs see Chapter IX, "Vines."

WINTERING HALF HARDY BULBS

Many half hardy bulbs from various parts of the world are available for summer bloom. The list includes lesser used bulbs such as Ixia, Sparaxis, Brodiaea, Calochortus (Mariposa-lily), Alstroemeria, Gloxinia, Incarvillea, Watsonia, Sprekelia and the more popular Montbretias, St. Brigid Anemones, Ranunculus, and Bulbous Iris.

They are usually handled as annuals, being planted in the spring and stored over the winter. It is only by intense cultivation in spring and early summer that they can be pushed into blooming.

They come from warmer countries where the summer is longer and the winter milder than ours. Because of the time we must wait to get them out in the spring, the blooming season of many of them becomes very short.

We show below a method (successful with many) of planting them in the fall and getting an early start in the spring.

Plant them in frames in soil as described for their needs elsewhere herein. The frames are four or more inches deep and must surround the bulbs well; about one inch remains above ground. A box of boards with a cleated slot to fit over this frame is placed above them after the ground is frozen. This box is filled with hardwood leaves and covered with boards to exclude the sun and water but admit the air to keep the leaves dry.

When severe weather is past this mulch is removed and the boards replaced with a sash. Be sure to give the ventilation necessary in all forcing frames. More boards are attached as the plant grows toward blooming size, and the protection is continued (especially at night) until warm weather is definitely established.

Some half hardy are mentioned in the list of outdoor bulbs and in addition the following are recommended:

Anemones and Ranunculus: Taken together because their culture is quite similar. Much used for cut flowers. Anemones grow 8 to 12 inches; and prefer the sun; Ranunculus are taller and do best in partial shade. They are half hardy and should be wintered in a frame.

Plant in early November so that no top growth will be made before

WINTERING HALF HARDY BULBS

POULTRY WIRE TO HOLD MULCH IN PLACE

TEMPERARY FRAME TO SHELTER BULBS

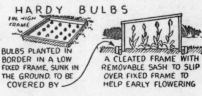

BULBS PLANTED IN BORDER IN A LOW FIXED FRAME, SUNK IN THE GROUND. TO BE COVERED BY—

A CLEATED FRAME WITH REMOVABLE SASH TO SLIP OVER FIXED FRAME TO HELP EARLY FLOWERING

spring. Tall top growth will winter-kill or be smothered by mulching, weakening or killing the plant. Spring planting means later blooming. Cover three inches deep, six inches apart. (See indoor culture, Chapter XXII.)

Ixia and Sparaxis: Gorgeous plants —see that soil is well drained or they will winterkill. See cultural directions for Cape Bulbs under House Plants, Chapter XXII.

Alstroemeria (Chilian-lily): A very fine lily-like flower, rose-white to deep orange, flowering from July to September, stems two feet high. Excellent for the cutting garden, fairly hardy. May be planted two feet apart, six inches deep in October or early spring. See Protection for Half Hardy Bulbs, above, also cultural directions under House Plants, Chapter XXII.

CHAPTER XIII

THE ROCK GARDEN

Flower in the crannied wall,
I pluck you out of the crannies;
Hold you here, root and all, in my hand,
Little flower—but if I could understand
What you are, root and all, and all in all,
I should know what God and man is.
—TENNYSON.

Rock gardens are unique in that they maintain our interest the year around. Some of the plants bloom as early as February and some as late as December. Because it takes so little space and is readily adapted to any contour a rock garden fits into many a home setting. Combined with water gardening in a small pool it is one of the most interesting of garden features. While few of the plants may be used for cut flowers, a careful selection will insure a continuous

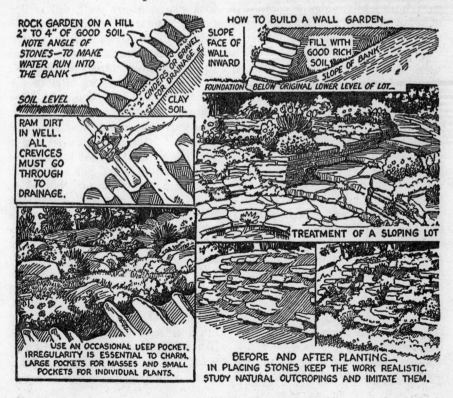

ROCK GARDEN ON A HILL 2" TO 4" OF GOOD SOIL NOTE ANGLE OF STONES—TO MAKE WATER RUN INTO THE BANK

2" CINDERS OR GRAVEL FOR DRAINAGE

SOIL LEVEL

CLAY SOIL

RAM DIRT IN WELL. ALL CREVICES MUST GO THROUGH TO DRAINAGE.

HOW TO BUILD A WALL GARDEN

SLOPE FACE OF WALL INWARD

FILL WITH GOOD RICH SOIL

SLOPE OF BANK

FOUNDATION BELOW ORIGINAL LOWER LEVEL OF LOT

TREATMENT OF A SLOPING LOT

USE AN OCCASIONAL DEEP POCKET. IRREGULARITY IS ESSENTIAL TO CHARM. LARGE POCKETS FOR MASSES AND SMALL POCKETS FOR INDIVIDUAL PLANTS.

BEFORE AND AFTER PLANTING. IN PLACING STONES KEEP THE WORK REALISTIC. STUDY NATURAL OUTCROPINGS AND IMITATE THEM.

bloom, and the foliage of many of them is as beautiful as the flowers themselves. In order to be at its best a rock garden should be almost covered with plants; a mound with a few petunias is not a rock garden; it is more likely to be an eyesore.

The first essential to success is the careful selection of the site. This should be a sunny location since but few plants suitable for a rock garden thrive in shade. If no slope is available a low mound may be constructed against a wall in the corner or at the edge of garden plan. Mounds made in the center of a lawn should be avoided. Drainage is absolutely necessary for success. Our illustration shows how to treat a rock garden on a hill, which is composed of heavy clay soil. In this instance the topsoil should be stripped off, if it is worth saving, and composted with some good humus or well-rotted manure; work in some sand and have the soil perfectly light and friable before using.

Remember, you cannot reach under the rocks and condition the soil when it has once been placed. See that it contains plenty of vegetable matter before using. If necessary, bring in a load or some barrowfuls of rich soil with which to build a rock garden "for keeps." It is better to build one square yard with the proper soil than a larger one with the improper soil. Avoid excessive chemical fertilization. See that the stones extend back into the soil and are tilted at a slight angle so that any rain falling on them will run back into the ground.

Place the stones irregularly with good size pockets of soil between.

Leave out a stone once in a while to make the larger pockets. Irregularity is essential. A rock garden must not look like masonry wall, unless you are building a wall garden, and even then, broken courses add to the charm. Enough stone must be used to keep the ground from washing, but by using smaller pieces of stone between to block these washes a large amount of dirt can safely be exposed. The idea is to use as few stones as possible for the effect desired and to use this material so that it looks like a natural formation. For instance, a limestone rock garden in connection with a pool and waterfall should look like the ledges in creek beds, while a hillside rock planting should look like the natural outcropping of limestone in hills.

A wall garden is essentially artificial and need not be an imitation of any natural setting. However, an appearance of ruggedness and rustic effect is essential; it must not look like a brick wall. Decide what you want the rock work to look like; spend your efforts toward that end.

The material to be used will, of course, depend upon what is readily obtainable. Limestone or well-worn rock of any kind is very good. However, it should not be so soft that it will crumble away in a few years. Boulders properly handled make a good moraine garden, but they should not be used for ledge effect. Avoid absolutely broken concrete and building rubbish. Do not build a rock garden if you feel it necessary to use these materials. Better, in every way, to raise the plants without the use of stone.

After drainage the next essential is firm soil. The soil between the crevices should be firmly compacted. Some plants have a tendency to work themselves out of the ground, or expose their roots.

Small pieces of stone left from the construction work should be saved and placed around the roots of plants, both to conserve the moisture and to keep them in the ground. Additional soil must be added from time to time to protect the root systems.

As to the selection of plants: Shade plants will bear sunshine, whereas, sun-loving plants will not do well even in partial shade. It is, therefore, necessary that the major part of the area be in the open, and that a careful study be made so as to plant only shade-loving plants in the unexposed portions. Most plants do not like lime, and this should be avoided, although a mulching with limestone chips firmed into the top part of the exposed soil has a tendency to keep it from drying out and adds to the naturalizing of the plant. Some rock garden plants like moderately alkaline soil and others acid soil. Ordinary soil will do for the alkaline-loving, but the acid-loving plant should have soil composted with peat moss or treated with Aluminum Sulphate.

Visit places where rock or alpine plants grow, or are offered for sale in bloom. Consult the grower as to whether the plant is a rampant or a slow grower. Attempt to group them according to foliage, color of bloom and also as to whether the rampant growers will crowd out the slow-growing plants. Trailing plants should have room to spread or hang down from projecting ledges. Do not be afraid to weed out the quick growers and keep them from strangling the others.

BUILDING A WALL GARDEN

The best time to build a wall garden is in the late summer or early fall.

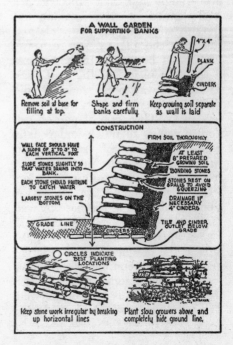

A WALL GARDEN
FOR SUPPORTING BANKS

Remove soil at base for filling at top.

Shape and firm banks carefully.

Keep growing soil separate as wall is laid

CONSTRUCTION

WALL FACE SHOULD HAVE A SLOPE OF 2" TO 3" TO EACH VERTICAL FOOT

SLOPE STONES SLIGHTLY SO THAT WATER DRAINS INTO BANK.

EACH STONE SHOULD PROTRUDE TO CATCH WATER

LARGEST STONES ON THE BOTTOM

GRADE LINE

CINDERS

FIRM SOIL THOROUGHLY

AT LEAST 8" PREPARED GROWING SOIL

BONDING STONES

STONES REST ON SPALLS TO AVOID SQUEEZING

DRAINAGE IF NECESSARY 4" CINDERS

TILE AND CINDER OUTLET BELOW GRADE

CIRCLES INDICATE BEST PLANTING LOCATIONS

Keep stone work irregular by breaking up horizontal lines

Plant slow growers above and completely hide ground line.

The work then will have a chance to settle during the following winter and any damage can be repaired before the plants become too large.

The plants will also have the cool fall weather to adjust themselves to their new environment and be ready to make a fine display the following season.

To get the best effect, rocks must come into the garden in a natural-appearing manner. If you have a gentle slope, which supports an easily grown lawn, do not deliberately cut it up to form a rockery or wall.

If, however, you have a sudden change of grade or a steep bank, which washes and is hard to keep presentable, it may be best to turn it into a wall garden.

Study the entire situation from every angle and then proceed on a well-planned program, staking out the site, collecting the materials, and selecting the plants. You can use larger and better established plants if they are placed as the wall rises. The wrong way to use stone is to dig holes in a slope and try to insert a few rocks. This type of garden seldom amounts to much and usually ends up in an unsightly mess. A good wall or rock garden must be built from below the ground up to the top.

The higher the wall the larger the stones should be at the base. A wall three feet high may have stones 12 inches square if there are some thick ones at the bottom and a few larger ones to use as bonding stones. Five feet is the maximum height at which these planted walls look or act well. The taller ones need stones 18 inches

square for at least half their height. It will be readily understood that stones at the top do not need to be as large and heavy as at the bottom.

The soil in which the plants grow should be open enough to allow excess water to drain through readily, but must hold water properly for plant use during dry spells. This writer has produced beautiful results with either a base of black soil from the woodland or good, dark, friable loam from the garden. This is spread on the ground in a three-inch layer and over it is spread one-inch of ⅜-inch screen stone chips. Now comes two inches of fine-texture peat moss. As this is acid it must have about one-half pound of lime to the bushel. Domestic peat or pure leaf mold is just as good. An inch of sand completes the formula. Mix all of it together well. Good soil can be bought by the load and stone chips, lime, and sand can be ordered from a building supply house. Make up plenty of this soil mixture; any left over is fine for dressing other beds or plantings.

Any form of rock gardening requires more drainage than ordinary plantings. Also, all structures should have solid foundations. In the case of a wall on ordinary soil we are able to somewhat combine these two. Dig down approximately a foot and lay a tile on the firmly compacted bottom. This tile should run the length of the wall, but if no outlet is available at either end it should be connected with one to the front. Compacted cinders should be placed over this to approximately four inches below the grade line.

If you are building against a clay

bank or location damp in ordinary weather, a four-inch layer of cinders should run up this bank as shown in our picture. The first stone should be a large, heavy one and should set at least four inches below grade on top of the cinders. If the soil is loose sand or gravel, the first stone should be set on a concrete footing, one foot below grade, and built up with other stones set in cement mortar to the soil level.

The other building details are explained in the pictures. First, grade your banks and firm them well. Then start the building, compacting the soil by pounding it in place behind each stone as it is laid. To keep materials separate use a board as shown. Fill in one side of the board with cinders and on the other with soil. After tamping each side well remove the plank and tamp again. This method can also be applied to keep growing soil from mixing with the soil used for filling.

No. 1. Vigorous Plants for the Beginner's Rock Garden

Achillea tomentosa (Yarrow)
Alyssum saxatile (Goldentuft)
Anchusa myosotidiflora (Bugloss)
Aquilegia nivea (Columbine)
Arabis alpina (Rock-cress)
Asperula odorata (Woodruff)
Campanula carpatica (Bellflower)
Cerastium tomentosum (Snow-in-Summer)
Dianthus caesius (Cheddar Pink)
Dianthus deltoides (Maiden Pink)
Gypsophila repens (Creeping Gypsophila)
Helianthemum mutabile (Sunrose)
Heuchera sanguinea (Coral Bells)

Iberis sempervirens (Candytuft)
Iris pumila
Myosotis scorpioides (Forget-me-not)
Nepeta cataria (Catnip)
Phlox subulata (Moss-pink)
Primula polyantha (Primrose)
Polemonium reptans (Creeping Polemonium)
Saponaria ocymoides (Rock Soapwort)
Sedum album (White Stonecrop)
Sedum ellacombianum (Stonecrop)
Sedum reflexum (Stonecrop)
Sedum spurium coccineum (Stonecrop)
Sempervivum soboliferum (Hen and Chickens)
Sempervivum tectorum (Roof Houseleek)
Teucrium chamaedrys (Germander)
Thymus serpyllum (Thyme)
Tunica saxifraga (Coatflower)
Veronica incana (Speedwell)
Veronica teucrium (Speedwell)
Viola cornuta var. Jersey Gem

No. 2. Choice But More Difficult Rock Plants

Aethionema pulchellum (Stonecress)
Anemone pulsatilla (Pasqueflower)
Aubrietia deltoidea (Purple- or False-rockcress)
Bergenia cordifolia
Campanula garganica (Bellflower)
Campanula rotundifolia (Harebell)
Ceratostigma plumbaginoides
Dicentra exima (Wild Bleeding-heart)
Hypericum repens
Mazus reptans
Myosotis alpestris (Alpine Forget-me-not)

Papaver nudicaule (Iceland Poppy)
Primula japonica (Japanese Primrose)
Saxifraga macnabiana
Sedum dasyphyllum (Stonecrop)
Sedum middendorfianum (Stonecrop)
Sedum sieboldi (Stonecrop)
Sempervivum arachnoideum (Spiderweb Houseleek)
Sempervivum blandum
Silene alpestris (Alpine Catchfly)
Silene maritima
Talinum calycinum
Thymus serpyllum var. languinosus (Creeping Thyme)
Trollius laxus (Globeflower)
Veronica pectinata (Speedwell)
Viola pedata (Birdsfoot Violet)

No. 3. Dwarf Shrubs for Rock Gardens

Abelia grandiflora
Berberis thunbergi minor (Barberry)
Cotoneaster horizontalis
Potentilla fruticosa (Cinquefoil)
Stephanandra flexuosa

No. 4. Dwarf Evergreens for Rock Gardens

Chamaecyparis obtusa nana (Dwarf Hinoki Cypress)
Daphne cneorum (Garlandflower)
Euonymus radicans (Evergreen Wintercreeper)
Euonymus radicans minimus (Dwarf Wintercreeper)
Juniperus horizontalis (Creeping Juniper)
Pinus mugo compaeta (Swiss Mountain Pine)
Taxus cuspidata nana (Dwarf Japanese Yew)

No. 5. Plants Suitable for the Shaded Rock Garden

Most rock garden and alpine plants demand virtually full sun, thereby indicating that a sunny situation is best for the average rock garden. Circumstances, however, may be such that the garden must be placed in the shade, and then the following plants, a number of them native wild flowers, will be found satisfactory:

Adonis vernalis (Spring Adonis)
Ajuga reptans (Carpet Bugle)
Allium moly (Lilyleek)
Anchusa myosotidiflora (Bugloss)
Anemone canadensis (Meadow Anemone)
Aquilegia coerulea (Colorado Columbine)
Arabis alpina (Rock-cress)
Arenaria balearica (Corsieau Sandwort)
Arenaria montana (Sandwort)
Asarum canadense (Wild Ginger)
Asperula cynanchica (Woodruff)
Asperula odorata (Sweet Woodruff)
Asplenium trichomanes (Maidenhair Spleenwort)
Camassia esculenta (Camass)
Campanula rotundifolia (Bluebell)
Cypripedium parviflora pubescens (Lady's Slipper)
Delphinium tricorne (Larkspur)
Dentaria diphylla (Toothwort)
Dicentra eximia (Fringed Bleedingheart)
Dodecatheon meadia (Shooting Star)
Epimedium macranthum
Hepatica triloba
Hosta (Funkia) (Plantainlily)
Helleborus niger (Christmas-rose)
Iris cristata (Crested Iris)
Mentha requieni (Mint) (moist soil)

Mertensia virginica (Virginia Bluebells)
Mitchella repens (Partridgeberry) (acid soil)
Myosotis scorpioides semperflorens (Forget-me-not)
Oxalis violacea (Violet Woodsorrel)
Pachysandra terminalis (Japanese Pachysandra)
Phlox divaricata (Blue Phlox)
Phlox subulata (Moss-pink)
Polypodium vulgare (Common Polypody)
Polystichum acrostichoides (Christmas Fern)
Primula (Various) (Primrose)
Pulmonaria saccharata (Bethlehem Lungwort)
Sanguinaria canadensis (Bloodroot)
Saxifraga umbrosa (Londonpride Saxifrage)
Saxifraga virginiensis (Virginia Saxifrage)
Sedum nevi (Stonecrop)
Sedum pulchellum (Stonecrop)
Sedum ternatum (Stonecrop)
Silene caroliniana (Wild-pink)
Silene virginica (Fire-pink)
Trillium grandiflorum (Snow or Large-flowered Trillium)
Trollius europaeus (Globeflower)
Viola (Various) (Violet)

No. 6. Lime-loving Rock Plants

Anemone alpina
Anemone hepatica (Windflower)
Anemone pulsatilla (Pasqueflower)
Aquilegia alpina (Columbine)
Aubrietia deltoidea (Common Aubrietia)
Campanula caespitosa (Bellflower)
Dianthus alpinus (Pink)
Erinus alpinus (Alpine Liver-balsam)

Gypsophila repens (Babysbreath)
Leontopodium (Edelweiss)
Saxifraga species
Sempervivum (Houseleek)
Silene acaulis (Cushion-pink)

No. 7. Ground Cover Plants for Rock Gardens

Ajuga reptans (Carpet Bugle)
Arabis alpina (Rock Cress)
Campanula carpatica (Bellflower)
Cerastium tomentosum (Snow-in-summer)
Dianthus deltoides (Maidenpink)
Euonymus radicans minimus
Myosotis scorpioides
Nepeta mussini (Catnip)
Phlox subulata (Moss-pink)
Saponaria ocymoides (Rock Soapwort)
Sedum album (Stonecrop)
Sedum spurium (Stonecrop)
Thymus serpyllum (Thyme)
Veronica filiformis (Speedwell)
Veronica pectinata (Speedwell)
Veronica teucrium (Speedwell)

No. 8. Bulbs for the Rock Garden

Camassia esculenta (Camass)
Chionodoxa lucileae (Glory-of-the-snow)
Colchicum (Autumn Crocus)
Crocus (Crocus)
Eranthis hyemalis (Winter-aconite)
Fritillaria meleagris (Guinea Hen Flower)
Galanthus nivalis (Snowdrop)
Lilium tenuifolium (Coral Lily)
Muscari botryoides (Grape-hyacinth)
Narcissus (smaller varieties, especially Poet's and Jonquils)
Puschkinia scilloides
Scilla bifolia (Squill)

Scilla hispanica (Spanish-bluebell)
Scilla nonscripta (English-bluebell)
Scilla siberica (Siberian Squill)
Tulipa clusiana (Lady or Candy-
stick Tulip)
Tulipa greigi
Tulipa kaufmanniana

No. 9. Rock Plants for Walks and Stepping Stones

Arenaria balearica (Corsican Sand-
wort)
Arenaria verna (Tufted Sandwort)
Cymbalaria aequitriloba
Herniaria glabra (Burstwort)
Thymus serpyllum (Creeping
Thyme)

Thymus serpyllum coccineus
Thymus serpyllum lanuginosus
Veronica filiformis (Speedwell)
Veronica repens (Creeping Speed-
well)

No. 10. Rock Plants for Wet Ground

Coptis trifolia (Goldthread)
Mentha requieni (Mint)
Mimulus ringens (Monkeyflower)
Myosotis scorpioides
Primula japonica
Sedum pulchellum (Stonecrop)
Sedum ternatum (Stonecrop)
Veronica filiformis (Speedwell)
Viola blanda (Sweet White Violet)
Viola palustris (Marsh Violet)

CHAPTER XIV

THE WATER GARDEN

O star on the breast of the river!
O marvel of bloom and grace!
Did you fall right down from heaven,
Out of the sweetest place?

—BUTTS.

Today almost everyone wants a water garden. Nothing gives as much in results for the time expended as this type of gardening. Requirements are few; sunshine for the full day, rich soil and water. Running spring water should be avoided in any great quantity, as it chills the pool and retards the growth of the plant. Waterlilies are the most adaptable of plants. In five-inch pots they will start in spring, bloom and then go dormant in cold weather the same as lilies planted in larger soil containers. The difference is in the size and number of leaves and blooms.

The first thing which must be determined is the kind and the shape of the pool. This depends entirely upon the amount of effort and expenditure which the owner is willing to put forth. A very interesting garden can be made of two barrels which will support two lilies, full size, and two tubs of shallow water plants. Procure two large, solid barrels, old vinegar barrels if possible. Soak with a strong solution of sal soda to neutralize the vinegar in the wood. Mark around each barrel where you are going to cut it into two and staple a hoop of heavy galvanized wire just below the cut as shown on the next page. This will give you a deep tub and a shallow tub. Repeat with the second barrel and then sink the tubs in the ground so that the tops are just below the level of the ground and about six or seven inches apart. Edge each with stone to conceal the wood, and make a small rockery between the tubs.

The formal pool is one that follows an exact symmetrical pattern. This may be constructed by first digging a hole a little larger than the size of the pool, then erecting wooden forms much like those for a house foundation. Any round portion of the pool may be made with sheet metal forms reinforced with wood. It is advisable that all pools be thirty inches at the deepest part—never less than two feet. Fish will winter at this depth without protection. The side walls should be at least six inches in thickness and it is better to have them eight inches at the bottom. The bottom of the pool should be made six inches thick and should be sloped toward the middle and one end, so that when you empty or clean it, all the water will run to one point.

For many years, pools have been constructed with no further reinforcing than a close mesh hog wire netting. However, this is a precarious practice and although concrete reinforcing is a little intricate, most authorities recommend that three-eighths inch deformed reinforcing rods be used and spaced eight inches apart to form a network. These should be wired into the forms so as to be in the center of the concrete when poured. Care must be taken that all bars are well covered with concrete. As the top of the pool receives the most severe strain due to the pressure of ice in the winter, it is well to run two half-inch reinforcing bars around the entire pool. Place them about three to four inches from the top and keep them close to the outside surface of the wall, being sure that they are covered at all points with at least one inch of concrete. Strengthen the joints by allowing the rods to run past each other about six inches. About eight inches from the top, poke into the wall through the forms some pieces of reinforcing about ten to twelve inches long. On these may be constructed around all or a part of the pool a shelf or a ledge to form pockets of soil for shallow water aquatics.

For the amateur, the informal, irregularly shaped pool is the ideal. It is the least expensive and can be constructed without forms. Reinforcing is necessary for any good pool. First, mark out the shape of your pool with stakes, connecting them with a piece

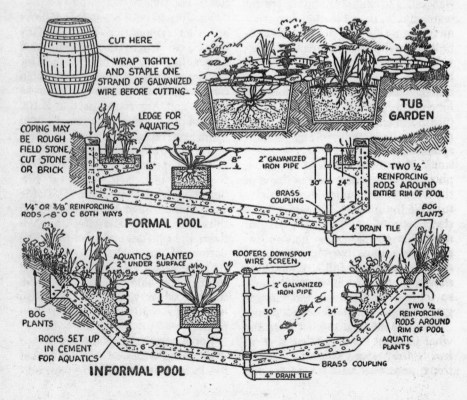

of twine or rope so that you can visualize the pool and how it will fit into the contour of your ground. Dig a hole with sloping sides and firm them and the bottom down smoothly with a tamper so as to form a good foundation for the concrete. Wet slightly with a broom dipped in a bucket of water and finish off smooth, troweling with the back of a spade. Then install reinforcing rods as advised for a formal pool. Make pool six inches bigger all the way around than the size of the pool desired and at least six inches deeper.

Best results are obtained with a mixture of one part Portland cement, two parts sharp sand and three parts washed gravel. Use just enough water to make a stiff mix. A sloppy mix destroys the effect of the cement. Better too dry than too wet.

For filling a small pool, a garden hose is usually sufficient. Therefore, no water connections need be made. However, in pools of fair size, an overflow is essential. This may be piped with sewer tile into a downspout connection on the house. In small pools, the water may be siphoned out with a hose by attaching the hose to the faucet of a laundry tub; fill the hose with water until it starts running into the pool, then remove the end from the faucet and allow it to drain into the tub. In the drawing opposite, the overflow is shown jointed in eight-inch lengths so that water level can be lowered gradually to facilitate cleaning.

What shape to make the pool and what to plant is many times a problem to the water gardener. The first thing necessary to a decision here is a little knowledge of the habits and needs of different plants.

On page 224 we show four types of formal pools with various plants suggested and identified on page 225. A novelty island pool illustrated is reached by stepping-stones. If this island is made into a rose garden bordered by such plants as alyssum it serves two purposes by giving the open location required by the roses as well as the scenic effect of the pool.

The lower diagram shows how to add a bog garden to your pool without disturbing the planting. The tub or pan may be used in the ground outside of the pool or in the pool itself.

Waterlilies need space to spread. Three feet all around the plant is the minimum and five feet each way is better. Plant everything on ledges or in boxes and prop them up with stones to the proper water depth.

This will enable you to have bog plants, shallow water aquatics, and deep water plants all in one pool. Plant lilies in strong boxes, two feet square and one foot deep or tubs made of old barrels (see page 221); first soaking the barrels with sal soda to remove acid. Eight inches below the surface is the right depth for lilies. Bog plants should have the bottom of the containers in water and shallow aquatics should be two inches under water.

A few fish should be placed in the water as well as frogs and snails. These scavengers keep out mosquitos and purify the pool.

As already advised, do not have running water in your pool to any great extent if you wish results. The plants thrive best in still, warm water.

Fountains or falls should be constructed to make a maximum of fuss with a minimum of water. A trickle of water falling eighteen inches or more gives the effect of motion desired, the same as a larger volume. Replace the evaporated water by spraying the plants after the sun has gone down in the evening. They appreciate water from the top the same as other plants. If green scum accumulates, sweep it off into the overflow pipe with a hose spray. It will soon go away. Wash off any plant lice from the leaves with a strong hose spray. If this is done in the morning, the fish will destroy many of them.

Hardy waterlilies and other aquatics may be set out any time in the spring after the weather starts to warm up and danger of freezing is over. Tropical plants, however, should not be planted until from the 20th of May to the 1st of June. If it is possible to plant them a little closer to the surface when they are small, they may be lowered as they grow larger and develop more rapidly. However, this is not necessary.

For soil to fill the boxes, three parts good garden loam mixed with one part well-rotted cow manure, plenty of bone meal and some blood meal is best. If manure is used, it should be composted with the soil several months before being put into the boxes in order that fermentation will

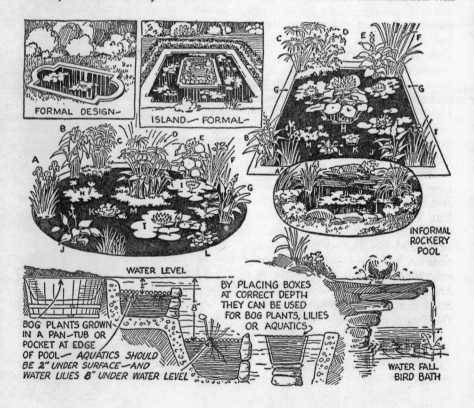

FORMAL DESIGN

ISLAND — FORMAL

INFORMAL ROCKERY POOL

WATER LEVEL

BY PLACING BOXES AT CORRECT DEPTH THEY CAN BE USED FOR BOG PLANTS, LILIES OR AQUATICS

BOG PLANTS GROWN IN A PAN—TUB OR POCKET AT EDGE OF POOL — AQUATICS SHOULD BE 2" UNDER SURFACE—AND WATER LILIES 8" UNDER WATER LEVEL

WATER FALL BIRD BATH

be over at that time. Do *not* use humus or sour soil.

Blood meal or some chemical fertilizer may be added during the plants' growing season by lowering the water to the top of the tub, making holes with a piece of pipe, inserting the fertilizer, and covering these holes with sand. This will encourage the plants to make new growth.

Waterlilies should be planted with the crown of the plant even with the surface of the soil. Cover the soil in the containers with about one to two inches of pebbles or sand but do not smother the plants with it. This will keep the pool clean.

The difference between annual and tropical plants must be understood if you are to have a really nice garden. Tropical plants are the most easily grown and give, under favorable conditions, much larger and more colorful blooms than the hardy. If you are going to the trouble to make a nice pool, a small expenditure each year will make it more beautiful and be more satisfactory than trying to run it on a strictly hardy plant basis.

The illustration on page 224 shows how plants look in the water and the sketches are more for identification than for proper setting. While shallow water aquatics may be grown out in midpool it is best to keep them close to the edges. Plants illustrated are, *Round Pool:* A—Water Iris; B—Arrowhead; C—Papyrus; D—Pickerel Rush and Umbrella-plant; E—Lotus; F—Flowering Rush; G—Pickerel-weed; H—Water-poppy; I—Waterlily; J—Velvet Leaf; K—Shell Flower; L—Water-hyacinth; M—Parrot Feather. *Rectangular Pool:* A—Water Iris; B—Arrowhead; C—Papyrus; D—Primrose-willow; E—Velvet Leaf; F—Cat-tail; G—Waterlily; H—Sacred Lotus of the Nile; I—Flowering Rush; J—Pickerel-weed; K—Shell Flower; L—Water-hyacinth.

Plants recommended for trial are: *Tropical Lilies, Night Blooming,* Juno (White), Rubra Rosea (Rosy Carmine), Bissett (Pink), *Day Blooming,* Panama-Pacific (Purple), Blue Beauty, August Koch (Blue), General Pershing (Pink). *Hardy Lilies:* Chromatella (Yellow), Marliac Rose, Gloriosa (Deep Red), Gladstone (White). *Annual Plants for Shallow Water:* Parrot Feather (bog ground cover), Water-hyacinth, Water-poppy, Primrose-willow, Papyrus, Japanese Lotus (White), Egyptian Lotus Single (Pink), Azolla and Duckweed (tiny, floating), Wild Rice (self-propagating from seed; grows 10 to 12 ft. tall). *Perennial Plants for Shallow Water:* Variegated Sweet Flag, Primrose Creeper, Cat-tail, Giant Arrowhead, Yellow and Purple Water Iris, Forget-me-nots (in pots just touching top of water), Flowering and Pickerel-weed, Water Arum.

For the damp ground at the edge of the pool use Forget-me-not, Parrot Feather, Marsh Marigold, Water Iris, Cardinal Flower, Sweet Flag and Pickerel-weed. (See lists in Chapter X, "The Flower Garden.")

CHAPTER XV

THE VEGETABLE GARDEN

Considering that perhaps the outstanding advantage of living in the country, a small town, a village or even a city suburb is that we can have a garden, it seems strange to me that so many of us limit our plantings to lawns, flowers, and other ornamentals and rely largely, if not wholly, upon canned goods, frozen foods and vegetables that we buy in markets and stores or from hucksters and market gardeners. Of these four sources, the last two are the more desirable because their products are likely to be fresher than those of the others. But all four are open to the objection that practically all the produce they sell is such as will withstand rough handling and necessarily of tougher fibre than similar goods which, grown in home gardens, do not have to be shipped or handled much.

Why Grow Our Own Vegetables?

No matter how varied an assortment modern markets can offer nowadays, and no matter how high the quality of the frozen foods that are becoming increasingly available, there are four outstanding reasons for devoting a moderate amount of our garden space to home grown crops. First, a garden can supply us with fresher vegetables than we can buy; second, it can give us most vegetables in the finest stage of development, impossible when they are bought; third, we can grow higher quality varieties than commercial growers usually attempt; and, fourth, we can grow kinds that we never, or rarely, see offered for sale.

Freshness is of prime importance in all plants whose leaves we eat raw, as lettuce, endive, garden cress. We can have them on our table before they would be large enough to gather for sale; indeed, the thinnings are as good as the more mature crops, if not better. And we can use them within a few minutes of their being gathered, while they are plump and crisp and full of the delicate, evanescent flavors that make them delicious as well as beneficial in the menu.

Stage of development, also important with salad plants, is even more so in the case of vegetables whose fruits we eat. Only the home gardener can put on his table tomatoes that have attained full ripeness on the plant; cucumbers firm with moisture and whose seeds are still soft; muskmelons gathered at just the right moment (when little cracks show between the stems and the fruits), then ripened for a day or two before being chilled and served; garden peas and sweet corn, neither immature nor too old, whose sugars and aromas have not been lost in their short journey from garden to stove to table. These two vegetables especially lose their deliciousness rapidly between gathering and using, because their sugars change into starch and other tasteless compounds. Asparagus, too, we can "snap off" so that every particle is edible instead of just a green bud at the end of a tough, woody stalk.

High quality is rarely found in commercial varieties because it is generally associated with fine texture and thin skin which do not make good shippers; it is also often found in varieties characterized by small size, long (or irregular) period of ripening, or relatively unattractive appearance, such as commercial growers are not interested in. But since we eat not only to sustain life, but also to get reasonable pleasure while doing so, we can well confine our selection of sorts to grow to those definitely suited to the small, amateur garden.

When seed catalogues do not specifically point them out, we can recognize the commercial kinds (and avoid them) by descriptive words and phrases that suggest business returns. Such, for instance, as "immense cropper," "highly prolific," "excellent shipper," "stands up well," "extra early," "long keeper," and so on. We will look instead for varieties said to be "ideal for the home garden," "with long season of ripening," "when served, everybody wants more," "of fine texture," "exquisite richness," "high, aromatic flavor," and the like.

As to actual kinds of vegetables, here adventure enters into gardening, for among those we have never been able to buy, we may discover some worthy acquisitions to our diet. Though I had seen broccoli listed in seedsmen's catalogues for decades, I never grew it, saw it growing, or even ate it until two or three years ago; now it is one of my regular annual crops. The so-called Jerusalem artichoke (a native American plant!) is never seen in the markets, I imagine, and rarely in gardens; yet it is one of the most delectable of vegetables escalloped or steamed and served with hollandaise or cream sauce. How many gardeners have tried the newer Chinese vegetables—chi-hi-li or celery cabbage; pe-tsai or Chinese cabbage, and wong-bok, which as yet has no American name? Have *you* ever grown the Italian introductions, finocchio, pomodoro, rucola, cicoria, basilico, escarolle or fagiuli? Why not buy a packet of seed of one or more of them this year and follow the directions printed on it? You may discover something!

When making up a list of vegetable kinds (*not* varieties) to grow, it is a good plan to follow a typical seed catalogue index so as not to overlook any. You might use a filing card for each kind and under the name (bean, corn, pea, etc.) write the variety or varieties you plan to grow and any cultural notes. Your choice will depend on: First, the family appetite; second, the amount of space the plants require (you'll probably omit winter squash and pumpkin); third, those that you can obtain in just as good quality elsewhere—onions, potatoes and winter cabbage; fourth, your ability and willingness to meet the requirements of certain fussy sorts or others especially susceptible to pests or diseases.

Some Good Garden Practices

In amateur gardening especially, anything that will save time, space or work is well worth adopting. Here are some methods that I have found of special value in my small area, some of them regular practices of successful market gardeners:

In small gardens, the various distances between rows usually recommended by professional writers will cause more bother than benefit however economical they are when several hundred rows of each vegetable are grown. Instead, the unit system of measurement between rows will save both time and space for you. It consists of using the narrowest recommended distance for small growing crops as the basis for all other distances. Radishes are often sown in rows only nine inches apart, so this distance, even though rather narrow, can be used. Crops that require more space are set twice, thrice or more times this basic distance apart. Perhaps the greatest advantage of this plan is that it avoids the necessity of changing the setting of blades and teeth on a wheelhoe in cultivating.

In large gardens it is often convenient and advisable to group the vegetables so the long season kinds are in one area, the short ones in another; those that require similar culture, and those that mature at about the same time by themselves, and so on. In a little garden this sort of thing is less effective because there may be space for only one row of each kind. In such areas some sort of "double cropping" method as used by commercial growers will be more serviceable. There are four of these.

Companion cropping is a system in which two (or more) crops that reach edible maturity at different times are sown or planted out in alternate rows, or as alternate plants in the same row. For instance, in early spring spinach and beets may be sown with their rows side by side, alternating; or lettuce plants can alternate with cabbage plants in the main rows with rows of radishes between. In the former case the spinach will be gathered in late May or early June leaving the beets in full possession of the ground; in the latter case the radishes will all have been gathered within six weeks, and the last of the lettuce a week or two later, after which the cabbages have the ground to themselves.

The same plan may be used in late spring or early summer with tender vegetables, tomato plants or sweet corn alternating with bush beans, for instance; or a crop such as pepper or eggplant that would be killed by the first frost alternating with a hardy late one, as winter cabbage or brussels sprouts. Another combination would be of a long season, hardy kind (parsnips) with a short season hardy kind (carrots).

Succession cropping is the plan by which quick maturing crops are sown or planted in an area by themselves, and, after being gathered, are replaced by another crop. Spinach or early spring peas might be followed by bush beans sown in late spring or early summer, and these in turn by turnips or winter radish sown in midsummer for autumn and winter use. This would make possible three crops in one season from the same area. Sometimes companion and succession cropping methods are combined, as when radishes, lettuce and early cabbage are followed by a midsummer sowing of rutabagas, carrots or round beets, a four crop combination.

Partnership cropping is illustrated when pumpkins, winter squash, cucumbers or melons are sown in a patch of sweet corn, or when a late maturing corn and pole beans are sown together, the latter climbing up and being supported by the former.

Marker cropping consists of dropping radish (or other quick-sprouting) seeds at three or four-inch intervals in rows of such slow sprouting seeds as parsnip and carrot, or those whose seedlings are difficult to see when they first come up, as onion and beet. The radishes, appearing above ground quickly, indicate exactly where the rows are so that cultivation may be started without delay and the first crop of weeds destroyed while very young.

Grouping the Vegetable Kinds

Before we can make a workable plan that will combine the advantage of these cropping systems, we must group the various vegetables according to the times their seeds must be sown or their plants (previously started in a greenhouse, hotbed, coldframe or elsewhere) set out.

We must also bear in mind the time each will require to reach edible maturity, the amount of space each one will need, and the amount of watering and feeding it normally re-

Store or garden?—Compare prime vegetables with jammed crates.

Good shipper and keeper, huge yields, easy to grow.

Extra fine quality delicious, best for home garden.

"Companion cropping—C=cabbage L=lettuce, R=radish

Put tall crops at north end—Run narrow row crops N and S.

"Partnership" cropping—Late corn supporting pole beans.

quires. All this is less complicated than it sounds!

Here is one grouping according to the time the crop occupies the ground:

Annual Crops: 1. *Early spring to late spring:* Forcing radish, early lettuce, onion sets, peppergrass (or garden cress), mustard, fetticus (lamb's lettuce, or corn salad), orach, spinach. 2. *Long season vegetables,* early spring to late fall: Parsnip, salsify, scorzonera, chickory, chard, celeriac, leek, parsley. 3. *Early spring to midsummer or early fall:* Beet, early cabbage, long rooted radish, carrot, onion, kohl-rabi, early celery, pea, turnip. 4. *Late spring to early fall* (killed by frost): Tomato, okra, pepper, eggplant, sweet potato, bean, muskmelon, watermelon, pumpkin, squash, husk tomato (ground cherry), martynia, luffa, zit-kwa, gherkin. 5. *Midsummer to late fall:* Turnip, rutabaga, beet, carrot, kohlrabi, broccoli, brussels sprouts, kale, cauliflower, endive, late cabbage, late celery. 6. *Late summer to late fall:* Lettuce, spinach, round seeded pea, winter radish, forcing radish, mustard garden cress, onion sets. 7. *To be sown in late summer or early fall for late fall or early spring use:* Dandelion, spinach, fetticus, sorrel.

Perennial Crops: Besides the annual crops mentioned there are several perennials, asparagus and rhubarb being the best known in home gardens. Others are French (or globe) artichoke, dock, cardoon, sea kale and Jerusalem (or American) artichoke. They belong in a separate class because they occupy the same area permanently. But, even so, they need not exclude quick maturing partnership crops which can be sown broadcast among them in early spring, and allowed to take their chances; these mature and are used before the perennials need the space. Among those often grown in asparagus beds (and why not among other perennials?) are spinach, lettuce, radishes and early turnips. If, in late summer, seed of spinach or corn salad is scattered over the asparagus bed, enough of the hardy seedlings should survive the winter to give an early cutting the following spring several weeks before a spring-sown crop could be expected.

The Vegetable Garden Plan

After trying various ways of making and using a plan, I find the following the most convenient and time-saving. Like most simple things it is harder to describe than to do.

On narrow strips of paper write the names of the vegetables to be grown in each row; the number of days they will take to reach usable size, and the approximate dates they should be sown. Use a different colored paper for each group of vegetables, blue for long season; yellow for short season, early sown; red for hot weather crops, and so on. When all are written, arrange and re-arrange them on a table until you have worked out a feasible plan like those illustrated. It will help if you first place the long season, earliest sown crops at one side of the area at twice the unit distance decided on. Between these rows alternate the short season early kinds, the "companion" vegetables, that will mature and be gathered in late spring or early summer while the others are still growing.

When the slips for these earliest sown kinds have all been placed, continue with the slips for the next series of sowings or plantings and arrange them similarly—the long season ones alternating with the short. Proceed thus until you have placed all the slips, with the "tender to frost" crops at the far side. In each case where a "marker," "partner" or "succession" crop is to be used, place the slip representing it temporarily on the main crop for that row.

After testing the workability of the arrangement by studying each row in relation, first, to what it is to contain during the whole growing season, and second, to the row on each side of it, you can make an actual plan from the slips, either by rewriting the names or pasting the slips on a large sheet of paper or cardboard. Because such a sheet is likely to be misplaced, is hard to handle out of doors, and is almost sure to blow away on a windy day, a good scheme is to draw the outline of the garden to scale on a large broad board and rule parallel lines the unit distance apart to represent spaces between rows. If done with waterproof ink this need not be done again for several years. Then you can paste the named slips exactly as you have arranged them on the table, using rubber pasting cement if possible, so that they can be removed without tearing if need arises. A hole bored in the middle of one side will make it possible to hang the plan up out of the way when not in use. The smooth, hard surface is good to write on when you want to make notes to guide your future operations. Later you can copy both plan and notes into your garden record book for permanent reference.

Crop rotation is less practicable in small gardens than in large scale farming. Nevertheless, whenever possible, group the plants that require similar cultural treatment and shift them about from year to year. The following groups can succeed one another in different seasons (or parts of the same season) according to convenience; do not let one crop of a group follow another of the same group.

1. Beans, garden peas.

2. Corn, tomato, eggplant, pepper, ground cherry (or husk tomato).

3. Brussels sprouts, broccoli, cabbage, celery, chard, collard, cress, dandelion, endive, kale, kohl-rabi, lettuce, mustard, New Zealand spinach, orach, spinach.

4. Cantaloupe, cucumber, gherkin, okra, pumpkin, squash, watermelon.

5. Beet, carrot, chicory, endive, garlic, leek, parsley, parsnip, radish, rutabaga, salsify, scorzonera, shallot, turnip.

Try to have a following crop as different as possible from the preceding one. If the two are botanically or culturally related (as mustard, cabbage and turnips), insects and plant diseases that attack the first are likely to be more troublesome on the others. Also, if a series of, say, root crops is grown, they tend to use up certain kinds of plant food, so that the last in the series may be partially starved.

Making the Vegetable Garden

The Site: When choice is possible, this should be fully exposed to the sun and longer from north to south than from east to west. For if the rows can run north and south and the long way of the area, this will favor the even distribution of sunlight and also reduce the number of necessary turns with the wheelhoe at the ends of the rows when cultivating. Always the plot should be well drained, because vegetables fail to grow well in poorly drained ground and because slow evaporation of excess water keeps the ground cold and "late" in spring and more subject to drouth in dry weather. If it can be higher than the adjacent ground so much the better; this will favor the "drainage" of cold air to the lower levels and often prevent damage by late spring and early autumn frosts.

Southern and southeastern exposures are earlier than western and northern slopes because they are warmer, especially when high ground to the north and west protects them from prevailing winds. Snow soon disappears on such slopes, excess water quickly drains away, and planting may start a week or two weeks earlier than elsewhere. Furthermore, crops normally mature earlier in such locations. However, if well drained as to air and water, and shielded from cold winds by high ground, woods, windbreaks or hedges, level land is nearly as early.

Soils: The best soils for vegetable gardens are loams, that is, combinations of sand, clay and humus. These hold moisture and fertility better than sands, and are more easily worked than clays. They can be built up by adding humus-forming materials such as manures, compost, leafmolds or green manures; or in case of stiff clay, as follows: In late autumn spread fresh manure (a two-horse load to 2,500 sq. ft.) and plow or dig it under, leaving the ground rough; during winter, add an inch of sifted coal ashes, preferably on the snow; in spring, smooth down the clods, add hydrated lime or wood ashes (about a pound to the square yard) and rake in before fitting the soil for planting. Repeat the program annually (except that lime need be added only once every five years) until the soil is rich and friable.

The best source of the valuable humus is stable manure because it is full of bacteria that help release plant food and because, in decaying, it also supplies plant food elements discarded by animals. If a local supply is not available it can be bought in dried, pulverized, easy-to-use form that is also free of weed seeds. When you want to improve a heavy clay, turn under fresh manure in

Laying out a garden—Sheet of paper on drawing or bread board—Use loose strips of paper to represent different crops.

How to dig light and heavy soils

Dig deep for root crops. Simple way to store celery

Always firm soil well after sowing seed with board or by treading—especially in light soils.

Thin out seedlings to permit good growth. — Thinned out plants can be cooked and eaten too.

Tillage is essential—use wheel hoe with different interchangeable parts—or any of various kinds of hoes

For small gardens hand weeding is practical— Here are types of hand weeders.

P.E. BAUER

autumn so it can decay over winter; when a light soil is to be enriched, apply well decayed manure in spring as the plant food in it will quickly become available.

Green manures are crops (grains, roots, etc.) grown solely to be turned under while green and soft to improve the soil. If sown after midsummer, they are generally called "cover crops" because they protect the ground against winter washing and excessive leaching of plant food. Crops used for these purposes are of two classes: those that gather nitrogen from the air and add it to the soil, and those that cannot do this but merely protect the surface and conserve what food is already present. Crimson clover (sow an ounce to 200 sq. ft.), winter vetch (an ounce to about 60 sq. ft.) and Canada field peas (an ounce to about 40 sq. ft.) are the most suitable nitrogen-gathering crops for home gardens. Sow them on any vacant land from July until mid autumn. Crops of the other type include: Buckwheat (1 ounce to about 60 sq. ft.), rye, barley and oats (an ounce to about 30 sq. ft.), and turnips or rape (1 ounce to 1,200 sq. ft.). A good combination is buckwheat, crimson clover, rye and winter vetch sown all at once in mid July, either on empty ground or between rows of late vegetables. The first frost will kill the buckwheat, and perhaps the crimson clover won't live over winter, but the rye and vetch will; and they will continue growing in spring until dug or plowed under.

Artificial manure, to take the place of or supplement the real thing can be made as follows, according to Missouri Experiment Station Bulletin No. 285 (now out of print): Heap straw, cut weeds, lawn clippings, and other waste vegetable matter in loose, flat-topped piles, five or six feet high on ground fully exposed to the weather. On top of each 4 to 6 inch layer, sprinkle evenly a mixture of 45 per cent ammonium sulphate, 40 per cent finely ground limestone (*not* burnt lime!) and 15 per cent superphosphate at the rate of seven or eight pounds to approximately 100 pounds of the vegetable material. Wet the pile as it is built and often enough thereafter to keep it moist, and the material will usually decay in three or four months, especially if it is forked over once or twice so as to throw the outside layer into the interior. The resulting compost is well worth making to improve the soil, to get rid of waste vegetable matter, and to avoid paying for as much high priced fertilizer as would otherwise be needed.

Commercial Fertilizers: As already noted (Chapter II) commercial fertilizers are organic and inorganic. Various materials of each type are often bought separately and mixed for use in farming and commercial vegetable growing, but it is generally advisable and more convenient in small gardens to use prepared plant foods, that is complete, balanced mixtures carrying analysis figures showing the percentage content of nitrogen, phosphates, and potash. Fertilizer recommendations are usually made on an acre basis. To find the corresponding amount to apply to a small garden, divide the number of square feet in an acre (43,560) by the recommended amount to apply (say 1,000 pounds). The answer (43 and a fraction in this case) is the number of square feet on which one pound of the mixture should be spread.

Soil Preparation: Land that has been in sod for several years should be manured, plowed or dug in mid autumn and left rough over winter to break down the turf and destroy many insects. In spring, level the clods or furrows as soon as the soil is dry enough to work. The depth of the digging or plowing must depend upon the depth of the soil; avoid bringing up too much of the sub-soil at any one time, but increase the depth of the surface layer gradually. Double digging or trenching is always good practice.

Cultivated ground can be prepared in fall (best for heavy soil) or in spring when [*continued on p. 236*]

VEGETABLE

QUICKLY MATURING

Name	Seed Required for 50 ft. Row	Time to Start Seed in Hotbed or Green-house	Time to Transplant Seedlings to Garden	Time to Sow Seed in Open Garden	Rows Apart (in feet)	Plants Apart in Row (In.)	Depth of Plant-ing (In.)	Degree of Hardiness
Beans—(Bush)	½ pt.	....	....	April–May	1½–2	4	1½	Tender
Beans—(Pole)	½ pt.	....	....	May	4	36	1½–2	Very tender
Beans—Lima (Bush)	½ pt.	....	....	May 15	1½–2	4	1½–2	Very tender
Beans—Lima (Pole)	½ pt.	....	....	May 15	4	36	1½–2	Very tender
Beets (Early)	1 oz.	February	April	April	1½	4	½	Hardy
Beets (Late)	1 oz.	....	....	June–July	1½	4	½	Hardy
Carrot (Early)	½ oz.	....	....	April	1½–2	2–4	½	Hardy
Carrot (Late)	½ oz.	....	....	July–August	1½–2	2–4	½	Hardy
Chard (Swiss)	1 oz.	....	....	April	1½	6–8	¾	Hardy
Cress		....	....	April–May	1–1½	2–3	½	Hardy
Dill		....	....	April	1½	4–6	½	
Endive	¼ oz.	....	....	April	1½–2	8–12	½	Tender
Lettuce	¼ oz.	Feb.–Mar.	April 15	April	1½–2	8–12	¼	Hardy
Mustard	1 oz.	....	....	April	1½–2	8–10	½	Tender
Onions (Sets)	1 qt.	....	....	April	1–1½	2–3	½	Hardy
Peas	1 lb.	....	....	April	6–8 Double Row	6	2	Hardy
Potato (Early)	4–5 lbs.	....	....	April	3	6–8	4	Hardy
Radish	½ oz.	Feb.–Mar.	....	April	1½–2	1–3	½	Hardy
								ALL SEASON
Artichoke, Jerusalem	4–5 lbs.	....	....	April	3–4	24–36	4	Tender
Broccoli	¼ oz.	....	....	April–May	2½–3	24	½–1	Hardy
Brussels Sprouts	¼ oz.	March	May	April	2½–3	18–24	½	Hardy
Cabbage (Early)	¼ oz.	Feb.–Mar.	May	April	2–3	24	½	Hardy
Cabbage (Late)	¼ oz.	....	....	May	2–3	24	½	Hardy
Cabbage (Savoy)	¼ oz.	....	....	May	2–3	24	½	Hardy
Cardoon	¼ oz.	Feb.–Mar.	May	....	3	18	½	Tender
Cauliflower	¼ oz.	Jan.–Feb.	May	....	2–3	15	½	Tender
Celeriac	¼ oz.	March	May	April	2	9	¼	Hardy
Celery	¼ oz.	Feb.–Mar.	May–June	April	2–3	6–8	¼	Hardy
Chicory	....	....	....	April	1–2	10–12	½	Hardy
Collards	¼ oz.	Feb.–Mar.	....	May	3	24–36	½	Hardy
Corn (Sweet)	½ pt.	....	....	May	3	24–36	1	Tender
Cucumbers	½ oz.	....	....	May–June	3–4	36–48	1	Tender
Egg Plant	¼ oz.	Feb.–Mar.	May	....	3	24	½	Tender
Kale (see Broccoli)	(above)	....	....	....	....	....	....	....
Kohl Rabi	¼ oz.	....	....	April	1½–2	8–12	½	Hardy
Leek	½ oz.	....	....	April	1¼–2	4–6	½	Very Hardy
Muskmelon	¼ oz.	....	....	May	3–4	36–48	1	Tender
New Zealand Spinach	¼ oz.	....	....	May	3	12–18	½	Hardy
Okra	1 oz.	April	June	May	3	12	½	Tender
Parsley	½ oz.	....	....	April	1	4–6	½	Hardy
Parsnip	¼ oz.	....	....	April	1½	4	½	Hardy
Peppers	¼ oz.	Feb.–Mar.	May	May	2	24	½	Tender
Potato (Late)	4–5 lbs.	....	....	May–June	3	6–8	½	Hardy
Pumpkins	½ oz.	....	....	May	4–5	36–48	4	Tender
Rutabaga	½ oz.	....	....	April	2½	8–12	1	Hardy
Salsify	1 oz.	....	....	April	1½	4	½	Hardy
Spinach	1 oz.	....	....	April	1–1½	6	½	Hardy
Squash	½ oz.	....	....	May–June	4–5	48–60	½	Very Tender
Sweet Potato	50 roots	March	May–June	....	3–5	14	3–4	Tender
Tomato	¼ oz.	March	May	....	2½–3	30–36	½	Tender
Turnip	½ oz.	....	....	April	1½–2	3–4	½	Hardy
Watermelon	1 oz.	....	....	May	8–10	80–90	1	Tender
								PERENNIAL
Artichoke, Globe	½ oz.	Feb.–Mar.	....	....	3–4	24	½	Hardy
Asparagus	40 plants	....	May	April	1½–3	14	4–5	Hardy
Dandelion	½ oz.	....	....	May	1½	8–10	½	Hardy
Horseradish	50 roots	....	....	April	2	8–12	2	Hardy
Rhubarb	25 roots	....	....	May	2½–3	24	¾	Hardy

By Permission of the American Fork & Hoe Co., Cleveland, Ohio.

PLANTING CHART

PLANTS

Successive Planting (Days Apart)	Days to Mature	Important Suggestions
14 days to July Season	60	Early plantings can be followed by Fall vegetables.
	60	Longer bearing than above. Use poles 6–8 ft. long, plant 6 seeds per pole and later thin to three.
10 days to July Season	60	Cultivate as for Bush Snap Beans above.
	60	Plant and thin as for Pole Snap Beans above.
14 days	40–70	Late plantings for Winter use should use turnip varieties.
. . . .	90	Before freezing, dig and store in cellar or pit.
14 days	100	Hoe deeply and frequently—keep clean of weeds.
. . . .	120	Give plenty of water and keep soil well cultivated.
20–30	60–70	Can replant until September for Fall and Winter use.
14 days to Sept.	35	Easily grown in Winter in greenhouse, hotbed or window box.
. . . .	. . . .	
Fall use in June	100–120	Tie outer leaves over center bud when 6 to 8 inches long.
August	70–90	Fertilize heavily—plant on rich soil and supply abundant moisture.
7 days	30–40	Can be grown in window boxes in Spring.
14 days	50–60	Till top soil frequently and keep free of weeds.
7–14 days	60	Do best in cool weather, so plant as early as possible.
June for Fall	90	Apply fertilizer between rows several times during season.
7–10 days	30	For Fall use long, white varieties.

PLANTS

Successive Planting (Days Apart)	Days to Mature	Important Suggestions
. . . .	5–6 mos.	Plant 3 or 4 small tubers in a hill.
. . . .	4–5 mos.	Winter crop may be started in May.
14 days	5–6 mos.	When small sprouts begin to appear—Cut large leaves off to favor sprouts.
. . . .	4–5 mos.	
. . . .	4–5 mos.	Fertilize and cultivate freely—Hill up slightly as growth progresses.
. . . .	4–5 mos.	
. . . .	5–6 mos.	Leaves bunched for blanching in early Fall.
. . . .	4–5 mos.	Never allow plants to become checked in growth.
. . . .	5–6 mos.	Blanching not required—Roots remain in ground until wanted.
. . . .	5–6 mos.	See "Vegetable Guide" for information on blanching.
. . . .	6–7 mos.	Then raised and transplanted in trench and covered with manure—After 4 to 5 weeks ready for use.
June	3–4 mos.	Stands hot weather better than cabbage or kale. Grown widely in Southern States.
10 days to June	2–3 mos.	Deep soil and frequent cultivation makes best crop.
. . . .	2–3 mos.	Plant in low hills for perfect drainage while young.
. . . .	4–5 mos.	Grow best in well drained, warm soil.
. . . .	2½–3 mos.	Quite hardy and does well where cauliflower cannot be grown.
. . . .	3–4 mos.	Plant in open furrow 5 or 6 inches deep—Draw in earth as plants grow to level of garden.
. . . .	3–4 mos.	Plant in hills, 10 to 12 seed, thin to 4 plants.
. . . .	3–4 mos.	Soak seed 2 hours in hot water.
June	3	Requires frequent cultivation until plants cover the ground.
May–June	3–4 mos.	Seed germinate very slowly—mark rows with radish seeds.
. . . .	4–5 mos.	Better flavored if subjected to early frosts.
. . . .	4–5 mos.	Top dress soil between rows when plants 6 inches high.
. . . .	4–5 mos.	Dig before hard freezing.
. . . .	4–5 mos.	Plant on hills and cultivate as for cucumbers.
. . . .	4–5 mos.	Pull roots before freezing, cut off tops and store in cellar.
. . . .	4–5 mos.	Dig roots in Fall or Winter as required.
. . . .	3 mos.	Apply nitrate of soda between rows to stimulate growth.
. . . .	2–4 mos.	Winter squash may be planted later and stored for use in moderately warm, dry place.
. . . .	5–6 mos.	Dig when vines have been killed by frost.
June	4–5 mos.	Protect from frost when first set out in garden.
June–July	2–3 mos.	Crowding or weeds make poorly flavored roots.
. . . .	4–5 mos.	Top dress with fertilizer high in nitrogen and potash.

PLANTS

Successive Planting (Days Apart)	Days to Mature	Important Suggestions
. . . .	Aug.–Sept.	If crowns get too large after two or three years—divide and reset.
. . . .	May–June	In northern states mulch asparagus to prevent heaving of the roots during winter.
. . . .	Sept. (1st yr.)	Blanch by covering with straw or leaves.
. . . .	. . . .	Tends to become rank weed—cultivate closely and root out volunteers.
. . . .	2nd Spring	Keep blossom stalks cut back—flowers and seed exhaust plant.

[*continued from p. 233*]
it has lost the glistening wet appearance, or when a squeezed handful does not wet the hand but breaks apart at a slight touch. When seeds are to be sown or plants set out, especially in dry weather, dig and rake the ground anew, fitting only as much as can be planted that day.

Seasonal Vegetable Garden Activities

Seed Sowing: In spring seed can be sown about four times its diameter, then lightly firmed in with the head of a rake; later, in dry weather, sow deeper and press more firmly. Large seeds (peas, beans, etc.) will sprout well if, after tramping the rows firmly, you cover them with loosely raked soil to serve as a mulch.

Soon after sowing, use the steel rake very lightly over the entire bed; within a week repeat the raking *in the direction of the rows,* but preferably with a bamboo or metal broom rake. This is to kill millions of tiny weed seedlings and also to break the crust to let the vegetables through. As soon as the plants have developed their second or third true leaves, thin them to the required distance for good development. Some of the thinnings can be transplanted to fill gaps in the rows or to make new rows; or if large enough, they can be eaten, especially those of beets, lettuce, etc.

Setting Out Plants: In cold climates, some vegetables are always started under glass or in sheltered beds, and transplanted when they reach suitable size and when conditions in the open are favorable. Sown in flats, the seedlings are "pricked out" to stand two inches apart each way in other flats as soon as they can be handled; then, after being gradually "hardened" they are planted outdoors, the soil being well firmed around them. The more tender and "fussy" kinds—eggplant, pepper, etc.—are often pricked out into small clay or paper boxes to lessen the disturbance of their roots in later transplantings. If cutworms are feared, wrap a "collar" of paper around each stem so it will extend an inch above and below soil level when setting out the plants.

Following the light raking already described, cultivation of the soil between rows and plants should be carried on frequently to kill weeds and especially to maintain a dirt mulch which tends to prevent loss of soil by washing, to facilitate the entrance of water into the ground, and to prevent its loss by evaporation. Until the foliage shades the ground, stir the soil after every rain (as soon as a crust has formed and dried) or, in dry spells, every week or ten days. For a garden 50 by 50 feet or larger, some form of wheelhoe is a great time and labor saver; for a smaller plot the Dutch or scuffle hoe (worked while walking backward) and other similar hand tools are excellent because they obviate walking on the freshly loosened ground.

Watering: If artificial watering seems needed, ordinary sprinkling with hose and nozzle is futile for reasons already explained. Real watering should drench the ground a foot deep or more, and be followed as soon as possible by cultivation. Actually, an occasional such soaking will not call for as much water as daily sprinklings, but will make much better use of it. The principle of overhead irrigation as used so generally on truck farms can be applied in miniature in various ways in the home garden.

Crop Protection: Control of plant

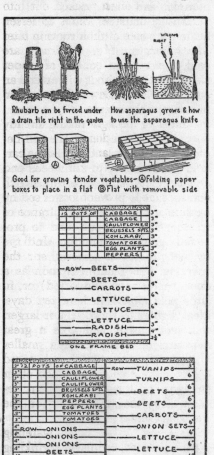

Rhubarb can be forced under a drain tile right in the garden

How asparagus grows & how to use the asparagus knife

Good for growing tender vegetables—Ⓐ Folding paper boxes to place in a flat Ⓑ Flat with removable side

ONE FRAME BED

TWO FRAME BED FOR LARGER GARDEN

A good layout of early planted vegetables for hotbed (or cold frame) gets a big start on the spring season. Radishes, lettuce, & early root crops can be eaten from frame— others are set out in garden.

R.E.BAUER

enemies begins with "sanitation," that is, the disposal of weeds and crop residues that harbor plant diseases and insects between seasons.

Shepherd's purse and wild mustard are early spring hosts for cabbage butterflies, old cabbage stumps are feeding grounds for plant lice, and so on. Rotating crops helps to prevent the spread of various soil borne diseases, club root of cabbage and related plants, scab of potatoes and beets, etc.

Use repellents, such as naphthalene flakes or tobacco dust, in the soil around cucumber and melon plants to drive away cucumber beetles; hydrated lime and Bordeaux mixture to repel flea beetles on beets and potatoes, and so on. Spray and dust intelligently or you will waste money, materials and time without getting results. Consult Chapter XVII for general principles and suggestions and if particularly troublesome problems arise, appeal for advice to professional growers in your neighborhood or to your county agent or state agricultural experiment station. It is always wiser for the amateur gardener to use commercial brands of sprays and dusts than to attempt to make his own mixtures. Reliable manufacturers keep their brands up to standard, or they couldn't continue in business.

The Harvest: When crops reach usable size, gather the edible parts and remove the rest to the compost heap because, left in the ground, it only wastes plant food and water. Then prepare, plant, or sow the vacant ground to some other crop so as to keep it actively producing something other than weeds all season long, whether vegetables or a cover crop. Harvesting really starts when lettuce thinnings and peppergrass cuttings can first be used in early spring, and continues until the last turnips, cabbage, celery, etc., are gathered for winter use. As most crops of various kinds mature more rapidly than they can be consumed, a part of each can usually be canned or dried for use during winter. Spring, summer and early fall crops specially desirable for canning include baby beets and carrots; tender peas, stringless beans and limas; sweet corn just past the "milk" stage; summer squash while the seeds are soft; okra, while soft, to add to soup stock; cucumbers and onions, for pickles; tomatoes, alone or with spices and other vegetables to make catsup, chutney, relish, etc.

Storage of home garden vegetables is generally limited to late fall crops that can, under favorable conditions, be kept for weeks or months. They fall into four classes: 1. Those that may be left in the ground over winter without injury, as parsnip, salsify, scorzonera, Jerusalem artichoke. 2. Those which, when dug, must be kept cold, dark and not too dry, as beet, carrot, turnip, potato, cabbage, cauliflower, brussels sprouts, celery, leek, eggplant, pepper, winter radish, rutabaga. 3. Those that must be kept cold and dry, onion, garlic. 4. Those that must be kept warm and dry, pumpkin and winter squash.

House cellars in which there are heaters are suited to only group four. The others must go in a separate cold, moist cellar or out of doors. Celery, leeks, cabbage, cauliflower, and brussels sprouts can be "planted" in boxes; root crops are best stored in crates or baskets placed on the floor. One convenient scheme employs a cold frame deep enough to hold cabbage, etc., hung upside down, celery and leeks "planted," and root crops in onion crates, peach baskets or bushel hampers. In severe weather such a frame must be protected against freezing temperatures by mats, quilts, or some other thick covering. For "planting material" indoors, or in a vegetable pit, granulated peat moss kept barely moist is ideal, lighter to handle than sand or soil, inexpensive, and able to hold moisture for a long time.

EDITOR'S NOTE: In the table on pages 234, 235, Jerusalem Artichoke, an all-season plant should be designated as *Hardy* in column nine, instead of "Tender." Any tubers left in the ground will survive the winter and start into growth in the spring.

Also the Globe (or French) Artichoke, among the perennial plants, should be described as *Tender*, instead of "Hardy." Actually it is a perennial only in mild climates or if given heavy protection over winter.

CHAPTER XVI

FRUITS AND BERRIES

All the reasons advanced for growing vegetables apply, and with even greater force, to growing fruits in home gardens. Moreover, fruit plants have other than food producing values. They cost no more, generally speaking, than shrubs, trees and vines that are planted solely for ornament. Yet, most of them are attractive enough in foliage and flower to deserve ornamental positions in the garden; they are as easy to manage, and their enemies are better understood and more easily controlled. And above all is the physical benefit and pleasure a family can take in "fruit from our own garden." Apricot trees are conspicuous with their glorious rose-pink flowers in early spring; the large-flowered varieties of peaches soon follow; then come the Japanese plums, the European varieties, sweet and sour cherries, apples and pears. All these can be used as specimen or shade trees except along the street front. The bramble fruits may serve as hedges along a fence or in place of it.

For an informal, unclipped hedge about five feet high the black raspberry is excellent because it "stays put" (whereas red raspberries spread to adjacent ground by developing suckers from their roots); it bears snowbanks of bloom in May and delicious fruit in July. Dwarf fruit trees trained as cordons or espaliers are excellent for beautifying unsightly walls or they can be grown on trellises like grapes. Grapes may replace such vines as kudzu, akebia and actinidia on verandas, pergolas and summerhouses. Even strawberries in well tended beds are pleasing to look at throughout the growing season.

The objection that one "must wait so long" before getting fruit can be answered two ways. First, no matter how long one waits he will *never* get any fruit from an elm or a spruce, a Dutchman's pipe vine, a forsythia bush or any other "purely ornamental" plant. Second, the waiting period is not "so long" after all. For instance, everbearing strawberry plants set in early spring will start to bear in July and continue more or less regularly until cold weather stops them. Regular varieties will bear abundantly the following summer. Bush fruits and grapes will start the year following planting and give increasing annual yields for several years. Nectarines, peaches, sour cherries, plums, apricots, and summer varieties of apples and pears generally bear fruit the third summer, while even sweet cherries and the slower maturing varieties of apples and pears usually begin the fourth or fifth, especially if on dwarf stock.

As a specimen for a prominent position few shrubs equal a well grown quince bush in full flower; none approach it in early autumn when laden with golden fruit. One bush is sufficient both as a specimen and as a source of fruit for a family of ordinary size. In soil naturally or purposely made acid, blueberries (huckleberries) may be grown in the garden. Their foliage is glorious in its autumn color and during winter the red branches are conspicuous. Some of the new, improved varieties developed by Miss Elizabeth White of New Jersey ripen successionally over a period of about two months.

Only in large gardens is there space for sweet cherries because mature trees often spread to fifty feet, whereas sour cherry trees rarely reach half that diameter and are easily kept within bounds by judicious pruning. Standard apple and pear trees also are too large for the small garden, but dwarf trees are easily adapted to small quarters whether in natural, round-head form or trained as pyramids, globes, or espaliers.

Choosing and Buying Plants: In choosing varieties for the home garden always select those of high quality and that are popular in the locality, even though the stock may have to be bought from a nursery some distance away. Choice varieties not obtainable in nurseries may be had by grafting or budding them on sturdy-growing commercial varieties or seedling trees. These processes are simple, so if space is limited one tree may be made to bear several to many varieties. Scions or buds of desired varieties may be secured through exchange or purchase from owners.

State experiment stations generally know who has trees of desired kinds and will gladly aid searchers. A few nuseries offer trees already grafted or budded with three to five varieties, but these may not be the sorts best adapted to the buyer's needs.

Among the most widely successful fruit varieties of high quality which can generally be bought from nurseries, even though the fruit is not often found in markets or stores, are those listed on page 251 as a guide to help amateurs in making their selections. If you want to grow really *new* varieties, you should join the New York State Fruit Testing Co-operative Association, whose object is to discover how such novelties behave in various parts of the world. For his $1.00 dues, each member is entitled to a premium plant of his own choice from the seasonal list, and he may buy at cost as many other plants as he desires. Write the secretary at Geneva, N. Y., for details.

Among the common mistakes made when buying fruit trees one of the most unfortunate is the purchase of large trees under the supposition that they will produce fruit earlier than younger ones. For one thing, such trees are often "leftovers," and when they are dug, the roots may be so badly damaged that they recover slowly. Smaller trees, two or even one year old, given the same care, usually start to bear sooner. Commercial fruit growers almost never plant trees older than two years; in fact, one year trees are generally preferred because the branches can be developed where the planter wants them to be.

Fruit Growing Practices

Building Strong Trees: When you buy a fruit tree, insist upon one whose straight stem has never been cut or broken. If its branches are far apart on the trunk with the three largest pointing in different directions, you will have no difficulty in developing a symmetrical, strong specimen. Next best is a "whip," or branchless, yearling tree on which, by suppressing undesired shoots and encouraging well placed branches, you can develop a symmetrical tree.

Always avoid a tree with a Y-crotch formation—two erect stems of equal size and vigor. If both grow, they will sooner or later split apart. But this fault can be corrected (1) by cutting back one branch severely and the other little or not at all; (2) cutting back one to a six-inch stub which is left for two or three years then removed cleanly (this plan is best with newly planted trees); (3) if the tree is a sapling with a well established root system, not a newly planted one, you can cut off one branch at once, at its base.

Most fruit trees, bushes and vines are dug in autumn and stored for spring delivery. It is well to order by January while stocks are complete. Before you sign for a delayed shipment of nursery stock insist on a "bad order receipt" from the express, freight or mail agent. Send it to the nursery company at once with a statement giving the facts and describing the condition of the plants. A month or six weeks later report on their performance and, if necessary, file a claim for replacement.

Unpack nursery stock in a shel-tered, shaded place. Examine the roots and prune back to sound wood any that are broken or scraped.

In planting, make the holes amply large and even deeper than seems necessary. Throw the upper layer of good soil in one pile and in filling the hole put it in first, around the roots. Never place manure or chemical fertilizer close enough to burn them. Organic fertilizers—bone meal, cottonseed meal and dried blood—are safe to mix with the soil and damp peat moss will help the roots to start growth. Break the soil up so it will sift down among the roots and when they are covered, pack it thoroughly by tramping. When the hole is full, leave a bowl-like depression in which to apply water during dry spells.

After planting, cut back the top one half or more so as to create a balance between it and the root system. When doing this, loosen the wires holding any labels or hang them by large loops around the trunk or a main branch.

Here are proper distances (in feet) to allow between plants based on the space a full grown plant will cover:

Apple, Standard, 30; Apple, Dwarf on Doucin roots, 20; Apple, Dwarf on Paradise roots, 12; Apricot, 20; Blackberry, 8; Blueberry, 8; Boysenberry, 8; Cherry, Hybrid Bush, 6; Cherry, Sour, 20; Cherry, Sweet, 30; Currant, 5; Dewberry, 6 to 8; Gooseberry, 5; Grape, 8; Loganberry, 8; Nectarine, 20; Peach, 20; Pear, Dwarf, 15; Pear, Standard, 25; Plum, 20; Quince, 15; Raspberry, Black, 6; Raspberry, Purple, 8; Raspberry, Red, 5; Strawberry, 2; Youngberry, 8.

Site: When planning a garden for fruit, choose the site—if choice is offered—with even more care than you would locate a vegetable garden. (See Chapter XV.) Exposure is especially important. Avoid eastern and southern slopes for apricots, peaches and nectarines because in such places the flower buds are likely to swell early and be injured by spring cold snaps. Or plant these trees on northern and western sides of buildings and walls. Other tree fruits, grapes and berry plants are hardier and blossom later.

Soil: Fruits can often be made to thrive in soil where a vegetable garden would fail. In such cases make the holes extra large and deep, cover the bottoms liberally with bones, and fill them at planting time with a mixture of equal parts good soil and damp peat moss, dusted with a handful of bone meal to each three or four shovelfuls.

Feeding: The first year after planting the feeding roots extend only a little way from the base of the plant, but thereafter they forage farther and farther in all directions, the main root branches becoming mere carriers of moisture and food. Hence, manure and fertilizer should be applied to an encircling zone that extends from about half way between the trunk and the limit of the branch spread to about twice that distance. Where the ground is kept cultivated or well mulched, the applications of manures and fertilizers recommended for the vegetable garden are satisfactory, but on sod land they should be doubled so both the grass and the fruit plants will be fed. Clean cultivation is preferable for

Diagram showing how 25 dwarf trees of six kinds can be grown in the space (20 x 20 ft) required by one standard apple tree—indicated by dotted circles.

⊙ = dwarf apple
◉ = " pear
✕ = " peach
▲ = " cherry
◻ = " plum
• = " apricot

If trees grow to such size as to unduly crowd, some can be removed after a few years.

Espaliered dwarf trees

Simple Cleft Grafting

Good blackberry Trellis
young shoots
Fruiting Area

Trellis for dewberry
fruiting canes
young shoots

tree and bush fruits grown in rows; but if they are planted along fences, heavy mulching is usually better as it conserves moisture, keeps down weeds, and adds humus.

How to Gather Fruits: Tree fruits should never be pulled off the trees so as to break the twigs or wound the fruits. Proper ways are as follows: *Apple.* Hold the specimen in the palm of the hand, the stem firmly between fingers and thumb, and give a twist. If it is ripe enough, the stem will separate from the twig without damage to either. *Pear.* Hold as described for apple but raise specimen through an arc of about 30°. If the stem does not separate readily at the point of union with the twig, it is not ripe enough; leave it on the tree.

Pest Control in the Fruit Garden

Principles of spraying and dusting

are the same here as explained in Chapters XV and XVII, but a few additional suggestions will be in order. It has been demonstrated that scale and other insects that hatch in early spring from eggs laid on plants the previous fall can be most readily killed by spraying with a "dormant" or "winter-strength" lime-sulphur solution, or a miscible oil emulsion, just when the leaf buds begin to swell. At this time the shells of the eggs and the protective covering of hibernating scales become softer and more porous so the spray penetrates them more readily. Overwintering fungi can also be destroyed by lime-sulphur, so the one spray at the time specified will be doubly effective. Arsenate of lead can be added to poison the first to appear of the chewing insects which, somehow, seem to know just when the first tender leaflets are going to be ready for them.

Herewith a few directions for the protection of special fruits:

Apple and Pear: The codlin moth lays eggs on the newly formed fruits. The larva or grub, which makes them "wormy," usually eats its way in at the blossom end and, once inside, it can't be checked. Therefore, a spray or dust poison must be applied before the calyx closes, which is a week or ten days after the flowers fall. Leaf-chewing insects, such as canker worms, are controlled by this same treatment; but plant lice and other sucking bugs must be killed with a nicotine, rotenone or other contact spray or dust. Borers in trunk and main branches must be cut out if not too deep, or destroyed by thrusting a flexible wire into their burrows in August or September when their presence is indicated by sawdust-like castings at the entrances. Fire blight of apples, pears and quinces, which blackens leaves and kills twigs and branches, is a bacterial disease that cannot be controlled by spraying or dusting. Diseased parts must be cut out and burned with sanitary precautions. Write your state experiment station for detailed directions.

Peaches and other stone fruits are made wormy by curculios (snout-beetles) which make crescent-shaped wounds in the fruit and lay eggs beside them. However, the adults feed on the foliage before the flowers open, so the trees should be sprayed with a stomach poison while the leaves are developing, again after most of the "shucks" have fallen from the young fruits, and once more a week later. If the trees are in a chicken yard, or if chickens can be confined beneath them in spring, the fowls will devour many of the insects, especially if the trees are soundly thumped with a carpet-covered sledge hammer early in the morning to jar off the adults while cold and sluggish. Later, the chickens (and birds, too) will eat many of the larvae that crawl out of the fallen fruit before they can burrow into the ground to pupate.

These trees, especially peaches, are also attacked by a particular kind of borer which usually enters at or a little below the ground surface, where a mass of soft gum and sawdust-like "frass" reveals the injury. Carefully scrape it and the soil away to find the small entrance hole. Then cut the bark with a sharp knife to find the burrow and the worm. Repeat a couple of weeks later to locate any that may have been missed. Early November is the best time to do this. If borers are bad, it may be necessary to protect trees by fumigating the soil around them with paradichlorobenzene which can be bought, with directions, at seed stores. Diseases of these fruits can be controlled by prompt spraying or dusting with fungicides.

Cherry and Plum branches and twigs attacked by "black knot" must be cut off and burned as soon as the swellings are noticed to prevent the spread of this disease.

Currant and Gooseberry foliage is eaten by green worms which should be poisoned by spraying or dusting upward from near the ground so all the foliage will be covered. Start as soon as the first leaves open and keep it up; but after the bushes flower, use only a non-poisonous spray or dust such as a pyrethrum or rotenone preparation. Plant lice which sometimes cause currant leaves to curl up must be sprayed with a contact poison before they become enfolded and hidden in the leaves. As old stems serve as breeding quarters for borers, cut out and burn any that have borne three crops.

Raspberries and their kin are attacked by various chewing insects for which use lead arsenate up to the time the flowers drop, then a non-poisonous spray or dust. Borers in the growing shoots cause wilting. Cut infested parts and burn.

Grapes have several leaf eating enemies easily controlled by early lead arsenate sprays. Plant lice on the tips of shoots can be destroyed by dipping the shoots in a nicotine solution or cutting off and burning them.

Fruits for Home Gardens

Apple: Before you plant even one standard apple tree, make sure you can spare the space it will need—a circle at least 40 ft. in diameter. If you can't, plan to use dwarf trees which are often planted 10 ft. apart. However, it is better to set apple (or pear) trees 20 ft. apart and put smaller growing, shorter lived kinds alternating in each direction between them—peach, nectarine, apricot, plum and cherry. In this way 25 dwarf trees can go in the space one standard apple tree would need, as shown in the illustration. As they become crowded, take out the shortest lived kinds first. In any case, it is advisable to devote the surrounding ground, while the trees are small, to annual vegetables or strawberries; or else to keep the ground in a two foot circle around each tree cultivated clean so as to reduce the danger of attacks by borers.

When the trees begin to bear fruit, watch for these signs of special food needs: small, yellowish leaves and short, spindling shoots mean insufficient nitrogen; in that case give each four year old tree about a pound of nitrate of soda in spring and increase the amount by a quarter pound for each additional year. Dark green leaves and long, sturdy growth indicate plenty of nitrogen but a possible lack of potash and phosphorus, so give a four-year tree about a pound of potash and 1½ pounds of superphosphate. When the trees reach full bearing, they will need twice as much potash and four or five times as much phosphate.

Apricot: The beauty of its blossoms entitles the apricot to a place in every home garden, but in addition, its early varieties ripen fully six weeks ahead of good peach varieties and its delightful flavors differ from those of all other fruits. Many Easterners know only the commercial, California product, picked before it is ripe; if they could once eat freshly gathered ripe dessert varieties, they would doubtless decide to plant some. Contrary to popular belief, the tree is hardy, though buds, blossoms, or newly set fruits are sometimes injured by spring frosts if located with an easterly and southerly exposure. They want deep, rich soils, well drained below as well as on the surface. Plum roots make the best, strongest stock to graft on; peach roots are all right on light, well drained soils, but must be watched for peach borers; almond makes a poor stock, so don't buy apricots grown on it.

The fruit usually sets heavily and should be thinned in early June so that the specimens left will not touch when mature and develop brown rot, for which preventive sprays with a fungicide should be given. The chief apricot pest is the curculio. For proper treatment see under peaches on page 243.

Blackberry: Only in the home garden can the blackberry be allowed to reach full ripeness and deliciousness. Plant choice varieties, give the plants the limited attention they need, wait to gather the fruits until they will drop into your hand at a touch, eat them within an hour, and

Tip rooting in the black raspberry.

Right and wrong way to prune twigs.

Well pruned grape vine— 4 cane Kniffin System

Advantage of thinning fruit

Rabbit guard around tree

Does spraying pay?

The right time for the first spring spray.

Handy hook for supporting grapes or brambles on trellis

It may pay to protect grapes from birds & Japanese beetles

Advantage of letting strawberry runners root in 2£ pot

you will never regret allowing space for them. But if you don't boss *them* they will boss *you!* For blackberries send up "suckers" or new stems from their roots and unless you *pull them up* when they are about ten inches tall they will create an impenetrable, thorny jungle. Cutting the shoots simply tends to make more suckers grow from the stumps.

Blackberries like deep loams with plenty of humus, but not over-rich; otherwise they develop sappy growth that falls prey to severe cold. Each spring reduce the canes in the rows to one every foot or so by pulling up the others; then either pinch off the tips of the growing stems when they are 30 inches tall to make them branch low, or fasten them to a wire when about three feet high. Better than one wire are two wires, stretched the length of the row and fastened to cross pieces nailed to posts set 25 or 30 feet apart. Young stems can be fastened to one wire one year and allowed to fruit the next season, while new stems are being fastened to the other wire. Cut the canes close to the ground as soon as they have borne, and burn them. In spring, shorten the branches of bushes trained the first way to about 18 inches, or cut back the canes of unpinched plants to about 3½ feet. Blackberries start to bear the second season; if cared for they should continue to bear for ten or fifteen years. When they begin to fail, start a new plantation.

Blueberry: In order to thrive, blueberries must have acid soil; also, specific fungi must be present on their roots to create certain necessary conditions, and self-sterile varieties must have others planted near by to insure fruit setting. Other essentials are sandy soil amply supplied with peat or humus, and continuous moisture in summer. Plants can be set 8 by 8 feet apart, or 8 by 4 feet if every other plant is transplanted when it begins to touch adjacent plants. Keep cultivated, but only 2 inches deep; the root system is shallow. Some fertilizer is helpful beginning about the third year after planting. Cut old barren stems back to ground level during the dormant season and do any transplanting in spring. Move with all the soil possible and minimum delay and cut the stems to ground level to encourage new shoot development.

Plant only named varieties, not seedlings; the following are recommended: Cabot, Concord, Jersey, June, Pioneer, Rancocas and Rubel.

Boysenberry, a combination of loganberry, blackberry and dewberry, resembles the last named and should be handled like it. The fruit is claimed to be the largest berry grown.

Bush Cherry: This low-growing, hardy shrub, native to the Great Plains, bears large, sweet fruits, especially good for cooking. The named natural varieties have been supplemented by many hybrids developed by Professor N. E. Hansen of North Dakota, which are a boon to gardeners in cold regions. Prune and train like the currant and stimulate the growth of new shoots by rigorous reduction of old stems. To insure cross pollination and fruit production, plant several varieties.

Cherry: Tree cherries are of two classes: *sweet,* borne on large trees; and *sour,* on small ones. An intermediate group of hybrids called "dukes" bears fruit of halfway tartness on smallish trees. These hybrids, the best of which is May Duke, are mostly self-sterile and should be planted with both sour and sweet varieties to insure pollination.

Sweet cherries do best in lighter soils than the sour kinds prefer and require more space—30 feet as against 20 or less. But sour cherries are the hardier and more adaptable, succeeding from Newfoundland to British Columbia, and over most if not all of the United States. Sweet varieties are either soft-fleshed (called hearts) or firm flesh (bigarreaus). The sour kinds are generally grouped together though some, with clear juice, are called amarelles and others with colored juice, morellos.

Currant: This hardy plant, properly treated, should produce ten or more pounds of large, luscious fruit annually. It thrives in strong, well drained but moist loams; as its roots are close to the surface, cultivation must be shallow; it is a gross feeder, so manure can be used freely. If it cannot be had, supply nitrogen or plant foods. Buy one or two year plants and set them at least 5 feet apart. Keep weeds from crowding the bushes and reducing the yield of fruit.

After stems have borne three or four times cut them off at the ground and burn them immediately. In spring cut out all the young, light colored shoots but the two strongest. Thus each bush should start the season with eight stems, the two oldest of which are removed in midsummer after bearing.

Pick the fruit when it is dry or it will spoil quickly. Shallow trays with perforated bottoms are better than close bottomed boxes to pick into because they prevent heating and spoiling. Half-mature currants make excellent tarts and pies; mature, but not over-ripe ones are best for jelly; for dessert use, best leave them several weeks longer until fully ripe.

Dewberry: A trailing plant that resembles one relative, the blackberry, in its fruit, but that multiplies, like the black raspberry, by rooting tips. Its fruit ripens between the strawberry and the blackberry seasons. As some of its thirty odd varieties are self-sterile, at least two kinds should be planted in close proximity.

Moderately fertile, light, well drained loams suit it best. Plant early in spring slightly below ground level to allow for soil settling, but not so the crown is covered. Plants to be trained on stakes should stand 5 by 5 feet; those to be grown on trellises, 3 feet apart in rows 6 feet apart. Clean cultivation and cover cropping are essential and any feeding should be done in mid to late autumn or early spring.

The favorite way to train the stems is to let the young ones sprawl lengthwise of the rows out of the way of tillage tools or the pickers' feet, the first year. The following spring they are fastened to posts or trellises with wires 18 and 30 inches from the ground; or as described under Blackberry, but lower. As soon as a cane has fruited, it is cut and burned.

Gooseberry: Managed like Currant, which see.

Grape: No other fruit plant has so wide a range, is so tolerant as to soil, so quick to begin bearing, so easy to manage, so bountiful a producer of a many purpose fruit over so long a season. But to handle grapes successfully, we must understand their natural habits and treat them accordingly. (1) All fruit is borne on green shoots that grow in spring from buds formed the previous year; never on the woody "canes." (2) The tendency is, therefore, for the bearing parts to get farther away from the roots each year and to become less productive; pruning must be done to prevent this. (3) Winter pruning should reduce the tops about 75% (a) by cutting off completely all puny and rank canes which never would bear, and (b) by shortening the normal canes at least 50%.

After planting first-class, two-year vines, cut off all puny growths and reduce the strongest stem to three good bud-bearing joints. Allow a shoot to grow from each bud until (about June) the strongest becomes woody at its base; then shorten the other two to one joint apiece with a leaf at each joint. The strong shoot will become stronger, and the next year, develop side shoots, some of which should bear fruit. The following winter shorten this main stem a third to a half and cut off all other growths. The second winter either cut back all the one-year canes on this main trunk to "spurs" of two or three joints and allow the buds on these to produce bearing shoots; or cut off all but the two strongest canes, leaving these to become "arms" to be stretched on a trellis or other support. Plants should be set 8 or 10 feet apart and posts 30 feet. Most trellises are of two or three wires, the lowest 24 inches from the ground, the others 18 to 24 inches higher.

Loganberry: This cross between the wild, California blackberry and a red raspberry has the trailing dewberry habit and bears large, purple fruit, tart even when fully ripe. It is too tender to be grown where winter temperatures reach zero. Plants are set 8 to 10 feet apart and propagation and training are as for the dewberry.

Mulberry: Too large for small gardens, and unsuited for use on lawns or near walks and drives because the soft, purplish-black fruit falls readily and messes up the ground beneath, this tree is fine for planting in poultry yards where the fowls eat the fallen fruit and the insects attracted to it, and also for decoying birds away

from the more valued cherries and raspberries. There are several delicious, large-fruited varieties, excellent for dessert, juice, or wine making and canning with other tart fruits. New American is best for the North; Downing, from Philadelphia southward; Stubbs and Hicks, in the South; Gorgeous and Monarch (white-fruited) for the Central West. The fruit of the Russian Mulberry is attractive only to birds.

Nectarine: This is a name for smooth skinned peaches which are managed the same as the more familiar "fuzzy" peach.

Peach: Though the life limit of peach trees is popularly rated at about ten years, it can reach 20 or 30 if careful attention is given to curculio control as directed on page 243. Every home garden should have at least one tree each of five varieties whose fruit will ripen over practically two months. Peaches thrive in any well drained location, but best on light, moderately fertile soils. Never grow peaches in sod as this favors borer attacks. Keep the ground cultivated around the trunks even when the trees are planted on a lawn. Avoid over-feeding with strong manures and fertilizers, but don't be afraid to apply plant food rich in potash and phosphoric acid when the trees are in bearing.

Peach varieties are grouped as freestone (best for dessert); clingstone (best for canning), and semicling. Some are white fleshed, some yellow; they range from early to late.

Pear: Though as hardy and almost as tolerant of soils as the apple, the pear does best in well drained, heavy loams. Avoid the use of manures and rich fertilizers as lush growth is more subject to the fire blight disease.

Pears are grown both as standards (on pear roots) and as dwarfs, grafted on quince stock. The varieties Angoulême, Easter, Louise Bonne, and Vicar of Winkfield are better as dwarfs than otherwise; the opposite is true of Bartlett, Été, Lucrative, Onondaga, and Seckel.

Plant in late autumn or early spring because late spring planting may damage swollen buds and both weaken and retard the development of the tree. A good number of main limbs and branches is desirable so that if some are hit by blight, others will remain to carry on. Keep weak, puny shoots cut off the main branches and disinfect the wounds.

Do little or no pruning until the trees have begun to bear; thereafter, the annual growth can be shortened 30 to 50 per cent each year to reduce the amount, but improve the quality, of the fruit.

Plum: Cultivated plums having been derived from several botanical species, vary in their characteristics and adaptability to soil and other conditions. As some varieties are self-sterile, get the advice of your state experiment station as to which kinds to grow. Also, buy trees from comparatively near-by nurseries as they will be better suited to your region. In general, all require well drained soil, but European varieties do best in heavy loams, while American and Japanese sorts prefer gravelly and sandy types.

After developing the main branches (as suggested under Building Strong Trees) the less pruning you do, the earlier the trees will start bearing.

Under favorable conditions trees, in the East, may continue fruitful for 30 to 40 years; in the Central States, half as long is good performance. Thinning is important, especially with American and Japanese varieties.

Quince: Because it is even more susceptible to fire blight and borers than are apples or pears, quinces should be treated as bushes rather than as trees so new stems can be grown to replace those attacked by those enemies.

Contrary to some recommendations, the quince does not favor a damp, cold soil, but grows best, yields best and lasts longest in well drained, deep, warm, but only moderately fertile, soil. As the roots spread widely, set plants not closer than 15 feet and cultivate shallow to avoid damaging the roots.

Quince flowers are borne at the tip of short shoots, so unpruned bushes become crooked and choked with worthless wood. The aim in pruning should be, therefore, to cut out worthless and superfluous twigs and branches *while the plants are in flower or even after the fruits have set.*

Raspberry: Varieties of raspberry are red (sometimes yellow) fruited, which propagate asexually from roots or root cuttings; black fruited, which increase by the rooting of young branch tips; and purple-fruited hybrids which may follow either parent, or both, in manner of propagation. All kinds bear fruit on biennial stems which die after bearing fruit and should then be removed and burned without delay.

Wherever wild raspberries grow it

is safe to plant cultivated ones, choosing, if possible, deep, well drained, fertile loams, rich in humus. Varieties that propagate from roots may be planted in the fall but those grown from tips are best set out in the spring. In general, early spring planting is best. Set black varieties not less than 5 feet each way and keep three to five stems per plant after the plants are established. Reds may be set as close as 2 feet apart in the rows which are generally kept 6 feet apart. Purple kinds vary, Columbian needing not less than 8 feet and Royal Purple only 5 or even 4. Training is as described under Blackberry, except that, with the reds, pinching the young stems is not favored.

Strawberry: Like the brambles, this is pre-eminently a home garden fruit. Its culture is as easy as that of most vegetables. After fitting the ground in early spring, set plants at distances varying from 18 to 24 inches in rows which may be that close if tilled by hand but must be 3 or 4 feet apart for horse cultivation. Row spacing also depends on whether they are to be grown in "hills," "hedges," or "matted rows." Take care in setting not to cover the crown of a plant nor to leave it so high that the roots are exposed to the air. Summer planting may be done when the plants can be had near by and when special care can be taken to keep the soil moist until autumn rains occur. Pinch the flowers from spring planted regular varieties the first season to build up the plants; do the same with everbearing kinds until late June or early July.

Beginning in June, the plants will send out "runners" which, if allowed

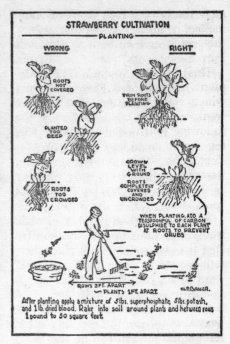

STRAWBERRY CULTIVATION
— PLANTING —
WRONG   RIGHT

ROOTS NOT COVERED

TRIM ROOTS BEFORE PLANTING

PLANTED TOO DEEP

CROWN LEVEL WITH GROUND

ROOTS TOO CROWDED

ROOTS COMPLETELY COVERED AND UNCROWDED

WHEN PLANTING, ADD A TEASPOONFUL OF CARBON DISULPHIDE TO EACH PLANT AT ROOTS TO PREVENT GRUBS

ROWS 3FT. APART
PLANTS 1FT. APART   W.R.BAKER.

After planting apply a mixture of 5 lbs. superphosphate, 5 lbs. potash, and 1 lb. dried blood. Rake into soil around plants and between rows 1 pound to 50 square feet.

to, will take root and become new plants. The first rosette on a runner makes the best plant because it has more time in which to grow before winter. By anchoring rosettes where wanted, rows can be kept narrow; by cutting them off before they root the original plants can be developed into hills (which produce the largest, finest fruit but less of it); by allowing them to root promiscuously, you develop "matted" rows which produce smaller berries but in greatest number.

Clean cultivation is essential, both to maintain moisture and keep down weeds. Since this means much hand work, the hill system is desirable because it permits more use of hoes and long-handled cultivators. Commercial growers often plow under their beds after gathering one full crop. Others mow the foliage (not too close) immediately after the harvest, loosen the mulch and allow it to dry, and burn the bed over rapidly.

This destroys weeds, insects and plant diseases, but not the plants which start into new growth in a week or so and bear a fair crop the following year. A home garden planting should, with care, continue productive for several years. Some varieties of strawberry are self-sterile or as the catalogues say, "imperfect" or "pistillate."

However, few strawberry specialists offer these varieties because the "perfect" ones are considered more satisfactory.

Strawberry plants, being rather shallow rooted, need protection during winter to prevent their being heaved out of the ground by the alternate thawing and freezing of the soil. A heavy mulch of marsh or salt hay, shredded corn stalks, buckwheat straw, or other material free of weed seed should be applied when the ground has frozen hard enough to bear a loaded wheelbarrow or wagon. Uncover the plants in spring as soon as they show signs of growth and rake the mulch between the rows to check evaporation of moisture and also to keep the fruit from getting mud spattered.

Wineberry: This Oriental, moderately hardy bramble propagates like the black raspberry and bears brilliant scarlet, usually rather insipid berries which are, however, highly popular with birds.

Youngberry: A comparatively new, dewberry-like plant that bears abundant maroon or wine colored, nearly seedless raspberry-flavored fruits highly valued for dessert, jams and juice. Its hardiness has not been fully tested.

Planting and training are the same as for the dewberry. There is a thornless variety which is considered hardier and more prolific than the type.

HIGH QUALITY FRUIT VARIETIES FOR HOME GARDENS

Apples

Williams	Delicious
Primate	Grimes Golden
Early McIntosh	Northern Spy
Sweet Bough	Esopus Spitzen-
McIntosh	berg
Wagener	Newton Pippin
Fall Pippin	

Crab Apples

Transcendent	Hyslop
Excelsior	Whitney

Pears

Bartlett	Seckel
Tyson	Beurre Bosc
Comice	Anjou
Howell	Lawrence

Peaches

Greensboro	Morris White
Rochester	Carman
Belle of Georgia	Hiley
Elberta	Champion
(canning only)	Fox
Frances	Fitzgerald

Plums

Abundance (Jap.)   French Damson
Reine Claude   (Eu. Canning
 (Eu.)   and Jam)
Italian Prune   Burbank (Jap.)
 (Eu. Canning   Golden Drop
   and Jam)   (Eu.)

Cherry, Sweet

Black Tartarian   (New variety
Napoleon   well spoken
Windsor   of)
Sweet September

Cherry, Sour

Early Richmond   English Morello
Montmorency   Chase

Apricot

Montgamet   Alexander
Moorpark   (Russian)
             Alexis

Quince

Orange   Champion

Currant

Perfection   Wilder
Red Lake   White Grape

Gooseberry

Downing   Red Jacket
Chautauqua   Columbus
Whitesmith   Poorman

Raspberry

Bristol (Black)   Latham (Red)
Logan (Black)   Marcy (Red)
Plum Farmer   Newburgh (Red)
 (Black)   Indian Summer
Columbian   (Fall bearing,
 (Purple)   red)
Marion (Purple)   Ranere or St.
Sodus (Purple)   Regis (Fall
Chief (Red)   bearing, red)
Cuthbert (Red)

Blackberry

Lucretia   Alfred (New)
 (Dewberry)   Rathbun
Eldorado   Brainerd (New)
Early Harvest

Grape

Portland (White)   Brighton (Red)
Ontario (White)   Catawba (Red)
Niagara (White)   Delaware (Red)
Golden Muscat   Moore's Early
 (White)   (Black)
Agawam (Red)   Fredonia (Black)
Vergennes (Red)   Concord (Black)
Brilliant (Red)   Barry (Black)

Strawberry

Premier   Dorsett
Fairfax   Catskill
Big Joe   Gandy
Ambrosia   Orem
Aroma   Chesapeake
William Belt   Aberdeen
*Mastodon   *Gem
*Green Mountain   *Wayzata

---

* *Everbearing varieties.*

CHAPTER XVII

PLANT DISEASES AND PESTS

*There was a little robin, whose head was
  always bobbin',
Who remarked as he gobbled up a worm;
"I have eaten all his brothers and ninety-
  seven others,
But, Golly! how they tickle when they
  squirm!"*

It would be a nice thing if the birds could take care of all our garden pests. There is no doubt that they do a considerable amount of good and the true gardener will protect them in every way possible. In the chapter on Trees, we suggest means of keeping cats and squirrels from climbing trees and robbing their nests. Bird houses may be provided and prove a decorative and interesting feature of the garden.

The subject of garden enemies is often bewildering to the amateur. The multiplicity of sprays and cures seems to be endless, but this is not the case. Pest control is relatively simple and when it is practiced as a preventive measure, it is comparatively easy to keep plants healthy.

An understanding of the kinds of garden foes with which we are to deal will make easy the selection of our weapons. These foes are first divided into three classes: weeds, diseases, and animal pests, such as rodents, insects and some minor groups. Many specific directions for control

are given in the preceding chapters, but will bear repeating here for the purpose of getting a complete picture of the pest problem.

Insects: Most insect injury results directly or indirectly from the insect's attempts to secure food. Some insects are most destructive in adult stages, others in larval (worm) stages. Feeding habits generally determine the control methods.

Three general classes of insects are:

1. Chewing or biting insects, which get their food supply by eating plant, flower or fruit. These are controlled generally by placing a stomach poison (such as lead arsenate) on the foliage or fruit. The insect is killed when it eats the poison. In this class of insects are: Beetles, bulb fly larvae, caterpillars, cutworms, grasshoppers, leaf tiers, leaf rollers, rose chafers, slugs, bagworms, etc.

2. Some types of animal pests hide in the soil and are eradicated with poison bait. Grasshoppers are also killed in this way. Ants get their chief food supply from the honeydew of insects, such as aphides, mealy bugs, etc. They protect these insects and are known to move them about and thus aid in spreading them. This applies especially to the aphides in the soil which attack the roots. If insects

are controlled there will be fewer ants, and if ants are controlled there will be fewer insects.

Other insects which operate underground or which for other reasons cannot be controlled by either method described above are generally controlled by use of fumigants or disinfection methods described later.

3. Sucking insects, which get their food supply by sucking the plant juices. As they do not eat the plant parts, poisons are of no value in their control. They are killed, however, by "contact insecticides" which clog their breathing pores or penetrate to their vital organs.

In this class of insects are the: Aphis (plant louse), cyclamen mite, chrysanthemum midge, greenhouse orthezia, lace bug, leaf hopper, mealy bug, red spider, rust mite, scale, thrips, white fly, etc.

Diseases: Plant diseases may be divided into three general groups: Bacterial, fungous and virus diseases.

1. Fungous diseases are most important to the home gardener. They can generally be controlled with Bordeaux mixture or sulphur. These diseases include: Brown rot, black spot of roses, leaf spot, mildew, mold, rust, shot hole fungus, etc.

2. Bacterial diseases are difficult to control. Successful controls have been discovered for only a few.

3. Virus diseases are not fully understood and little is known about their control. They are frequently transmitted by insects and in such cases control of the insect will control the disease.

Treatment of plant diseases may be roughly divided into four methods:

1. Disinfection of seed or soil before planting.

2. Spraying or dusting plants as a preventive.

3. Spraying or dusting to cure diseases.

4. Controlling insects that spread diseases.

While some diseases may be controlled after they appear, better and more economical control is generally secured by preventive methods.

Control: One of the first steps in the control of insects or disease is to keep the garden clean. Any plot which is allowed to grow over with weeds will multiply your troubles. Carefully gather and burn all diseased leaves, pull out sickly or wilted plants and clean up and destroy any stalks of last year's garden.

As previously explained, the digging of the garden in the fall or winter to allow it to freeze not only breaks up the ground, but exposes many soil pests to freezing temperatures as well as the sun and birds.

Sometimes it becomes necessary to cut back portions or all of a plant in order to get rid of borers or pests of this kind. Pussy willows and other quick-growing trees are sometimes so badly infested that this is the only means of control. Often it is necessary to cut them off close to the ground. In this case, all leaves and rubbish must be raked up and burned immediately. It is also well to sprinkle the soil completely with gasoline (it can be spattered about with a whisk broom) and burn it over with a quick hot fire. It should then be spaded up and fertilized so that the plant may have a chance to recover its growth. The fire must not be allowed to get hot enough to injure the plant's stem or roots.

The most important part of pest control is prevention. Keep a daily watch upon your plants and see that they do not become badly infested. Disease is easy to prevent, but hard to cure. Spray or dust as a matter of routine to keep your plants growing well.

Methods: Protecting the home garden from insect and disease attacks does not demand expensive equipment. In most cases one has the choice of spraying or dusting as a method to use. Each method has its merits and the choice will depend upon the preference of the individual. Some advantages of each method are:

Spraying: Material adheres to foliage better than when dusted and fewer applications are necessary to protect crops. Can be done under weather conditions, such as light wind, which makes dusting impracticable. Less material is wasted in spraying than in dusting. The control of some diseases and insects by dusts has not been as fully worked out as for spraying methods.

Dusting: Less time is required for applying the material than for spraying. Less labor is required for dusting, and less inconvenience in handling the hand duster than the hand sprayer. There is less danger of burning tender foliage than spraying, and it is more efficient in killing aphides that attack leaves of low-growing crops, where it is impossible to force liquid spray against the bodies of the insects.

Whether spraying, dusting, or a combination of both methods is fol-

lowed, good equipment should be provided, and thoroughness of application is essential if control is to be secured. It is also necessary to cover the entire plant, both the stems and underside of the leaves as well as the top. A partial killing off of the pests is of little advantage, as they reproduce so fast that the condition soon reverts to its original state unless a thorough job is done.

Equipment: Protective equipment necessary for a garden depends upon its size and labor available. Every garden should have a dust gun and a hand or atomizer spray. These should be of fairly good quality.

A dust gun costs from $1.25 to $25.00. The gardener should select one which is guaranteed by a reliable dealer and see that it is fitted with a metal spot or deflector to force the dust against the undersides of leaves of low-growing plants when necessary.

Hand sprays can be purchased for from ten cents up, but the cheap ones last but a short time and are wasteful of material because they do not give the fine mist necessary to coat economically. They are also less efficient as they do not have enough force for the use of contact sprays.

A knapsack sprayer is very useful for the ordinary garden, because it can be pumped up in advance and the gardener may devote his entire attention to the proper application of the material. In covering any large amount of garden area it will save much time as well as labor.

Before going into the large types of spraying equipment, it is necessary to consider the matter of labor of the proper kind. If the gardener wishes to experiment and to carefully do the work himself, anyone who can work the plunger will do for an assistant. This will no doubt save a considerable part of the spraying cost. But if the work must be entrusted to unskilled, disinterested labor, it would be better to secure the services of a competent expert. Reliable nursery and tree expert firms have spray

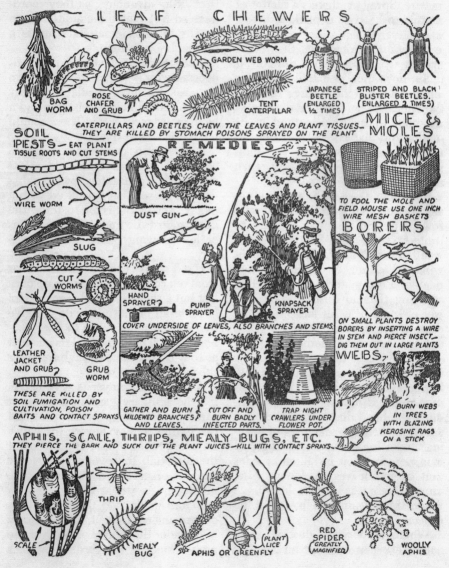

INSECTS AND REMEDIES

LEAF CHEWERS

GARDEN WEB WORM

BAG WORM

ROSE CHAFER AND GRUB

TENT CATERPILLAR

JAPANESE BEETLE (ENLARGED ½ TIMES)

STRIPED AND BLACK BLISTER BEETLES. (ENLARGED 2 TIMES)

CATERPILLARS AND BEETLES CHEW THE LEAVES AND PLANT TISSUES—THEY ARE KILLED BY STOMACH POISONS SPRAYED ON THE PLANT

MICE & MOLES

SOIL PESTS — EAT PLANT TISSUE ROOTS AND CUT STEMS

WIRE WORM

SLUG

CUT WORMS

LEATHER JACKET AND GRUB

GRUB WORM

THESE ARE KILLED BY SOIL FUMIGATION AND CULTIVATION, POISON BAITS AND CONTACT SPRAYS

REMEDIES

DUST GUN

HAND SPRAYER

PUMP SPRAYER

KNAPSACK SPRAYER

COVER UNDERSIDE OF LEAVES, ALSO BRANCHES AND STEMS.

GATHER AND BURN MILDEWED BRANCHES AND LEAVES.

CUT OFF AND BURN BADLY INFECTED PARTS.

TRAP NIGHT CRAWLERS UNDER FLOWER POT.

TO FOOL THE MOLE AND FIELD MOUSE USE ONE INCH WIRE MESH BASKETS

BORERS

ON SMALL PLANTS DESTROY BORERS BY INSERTING A WIRE IN STEM AND PIERCE INSECT—DIG THEM OUT IN LARGE PLANTS

WEBS

BURN WEBS IN TREES WITH BLAZING KEROSENE RAGS ON A STICK

APHIS, SCALE, THRIPS, MEALY BUGS, ETC.
THEY PIERCE THE BARK AND SUCK OUT THE PLANT JUICES—KILL WITH CONTACT SPRAYS.

THRIP

SCALE

MEALY BUG

APHIS OR GREENFLY

(PLANT LICE)

RED SPIDER (GREATLY MAGNIFIED)

WOOLLY APHIS

service available at reasonable prices in almost every locality.

The working parts of the sprayer should be kept in good condition. A little lubricant placed upon the plunger of the air pump will keep the washer from drying out. It is a simple matter to replace these washers with new ones. The nozzle must be cleaned frequently and should be equipped to deliver a fine mist-like spray.

Spray Thoroughly: We wish to emphasize again that thorough coverage of the plant with the spray material is essential to successful pest control. This is particularly true when contact insecticides are used, as the insect to be killed must be hit by the spray material. Insects missed soon reproduce and give rise to a new infestation. Spray both sides of every leaf and twig.

Caution: The strength of the spray materials now available has been determined carefully in their manufacture, and if any burning of the foliage appears the cause is usually the manner of application. Perhaps you were careless with proportions in mixing and had the solution too strong. Then, too, spraying should not be done when the temperature is extremely high or when the ground is dry and the plants wilted. Under such conditions the plant may draw in through its leaves some of the poisonous material. **Remember,** a number of sprays and dusts are poisonous to man and other animals and should be kept under lock and key or on a shelf inaccessible to children.

Avoid inhaling vapors or dust, conveying any of the materials to the mouth, or permitting them to come in contact with sores or injuries. Always wash the hands after handling or applying these chemicals. In treating plants, thoroughly coat the infested parts, but do not use so copiously that quantities of the material will coat the ground beneath. After spraying, destroy or plainly label and securely store in a cool, dry place any remaining material. Carefully clean and dry the spraying apparatus and destroy or properly dispose of any residue.

MATERIALS TO USE

There are so many proprietary materials on the market that it is bewildering to the amateur just what to use. Many have real value for the money expended, but a great many do not justify their price.

Many insecticides do not possess any particular advantage over arsenate of lead to kill insects, and the same may be said of certain fungicides as compared with the long used copper and sulphur preparations. Many of the following materials can be bought packaged by reliable nationally advertised firms at reasonable prices. This is better than buying in bulk. Cheap materials do not pay.

In many sprays, soap or some other material is added as a spreader to keep the mixture from "crawling off" the plant surfaces. Care must be exercised in mixing to use the proper amounts and the directions here and after given as well as the directions on the package should be carefully considered.

Arsenate of Lead: Arsenate of lead is the most used and best known material for killing leaf-eating insects.

It is sold usually in the powder form, which is well adapted for the small garden because it can be used either as a dust or spray. When used as a spray it is best to mix the required amount of powder in a little water before applying, then dilute with the proper amount of water for the insect to be killed. It can also be had as a paste.

Arsenate of lead can be combined with Bordeaux mixture or sulphur to control both insects and diseases.

Barium Fluosilicate: Barium fluosilicate is another stomach poison used for dusting in the same way as arsenate of lead. It is also especially effective on beetles difficult to kill with arsenate of lead. For use, mix with five times as much (by weight) hydrated lime.

Bordeaux Mixture: This mixture of copper sulphate and lime was, for years, the most widely used spray for protecting garden crops against fungous diseases. It is used in different strengths for different purposes, and these strengths are indicated by directions on the package.

Calcium Arsenate: Calcium arsenate (arsenate of lime) is sold as a white powder similar to arsenate of lead. It has slightly stronger killing power than arsenate of lead due to a higher percentage of arsenic oxide, but must be used with lime to prevent foliage burning on most vegetables and ornamental plantings. It is recommended as a safe spray when used with one and one-half times its weight of hydrated lime, or in Bordeaux mixture.

Nicotine Sprays: Concentrated tobacco (nicotine sulphate) solution for spraying plant lice is sold under several trade names. This can be diluted to the proper strength with accuracy, and is very toxic to plant lice at a strength of one part to six hundred of water or one and one-half teaspoons to one gallon of water.

The spray kills only when it comes in contact with the bodies of the insects, hence must be directed against both sides of the leaves. It may be combined with arsenate of lead for controlling both aphides and leaf-eating insects. It can also be used with Bordeaux mixture. When nicotine sulphate is used, soap should be added at the rate of one cubic inch to each gallon of water, or two to three pounds to fifty gallons. Dissolve the soap in a little hot water before adding to the spray. In a nicotine-Bordeaux combination spray, omit the soap except on grapes and potatoes.

Nicotine Dust: A finely powdered material containing a small percentage of nicotine sulphate mixed with a sulphur, talc, lime or other carrier is now sold under trade names or as nicotine dust. This mixture is serviceable for killing plant lice and other soft-bodied insects, provided the material carries enough nicotine and the dust can be brought in contact with their bodies. Results with the factory-made product have been variable, due apparently to the oxidation of nicotine in the stored product.

Massey Dust: Many combinations of spray materials control more than one pest. For instance, a highly efficient dust to prevent black spot and rose mildew and control insects was perfected by Dr. L. M. Massey. You can make it by mixing nine parts of dusting sulphur and one part of arsenate of lead. Tobacco dust may be added to it to control aphides. Thus we have sulphur for control of fungus, arsenate of lead for leaf chewers and tobacco dust (nicotine) for aphides. This mixture is also suitable for some perennials. Many expensive rose dusts are for sale, but few are better than this. Several rose dusts are sold having this same formula some of them are colored green so as to be less noticeable on foliage.

Miscible Oil: Miscible oil is an oil that can be used for spray because it breaks up and forms an emulsion with water. It is used for control of scale insects on dormant plants, also for summer spraying for scale and red spider.

Pyrethrum Sprays: There are now offered for sale commercial sprays containing pyrethrum extract as a killing agent. This material, like nicotine, is very toxic to insects when it strikes them and kills by paralyzing them.

Some plant lice are killed by dilutions of these materials at a strength of one part to eight hundred of water; other species of plant lice require stronger solutions as do insects such as the rose bug, blister beetle, and striped cucumber beetle. We recommend that the grower follow strengths recommended by the manufacturer. Some of the pyrethrums require mixing with soap in solution, while others have the spreader incorporated with them.

Insects must be hit by the liquid, and there is no lasting protection secured by covering the foliage with spray as is the case with arsenicals. Pyrethrum sprays are especially adapted to use on small plantings where expense is no item and on flowers where staining of the foliage or bloom would be objectionable. These materials leave little or no stain and are not unpleasant to apply. Many commercial pyrethrum sprays are liquid soaps, a most efficient form.

Poisoned Bran Mash: Poison bait for cutworms and grasshoppers may be made of one-half teaspoon of Paris green or white arsenic, one pint of bran, one tablespoon of syrup, one-half pint of water and one-fourth ground orange or lemon.

Mix the bran and Paris green dry, stir the syrup and finely ground fruit into the water. Pour the sweetened liquid over the poison bran and mix thoroughly so that it is crumbly, but not sloppy. Scatter this around the plants in the evening and keep away poultry or pets. It may be concealed under a pan or flower pot. Apply in early morning for grasshoppers. These insects die slowly after feeding.

Rotenone: The rotenone sprays, relatively new, are very similar in action to the pyrethrum sprays and the two are often combined. Rotenone is a stomach poison, as well as a contact insecticide.

Sulphur Dusts: There are on the market, especially in fruit sections, a large number of sulphur dusts. These are excellent fungicides and can be obtained in a new wettable form (colloidal). On evergreens it acts as a fumigant to destroy red spider. The sulphur used for dusting purposes should be finely ground so that a large portion of it will pass through a 300-mesh per inch sieve.

Various formulae may be obtained. Thus a 90:10 sulphur-lead arsenate dust would mean ninety parts of sulphur and ten parts of arsenate of lead. Get fine dusting sulphur from your seedsman.

Tobacco Dust: Finely ground tobacco, sometimes called tobacco stem meal, has many uses in the garden. It can be safely worked into the soil around asters or other plants infested with soil pests, may be scattered upon the surface of the ground and is excellent mixed with peat moss or homemade compost when used as a mulch. Tobacco seems to be a more reliable source of nicotine for dusting than the chemical product.

PREVENTIVE MEASURES

Seed Disinfection: In previous chapters we have recommended the disinfection of bulbs and seeds with both hot water and corrosive sublimate. It is not necessary to disinfect all seeds, but it is well for the amateur to know how to do it when he finds it recommended in planting instructions.

Corrosive sublimate, which is a deadly poison, is used as a seed disinfectant, and also for controlling maggots and root pests. The most convenient form of this material for use in small quantities, as for disinfecting seeds, is that of tablets. Each tablet contains 7.3 grains of corrosive sublimate, and when dissolved in a pint of water gives a 1:1000 solution, which is the strength ordinarily used. For larger quantities, the powder is more economical. One ounce should be dissolved in 7½ gallons of water.

Corrosive sublimate should be used only in wooden or earthen vessels, since it corrodes metals. It should also be kept from rings, wrist watches, etc. It is very poisonous.

Soil Sterilization: Some soil fungi and bacteria which infect young seedlings can be best killed by soil sterilization. Young seedlings may be attacked and killed before they come through the soil. This is not due to poor seed, but to the sudden rotting by a fungous disease called "damping off." It is usually due to hot confined atmosphere and is generally discussed in Chapter XIX on Propagation and elsewhere.

Soil is disinfected in large quantities by the use of steam or by baking, but for the amateur, organic mercury compounds and formaldehyde dusts are best.

In greenhouse flats or small boxes where the soil is 2½ to 3 inches deep, 1½ ounces of a 6% formaldehyde dust are required per square foot of soil surface. Where a number of boxes or benches are to be filled, the dust should be used at the rate of one-half pound per bushel of soil. The dust and soil should be thoroughly mixed by shoveling over several times. The flats or benches should be filled with soil, the seed sown and the soil well watered immediately after seeding.

For larger seedbeds out of doors the upper surface may be sterilized by burning brush over it or by using formaldehyde, one pint to six gallons of water, and applying one to one and one-half gallons of this solution to each square foot of seedbed. The soil should be first loosened so that the solution may penetrate readily. A sprinkling can may be used to apply the solution. After application, cover tightly for 12 to 24 hours with damp sacks, canvas, or boards. After uncovering, the soil should be stirred several times to permit the fumes to escape. Plant after ten days to two weeks.

Dormant Sprays: A good scheme for keeping the garden free from attack is to inaugurate a calendar system for spraying. Scales are the small sucking insects which infest the stems and branches of most plants, hiding under either hard or soft protecting shells. They are killed by a spray applied during March while the plant is dormant. Dormant spray consists of lime-sulphur or miscible oil. If the lime-sulphur is used it should be purchased in solution and applied as directed. Miscible oil is the cleanest and best for the amateur.

Some types of scale, such as the mealy bug, are easily recognized by the mealy covering with which it surrounds itself; others require closer inspection.

It is well to spray all dormant trees, shrubbery and evergreens each year. Certain evergreens, such as Colorado and Koster's blue spruce, may be temporarily injured by the miscible oil spray, but if the application is made before growth starts they will quickly recover.

The oil spray has the advantage that it does not stain paint. Lime-sulphur will cause black spots if blown against a white house, garage, pergola, etc. This is quite an item in the windy month of March or any other month. The oil also helps to control red mite and red spider.

Perennials and Roses: Do not wait for such perennials as delphinium, phlox, peonies and others to become infested with mildew, but start spraying the crowns of plants with Bordeaux mixture even before they start through the soil. Such spraying should be repeated every ten days in early spring, but may be done less often as the plants mature. Later spraying is objectionable because it discolors the foliage. However, use Massey dust weekly on roses.

Massey dust may also be used upon perennials and with tobacco dust will usually keep them free from disease and insects. It may be necessary to use a nicotine spray on nasturtiums, roses and other plants to control aphides, but this need not be done until it is found that the combination spray does not control them.

Summer Spray: If the leaves of your trees and shrubbery have parts eaten away or holes cut in them, they are being attacked by leaf chewers and need one of the poison sprays before mentioned. Trees and shrubbery which were infested the previous year should be sprayed as soon as the leaves have fully formed.

A good summer spray is miscible oil and arsenate of lead mixed as per directions on the package.

Rusty evergreens in the summer usually indicate red spider injury. This pest multiplies very rapidly during hot, dry weather. Oil spray is the best remedy, dusting with sulphur the second best, but the two should not be combined. The sulphur seems to kill the pest by its fumes which are given off during the warm weather.

If mildew or fungous growth is noticed on the leaves of trees and shrubbery, it may be well to incorporate Bordeaux mixture in the spray, but this is seldom necessary.

CURATIVE MEASURES

Ants: See control in Chapter III, Lawns.

Aphides: Aphides are the small insects—green, red, black, yellow and white, usually found in clusters on stems or leaves. They are killed by contact spray—nicotine or pyrethrum extract, one and one-fourth teaspoons to one gallon of water or as directed on the package. Make a mild soapsuds of the water before adding the chemical. They may also be controlled by adding nicotine to other sprays or dusts. Pull off curled leaves in which they hide.

Bagworms: These worms, chiefly infesting evergreens, hatch out in the spring and make a bag or nest of silk and twigs which they drag around with them while eating. Handpicking is most effective, but arsenate of lead (ten teaspoons to a gallon of water) applied about May 1st will save much damage. The arsenate may be applied with a summer oil spray or mixed with the dusting of sulphur used to control red spider. This mixture is not so economical, but easier of application. When the worms mature they fasten the bags to twigs and retreat inside them to pupate. Therefore pick off the bags whenever seen and burn them, and remember to spray early the following season.

Borers: Borers cause tops of plants to wilt or break off above the surface of the ground. In early stages they are killed by inserting fine wire into the stalk. In advanced stages there is no cure on smaller plants. On trees, try the wire method or if the tree is healthy dig them out, if not too deep, with a thin-bladed knife, afterward sealing the hole with grafting wax or tar. In deep drills, squirt special borer-killing preparations in the holes and immediately plug them with grafting wax, putty or wet clay. The best protection against borers on trees is to carefully coat over any injuries to prevent their entrance.

Chewing Insects: If the foliage of your plant is being eaten, use an application of arsenate of lead (ten teaspoons to the gallon of mild soapy water) or dust with one part arsenate to ten hydrated lime. If the offender is discovered to be a blue-black beetle, which the arsenate does not kill, use barium fluosilicate, one part to nine parts flour, dusting in the morning before the dew leaves the plant. They may be killed with a pyrethrum contact spray (three teaspoons to one gallon of soapy water) provided the spray touches them.

Chiggers: Chiggers do not properly belong in the discussion of plant troubles, but they are sometimes very troublesome to the gardener. An easy and sure way to avoid attack is to roll down the stockings to below the tops of the shoes and dust thoroughly with sulphur from a perforated can. At a picnic or to rid the lawn of any such pests, the dusting of the area to be used with flowers-of-sulphur applied with a dust gun, usually proves very effective.

Cutworms: When plants are cut off at the ground the most probable reason is a night crawler, known as cutworm. They are rather difficult to find, but are eradicated by the poison-bran bait previously described.

Dogs: Dogs and other animals

sometimes injure plants and become a neighborhood nuisance. Certain scents are repugnant to some animals even when so faint as to hardly be noticeable to man. This principle has been used recently in preparing a number of sprays to keep dogs away from trees, evergreens, or shrubs. A nicotine spray made at ordinary strength without a soap spreader may be used.

Grasshoppers: Use poison bait, sprinkle in the morning.

Mildew: White or grayish powdery spots on foliage are the indication of mildew. This is a fungous growth and is controlled by dusting with sulphur alone, or combined with materials to control other pests. Start in June and repeat twice a month throughout the season. Is controlled on roses and other plants by the use of Massey dust.

Rabbits: These rodents do greatest damage to trees and shrubs in winter by gnawing the bark when their normal food supply has been cut off by deep snow. A preventive spray of whale or other fish oil can be used in the fall on trees and shrubs. Success has also been reported with the use of a standard commercial powder for insect control, which contains sulphur, copper, carbolic acid and arsenic. Complete coverage of plants is not necessary, as one taste will drive them away. This is a good summer control also when, if not fenced out, rabbits will do much damage in vegetable gardens and among young seedlings of many ornamentals. The New York *Times* has suggested a spray to repel rabbits as follows: Cover 1 pound of commercial aloes with a small quan-

tity of commercial alcohol until dissolved; strain into 4 gallons of water. This has to be renewed after a rain. Protection can be given to newly planted trees by a collar of tar paper fastened with stovepipe wire. Wire netting will protect specimen shrubs. See also "Dogs."

Red Spider: Red spider infests evergreens, phlox, English ivy and many other plants, causing them to turn light gray and brownish. The underside of the leaves become dirty or dusty looking, although no insect is visible. Arborvitae and other evergreens apparently dry up. This spider is a microscopic mite which does not yield to poison. It is killed by spraying with miscible oil, dusting with sulphur, or coating the plant with glue solution.

Dissolve one-half pound of cheap ground glue in a pint of hot water, then add five gallons of warm water and apply when cool once a month from June to August. Most plants respond best if the glue is washed off with a hose one week later. The oil or sulphur is the better spray for evergreens and most perennials.

Root Lice: Root lice attack many plants, especially asters, causing them to become stunted in growth with weak, yellowish foliage. They may, most times, be prevented by incorporating tobacco dust in the soil at planting time and making another application when the plants are half grown. They may be killed by forming a basin of soil at the foot of the plant and the application of a half pint of nicotine sulphate mixed with one teaspoon to the gallon of water, or by thoroughly soaking the ground with strong tobacco water.

Root Rot: When plants rot off at the ground it may be caused by this disease. There is no cure for advanced stages, but, in earlier stages, it may be overcome by soaking the ground with corrosive sublimate (one tablet to a quart of water).

Rust: When brown spots appear on the bottom of leaves, such as snapdragons and hollyhocks, they may be controlled by dusting with sulphur or spraying with Bordeaux mixture.

Scale: Scale has been previously described and may be discovered on lilacs, poplars, and ash trees especially. There are many types of scale, one of the most common being the shape of an oyster shell. It is controlled by a dormant spray of oil or lime-sulphur.

Slugs: Slugs usually leave a silvery streak across the soil as they feed upon garden plants, usually seedlings, iris and rock plants. They do not like lime and a dusting will usually keep them away. Poison dust of one part barium fluosilicate to ten parts flour is also effective. They are night crawlers and at that time may be sprayed with pyrethrum (two teaspoons to one gallon of soapy water); but they must be hit by it. For this method it is best to use a flashlight after dark.

Thrips: These are small insects about one-sixteenth inch long in various colors which produce bleached spots on gladiolus and other flowers and also cause defective bloom. They may be controlled by spraying with nicotine and pyrethrum (two teaspoons to one gallon of soapy water) or with a mixture of tartar emetic 4½ teaspoons, brown sugar, 1⅓ cups, water 3 gallons, once a week until eradicated. They hide in the fold of the gladiolus leaf and it is better to dip the bulbs as described in Chapter XII.

Wilting: This is a plant disease carried in the soil. It is overcome by planting in new soil each year and the disinfecting of seed. China-asters are especially subject to it and only seed of special resistant strains or varieties should be used in wilt infested sections.

Wireworms: Wireworms are not worms at all but slender larvae of a beetle. They attack tubers, roots and other vegetable matter in the ground and are controlled by good tillage and soil fumigation.

Yellows: This is another disease of China-asters and is carried to them by leaf hoppers from neighboring weeds. The cure is to remove all perennial weeds from the neighborhood or to grow the asters in cloth houses to keep out the insects.

EDITOR'S NOTE: This chapter deals with fundamental problems and practices and suggests remedies and methods that are still effective and that can well be employed in home gardens. However, modern scientific research and discovery are constantly supplementing them with new materials and methods designed to accomplish the same ends more easily, quickly, and effectively. For information about them see "GARDEN MAGIC MARCHES ON," page 439.—E.L.D.S.

THE CONTROL OF INSECT PESTS AND PLANT DISEASES

From Bulletin 76, OHIO STATE UNIVERSITY by T. H. Parks and A. L. Pierstorff.
(Diseases are listed in italics)

Crop attacked	Insect or disease	Description	Remedy or prevention	When to apply
ALL OR MOST GARDEN PLANTS	White grubs	Large, white larvae with hard, brown heads. Live under the surface of soil	If grubs are discovered in the seedbed, sow more seed and thin out later Plow or spade deeply in October, garden soil known to harbor white grubs Grub-proof lawns with 5 to 10 lbs. lead arsenate per 1000 sq. ft. spread evenly and watered in.	(See remedy)
	Wireworms	Long, slender, yellow or brown larvae living in the soil	No remedy, except prevention Avoid planting potatoes, sweet corn, or root crops in soil known to contain these worms Rotate garden crops Spade or plow deeply in the fall	(See remedy)
	Grasshoppers	Need no description	Poisoned bran mash	When grasshoppers first appear
	Damping-off	Seedlings rot off at surface of ground	Sterilize seed and soil Plant seeds thin in rows Keep surface of soil stirred after seeds come up. Water thoroughly at longer intervals. Give as much sunlight and air as possible.	Before planting After seeds come up
ASTER	Blister beetle	Black or gray elongate beetles ½ to ⅝ inch in length which frequently appear in large numbers and ruin the flower and buds	Spray beetles as soon as they appear with strong pyrethrum spray. Strike insects with spray. Repeat as new beetles appear	When beetles first appear and as long as they are present
	Leaf beetle (12 spotted)	Greenish-yellow beetles, ¼ inch long, with twelve prominent black spots on wings. Eat holes in leaves	Spray plants with arsenate of lead 4 level tablespoons in 1 gal. (1 pint to 8 gals.) of water; or Use pyrethrum spray as for blister beetles to avoid stain on flower if asters are ready to cut for market or ornament	When beetles are first seen As long as beetles are present
	Root aphides	Bluish green plant lice attack the roots causing growth to stop and leaves turn yellow	Destroy ants which foster these aphides Work into the soil about the roots fresh tobacco dust, or Loosen soil about portion of roots and pour into it nicotine sulfate solution at strength of 1½ teaspoons to a gallon of soapy water	When insects are found
	Striped stalk borer	See Dahlia	See Dahlia	
	Leaf hoppers	Small yellowish-green insects that suck sap from under surface of leaves. Winged ones fly away upon least disturbance. Young run sideways across leaf Insects transmit "yellows" disease	Spray both surfaces of leaves with Bordeaux mixture 3–5–50 and nicotine sulfate 1½ teaspoons to 1 gal. of soapy water or Spray insects with pyrethrum spray	When insects are first noticed. Repeat at 7- to 10-day intervals Repeat as above

Crop attacked	Insect or disease	Description	Remedy or prevention	When to apply
ASTER	*Wilt*	Plants wilt. Lower leaves turn yellow. A ring of brown dots inside of stem just beneath the "bark."	Select seed from healthy plants or sow seed in sterilized soil Grow wilt resistant varieties which are now on the market Plant in new location	Before seed is sown
	Yellows	Plants turn yellow, are much dwarfed and the flower heads open unevenly or only partially and have a greenish cast	Pull up and burn diseased plants. Keep weeds down Spray at 7- to 10-day intervals with Bordeaux mixture 3–5–50 to prevent leafhopper feeding or Grow plants under insect proof cheesecloth cages	As soon as diseased plants are noticed
CHRYSAN-THEMUM	Aphides	Green or black plant-lice that cluster on stems and branches	See Aster	
	Blister beetle	See Aster	See Aster	
	Striped stalk borer	See Dahlia	See Dahlia	
	Wilt	Plants wilt and die. Lower part of stem turns black	Plant in new location	
DAHLIA	Striped stalk borer	Borer enters stem through a round hole and tunnels the center, causing wilting	No effective remedy after infested Keep coarse weeds and grass cut near flowers Destroy wilted stems	Until August 1
	Blister beetle	See Aster	See Aster	
	Tarnished plant bug	Brown plant bugs about ¼ inch long that fly away rapidly. Bugs puncture and deform flower buds	Difficult to control Strike bugs with pyrethrum spray	When first observed
	Leaf hopper	See Aster	See Aster	
	Rose chafer	See Rose	See Rose	
	Stunt (Mosaic)	Plants stunted, bushy, and foliage yellowish green	Dig up and discard infected clumps if the cause of stunt is not due to insects, rotted tubers or poor growing conditions	As soon as noticed
	Stunt (Insects)	Plants bushy and dwarfed. Foliage bears leaf hoppers	See Leaf hopper	
EVERGREEN (Arborvitae)	Bag worm	Brown larvae encased in a small conical bag or covering made of fragments of leaves. Feeds on foliage	Hand pick and destroy bags with larvae On larger plantings, spray with 4 level tablespoons of arsenate of lead or calcium arsenate in 1 gal. of water	When insects first appear
	Red Spider	Very small mites that feed upon foliage causing "rusty" appearance of same	Dust plants with powdered sulphur or Spray plants with 1 pound of glue dissolved in hot water plus dry lime-sulphur 2½ oz. and dilute to 10 gallons	When insects first appear

THE CONTROL OF INSECT PESTS AND PLANT DISEASES

From Bulletin 76, OHIO STATE UNIVERSITY by T. H. Parks and A. L. Pierstorff.
(Diseases are listed in italics)

Crop attacked	Insect or disease	Description	Remedy or prevention	When to apply
GLADIOLUS	Thrips	Very small active, black insects that feed under leaf sheath, causing plants to be stunted and flowers deformed	Plant only sound, uninfected corms. If plants become infested, spray with 1 tablespoon of Paris green and 2 lbs. of brown sugar in 3 gals. water. Or tartar emetic spray. Frequent drenching of plants with a stream of water affords some relief. Fumigate infested corms	Spring. As soon as thrips are noticed and repeated weekly until flowers show
	Penicillium rot	Lesions brown outside, gray within. Causes a porous rot throughout corm	By avoiding injury through digging, this disease can largely be eliminated. Sort out all rotting corms in storage	
	Scab	At first small brown spots on leaves; later elongating and turning black. Base of leaf may rot off or entire top die	Avoid injuring corms at harvest time. Remove all husks before planting. Discard all corms which show any spotting. Plant in soil which has not grown gladioli. Treat corms in a solution of corrosive sublimate 1 to 1000 for 2 hours	Before storing. Just before planting
	Hard rot	Spots on leaves reddish brown sometimes with purplish margins. Minute black dots in center of older spots. Lesions on corms in fall are minute, appear water soaked reddish-brown to brownish-black in color	Rake up and burn all dead tops left on ground. Also follow remedies suggested under scab	After harvest
	Dry rot	Stems may rot off below the surface of the ground. Lesions on corms are minute reddish-brown circular spots later increasing in size with sunken centers, definite margins and the color deepening to black	Follow suggestions for *Scab* and *Hard rot*. In addition dig up and destroy any infected plants	During growing season and at harvest time
IRIS	Iris borer	Large cream to pinkish colored caterpillar spotted on sides. Tunnels through larger roots, causing them to decay and plants to die	Destroy old top growth in early spring. Cut away and remove leaf fans showing early feeding work, which removes young borer with it and prevents root damage. Reset plants every second year soon after bloom	Early spring. May or early June
PEONY	Rose chafer	Long-legged yellowish-brown beetles about ½ inch long that feed on blossoms and leaves	See Rose	
	Ants	Cluster on flower buds	These do no harm to buds but feed on sweet secretion	

Crop attacked	Insect or disease	Description	Remedy or prevention	When to apply
PEONY	*Botrytis bud blight*	Blasting of young and old buds. Young shoots have brownish water soaked lesions at ground line	Remove and burn diseased portions. Spray plants with 4–6–50 Bordeaux mixture as soon as shoots show in spring	As soon as noticed
	Root rot	Crown and larger roots rot	Dig up and destroy badly rotted plants. Slightly rotted roots may be cut away and healthy portion planted in new location	As soon as noticed
ROSE	Rose slug	Slimy, green slugs that feed upon the upper surface of rose leaves, skeletonizing them	Spray or sprinkle with hellebore, 1½ oz. to 1 gal. water or Arsenate of lead (pwd.) 3 level tablespoons to 1 gal. water (½ pt. to 5 gals.) Drench frequently with water from hose	When slugs appear
	Rose chafer (rose bug)	Long-legged yellowish-brown beetles about ½-inch long that puncture young buds and leaves	Spray with arsenate of lead (pwd.) 5 level tablespoons to 1 gal. water sweetened with sirup 1 pt. of arsenate of lead to 6 gals. sweetened water or Spray beetles with strong pyrethrum spray or Spray or dust with fluosilicates	When beetles appear
	Leaf hopper	Small, greenish-white, active insects that suck the sap from underside of leaf. Cause leaves to have white speckled appearance	Spray with nicotine or pyrethrum solution as for rose aphides. Be sure to wet the underside of leaves or Dust insects with nicotine dust	When insects appear
	Leaf roller	Pale green caterpillar with brown head which rolls up and lives in fold of leaf	Collect and burn infested leaves containing these worms Spray with arsenate of lead (pwd.) 3 level tablespoons to 1 gal. water (½ pt. to 5 gals.)	When damage is first noticed
	Aphis or plant louse	Small, sluggish, green plant lice which mass upon the buds and stems, and suck the sap	Spray insects with nicotine sulfate 1½ teaspoons to 1 gal. soapy water or Pyrethrum spray directed against the lice or Dust insects with nicotine dust	When insects first appear
	Ants	No description needed	Ants on stems and buds do no direct damage to roses but feed on honey-dew secreted by aphis For control, see under Grass	
	Leaf cutting bee	Bee which cuts out circular pieces from leaf	No remedy known. Damage is not usually severe	
	Black-spot	Large, circular, black blotches on leaves	Dust thoroughly with 90-10 sulfur-manganar or 90-10 sulfur-lead dust or Spray with 4–6–50 Bordeaux mixture	Before disease appears, if possible Repeat at 10-day intervals
	Mildew	Leaves covered with white powdery growth, often dwarfed and deformed	Same as for black spot	When disease first appears
	Brown canker	Small purple spots on stems or petioles of leaves. Later light colored in center, with purplish margin. Similar spots on leaves and petals	Cut out and burn large cankers Spray 5 to 6 times with Bordeaux mixture 4–6–50	As soon as noticed Start with new growth in spring

CHAPTER XVIII

EQUIPMENT

*The failures of life sit around and
    complain,
    That the gods haven't treated 'em right.
They've lost their umbrellas whenever it
    rains
    And they haven't their lanterns at night.*

The above, quoted from memory (perhaps incorrectly), serves as a caustic comment on the boy-scout-like virtue of preparedness.

Good garden work needs good tools and materials but we do not advise rushing into quantity purchases without careful consideration. First have a place to keep them, then buy the tools, or if you have them, get them clean and sharp. Perfection was never achieved in a minute.

A little experience will prove to the amateur that clean, sharp tools are far easier to use than those which have been neglected.

GARDEN TOOLS

Our illustration shows (1) a planting shovel which is small and very handy around the garden. The spading fork (2) is much easier to handle and does better work than a regular spade. A speedy cultivator (3) will help keep the perennial beds and the rose garden in shape with very little labor. The bow rake (4) has two uses; it takes the rough stuff off the lawn and is much handier than the regular rake in garden cultivation. The weed spud (5) should be used for such weeds as plantain, dock and other surface-rooted weeds which

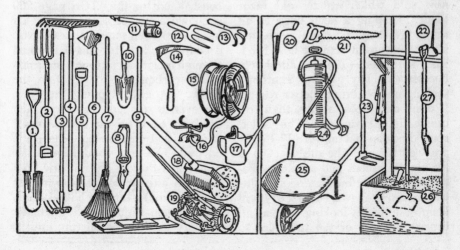

can be eradicated with one removal. This tool is not good for dandelions, unless they are worked over a dozen or more times a season. The dandelion will sprout from the old root and make more plants when cut. The broom rake (7) should be used to remove rubbish from the lawn; don't use it to remove grass clippings, but allow them to go back into the soil, replacing vegetable matter. Shears (8) are something every gardener should have and use. Proper pruning makes good plants. A home-made tamper (9) is fine to smooth out the newly dug garden bed or to level up the lawn in the spring. Dozens of uses can be found for it about the garden. The hand fork (12) the trowel (10) the hand cultivator (13) should be kept in the hand box at all times within easy reach to remove that weed or break up the soil around the backward plant. The hand sprayer (11) may be enough for you to use, but the knapsack sprayer (24) can be pumped up and carried about the garden with a generous supply of spray. A good edging sickle (14) is now sold which utilizes old razor blades, keeping a keen edge at all times. Nothing is more neglected about the garden than the hose (15). The sprinkler (16) is absolutely necessary in any garden. Thorough soaking always brings better results, if done only occasionally, than frequent light sprinkling. The roller, sprinkling can and mower (17-18-19) are well known. The dibble (20) is for planting seeds and seedlings. Potato hoe (23) is fine for deeper cultivation and the lawn edger (27) will keep your walks looking trim at all times. The rest of the tools are so well known as to need no comment.

The first thing we need is a place to store them when not in use. If you have an easy entrance to your cellar from your garden, this problem is soon solved. A garage built a little larger than is necessary to care for the car and the automobile tools, also soon solves the problem. However, if neither of these is available, a small rain-proof shed may be concealed in the shrubbery, not forgetting what it will look like when the leaves are off. It should be waterproof not only as to the roof, but also at the sides. Small tools may be stored in a hinged top box full of oiled sand. This may form one of the seats in the garden house.

No matter where you store tools, cleaning cloths should always be provided to care for them after each use. First you need an oily cloth and then a dry cloth. It is surprising how much easier they are to use, how much more satisfaction they will give if they are kept clean.

Of course the most desirable place to keep tools is in a rack especially constructed for them. On page 269 is shown a box of sand over which has been poured some oil. Crank case drainings will do for this if strained through a cloth so as to get out some of the carbon which will stain the hands. The cost of oiling the sand, however, is so small, being only ten or fifteen cents for the entire time it is used, that the use of clean oil is advised. The sand should be rather coarse and thoroughly sun dried before you attempt to mix it with the oil. Mix about a third or half as much sand as you require and gradually add dry sand to the mixture until it has a dry oily feeling. Too much oil should not be used as it will make the tools greasy and hard to handle.

Tools plunged into this oily sand are not exposed to the air and therefore do not rust. In addition, there is a constant film of oil upon them and they are very easily cleaned after use. Sickles, scythes, shears, etc. will stay sharp much longer if not rusty.

Of course tools which have working parts, such as the lawn mower, must be kept free from sand. Only the blade of the shears should be forced into this sand which must not get into the pivot or friction surface of the shears. Keep this pivot well oiled and wipe sand from the shears before using them.

This box should be not less than 12 inches wide and 12 inches deep and a little more will help. The construction of a rack or guard rail above the box to keep tools from falling down will avoid annoyance. Above this rack may be constructed the spray shelf mentioned later on.

To start with in carrying out this tool program, we should first soak them in water and scrub them well. Metal parts should be cleaned with a wire brush and then rubbed with sandpaper, or emery paper. Coarse emery powder and oil used on a piece of old carpet will soon brighten them up. Sandpaper is now manufactured that may be used while wet and this helps considerably. There are also manufactured rust removers and penetrating oil which do this job very well. These things cost very little money and save a lot of labor. If your hardware dealer cannot supply you, inquire at a mill supply house.

Wooden handles should be scraped with a wood scraper or piece of glass to get the old paint and rough splinters off of them; then carefully sand them and paint them some bright color. Red or yellow wagon paint is best. This identifies them as your property and makes them easy to find when left lying on the lawn. It will also keep them from being appropriated by forgetful neighbors.

The Garden Hose is a much abused tool. Do not allow it to kink when you are pulling it or do not run over it with a heavy wheelbarrow or leave it lying about in the hot sun of summer. Nothing is so hard on rubber as heat and oil. Many types of reels are now in use which can be attached to the side of the house in the shade or rolled along the ground, making it easy to care for the hose. In storing hose for the winter be sure that all water is fully drained and that no water freezes in it. It should always be loosely coiled.

Sprayers: No one can have a successful garden unless they wage effective war on insects and plant diseases. All spraying machines must be washed out with clean water after use, and the nozzle should be examined to get out any particles of grit which are bound to choke it.

If you use a rubber bulb syringe spray, examine it frequently for grit and keep it away from hot sun or steam pipes. In the spraying equipment, the leather washer in the pump needs frequent attention. Remove this washer, clean and oil it frequently. It will save time in the end. If the washer has hardened so that it will not respond to the oil treatment, secure a new one from your hardware dealer or seed store—they have them in stock. Examine all attachments to the sprayers. See that they do not leak air.

It always pays to buy a good sprayer in the first place. A ten or fifteen cent sprayer will do the work for a while, but will be the most expensive in the end.

The Lawn Mower: The care (or lack of care!) given the lawn mower is sometimes disheartening. The curving blades of the mower rotate against the bottom knife which is fixed and should just touch it evenly all along. If they do not touch, the grass cannot be cut, while if they are too tight it will be difficult or impossible to push the machine. If the mower will cut a piece of newspaper inserted between the blades it will cut grass. Try it with slips of paper at various points. Adjustment is made by two opposing screws which moves the bottom blade up or down.

The revolving blades are driven by gears which are located on the inside of the driving wheels which roll upon the ground. These gears frequently become full of dust or dirt, making them hard to operate. Loosen the screw on the center of these wheels and remove them one at a time. In some cases it is necessary to remove a nut. A little examination will disclose how. After removing the wheel flush out the interior with kerosene which you can apply with a regular squirt oil can. See that each individual tooth and gear is clean and that each movable part is working evenly. If you remove any of the gears, do so one at a time and note carefully just how you take it out so

as to get it back in exactly the same position. The part which you found packed in cup grease should be repacked with cup grease, after which the mower should be assembled and lubricated thoroughly with good grade medium body machine oil.

When the mower leaves ridges of uncut grass, it needs adjustment. No amount of oiling and cleaning will make it cut. Cleaning and oiling merely save effort in propelling the mower. If the blades seem to be dull, they can be sharpened by applying coarse valve grinding compound on the stationary blade, and then running the mower backwards. (Some mowers cannot be reversed.) The knives may be touched up a bit with a file, but care is needed to avoid filing them unevenly. If the blades are badly worn or nicked, it is best to take them to a professional who uses a machine especially designed for sharpening them. Rust is the greatest enemy of the lawn mower and frequent painting will lengthen its life. Bronze or aluminum paint applied with a small brush is the thing for this. The wooden roller determines how long or short the grass shall be cut; it may be raised to make a longer cutting and lowered for a shorter one. Again care must be taken that this adjustment be made evenly on both sides. (See illustration under "Lawns," page 52.)

Quality: With tools as in everything else, quality pays. Buy only the best of tools and do your best to keep from lending them to your friends and neighbors. A man who is not interested enough in gardening to own the necessary tools will not take proper care of yours. If you are

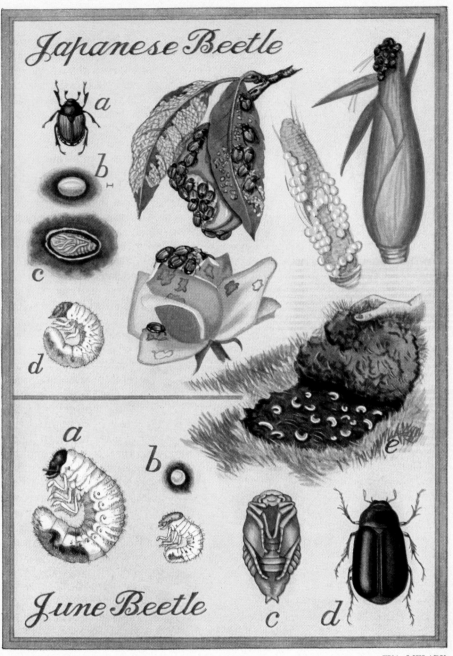

EVA MELADY

JAPANESE BEETLE: (a) *adult, with injury on peach, rose, and corn;* (b) *egg in soil (enlarged);* (c) *pupa in soil;* (d) *grub;* (e) *grubs with damage to turf.* **JUNE BEETLE:** (a) *white grub (larva, full size);* (b) *egg (enlarged), and larva;* (c) *pupa;* (d) *adult.*

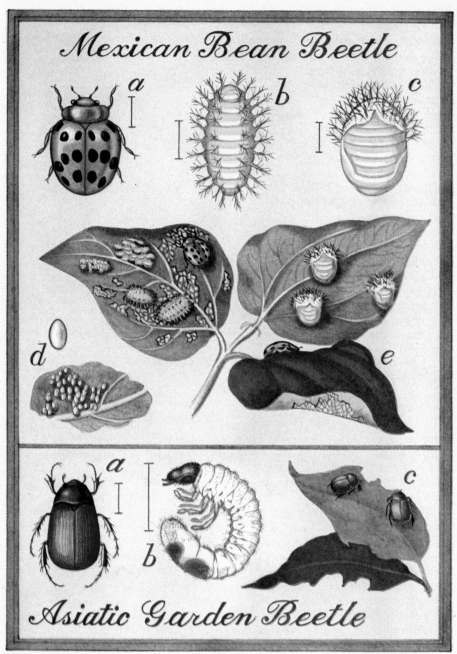

Mexican Bean Beetle

Asiatic Garden Beetle

EVA MELADY

MEXICAN BEAN BEETLE: (a) *adult;* (b) *grub (larva);* (c) *pupa showing larval skin pushed back at one end;* (d) *egg cluster on back of leaf and single egg (enlarged);* (e) *bean leaf showing beetle in all stages and feeding pattern (skeletonization).* **ASIATIC GARDEN BEETLE:** (a) *adult;* (b) *grub;* (c) *beetles, natural size, feeding on foliage.*

forced to lend your tools make a note of it and ask for the return of them within a very short time.

The maxim for every gardener should be, "I buy the best of tools and keep them in the best of condition."

The Hand Tool Box: Anyone would question the efficiency of a doctor who was to visit the sick without equipment. The joke about the plumbers trips to the shop is an old one. The gardener, however, may make hundreds of trips to his tool supply without ever questioning or planning a better arrangement.

Good tools are useless if they are not handy. In our trips of inspection, a snip here, a little spraying or dusting there or even tying up a plant is but the work of a minute if the materials and tools are with us. If we have to walk back to get them the work is delayed until tomorrow (which never comes) or forgotten until too late.

In gardening, as elsewhere in life, success comes from knowing what you are doing and doing what you are knowing. "Do it now," is a good motto if backed up with knowledge and forethought.

The best preventive of procrastination is the hand tool box or first aid kit shown on page 275. Ideas are quickly recorded in the cheap, loose-leaf student's note books which are sold with semi-waterproof covers almost everywhere. With the means of measuring and staking, the border can be replanned in a moment of inspiration which may never return.

The box is made of one-half inch poplar and contains the lightest of tools. Keep it with you at all times.

SAVING LABOR ON THE HOME GROUNDS

RIGHT— BLADE ENGAGES OBJECT TO BE CUT AT A SLANT
HOW TO USE A GRASS WHIP

WRONG— BLADE HITTING AT RIGHT ANGLE HAS TENDENCY TO KNOCK OBJECT DOWN RATHER THAN CUT.

RIGHT— WRIST MOTION DRAWS THE BLADE ALONG THE GRASS CUTTING IT OFF
TIPS FOR USING A SICKLE

WRONG— LONG ARM STROKE BREAKS THE GRASS AND KNOCKS IT DOWN

THE RUBBER-TOOTHED RAKE— WILL NOT TEAR THE SPREADING TURF

THE BROOM RAKE - BEST USED AS A BROOM WITH LITTLE DISTURBANCE TO GRASS

Its usefulness will grow upon you and fascinate you.

SOME NEW USEFUL TOOLS

Every year sees new gadgets and labor-saving devices put on the market and offered to the amateur gardener. Many of them are well worth while and will help him in his work around the grounds. But some don't always measure up to expectations, and there is such a thing as overdoing the purchase of new things. For this reason we do not recommend the purchase of every gadget offered to lighten garden care, but we are going to mention a few which may prove useful. Our motto in the purchase of garden tools is always that old saying:

"*Be not the first by whom the new is tried*
Nor yet the last to lay the old aside."

One thing which makes for tiring exercise on the lawn or garden is the necessity of stooping or kneeling, therefore anything which saves this is greatly to be desired. Perhaps the most useful tool which has been perfected in recent years for the lawn is the grass whip illustrated on page 273, which has achieved a well-deserved popularity.

Every home has a sickle, but not many are ever found in shape to use after a few usings. To overcome this, some one has invented one that has an edge renewable by the insertion of discarded safety razor blades of the double cutting type. This kind of tool is useful for cutting grass when it becomes too tall for the mower, but it is not so good for cutting heavier weeds. Few people use such tools advantageously.

Take the use of the sickle, for instance, most users draw back the arm and strike the grass in such a manner that the blade is brought into contact with the grass at right angles to the blade with considerable force. This has a tendency to knock the grass flat instead of cutting it off. Cutting requires that the blade be drawn across the object to be cut and a wrist motion is much more effective. We have tried to illustrate this in the sketches of sickle and grass whip.

A very important thing in the culture of a fine lawn is raking. Blue grass, which forms the backbone of lawn grasses over much of the country, has a creeping tendency and gains density by spreading sidewise. In the early spring combing the lawn with an iron-toothed rake is beneficial for it pulls out all the dead grasses and frees the ground for occupation by the spreading lawn grasses. When the blue grass spreads and starts new stools or tufts, harsh raking will break connections with the main plant and possibly cause the newly sprouting growth to die out before it becomes self supporting. To offset this, there is now sold a rubber-toothed rake, which will gently comb out all loose material, but will slip over anything which resists it. Among the best tools for removing cuttings from the lawn is the well known broom rake, made in bamboo and also of steel. It may be used in the manner of the regular garden rake, or with a sidewise sweeping motion, which makes the operation somewhat easier.

The cart illustrated is a recently introduced means of removing refuse from the lawn or garden with the least possible labor. If you are interested your seed store can probably obtain one for you, or you will doubtless find it advertised in garden magazines.

SERVICE PLOT

The writer's success in the use of the hand box gave him the idea of the service plot. Why not a laboratory—a kitchen, if you please, to supply the garden needs?

On page 280 we show such a spot; it may be hidden behind shrubbery, a fence, or in some manner to screen it out of the general landscaping scheme. Here we put a handy toolhouse to hold the larger tools and materials so that they too may be readily accessible at all times. A shallow cellar below (4′ is a good depth) will hold rotting manure in barrels,

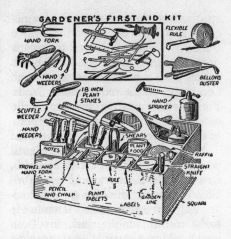

GARDENER'S FIRST AID KIT

HAND FORK
FLEXIBLE RULE
HAND WEEDERS
BELLOWS DUSTER
18 INCH PLANT STAKES
HAND SPRAYER
SCUFFLE WEEDER
HAND WEEDERS
NOTES
SHEARS
PLANT FOOD
RAFFIA
TROWEL AND HAND FORK
STRAIGHT KNIFE
RULE
PENCIL AND CHALK
PLANT TABLETS
LABELS
GARDEN LINE
SQUARE

a bale of peat moss, or a sack of humus. Do not cement the floor but put down six inches of clean washed gravel or cinders and a rather tight removable wood floor on top of it. This will keep it dry.

A concrete compost pit 4 x 4 and 4 or 5 ft. deep will hold a lot of leaves while rotting into leaf mold. These are packed into tight, six inch layers and treated with a generous dusting of lime and ¼ pound of sulphate of ammonia to the square foot. About two inches of soil is placed over them and the process repeated. The pit being waterproof facilitates keeping the leaves wet which is the important thing in making leaf mold. It also avoids, to some extent, losing the fertilizing elements from the compost.

The blossoms of almost all plants are increased in size by the application of liquid manure at blooming times. As it is applied, diluted to the color of weak tea, a little of it goes a long way. Try to find a sound wooden barrel, soak it over night with a solution of two pounds or more of sal soda to neutralize the acid (if it held vinegar). Suspend a bushel of fresh horse or cow manure in a sack in it, provide a wooden lid and you have a plant food factory that will last for years, if you keep water in it in summer and drain it to about two inches in winter. Paint the outside with black asphaltum to preserve it against rotting.

A small concealed bed is a handy thing to have in the garden. Here we may make a kitchen green garden and plant those things which grow themselves such as a clump of mint for sauce, etc.; clumps of chives, parsley, rhubarb, etc. Flowers for cutting, bulbous iris, cosmos, etc., many times are not sightly enough for the open border, yet we want them. Annuals or summer flowering bulbs in pots started here are easily transplanted to fill the bare spots in the border left by earlier flowering varieties. Plants raised from seeds or cuttings may be hardened to full sun under slats; spring flowering bulbs may be heeled-in to ripen their foliage; shrubbery may be heeled-in until ready for permanent planting and so on for numerous other uses, "ad infinitum."

The use of a small propagating bed for an abundance of plants is explained later. It may be combined with a coldframe by replacing one of the sash with a slatted frame made of lath. Leave a little room, however, in case you decide to have a separate bed for propagating.

The service plot should always contain a seat. One of those light movable slat affairs is good. Upon this the gardener catches a few moments of ease while doing his heavy thinking or planning, or when checking notes or supplies. Visitors, too, will find it useful for repose while giving back seat directions to the gardener.

The Coldframe: To the average gardener hotbeds and coldframes are synonymous. This is not the case. This gardener has found that unless you have full time attendance it is best not to attempt a manure-heated hotbed. There are too many temperature requirements, too much opening and closing of sash at times which are inopportune.

The coldframe, however, is merely a glass-topped box set in or upon the ground which, while protecting the contents from wind and frost, is heated by the sun in the daytime and this heat may be retained at night by a mat covering.

Its uses are so many that we hesitate to try to name them. Every gardener will find it adaptable to some need. It has been estimated that the flowering season may be prolonged outdoors for sixty days by using it to start flowers earlier and to mature the late ones in the fall. Spring flowering bulbs potted for winter bloom may be easily plunged (buried) here, to be used all winter indoors just as we use fruit and vegetables from our preserving cellars.

For wintering the half hardy plants such as foxglove, campanula, kniphofia (Red Hot Poker) etc., its value cannot be overestimated. Pansies, violets, geraniums and other plants may be wintered and grown here with little or no protection. No housekeeper will object to growing winter onions, parsley, etc., for seasoning, all winter, not to mention the early onions, radishes, lettuce,

etc., whose flavor cannot be duplicated in stores.

The messy business of trying to start seedling plants indoors in the spring is to a great extent made unnecessary by a coldframe. Seeds started early may be hardened to fit outdoor conditions and the chances of success are multiplied many times.

A practical selection of plants which can easily be started in coldframes in March would include: China asters, coreopsis, cardinal flower, chrysanthemum (annual), early cosmos, dahlia, larkspur (annual), phlox (annual), snapdragon, stock (ten weeks), sweet William, etc. Experience will find many more.

Location: Both hotbeds and coldframes should be located in a sheltered place, where they will be protected from north and northwest winds by shrubbery, a fence, building or higher ground. They should also be placed on ground with a southern and an eastern exposure, so that the plants will receive the maximum amount of light and heat. The frames should be handy to the house and garden, so that they can be given constant attention, for this is necessary to obtain true success. The soil in and about the frame should be well drained. The water supply should be close to the frame, for watering is an essential factor in the production of good plants. Be careful not to locate in a damp spot unless you first drain it thoroughly with farm tile.

Construction: Do not be in too big a hurry to construct your coldframe of concrete. A wooden one will last for years. After you have used it for a while you may want to move it.

The frame may be constructed upon top of the ground but a better way is to dig a pit and extend the wooden frame to the bottom; then after conditioning the soil replace it in the pit. The wooden frame insulates the soil in the bed from the surrounding conditions and enables you to more easily control it.

The frame should be made of tight boards and it is better to bank the soil around as a further protection. The sash comes in standard size 3 ft. wide and 6 feet long. Half size sash 3 x 3 ft., are made for small frames. They are the best to use if they are to be handled by women or children. They can be purchased ready made, which is cheaper than made to order. They must be painted each year and stored on end, in the shade, where it is fairly dry, when not in use, as the sun and continual moisture rot them.

The sash are made as light as possible for handling and because of this sag quickly. They must be supported by a 2 x 4 on edge at each end of the frame and by 2 x 4 bars set flat between each two sash. The sash are allowed to rest upon these bars one inch on either side. Upon the bars are nailed one inch strips to keep the sash from interfering when moved and to make them fit tight. Close fitting is essential as a slight draft at the wrong time will harm the plants.

Soil: Coldframe soil depends upon the use to which the frame is being put. For growing more mature plants, fertility is necessary, but for starting seed and maturing seedlings a rich soil is a detriment. A well developed plant usually thrives in rich soil which is liable to burn the roots of younger plants. Seeds and cuttings must first have their roots developed in what is known as a sterile medium, usually poor soil with plenty of sand for drainage and peat for holding moisture sterilized by hot water or baking to destroy weed seeds and disease spores. This causes the roots to forage for food developing sturdy growth.

Whatever the use, the soil at all times must drain well. The enemy of all propagation, indoors or under glass, is a fungous disease referred to as "damping-off." This is caused by an excess of moisture in soil and air. The soil must be allowed to hold only what can be absorbed by it, and the excess run off freely. Sand or ashes must be mixed with it to make it break up easily when compacted, while damp, into a ball. Stiff soil is cold soil; we need soil that warms readily in spring.

Atmosphere: When wintering plants in a coldframe the sash may be left on most of the time but when young plants are being raised, ventilation is necessary every day. The air is damp and confined and the weather changeable. This results in the fatal damping-off. Steam or moisture upon the glass is a danger signal. Open the sash on a tiny crack for a short time in cold weather and more in warmer. Always open on the side away from the wind.

Watering: Indiscreet watering will cause loss. On sunny days water each day in the morning so that plants dry off before the cold of night. Going to sleep wet is bad for them. In cloudy weather they may need watering only once every two or three days, but always do it in the morning.

Covering: For sudden changes or cold nights late in spring, it is well to have a mat made of an old rug, quilted burlap bags, etc., to cover the entire frame. Tie it down but be sure to remove it during the daytime. Strong mats, made for the purpose can be purchased.

Forcing Boxes: Emergency forcing boxes can be readily improvised from almost anything. For instance, a barrel set over a rhubarb plant and covered with an old sash forces long tender stalks; and soap boxes covered with glass serve for protection during a late spring freeze.

Forcing boxes generally require considerable and constant attention by the grower. Because of the small volume of air which is inclosed, ventilation and watering must be watched closely. As soon as there is any indication of moisture on the inside of the glass, a little ventilation should be given. Gradually, as the season becomes warmer and the plants hardier, the ventilation should be increased until the glass can be left off during the day and finally all the time. After the warm weather sets in the boxes should be removed and stored in a dry loft or basement. The commercial forcing boxes are quite expensive, so that it is advisable to make them at home during the winter months, when gardening is at an ebb.

HOTBEDS

A hotbed is heated from below by the fermentation of manure or otherwise. It is a miniature greenhouse. On page 280 is shown the construction and much of the information offered above is applicable to it. The following instructions give brief directions but more should be obtained from garden books obtainable at your public library or from literature that any good greenhouse manufacturing company will send.

Manure and Its Handling: A good deal of the success with hotbeds is due to the careful selection of the manure. Cold manure, like that of cows and pigs, should never be used because it will not heat. Horse manure is best, but in this case at least one-third of the bulk should be straw. If pure manure is used, it will pack too tightly when firmed, so that it will not heat. If possible, the manure from grain-fed, straw-bedded horses should be used.

The manure to be used should be hauled at least two weeks before it is to be used. It should be piled in a flat, compact pile, three to five feet high, and of a convenient width and length. If the weather is cold or the manure refuses to heat, add considerable water and firm the pile. When complete, the pile should thoroughly heat in four or five days, after which it should be turned so as to put the cool manure on the inside and the hot manure on the outside. By so doing a very uniform heating will be obtained. After about another week the pile will again be thoroughly heated, so that the pit can be filled.

Filling the Hotbed: In filling the hotbed, place the manure in the bed in layers six inches deep. As each layer is put in the pit it should be thoroughly tramped, so that it is firm, especially in the corners and along the sides of the bed. It is essential that the manure be well tramped, otherwise it will not heat and the bed will be useless. Also the bed will settle less if the manure is well firmed before the soil is placed in the frames. When the pit has been filled to the level of the ground with well-tramped layers of manure, the sash should be placed on until the manure has thoroughly heated. The soil should then be placed in the pit to a depth of six inches, if crops are to be grown to maturity; four inches of soil will be sufficient for starting early plants. The soil should be a finely pulverized garden loam, which has been well leveled and packed.

The Temperature: The temperature rises rapidly for several days, often going above 125 degrees F. After the temperature of the manure has dropped to 85 or 90 degrees, the bed will be ready to plant. To take the temperature in hotbeds, a plunging thermometer should be used. This consists of a metal, brass, or iron point which encloses the thermometer bulb. The whole is mounted on a wooden handle, which protects the glass from any possible injury. Such thermometers can be purchased for about a dollar and a quarter from supply houses. In taking the temperature, thrust the thermometer through the soil into the manure, and read the temperature when the thermometer is in place.

Care of the Hotbeds: *Watering:* The soil in a hotbed should be kept moist without soaking the manure. If the manure is soaked, it will cause uneven heating besides cooling the bed, so that the heat is spent sooner than it would be by judicious watering. Occasional thorough waterings are much better than frequent light sprinklings. It is advisable to water on mornings of bright, sunshiny days, and never on cloudy days or late in the day. Late watering lowers the temperature at a critical time and leaves the foliage wet for overnight. Both of these conditions foster disease, especially "damping-off," which is the most serious disease in the frames.

Ventilation: Ventilation is absolutely essential to supply the plants with fresh air, to reduce the humidity, and to control the temperature within the bed. A very good indication of the need of ventilation is the amount of moisture which collects on the inside of the glass. A little air should be given the beds each day, gradually increasing the amount until the sash can be left off during the day. A week or ten days before the plants are set in the field the sash should be removed day and night, so that the plants are thoroughly hardened.

Cultivation: If seeds and plants are in drills or rows, it is desirable to cultivate between rows and plants. Cultivation keeps the weeds down, makes a surface mulch, and lessens the amount of disease in the beds.

Advantages of Using a Hotbed: (1) Crops can be matured in sections where the season would otherwise be too short.

(2) There is less danger from fall frosts, in the open, than there is from spring frosts.

(3) By advancing the season, two or more crops can be grown on the same land.

(4) Weeds are less difficult to handle when good-sized plants are set out.

(5) Many insect pests and plant diseases are avoided.

(6) Larger crops can be produced.

(7) Crops mature earlier.

The Electric Hotbed: Electricity is now the key to modern hotbed operation. It does away with the delay and mess of using fresh manure, which, incidentally, is becoming harder and harder to obtain in cities, suburbs, etc. It is easy and inexpensive to install, and it provides steady heat where most needed (just below seeds of plants) and, with the help of a simple automatic thermostat, to whatever extent is desired. Assuming that an ordinary light socket is close by the hotbed, or that you can rig up (or have rigged up) the neces-sary wiring, all that is needed is (1) a length of lead-covered heating cable to be laid back and forth on a bed of sand in the hotbed and covered with another layer of sand and then the soil; (2) the thermostat which shuts the current on when heat is needed and off when it is not; (3) a soil thermometer connected with the thermostat and inserted in the soil. The whole business can be bought of most good seed stores, dealers in electric equipment, or greenhouse manufacturing firms for a few dollars and should last a good many years. For full information about electricity in modern garden-

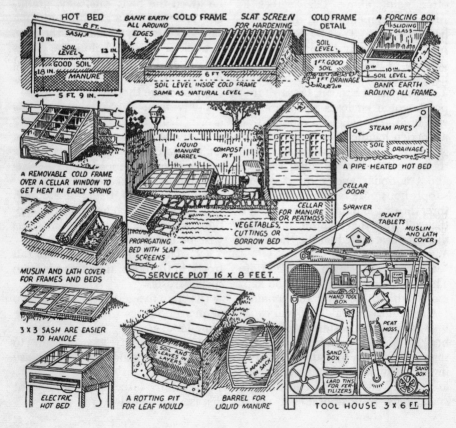

HOT BED — COLD FRAME — SLAT SCREEN FOR HARDENING — COLD FRAME DETAIL — A FORCING BOX

A REMOVABLE COLD FRAME OVER A CELLAR WINDOW TO GET HEAT IN EARLY SPRING

A PIPE HEATED HOT BED

SERVICE PLOT 16 X 8 FEET.

MUSLIN AND LATH COVER FOR FRAMES AND BEDS

3 X 3 SASH ARE EASIER TO HANDLE

ELECTRIC HOT BED

A ROTTING PIT FOR LEAF MOULD

BARREL FOR LIQUID MANURE

TOOL HOUSE 3 X 6 FT.

ing write to the nearest headquarters of any big utilities (light and power) company, or to your state experiment station for bulletins on the subject that it or other nearby stations will send you.

As a summary let us consider:

Some Things to Remember in Operating Coldframes and Hotbeds: Be careful to keep all drains and gutters around or above the frames free from snow and ice. Otherwise, a sudden thaw may soak or even flood the soil in the frames with bad results.

Give ventilation frequently, even if temperature inside does not make this necessary. Fresh air is important to health of plants and it discourages disease and bugs. Too much ventilation, however, will chill your plants and retard growth; on the other hand caution is also needed in giving them too little fresh air. This error may cause you to find your plants "cooked," which will cause them to be soft, and will also prevent that vigorous growth which is one of the

delights to users. In cold weather, the sash raised a crack at the back during the middle of the day will give sufficient ventilation as a rule.

When the weather moderates, elevate the sash on short supports or else slide them down. Some experienced growers advise raising the sash on the leeward edge, that is, the side or end opposite to that from which the wind is blowing.

Slat shades are part of the successful grower's coldframe equipment. They serve to prevent the wilting of young plants when first transferred to the frames from hotbed or indoors by shading them from the direct rays of the sun, which is often too hot for them. They also serve to encourage the plants to make vigorous root growth instead of excessive top growth before the roots are sufficiently developed to support it.

It is best to not rush their natural growth, otherwise you may find yourself with lank and shallow-rooted plants.

EDITOR'S NOTE: Some of the most interesting progress in home gardening has been in the application of scientific principles and the development of mechanical devices aimed at the saving of time and energy. Recent developments in this field are discussed in "GARDEN MAGIC MARCHES ON," page 439.—E.L.D.S.

CHAPTER XIX

PROPAGATION

Old Mother Nature doesn't fret
Old Mother Nature always knows
When skies are gray and fields are wet;
What's underneath the wintry snows.
　　　　　　　　—Douglas Malloch.

•

One of the most interesting parts of gardening is propagation. It is a never-failing source of wonder to the thinking person what can be accomplished with a few seeds or cuttings from plants. It is not only interesting but profitable for the amateur to raise annuals, perennials and biennials, but the raising of trees, shrubbery, etc., should be treated more or less as a hobby, as the average home place is too small for the rather extensive nursery operations necessary.

Propagation covers the raising of plants from seeds, divisions, cuttings and layers. For the more expert, budding and grafting should be added, but this work, while quite interesting, is something that requires more study than the average amateur may be willing to give.

Special instructions are given for the propagation of various plants in their respective chapters, and it is always well to investigate the cultural directions to learn plant preferences as to acid soil or other matters before attempting to raise them.

SEEDS

Most people think of seed as being something that is sown only in the spring. This is not the case, for many perennials and biennials grow best if sown during the summer. Other perennials seem to need the freezing effect of winter before germinating and are planted in the fall. In general, there are two phases of seed sowing—that done outdoors, in the ground, and that done "under glass" in hotbeds, coldframes or flats or pots in a greenhouse.

Seed Quality: Poor seeds are expensive at any price. The labor and care needed to raise any plants justify paying a few cents more per packet. Cheap seeds are cheaply grown, while good seeds from reputable seedsmen are grown in special soil under expert attention. No wonder they outdo home-gathered or bargain price products.

Seeds Indoors: By sowing seeds indoors early in the spring we are able to gain from four to six weeks over those sown outdoors directly in the beds where they are to bloom. Almost any sort of receptacle will do for starting the plants. If you only have a few seeds a large flower pot or bulb pan is the best and easiest handled receptacle, although any pot or kettle with a hole or holes in the bottom to provide ample drainage is permissible.

If the pots are new they must be soaked in water for a couple of days before using—boiling them for an hour will serve the same purpose. First cover the hole in the bottom of the flower pot with several pieces of broken pot and add an inch or two of coarse gravel or small cinders for drainage. Many people prefer to place over this a thin layer of sphagnum or peat moss and then add the carefully prepared soil in which to plant the seed. This soil should consist of good garden loam, clean sharp sand and peat moss, humus or leaf mold in equal parts. If you do not have good garden soil buy a bushel or so for the purpose from a florist. It should be screened through a ½″ wire riddle and firmed down into the pot with the bottom of another pot until it is about 1″ from the top. It is now watered thoroughly and the best way to do this is to set the pot in a pan of water deep enough so that it is submerged two-thirds of its depth.

Wait until dampness shows on the surface of the soil, then set it aside for an hour or two until the surface has dried somewhat, when the seed may be planted in rows or broadcast, being careful not to have it too thick. Fine soil is then sifted over the seeds through a piece of fly screen.

The usual rule is to cover with soil about three times the diameter of the seed, but many of the finer seeds may be pressed into the soil and not covered at all except with a sheet of newspaper to keep them from drying out. Another good way to do this is to cover the pot with a piece of cloth.

Flats are shallow boxes of almost any size, but handiest when 9″ wide and 12″ long by 3″ deep. They may be made of almost any scrap lumber if the bottom is thoroughly pierced for drainage. A good and inexpensive way to make them is to use two pieces of ⅞″ board for the ends, which should be 9″ x 3″. The balance of the flats is composed of lath, spaced ¼″ apart. No holes for drainage will be necessary in this case.

The bottom of the flat should be covered with broken flower pots or clean cinders about ½ to 1″ thick; then proceed as instructed above in filling the flower pots. Plant the seeds

PLANTING SEEDS INDOORS

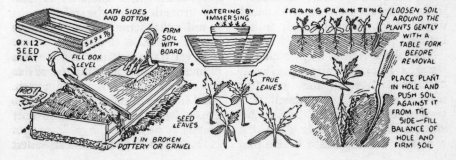

9 x 12 SEED FLAT — LATH SIDES AND BOTTOM — 3 x 9 x ⅞ — FILL BOX LEVEL — FIRM SOIL WITH BOARD — WATERING BY IMMERSING — TRANSPLANTING — LOOSEN SOIL AROUND THE PLANTS GENTLY WITH A TABLE FORK BEFORE REMOVAL — TRUE LEAVES — SEED LEAVES — 1 IN BROKEN POTTERY OR GRAVEL — PLACE PLANT IN HOLE AND PUSH SOIL AGAINST IT FROM THE SIDE—FILL BALANCE OF HOLE AND FIRM SOIL

in rows rather than broadcast, as it makes them easier to identify when weeding. Cover the box with a pane of glass; it is always well to raise it ¼" on one end after the first day and wipe off moisture daily. A piece of newspaper laid over the glass will keep the seeds from drying out until they have germinated. Be sure to soak the ground in the flat before seeding, not afterwards, and to sift the topsoil through fly screening.

Label all rows and try not to have too many varieties in a receptacle. Plant those varieties which will mature for transplanting at the same time. It cuts down general care.

As soon as a fair number of seedlings appear it is necessary to remove the paper as well as the glass, and place the container in the light, but out of the direct rays of the sun. The temperature should be about 70 while the seed is germinating and about 50 to 60 thereafter. The lower temperature makes the plants more stocky and vigorous. Watering after the seed has germinated should be even more carefully done than before. A rubber bulb plant syringe is best for this purpose and the water should be at room temperature. The soil should not be allowed to get too wet but should be kept from getting really dry. Do not water unless the surface appears dry, then give enough water to go clear through to the bottom.

The plants started in pots may be watered from below as previously described. When the moisture reaches the top, drain them. It is always best to water in the morning and let the plants go to sleep dry. As the plants increase in size they

should be thinned out by removing some from the soil. Do not break them off. If the remaining plants show signs of sluggishness, put them closer to the window and thin them out some more.

Damping-off is the chief enemy of indoor plant culture. It is a stem rot caused by a fungus that grows best where there is too much moisture and lack of ventilation. A light sprinkling of hot sand or powdered sulphur sometimes helps to keep this in check. Sometimes soil sterilization is used to prevent it. Formaldehyde and a number of mercurial disinfectants are offered by seedsmen, and should be used according to directions given in Chapter XVII. The seedlings should not be exposed to the direct rays of the sun until well advanced, after which they may be hardened gradually, being shaded from the direct noonday rays.

Contrary to popular belief, transplanting helps the development of the young plant. Shifting it to new pots, pans or flats indoors will help harden it off for its outdoor debut. Soil may be prepared much in the manner as for planting seed. Do not fertilize the young plant until it has a good hearty start. Plants may be lifted from the soil with a pointed stick, teaspoon or kitchen fork, and the ground should be fairly moist in order that some soil may be taken up with them.

Never transplant into soil too rich in humus, or into pure humus, as this is likely to cause a fungous growth. Sand in the soil induces rapid drainage which is the best preventive of fungus.

Plants should not be transplanted

until they have developed their first pair of true leaves. Do not become confused because the seed leaves which some plants put out do not look familiar; and above all, do not mistake them for weeds. Be sure to firm the soil carefully about the roots. Loose planting is dangerous.

After the plants have obtained some growth, cultivate them. They may be hardened off by placing the flats in a coldframe before moving outdoors. Do not be afraid to transplant them two or three times before reaching their permanent location. Poppies, Candytuft, Sweet Alyssum, Cornflowers and Portulaca (Moss Rose) are flowers which must not be transplanted, but sown directly where they are to bloom. They are sometimes used as ground covers and are then broadcast over the garden bed between other plants.

Outdoor Seeding: Every garden should have a propagating bed in which plants raised indoors are hardened before being set in permanent locations. Annuals may be planted directly here in the spring, following somewhat the instructions given for indoor sowing, but cover with burlap instead of glass to conserve moisture during germination.

Many uses will be found for such a seed or propagating bed, as explained later, but not the least of these is raising perennials and biennials from summer sowing. Perennials are raised during the summer for blooming the following season and a number of seasons thereafter. Some, if sown in the spring, will bloom the same year if planted early enough, and for this reason are handled as annuals. (See pp. 140–50.)

Biennials differ from perennials in that they bloom the second year from seed, but only for a single season. Many people complain of their plants disappearing or "running out." Foxgloves, Canterbury Bells, Pinks and some Columbines are constantly doing this fadeout. These must be sown each year in midsummer so that a continuous supply is on hand for the following year. As most of them retain some of their foliage through the winter, they need special protection as described in Chapter X, "The Flower Garden." They also may be wintered in the coldframe or propagating bed properly covered.

While perennial seed may be successfully planted any time between June and September, most authorities consider June the best month. This gives time for hardy clumps to develop before winter, and they will be ready to bloom the following spring.

The most essential things are shade, moisture and drainage. Dry seeds will not germinate. Rich soil is not necessary and in fact an excess of nitrogen may be harmful as it causes a rapid, soft top growth which will not stand transplanting well.

After the plant has appeared above ground it is necessary to protect it from the sun and from drying out but ventilation is necessary to prevent damping-off. If the following rules are followed success is reasonably sure:

First locate a sunny fence corner. Measure a bed about three feet wide by six feet long or smaller. This will raise a lot of plants and yet be easy to reach to tend them. If the bed is of ordinary lawn soil, dump on it one wheelbarrow load of sand and one of sifted leafmold, sedge peat humus or finely granulated well-weathered peat moss. Do not use coarse peat moss as it comes from the bale. It should sift easily through one-quarter inch sieve. If the soil is bad clay, these materials must be increased enough to make it friable yet able to hold moisture. It must break up easily even when wet. Baked, cracked soil will not raise plants easily. Some gardeners make the top three inches of the bed of a compost of equal parts soil, sand and humus. This insures proper moisture condition. Also it is good policy to raise the bed four to six inches above grade.

Cultivate the soil deeply and be sure it drains well and that the surface is fine and level. Construct a frame as illustrated providing various degrees of shade for special conditions. Do not think it is complicated; it is not. A little forethought will insure success.

The day before planting seeds soak the bed until the water penetrates eight inches deep. Allow it to remain uncovered until the topsoil is readily friable and then sow the seed in rows four to six inches apart.

Seeds large enough to be handled may be sown two or three inches apart. Most gardeners sow small seed too thickly and waste it by the neces-

SUMMER SOWING OF PERENNIALS

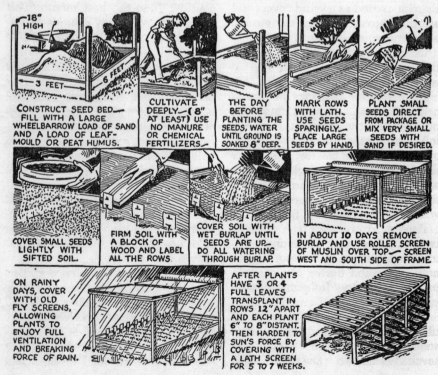

sary thinning which follows. Mix the seed with fine sand if necessary, but make it cover the space. Sow in rows —it enables you to tell seedlings from weeds while the plants are small.

Sift soil lightly over seeds. Firm well with a smooth block. Water lightly and cover with burlap pegged down to the soil. Water this burlap often but lightly. In about ten days most of the seedlings will have appeared; then remove the burlap and cover the frame with a muslin shade, watering the seedlings gently each day with fine spray.

If a hose is used, the long "flaring rose" type nozzle, preferred by growers, is the safest. Water pressure should be cut low, but not to the dripping point. The French and English pattern sprinkling cans are also satisfactory as they are equipped with fine roses and are practically dripless. Great loss can result from the drip of an ordinary sprinkler while the seedlings are small.

As soon as the seedlings have three to four leaves, transplant them to a nursery bed of well-drained soil mixed with sand and rotted manure or other vegetable matter. Care should be taken to remove plants when soil is damp but not wet. A little soil around the seedling roots will retain the fine feeding roots.

Nursery rows should be about twelve inches apart and the plants 6 to 8 inches apart in them. Fill each hole with water before planting and pull a little dry dirt around each plant after it is set.

Plants should be protected from direct, prolonged sun by the slatted screen until they are about six or seven weeks old. Cultivate these transplants often and fertilize lightly until well established.

Do all watering in early morning or late evening during hot weather. Early evening watering may cause a steam which seems to scald the young plants.

BEGINNER'S DOZEN

These plants grow easily from seed and are important in the garden make-up. It is an advantage to have a stock of them growing on.

The biennials (B), are needed in quantity to fill in during late May or June, when the early perennials are resting, and the later ones, and the annuals, are not blooming.

Young plants of the "variables" (V), will quickly replace any of the older plants that are lost. One-year-old delphinium and pyrethrum plants will bloom in August.

It is thrifty to grow from seed as many rock or edging plants (R) as possible. Typical perennials (P) are Coreopsis and Sweet Rocket. They are staple fillers and easy to handle.

B—Althea—Hollyhock

V—Aquilegia—Columbine

B—Campanula medium—Canterbury Bells

R—Cerastium tomentosum—Snow-in-Summer

P—Coreopsis—Tickseed, doubles

V—Delphinium, Chinese and hybrids

B—Dianthus barbatus—Sweet William

B—Digitalis—Foxglove

R—Linum perenne—Blue Flax

R—Nepeta mussini—Catmint

V—Pyrethrum—Painted Daisy

P—Hesperis—Sweet Rocket

Miscellaneous Seed Information: There are many methods of starting seeds besides that described above. Some authorities recommend that small seeds be placed upon a piece of dampened cloth until they sprout when they are transplanted into the loose soil. Others recommend raising them directly in peat moss or clear sand which has been sterilized. See Chapter XXIII.

Some plants take so long to grow from seed to the blooming period that it does not pay to attempt them. Others have shells so hard that they must first be notched or ringed with a knife before planting. It is a safe procedure to figure that large seeds, ranging from Nasturtium to Lima Beans, will stand soaking over night to soften their shell for rapid germination. Small seeds may be softened by soaking them in water and then draining them upon a cloth, allowing the cloth to dry before attempting to remove the seeds.

Common sense should teach us that in seeding, soil should be finely pulverized. When we consider that the tiny seedlings must push aside everything in their path, we should not expect them to be strong enough to move great stones or lumps of clay.

The following is the summary of the Ohio Experiment Bulletin No. 487, regarding the propagation of seeds:

1. Seeds germinate satisfactorily if held at the temperature at which the crop makes satisfactory growth.

2. Moisture is commonly the limiting factor in the proper germination of seeds. Too much moisture causes rots and damping-off of the seedlings that have started.

3. A satisfactory medium for seed sowing should hold sufficient moisture for proper germination, should not crust over easily on drying, and need contain very little mineral salts (fertilizer) if the seedlings are to be transplanted.

4. A mixture of one-half sand and one-half moist, good quality granulated peat moss makes a satisfactory soil medium for starting seeds. Several materials have been found satisfactory, however, if given the proper environmental conditions.

SAVING AND TESTING SEED

Many gardeners like to save seeds from their own plants from season to season. But soil and weather conditions vary and home gardeners are not able to give the constant attention which is given in professional seed growing under ideal conditions and combined with the best of storage. In using home-grown seed a germination test is an excellent thing as it will enable us to know what percentage of our seeds will become plants.

Some seeds do not grow unless planted within a very short time of their ripening but most of our annual plants will retain their vitality for several years. The only way for the gardener to know what results will be with seeds held for more than one year is to test them. This may prevent him from wasting time by sowing seed of low germinating power. Germination tests will also help you check the claims of various seed firms and decide which are giving you the best value.

Tests usually recommended for home gardeners require two shallow dishes. A little moist sand is placed in one and over this is spread a piece of flannel which has been sterilized by boiling. White blotting paper may be used if new sheets are taken for each test. The edges of the flannel or paper should be turned down along the sides of the dish so that they reach the bottom and act as a wick to bring up the moisture. The sand and cloth or paper should be thoroughly moistened before being placed in the dish.

If blotting paper is used, mark it off into squares with a pencil and mark flannel with pieces of colored cord. Either number or label each square and sift on to it a few of the seeds selected at random. Spread them out evenly and, of course, use only one kind of seed in each division.

Cover with another dish so that it is almost air tight and place the test near the heater where the temperature is about seventy to eighty degrees at all times. If you have carried the fabric to the bottom of the dish, it may be easily kept moistened by pouring a little water in the side of the dish without disturbing the seeds. Too much water will cause the seeds to mold.

As they germinate, they should be removed to keep them from drying out the cloth and spoiling the tests of the slower seeds. If mold appears, scrape it off to keep it from spreading and start a new test in another dish. Make a record for each square, showing the number of seeds planted and the number germinated.

Some seeds do not test well in this manner and if your results are not satisfactory, try to find the cause be-

fore condemning them. Aquilegia, Delphinium, Larkspur, Lupines, Lantana, Primulas, Verbena and Violets and some others do not respond well to this procedure and should be tested in a seed pan full of soil covered with glass and dark cloth. Remember, some seeds take a long while to germinate. Consult the germination table on pages 294–97.

VEGETATIVE PROPAGATION

Division: Propagation by division is discussed for special plants in a number of chapters. Some plants divide more easily than others. Old perennials make good new ones if care is used.

Do not get the new clumps too small and be sure to include in them vigorous parts from which new plants will start. Old dead centers should be discarded. Examine the plants each year and those which have dead centers should be divided. Replant immediately.

Plants from Summer Cuttings: While raising plants from seed is the normal, easiest and most satisfactory way to propagate, it sometimes becomes necessary to propagate by cuttings and root division. Many plants if grown from seed will not flower true to color, size and growth characteristics of the parent plant. This is due to cross pollination or other causes, but cuttings and roots are not so affected and will come true to variety.

Also in most instances a larger plant can be produced in a shorter time from a cutting or division, and the process forms a source of fascinating enjoyment for those interested in plant experimentation. It is comparatively simple and not the mysterious process generally supposed.

Slips used in summer propagation are called softwood or greenwood cuttings and are used for certain perennials, annuals and shrubs. A partial list of those best suited for this purpose are: Antirrhinum, Arabis (Rock Cress), Aubrietia (Purple Rock Cress), Black Currant, Calceolaria, Chrysanthemum, Dianthus (Hardy Carnation, Pinks, etc.), Dahlia, Golden Elder, Golden Privet, Gooseberry, Iberis (Candytuft), Loganberry, Myosotis (Forget-me-not), Own root roses, and Violas.

If but a few new plants are desired many of the plants in your garden and rockery can be increased by layering. This is the process of rooting a branch without detaching it from the parent. Many plants propagate themselves by this method.

A branch is notched and this notch held open by a small pebble or by bending the stem. It is then stapled to the ground by bent pieces of heavy wire and well covered with earth. Kept watered, it is severed from the main plant when well rooted. Plants which may be easily layered are Dianthus, Nepeta, Sedum, Thyme, Veronica, Forsythia suspensa, Climbing Roses and most creeping plants.

Delphiniums are sometimes reproduced by a similar process called "Ringing." More stems are allowed to grow than are desired for bloom. In July these stems are bent down upon light, damp soil, a little soil is scattered over them and kept shaded. Roots form at the joints which are later separated as new complete plants.

When making cuttings for propagation cut the shoots from sturdy plants which have finished blooming. Iberis and Arabis may be taken with a piece of the old stem (mallet shape); other plants, if large enough, may be cut with a heel which is a small oval piece of the outside of the old stem about one-half inch long. This is cut with a straight knife and must not be torn or pulled away from the stem of the new shoot. Roots form very quickly from heel cuttings. Small creeping plants may be cut eight or ten joints long and buried two-thirds their length. Care must be taken not to get shoots too long as weak leggy plants will result. The best length for softwood cuttings is three to six inches. About half the leaves and all flower buds should be removed, cutting carefully without tearing.

If a heel is not obtainable choose a terminal or lateral shoot which snaps when bent. If it crushes do not use it as it will root slowly. Cut at the base of a joint except in the case of willows and clematis which root better if cut halfway between joints. Set about one to one and one-half inches deep. Carnations are set shallow both in the rooting medium and when transplanted.

Cuttings when taken from the parent plant have no roots and therefore do not need nourishment. What they want most quickly is roots. Clean sharp sand is the best rooting medium, any humus or decayed vegetable matter in the soil may lead to the fatal damping-off. This is the enemy of all propagation and is usually caused by too much moisture stimulating activity by the wrong soil bacteria. Because of this danger, new sand should be used for each propagation.

Rooting seems best carried on in a slightly acid medium so we can first water the sand with a weak solution of vinegar (acetic acid); one teaspoon of vinegar to each gallon of water.

Propagation is hastened under ideal conditions created by bottom heat. This is applied in a hotbed by the fermentation of manure or by the new electrical cables and in a greenhouse bench by steam pipes or an electric heating cable placed underneath. By late July the ground in most localities is sufficiently warmed to permit rooting cuttings in it.

Propagating may be done in two or three inches of sand in a coldframe or in a Wardian Case constructed of glass as shown just below. However, for the amateur, a box 8 inches deep (a soap box will do), open at the bottom and top is best. A small box will handle many cuttings.

SOFTWOOD PROPAGATION

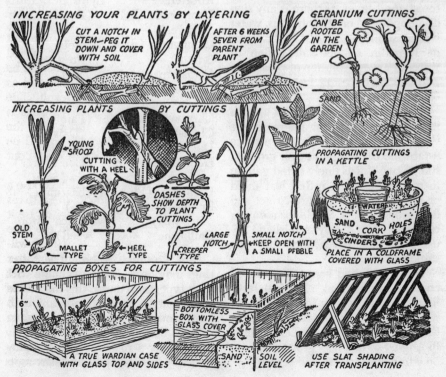

INCREASING YOUR PLANTS BY LAYERING

CUT A NOTCH IN STEM—PEG IT DOWN AND COVER WITH SOIL

AFTER 6 WEEKS SEVER FROM PARENT PLANT

GERANIUM CUTTINGS CAN BE ROOTED IN THE GARDEN

INCREASING PLANTS BY CUTTINGS

YOUNG SHOOT

CUTTING WITH A HEEL

DASHES SHOW DEPTH TO PLANT CUTTINGS

OLD STEM

MALLET TYPE

HEEL TYPE

CREEPER TYPE

LARGE NOTCH

SMALL NOTCH KEEP OPEN WITH A SMALL PEBBLE

SAND

PROPAGATING CUTTINGS IN A KETTLE

WATER

SAND CORK HOLES

CINDERS

PLACE IN A COLDFRAME COVERED WITH GLASS

PROPAGATING BOXES FOR CUTTINGS

6"

A TRUE WARDIAN CASE WITH GLASS TOP AND SIDES

BOTTOMLESS BOX WITH GLASS COVER

SAND

SOIL LEVEL

USE SLAT SHADING AFTER TRANSPLANTING

Remove the soil three inches deep and set the box in this excavation, fill to soil level with clean, sharp sand and soak with vinegar solution as before mentioned. Allow to stand an hour or two and then wet sand thoroughly with clear water and tamp firmly.

Now set the cuttings about two inches apart each way, carefully label and water. Cover the box snugly with a piece of glass. Shade the box with paper or cloth and keep closed for about ten days, opening it to give light and fine spray sprinklings, but ONLY if the top of the sand shows signs of drying out.

After the ten days the glass is raised during the mornings, shade being maintained and the sand kept moist at all times. If there is any sign of damping-off or other fungus, water with a solution of three tablespoons of formalin to one-half gallon of water or a weak solution of potassium permanganate, using just enough to color the water pink.

When plants show signs of growth remove the glass but maintain the shade until good root systems are established. Transplant to a growing soil of two-thirds finely sifted garden loam and one part rotted leaf mold or sedge humus. Be sure to get soil firm around roots. Shade for a day or two and then apply semishade by using the slat cover until they can stand full sun.

Water well and keep soil loosened on top. Apply weak chemical fertilizer (one tablespoon to one gallon of water) to the plants after they have three or four new leaves. Do this only in August so that new growth will not be stimulated late in the season.

Mulch after the first good ground freeze with hardwood leaves six inches deep, held loosely in place by boughs or poultry netting. Of course such tender plants as Geraniums, etc., must be lifted and potted for house culture as they will not stand a winter in the open in most parts of the country.

The following is quoted from Ohio Experiment Station Bulletin No. 525:

Perennials Propagated by Stem Cuttings

Arenaria (Sandwort)
Artemisia (Wormwood)
Aster (various)
Aubrietia
Campanula (Bellflower)
Campanula (dielbata)
Cerastium tomentosum (Snow-in-Summer)
Chrysanthemum
Clematis
Daphne
Delphinium (Larkspur)
Dianthus (Pink)
Epigaea(Trailing-arbutus)
Gaillardia
Helenium (Sneezeweed)
Iberis (Candytuft)
Lupinus (Lupin)
Lythrum salicaria (Purple Loosestrife)
Myosotis (Forget-me-not)
Phlox
Pyrethrum (Painted Daisy)
Rudbeckia (Coneflower)
Salvia (Sage)
Verbascum (Mullein)
Veronica (Ironweed)

Leaf Cuttings: Although leaf cuttings may be used to advantage with such types as sedums, this method of reproduction is relatively unimportant in outdoor gardening.

Root Cuttings: Root cuttings may be used as a means of propagating some perennials. Medium fleshy roots are cut into 1- or 2-inch pieces and placed in soil in shallow flats in the greenhouse or planted in well prepared beds outside. Root pieces should be placed close together, but not overlapping, and covered with about ½ inch of soil. When two or three leaves have been produced, the new plants may be potted or planted directly outside in beds.

Perennials Propagated by Root Cuttings

Anchusa (Bugloss)
Anemone
Ascelpias (Butterfly-weed)
Bocconia (Plume-poppy)
Ceratostigma
Coronilla vera (Crown-vetch)
Dicentra spectabilis (Bleeding-heart)
Echinops (Globe-thistle)
Gypsophila paniculata (Babys-breath)

Oenothera (Evening-primrose)
Papaver (Poppy)
Phlox
Polygonatum (Solomon's Seal)
Romneya (Canyon-poppy)
Stokesia (Stokes-aster)
Thermopsis
Trollius (Globe-flower)
Yucca (Adam's-needle)

Hardwood Cuttings: Hardwood cuttings are usually taken eight inches long when the plant is dormant, but not during freezing weather. We cannot control them as we can seeds and softwood propagation and they are pretty much of a gamble.

The wood should be one year old, firm, strong and free of leaves. Each should have two or more eyes or nodes and be plump and thick. Thin branches have little food in them. There should be an eye at the top of each cutting.

We illustrate the method of handling the cuttings. After the ripened wood cuttings have been made and tied in a bundle they are buried in damp peat moss and stored in a temperature of about 45° until they have formed calluses. The time necessary for this formation varies somewhat, but generally speaking the process will take all winter. The peat should be damp enough to keep the cuttings from drying out, but not wet enough to wet them.

When the cuttings are removed from the storing medium in the spring their butt ends will show more or less complete rings of callus. It is from these calluses that the roots will start when suitable growing conditions in soil are provided. The illustration shows the method of planting the callused cuttings in nursery rows outdoors. It will be noted that [continued on p. 298]

CUTTING AND BUNDLING YEAR OLD WOOD.

BURIED IN DAMP PEATMOSS AND STORED IN A TEMPERATURE OF 45° UNTIL THEY HAVE FORMED CALLUSES

IN THE SPRING THEIR ROOTING END WILL SHOW RINGS OF CALLUS FROM WHICH ROOTS WILL START TO GROW.

PLANT OUT DOORS IN SPRING - SET VERTICALLY DEEP IN THE SOIL WITH CALLUSED ENDS DOWN.

NEW YOUNG PLANTS.

PERENNIAL SEEDS
TIME FOR GERMINATION

Germination Time Varies with Temperature and Moisture Conditions

Proper Name	Common Name	Germination Days	Proper Name	Common Name	Germination Days
S—Achillea ptarmica	The Pearl	10	S—Heuchera	Coral Bells	15
F—Aconitum napellus	Monkshood	150-190	S—Hibiscus	Giant Mallow	10
F—Adonis amurensis	Bird's Eye	100-175	S—Iberis sempervirens	Candytuft	15
S—Alyssum saxatile	Basket of Gold	5-10	S—Incarvillea	Hardy Gloxinia	20
S—Althaea	Hollyhock	10	—Iris kaempferi	Japanese Iris	25
S—Anchusa italica	Drop More	25	S—Lathyrus	Everlasting Pea	40
S—Anemone	Windflower	20	S—Lavandula vera	Sweet Lavender	25
F—Anthericum	St. Bernard's Lily	20	—Lepachys pinnata	Thick-scale	20
S—Aquilegia	Columbine	15	F—Liatris	Gay Feather	15
X—Arabis	Rock Cress	15	X—Linum perenne	Flax	15
S—Armeria	Sea Pink	15	F—Lobelia cardinalis	Cardinal Flower	50
S—Aster	Michaelmas Daisy	15	S—Lupinus polyphyllus	Lupin	25
S—Auricula primula	Primula	50	X—Lychnis chalcedonica	Campion	10
—Baptisia	Wild Indigo	50	S—Lythrum roseum superbum	Rose Loosestrife	25
F—Bellis perennis	English Daisy	10	S—Malva	Mallow	20
F—Bocconia cordata	Plume Poppy	20	S—Matricaria	Mater	12
S—Campanula carpatica	Harebell	15	S—Mertensia	Blue Bells	12
S—Campanula medium	Canterbury Bell	15	X—Myosotis	Forget-me-not	10
—Campanula calycanthema	Cup and Saucer	20	S—Nepeta	Catnip	20
S—Campanula persicifolia	Peach Bell	15	S—Nierembergia	Cup Flower	30
S—Campanula pyramidalis	Chimney Bell	15	F—Oenothera	Evening Primrose	150
			S—Papaver	Poppy	15
			F—Pardanthus	Blackberry-lily	20

F—Catanache coerulea	Everlasting	12
—Centaurea macrocephala	Rays of Gold	20
S—Centaurea montana	Cornflower	15
S—Centranthus	Valerian	15
X—Cerastium	Snow-in-Summer	50
S—Cheiranthus cheiri	Wallflower	10
S—Chrysanthemum leucanthemum	Shasta Daisy	20
F—Cimicifuga	Bug Bane	25
X—Coreopsis	Tickseed	10
F—Delphinium chinense	Larkspur	25
F—Delphinium hybrids	Larkspur	20
S—Dianthus barbatus	Sweet William	10
S—Dianthus deltoides	Maiden Pink	20
F—Dictamnus	Gas Plant	150
S—Digitalis	Foxglove	10
F—Funkia	Plantain Lily	150
X—Gaillardia grandiflora	Blanket Flower	15
S—Geum	Avens	15
S—Gypsophila paniculata	Baby's Breath	15
S—Helenium	Sneezewort	10
S—Helianthemum	Sun Rose	30
S—Heliopsis	Sunflower	15
F—Helleborus	Christmas-rose	100
S—Hepatica	Liver Leaf	30
S—Hesperis	Sweet Rocket	15

S—Pentstemon	Beard Tongue	60
S—Phlox decussata	Phlox	160
S—Physostegia virginica	False Dragon Head	10
S—Platycodon	Ballon Flower	15
X—Polemonium	Jacob's Ladder	150
X—Polygonum	Knotweed	30
X—Potentilla	Cinquefoil	20
S—Primula officinalis	Cowslip	50
—Primula vulgaris	English Primrose	150
S—Pyrethrum hybridum	Persian Daisy	15
X—Pyrethrum uliginosum	Giant Daisy	18
S—Rudbeckia	Coneflower	15
S—Salvia azurea	Sage	25
S—Scabiosa caucasica	Blue Bonnet	25
S—Sedum	Stone Crop	20
F—Sidalcea	Indian Mallow	20
F—Silene	Catchfly	25
X—Silphium	Compass Plant	18
S—Statice latifolia	Sea Lavender	50
S—Stokesia cyanea	Stoke's Aster	25
S—Thalictrum	Meadow Rue	20
S—Tritoma	Red Hot Poker	30
F—Trollius	Globe Flower	25
X—Tunica saxifraga	Goat Flower	10
S—Valeriana	Valerian	15
S—Veronica	Ironweed	25
S—Viola cornuta	Pansies	10

S—Indicates which can be sown in summer.   F—Plants best sown in fall.   X—Plants sown in spring, most of which bloom the first year.

ANNUALS
HOW LONG TO GERMINATE

Proper Name	Common Name	Germination Days
Acroclinium	Everlasting	8-10
Agathea	Blue Daisy	18-20
Ageratum	Floss Flower	8-12
Amaranthus	Amaranth	20-25
Antirrhinum	Snapdragon	20-25
Arctotis	African Daisy	15-20
Argemone	Mexican Poppy	20-25
Aster	Asters	8-10
Balsam	Lady Slipper	10-12
Begonia	Begonia	15-20
Brachycome	Swan River Daisy	20-25
Browallia	Amethyst	18-20
Calceolaria	Slipper Flower	15-18
Calendula	Pot Marigold	10-12
Calycanthema	Cup and Saucer	11-15
Calliopsis	Tickseed	10-12
Campanula	Canterbury Bells	12-15
Canna	Canna (Indian Shot)	25-40
Carnation	Marguerite Carnations	8-10
Celosia	Cockscomb	20-25
Centaurea	Bachelor's Button, Sweet Sultan	5-20
Cerastium	Snow-in-Summer	8-10
Chrysanthemum	Chrysanthemum	5-8
Lantana	Lantana	15-20
Linum rubrum	Scarlet Flax	15-18
Lobelia	Lobelia	8-10
Lupinus	Lupin	25-30
Marigold	Marigold	5-8
Matricaria	Feverfew	20-25
Matthiola	Evening Stock	8-10
Mesembryanthemum	Ice Plant	5-20
Mimosa	Sensitive Plant	8-10
Mirabilis jalapa	Four O'Clock	12-15
Myosotis	Forget-me-not	15-20
Nasturtiums	Nasturtiums	8-15
Nicotiana	Flowering Tobacco	20-25
Nigella	Love-in-a-Mist	10-15
Primula	Primrose	10-25
Papaver	Poppy	15-20
Passiflora	Passion Flower	50-60
Peas, Sweet	Sweet Peas	15-20
Pelargonium	Geranium	20-25
Petunias	Petunia	18-20
Phaseolus multiflorus	Scarlet Runner Bean	8-10
Phlox drummondi	Phlox	20-25
Portulaca	Moss Rose	18-20
Primula	Primrose	10-25

Cineraria	Cineraria	5-8
Clarkia	Clarkia	8-10
Cobea scandens	Cup and Saucer Vine	15-20
Coleus	Flame Nettle	20-25
Cosmos	Cosmos	5-15
Datura	Trumpet Flower	15-18
Delphinium	Larkspur	15-20
Dianthus	Pinks	5-8
Gaillardia	Blanket Flower	12-15
Gloxinia	Gloxinia	15-20
Gourds	Gourds	15-25
Gypsophila	Baby's Breath	15-20
Helianthus	Sunflower	15-20
Helichrysum	Strawflower	5-10
Heliotrope	Cherry Pie	10-15
Iberis	Candytuft	5-8
Impatiens	Zanzibar Balsam	8-12
Ipomea	Moon Flower	5-8
Kochia	Ball of Fire	15-18
Rhodanthe	Swan River Ever-lasting	10-12
Ricinus	Castor-oil Bean	15-20
Salpiglossis	Painted Tongue	15-20
Salvia splendens	Scarlet Sage	15-25
Scabiosa	Pin-cushion Flower	18-20
Schizanthus	Butterfly-plant	20-25
Stocks	Cut-and-come-again	10-15
Thunbergia	Black-Eyed Susan Vine	8-10
Verbena	Verbena	8-10
Verbena, lemon	Lemon Verbena	8-10
Verbena venosa	Heliotrope Verbena	10-15
Viola tricolor	Pansies	8-10
Viscaria	Campion	10-12
Wall flower	Wall Flower	8-12
Xeranthemum	Everlasting	8-10
Zinnia	Zinnias	5-8

[*continued from p. 293*]

they are set vertically and quite deep in the soil with their callused ends down. In this position they will develop both roots and new top growth.

The soil and care for planting outdoors should be provided substantially as previously described for softwood transplants. All shrubs should be transplanted several times before they are placed in their permanent locations.

Hormone Treatments: Scientific progress has in recent years developed materials of much value to gardeners because they stimulate the rooting of cuttings of plants formerly hard to propagate in this way, and hasten the rooting time of easily handled kinds. They are called hormones or growth-producing substances and are obtainable in concentrated liquid form or as powders at seed stores and other garden supply houses. Following directions supplied with them, the gardener merely soaks the base half inch or inch of his cuttings for a certain time, which may range from a few to 24 hours, then plants them in the usual way. Or, if using a powder type hormone, he sticks the moistened base end of each cutting in the powder, taps it to shake off any excess, and plants it immediately with the rest adhering. The prompt vigorous root growth that follows will not only help insure a better stand of new plants, but will also enable the plants to make rapid growth and attain planting out size in short order.

Shrubbery from Seed: Some shrubs best raised from seed are: Japanese Barberry, Regel Privet, Ibota Privet, European Privet, Arrowhead (Viburnum dentatum), Wayfaring tree (Viburnum lantana), Nannyberry (Viburnum lentago) and European Cranberry bush (Viburnum opulus).

The seeds should be gathered in the fall and do best if buried in moist sand or peat moss over the winter at a temperature of 32° to 50°. Plant out of doors as early as possible in spring. They may also be planted directly outside when gathered in the fall.

Start transplanting the second year. It takes longer to develop shrubs from seeds than from cuttings, but plants from the foregoing list are much superior if grown from seed.

EDITOR'S NOTE: Many interesting developments have taken place in recent years in the plant propagation field. Although in most cases they have aimed at increasing the efficiency of commercial plantsmen in producing more and better plants for their customers, many of them are of interest to the enthusiastic amateur and, in a number of cases, the methods that have been devised can be used by the amateur gardener either as originally worked out or in some modified form especially adapted to home garden conditions.

Some of these developments are described in "GARDEN MAGIC MARCHES ON," page 439.—E.L.D.S.

CHAPTER XX

THE AMATEUR'S GREENHOUSE

Unconscious of a less propitious clime
Here blooms exotic beauty warm and snug,
While the winds whistle and snows descend.

Many people believe a greenhouse to be a luxury but once having owned one, they usually change their minds. Of course, there are many greenhouses which are expensive to build and operate, but the amateur who is handy with tools may easily erect one at small cost.

Another opinion is that the process of raising plants in a greenhouse is something intricate and mysterious. Anyone who has been successful with plants out of doors may, by altering the principles slightly, apply his knowledge to gardening

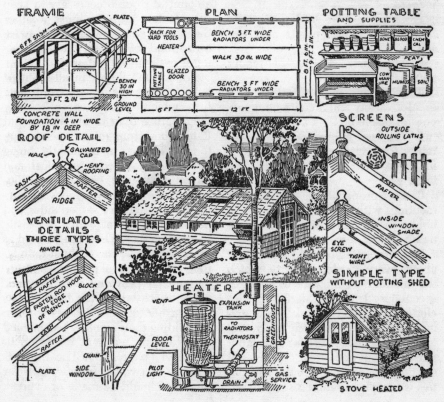

under glass. Many of the cultural operations are the same.

It must be understood that a greenhouse is not always a "hot house," as it is sometimes called. As pointed out in Chapter XXII on "House Plants," plants do best at temperatures slightly lower and with much higher humidity than is usually maintained in our living rooms.

In a small greenhouse it is comparatively easy to regulate temperature, humidity and ventilation. Light is more difficult but it too yields to the application of common sense.

The amateur uses a greenhouse chiefly for the following reasons:

1. Raising plants for winter use indoors.

2. Carrying over garden plants to be used as "stock" plants next season.

3. The early starting of tender plants from seed.

4. Increasing the possibilities of a greater variety and a continuous succession of bloom.

5. The easy culture of small vegetables for winter use on benches or in pots and boxes beneath the benches.

6. For propagating, and experimenting with various plants as a hobby for the purpose of developing new varieties, etc.

The foregoing should constitute about every garden activity which the amateur would care to enter. A greenhouse is doubly useful if it includes a shed and a work bench, giving easy access to both tools and materials. This saves time and labor in the various activities. The muss of starting seeds indoors under difficulties is completely unnecessary.

Greenhouses are of many types. Some are merely lean-to structures against the house, garage or other building. Others are electrically heated, but the type most adaptable to the ordinary city lot is a single span type (see page 299). This can be very simple, or complete. It can be heated by a stove, fired with coke or special coal, at a cost of only a few dollars a year. Other types have miniature hot water or steam systems heated by a small coal or coke fired boiler. Still another type is the gas-heated variety shown in the illustration on page 299.

This should dispel any doubt in the mind of the gardener as to the amount of trouble necessary to keep the plants warm. In most weather the boilers need be fired but twice a day, and, of course, the gas heating is easily made automatic.

For anyone who can afford it, it is best to buy the greenhouse from a firm which specializes in making them rather than to attempt to put it together from miscellaneous materials. There are constantly being offered, at low cost, practical and attractive houses of new and improved design. They come with complete sash sections, sloped sides and pointed roof, all of which are easily bolted together. They can be used as portable cold houses without foundation, or built on a permanent foundation and provided with benches.

For those who wish to cut costs still further, or desire the experience of building their own, we recommend the erection of one of the types illustrated (page 299). The frame is entirely of two by fours, which for long life should be made of cypress.

However, ordinary lumber will do very well if properly painted. Hotbed sash (stock size 3′ x 6′) forms the glass roof and panes of glass, held in place in the 2 x 4 frame by strips of quarter-round mold, are used for the side glazing where it does not have to open.

The lower or solid part of the structure is inclosed by tacking roofing paper directly to the studs and nailing the tongued and grooved material on the top of it. For further insulation, it is well to close up this space at the bottom and pack it with mineral wool; or good results may be obtained by insulating with roofing paper of the same kind as is used on the outside.

For appearance sake the exterior may be stuccoed or covered with slate-surfaced roofing, which will further insulate it. Or a good substitute for stucco is awning duck or canvas which will last indefinitely if painted every year or two. It may be stripped with lattice in the corners or to obtain any decorative appearance desired.

With a view to preserving the frame it is well to place the house upon a concrete foundation. As the weight to be placed upon the foundation is not considerable, it need not be a very rich mixture and no particular care need be taken with it except to see that the ground on which it stands is firm and the top level. It should extend from one to one and one-half feet in the ground and can be made by pouring a carefully excavated trench full of concrete, or by the use of forms. If it is brought up three or four inches above the ground it will save the framework

from exposure to moisture. Of course the entire bottom part of the greenhouse might be cast of concrete, but this would necessitate form work and expense which we are attempting to eliminate.

It would be best to have the sill or bottom members of the frame made of cypress and all of the frame should receive two coats of good ready mixed paint before being placed together. If this is not feasible, paint each side of the joint heavily when nailing in place. The high humidity in the greenhouse quickly rots lumber unless thoroughly protected. The hotbed sash should also be painted two coats before being placed in position.

It is necessary that the roof does not leak. Cold water dripping upon the plants is very injurious. Therefore, in placing the sash the rafters (which have already been painted) should be coated with a mixture of white lead and oil (not too thick) and the sash nailed on while this is wet.

The sash should be butted together on top of the rafters and any cracks completely filled with putty. On top of this joint should be firmly nailed a cypress lattice strip which should also be bedded in white lead.

The entire structure should now be given a third coat of paint. It is best for the amateur not to mix his own paint, but to purchase a well-known brand of the best grade obtainable. It is much more important that high-class paint be used on a greenhouse than almost anywhere else.

The life of such a house without proper painting precautions is from five to eight years; kept properly painted and caulked it will last indefinitely. We show structural details on page 299.

Where the sash come together above the ridge, tack a piece of heavy roofing paper. This is both for insulation and to keep out water. The amateur may get along with this alone, but it is better to place on top of it a piece of sheet metal. This can be purchased from a roofer in a stock form somewhat as shown; it then should be nailed to the sash through the roofing, which may then be trimmed off evenly.

Every greenhouse needs a workshop where potting can be done without using the valuable space under glass. For this reason most of them have a potting shed in which there is a bench similar to that described in Chapter XXII, above barrels, galvanized cans or discarded oil tanks to contain the necessary planting material. Fifty-pound lard tins protect the various fertilizers from rats or dampness and shelves should be arranged to hold pots, labels, stakes, etc. The boiler for the heating system is also installed here and, if the shed is large enough, it may contain all of the rest of the garden tools and paraphernalia.

Where a stove is used for heating, it should, of course, be located at the north end of the greenhouse and not in the potting room. The interior of the house consists of two benches, three feet wide, between which runs a thirty-inch walk, which may be paved with stone, concrete or brick; otherwise, it may be advisable to use a wooden walk to protect the gardener from the dampness of the soil. The benches should be well sup-

ported and fastened to the frame three feet from the ground. The legs must be placed upon a concrete foundation or flat stones so that they will not sink into the ground when loaded.

Water must be provided; it may be piped from the house service line in a trench putting it below frost line. Gas may run in the same trench if it is desired to use it for heating. A gas plate in the potting room is excellent for heating water for washing old flower pots or boiling new ones.

If gas is to be used for heating, a good system for the small greenhouse is to use a fairly large size copper coil water heater. This, equipped with a thermostat, can be obtained from almost any plumber. This will operate a hot water heating system by using ordinary wall radiation hung beneath the benches. Secondhand radiation is all right for this purpose if guaranteed when purchased. The thermostat is placed upon the return to the heater and the temperature of the water can be regulated automatically in this manner.

Keep a record of its performance during different kinds of weather for a short time and you will know how to set the thermostat to maintain a proper greenhouse temperature.

If you are able to adjust the temperature of the water it is always better to have as much radiation as possible. This is economy during mild weather and a necessity under extreme conditions.

The heater, of course, must be installed in the potting room and the door between must be kept closed when it is in operation. Gas in any form is deadly to plants. While this is not the most economical type of heater the writer used one in his own greenhouse for a number of years with very satisfactory results and amazingly small gas consumption. Probably the cheapest ways to heat are by using coal, coke, or oil.

A small stove with coke for fuel requires attention but twice a day, night and morning. With experience a fire can be held for sixteen hours. The stove is located in the north end of the house and when the plate is built high enough, the pipe is slung from the ridge, running the complete length of the house and out the south end above the door. If a damper is located in the pipe near the south end, the maximum amount of heat is preserved.

Another requisite of every greenhouse is ventilation. In summer time it becomes very warm and it is necessary to abandon the house unless openings are easily available. A very simple way to do this is to hinge one of the sash on top of the plate as shown in cut on page 299. The sash is slipped away from the ridge about two or three inches and a board inserted in its place to hold the galvanized ridging. The sash is raised or lowered by a perforated piece of heavy strap iron with holes to slip over a heavy nail or screw set in the side of the rafter.

It might seem more feasible to hinge the sash near the ridge and raise it from the bottom, but this would allow the draught to blow directly upon the plants on the bench and would not permit the escape of hot air at the highest point of the house. It might also admit enough direct sunlight to scorch certain plants.

The second type of ventilation which we show is made by removing about one-half of the glass in a sash, nailing in a cross member at the end of the remaining glass and placing another on top of this. This sash is hinged near the ridge because sun will seldom reach the plants through it and it is high enough to permit adequate ventilation. It is opened and closed by a rod or strap ending in a hook which may attach to a screw eye on the bench.

There should be two of these ventilators, one on either side of the roof, so that they may be opened on the side which will cause the least draught, according to the way the wind is blowing.

As it is necessary to keep the roof from dripping water upon the plants, it must be made as tight as possible. A lattice strip should be nailed about the edge of the movable sash to lap over the joining sash, but should it be found impossible to keep the movable sash from dripping, an inconspicuous metal gutter may be easily nailed to the rafter to carry the water away from the plants to the floor where it will do no harm.

In warmer weather additional ventilation becomes necessary and the side windows above the bench should be equipped with sash as shown, hinged at the bottom to open outward on a chain. Care must be taken to provide strong hooks on all movable sashes, especially those in the roof, as a windstorm not only will injure the sash but may ruin all the plants.

We show the end of the greenhouse fitted with another hotbed sash. This sash should be attached with hooks and weather-stripped so that it may be fastened tightly in winter and removed, if necessary, in warmer weather. Light is essential to all types of plants, but many can be raised for at least part of their existence on shelves beneath the benches. This sash provides more space of this kind. A full-glazed door may take the place of this and be installed on hinges to open out if desired.

The amateur has often wondered why a greenhouse is first made of glass to let in the sun and then covered with whitewash to keep it out. The reason is that a number of plants will not stand direct sunlight.

As we have discussed in outdoor gardening, young plants and many mature plants need shade or partial shading. Foliage plants, begonias, cyclamen, etc., must have constant shade. Roses, sweet peas and some others will stand clear glass.

Many growers spray the outside of the glass with whitewash. This is done in the early summer and is supposed to weather off before winter. Others smear the inside of the glass with clay, soaking it off with a hose whenever desired.

Many modern greenhouses have slat curtains working on the outside with cords to cast alternate shade and shadow on the plants. We illustrate a method of making such a rolling screen, using lath and wire on page 299.

Lath should be made to roll up as close to the ridge boards as possible, so it will not cast any shade when this is not desired.

We show another method of providing shade without smearing up the glass, that is, the use of a roller window shade which is supported by three tightly stretched pieces of stovepipe wire. The roller end should be attached upon the ridge rafter and an eccentric shade pulley on the plate will hold it wherever desired. In case it is found that the shade cloth is too easily injured by dampness it may be replaced with coarse muslin.

LOCATING

We have been discussing the erection of a single span type house at a distance away from the residence. The advantage of this is that light can be obtained all around it, but it has the disadvantage that it must be visited during unfavorable weather. Many greenhouses are attached to the house or garage.

One disadvantage of this is that it is usually hard to get proper light. It seems at first glance that there would be a considerable advantage in using the heat from the house, but upon study it will be noticed in greenhouse management, plants need their maximum temperature at night when the house heating system is allowed to run low.

During the day the greenhouse has the advantage of the heat from the sun, but if not watched it will go too low at night.

The best method of locating is to run the house east and west with the potting shed on the east end, although this is not absolutely necessary. In this manner one side of the roof is exposed to the southern sun and will also receive the western light most of the day. The sun-loving plants can thus be placed on the

Anyone's window sill can be a cheerful garden if the plants are well chosen and if they are not crowded so close together that individual characteristics are lost. The brilliant Poinsettia reflects holiday spirit.

Here is the way even a small home greenhouse can look in February or March. Yellow Snapdragons, Daffodils, pink and white Hyacinths, white Lilies, blue Cinerarias are among the flowers that stand out most prominently.

north bench where they will get the most light.

SIMPLE LEAN-TO GREENHOUSES

We are now going to describe two simple, quite inexpensive lean-to greenhouses that almost anyone handy with tools can construct against the wall of his dwelling or garage. The first of them is built against the south side of the house and, if possible, with a southwest exposure so that it gets the morning and the greater part of the afternoon sun. Because, as noted, plants do better with a temperature of about 40 to 60 degrees, but need a humidity which should run 75 per cent as against 20 per cent to 30 per cent in our living rooms, there is no attempt to pave the floor. The desired humidity is obtained by spraying the floors, benches, and plants, and everything is arranged to evaporate water. The only masonry consists of a foundation of rows of concrete block bedded in the ground and holding the wood a couple of inches off the ground to protect the lumber from carpenter ants or from termites.

The framework is made of 2 x 4's joined together as shown in our illustration. The bottom 30 to 36 inches of the house is clapboard and lined on the inside with sheathing. The space between is filled with shavings or better still some of the rock-wool insulation available for this purpose.

This protects the house at the bottom where the cold air is most apt to enter. The only millwork consists of a door and a ventilating window in the roof. A large cellar sash can be used for this, while the door can

be almost anything glazed or unglazed. Almost any lumber mill will give you a price on the whole thing, or a wrecking company will be somewhat cheaper, although it will need more work to make it presentable.

No glass is used except on the sash but a flexible material which admits the light is tacked directly to the 2 x 4's and the edges covered with screen

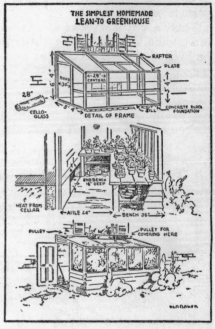

mold. The material, known as Cello-glass, has been in general use for a good many years. Any lumber or hardware dealer can get it for you. It is tacked on, much in the manner of fly screen, and is as easy to apply.

The second house, though also simple to build, is a little larger and more substantial. It is a glazed lean-to greenhouse made up of multiples of hotbed sash. These sash come (standard) three feet wide by six feet long, and also in half sash three by three. The frame should be constructed so that sash of these dimensions center on its members.

Our pictures show roofs made of two of these sash but this can be increased to any size provided it is in multiples of these measurements. The larger size may be used for the ventilating sash in the roof and be hinged to the smaller sash which is fixed in a permanent position.

There are two ways of using sash in building this house. The first is to build it all of hotbed sash as illustrated. This has the advantage of having light under the benches which increases the space available for raising seedlings until time to harden them off in the spring. It is also use-

ful for shaping and perfecting the blooms of bulbs forced for indoor use and provides a safe and convenient place to put house plants during their resting period.

The other type is built with the lower part solid about 36 inches from the ground and the upper part made of sash. This has the advantage of making it possible to insulate the lower part (as described above) and of being more solidly constructed. The sash in the sides of this house need not be hotbed sash, but can be any kind of sash of suitable size which will fit. These can be stock sash and obtained cheaply from any mill.

A happy combination of these two plans is to use the one with a solid bottom and insert a sash or two

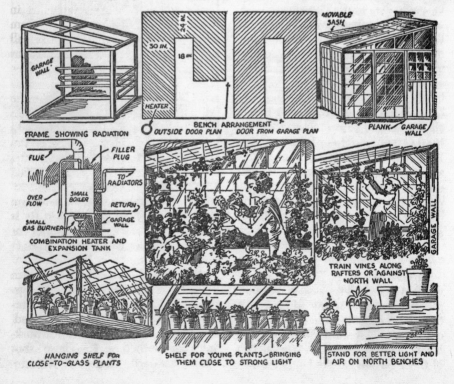

FRAME SHOWING RADIATION

BENCH ARRANGEMENT
OUTSIDE DOOR PLAN   DOOR FROM GARAGE PLAN

MOVABLE SASH

PLANK   GARAGE WALL

COMBINATION HEATER AND EXPANSION TANK

TRAIN VINES ALONG RAFTERS OR AGAINST NORTH WALL

HANGING SHELF FOR CLOSE-TO-GLASS PLANTS

SHELF FOR YOUNG PLANTS—BRINGING THEM CLOSE TO STRONG LIGHT

STAND FOR BETTER LIGHT AND AIR ON NORTH BENCHES

below the level of the benches for the special uses described.

As shown, this type of house is designed to be located against the wall of a house or detached garage. If entrance can be arranged from the house or garage, it will save quite a little inside bench space. However, it must be remembered that the house should face south or better a little southwest to take advantage of the maximum sun.

Heat from the cellar ceiling may be obtained by locating the house over a cellar window. However, the furnace fire is banked at night, the time when the greatest heat should be furnished, after the sun has gone down. So if this method is used, emergency heating apparatus should be on hand for severe nights in the shape of a round wick, old-fashioned kerosene lamp or regular portable kerosene heater. These set on the floor will answer. An electric heater will also cost but a cent or two a night.

In no case must a gas flame be used in the greenhouse itself, but a heater for heating by hot water can be located in another building and heated with gas. In the system pictured the boiler is a 10 to 20 gallon tank and care must be used to have a pet cock in the radiation at the highest point to let out accumulated air from time to time.

MANAGEMENT

In Chapter XXII, "House Plants" we have much to say concerning plants indoors which would apply to their culture in the greenhouse. The culture of a great many bulbs and house plants is described there but all of them can be handled easier under these more favorable circumstances.

The thing which makes a greenhouse more adaptable is the ability to get not only temperature when we need it, but also humidity. This is done by syringing and watering with a hose and, as is frequently observed, it should be done in the morning to give the plants a chance to dry off before the night. Do not keep the plants soggy but do not be afraid to water thoroughly when they start to dry out. Soak the floor and the benches as well as the plants.

Even in extreme cold weather a little air is necessary and this can be increased as conditions permit it. Some air must be given daily. Confined conditions breed disease, which is hard to check.

Do not pack too many plants in small space. Allow them to have room to spread. A little arrangement will make possible many things. Vines, for instance, can be trained along the rafters on the north side where they will not shade other plants. In the early stages, flats of seedlings will do well in the partial light underneath the benches, saving the room on top until they are ready to be brought up.

Chapter XIX on Propagation covers raising seeds indoors, and instructions for summer propagation also apply to the greenhouse. It is much easier to get bottom heat for propagation in a greenhouse than out of doors.

With these instructions anyone can be successful in raising simple plants. However, we would advise further reading; books by experienced, practical growers like F. F. Rockwell and the late Ernest Chabot can be bought or found at libraries.

And some agricultural experiment stations offer bulletins on greenhouse management. Excellent technical, specific directions are contained in an older book called "Fritz Bahr's Commercial Floriculture," which is well worth studying if obtainable.

Let us take up the various uses of the greenhouse previously mentioned:

1. *Wintering plants for use indoors.*

The greenhouse enables us to bring the plants in before frost and after a short resting period, bloom them again for house use. Bulbs can be raised to the blooming period and taken inside in relays. Foliage plants can be used indoors and taken back to the greenhouse for a vacation or build-up period. Roses will bloom all winter as well as many annuals if handled correctly.

2. *Stock plants can be carried over for next season.*

A great many plants, such as fuchsias, salvias, chrysanthemums, geraniums, and many perennials can be carried over beneath the benches as a mere ball of roots. Early in spring they can be brought to the top and watered into growth from which cuttings are taken for a wealth of plants during the summer. Cuttings may be taken from one or two dahlias so that a number can be grown from a single tuber.

3. *Raising plants from seed.*

This is thoroughly discussed under propagation. Many plants can be raised from seed to flower indoors in winter. It is interesting to experiment with most of the garden favorites. Morning glory vines, for instance

(large varieties), may be brought to bloom in the greenhouse to decorate our windows or table. And, of course, several weeks can be saved in spring by starting tender plants from seed long before they could be sown outdoors.

4. *Increasing possibilities of variety and succession of bloom.*

Many plants are not possible in our garden unless they are first started indoors and the mess of doing this in the house discourages us from the attempt. Many bulbs can be brought to flower in early spring by starting them under glass and prolonging the season of their bloom. Try forcing violets and various wildflowers from the woods.

5. *The easy culture of small vegetables for winter use on benches or in pots and boxes beneath the benches.*

Small vegetables grow so readily in the greenhouse that they may be said to almost grow themselves. Lettuce, peppergrass, onions, parsley, sage, mint, carrots, radishes, spinach may be grown on top of the benches in very small space. Tomatoes may be raised in pots in late March and transplanted to nail kegs when the weather opens up in April. They require extremely warm temperatures which is easily possible as the weather moderates in April. Beneath the benches asparagus and rhubarb will grow after a short resting period and, if an enriched wet spot can be maintained, much better watercress may be grown than is obtainable by purchase. Mushrooms require more care, but are raised quite readily beneath the benches.

One of the chief things to be remembered about plants is that they have a resting period. They must not be expected to bloom twelve months in the year. When they begin to show signs of weariness under favorable conditions, it is time to let them dry out and to remove them to a less favorable part of the house.

The remedies for insect pests are much the same indoors as out. Chewing insects can be killed with arsenate of lead, and the aphides or plant lice by a contact spray of nicotine sulphate. We have an additional remedy not possible out of doors, that of fumigation. This is done by burning strips of prepared paper, or the use of a fumigator. Do not wait for pests to get a foothold; fumigate upon the appearance of the first green fly or aphis. Keep a clean house. Scale can be cleaned from the stems of plants with a little alcohol on a cloth or piece of cotton, but it is better to use a spray. If you wash off the plant leaves frequently, you may not be bothered with red spider.

Damping-off, as explained in the chapter on Propagation, yields to various treatments. Soil sterilization is covered in Chapter XVII.

A WINDOW GREENHOUSE

To get an early start and a longer season of bloom, we may start seeds indoors. Their chief need is clean soil receptacles, sterilized soil and proper temperature and humidity after germination. Low temperature makes stocky, well-rooted plants but it is almost impossible to get in the house. The boxes shown below may be hung against the window frame with gate hooks or corner irons and weather stripped around the edges to keep out cold. Ventilation helps prevent disease and these boxes are easily ventilated on warm days by raising the hinged sash and warmed from the house by operating the window sash. A thermometer hung in the box checks temperature and frequent sprinklings insure necessary humidity. One large greenhouse concern offers a strong, metal-frame "bay window" complete with shelves, screened ventilators, etc., that can be bolted to the house right over a regular window.

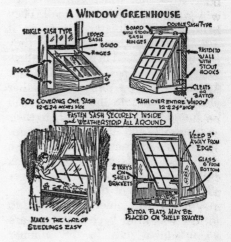

A WINDOW GREENHOUSE

CHAPTER XXI

WINDOW BOXES

Although we hear much of interior decoration, few people realize the possibilities of improving the appearance of the exterior of the house by the use of vines and window boxes. They may be made to soften severe lines or to add gay colors to brighten sombre shades.

The box need not always match the architecture of the house, in fact, this would sometimes be impossible, but it should harmonize and not be painted a color which clashes.

Do not make them too small. They will appear to better advantage if they are many times as long as they are wide. If placed in a window allow them to extend past the opening four to six inches on either side rather than fit them into the sill. This will be found to add considerably to their appearance and they may be supported on brackets attached to the wall. If a box is placed on a porch rail, it is better to have the larger portion outside of the rail.

One of the chief objections to flower boxes has been that they are an ornament only in the summer time. They can be made attractive in winter as well by the use of small evergreens and vines, or they can be made removable to be stored away during the winter.

A window box should be made of redwood or cypress, both famed for their lasting quality. Ordinary clear yellow pine will last a long time if carefully painted. All joints should be thoroughly painted before the box is put together (at least two coats) and brass screws should be used instead of nails.

Soil requirements are the same as for house plants, and boxes which are not designed to be sub-irrigating, should have plenty of drainage and about two inches of coarse gravel in the bottom. Over this should be placed enough sand to cover it well. In this type of box, watering is required almost daily, for if the soil is allowed to dry it will shrink away from the sides of the box and the plant will suffer.

We illustrate two sub-irrigation types. Sub-irrigating boxes may be purchased in most stores, but they can also be made as shown. The two inches of gravel in the bottom should be very coarse and well covered with sand to keep the soil from washing down into it and destroying its usefulness. The watering spout shown and the watering slot on the side-irrigation type permit the entrance of some air as well as water which is highly beneficial to the plants. This type of box need be watered only once a week, except in extremely warm and dry weather.

No watering from the top is neces-

WINTER   WINDOW   SUMMER
BOXES

INSIDE MEASUREMENTS 8 IN WIDE BY 8 IN DEEP

FOR ENGLISH OR SWISS TYPE HOUSE

FOR COLORED SHINGLE HOUSE

2 SUB-IRRIGATING TYPES

2 IN. GRAVEL — SOIL

WATERING SPOUT

NOTCH

WATER HERE — SOIL

SAND OR GRAVEL

12 IN.

14 IN.

METAL PAN SHAPE OVER BOX

2" PEBBLES

BOX WITHOUT SUB IRRIGATION

MUST HAVE 2 IN PEBBLES IN BOTTOM & PLENTY OF DRAINAGE HOLES.

BEND OVER

AND FLATTEN.

COLONIAL - DECORATIVE

COLONIAL - PLAIN

LATTICE DESIGN

PIONEER - RUSTIC

LOG CABIN - RUSTIC

STUCCO COVERED OR WOOD BOX WITH SILHOUETTE CUT-OUT DESIGN OF METAL.

MAKING A CONCRETE WINDOW BOX.

BEND DOWN

WIRE BOX TIGHTLY.

USE TAPERED WOODEN BOX OR METAL CORE.

POUR 1/2 OF BOTTOM OVER CORE — LAP MESH OVER CONCRETE AND COMPLETE POURING

CUT DESIGN FROM CARDBOARD OR FIBRE. TACK ON TO INSIDE OF MOLD — OIL ENTIRE INTERIOR BEFORE POURING CEMENT.

CAST BOX UPSIDE DOWN

TO RE-ENFORCE CONCRETE USE 1/2 IN. GALVANIZED IRON WIRE MESH.

KEEP WIRE MESH IN CENTER OF CONCRETE. TAMP FIRMLY ON BOTH SIDES.

REMOVE FORMS & LIFT OUT CORES.

sary, but the soil should be examined from time to time by digging down into it a little to see when watering is needed.

This box may be made fairly water tight by puttying the joints but it is very simple to install a metal pan (three or four inches deep is all that is necessary) made without soldering by the method illustrated on p. 311.

If the soil is carefully selected and prepared, and reworked with some sheep manure each year, the box need not be refilled for several years. Liquid manure, applied as previously instructed, adds to the bloom. A little chemical plant food or, still better, plant tablets, may be given once a month but care should be used not to apply it until the plants are well established and then not to overdo it.

A wide variety of plants are available and the simple favorites are many times the best. The writer has had beautiful boxes consisting of asparagus ferns, geraniums and petunias. Some of the ruffled type petunias are susceptible of considerable

stimulation. One box, located where it had shade in the late afternoon only, had plant tablets applied monthly. The petunias developed a number of stalks which bloomed vigorously, trailing over the side of the box two to three feet. Many times fifteen to twenty large blooms could be counted on a single plant.

Select the plants to fit conditions of sun or shade. Even partial shade affects them.

For sunny exposure use:

Upright—Lantana, Petunia, Nasturtium, Dwarf Marigold, Heliotrope, Geranium, Everblooming Begonia, Candytuft, Sweet Alyssum, Ageratum, Coleus and Dusty-miller.

Trailing—Trailing Geranium, Trailing Lantana, Asparagus plumosus, Asparagus sprengeri, Vinca, German Ivy and English Ivy.

For boxes in the shade:

Upright—Begonia, Viola, Fuchsia, Forget-me-not and almost any fern or foliage plant.

Trailing—Same as sunny box.

CHAPTER XXII

HOUSE PLANTS

He has no yard behind his house,
No garden green to till,
And so he works the hothouse plan
Upon his window sill.

—OLD SONG

The cultivators of house plants indoors are divided into two classes: Those who raise them for love of the plants and those who have a few plants for indoor decoration. As these classes overlap to some extent, we will attempt to cover most of the phases of indoor culture, leaving it to the individual to choose the information best suited to his needs.

The chief requirements of house plants are:

1. Light.
2. Suitable potting.
3. Watering (soil moisture).
4. Moist air (temperature and ventilation).
5. Care of leaves.
6. Food.
7. Protection against pests.

With the exception of number four, all of these requirements are simple. We will therefore reserve it for discussion until last.

Light: Unless otherwise directed, it is safe to say that all blooming plants should be placed in the sun for at least a part of the day and turned often for even bloom. During our dark winter days there is little chance of many indoor plants being injured by too much sun. Ferns, vines and foliage plants do well at north and east windows but flowers are the result of exposure to the south and west sun. Ivies and several other plants will thrive away from windows but all must have light.

Potting; Repotting: Suitable potting is largely a matter of knowing how. We show (page 316) pot sizes —in inches and by name. Two-inch pots are sometimes called "thimbles"; two and one-half inch, "thumbs"; four and one-half inch "48's," six inch "32's," etc. Fern or azalea pots are made for plants with relatively shallow roots and are three-quarters as deep as the regular size; a special shallow pot called a "pan" is made in various sizes for potting bulbs, but is useful for other purposes. Some pots are also made with special bottom aeration for azaleas, cyclamen, etc.

A very common error is made in potting by the beginner. Ordinarily one would think that the larger the amount of soil the better for the plant. This is not the case. Flowering plants to give the best bloom must become "pot bound"; that is, their roots must pretty well fill the soil mass in the pot. But then, they must receive plenty of food.

Contrary to previous belief, experiments have proven that glazed decorative pots are satisfactory receptacles. If watering is carefully done, some plants, such as succulents and moisture-loving kinds, even do well in pots without bottom drainage holes.

Most plants, however, need potting as shown on page 316.

It will be readily seen that clean pots are essential. All clay, scum or dried slimy substances which would tend to stop the ready passage of air and water must be removed by washing and scrubbing with sand, if necessary. Pots seem to acquire alkali in the process of manufacture which injures the plant roots. For this reason you should soak new ones for a few days or boil them for a little while before using.

More attention should be paid to the condition of the soil than to its richness. Soil which has sufficient drainage and enough humus to hold moisture can easily be supplied with food by top dressing. This means applications of fertilizer in liquid or solid form from above.

Good garden soil is not fine enough for potculture so we take two parts of soil well worked and friable and add to it one part of sand and another of finely ground peat moss, peat humus or sifted leafmold. Florists like to use well rotted cow manure, or sod taken from a pasture and composted. Both are excellent but not essential. These ingredients sifted through a rather fine screen should be mixed with fine bone meal.

It is best for the gardener who expects to do any great amount of gardening to have a potting bench. Having things handy makes tasks light. The equipment consists of a strong table, some barrels to hold sifted soil, sand and peat moss; some 50 lb. lard tins with covers (these can be purchased from a meat shop for a few cents each) to hold dried cow manure, sheep manure, bone meal, etc. The bench can be an old kitchen table with the legs lengthened six or seven inches to make stooping unnecessary and a few boards nailed to the back and sides at the top to keep the soil from spilling off. A table 3 x 3 feet can easily be made of scrap lumber. Thirty-six or -seven inches is a good height for most people.

Where there is no garden house, it is well to appropriate a space 6 x 8 feet in the corner of the garage or cellar for this purpose. This confines the mess and the gardener has a chance to vary his outdoor tasks on brisk chilly days when prolonged outdoor occupation is uncomfortable.

The potting itself is simple. First, we place over the drainage hole two or three pieces of broken pots. This is important; break up a few pots if necessary or get some at a florist's. Over this it is wise to place a three-quarter inch layer of one-half inch cinders or pea sized charcoal, topped by a thin layer of leaves or peat moss (not over one-quarter inch thick). Now put in the growing soil loosely. Do not push it down. Jar the bottom sharply against the table to settle it. When it is full enough, place the plant in position, spreading the roots over the soil toward the pot sides. More soil is now added until the pot is about full. Firm well with the thumbs about the plant roots. Now water and allow the soil to settle. When fully compacted by watering, the soil should be from one-half to an inch below the top of the pot according to its size. This will facilitate future watering. Keep in a shady place a few days until new root growth starts.

When we talk of potting we mostly mean repotting or shifting from one container to another. Most repotting is to obtain proper rooting. To see when this is necessary, we first water well, then remove the soil from the pot by inverting and striking it upon a table while holding the soil and plant with the other hand. Our illustration shows conditions which call for different sized pots. Sometimes a pot becomes so root-bound that the pot must be broken to get it out. This is better than injuring the roots by cutting. Do not be in a hurry to repot. Geraniums and many other plants bloom best when slightly pot-bound. Pandanus is still well potted when it thrusts its roots to the top of the pot.

There is no hard and fast rule as to when to repot. The seedling may require several changes each season while larger plants (Chinese rubber plants, etc.) need it only once every two years. Most plants need repotting in the spring and a yearly examination of the roots is wise. After the long winter indoors the favorable conditions of summer enable them to recover from the shock better than they would at other times.

Do not hesitate, however, to repot when the plant needs it. A three-day period in the shade usually gives the healthy plant a chance to recuperate. Sometimes the need for change is shown by a slight yellowing of the foliage and a forcing of the roots through the drainage hole. Such roots should be combed with a strong fork and broken ends cut off clean.

If upon examination the ball shows no roots at all but only a sticky mass of mud, the soil should be removed, even washed off the roots, and the plant repotted in good, clean soil. This condition is a general indication of consistent overwatering and the need of a smaller pot.

If the ball reveals a mass of fine roots around the edge and they seem to be getting out of bounds, a larger pot is indicated. For fast, hearty growers, a pot two inches bigger may be required; for the slower growing, one one inch larger will be sufficient.

Summer Care: After the spring renovating the plants should have a chance to renew their vitality in the fresh air. Open sun for the bloomers (slight protection for begonias), semishade for many foliage plants and the more dense shade for the ferns. Do not overlook summer watering and pest inspection and before taking indoors examine the soil for worms and treat as later described.

It is advised for most plants that they be plunged (still in their pots) outdoors during the summer. Bury to the rim placing a concave piece of pot below the drainage hole to keep it open. When ready to bring indoors, knock the soil from the pot and wash it outside and around the rim so that it starts the winter clean.

Geraniums which have bloomed all winter should be discarded in the spring as soon as three-inch cuttings have been taken off for rooting in the coldframe or propagating bed. Such shrubbery plants as flowering almonds, lilacs, wisterias, hardy roses, hardy azaleas, etc., which have been forced for indoors, should have their roots loosened and spread before they are placed in permanent locations outdoors. They rarely do well as house plants for the second season unless given special care.

Watering: Watering may be divided into two distinct parts: moistening the soil and cleaning the leaves. These should not overlap.

It is stated that more plants die from overwatering each year than from any other cause. General rules are misleading but the idea is to water well but not so often. Get enough water on the plant to thoroughly moisten all the soil in the container. Excess water must be allowed to run off freely. Plants do not like what florists call wet feet. Jardinieres are dangerous if the plant is allowed to stand in water or if stale water is allowed to remain, to breed fungous

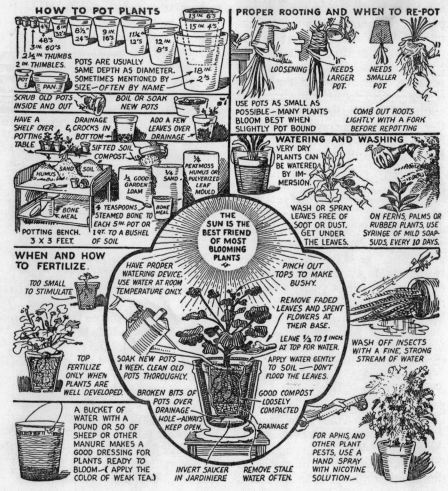

growth. Change it often. There are exceptions to this rule, but not many. Fast-growing plants stand soggy conditions better than slow-growing ones. Examine the soil for about one-half inch below the surface to see if it is dry before applying more water. Larger pots require less frequent watering than smaller ones because the larger volume of soil dries out more slowly.

Daily watering is not necessary but daily inspection is. Some florists can tell by rapping a pot with the knuckles. They use the system advanced by the Southern boy for testing the ripeness of watermelons. He stated, "If they goes 'pink,' they is green, but if they goes 'punk' they is ripe." A rap on a pot which gives out a hollow sound indicates dryness, but a solid sound indicates that the soil is pressed tight against the sides of the pot by the expansion which sufficient moisture gives to its contents.

Never sprinkle the topsoil but apply the water directly to it until it runs out the bottom. Sometimes a pot may be so dried out that the soil is cracked or shrunk away from the sides. In this instance the top water will run through to the bottom without the thorough wetting of the soil. We then must place the pot in a bucket of water so that it will enter from the bottom until complete moistening takes place. Do not let water come over the rim of the pot.

Care of Leaves: Never pour the water over the foliage of the plant but apply a fine misty spray with a bulb syringe sprinkler every ten days to flush off soot and dust. Any with smooth, strong leaves should be washed with lukewarm water and mild soapsuds once a month, using a soft sponge. For ferns and palms and rubber plants mild soapsuds is used every ten days as a spray instead of just plain water. Be sure to get the under side of the leaves in wetting and washing and do the job in the morning so that they have a chance to dry before night. Protect from direct sunlight while wet. Plants with hairy foliage (African-violets, etc.) do not like water on their leaves at all.

All dead or yellowed foliage should be removed flush with the stem and all flowers cut off as soon as they have passed their usefulness as ornaments. Pinch out the top of geraniums and cut back such plants as begonias, which are inclined to become straggly, to make them bushy and to stimulate better blooming.

Food: Feeding of plants requires thought and knowledge of their needs. Plants with heavy roots require a heavier, more loamy soil; plants with fine fibrous roots need a more open, sandy soil. For quick-growing plants a quart of sheep manure or dried cow manure may be incorporated in each bushel of soil. For slow-growers a quart of bone meal is better. This figures from one to three tablespoons to each 5-inch pot. The bone meal can be applied to any potted plant (except azaleas and other acid soil plants) as it is safe and beneficial.

The use of liquid manure must also be understood. A few handfuls of cow, horse or sheep manure in a bucket of water makes a good top dressing for healthy plants about to bloom. Applied to a sickly or dormant plant, it does no good and may harm rather than benefit. First pot, water and sun your plant until it starts active growth, then gradually feed it until it flourishes. Dilute the liquid manure to the color of very weak tea and then apply the same as other waterings. Quick-growing plants may have it every ten days; slow-growers, once every thirty days.

A solution of chemical plant food, one tablespoon to three gallons of water, may be applied as a substitute for liquid manure. Plant tablets are excellent, especially on plants used for window boxes, as geraniums, petunias, lantana, vinca, etc. Press down into the soil close to the stem and wet thoroughly. Never use either liquid or dry plant food upon dry soil. Water first, then fertilize. Never permit plant food to touch leaves.

Loosen the soil carefully on the top of the pot as frequently as possible. This admits air to sweeten the soil. Never use lime on house plants unless specifically directed to do so.

Beefsteak, oysters and castor oil are not plant foods and do some harm to the plant as well as being offensive to everyone near them.

Pests: Surface spots on foliage indicate fungous troubles. A good spray for them is a solution of one ounce of liver of sulphur (potassium sulphide) in three gallons of water. Hit under side of leaves, too. Dusting with this is a safe remedy for mildew. Separate diseased plants from healthy ones and in severe cases destroy them.

Control aphis with a solution of nicotine sulphate as directed on the container. Mix with soapsuds.

Washing strong-leaved plants with a hose spray and syringing of others usually destroys red spider, scale, mealy bugs, etc. If it doesn't, a spray of miscible oil will do so.

Angle worms sometimes get into the pots, especially after summer plunging. A few matches stuck into the soil are said to kill them, but a better method is a piece of lime a little bigger than your fist in a gallon of water. Crush, stir and wait until the mixture settles, then bottle for use at any time. An application or two will drive the worms to the surface so you can remove them. If azaleas or hydrangeas are treated, it is better to soak the soil immediately afterward with a solution of one ounce of aluminum sulphate to a gallon of water to neutralize the alkalinity.

Humidity and Temperature: Many flower-lovers have been disappointed with indoor blooms because of the hot, dry condition of the air in their living rooms. When it is just hot enough to be comfortable for us, steam heat becomes a deadly thing for the plants.

A dry heat of 75 degrees is the top for plants indoors and the list which will stand this much is quite small. Bulb plants in bloom last much longer at 65 to 68 degrees and tropical ferns and poinsettias do well at this rate.

Most plants thrive at from 55 to 65 degrees. How to attain this in our homes is a problem. Most people would feel decidedly chilly at this temperature.

It is generally thought that plants need an even temperature maintained at all times. Such is not the case. Cool rooms are better than those constantly warm but if the temperature is high in daytime it is a decided benefit and flowering is prolonged if we reduce it at night. Not, however, less than 55 degrees. They must not be allowed to freeze, and drafts and sudden changes must be prevented. Our grandmothers who covered the plants with cloth or newspapers when the fire in the stove was permitted to run low, had the right idea.

Another thing needed is humidity. For our own health we should use all the devices possible to obtain it in winter. Few homes unless air-conditioned have it to a sufficient degree. In greenhouses and conservatories humidity is attained by spraying leaves, benches, floors and the plants themselves. Tests in well-managed greenhouses indicate that the humidity runs 75% to 85%, while in the average living room it runs 20% to 30%.

This condition can be somewhat overcome by pans on radiators, boiling water on stoves and keeping water pans filled in hot-air furnaces. Some furnaces have devices which allow for a constant drip of water upon a hot place on the fire bowl. This is best of all.

A Window Conservatory: We illustrate a window sill conservatory which, while it is far from perfect, will provide humidity and a moderate temperature. It somewhat isolates the plants from the room heat and its area is cooled by radiation from the window glass. Humidity is supplied by dampened peat on its floor.

Our details call for the most simple form, but more interesting designs can easily be worked out in the shape of miniature conservatories. Use light sheet metal angles enameled in light green or white to form the frame, and celluloid in place of glass for curved surfaces, upon which can be painted the lesser divisions.

Our simple form is made of single strength glass, held in place by a one-inch hardwood frame. The bottom should be six inches deep, filled with peat moss in which to sink the pots. A hinged sash or front door is held at different positions by the use of a nail and chain for ventilation. The box open at the window side is left at least one inch from the window pane and another two-inch space over the front door sash allows for ventilation in normally cool weather.

A few newspapers are placed against the window glass on excessively cold nights to prevent drafts

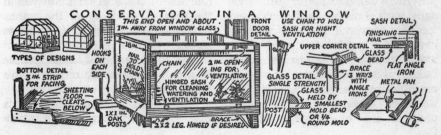

CONSERVATORY IN A WINDOW

TYPES OF DESIGNS

THIS END OPEN AND ABOUT 1 IN. AWAY FROM WINDOW GLASS

FRONT DOOR DETAIL

USE CHAIN TO HOLD SASH FOR NIGHT VENTILATION

SASH DETAIL

FINISHING NAIL

BOTTOM DETAIL 3 IN. STRIP FOR FACING

HOOKS ON EACH SIDE

18 IN. WIDE

NAIL TO HOLD CHAIN

CHAIN

2 IN. OPENING FOR VENTILATION

HINGED SASH FOR CLEANING WATERING AND VENTILATION

UPPER CORNER DETAIL

GLASS BEAD

GLASS DETAIL SINGLE STRENGTH GLASS HELD BY SMALLEST MOLD BEAD OR 1/4 ROUND MOLD

BRACE 3 WAYS WITH ANGLE IRONS

FLAT ANGLE IRON

METAL PAN

SHEETING FLOOR CLEATS BELOW

1X1 IN. OAK POSTS

2 X 2 LEG. HINGED IF DESIRED

BRACE

POST

and the front door sash of the frame is left open on the chain at nights when the heat goes down, to give extra ventilation and maintain evenness of temperature. Do not keep the box too tightly closed. A little experimentation will tell how to ventilate. Be observant.

A waterproof pan should be provided for the bottom to avoid damage to floors. We show how to make this out of sheet metal without soldering. It also can be made of heavy rubber type roofing paper.

Place an inch of coarse gravel in the bottom beneath the peat moss and take care not to water too freely so that the pots set in water. Keep their feet dry.

Timothy seed sown upon the peat will give a novel effect of a lawn between the plants. As it dies, stir the peat and repeat the sowing. It germinates quickly if kept moist.

Pink begonias, geraniums in many colors and the lavender of the heliotrope combine with the flowering bulbs. Glasses of water support miniature water plants, especially the graceful parrot feather, and small-leaved ivy, wandering jew, etc., which can be depended upon to travel over spaces between pots.

Lily of the valley pips just out of storage fill small hidden pots or may be planted directly in the wet peat.

Syringe daily, or better still, twice daily with a rubber bulb purchased for that purpose. It will prolong bloom. Be careful to avoid those plants that do not like to have their foliage wet: cyclamen, gloxinias, primulas, African-violets, some varieties of begonias, etc. It is always poor practice to deluge the leaves of the plant when watering for soil moisture.

If too much water accumulates in the bottom of the pan, siphon it out with a small piece of rubber tubing. A little water is all right if not allowed to grow stagnant. It should always be well below the top of the gravel.

A small tin tube or a short piece of ½-inch iron pipe (a 6-inch nipple from any hardware store) can be inserted in the peat and pebbles at a front corner and through this can be seen the depth of water. A small rubber tube for siphoning can also be used here without disturbing the peat.

Other Methods: The window conservatory is not the only means available for culture of house plants. A shelf or table with a ledge to hold dampened peat and lined with roofing paper may be used in a cool room. An upstairs hall window, free from drafts, a sewing room or a spare bedroom can usually be kept cool. The shelf or table can be moved out into the hall when the room is ventilated for sleeping at night.

Plants may be brought from the conservatory or cool shelf in the daytime when desired for living room decoration, to be returned at night for recuperation.

A deep pan with water in the bottom may have a grille upon which the pots set well out of the water. Evaporation keeps them somewhat humid.

Next to these a shelf in the kitchen is best. The temperature often rises but the humidity is usually better.

Ventilation: Do not forget that fresh air is essential to all plants. See that they get some of it by opening the window farthest away from them if for only a few minutes a day. Thoroughly ventilate an adjoining room and then open the door into the one containing the plants. No harm will be done even if the temperature goes down to 50 degrees, if no drafts are allowed.

Natural gas is the worst enemy of house plants. Even a small amount of it in the air is almost fatal. If you heat your rooms directly with open gas stoves, plant culture is almost an impossibility.

No Noxious Gases from House Plants: Just laugh when anyone tells you that plants in sleeping rooms are detrimental to health. If plants gave off this much injurious gas the human race would have been exterminated long ago.

Display an Arrangement: Many stands for the display of plants indoors are ghastly things. When we combine grace of line with the grace of the plants we achieve the truly artistic.

A wrought iron stand to hold pots can be made to look like an iron tree. It can be easily moved to the window for light and back again for decoration. Anyone handy with tools can make such a stand to hold small watertight, ornamental vases in which the pots are set. A few scrolls of strap iron and a piece of hammered pipe, held together with bolts or rivets, need only careful design to add to the room decoration. Wall brackets can be made in the same way for hanging at the windows or elsewhere in the room.

Ivy grown in a small plant box (page 325) and trained over a light scroll, makes a fine screen or windbreak for house or porch. Castors on the box facilitate moving it indoors or out.

At a window we can keep plants on a tray to brighten the whole room with bloom, but why waste the space beneath it? We illustrate an easy way to utilize it for a storage rack for magazines. With small changes it can be adapted to the storage of the watering can and the things necessary for the care of plants. Fitted with drawers instead of a bin, there is no end to its usefulness. (See illustration, page 325.)

Ivy can be trained as window drapery with beautiful effect, but do not combine plants with cloth drapes. Set the pots upon the window sill and fasten the vines directly to the sash or frame, using thumb tacks and, if necessary, small loops of neutral colored paper held by thumb tacks or pins. All the care that is necessary is to take it down and wash off the leaves with soap and water once a month. Rap upon the pots daily to test them, and keep them moist. The smaller varieties of English ivy are best. It resents, the least of all plants, the hot, dry air of our living rooms; but watch out for red spider.

A List of Plants: We offer here a list of plants taken from a bulletin issued by The Ohio State University, prepared by Irwin Klein, floricultural specialist, but have omitted some plants which we describe more fully elsewhere.

Foliage Plants

CAST-IRON PLANT (*Aspidistra elatior*). This plant easily rates as the most tolerant house plant. It will live for months without direct sunlight; it doesn't object to too much or too little water, and it can withstand fluctuations of temperature. Because of its extreme tolerance the plant is put to many uses.

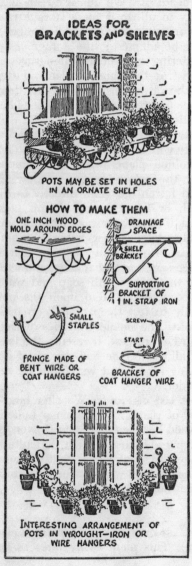

IDEAS FOR
BRACKETS AND SHELVES

POTS MAY BE SET IN HOLES
IN AN ORNATE SHELF

HOW TO MAKE THEM

ONE INCH WOOD
MOLD AROUND EDGES

DRAINAGE
SPACE

SHELF
BRACKET

SUPPORTING
BRACKET OF
1 IN. STRAP IRON

SMALL
STAPLES

SCREW

START

FRINGE MADE OF
BENT WIRE OR
COAT HANGERS

BRACKET OF
COAT HANGER WIRE

INTERESTING ARRANGEMENT OF
POTS IN WROUGHT-IRON OR
WIRE HANGERS

The leaves are large with long petioles arising from the rhizome. The drooping leaves give the plant a somewhat graceful appearance. Insects seldom attack it. An occasional bath will make it appear attractive at all times.

WANDERING JEW (*Tradescantia fluminensis*). This is a trailing vine of succulent growth with green leaves, often purplish beneath. Its requirements are few; plenty of moisture, a fair amount of sunlight, and approximately 60° temperature. Any type of soil will do; in fact, it will grow well in water. It is easily propagated by cuttings, placed in water, sand, or soil.

ENGLISH IVY (*Hedera helix*). Another popular plant, perhaps because it does well in places receiving little sunlight and heat. It makes rapid growth under normal conditions and can be trained to supports for unusual effectiveness. If a bushy plant is desired, the ends of the branches should be pinched off. These removed branches may be used as cuttings to propagate new plants. Occasionally aphids attack the young foliage. A spray of nicotine sulphate will hold the insects in check. The variegated so-called Mexican and California ivies are attractive but not as vigorous as the ordinary kind. A number of new varieties, self-branching or semi-erect, are worth a trial; among them are Albany, Hahn's Miniature and Self-branching, Merion Beauty, and Sylvanian.

BOWSTRING HEMP (*Sansevieria*). Two popular forms of this plant are: S. *zeylanica*, banded with lighter green; and S. *trifasciata* var. *laurenti*, whose leaves have yellow edges.

Either will exist under trying conditions. The leaves which arise from the base are of a fleshy, tough texture. They are propagated by division or leaf cuttings; however, the *laurenti* variety will not come true to color from cuttings.

EAST INDIAN HOLLYFERN (*Polystichum aristatum*). This is one of the most tolerant of all ferns for the house. It is very easily grown, requires moderate amounts of water, and prefers shade. The plant grows 12 to 18 inches tall and each leaf is 12 to 24 inches long and 10 inches wide. Although coarser in appearance than the Boston fern, it is very vigorous in habit and stands rough treatment.

RUBBER PLANTS (*Ficus*). These are popular with most people. They are sensitive to overwatering and prefer partial shade. A temperature of 60–65° is best. All rubber plants will do best outdoors during the summer. Frequent sponging will remove dust and eliminate clogging of the breathing pores. *Ficus pandurata* (Fiddleleaf) with its large, fiddle-shaped and deeply veined leaves, is somewhat more attractive than the common *F. elastica*.

CREEPING FIG (*Ficus pumila*). This is a dainty trailing plant with small leaves close to the stems which cling to wall surfaces. The dense growth and rich green color make it desirable. It is native to Japan and China.

PALMS. Many of these decorative evergreens are frequently used as house plants. All require a temperature of about 60–65° F. Although they require plenty of moisture during the summer they will suffer if overwatered in winter. Most palms

do best if not repotted too frequently. *Howea belmoreana* is a graceful plant with rather broad fan-shaped leaves. The leaves of the Phoenix are finer and more graceful. In its native habitat this species produces dates. *Areca lutescens* is a rapid grower with feathery foliage on long yellow stems.

NORFOLK ISLAND PINE (*Araucaria excelsa*). This plant is a beautiful evergreen, a fairly rapid grower, and quite tolerant. As a small plant it makes an excellent table centerpiece. It requires a medium rich soil and a temperature of 60° F. During the summer it thrives in partial shade.

GRAPE-IVY (*Cissus rhombifolia*). An excellent trailing, evergreen plant with three-parted leaflets. Each leaf is about 4 inches long. New plants are grown from cuttings.

ST. BERNARD-LILY (*Anthericum liliago*). An herb that grows rapidly from stolons like the strawberry plant. Because of its rapid growth and trailing habit it is very useful for hanging baskets. Propagation is most easily effected by stolons, although it is sometimes perpetuated by division or seeds. Usually, the plant does not suffer from the effects of overwatering.

COLEUS. Among these plants, *Coleus blumei* is the most commonly cultivated species. To produce a bushy, well-balanced plant the stems require frequent pinching to encourage branching. Full sunlight, high humidity, and a temperature of 60° F. are the cultural requirements. The easiest method of propagation is by cuttings, although seeds germinate readily and provide many interesting variations in pattern. Mealy bugs are the worst enemies of this plant. Frequent washing and syringing will help to keep the insects in check. Touching the insects with a wisp of cotton dipped in alcohol insures instant death.

UMBRELLA PLANT (*Cyperus alternifolius*). A peculiar looking plant which derives its common name from the appearance of the foliage, a long petiole with leaves (blade) arranged similarly to the ribs of an open upright umbrella. It is native to Africa and therefore needs a warm temperature (65° F.) and plenty of water. Fertilize occasionally. Sometimes mealy bugs are a serious pest.

PHILODENDRON. This is a very interesting and rapidly growing vine, although not quite so tolerant as the English Ivy. The leaves are large, bright green, and somewhat heart-shaped. It requires a fair amount of sunlight and much moisture; in fact, stems are frequently placed directly in water in ivy bowls, where they root and thrive if nutrients are occasionally supplied. A variegated form is interesting but harder to grow.

BABY'S TEARS (*Helxine soleiroli*). A dainty creeping plant with very small leaves, forming a dense mat. In some homes it may be found on kitchen window sills where the high temperature and abundance of moisture are particularly favorable for its development. It thrives in partial shade. Avoid excessive watering during the winter.

SILK-OAK (*Grevillea robusta*). Not a particularly showy plant, but a very rapid, vigorous grower. In its native land of Australia it becomes a tree 150 feet tall. As a pot plant it produces a slender stem with long horizontal branches and feathery fern-like leaves. The usual method of propagation is by seed.

PERIWINKLE (*Vinca minor*). An excellent vine for window boxes and wall vases. The variety with variegated foliage is most attractive.

LEOPARD PLANT (*Ligularia kaempferi*). This plant is used chiefly for its spotted foliage of white, yellow, or pink. New plants are started by cuttings or division.

BOSTON FERN (*Nephrolepis exaltata bostoniensis*). One of the most popular house plants, although many people find it difficult to grow satisfactorily. Ferns are sensitive and require a temperature between 65 and 70° F.; lower or higher temperatures may cause poor growth. Poor drainage, together with overwatering, will turn the leaves yellow. Oversized pots create excessive moisture in the soil. High humidity (air moisture) is essential, which may be provided by frequent washing of the leaves. A partial shade is preferred to direct sunlight. All ferns are propagated by runners or division. Be on the lookout for white flies, aphids, and scales.

ASPARAGUS-FERN. This plant is a native of South Africa. The species *A. sprengeri* and *A. plumosus* are the two most common types used as house plants. Both produce long fronds which occasionally bear red to black berries. Overwatering and a hot, dry atmosphere will cause the leaves to drop.

HOUSE HOLLYFERN (*Cyrtomium falcatum*). This interesting plant has dark green, glossy, pinnate leaves. The fronds are long and graceful.

DUMB CANE (*Dieffenbachia se-*

POPULAR HOUSE PLANTS

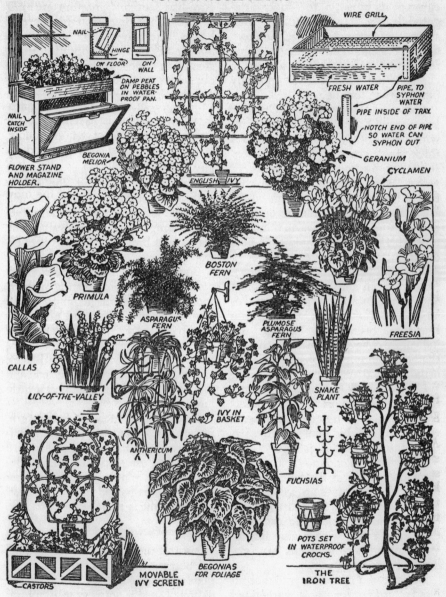

NAIL

HINGE

ON FLOOR

ON WALL

DAMP PEAT ON PEBBLES IN WATER-PROOF PAN.

NAIL CATCH INSIDE

FLOWER STAND AND MAGAZINE HOLDER.

BEGONIA MELIOR

ENGLISH IVY

WIRE GRILL

FRESH WATER

PIPE, TO SYPHON WATER

PIPE INSIDE OF TRAY.

NOTCH END OF PIPE SO WATER CAN SYPHON OUT

GERANIUM

CYCLAMEN

PRIMULA

BOSTON FERN

ASPARAGUS FERN

PLUMOSE ASPARAGUS FERN

FREESIA

CALLAS

LILY-OF-THE-VALLEY

IVY IN BASKET

ANTHERICUM

SNAKE PLANT

FUCHSIAS

MOVABLE IVY SCREEN

CASTORS

BEGONIAS FOR FOLIAGE

POTS SET IN WATERPROOF CROCKS.

THE IRON TREE

guine). Grown as a potted plant because of its broad, 5- to 7-inch variegated leaves, it is propagated from short stem cuttings, planted horizontally in sand. The common name refers to the fact that if a stem is chewed, the juice will temporarily paralyze the tongue.

JADE- or WAX-PLANT (*Crassula arborescens*). A slow-growing plant with very fleshy, oval leaves, and a thick stem, growing well in partial shade with moderate amounts of water. Most Japanese gardens contain at least one of these plants which are propagated from the tip cuttings or the fleshy leaves. A warm temperature with moderate humidity is necessary.

NANDINA (*Nandina domestica*). An evergreen shrub native in China and Japan. As a house plant it makes an excellent specimen with its thin branches, bright red berries, and delicately colored leaves. It thrives in shady or sunny positions. Seed is the usual method of propagation.

COPPER-LEAF (*Acalypha macafeana*). A colorful plant, with copper-colored leaves as its name implies. It is propagated by heel cuttings. A temperature of 65° F. is best.

SCREWPINE (*Pandanus*). The most common species of the Screwpine is *P. veitchi*. The leaves are long, variegated, sword-like, with sharp teeth on the margins. It objects to excessive moisture in the winter and insufficient sunlight. New plants are produced by offsets.

DRACENAS (*Dracaena*). Beautiful plants, grown for their variegated foliage. The genus Cordyline is similar to Dracaena, differing only in the flower parts. *D. fragrans* (Corn-

plant) is most common, with its large corn-like leaves. *Cordyline australis* (*indivisa*) has long, drooping, narrow leaves. The leaves of *D. godseffiana* appear in whorls or opposite on the stem, 3 to 4 inches long, with numerous white spots; flowers are greenish yellow. *C. terminalis* has large leaves (12 to 30 inches long by 3 to 4 inches wide) in many colors. *D. goldieana* is a fine foliage plant with its broad, rounded leaves (7 to 8 inches long and 4 to 5 inches wide) of white and green bands. Sponging the leaves with water at frequent intervals will improve their growth. Moderately warm temperature is necessary. The leaves will brown at the tips if overwatered.

BIRD'S NEST FERN (*Asplenium nidus-avis*). This interesting plant is sometimes grown as a house plant. The leaves are broad and of a delicate green color. The arrangement of the leaves suggests a nest for birds. Strong sunlight will spot the leaves, and too much moisture may cause a loss of color. It likes peat and a little lime.

Small plants such as *Pteris fern, Peperomia maculosa, Mesembryanthemum, Pilea microphylla* (*Artillery Plant*) find use as potted plants. Because these plants are fairly slow growers, small-sized pots are best. Full sunlight is required.

Flowering Plants

Most of the flowering house plants are best grown if purchased as small plants from the florists. Home germination of seed is not very satisfactory.

AZALEAS, INDIAN. These are usually available in the earlier varieties at Christmas, and the later at Easter.

They require ample water, a fairly cool spot, and abundant light. After the blooms fall, they should be moved into a warmer place, and given more water on soil and foliage. In May, they can be set out, still potted, in the shade, and kept moist, so that new foliage will mature. In September, when brought inside, a cool sunny window and water will help bring them into bloom in November. Empress of India is a recommended variety.

LEMON, ORANGE, AND GRAPEFRUIT. These are the most common citrus plants used as house plants. Of all flowering plants these are the most tolerant. They thrive in the high temperature of the average home. Although tolerant to partial shade they grow better in full sunlight. Overwatering is objectionable only during the winter. They react favorably to additions of complete fertilizers at regular intervals. On mature plants scales are troublesome occasionally.

GARDEN BALSAM (*Impatiens balsamina*). An old-fashioned plant popular with most people. The stems and leaves are quite succulent and the flowers, of various colors, are borne close to the stems. Pinching the terminal growths keeps the plant bushy and shapely. It thrives in a fertile soil in direct sunlight when supplied with plenty of water. It can be perpetuated by seeds or cuttings.

CIGAR-FLOWER (*Cuphea platycentra*). A native of Mexico. The flowers resemble a cigar, with their bright red calyx and white mouth with a dark ring at the end. It is easily grown in the house and is propagated by seeds.

GERANIUM (*Pelargonium*). In-cludes many species, such as the Fish Geranium, one of the most common house plants. The Lady Washington Pelargoniums are smaller leafed, many flowered, white to red with black blotches on the two upper petals. Madame Sellori, a variety of the Fish Geranium, is characterized by its variegated leaves. All species prefer plenty of sunlight and an abundance of water, although overwatering during the winter may cause the leaves to drop. A temperature between 65 and 70° F. increases flower production. Applications of fertilizer in fall and spring will improve the quality of the foliage and flowers.

ROSES (*Rosa*). Many species make good house plants if given proper attention. A temperature of 60° F. is most desirable. When the plants are in flower a lower temperature and less water are essential. In the spring they may be planted out into the garden. Red spider is the most serious insect to fight. Frequent washing and syringing with water will give satisfactory control when applied during bright, sunny days. Dust with sulphur to prevent the spread of mildew, a white powdery growth which appears on the leaves.

POCKET-BOOK PLANT (*Calceolaria hybrida*). A very attractive plant. The flowers are shaped like a well-filled purse, and are of many brilliant colors. Good drainage is essential. A good fibrous loam soil will produce quality plants if grown at a temperature not above 50° F.

POINSETTIA (*Euphorbia pulcherrima*). This is the favorite Christmas flower. While the plant is in bloom, refrain from adding much water.

During its growing season it requires a temperature of 65° F. and plenty of sunlight. Avoid sudden chills. The plant is propagated by cuttings taken in early summer from plants carried from the previous winter. If the flower is cut from the plant, dip the end of the stem into boiling water or sear with a flame to prevent bleeding. The showy red, white, or pink parts are bracts, or modified leaves; the small green-yellow flowers cluster in the center.

HYDRANGEA (*Hydrangea*). This beautiful plant seldom makes a good house subject because it is so hard to satisfy its needs in the ordinary home. It requires a cool temperature, an abundance of water, and an acid soil. If hydrangeas are desired in the home it is best to secure the plants from a florist while they are in flower. In spring transplant to a place in the garden having an acid soil. Protected the first year with a mulch they overwinter well outdoors. To be used again as a house plant they require a light freezing before being lifted. Keep the plants in a cool place until December and then force into growth.

GLOXINIA (*Sinningia speciosa*). An interesting plant. The flowers are large and bell-shaped, in velvety colors of violet, to red, or even white. It requires a warm, humid atmosphere and partial shade. After blooming, the tubers should be stored in a cool place until February when they may be started into growth. Be careful not to wet the foliage. Flowering plants can be produced from seeds or cuttings in about twelve months.

AGERATUM, HELIOTROPE, LANTANA. These are all grown occasionally as house plants. They require full sunshine, a moderate amount of water, and a temperature of 60–65° F.

For additional varieties and care see Calendar for each month (page 374).

CACTI

The growing of cacti in small bowls is popular with many people. Their peculiar shapes and habits of growth attract attention. Very few of the cacti will bloom in the average home, but in their native habitat their flowers are extremely beautiful. A useful exception is the Christmas or Crab Cactus (*Zygocactus truncatus*), whose jointed drooping stems are tipped with red flowers, which blossoms from December to February.

Most species will grow in a sandy soil, and but little water is required by them. An occasional sprinkling of water over the plant will suffice. A temperature of 65–70° F. is desirable.

HANGING BASKETS

Round bottom wire frame baskets are used for hanging baskets, as a rule, although rustic wood and pottery are used occasionally.

Before filling the wire or wooden baskets it is necessary to line the sides and bottoms with sheet moss to retain the soil.

Because the baskets are hanging overhead and somewhat out of sight, their proper water requirements are often overlooked.

Plants that are effective in a hanging basket are English Ivy, Sprenger's Asparagus, Wandering Jew, Coleus (Trailing Queen), German Ivy, Thunbergia alata, Moneywort, Trailing Honeysuckle, and Trailing Lantana.

ANNUALS AND PERENNIALS USED AS HOUSE PLANTS

Many annual flowers are used as house plants. Several kinds, including the snapdragons, marigolds, ageratum, calendulas, and zinnias, mature early in the garden and drop their seeds to the ground. The resulting seedlings may be transplanted to small pots and grown as house plants. Frequently the older plants may be potted if they are severely pruned back to stimulate new growth. In fact, nearly all house plants will be more sightly if the branches are cut back. A more balanced and shapely plant will result from this practice.

A few perennials, in small clumps, do well in the house. The kind to select are those which bloom continuously throughout the summer, as gerberas, gaillardias, pinks, and hardy chrysanthemums. Perennials like delphiniums, phloxes, campanulas, coreopsis, poppies, aconitums, and larkspurs require comparatively long rest periods, and therefore do not make good house plants. If some of the latter group are allowed to freeze, then lifted some time after January, potted, kept in a cool place for about a week, and then gradually removed to a warmer location, the plants can be forced successfully into bloom.

BULBS INDOORS

In the cultivation of house plants, indoor bulbs are the most easily raised and maintained as well as the surest to bloom.

Spring Flowering Bulbs: Spring flowering bulbs for winter bloom belong to the group of garden bulbs which are planted in the fall and bloom in the spring. They are sometimes referred to as Holland bulbs or Dutch bulbs and the process of raising them to bloom indoors in winter is called "forcing."

To most amateurs the word forcing means something intricate and technical. It means quick growth at high temperature. Bulbs for indoor bloom are raised at low temperature and very slowly. The process is so elementary that a child can master it easily.

The most simple type is the colchicum, sometimes called "autumn crocus," which has its foliage in the spring, the flowers coming directly from the ground in the fall after foliage has gone. In the house it is almost impossible to keep it from blooming. Placed away from sun its blooms are white; in the sun they are lilac. It will bloom on a window sill without water or soil in winter and can then be planted outside in early spring.

Paperwhite narcissus will bloom after a fashion if merely kept in a bowl of pebbles and water, but finer blooms, lasting three or four weeks, can be had by placing the bowl in a closet or dark cellar for three weeks to develop roots, and out of the sun for another week while leaves develop.

Spring flowering bulbs such as hyacinths, tulips, narcissi, crocuses and a host of other small bulbs force easily if you follow the rules.

As previously explained a bulb is a bud and needs only warmth and water, and the means of absorbing water (roots), to develop its bloom.

In natural planting of spring flowering bulbs, we bury them in the ground in the fall where they develop roots for rapid spring top growth. The soil then is cool and moist. In the spring they develop sprouts best under a light mulch of leaves and the lesser sunlight. Their blossoms follow with warmer weather and brighter skies.

In forcing we must try to imitate as much as possible these conditions and we do so by following these rules:

Rule No. 1: Roots must be developed before any other growth. The secret of success is a pot full of roots. We do this by removing all light and keeping the temperature down, imitating autumn soil conditions.

A garage attached to the cellar, an unheated fruit cellar, coal bin under a porch, separated from the furnace room, make good, cool places as they maintain a temperature of about 50 to 60° all winter. By far the best and easiest place is out of doors in a cold-frame.

Rule No. 2: Slow stem growth should precede bloom. Bulbs placed in direct sunlight immediately after being brought from the dark develop too fast (soft growth), the foliage flops over and the stems may be unable to support heavy bloom. Keep them shaded for a short time.

Rule No. 3: Place in a sunny window and turn daily for even bloom.

Rule No. 4: Flowering is prolonged by moisture in the air. Outdoors they develop in cool temperature, 65° or less, and moist spring air. For your own health and that of the flowers, keep the air moist.

Rule No. 5: Perhaps this should be rule one. It is always best to buy good named bulbs. They do not need to be exhibition size or expensive. Large size, especially in hyacinths, many times indicates age rather than vigor. Bulbs well rounded and firm, two inches or more through (in the larger kinds) are usually satisfactory. Some dealers feature bulbs especially prepared for forcing. They should be better than those used outside.

Spring flowering bulbs are forced in water alone, in pebbles and water, in fiber and in pots of soil, but the above rules apply to all of the methods.

Hyacinths in Jars of Water: Regular hyacinth jars are for sale at your seedsmen. Quart food jars do just as well. Add charcoal to keep the water sweet and an inch or so of pebbles in the bottom to give the jars stability. Fill them up with water and place the bulb on top. If it is too small to sit on the opening, three or four toothpicks or small pieces of wire stuck into it will hold it just above the surface of the water. Do not let it touch or the water may become slimy and the bulb decay.

Put the jars in dozen lots in cardboard cartons just slightly deeper than is necessary to hold them so that the air may circulate over the top of the bulb. Poke some holes in the sides to let in air and close the four lids of the cartons loosely to keep out all light, yet admit air. Put them in the darkest corner of your garage and cover loosely with several thicknesses of newspaper to keep light out of air-holes.

It is well to place the cartons upon boards held away from the cement floor by bricks. Contact with the floor seems to hold them back. Examine them once in a while and add tepid water if necessary. Temperature should stay between 40° and 50°.

In about eight to fifteen weeks roots will have reached the bottom of the glass and some of the best developed ones may be moved to a warmer place (55° to 60° is best), and covered with a paper cone until a sprout about five inches long has formed. The foliage will be sickly, but upon removal of the cone it will turn bright green. Then set in a sunny window to bloom, and turn daily for even growth.

Good results can be had by merely bringing the jars as needed from the cool cellar into a dark corner of a slightly warmer one until top growth is started and then to a sunny window.

A hundred jars or more can be rooted in this manner to be brought upstairs as needed and a succession of bloom is obtained from January to April, growing better as the season advances. Cover the jars with crepe paper jackets for appearance and supply with a wire stake to support the bloom.

Young hyacinth bulbs force easiest, Roman hyacinths easiest of all.

There is no reason why hyacinths should be planted only in glass containers other than economy. If you wish to go to the trouble of securing a number of glazed pots or vases, very presentable ones can be obtained for ten or fifteen cents each. They should hold over a full pint and better still about a quart. Forcing in fiber or peat are excellent methods and just about as easy as in water.

Narcissus in Water: Paperwhite narcissus bulbs and Chinese sacred-lilies (which are really a variety of narcissus) can be forced in a bowl of pebbles, easiest of all the bulbs. In fact they will give some degree of bloom if the bowls are merely placed in the light.

They do best, however, if placed six or more in a glass bowl, which is set away in a dark closet, or better still in a cool, dark spot in the cellar, for three or four weeks. This has a tendency to hold back top growth until roots are established. When brought into the open keep away from direct sun for a few days until the tops turn bright green.

It takes about five weeks from the

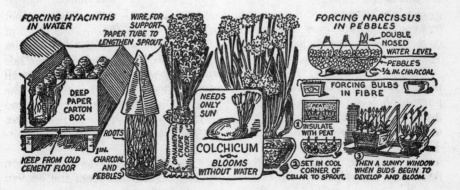

FORCING HYACINTHS IN WATER — WIRE FOR SUPPORT — PAPER TUBE TO LENGTHEN SPROUT — DEEP PAPER CARTON BOX — ROOTS — KEEP FROM COLD CEMENT FLOOR — 1 IN. CHARCOAL AND PEBBLES — ORNAMENTAL CREPE TUBE — NEEDS ONLY SUN — COLCHICUM BLOOMS WITHOUT WATER — FORCING NARCISSUS IN PEBBLES — DOUBLE NOSED — WATER LEVEL — PEBBLES — ½ IN. CHARCOAL — FORCING BULBS IN FIBRE — ① INSULATE WITH PEAT — ② SET IN COOL CORNER OF CELLAR TO SPROUT — ③ THEN A SUNNY WINDOW WHEN BUDS BEGIN TO DEVELOP AND BLOOM.

time bulbs are started for them to begin to bloom. If water level is retained, cold drafts kept away, and they are kept in a temperature of about 60°, the blooms will last at their best for two or three weeks.

Paperwhite bulbs bloom best if started about December 1st. They seem to need a curing period after being dug. If you get them sooner expose them to the sun on a window sill for a week or two.

Get colored pebbles of proper size from your seedsman and use two-inch firm round bulbs with a single sprout or neck. Double sprouts do not do as well.

Chinese sacred-lilies need more humidity than paperwhites and it is best to try them in a kitchen window where there is moisture in the air. Make a cut crosswise through the outer skin one inch from the top of the main bulb. Additional flower stems will come from it.

Growing in Fiber: Prepared peat moss or prepared fiber are for sale at all seed stores. This method is far superior to the other (water) method and can be successfully used on a much wider range of bulbs. It is not as good as forcing with soil but is cleaner in the house.

The bowl can be water tight so as to avoid possible injury to furniture or it may be a regular squat bulb pot (called a bulb pan) in a saucer.

The fiber or peat is treated with plant food so that it serves the purpose of holding the water for the bulbs and at the same time providing nourishment for roots and flowers.

If the receptacle is water tight put a layer of charcoal in the bottom, press down firmly but not hard a

layer of fiber and place the bulbs in position. They should be about one-half their diameter apart and the peak of the bulb should be just below the top of the bowl.

Now press fiber gently but firmly into place so it covers all but the tips of the bulbs which should leave it one-half inch from the top of the vase. Pour on water slowly until the fiber has reached full absorption and let it stand about one-half day. Tilt the bowl and drain off all water not held by the fiber; they want to drink, not to swim.

If the plants are raised in a bulb pan the surplus water will drain off into the saucer and water may be added from time to time to freshen the planting, which will make the charcoal unnecessary.

The same process of forming roots first is used with fiber as with the water method. Put bulbs in a well-ventilated place in the dark at a temperature of forty to fifty degrees for several weeks until they are two or three inches high. Water them occasionally, pouring off surplus as before described. If you have no cool place, put them in a box and surround them with a layer of three or four inches of peat moss, slightly damp. This is a fine insulation against heat and drying out.

When the bowls are filled with roots, bring them into the lesser light until the sickly tops turn bright green, then they may receive bright sun for blooming.

Hyacinths, tulips, narcissi, crocuses, callas, freesias, muscari, scillas, snowdrops, spireas, and Easter lilies are particularly adapted for fiber growing. Place a paper cone as before described over hyacinths and tulips, before exposing to the sun, to stimulate top growth.

A better way to develop roots in fiber is to bury them outside (called plunging), which is described later. By this method they may all be prepared at once and brought in as needed, while with the cellar method it becomes impossible to suppress the top growth and they may all start into growth at the same time.

Forcing Bulbs in Soil: Prepare soil by mixing two parts good garden soil with one part commercial humus or peat moss (mix the two together if you have them), and enough sand (it will usually take one part sand to three parts soil mixture) so that you cannot pack the soil into a ball when squeezed wet. Have it damp but not wet. Sift it through a coarse riddle as you need it, first adding a five-inch pot of fine steamed bone flour to each bushel of soil.

If the pots are new they should be thoroughly soaked for at least a week. They will dry out your bulbs if this is not done. If they are old clean them, or, if necessary, scrub off all mold with sand or a fine wire brush. Dry before potting.

Place a piece of broken pot over the drain hole and fill the pots lightly. The bulbs must be placed as the pots are filled, not screwed in afterwards. They should be just even with the top of the soil which should be one-half inch from the pot rim. Do not pound soil into the pots, but fill them and tap once or twice to settle. The roots will strike down more easily in loose soil. They must have room to grow or they will force the bulb from the soil.

After a thorough watering they are ready to take to the cool cellar. Do not set them on the cement floor but bed them in sand or peat moss and if it is warm or dry cover them with sand or pack them in a three-inch layer of peat moss. The root development takes for miniature hyacinths at least eight weeks, first size hyacinths ten to twelve weeks, tulips ten to twelve weeks and narcissi (except paperwhite) twelve to fifteen weeks.

The easiest and best way to root them is out of doors. This is known as "plunging." It is more natural and has the advantage of holding them dormant. As one writer tells, "pots in cold storage are much the same as pantry shelves filled with groceries

FORCING IN POTTED SOIL

NEW POTS MUST BE SOAKED IN WATER FOR A WEEK BEFORE USING.

SCRUB OLD POTS CLEAN WITH SAND OR A FINE WIRE BRUSH BEFORE USING.

DAMPEN WELL WHEN MIXING

RUN THRU COARSE SCREEN

PEAT OR LEAF MOULD — GOOD SOIL — SAND

ADD 5 IN. POT OF FINE STEAMED BONE TO EACH BUSHEL

HERE IS THE SECRET FOR SUCCESS

A POTFUL OF ROOTS BEFORE TOP GROWTH STARTS.

LILY OF THE VALLEY

SHORTEN ROOTS TO 3 INCHES

PLANT 6 TO 8 IN A 5 IN. POT — PLACE IN PEATMOSS. KEEP IN A WARM PLACE.

TO FORCE TOP GROWTH INVERT A POT OVER ROOTED BULBS.

OUTDOOR ROOTING PITS

PLUNGING IN A COLD FRAME.

SASH

PEATMOSS SOIL CINDERS SOIL SOIL

PLUNGING IN A PIT. LEAF MULCH NATURAL SOIL LEVEL 12 IN. SOIL 3 IN. SAND CINDERS

and canned food, ready for use as needed."

The method is simple. Some people merely dig a trench, one spade deep, near a sheltered foundation wall. In the bottom of this is placed two inches of coal ashes and the pots set upon it. The soil is tucked in around the pots to keep the mice from making it their winter home and a layer of two inches of sand placed over them. The balance of the soil is then piled over it and the top mulched with about a foot of leaves or six inches of peat moss held in place with boards.

By far the easiest way to plunge is in a coldframe. An excavation is made in the loose soil, the pots set on ashes, filled around and covered with the soil. A heavy layer of peat moss about one foot thick is placed over them. The frame is not covered with the sash until severe weather. The ease with which the peat can be removed for examination makes this arrangement attractive.

The orthodox method recommended by most writers is to bury the pots in a pit deep enough to contain them when set upon two inches of cinders and covered with two inches of sand and ten inches of soil. A mulch of leaves is placed over this when the ground is frozen.

At the end of the time for rooting the pots must be uncovered and examined. They may be knocked loose by gently tapping the inverted pot. If the roots are well distributed through the soil, you will know they are fully developed. The best developed should be brought indoors as needed and placed in a temperature of 50° for the development of top growth.

Lily of the Valley: Valley lilies are not really bulbs. Their roots and crowns together are called "pips," and are excellent for indoor forcing. If you want to secure them from your own bed after freezing, discard the pointed crowns and select only the older, thicker crowns which end in a stubby blunt point. Lopsided crowns with a bulge on them must not be used.

It is much better to purchase them from your seedsman as they are sure to bloom, while those dug from your garden are doubtful. Professional growers know best how to grow them for forcing.

One writer says they are as reliable as an electric clock and that she did not start them in the dark at all but planted them in peat moss or pebbles because she liked to see their leaves unfold. The results are not as good this way but it is less trouble.

The prescribed way is to place half a dozen or more in a five-inch flower pot, with tips just above the surface after cutting the roots back to about three inches. Soaking the pips in warm water (90° or 95°) for several hours will help develop the foliage.

They can be raised in deep vases of fiber without drainage, or potted in soil, sand, peat moss, or fiber and then watered well. Pots must never be allowed to dry out. Place them in a cool, semi-dark place until sprouts start and then bring into a hot place until ready to bloom. On top of a mildly warm radiator is not too hot, but keep them wet.

Another method is to set them, after potting and watering, out of doors for ten days to freeze and then bring them in to thaw out gradually and place on top of the furnace or radiator, packed in a box of damp peat moss. Keep it damp by placing a glass over the top of the box and wiping it dry often. Remove it in about a week and they will grow vigorously.

Try these methods then practice the one you like best.

CAPE BULBS

These plants get their name from their habitat near the Cape of Good Hope in southern Africa. They include both bulbs and corms, such as freesias, ixias and oxalis. Anemones and ranunculus are not cape bulbs but require the same culture, so we include them here.

They require a light, cool spot 40° to 55° after potting to develop root and top growth at the same time. After this they are brought into a slightly warmer room for blooming. They are small plants and require but small containers—four- or five-inch pots. Water given them should be at room temperature.

Anemones and Ranunculus: Plant in deep pots, covering the roots two to three inches. Start potting in September and continue at monthly intervals until February for succession of bloom. Use rich soil—six or eight bulbs in a pan if you wish—place in a cool, fairly light cellar—keep moist but not soggy until top growth begins. When brought to a sunny window give more water and keep some standing in the saucer. The foliage of the anemone is fern-like and attractive and it flowers successively until through blooming. Allow the bulbs to ripen naturally and then keep them in sand or peat to prevent

drying out until needed. Plant spent bulbs outdoors in fall or spring and use fresh bulbs for indoors each year. (See Outdoor Culture, Chapter XII.)

Freesias: New colored hybrid varieties make this fragrant plant more attractive than ever. They will bloom from fall until spring under careful management. Large bulbs bloom sooner than small ones which may take until April.

A succession of bloom is obtained by pottings every three or four weeks from September 1st to October, but they may be potted as late as February provided cormels have not started to form on top of the old ones. They should bloom in ten to fourteen weeks. Bulbs are said to grow better if dried for two weeks in a sunny window. They may be planted all at one time and held back until needed in a coldframe or pit. They are tender and must never be put in freezing temperatures.

Plant six to a deep bulb pan two inches apart and cover tips not over one inch with soil made of garden loam, humus and sand in equal parts. If peat moss is used it must be finely pulverized. Moisten the soil (not wet) as mixed and press the bulbs gently to proper depth. Place in a cool light spot (about 50°). When sprouts show bring into room where temperature stays over 50° and under 70°. Keep close to, but not touching, the window, and avoid drafts, set away at night when the temperature should be higher than in the daytime.

As the buds show, give a little weak, very weak, liquid manure when watering. Water frequently (not cold) after sprouts start, avoiding water soaked soil, and support blooms with thin stakes of wood or heavy wire.

One method recommended is to pot them in soil in which some other plant has been grown the previous season. Then leave them out of doors until freezing weather, and put them in a sunny window to bloom, which will take place in four or five weeks. Water well at all times. Care must be taken not to leave out too long.

After flowering, pots can be dried out gradually and natural growth completed until the foliage yellows. Bulbs are placed in a frost-proof sunny location to ripen, then stored until potting time. Storage is considered difficult and it is better to buy the few bulbs needed, each year.

Oxalis: A dwarf trailing plant producing an array of dainty cup-shaped flowers; much used for hanging baskets and window boxes. Leaf is similar to that of clover or shamrock. Comes in pink, lavender and white. Planted in spring outdoors, it is used for an edging flower to be dug before frost.

Put three or four bulbs in a four-inch pot covered one inch deep and place at once where it is to flower, where it will bloom in a few weeks and continue through the season. Water sparingly but keep soil moist. It has a rest period for a couple of months when the leaves will die. Dry out by gradually withholding water and put in a warm place (need not be dark) for a couple of months. In July or August pot the new bulbs which will be found at the end of the roots in the bottom of the pot.

Ixia and Sparaxis: Fairly hardy bulbs outside but good for inside also. The first is sometimes called African corn-lily, and the second harlequin-flower. Beautiful flowers in many colors with attractive foliage growing eighteen inches to two feet high. Plant outdoors in October or November and protect thoroughly, or plant in early spring, three inches deep and three to four inches apart.

Indoors, pot in September or October and give excellent drainage (ashes or sand in soil). Allow to root in a cool, light spot as described for anemones, freesias, etc.

MISCELLANEOUS BULBS FOR INDOORS

Alstroemeria (Chilean-lily): Pot in August or as soon as possible, two inches deep, with sand about bulb. Root in coldframe or pit and bring directly to best sunlight. Water moderately but often while growing. Dry out after blooming to ripen until required for repotting. (See Outdoor Bulbs, Chapter XII.)

Amaryllis or Hippeastrum (Star-lily): Perhaps nothing will give the amateur greater pleasure than this lily-like, easily managed plant. It is essentially a window garden plant, producing under the simplest conditions one to three spikes and three to six blooms above broad, strap-shaped leaves. Improved hybrids in many colors have increased its popularity in recent years.

Plant bulbs as soon as received, usually October and November (any time before January), in pots one inch greater in diameter than the bulbs. They will not bloom if the pots are too large. Only the lower thick part is covered with soil; the long neck must be fully exposed. Use two parts good soil, one of rotted cow manure and some bone meal both fine and coarse. Mix this thoroughly, and water sparingly until growth is well started, but supply generously thereafter. Be careful of drainage. Keep them in a cool, shaded place but bring into light at first sign of growth.

They need plenty of sunshine and liquid manure each week during the growing season. Flowers may appear before leaves as most of the foliage is produced after blooming. Take good care of the leaves after flowering if you want bloom again next year. They vary greatly in time of flowering, some buds appearing in January, others not blooming until spring.

Repot in summer if well established, using only slightly larger pots and plunge the pots into soil, in the open where they will get plenty of sunlight. When the leaves begin to turn yellow or frost checks them, gradually decrease watering and store pots in cool cellar. Look them over occasionally. Bring to light and water regularly when they show signs of life.

Repotting is beneficial but not necessary as they will thrive for years with applications of liquid manure or even chemical plant food in solution. The best time to repot is after the flowering, before new foliage appears; but no harm is done by potting in the fall at the close of the dormant season. Some writers recommend leaving them in the pots until they break them. Refertilizing is done by removing some soil from the pots about the bulbs and replacing it

with good soil, cow manure and bone meal.

Tuberous Begonia: They may be started from February to April. Pack them in peat moss level with the surface or on the surface, smooth side down (concave side up). Keep damp, not wet, and place in a warm, shady place until new growth starts. Then, for rooting, put each tuber in a four-inch pot of compost of garden soil (humus, dried cow manure and some sand) finely screened, rich and loose. Do not break roots when potting. Grow in temperature of 50° to 60°; protect them from too much sunlight, and change to pots six inches or better as soon as roots fill the smaller ones.

Soil for second potting is two parts

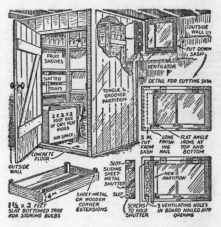

A cellar cool-closet can easily be made for wintering bulbs or for rooting them for forcing. It is also excellent for storing fruit or vegetables. A three or four by five foot cupboard gives a lot of storage. Use a corner so that the two concrete walls may help moderate the temperature. Cover the partition with wallboard if your cellar is hot. Bulbs, apples, etc., keep well in slat-bottomed trays but they keep better in boxes of dried peat moss and potted bulbs root well here also.

fine leafmold or leaf woods soil, one part humus, some sand and a generous dusting of bone meal and dried blood. Have three-fourths inch of pot rim exposed for watering, which must be done often. Good and prompt drainage is necessary. Always plant tubers near surface. Pinch buds until plants are vigorous. Keep protected from direct sun. Apply weak liquid manure when well established.

Semperflorens, the fibrous-rooted florists' begonia, is easy to grow. Beautiful semituberous begonias are featured by many florists (Melior, Glory of Cincinnati and Mrs. Peterson are excellent examples), but plants should be purchased as propagation is difficult and exacting.

Calla (*Zantedeschia* or *Richardia aethiopica*): This plant, often but wrongly, called lily, is really an aroid and related to the Jack-in-the-Pulpit of our woods.

Use a six-inch pot of rich, heavy soil, in the late fall, allowing about one inch of the root to remain above the surface. A compost of two-thirds good soil, one-third cow manure (very old) and a little sand to open it up is best. Do not place in the dark but root them in a slightly cool place (they freeze easily). As soon as new growth is shown move to a sunny window, water plentifully and regularly. A saucer of water under them is sometimes used.

Frequent applications of sulphate of ·ammonia, one-half ounce to the gallon of water, just before first bloom, makes them continue freely. They stand a warm temperature.

When the rest period approaches (June, July and August), gradually dry out and either plunge in soil or place pots on their side in a dry, shady place. Repot in September.

White and yellow callas are recommended for house culture or out of doors. Spotted callas are usually reserved for outdoor culture.

When a plant is in growing condition, warm water given several times weekly hastens flowering and increases number of blooms but may shorten the blooming period.

Cyclamen: One of the most deservedly popular house plants, flowering from Christmas to Easter. Most plant lovers have found that new purchases each year make shapely specimens as the best blooms come from seedlings about fifteen months old. Home propagation of seedlings is slow and difficult except in a greenhouse and last year's bulbs are very uncertain.

The young plants may be procured very reasonably in three-inch pots from August to November and repotted, as soon as received, in four-inch pots. As fast as pots become filled with roots move into five- and six-inch pots. They do well in any soil not too heavy, but the best is made of two parts garden soil, one part fine peat moss and one part sand with, to each bushel, one large single handful of coarse bone, dried cow or sheep manure and hydrated lime. Moisten before potting. For fine blooms pinch out flowering stems that rise above foliage, before November, to conserve strength of the plant, and after this time give a weak fertilized solution weekly.

They will continue to bloom for three months or more if flowers are pulled loose at the corm as soon as faded. Do not cut them; any parts of stems left will decay. Keep them in plenty of light but avoid noon sun. An even temperature is desirable; 40° to 50° will prolong the blooming season. Failure can usually be traced to neglect or constant exposure to hot, dry air.

Do not splash water on the plant when watering as the center of the bulb will decay if wet. Use water at room temperature and keep plant moist but not wet; empty saucer if water accumulates in it. A fine spray with a sprinkler bulb early in the day is beneficial; but keep the plant shaded until foliage dries. Wash leaves if dusty.

Gladiolus: Most failure of gladiolus to bloom indoors (coming blind) is due to attempts to grow at room temperatures. Unless a temperature of 45° to 50° can be maintained, especially at night, do not attempt them. Use only early varieties and plant in December or January, using four-inch pots; later shift to six-inch containers or boxes six inches deep. Plant three inches deep and start in full light; the same culture as freesia. Give water and drainage.

Gloxinia: Although they have the name of being difficult, these large plants with bell-shaped flowers are easily grown if understood. Colors are many and they get along well at a temperature of 60° to 70°.

They should be handled in the same general way as tuberous begonias, except that the soil requires more sand. Take care in watering to keep the foliage absolutely dry. Keep soil moist but not muddy. Bulbs are offered in February and March and bloom the following March.

EDITOR'S NOTE: Remarkable progress has been made in the discovery and development of new house plants and in ways to grow, feed, and care for them. Convenient, attractive containers of plastic and other materials, soluble plant foods and multipurpose pest controls in handy form, lighting and temperature-control devices have played a part in adapting cultural operations to modern home conditions and dimensions. See "GARDEN MAGIC MARCHES ON," page 439, for further discussion of these matters. But the fact that plant requirements have not changed is proved by the fact that success is often achieved under the simplest conditions—if they are right—just as our grandmothers' kitchens used to contain plants that any grower would be proud to produce today.—E.L.D.S.

CHAPTER XXIII

SOILLESS GARDENING

The subject of soilless gardening has, in recent years, aroused a great deal of interest and curiosity and been responsible for a great volume of discussion, written and oral. Under various names, such as chemical gardening, chemi-culture, water-, sand- and gravel-culture, hydroponics and others, it has been hailed as a marvelous new invention and the secret of mankind's future food supply. A lot of money has been spent on equipment and materials offered or recommended as essential to this "new" kind of gardening. And, as might well be expected when anything interests a great many people and makes an appeal to the public imagination, there have been all kinds of experiences with it, including both successes and failures.

Actually while, from one angle, the subject is new, from others it is very old indeed; and, fundamentally, it involves no principles of plant growing that have not been known for a long time. When we talk about feeding plants with essential food substances in solution (which is what all types of soilless gardening amount to), we are right back on the well known basis of all plant growth as already discussed in the early chapters of this book. Except for the carbon, hydrogen and oxygen taken out of the atmosphere by its leaves, a plant gets *all* its nutriment in the form of a very weak solution that it takes in through its tiny white feeding roots. Ordinarily this solution consists of the moisture contained in the soil (even in an apparently dry one it exists as a thin film around the soil particles), in which are dissolved the various salts and plant food elements as derived from the soil itself or added by the gardener in the form of fertilizers. If we substitute for the soil and its "soup" a systematically prepared solution of chemicals from which the plant can get what it needs, we have merely changed the method, not the operation. As a matter of fact, that is just what scientists, studying the growth habits and food needs of plants, have been doing in their laboratories for more than a hundred years. So really, the only new angle to this whole thing is the idea of applying this "solution culture" idea to commercial and amateur plant growing.

It was this application of a familiar scientific method, suggested a few years ago by Dr. W. F. Gericke of California, that caught the public fancy and gave rise to a vast amount of speculation and, at first, a lot of prophecies that were largely unfounded and considerably exaggerated. Because people are constantly looking for ways to "do things more easily" and get larger returns for smaller expenditures of money, time and effort, the claim that soilless gardening was immeasurably simpler, cheaper and more productive than orthodox soil gardening caused widespread excitement and raised many false hopes. In the wake of those who knew what they were talking about when they discussed growing plants in other substances than soil, came the usual over-enthusiastic theorists and profit-seekers whose activities served only to confuse the issue.

The Facts About Soilless Gardening

The facts as generally recognized now are about like this: (1) Soilless culture does offer certain possibilities and advantages if practiced intelligently; (2) as far as its practical, large scale operation is concerned, it is still in the experimental stage; that is, there is no short, simple formula or set of rules that can be followed under all conditions and with all kinds of plants and counted on to insure success; (3) it does *not* lessen the importance of, nor remove the necessity for, favorable growing conditions and the right sort of care. Indeed, there are some details of successful soilless gardening, such as the maintaining of the right solution and the correct degree of acidity, that gardeners might easily consider more difficult and "tricky" than anything called for in everyday outdoor gardening. You might say that it compares with ordinary cultural methods as the feeding of a family according to modern scientific methods and with the latest improved gadgets, compares with standard, old

fashioned, homespun cookery. Both supply the needs of the individuals, but by different methods—one "streamlined" as it were, the other according to time-tried experience.

So don't get the idea that the person who doesn't know how to make and care for a garden and who won't take the trouble to learn, is going to be able to grow good plants by taking up soilless gardening. Don't imagine that it takes the place of sunlight, correct temperature and humidity conditions, protection against insect pests and plant diseases, etc. Don't take any stock in rumors that with it families are going to grow their vegetables in cellars or kitchen closets, that every city apartment is going to raise flowers and food in tanks on the roof, that the ocean liners of tomorrow are going to carry their gardens with them 'tween decks. All that sort of thing is mere "horticultural hooey."

What we should realize is that the field is an interesting one full of possibilities for the home or indoor gardener who is willing to find out what it is all about and go into it in an intelligent, conservative way. Also that, for the commercial grower of various kinds of flowers and vegetables, it may hold real promise because it does away with some of the drudgery, such as preparing and replacing soil in beds and benches, repeated messy watering, etc., and permits keeping the growth of the plants under constant, exact control. However, in a commercial greenhouse it calls for a heavy investment in special equipment—tanks, beds, pumps, and the like, and also unremitting attention in keeping the easily upset conditions just what they should be.

This writer does not look for soilless gardening to take the place of the outdoor cultivation of home gardens; he would be sorry if it ever did. But he sees in it another fascinating phase of the big subject of plant growing from which the person who approaches it with understanding and an open mind can get much pleasure, interest and benefit.

Soilless Gardening in the Home

As the name implies and as we have already explained, soilless gardening means simply the growing of plants in some other medium than soil and the supplying of the necessary nutriment in the form of a prepared solution adapted to their particular needs. The plants may be supported in a layer of excelsior or other material in a wire-bottomed tray over a tank which contains the solution in which the roots are submerged. Or they may be planted in the orthodox manner in a pot, box or other container filled with clean sand, fine gravel or cinders which, having no plant food value, merely support the specimens. In such case the nutrient solution may be poured onto the container until it submerges the roots, then allowed to drain off, this operation to be repeated at frequent intervals; or it may be pumped into the container from below, and allowed to run back into a supply tank; or it may be applied to the surface of the sand drop by drop from an elevated reservoir so as to keep the roots supplied with food but not constantly wet; or, finally, it may be placed in the lower half of a special type of container and carried by what is called capillary action up through a "wick" of porous clay or other material to the sand in the upper part of the receptacle, in which the plant is growing.

The last described method is used in many types of so called "self-watering" flower pots now obtainable in seed stores, department stores, etc., usually with a supply of gravel, a small amount of concentrated solution, and complete directions. Yet this is but the revival in modern dress of an old time house plant accessory. Perhaps many of our readers can remember the self-watering window box of a score of years ago. This was a galvanized iron tank with a false bottom which left an inch or so of space below the customary drainage material and soil. This false bottom was pierced by several holes into which were thrust pieces of sponge extending into the space below and also into the soil above. Water was poured into the bottom space through a tube in one corner and carried, by the bits of sponge, up to the soil and the waiting roots. Except that the sponge has been replaced by better conveyors of the liquid, the plain water replaced by a nutrient solution, and the soil replaced by a neutral medium such as sand, there is no real difference between modern soilless culture equipment and that of a previous generation of home gardeners.

A Soilless Window Box

Speaking of window boxes, a simple type, designed especially for soilless or solution culture by Victor A. Tiedjens of the New Jersey Agricultural Experimental Station, is illustrated here, and could easily be made by a tinsmith; or the same idea could probably be carried out by any handy man used to working with metal. It consists of two parts, the plant box proper, water tight and of any convenient dimensions and either supplied with legs or made to rest on some solid support; and, hinged to it, a second box or tank large enough to hold enough solution to fill the first. The second tank should be so shaped that, when the solution is in it, the level of the liquid will be below the sand, gravel or cinders in the plant box. In the bottom of each container is a hole equipped with a short metal tube and the two tubes are connected by a length of rubber hose or flexible tubing.

To use the apparatus, you set the plants in the gravel or cinders in the window box taking precautions as outlined farther on. The solution is placed in the tank, and the latter is raised on its hinges until the solution runs into the box and floods the gravel. When all the solution has run into the box, the tank is lowered to its original position so the liquid can run back into it through the hose. This is repeated as often as may be necessary, usually once or twice a day, for two or three weeks; then the solution should be drawn off, a tankful of clear water poured into the plant box to flush the gravel clean, and the tank refilled with fresh solution. Use enough solution so that plant box will be level full when tank is completely empty. Mr. Tiedjens says that any recommended nutrient solution can be employed, but offers the following one to be made

of chemicals obtainable at a drug store or from a drug supply house:

To each gallon of water, add of—

16 percent super-
phosphate . . . . . . 1½ teaspoons
Potassium nitrate . ¼ teaspoon
Calcium nitrate . . . 1 teaspoon
Magnesium sul-
phate (Epsom
salts) . . . . ½ teaspoon
And, if the leaf tips begin to show
yellow, Ammonium sul-
phate . . . . ⅛ teaspoon

For further information about this apparatus, write to the Rutgers Endowment Foundation, Rutgers University, New Brunswick, N.J., which holds the patent rights.

Starting Seeds in Sand

The writer's first information about this whole subject came, even before publicity was given to Dr. Gericke's

SAND CULTURE OF SEEDLINGS:
(1) Wash sand clean in pail; use hot water; stir until all soil, silt, clay and rubbish are rinsed out

(2) Place sand in flat; level off sprinkle with ⅛ teaspoonful saltpeter in ½ cup water

(3) Sow seed, cover lightly with sand; then with sheet of glass and newspaper until seed sprout. Sprinkle when necessary to keep sand moist

TYPES OF CONTAINERS FOR HOME SOILLESS CULTURE

Soilless Window Box

Old fashioned "self watering" metal window box. Has false bottom of zinc with holes in which are pieces of sponge to serve as wicks. Water is poured through tube (A) into false bottom whence it rises through sponges to soil.

work, from a discussion of the Sand Culture of Seedlings, in a Bulletin (No. 380) issued in 1936 by the Connecticut Agricultural Experiment Station. This described a method of starting flowers and vegetables in washed sand in flats or other boxes, instead of in the soil or peat moss-soil mixture commonly used. Advantages claimed for it were, first, that it greatly lessened the chance of seedling losses from the damping-off disease; and, second, that the root growth was generally superior in sand to that in soil. Having used the method with marked success, we are glad to recommend it to any gardener wanting to get a jump on the spring season by starting his seeds indoors, whether in a sunny window, a hotbed, or a simple greenhouse or conservatory. The summarized directions as given in the Bulletin are as follows:

"1. Secure the desired amount of sand (as free from silt and loam as possible) from a sand pit, lake, river, seashore, or dealer in masons' supplies.

"2. Wash the sand in several changes of hot water (160 degrees F. or above) until it remains practically clean after stirring.

"3. Place the sand in *clean* wooden boxes or flats, or any sort of container that will allow a little drainage. Level off the surface to about 2 inches or more in depth.

"4. For each square foot of sand surface, dissolve about one-half teaspoonful of saltpeter (potassium nitrate) in about one-quarter pint of water and sprinkle over the sand. For a flat of ordinary size, this amounts to about one teaspoonful of saltpeter dissolved in a cup of water. For larger surfaces (as in a hotbed) add one ounce of saltpeter to three pints of water for each ten square feet.

"5. Drill or broadcast the seeds and cover lightly with more of the washed sand.

"6. Keep surface of sand moist by occasional watering (with a fine, gentle spray) until the seedlings are grown." (To conserve moisture, avoid the necessity for frequent sprinkling, and prevent the resulting leaching away of the nutrient materials, it is well to cover the surface of the sand with newspaper or cheesecloth and the box with a sheet of glass, until the seeds have germinated.)

"7. Avoid contamination of the sand by using clean water in watering. Do not add soil to the culture under any conditions. If seeds need more covering after they have sprouted, use only clean, washed sand for this purpose."

The one application of saltpeter in solution will usually suffice to support the seedlings until they are pricked off and transplanted to pots, other flats, a coldframe or elsewhere. However, if it is necessary to keep them in the sand longer than this, it would be advisable to give a second application of the solution. Of course, this is not a "complete" or "balanced" plant food solution and if the little plants are to be carried on in sand, gravel or any other soilless culture medium, they should receive one more suited to supplying all the needs of growing plants.

Nutrient Solutions

This brings us logically to the important subject of nutrient solutions upon which much has been—and probably will be—written. Here it should be emphasized that, as yet, no one solution has been discovered that is superior to all others and able to give the best results under all conditions and with all kinds of plants. The formula that one investigator may find very successful with one crop, may prove inferior to some other in experiments with the same crop performed by someone else. Fortunately, plants can adapt themselves to widely different circumstances, as is well proved by their ability to thrive in all kinds of soils and locations in different gardens. Furthermore, no solution long remains the same when plants are growing in it. They may take more of one substance than another; chemical changes may take place as its constitution changes; salts obtained from different sources may vary in purity, etc. This is the reason why care must be taken to maintain the right solution according to constant observation of the plants and frequent tests of its acidity.

The first purpose of any solution is to provide an adequate supply of those three vital elements in plant development—nitrogen, phosphorus, and potassium. But, as we know, these are only a part of what a plant must receive to make normal growth. So chemical salts are chosen that will supply the other elements as well, even those whose importance has only been recognized in recent years and of which only very small amounts are needed. These "trace elements" are usually combined in a secondary solution, a little of which

is added to the basic solution after it has been prepared. While the water used may slightly effect the solution, the average tap, well, or spring water, if suitable for drinking, will generally do for all practical purposes in home gardening.

From among the many formulas that have been given out by different scientists and experiment stations, we are going to suggest only two, both easy to prepare and of general all around adaptability. Anyone going deeply into the subject, will want to consult some of the various textbooks obtainable in which other special solutions for special conditions are described.

In the case of each of the following, there is to be added a small amount of the trace element or supplementary solution which we are calling Solution No. 3. These recommendations are from Dr. Charles H. Connors, of the New Jersey Agricultural Experiment Station, author of "Chemical Gardening for the Amateur."

Solution No. 1

Dissolve in one gallon of water—
½ teaspoon or 2.3 grams of Primary potassium phosphate
2 teaspoons or 8.0 grams of Calcium nitrate
1½ teaspoons or 4.2 grams of Magnesium sulphate
3 teaspoons or 14.5 grams of Solution No. 3

Solution No. 2

(Suggested as especially adapted for summer use when plants are growing more freely and can use more moisture; in winter, the amounts of salts given should be doubled.)

Dissolve in one gallon of water—

½ teaspoon or .32 gram of Primary potassium phosphate

2 teaspoons or 8.0 grams of Calcium nitrate

1½ teaspoons or 4.2 grams of Magnesium sulphate

¼ teaspoon or 1.0 gram of Ammonium sulphate

3 teaspoons or 14.5 grams of Solution No. 3.

Solution No. 3

(To be added to the nutrient solutions as noted above.)

1.0 gram of Manganese sulphate

1.5 grams of Boric acid

.5 gram of Copper sulphate

.5 gram of Zinc sulphate

1.0 quart of Water

Although for any serious attempts at soilless gardening it is desirable to use a special, freshly prepared solution of the type just mentioned, the beginner, satisfied to grow a few plants in the water culture containers or flower pots that we have spoken of, may prefer to start with one of the prepared mixtures now on the market. Some are sold in powder form, with directions for dissolving separately the contents of two or three packets, then mixing and diluting the resulting concentrates; others can be had in liquid form ready to be added to so many parts of water. None of these preparations are wholly efficient from the scientific point of view, nor are they as economical as solutions made from chemical salts bought in bulk. A few, that have been put on the market to the accompaniment of flamboyant claims

as to what they would do, have failed to live up to the promises made for them and have quietly slipped out of sight. But others more honestly made and marketed, are handled by reliable stores and usually give satisfactory results with ordinary house plants.

Handling Plants in Soilless Culture

Plants for soilless gardening may be started from seed, as above described, grown from cuttings as directed in the chapter on Propagation, or purchased while small from a grower. In either case, their roots should be gently washed free of all soil, peat moss or other foreign substance before they are planted. If tank culture is to be followed, let the roots pass through the wire netting so they will hang in the solution, and pack excelsior or some such material around the plants to support them. In the case of sand or gravel culture, spread the roots out in the container as you sift the material carefully around and over them, then soak it generously with the solution so as to settle it firmly.

In the constant-drip method, the plant is set in an ordinary pot with a drainage hole in the bottom and placed above a small pan or deep saucer to hold the liquid that drains through. Then a container full of the solution is placed a little above and to one side, either on a separate stand or on a bracket that can be hooked on the edge of the pot. One good arrangement consists of an ordinary mason jar inverted in a shallow saucer, like the drinking fountains used in chicken yards; from the liquid in the saucer a piece of wicking or a length of twisted gauze bandage runs over to the sand or gravel in the pot. A little experience will show just how wide a piece of bandage is needed and how tightly it should be rolled in order to convey just enough of the solution to keep the plant supplied.

Among the conditions that a plant must have is a supply of air for the roots, as well as the leaves. When the tank or solution culture method is followed, this air is provided by aerating the solution. A small air pump like those used in aquariums will do this nicely, or some of the solution can be dipped out with a pitcher and poured back so as to agitate the liquid. Another plan is to lift the whole tray and prop it up so that the roots are in the air instead of the liquid for half an hour; this can be done once every three or four days until the plants become too large and heavy, then some other scheme must be resorted to. In sand or gravel culture, the roots are sufficiently aerated between the floodings with the solution, and in the constant-drip method just described, the solution in its slow passage down through the pot carries enough air with it.

Plants to Grow

As far as plants to grow in soilless gardening are concerned, the method used is of less importance than the conditions in the room or greenhouse in which they are to be kept. If there is plenty of sunlight and if the temperature can be maintained evenly between, say, 62 and 75 degrees F., almost any of the popular flowering house plants can be tried. Primulas, Begonias, Cinerarias, Impatiens, Fuchsias, Lantanas and Geraniums are all good subjects, provided, as noted, conditions of light and temperature are favorable. Calendulas, Alyssum, Ageratum, Nemesia, Nemophila, Browallia and other garden annuals can be handled in this way, if the temperature is somewhat on the cool side. Commercial growers are doing well with such crops as Carnations, Sweet Peas, Gardenias and Chrysanthemums, so if you have even small greenhouse facilities, you might experiment with a few. Any of the commonly grown forcing bulbs— Paperwhite Narcissus, Chinese Sacred-lily, etc., are, of course, easy to handle, and others not so commonly grown in the house may succeed in sand or gravel because of the uniform moisture supply, notably, Gladiolus, Freesias, Ixias, and even Ranunculus and Anemone.

If there is less light, the familiar foliage plants are well adapted to soilless culture, including the reliable Aspidistra, Sansevieria, Aucuba, Dracena, Peperomia, the true and asparagus ferns, and a number of vines such as English Ivy, Wandering Jew, Periwinkle and the small-leaved Climbing Fig. Again it should be pointed out that soilless gardening of itself will not make any particular location any more favorable for a particular kind of plant; but if favorable conditions exist, it can be employed to get good results with moderate attention and care.

CHAPTER XXIV

CONCRETE IN THE GARDEN

There is nothing intricate about the use of concrete and a few mistakes are responsible for most failures. Many interesting improvements can be made about the home by the simple processes necessary for its use. It recommends itself at once to the home owner who has a little leisure, ingenuity and a zest for experiment.

Our first care should be for the materials. Concrete is made by mixing cement with sand and crushed stone or pebbles. The sand is called fine aggregate and the stone or pebbles coarse aggregate. The cement and sand form a sort of glue or mortar which goes into the spaces between the pebbles (called "voids"), uniting them into a stone-like mass. Therefore when we estimate our needs we cannot add together the quantities used as the sand and cement "disappear" to some extent into the voids. Our illustration shows how 7 cu. ft. of material mixes to form 4½ cu. ft. of concrete.

It will be seen at once how necessary it is for the cement to hold tightly to the particles of the aggregates. If there is clay or vegetable matter present, it is prevented from doing this. Therefore all specifications call for clean sharp sand and washed pebbles.

Large masses of concrete may use coarse pebbles or stone but small objects, such as steppingstones, slabs, garden pottery or furniture, should have fine pebbles usually called pea gravel or torpedo sand.

Also it is easy to see that if the cement is to hold the aggregates together, they must be mixed so that every particle is surrounded by it. We must thoroughly mix the materials together while dry, and then again after the water is added.

In recent years more and more stress has been laid upon the water content. A sloppy mixture makes weak concrete. Any water which runs out of the mold or form, carries with it cement needed to give the concrete strength. There are many reasons for the use of as small an amount of water as is possible.

In plants where pre-cast concrete building material is made, the mixture goes into the molds so dry as to resemble wet crumbly sand and is compacted into a mass by a series of tamping hammers. This results in high strength concrete. Along a new roadway we frequently see trucks from testing laboratories. They have been making various tests to see that the proper amount of water is being used.

The amateur should follow a middle course, having his mixture wet enough to form a pasty or jelly-like mass but not soupy enough to flow or run.

Mixing is best done by machine,

HOW TO USE CONCRETE IN THE GARDEN

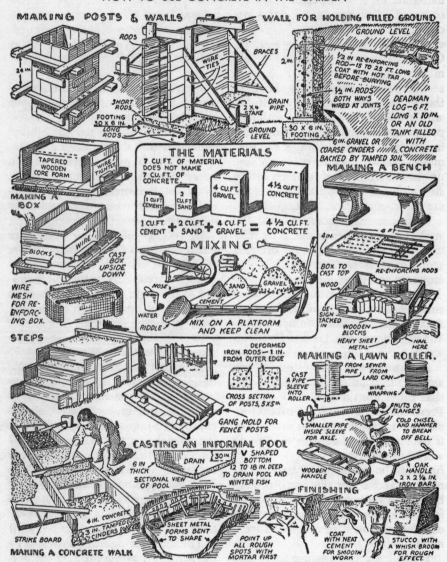

MAKING POSTS & WALLS

RODS

WIRE TIES

BRACES

DRAIN PIPE

2 X 4 STAKE

24 IN.

3 SHORT RODS

FOOTING 30 X 6 IN.

LONG RODS

GROUND LEVEL

WALL FOR HOLDING FILLED GROUND

GROUND LEVEL

½ IN RE-ENFORCING ROD—15 to 25 FT. LONG COAT WITH HOT TAR BEFORE BURYING

½ IN. RODS BOTH WAYS WIRED AT JOINTS

30 X 6 IN. FOOTING

2 IN.

DEADMAN LOG—6 FT. LONG X 10 IN. OR AN OLD TANK FILLED WITH CONCRETE BACKED BY TAMPED SOIL

6 IN. GRAVEL OR COARSE CINDERS

TAPERED WOODEN CORE FORM

WIRE TIGHTLY

MAKING A BOX

BLOCKS

WIRE

CAST BOX UPSIDE DOWN

WIRE MESH FOR RE-ENFORCING BOX.

STEPS

THE MATERIALS

7 CU. FT. OF MATERIAL DOES NOT MAKE 7 CU. FT. OF CONCRETE.

1 CU. FT. CEMENT + 2 CU. FT. SAND + 4 CU. FT. GRAVEL = 4½ CU. FT. CONCRETE

MIXING

NOSE

WATER

RIDDLE

SAND

GRAVEL

CEMENT

MIX ON A PLATFORM AND KEEP CLEAN

DEFORMED IRON RODS—1 IN. FROM OUTER EDGE

CROSS SECTION OF POSTS, 5 X 5 IN.

GANG MOLD FOR FENCE POSTS

MAKING A BENCH

4 IN.

4 FT.

RE-ENFORCING RODS

18 IN.

BOX TO CAST TOP

WOOD

DESIGN TACKED IN

WOODEN BLOCKS

HEAVY SHEET METAL

NAIL HERE

MAKING A LAWN ROLLER.

FROM SEWER PIPE

FROM LARD CAN

WIRE WRAPPING

CAST A PIPE SLEEVE INTO ROLLER

18 IN.

SMALLER PIPE INSIDE SLEEVE FOR AXLE.

NUTS OR FLANGES

COLD CHISEL AND HAMMER TO BREAK OFF BELL.

WOODEN HANDLE

OAK HANDLE

2 X 2¼ IN. IRON BARS

CASTING AN INFORMAL POOL

6 IN. THICK

DRAIN

30 IN.

SECTIONAL VIEW OF POOL

V SHAPED BOTTOM 12 TO 18 IN. DEEP TO DRAIN POOL AND WINTER FISH

SHEET METAL FORMS BENT TO SHAPE

POINT UP ALL ROUGH SPOTS WITH MORTAR FIRST

FINISHING

COAT WITH NEAT CEMENT FOR SMOOTH WORK

STUCCO WITH A WHISK BROOM FOR ROUGH EFFECT.

4 IN. CONCRETE

3 IN. TAMPED CINDERS

STRIKE BOARD

MAKING A CONCRETE WALK

but hand mixing is just as good if properly done. Lay the proportioned materials on a water-tight platform of boards; first spread the sand and cement in layers and cut them each way until no streaks of gray show. Over this spread the pebbles and mix thoroughly. It is well to have a second person apply the water (after the dry materials are mixed together) with a hose, gradually obtaining the proper moisture, or it may be applied in a depression or hollow in the top of the pile as it is mixed. When the process is completed every pebble should be coated with a mortar of sand and cement.

In the making of smaller objects such as boxes, benches, etc., it is more important than ever that the cement be fresh. Cement is very sensitive to moisture and if exposed to rain, fogs, dew or moisture of any kind it receives its first set or "hydration." This destroys its usefulness for fine work although it may work very well in walls or mass.

Its freshness may be tested by examining the sack when opened to see that there are no hard lumps in it. Fresh cement will feel slippery when rubbed between the finger tips. If it feels gritty it is all right for rough work but not for surfacing or making furniture, vases or flower boxes. Cement stored about the home should be kept in air-tight cans such as used food cans from your butcher or grocer. Nothing can restore spoiled cement.

When cement is used, mixed with water alone, it is called "neat." Neat cement is used for coating surfaces of pottery boxes and other objects which we wish to make very smooth.

Any cast which does not come out of the form well finished can be pointed up with mortar mixed as described later. A coat of neat cement will give a uniform color appearance. Cement paints are for sale in white and other colors for yearly freshening.

Sometimes a rough or pebbled finish is desired. In this case we use a very wet or soupy mortar and apply it by spattering it over the object. This is called stucco. Dip a whisk broom into the mortar and throw it in fine particles against the slightly dampened surface of the object to be covered.

All materials should be accurately measured. A large scoop shovel is good for this purpose. Also a pail may be used. Thus a standard mixture known as 1:2:4 would be measured: 1 pail of cement, 2 of sand and 4 of pebbles. A sack of cement contains approximately 1 cubic foot.

Forms are made of metal, wood and in some cases plaster of Paris. In mass work (walls, piers, etc.) it is important that the forms be strongly made. The extreme weight of the material causes great pressure against the form walls. If they are not well braced and wired together they will bulge and cause irregular work. They must be true and level. Spreader blocks are placed to keep the form faces the right distance apart; they are removed as the concrete is placed up to them. The wires are twisted as the form is made to true it up and keep the blocks in place. The weight of the mass as placed loosens them for easy removal.

Whether you are building a wall or

a vase, your finished surface will be no smoother than your forms. Good forms are not battered or rough. All of them should be coated with oil before placing concrete in them to prevent adhesion and to make their removal easy. If the form is to slide out of, or away from the concrete, it must be slightly tapered and if made of metal, it must be free from dents which would impede this process.

The concrete should be placed in the forms as soon as possible; in no case more than 30 minutes after mixing. In walls, etc., place it in layers six inches thick, thoroughly spaded. By spading is meant working with a spade or chisel board into the concrete against the forms up and down and to and fro, to remove any air spaces and force large pebbles away from the forms into the mass. This insures an even, dense surface when finished.

Concrete in smaller objects is thoroughly worked with a chisel-edged stick or trowel to see that all corners are completely filled and the coarser particles kept away from the faces of the form.

In making a lawn roller, a piece of iron pipe is cast in the exact center to act as an axle sleeve or boxing. A smaller piece of pipe threaded at each end is run through this to be used as an axle. Pipe flanges or nuts are used to fasten it tightly to the handle. Some prefer to cast the axle solidly into the concrete allowing it to turn in the handle.

Flat work such as walks and floors is not spaded. A foundation layer of cinders is tamped on ground which has been thoroughly compacted, and the concrete is placed and leveled off with a "strike board." This concrete is then firmed into place by tamping it lightly and finishing with a float or trowel. If a smooth surface is desired, it is finished with a steel tool which draws the water and cement to the surface. This is called "flowing it" or "floating it" to the top. This cement lacks wearing qualities so that excessive manipulation of the surface will cause hair cracks after the concrete hardens. A surface finished under a wooden float wears better and is not so liable to be slippery.

Having successfully mixed and placed the concrete it should be allowed to harden before removing the forms. In summer it takes from two to four days and in winter from four to seven days. It must never be allowed to freeze until it is thoroughly set. Heat hastens and cold delays setting; thus it can be hastened by using warm water and, in cases of smaller objects, adding a very small quantity of washing soda to the water.

Properly prepared concrete is one of the few things which harden with age. If it is exposed to the sun or wind the water necessary for its hardening will dry out too quickly causing cracking or shrinkage. The hardening is a chemical change which takes place slowly in the presence of water. Keeping the object damp for ten days to two weeks is good practice. The objects may be covered with damp straw or canvas and wet by sprinkling. Walks and flat surfaces may be covered with earth after hardening and small objects made very hard by immersing in water for four or five days. After the forms have been removed all rough spots should be pointed.

Sometimes if cement has been neglected while curing, the surface begins to powder or wear, as in the case of floors. This can be helped many times by washing away all dirt and particles with a stiff brush and applying a solution of water glass. Allow the surface to dry thoroughly and apply the water glass (sodium silicate of 40 degrees Baumé) in a solution of 3 to 5 parts water depending upon the absorbing qualities of the cement. Mix well and apply with a brush within an hour. When thoroughly dry, wash off and repeat the process three times, allowing it to dry after each operation. The silicate penetrates the concrete, contacting the alkalies, and making it very hard.

Re-enforcing is a rather intricate subject and in any considerable job should be designed by a competent engineer. It is done because concrete is strong under compression and is capable of bearing great loads but is comparatively weak in tensile strength. Steel rods properly placed increase its power to resist strains and keep it from pulling apart. Improperly placed they are wasted.

In most of the smaller objects we use ½ inch wire net re-enforcement to resist cracks due to shrinkage. Poultry netting or fine fence wire is also used. All joints should be lapped or run past each other and care must be used to keep the re-enforcing material equally distant from the two surfaces. In slabs the concrete can be poured into the molds and firmed down, after which the re-enforcing mesh or rods can be laid upon it and the rest of the concrete poured.

In walls or piers which do not have to stand any great strain but are re-enforced to avoid cracks or shrinkage, ⅜ inch deformed rods should be spaced eight inches apart each way to form a network. They should be wired together into place midway between the form faces as the forms are built. They must stay in exact position as the concrete is spaded around them.

The rod sizes can be increased slightly if the ground to be supported is filled but, if beams or walls are to be cast and are expected to hold great loads, it is better to hire an engineer to properly design the steel placement than to risk the loss of all the work.

A false impression is entertained by many that almost any kind of scrap wire or iron will serve as re-enforcing. Such wire is often rusty and greasy, in which case the concrete will not adhere to it. Wire purchased in coils is hard to handle. More certain results will follow the use of rods in larger work and clean bright mesh in smaller items.

All steel should be covered with at least 1 to 1½ inches of concrete to protect it from dampness and corrosion. Any hooks, bolts or rings, which are to be attached, should be set at once and not after the concrete has started to set.

All walks, steps, piers, walls, etc., must be placed on solid ground. Any settling will cause them to crack or fall. Footings should be placed under piers, walls, etc. If they have very much height it is well to re-enforce the footing by short pieces of rod eight or ten inches apart with a long bar connecting them at both edges and running the full length of the footing two inches from the outer edge.

This writer has had two unpleasant experiences with walls tilting over, due to filled ground. The ground in extremely rainy weather becomes a soggy, slippery mass and often will force a wall over, years after it is placed. To prevent this, all walls should have a drainage of six inches of gravel or coarse cinders against the unexposed side. Weep holes 2 inches in diameter should be arranged through the wall every two or three feet, level with the footing. Use iron pipe or tile. To be doubly safe on clay ground tie a deadman as shown in the illustration on page 350. Bury it several feet deep, use as long a rod as possible, and get back into solid ground if you can. Coat all buried metal parts with hot tar if you want them to last.

An engineer will perhaps smile at the above. He would design the wall to eliminate the deadman. This amateur knows something of this but thinks it too complicated for small work. The deadman scheme has never failed the writer.

Plastering or stucco is made of a rich mixture of sand and cement. For amateur purposes it should be a 1:2 mixture, that is, one part cement to two parts sand. It is used for waterproof plastering the inside of tanks or pools, for pointing up rough spots after form removal and for casting flower boxes, small vases, etc.

For larger objects such as steppingstones, slabs, benches, bird baths, fence posts, etc., we use a 1:2:3 mixture, meaning one part cement, two sand and three parts pebbles. The pebbles should be fine (torpedo sand or pea gravel).

Standard mixture is 1:2:4. The pebbles may be fairly large. This is used for walls, walks, structures, floors, foundations, pits, etc.

For further or more technical information apply to your cement dealer or get literature direct from The Portland Cement Association which has offices in New York and several other large cities. A most interesting book, "Color Cement Handicraft," by P. J. and P. A. Lemos, deals very clearly with cement for vases, tiles, etc.

STEPPINGSTONES

Steppingstones are in great favor. They do not divide a garden layout and make it seem smaller as a solid path does, and they have the advantage of lending color contrast against the green of the lawn.

If flat stones are not available, concrete slabs can be cast in the molds shown on the facing page. The forms for the ones which are cast directly upon the ground are made of heavy scrap sheet metal held by pegs. The joints are filled with dry sand to prevent their spreading. Do not finish too regularly or smooth. They are supposed to imitate stones.

The effect of stone can also be obtained in the following manner: crumble a long sheet of the heaviest brown paper into a barrel or tub of water and let it soak for a few minutes. Then spread it out carefully on a wood or concrete platform and set a single mold or multiple wooden molds upon it. The creases of the paper will make a pattern on the concrete as it hardens, that suggests

HOW TO MAKE WALKS AND STEPPINGSTONES

THE EDGES OF WALKS SHOULD BE EVEN

PACKED SAND

2" CONCRETE
2" PACKED CINDERS

3" GRAVEL
3" OF HARD PACKED CINDERS

TEMPORARY EDGING BOARD

PLACE STEPPING STONES ¼ IN. ABOVE SOIL SURFACE

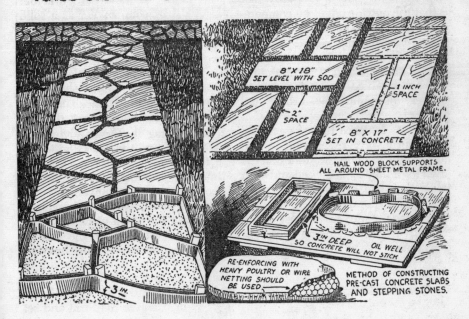

8"X 18"
SET LEVEL WITH SOD

1 INCH SPACE

2" SPACE

8" X 17"
SET IN CONCRETE

NAIL WOOD BLOCK SUPPORTS ALL AROUND SHEET METAL FRAME.

3 IN DEEP
SO CONCRETE WILL NOT STICK

OIL WELL

RE-ENFORCING WITH HEAVY POULTRY OR WIRE NETTING SHOULD BE USED

3 IN.

METHOD OF CONSTRUCTING PRE-CAST CONCRETE SLABS AND STEPPING STONES.

stone. For a walk, build an oblong mold of wood, the width of the walk and long enough to represent one section of the pattern desired. The finished blocks can be set on cinders or tamped ground and the joints filled with sand, or fine soil in which seed can be sown, or thyme and sedums planted.

By using molds of two different shapes and then using the slabs in as many different positions as possible the danger of monotony can be avoided. They should be laid just a trifle higher than the soil level and then tamped with a 2 x 4 to grade. Repeat the tamping several times after rains if necessary.

One important detail in laying steppingstones and in fact all walks, is that the outside edges be comparatively parallel. The path should be planned by placing a cord or a row of stakes before setting. If wide and narrow stones are laid at random it will not produce a pleasing design. Curves also must be broad and graceful.

The late Leonard Barron once told me about a way in which he got the curve right. He laid the stones on the lawn until they looked good and then when they had discolored the grass in spots, he dug out the sod in these spots and made holes just deep enough to permit sinking the steppingstones.

PRE-CAST CONCRETE WALKS

Irregular forms of heavy scrap sheet metal are stiffened with 2x4 blocks

Do not set stones according to edges. Balance their area on an axis.

Stepping stones do not cut up the lawn or dwarf it by divisions

Be sure ground is well firmed before laying stones

This gang-form for regular flag-stone blocks is shown in parts and assembled

Allow a two inch space between slabs for grass — one inch for cement.

The other walks shown are self-explanatory. Use care in laying walks on sand and cinders. The cinders must be of fine grade to support gravel. They must be soaked and thoroughly tamped several times before applying it. The sand must be compacted and the bricks imbedded in it. This method will last for some time but eventually will settle and become somewhat uneven.

If the ground is water-bearing or marshy, a four-inch agricultural tile should be used under the cinders. This is comparatively inexpensive.

THE WISH

. . . E're I descend to the grave
May I a small house and large garden have!
And a few friends, and many books, both true,
Both wise, and both delightful, too!

ABRAHAM CROWLEY

CHAPTER XXV

GARDEN RECORDS

Some years ago this writer decided that he must have some orderly means of preserving the fine fund of highly specialized information contained in the various garden magazines, seed and nursery catalogues, and other sources. After trying many systems, the scrapbook method shown here was selected as the most practical. The original collection has grown to fill many loose-leaf books.

You may obtain loose-leaf, ring-fastened books from your stationer's. A cheap book will not do, as the rings soon give way under the wear given a scrapbook.

Clippings are pasted on sheets purchased to fit the binder. If you use rubber cement instead of library paste or mucilage, the clippings may be removed or shifted about without tearing. It has the advantage of

FULL SIZE HIGH GRADE 8½ X 11 INCH RING BOOK WITH WATERPROOF COVER—(DO NOT USE THE STUDENT SIZE.)

USE 8½ X 11 INCH STOCK BOND PAPER SHEETS FOR NOTES AND PASTING IN CLIPPINGS.

CLIP OFF MARGINS OF MAGAZINE PAGES YOU DESIRE TO KEEP IN SCRAPBOOK.

A PUNCH FOR FULL MAGAZINE PAGES

HOW TO USE THE PUNCH

PUNCH HOLES WITH PENCIL

PASTE A CLOTH RE-ENFORCING RING AROUND TWO END HOLES

FILING SMALL BOOKS, BOOKLETS AND BULLETINS ARE KEPT FROM BINDING AT THE RINGS BY DOUBLED STRIPS OF CLOTH GUMMED TAPE.

TRELLISES AND ARBORS

MAKING AN INDEX

RUBBER CEMENT

PASTE CONTINUED PARTS ON REAR OF MAGAZINE PAGES YOU ARE-SAVING.

STOCK QUADRILLE PAPER FOR PLANNING RULED IN 3/16 IN. SQUARES. EACH SQUARE REPRESENTS A CERTAIN NUMBER OF FEET OF SPACE.

LETTER FIRST, THEN CUT

GUMMED INDEX TAB STRIP

PASTE ON TO STRONG PAPER DIVISIONS

BULBS LAWN WATER PLANTS ROCK PLANTS ANNUALS

drying instantly, and can be thinned with gasoline or benzol when it evaporates too fast. The small clippings or continued parts may be pasted on the backs of full-sheet articles, thus saving space. First clip out a complete article, then assemble it as closely as possible.

An average full-size garden magazine sheet with the margins clipped just about fits the book size. Insert this in the punch pattern, holding it firmly with the left hand. Now push a pencil through the holes, place a re-enforcing ring around each of the end holes, and it is ready for the binder.

There is always plenty of room at the outer edges of the book. For this reason we bind agricultural bulletins and other booklets less than full page width, with two pieces of doubled cloth tape pasted together. This can be purchased seven-eighths inch wide.

Anyone who has never planned a garden or other layout with quadrille ruled paper does not know how much easier it is. The paper is very inexpensive.

Gummed index strips come in twelve-inch lengths. Print them neatly, cut them off and attach to strong punched binder sheets. This facilitates getting the information into the book as well as out of it.

Rubber cement, blank pages, quadrille pages, cloth tape, index strips, etc., are for sale at all stationers and most 5 and 10 cent stores. Be sure to get standard 8½ x 11 inch paper and not the student size, which is smaller.

Do not put off clipping articles—they will be overlooked and lost. Do it as soon as you see them and then file them away promptly before they get mislaid or thrown away.

A PHOTOGRAPHIC RECORD

Someone has well said, "No business can succeed without adequate records." We might paraphrase this truism by saying, "No garden can be properly developed without records."

When you look upon a successful garden it is, most times, the result of evolution. After the gardener has planned the major features well, the small color combinations and the intricacies of height and foliage texture form a never failing source of interest. It is change and the ability to improve which keep our interest active.

As you stand before your garden in midsummer a dozen different ideas occur to you for improvement. The season is not right for change and by spring these ideas are far away. This is where records step in, records which enable you to repeat success as well as to correct mistakes.

In winter it is easy to sit down with "The Complete Book of Garden Magic" to find the reason for any condition in our garden. We then have the leisure precluded by the joyous summer tasks. The only catch is that the intimate details are not fresh in our minds.

The simplest method of bringing these two periods together is by a garden chart coupled with a few small photographs.

Too intricate, you say? That's the way it seemed to me until I talked with Edw. J. Hoffman, who has long made a specialty of garden and flower photography. He showed me that with the developing and printing of the pictures you can take, as close as your local druggist, chart making was not only simple, but inexpensive.

First, on a sheet of paper divide any planting into sections as shown in sketch on page 360. These sections should be the record of an area a little smaller than that covered by the photo.

By measuring the exact distance from the bed and using a tripod, the camera may be placed in relatively the same position for each successive photograph. This will give pictures of the same size which may be trimmed and joined to form a composite picture of the entire bed. Your entire grounds may also be made into a picture.

Below each photo is written a brief record of the section; the name of the plants with their difficulties and accomplishments. Thus the gardener is able to bring the garden indoors with him and the study of it at his leisure will impress upon his mind the things necessary to correct every failing.

How to Take Garden Pictures: A little knowledge of the use of your camera is required. In taking a picture of a moving object, shutter speed is necessary, so in bright light we open the stop or iris diaphragm to its wide opening (f.6.3) and use the fastest shutter 1/100 of a second. This does not however give the clear detail and depth of focus which we need for garden pictures.

By depth of focus we mean having the objects as clear in the background as in the front of the picture. To get this effect we reverse the action or snapshot method, using a smaller stop opening and a slower shutter.

Thus an excellent garden picture can be taken at 7:30 o'clock in the morning of a bright day with stop set at f.16 and shutter at $\frac{1}{25}$ of a second.

A photo is made up of black and white shades, on flat paper. Yet shading makes it appear to have depth or a third dimension. Shading also suggests color interest. The more delicate this shading the more convincing the picture. At noonday the shadows are most distinct, darkness appears black and white appears glaring, so for flower pictures in summer we chose the softer light of early morning (7 to 8) or evening (5 to 7) when the sun is low. This choice is a fortunate one for most gardeners have leisure at these hours.

The use of the camera is bound to lead the garden enthusiast into the field of flower portraits. This means further decreasing the diaphragm opening and slowing up the shutter. Time exposure sounds technical. It scared me for years. It simply means that the camera must be held steady while you operate the shutter.

We may get this steadiness by placing the camera on a box, a stone wall, a chair or a stepladder, but the best of all is the tripod. It allows so many angles unattainable in any other way. A great help in this sort of thing is a portrait attachment. This also had me bluffed until I found that it was only another lens to put over the lens of my camera and that it enabled me to slip up on objects to within thirty inches where the distance indicator on my camera said, "Don't come closer than six feet."

Getting closer to the object of course makes it bigger and gives increased detail. Using the attachment, when your camera is exactly 30 inches from the object, you must set your distance indicator at 6 ft.; when 33 inches away set it at 8 ft.; when 36 inches, at 10 ft.

Some cameras are arranged to give as slow an exposure as 1/10 to ½ second and of course these are best for this use but the ordinary camera will serve as well.

If you wish to take a picture with a box camera and not jar it, place it upon some solid object, focus it, then cover the lens with a book. Having set the stop for the smallest opening, open the shutter for time exposure. This is made by removing the book and quickly replacing it.

With other types of cameras a bulb or push pin cable is necessary to get steady time pictures.

A little practice will show how to time the exposure. In sunshine you can scarcely open and close the shutter fast enough. The size of the stop opening is the thing to watch. Use f.3.2 or f.4.5. If the print comes out too light it is under exposed, which means that the stop opening is too small. If it is too dark you have too large a stop opening.

The small stop opening gives sharp detail in the background and many times the photographer wishes to catch this also. However, if we are taking a picture of a beautiful specimen, we sometimes wish to accentuate it by shutting out diverting views.

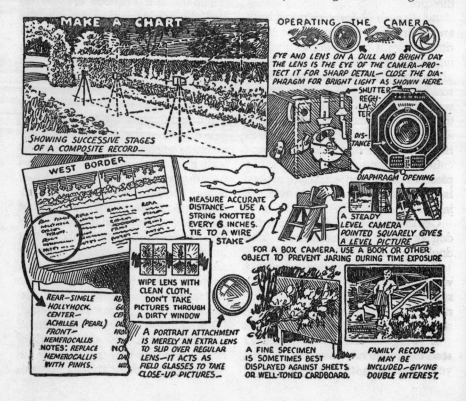

MAKE A CHART

SHOWING SUCCESSIVE STAGES OF A COMPOSITE RECORD—

OPERATING THE CAMERA

EYE AND LENS ON A DULL AND BRIGHT DAY THE LENS IS THE EYE OF THE CAMERA—PROTECT IT FOR SHARP DETAIL— CLOSE THE DIAPHRAGM FOR BRIGHT LIGHT AS SHOWN HERE.

SHUTTER REGULATER
DISTANCE

WEST BORDER

DIAPHRAGM OPENING

MEASURE ACCURATE DISTANCE— USE A STRING KNOTTED EVERY 6 INCHES. TIE TO A WIRE STAKE

A STEADY LEVEL CAMERA POINTED SQUARELY GIVES A LEVEL PICTURE

FOR A BOX CAMERA, USE A BOOK OR OTHER OBJECT TO PREVENT JARING DURING TIME EXPOSURE

REAR—SINGLE HOLLYHOCK. CENTER— ACHILLEA (PEARL) FRONT— HEMEROCALLIS NOTES: REPLACE HEMEROCALLIS WITH PINKS.

WIPE LENS WITH CLEAN CLOTH. DON'T TAKE PICTURES THROUGH A DIRTY WINDOW

A PORTRAIT ATTACHMENT IS MERELY AN EXTRA LENS TO SLIP OVER REGULAR LENS—IT ACTS AS FIELD GLASSES TO TAKE CLOSE-UP PICTURES—

A FINE SPECIMEN IS SOMETIMES BEST DISPLAYED AGAINST SHEETS OR WELL-TONED CARDBOARD.

FAMILY RECORDS MAY BE INCLUDED—GIVING DOUBLE INTEREST.

In this case we arrange it against properly smoothed cloth or soft-toned cardboard. If this board is held in place by a stake in the ground it is not necessary to remove the blossom from the plant.

The panchromatic film is a blessing to the amateur. It used to be that if you took a picture of a prize blue delphinium, the stalk would be dark and the bloom too white for realism. This was because the old style film was too sensitive to greens, reds, etc., while blue was too light. This is largely corrected by modern film; in addition, it records much faster.

Your picture will be exactly as you see it in the finder. If the scene shows level there, it will be straight upon the print. Have the camera level, stand directly in front of the subject and point the camera squarely at right angles. Oblique angles and tilting produce grotesque results.

Remove the back of your camera and look through the open shutter to see if it is clean. Polish the front of the lens; if it is cloudy take it to your dealer for complete cleaning. Don't take pictures through a dirty window.

Get accurate distances. Knot a piece of stout cord every six inches, fasten it to a stiff piece of wire to jab into the ground.

Get interest into the picture. A pet dog or child will make the record doubly pleasing.

Get out the instruction book that was supplied with your camera and study your particular type of apparatus. These instructions are few and simple.

If you get a kick out of a colored seed catalogue in winter, try coloring your photos with transparent oil paints. Expert work of this sort costs little. Enlargements are inexpensive.

HOW TO MAKE ZINC LABELS

Labeling of plants is important. It enables the gardener to distinguish plants of similar foliage and to avoid loss where unskilled labor is used. A wooden label soon loses its legibility and where something more permanent is desired, zinc labels supply this need.

The first requisite of a label is legibility. It should always be large enough to contain easily all the plant name. It is best to print the part of the name which you desire to be most prominent. The other classifications may be carefully written smaller.

Zinc in rolls or smaller lengths, may be secured from sheet metal supply houses or sometimes from tinners or roofers. The writer uses it two inches wide when attached to stakes, to label large plants, and one-half inch wide when used for strip labels which are sharpened on one end to force into the ground for their own support. The zinc is easily cut with tin snips or a cheap pair of scissors.

There are several methods of fastening the zinc to stakes. Where a strong piece of wire (for sale at hardware stores) is used it may be bent into a frame and either end of the zinc curled around it. It is no trick to tip it on the wire with two drops of solder. Have the label about ten inches above ground, and the stake six to ten inches in the ground. Bend a knee or kink in the stake at the ground level to steady it. If this is forced into the ground slightly, it will add to its stability.

To attach to wooden stakes, use brass or copper tacks or, better still, split-end copper rivets, used for fastening leather. The brass paper rivet sold by stationers is also good.

The strip label is used for marking low growing or creeping plants and in the greenhouse. Decide how much space the name will take. Allow 1½ inches to keep the soil from splattering the name, and 1½ inches to force into the ground. Point one end and after writing the name, crease the zinc slightly along the whole length to stiffen it.

To write upon the zinc, first wipe it carefully with a cloth or, better still, a bit of emery paper. Then, using a quill pen or a sharpened stick, write or print with ink prepared according to one of the following formulae. The writer has used the first mixture successfully:

Verdegris . . . . 1 oz.
Sal Ammoniac . . . . 1 oz.
Lamp Black . . . . 1½ oz.
Distilled Water . . . . . 1½ pt.
Shake well before using.

Another mixture recommended is ½ Butter of Antimony and ½ Hydrochloric Acid.

A long lasting label can be made by weathering the zinc by exposure for several weeks and writing upon it, with a lead pencil. Weathering can be hastened by soaking in strong salt solution for a few days.

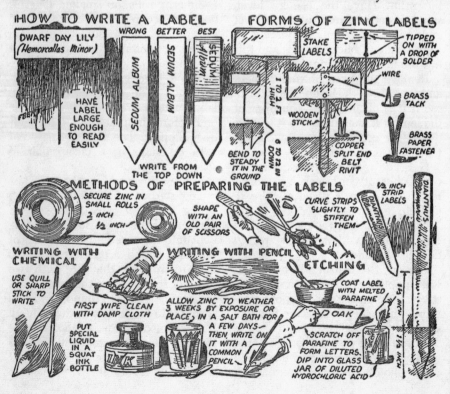

HOW TO WRITE A LABEL

DWARF DAY LILY (Hemorcallas Minor)

HAVE LABEL LARGE ENOUGH TO READ EASILY

WRONG BETTER BEST

SEDUM ALBUM

WRITE FROM THE TOP DOWN

FORMS OF ZINC LABELS

STAKE LABELS

1 TO 2 FT. HIGH

6 TO 12 IN. DOWN

BEND TO STEADY IT IN THE GROUND

WOODEN STICK

COPPER SPLIT END BELT RIVIT

TIPPED ON WITH A DROP OF SOLDER

WIRE

BRASS TACK

BRASS PAPER FASTENER

METHODS OF PREPARING THE LABELS

SECURE ZINC IN SMALL ROLLS
2 INCH
½ INCH

SHAPE WITH AN OLD PAIR OF SCISSORS

CURVE STRIPS SLIGHTLY TO STIFFEN THEM

½ INCH STRIP LABELS

DIANTHUS

WRITING WITH CHEMICAL

USE QUILL OR SHARP STICK TO WRITE

PUT SPECIAL LIQUID IN A SQUAT INK BOTTLE

INK

FIRST WIPE CLEAN WITH DAMP CLOTH

WRITING WITH PENCIL

ALLOW ZINC TO WEATHER 3 WEEKS BY EXPOSURE OR PLACE, IN A SALT BATH FOR A FEW DAYS—THEN, WRITE ON IT WITH A COMMON PENCIL

ETCHING

COAT LABEL WITH MELTED PARAFINE

OAK

SCRATCH OFF PARAFINE TO FORM LETTERS, DIP INTO GLASS JAR OF DILUTED HYDROCHLORIC ACID

¾ INCH

1½ INCH

For permanent labels etching is sometimes employed. The zinc is coated with paraffin and the letters scratched through to the metal. When the label is dipped in diluted hydrochloric acid, it eats into the zinc where the paraffin was scratched away. If the letters so formed are coated with the ink mentioned above, they will be legible for years.

EDITOR'S NOTE: The development of color film in 35 millimeter and larger sizes (which Mr. Biles did not have opportunity to work with) is one of the gardener's greatest aids in keeping a record of his flower and planting effects, and in sharing the charms of his garden with others. The operation of cameras in which color film can be used (some of which are quite inexpensive) is simple, and the processed pictures (transparencies) can either be projected on a screen (or studied through a magnifying viewer) or used as "negatives" for the making of color prints.

Excellent detailed instructions can be had from the large camera manufacturers, from dealers, and through classes, and there is at least one excellent book devoted exclusively to garden, plant, and flower photography.—E.L.D.S.

CHAPTER XXVI

FLOWER ARRANGEMENT

The use of flowers in the home can be a source of satisfaction and pleasure to the grower of flowers. It will enable him to see how they react to various backgrounds and lighting conditions. He will learn a great deal about combining colors, indoors and out, and the general arrangement of plants in the garden. The beauty he creates will add to his pride of accomplishment and be the crowning glory of his gardening career.

The study of flower arrangement in America has developed within the last two decades, along with the rise of the garden club movement. The latter may be said to have been stimulated largely by the great increase in available plant and flower material, through the efforts of hybridizers here and abroad, and the many plant introductions from the Orient.

The interest in flower arrangement is limited to no one class of people or section of the country. Exponents of various schools have arisen among artists and laymen, demonstration courses have been offered, and many valuable books written for either casual or serious study.

No matter what the individual viewpoint may be, all agree that flower arrangement or composition is a living art and subject to the principles of the graphic arts to which it is related. Where the painter uses canvas and pigments, the flower lover may create with living materials, a picture which contains all the elements of design—light and shade, color, composition, and line.

This use of flowers as the material in a composition is a thing apart from our enjoyment of them as individuals or grouped casually to emphasize their perfume or color, which is universal and cannot be supplanted. It enlarges their sphere of use and beauty and awakens a keener appreciation of their possibilities.

The fortunate gardener who is endowed with natural taste, the gift of "seeing right," may need little instruction in this new art, especially since he has a background of experience in handling plants. But that ability is a gift, and those not so endowed must go forward step by step, learning by study and experiment to build up appreciation and develop skill in composition. To be able to grow flowers, to know their habits of growth and the possibilities of their combinations with their neighbors in the garden, is a great privilege. To know how to transplant their beauty indoors so that none of it will be lost, rounds out the gardener's life.

The "American Way" of arranging flowers is still in a formative stage, but it gives promise of being a combination of two great schools of flower artists. These are the schools developed respectively by the Japanese, who work with living materials with emphasis on line to the sacrifice of color and mass, and by the great Flemish flower painters who used color and mass with little or no emphasis on flowing line as such. This union promises to be a happy one, admitting many variations, and easily adapted to our homes and manner of living.

Japanese Flower Arrangement

The creation of "living flowers" (Ike-bana) has been a part of the daily lives of the Japanese since the middle of the sixth century A.D. Its inspiration came with Buddhism from China in the use of temple flower offerings. It became a learned profession and a recreation for all classes, and it is still taught in the public schools of Japan. The original art, which was severe and limited in the use of materials, has been modified by the formation of various schools, a few of which are occidental in spirit.

The idea is the creation, with living materials, of a pattern or reproduction of a plant in its natural surroundings. Therefore the color of the vases and bowls used suggests the earth, while the water represents the surface of the soil from which the plant springs as one parent stalk. The individual blossom is considered of value, not for its own beauty, but as a part of the plant itself.

The basic motif of all Japanese groups—Heaven, man and earth—was not established until the seventeenth century which saw the full-flowering of the art. It has many modifications, but is based on the following: Heaven, standing, is the central branch, curving upward with its tip directly over its base. Its height will approximate one and one-half times the height of the vase, or the diameter of the bowl. Man, going, is half the length of Heaven, and follows the Heaven curve. Earth, running, is half the length of Man, and has a lateral curve opposite that of Man. Any other branches are considered attributes and are of uneven length. Skill in bending these branches or stems is acquired by long practice. All continue for several inches as a trunk or stem. Arrangements made according to this system are highly symbolical, and often seasonal to represent the wind-blown branches of spring, the open water of summer, and the stark trees of the winter landscape.

The influence of the Japanese on our flower arrangements of today is very apparent in our growing appreciation of the beauty of line in composition and in nature. This adds pattern and rhythm to our love of mass and color and inspires us to express our originality in the choice of plant material with which to carry out our ideas. We use bowls and vases designed (with the Japanese idea in mind) so as to allow the flowers room enough to show their habit of growth as well as to live and breathe. Our supports and holders have been evolved from those of Ike-bana, along with the principal tenets of its creed: do not overcrowd nor have a confusion of foliage with color in spots; do not allow stems to cross each other nor be of equal length; do not have regular spaces between the flowers, nor step them down evenly; use no inferior or wilted material.

Terms Used in Flower Arrangement

It is impossible to condense into a few pages what is needed for the beginner venturing into the arts. He will no doubt be confused by cryptic phrases and definitions, which when analyzed may simply mean that what he needs is common sense plus a wholesome imagination, a vase and a bunch of flowers of varying shapes and gradations of color. However we may well comment on some of the frequently used terms.

Arrangement, composition and **group** have similar meanings. Design, is the idea or pattern you have in mind to carry out. Line, to the artist is a visual path which follows the main outline of a composition and may suggest a circle, oval, triangle, rectangle or other shape.

Balance, or repose, gives a feeling of stability and can be emphasized by the size, shape and color of the container. Upon its apparent weight or bulk depends the proper height and width of the group. A metal or pottery bowl will allow for a much larger assembly than a transparent glass receptacle of the same size, because the pottery seems heavier.

Vertical axis, is an imaginary line drawn from the bottom of the vase to the top of the arrangement. It can be indicated by the massing of flowers along it.

Center of interest is the point where all visual lines converge and is usually on the vertical axis slightly above the top of the vase. At that point the largest and darkest flowers are assembled, or a heavy group of small ones, or the strongest foliage mass.

Rhythm, is the handling of line and color to carry the eye from part to part of the composition. It should stimulate an unconscious progress, and is served by line and color and the shape of the flowers.

Color harmony, is an agreement in tone or shade that satisfies the eye. Tints and shades prevail in flowers and are easier to combine than pure spectrum colors. When two of the latter must be used, as red and blue, the latter should predominate, and a few purple flowers be added to harmonize the whole. Harmony of analogy, is the use of the tones of neighboring colors on the color chart; harmony of contrast, is the use of the opposite or contrasting colors.

The study of pictures of flower arrangements will further define these terms and practice will fix them. It will take considerable training to enable the eyes to follow some of the more elusive elements.

Applying the Principles

In mass or full arrangements, group large flowers at the base and hide the edge of your container by means of overhanging leaves or blooms. Also in mass arrangements place the darker, heavier material at the base nearest the center. The most flagrant sin in mass arrangement is overcrowding. Do not use too many varieties of flowers. There is dignity and restraint in an arrangement of one variety in its own foliage. When you do use several varieties and colors, do not scatter them through the composition but try to hold color together, allowing no two colors to be equal in amount but having one color dominate and the others act as complement to it.

Line arrangements are more interesting than mass effects but much more difficult. A simple principle is to allow one gracefully curving stem or the tallest flower to become the center of the composition, being careful to keep the tip directly over its base. It may curve away from the base but must return at the tip. Upon either side of this (using but few flowers) are assembled the stems, rising in strong lines from a central source. None of these stems shall be precisely the same height, nor must they cross or parallel one another. Curves must be strong and definite.

All nature has taught man to expect an appearance of stability at the base. A tree or shrub is heavier there and a flower arrangement must be also. Strong lines at the base give this effect in line composition. The use of heavier mass at the base gives it in other arrangements.

In combining mass and line, avoid confusion. Use a little of both types but do not complicate them with a tangle of ferns, babysbreath or sprays of weak growth. They blur the lines and clutter composition. Bold and vivid contrast, strong and graceful lines always win over a fussy attempt at prettiness. If these materials are used they should be a studied part of it and not an afterthought. Make the composition logical.

The Container

This should be of correct size, neutral or harmonious in color, sec-

ondary in interest, yet an essential and recognized part of the whole composition. As has been noted, it assists balance in color, shape and size. It can also complete a color harmony by carrying out a deeper shade in the flowers or a contrasting one. In period groups and other exceptional cases, it may equal or dominate the flowers in value.

Early disciples of the art had great difficulty in finding usable bowls and vases, but the present task is to choose from the multitude of beautiful and practical containers in every medium, color, type. Designers have been swept up on the wave of enthusiasm and not only follow, but create styles and trends.

In selecting containers, consider your flowers, the type of house and its furnishings, and the places where the arrangements will be used. For example, in a hall, with cheerful, welcoming flowers, you can use brass, copper or bronze, with perhaps a tall jar for the floor for branches or other tall material. The living room will need light pottery and glass in occasional vases or as permanent mantel features. One lovely urn which may or may not hold flowers is appropriate and distinguished here. The dining room calls for silver, china and crystal, the bedrooms, quaint figures and vases in small scale for delicate flowers.

The flowers you like to have about you will suggest the medium. Roses like glass, silver and porcelains, which give an effect of increase in size and number. Since roses are one of the few flowers whose foliage stays fresh under water, it is nice to use glass for them. Try for fairly slender, soft stem green vases that will not need a flower holder. Peonies need large heavy pottery, heavy silver or pewter bowls or flaring vases. Iris go Japanese in low bowls of metal or pottery; or brass milk pans are perfect. Tulips look well in pitchers or tankards. Gladiolus and lilies require vases that repeat the classic lines of their stems; urns and jars are good types. The smaller gladiolus are delightful in bowls if you keep the majority of the stems in a horizontal position, and do not use too many. They will turn up at the tips and give added grace to the arrangement. Copper, brass and pottery are ideal for groups of summer flowers. The former has slight preservative value, and all keep the stems dark,

and the flowers last longer. Copper washed with tin is a lovely medium for any flowers. Wooden bowls can often be used for dried material and berries with good effect. Do not put summer flowers with soft stems in glass vases, asters, calendulas, chrysanthemums, dahlias and zinnias for example.

The ideal for every home should be at least: (1) One heavy large container for flowering shrubs, thick-stemmed flowers or foliage. This may be copper, pewter or pottery but should be unglazed and dull in tone. (2) One tall vase about a foot high for long-stemmed flowers. (3) Several vases ranging in size from five to ten inches high in various materials and colors. (4) One large shallow

½ IN. WIRE MESH HOLDERS CAN BE FORMED TO FIT ANY SIZE BOWL

½ INCH WIRE MESH

HEAVY LEAD STRIPS 1 TO 1½ IN WIDE MAY BE BENT INTO ANY SHAPE HOLDER

PERFORATED GLASS BLOCK

SUPPORTING WITH LEAD STRIPS

VASE WALL SUPPORT FROM REAR EDGE OF VASE WITH LEAD STRIPS OR WIRE

USING THE TWIN WIRE

SIMPLICITY IS THE KEYNOTE FOR THE WATER LILY DISPLAY

AN EXAMPLE OF SUBMERGED DISPLAY

AN OPEN COMBINATION OF MASS AND LINE

A BLACK BASE BENEATH A TRANSPARENT VASE WILL ADD WEIGHT.

A SIMPLE AND AN EFFECTIVE ARRANGEMENT

Here are just a few of the many prepared cuttings with which indoor plants may be increased at no cost. Among the kinds represented are: African-violets, Zonal Geraniums, Crotons, Christmas-cactus and Fuchsia.

Two examples of the way simple accessories, in the one case a ceramic bird and the other a charming figurine, can give colorful accent to the most unpretentious of flower displays

ARRANGEMENTS BY MRS. E. L. SCOTT (LEFT) AND MRS. JOHN POTTER

PHOTOGRAPHS, F. W. CASSEBEER

bowl about fourteen inches wide. (5) A few smaller bowls for dining tables, etc. (6) Where water lilies are available, a flat bowl of bronze or iridescent glass, three inches deep, about fourteen inches wide and having a basin of six inches with a four-inch almost flat lip or edge, is ideal for an aquatic arrangement.

Under-water or floating plants, sometimes make a charming table decoration. Roses and Sweet Peas will stand submerging and may be so displayed in crystal jars or globes. A strip of sheet lead around the stem will hold them upon the bottom. Water lilies will only float, so they are displayed with smaller specimens of their foliage in the flat bowl previously described. The smaller pads are arranged upon the flat sides, while a white and a colored flower float in the basin, separated by two diminutive leaves of Water-hyacinth or a spray of Primrose Creeper. Night bloomers will stay open better indoors. A little paraffin (barely warm enough to melt) dropped into the center will help keep other kinds open.

Locating Flower Arrangements

The first thing to consider when selecting the flowers is how you wish to use them. Some flowers have such an intimate appeal that they seem made to be looked into; others have a stately and dignified appeal —these are to be looked upon. Select your flowers to fit the use and location.

Violets, Lily-of-the-valley, Pansies, Water lilies and many Roses show to better advantage when looked into or down upon. These are examples of the intimate flowers and do well upon tables and lower locations. Gladiolus and Hollyhocks, are seen best when slightly above the eye and against a background. This does not constitute a hard and fast rule, but is only a general suggestion.

Color harmony also enters into selection. Colors must not clash with each other or with wall paper or furnishings. And last but very important, flowers must suit the container in which they are displayed. Both vase and flowers may be beautiful but they do not belong together unless they complement one another.

Place vases of tall flowers on tables or pedestal stands against a wall or in a corner; low bouquets on coffee or medium tables; vases in pairs on mantels. Yellow flowers will lighten a dark corner. Blue needs a strong light and, like purple, fades out in candlelight. White roses are the most formal for a living room, and any white flowers add gayety. Never use strong colors for a formal dinner; reserve them for buffet suppers and luncheons. Too much color at breakfast offends as many as it pleases; soft colors are always safe. Children like red, white and blue flowers in their rooms. Do not use strong colors or heavy arrangements in very warm weather. Bowls with water showing, soft colors, and the more delicate flowers add coolness.

Flower Holders

To the types of flower blocks and supports shown on page 368, should be added those of heavy metal with square meshes. They range in size from one and a half to six inches, and come in shapes to fit all types of containers. The pin point holders on heavy lead bases are suitable for all open water arrangements, and can be masked with stones, moss or small crystal balls. Both of these supports can be anchored to the bottom of a bowl with pieces of plastic clay when the bowl is dry.

Chicken wire in regular or one inch mesh is the best filler for baskets and other large pieces. It can be rolled or crushed in place and wired in or held firm with stiff fern or hemlock stems. Twigs and greens may be used for fillers in heavy pottery but are not as successful as wire. Strips of sheet lead have innumerable uses. The lighter weights can be wrapped around stems to hold them in place and may be hooked over the rear rim of the vase to support some stem. Heavier weight may be used to form an easily changed flower base. Lead is obtainable at most plumbers or supply houses and fine wire just the right size for supports is sold by stationers for fastening shipping tags. Holders should never be used in clear glass receptacles unless they can be masked with bits of fern without spoiling the effect of the flowers. Too much emphasis cannot be placed on the necessity of a firm base for any floral piece. Without it an arrangement has no unity, and extra flowers may have to be tucked in at the expense of the design.

Classes of Flowers

Any text on flower arrangement would be of little value if it failed to include some flower classification as a guide for use in selecting material for design work. The groups which follow are far from complete and may be supplemented by the lists in Chapters V, IX and X. Of necessity, they overlap, the rose, for example, being dominant, solitary, and fragrant.

Line flowers give outline and rhythm to composition, while the dominants add weight, color and mass. Solitary flowers may have unusual or distinguished design in themselves; those listed as delicate, show airy grace of line or form. The fillers give line and color as well as some degree of unity.

LINE: Anchusa italica, baptisia, buddleia, campanula, Celosia plumosa, delphinium, foxglove, gas-plant, gladiolus, hollyhock, larkspur, liatris, lupine, monkshood, penstemon, plume-poppy, salvia, snapdragon, spirea, tritoma, veronica, vitex.

DOMINANT: Aster, balsam, calendula, carnation, chrysanthemum, cornflower, cosmos, daffodil, dahlia, daisy, doronicum, gaillardia, hemerocallis, iris, lily, marigold, narcissus, peony, peruvian-daffodil, petunia, phlox, poppy, pyrethrum, ranunculus, rose, scabiosa, sweet william, thistle, tulip, verbena, zinnia.

SOLITARY: Amaryllis, anthurium, bird-of-paradise flower, gladiolus, iris, lily, orchid, poinsettia, rose, water lily.

DELICATE: Anemone, begonia, bleeding heart, blue bells, columbine, coral bells, cyclamen, forget-me-not, fuchsia, grape-hyacinth, lily-of-the-valley, pansy, salpiglossis, spirea, sweet pea, viola.

FILLER: Acacia, achillea, ageratum, artemisia Silver King, Euphorbia corollata, grasses, gypsophila, heather, meadow rue, Queen Anne's lace, statice, stevia, plume-poppy.

FOLIAGE: *Spiky:* aspidistra, dracaena, gladiolus, iris, yucca. *Soft:* meadow rue, maiden-hair fern. *Heavy:* canna, funkia, galax, leucothoë, laurel, magnolia, oak, rubber plant.

FRAGRANT: Buddleia, carnation, clematis, gas-plant, heather, heliotrope, hemerocallis, honeysuckle, lily, lily-of-the-valley, mignonette, nicotiana, petunia, pinks, rose, stevia, sweet pea, tuberose, valerian, viola.

FRAGRANT SHRUBS: Buddleia, clematis (bush type), currant,

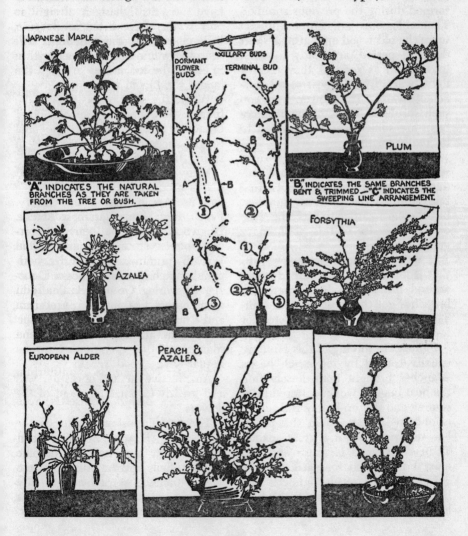

daphne, elder, honeysuckle, lilac, Magnolia glauca, mockorange, rose, strawberry bush.

Forcing Flowering Branches

When you begin to tire of winter it is time to brighten the home with flowering branches forced in water. The early blossoming varieties force the easiest. These are from buds formed during the previous summer. Their blossoms are borne directly upon the old wood and, after a short dormant period, are ready to burst into bloom as soon as they receive light, warmth and, most of all, sufficient water. The flower buds on such shrubs as Forsythia and Spicebush are sufficiently well formed to be really visible.

Many of the later flowering shrubs, such as Weigela and Lilac, are produced on green-growing shoots from buds formed the previous summer, but they are harder to force because of the necessity of this preliminary green growth.

It will be noticed in most shrubs that the flower buds are formed around the outer edges where the branches get the most light and air. These portions should be selected for forcing.

Failures in forcing of this kind are usually caused by too much haste. Branches brought immediately into the heat begin a weak scattered blossoming and dry up before full bloom is obtained. The sap in the plants has not risen to any great extent. Their chief need is water and this must be supplied for early forcing.

For the best results immerse the branches in tepid water (bathtub or laundry tub) for the better part of a day. Do not use hot water. Then place in jars of lukewarm water in a sunny window of a cool room for about a week. When the buds are about to burst, bring into a warm room for display. If the branches do not seem to respond, repeat the soaking for an hour or so.

The branches will absorb considerable water and care must be taken to have the water changed often. Use only water at room temperature. A little charcoal in the containers will keep the water sweet. After they are in bloom the cooler they are kept the longer the bloom will last.

When the bloom has faded the foliage will appear. If a succession of branches is brought from the cool room, succession and variety in spring bouquets are obtainable.

Many common and easily procured plants produce brilliant results. We may use Apple, Pear, Plum, Cherry, Peach, Red Maple, Japanese Maple, Dogwood, Forsythia, early flowering Spireas (thunbergi and Bridal Wreath—prunifolia), Flowering Almond, Witch Hazels, Lonicera, Deutzia, Flowering Quince, Azalea, and many others. Catkins from American and European Alder and Pussy Willow make attractive displays and sometimes the common Carolina Poplar gives good results.

An effective method of display will add greatly to our enjoyment of the flowers.

The first important matter is the receptacle. Transparent bowls or light-colored porcelain do not fit. Dark, rather heavy pottery is best. The Japanese use brass jars. We illustrate a method of trimming branches at the bottom of the narrow center panel on page 371. The Figure 1 indicates a primary or upright branch; Figures 2 and 3 indicate side branches.

The principal charm of branch arrangement is an open balanced irregularity. A crowded mass of blossoms is difficult to arrange artistically. The Japanese principle of "balance of inequalities" means roughly an equal amount of bulk or branch area on each side of the base—not in symmetrical form, however.

There are illustrated on page 371 examples of arrangements of sprays of several kinds of flowering shrubs and trees. In the Forsythia arrangement, the bold upward sweeping lines are complemented by the gently drooping branches. The charm of the blossoming fruit branches is their simple austerity. Branches should be trimmed and bent to sweeping irregularly symmetrical lines, as indicated by "C" in the upper part of the center panel. Crossed branches are permissible and the Peach and Azalea arrangement is an excellent example of this; but it is usually safest for the inexperienced worker to stick to the more open type.

See article "How to Keep Cut Flowers" on pages 407–08.

GARDEN CALENDAR

THE GARDENER'S JANUARY

Old Winter sad, in snowy clad,
  Is making a doleful din;
But let him howl till he crack his jowl,
  We will not let him in.
  —THOMAS NOEL.

January is a good month when it comes to planning. Soon the seed catalogues will come in. These are really pieces of fine literature for the gardener. Perhaps they bewilder you with the multiplicity of their offerings but if you really plan to be an enthusiastic gardener, you will use them carefully then file them away for future reference. Among the treasured articles in the writer's file are catalogues from firms all over the country. These are from years before he had any idea of putting his thoughts about gardening on paper.

If you should go into the various seed houses of the country during the summer you would see what vast amount of effort, time and patience go into the composition of these catalogues which are sent to you, free, so that you may select the offerings of the season.

Some of the catalogues which you will receive will offer new flowers, many of which are your old friends in new and improved garb. The garden magazines will give you the story of each year's newest offerings. Our idea is not to plunge too heavily into new offerings but to remember that wise old adage, "Be not the first by whom the new is tried, nor yet the last to lay the old aside." While trying out some of the new and more difficult offerings, have the major portion of your garden devoted to your old friends, tried, true and easy of culture.

GENERAL

Make an inventory of your garden supplies, tools, fertilizers, spraying material and other necessities. Order your seeds early and buy only the best quality, remembering what a saving they will make to you in labor, patience and satisfaction. Old edged tools should be gone over and sharpened for the coming season. New handles should be placed and friction tape wrapped about that split place which always pinches your finger. Paint the handles a bright color to find them easily in the long grass and to help you remember to take them in at night. Read Chapter XVIII and plan now for a successful campaign.

Dig up your garden if the soil is not frozen or wet and expose it to the beneficial effects of freezing which breaks apart the heavy clods causing them to crumble. The turning also exposes the eggs of many insect pests to the effects of sun, wind, freezing and the food-hunting winter birds, all of which help to thin out their ranks considerably. Save the coal ashes to dig into beds which need loosening. They do not have much fertilizing value, but are excellent ground conditioners.

Look over the stored tubers to see that they are not suffering from too much moisture or lack of it. Mix up some potting soil ready for the propagating of seeds indoors. Bring it inside so that it will thaw out and become sufficiently dry to work well. Also get some soil under cover out of doors so that it will be dry enough for use on seed beds. Read Chapter XII.

PESTS

Don't forget to spray for scale as advised in Chapters XVI and XVII. Brush cocoons from the bark of old trees and burn them off lightly with a blow torch, if necessary, to get into the close spots. Be sure to tap off the snow on the evergreens to keep the branches from breaking or bending out of shape and get ready to give them an oil spray some time before March 15th on a day when it is over forty-five degrees, without much chance for a drop in temperature at night. You will be surprised how it removes the whitish scale and keeps down red spider and other pests.

CONCERNING THE FLOWERS

ROCK GARDEN: Sunny days bring out life in the rock garden and a close watch should be kept, if the snow is absent as a protector, to see that the surface soil has not been washed away from the plant's crown. Press any lifted ones back in their pockets and sprinkle around more stone chips or gritty soil.

SEEDS: Seed sowing time will soon be here. Have you all the material ready—soil which has been screened, sand, stones or broken flower pots for drainage, moss, boxes, seed pans, label sticks, etc.? If not, better get them at once and have them in good order ahead of time.

BULBS: The bulbs outdoors sometimes poke their noses through the ground during a warm spell; in such case, cover them with soil or peat moss, or draw the covering of boughs or straw a bit closer. An excellent use for discarded Christmas trees is to cover such early adventurers.

HOUSE PLANTS

WINTER CARE: Soap and water work wonders with dust-clogged leaf pores of house plants. Don't forget to feed. Sheep manure made into liquid manure (use only after a thorough watering) or dug into the topsoil, bone meal, packaged plant foods—all will do the trick if applied regularly. Most potted plants like to get their moisture, as do their outdoor relatives, by drinking with their roots from below. Use a deep saucer in which to stand each pot for an hour or so. Too much overhead watering ruins the foliage.

Set blooming plants on the floor at nights during ordinary winter weather so that they may have a rest from the overheated rooms of the daytime. It is also good practice to pull down the shades behind the plants on the cold nights or if necessary cover them with newspapers so that they will not suffer from drafts. Remember to do your watering in the morning and let the foliage go to sleep dry.

CARE OF CHRISTMAS PLANTS

POINSETTIA: Protect the Poinsettia from draft, keeping it in a temperature of seventy degrees in the daytime and not lower than sixty-three at night. Water twice a day with tepid or slightly warm water from above. When it has finished blooming and begins to drop its leaves, set it aside and give it only enough water to keep it from drying out. In April, the plants are pruned back hard and repotted in a rich light soil. They are kept growing in a light position and in early June are plunged in the garden, where they may remain until late September.

BEGONIA: Christmas Begonias last for a long time in bloom if given reasonable care and temperature conditions similar to those advised for Poinsettias.

CHERRY: The Christmas Cherry is longlasting and less delicate than either Begonias or Poinsettias, thriving well in a cooler temperature and withstanding greater variations of temperature. During summer it can be planted in the open garden.

BULBS: If you have rooted bulbs, as previously instructed, you are now enjoying bloom aplenty but if you haven't, Lily-of-the-valley pips may be obtained from your seed store or florist. Their preparation for bloom is simplicity itself. Hyacinths, Chinese Sacred-lilies, Paperwhite Narcissus, Soleil d'Or, etc., may now be forced in bowls of water for the house. Bear in mind that it is a succession of bloom that is wanted, therefore, a fresh batch of these quick rooting bulbs should be placed in bowls for rooting every ten days. (Pages 331, 333.)

GREENHOUSE AND COLDFRAMES

COLDFRAMES: Tilt the sash on coldframes on sunny days to ventilate. But be sure to cover them up again at night. Look over the cuttings and young perennial plants which are being carried over. See that they do not lack for water. Use only warm water and then only on very mild days in the morning when they can be well ventilated before night.

PESTS: Greenhouse plants must be sprayed frequently with a strong force of water to keep the red spider in check. This is one of our worst greenhouse pests if neglected, yet easy enough to keep under control. It is a case of frequent inspection and prompt action when necessary.

METHODS OF OBTAINING EVEN DISTRIBUTION OF SEEDS—

FOR REGULAR DISTRIBUTION MIX ONE OUNCE OF FINE SEEDS WITH ONE-HALF PINT OF FINE DRY SAND

TAPPING SEED FROM A FOLDED PAPER

A QUILL NOTCHED INTO THE SIDE OF A CORK MAKES AN EXCELLENT SEED SOWER

THIS TYPE OF SOWER IS FOR SALE BY SEEDMEN

METHODS OF PREPARING SOME SEEDS FOR QUICK GERMINATION

SOAK SEEDS IN WATER OVER NIGHT FOR QUICK GERMINATION

POUR SOAKED SEEDS INTO A CLOTH ON DRAWBOARD OF SINK

IN SOME SEEDS GROWTH CAN BE HASTENED BY CLIPPING OR NOTCHING.

SOME SEEDS' ARE SO HARD A FIRE MUST BE BUILT OVER THEM TO CAUSE GERMINATION

MUSLIN

SMALL STICK   GLASS   PAPER

SEEDS WHICH LOSE THEIR VITALITY QUICKLY WHEN DRY—AND THOSE SLOW TO GERMINATE ARE "STRATIFIED" IN MOIST SAND—

START VERY SMALL SEEDS IN A BULB PAN COVERED WITH GLASS

GETTING STARTED IN FEBRUARY

*The north wind doth blow and we shall
  have snow,
And what shall poor Robin do then,
  poor thing?
He'll hide in the barn to keep himself warm
And hide his head under his wing, poor
  thing.*

—OLD SONG.

February may seem an off month for the gardener but we must remember that March, the busiest month of the year, is just ahead and start to anticipate. Start to do anything that will make spring tasks easier. Have you kept any of your New Year's resolutions in regard to your garden?

Have you sprayed your trees for scale with miscible oil or lime-sulphur solution?

Have you brought in and screened your compost to start seeds in flats?

Have you painted and sharpened your tools and made an inventory of your garden supplies?

Have you ordered your seeds and studied the shrubbery needs of your planting? If not, February is the time to do it when you have leisure to let it rattle around in your mind and be sure that it is the thing you want to do. Most gardens are spoiled by snap decisions which the gardener makes in the heat of a busy season.

GENERAL

This gardener must confess his greatest sin. He has a tendency to crowd too much into his garden. This is why he repeats the advice against this practice so many times. Study some of the principles of planting in making your plan this year and don't attempt too great a variety. If you must drag in exotic plants not hardy in the region in which you live, remember that they are museum pieces rather than the backbone of your garden and treat them as such. Don't let your garden become a collection of oddities no matter how great the temptation may be to have something different from your neighbors.

It is much easier to have your lawn mower taken care of now than it will be when you want to cut grass. You will then be in competition with everyone else and the service may be slow and uncertain. Instructions for ordinary greasing and adjustment are given in Chapter III. There are patent home sharpening devices which are said to work well when directions are carefully followed.

Now is the time to order arbors, seats or garden furniture, as well as to consider their repair and painting.

Plant stakes and labels are a necessary evil. If you expect to make some, get them ready now so that your staking may begin before your plant gets out of shape. Your seedsman can supply you with many varieties in wood, metal and bamboo which will save you a lot of trouble.

How about considering an irrigation system for your lawn and garden this summer? An inexpensive one is shown in Chapter II. Water is the life-giving force of the garden and many a plant dies because the gardener thinks it is just too much trouble to give it the attention necessary at the time it needs it. Even such a crude system as we illustrate will deliver the supply to the spot needed with minimum effort.

CONCERNING FLOWERS

BULBS: All the summer-flowering bulbs, such as Cannas, Dahlias, Gladiolus, etc., are subject to damage. See that they have not been started into growth by heat or dampness. They should be stored in a thoroughly dry place at a temperature of about forty-five degrees to hold them back. If the tubers have shriveled, place them in very slightly damp peat moss but keep them cool so that they will not start into premature growth.

ANNUALS: The time for selecting annual seeds is at hand. For all round general use and beauty, nothing can equal Petunias, Marigolds, Nasturtiums, Zinnias, Snapdragons. The Zinnias come in so many sizes, colors and shapes from the Lilliput to the Dahlia-flowered that a large space might be devoted to their culture without monotony. They do best, of course, when intermingled with plants of softer foliage texture.

On pages 150 to 155 you will find lists of annuals for almost any use. Also on pages 155 to 168 you will find an excellent list of annuals with descriptions. This last list is by Professor Victor H. Ries of Ohio State University and we also want to call your attention to the names of experts on page 141 who compiled many of these lists.

Because such a large collection is confusing, we will give here a few selections especially to be recommended in combinations which go together well.

BACKGROUND: Lavender Basket-flowers and Flowering Tobacco Hybrids in red, pink, etc. Lemon-yellow Marigold and burnt-orange Zinnias. Sulphur-yellow Marigold, maroon and yellow Calliopsis with pink and white Cosmos. Globe-amaranth (Magenta and White Everlasting), large type Zinnias.

MIDDLE BORDER: Of course, plants for the middle border must be selected with a view to what is immediately behind and in front of them. In front of the pink Flowering Tobacco and the Basket-flowers, we would place shell-pink Zinnias and blue Larkspur. In front of the lemon-yellow Marigold and burnt-orange Zinnias, we would place Annual Lupine, blue Cornflowers and Annual

Sweet Williams in variety. Rose colored Zinnias also go well in front of the Flowering Tobacco. Pink Feather Coxcomb does well in front of the sulphur-yellow Marigolds and white Cosmos as also do pink and white China Asters.

FRONT BORDER: Ageratum, China Pinks, California Poppies, dark-red Dwarf Nasturtiums, Petunias in many shades, Sweet Alyssum and Lavender annual Phlox.

WINTER BOUQUETS: Now, while it is still winter, is a good time to appreciate the value of everlasting bouquets for winter decorations. Some of these may be brought indoors from the shrubbery border or the woods, but the majority of them require careful planning in the garden. List No. 35 on page 154 gives the best plants. Many catalogues devote space to the descriptions of these plants. You will find some of them fit into your borders very well while others are too stiff or sturdy in their texture and must be grown to themselves. By all means include some of them in your seed order. Instructions for drying them are found in the May Calendar.

STARTING INDOORS: February 22 is the traditional time to plant the seeds which take a long time to germinate, such as Lobelia, Ageratum, Verbena, Petunia, Penstemon, Scabiosa, etc. Read instructions on pages 282 to 285. These will also help you get ready for the sowing of many other seeds for March.

HOUSE PLANTS

Sponge the leaves of house plants every week with clean water. Give them plenty of fresh air, but not direct drafts. Now that the turn of the winter has passed, use a little fertilizer on any house plants which have begun to show new growth. Do not try to force these before they start.

Do not try to keep Cineraria or Poinsettias active after they have finished blooming. Keep Jerusalem-cherry, Cyclamen, Erica, Azalea, Genista, and Heliotrope moist. Don't repot orange trees too often; keep pot-bound. Feed with bone meal once a month during the growing period. Put Freesia in the cellar when flowering is over; plan to repot from August to February.

Watch out for these pests inside: Red spider, aphids, white fly, mealy bug, and scale. For aphids and mealy bug use thick soapsuds and rinse off after an hour, or wipe off with a soft cloth dipped in soapsuds. Scale must be scraped off by hand with cloth or brush and the foliage rinsed off later. Red spider is very difficult to get rid of and very easy to acquire. Remember that it cannot live in moist, cool, conditions and that the underside of the leaf is especially affected. Wash the leaves often with water as a preventive and keep the air moist and cool. White fly sucks the plant juices. Use nicotine and soapsuds as for aphids or, if very prevalent, fumigate the window or room, using a nicotine fumigant from your seed store. This is a heroic treatment and may be carried on in a large box in your garage or cellar some warm day when windows can be opened to get out the fumes.

TREES, VINES AND SHRUBS

DESTROY INSECT EGGS: February is an excellent month to get your trees in shape for the growing season. Get some miscible oil spray from the seed store and get after the scale. Remember, this should be done before March 15th. See instructions for dormant spray, page 261. Brush cocoons off of bark but do not scrape so as to injure the tree. Collect and destroy the egg masses of tent caterpillars which are shiny rings of tiny eggs around the small twigs of fruit trees. Investigate anything that looks foreign to you on the tree and find out what it is so that you may destroy it, if necessary. Spray Lilacs with limesulphur for scale if badly infested.

PRUNING: Get all your trimming and shaping of shrubbery done as soon as possible. Avoid spring pruning of the trees which bleed, such as Elms, Maples, etc. This work is best done after the foliage is well developed, or left until September. Be careful to trim only the flowering shrubs which bloom late in the season as you will destroy the blossoming wood on the early flowering variety by pruning now. Pruning of shrubbery is largely to remove the oldest wood to induce new growth from the bottom. Read Chapter V and pages 72 to 74. Prune the Peegee and Snowhill Hydrangeas to very short stubs of branches.

NEW SHRUBS: Select the shrubs which you want to add to your planting, using the lists in Chapter IV.

EVERGREENS: Giving them a dormant spray now will help keep down the red spider as well as scale and other pests. Shake off with care any heavy snow which clings to them as the shape of the plant can be spoiled beyond remedy if it is left on too long.

GRAPES: Now is a good time to do the pruning. The fruit is borne near the beginning of shoots which will develop during the present season. These shoots come from last year's growth. In order to keep the strength of the plant from going into foliage instead of fruit, we must trim away the oldest wood leaving only some principal stems. Each of these old stems should retain two or six of the canes which grew last year. These last year's canes must be cut back to three to ten buds each.

BERRIES: Cut out the canes of Raspberries and Blackberries which bore fruit last year. On Currants, prune out the wood which is over three years old. Get supports of wire or tightly stretched wire fencing ready for the berries so that the new canes may be fastened to them for the best exposure to sun and air. Have you studied the merits of a fruit border? Raspberries, Currants, Gooseberries, Blackberries, Grapes—all these make excellent border plants for the garden if kept within bounds and upon sightly supports.

FRUIT TREES: Fruit trees should be pruned now. Of course, they will bear if they are not pruned, but will do much better if given care at this time. Good fruit is the product of intelligent pruning and spraying. The product of trees which do not have this care is usually wormy and knotty. Spray with lime-sulphur at dormant strength or use miscible oil if close to your house. All this pruning and spraying should be done before the sap starts to rise. Consider trying some dwarf fruit trees for bloom and fruit if your place is small.

HOW TO ATTRACT BIRDS

Birds are so much a part of the garden that the coming of the Robin in February or March seems to act as the gardener's first notice that spring is on its way. Almost everyone wants them in the garden but few know how to attract them.

Their chief needs are food and fresh water. During the early spring freezes, the need for water becomes acute and frequently they are seen flying about in search of it. A pan of warm water in their accustomed drinking place will solve this problem. The water in ornamental bird baths is too often allowed to become stagnant and worthless. Anyone who has seen them in summer about an automatic lawn sprinkler will be impressed with their desire for fresh, cool water. Food, consisting of a piece of suet wired to a tree limb, combined with seeds or at least crumbs and table scraps, will keep them coming back year after year if they are supplied with water and suitable nesting places.

A little knowledge of the various simple nesting needs of the more familiar types will keep them safe from their natural enemies. The size of the bird, the distance from the ground, the surroundings they like best and most of all the size and shape of home which they require must be carefully considered. Guards of metal twelve inches wide, tacked completely around the tree or pole six feet from the ground, will keep a cat from climbing as the cat cannot get its claws into the wood.

Wood is the best and easiest material to use. One-half inch poplar or pine is readily obtained at box factory or mill. Painting should be done several weeks before the house is to be occupied. Birds dislike newly painted houses. Colors should be rather somber. They do not wish to attract too much attention to their nesting places. Provision must be made for cleaning each year as few birds will clean house. Do not place nesting materials in the houses but upon the ground in the open nearby. A few strings, shredded rags or fine short pieces of raffia may help.

The Purple Martin seems to be the only one which does well in an apartment. He is the largest of our swallows and likes his house on top of a pole. Make a porch 4 to 6 inches wide on which the birds can rest in the sun. Do not have a railing upon it. This bird arrives in April, nests in May and stays until September. Close the boxes until April 1st to keep the sparrows out.

The House Wren will build in almost anything, but the entrance should never be larger than ⅞ of an inch or the young birds may be destroyed by a cat. This size also keeps out the undesirable sparrow. A perch is not absolutely necessary but is a help.

The Robin likes a sheltered shelf but open on three sides. A board nailed under the eaves serves well. This gives the mother bird protection from torrential spring rains while nesting. It is the best known and most sociable of native birds, building its nest where no other bird would venture. Its calls vary with the hour and season.

Give him pieces of apple, suet,

scraped meat (no salt) and crumbs and he will soon be perched upon the porch rail or doorstep. Those who object to his raids upon the cherry tree should plant other fruiting trees and shrubs. He much prefers these.

A Bluebird will build in a swinging house and a sparrow will not. As the sparrow is his enemy and frequently drives him from his home, this is important. It should be in place by March 15th as the bird nests in early April.

All houses except the Martin's should have partial shade. All houses need a number of ¼ inch holes bored just under the eaves for ventilation. For more information get U. S. Fish and Wildlife Service Conservation Bulletins 1 (Attracting Birds) and 14 (Homes for Birds), each 10 cents, from Supt. of Documents, Government Printing Office, Washington, 25, D.C.

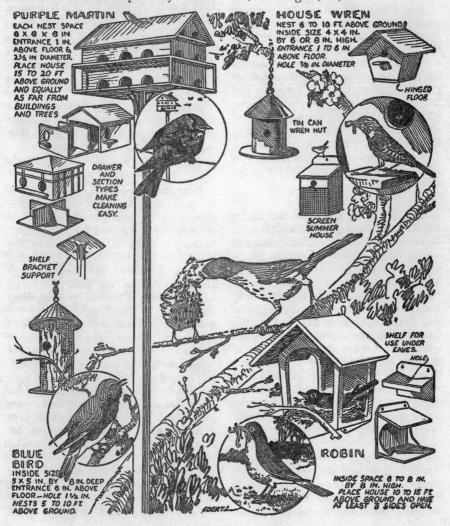

PURPLE MARTIN
EACH NEST SPACE 6 X 6 X 6 IN. ENTRANCE 1 IN. ABOVE FLOOR & 2½ IN. DIAMETER PLACE HOUSE 15 TO 20 FT ABOVE GROUND AND EQUALLY AS FAR FROM BUILDINGS AND TREES

DRAWER AND SECTION TYPES MAKE CLEANING EASY.

SHELF BRACKET SUPPORT

HOUSE WREN
NEST 6 TO 10 FT. ABOVE GROUND INSIDE SIZE 4 X 4 IN. BY 6 OR 8 IN. HIGH. ENTRANCE 1 TO 6 IN. ABOVE FLOOR. HOLE 7/8 IN. DIAMETER

HINGED FLOOR

TIN CAN WREN HUT

SCREEN SUMMER HOUSE

SHELF FOR USE UNDER EAVES.
HOLE

BLUE BIRD
INSIDE SIZE 5 X 5 IN. BY 8 IN. DEEP ENTRANCE 6 IN. ABOVE FLOOR—HOLE 1½ IN. NESTS 5 TO 10 FT ABOVE GROUND.

EBERTZ

ROBIN
INSIDE SPACE 6 TO 8 IN. BY 8 IN. HIGH. PLACE HOUSE 10 TO 15 FT ABOVE GROUND AND HAVE AT LEAST 3 SIDES OPEN.

THE BUSY MONTH OF MARCH

The garden seems more dear
Because I gave a drink
To thirsty flowers.
The birds that winter here
Sing sweeter in the spring, I think,
Because I made the barren hours
Less so with sustenance.
                                    —UNKNOWN.

One thing the successful amateur must learn is to know when to be in a hurry and when to restrain himself. With the first warm days of March it is a temptation to start to remove the winter mulches. That is the time for restraint. Someone has said that when you feel that it is time to uncover your plants, take a trip to Florida and do it when you come back. Better let them alone until all danger of frost is past. There are so many other things that you can do, that your energy should be devoted elsewhere.

It must be borne in mind that all instructions given in these Calendars must be mixed with brains. Fickle weather of spring makes absolute dates for planting, pruning, etc., an impossibility. Many operations can be done during February or March when spring is early and the weather dry, while the next year may find it impossible until later in the season. Then, too, this book has been written to cover such a wide range of territory that if we tried to give exact dates, some localities would find themselves attempting to work in snow-drifts, while others would wonder why they had not been able to do it long ago. Suit the work to the weather.

GENERAL

While it is best not to remove the mulch, it is always excellent practice to loosen it so that it will dry and allow the air to penetrate. A mulch is placed as a protection from wind and sudden changes in temperature caused by warm spring days, followed by cold drying nights, which heave the plants from the ground and damage their root system. When you do your early spring cultivation, rake off the rougher material to be burned or composted and dig all the finer mulch into the beds. It is well to let this matter rest until about April 1st in most localities, suiting the time to your location and climate. Always remember it is better to be too late with this removal than too early.

Fork over the compost pile. The rapidity with which it becomes compost depends a great deal upon keeping it moist and stirring it frequently.

PESTS

Dormant spraying may be safely done in most localities until March 15th. After that, the strength of the solution must be cut down considerably in order to keep it from injuring the swelling buds. The best time is a dull, still day when the weather is over forty degrees. Use lime-sulphur for fruit trees and Lilacs if they are far enough away from the house to avoid splattering paint work. This material oxidizes white lead and spots it. It may also discolor brick or stucco. I have found that shrubs near fences and hedges needing lime-sulphur, can have it applied to the branches with a paint brush—possibly this is not generally known. Miscible oil (from your seed store) is the best general purpose dormant spray. It will not injure buildings, walks, trellises, etc. Refer to Chapter XVII.

Any plants subject to mildew should be sprayed or dusted with Bordeaux mixture as they emerge from the dormant state. Roses, Phlox, Delphinium,

Peonies, etc., benefit from this treatment.

LAWN DON'TS

CONSTRUCTION: Don't delay any filling or changes. Thawing will help settle newly added soil and avoid more work in the summer.

ROLLING: Don't be in a hurry to roll your lawn with a heavy roller. Heavy rolling when the ground is wet compacts the ground so that clay soil puddles into a sticky, putty-like mass that makes it crack and bake in drier weather. It destroys soil texture. (See "Soil Texture and Structure," pages 29–30.) Light rollings are good to force any clumps of heaved sod back into contact with the soil but reserve heavy rolling, necessary to smooth the lawn, until a dry spell after the frost is definitely out of the ground. A water weight roller is a great advantage in regulating light and heavy rollings.

SEEDING: Don't wait until May to sow grass seed. Seed must be kept wet for at least two weeks to germinate and after that seedlings will die if dried out. Altogether it requires thirty days of moisture to grow successfully. This is easy if the seed is sown about March 15th but harder a month later. For resowing to thicken the turf of lawns in fair condition, use one pound (one quart by bulk) to each 600 square feet (10 x 60 ft. strip). Increase this if the lawn is in poor condition up to one pound to 250 square feet (10 x 25) for bare areas. Don't use seed unless it is guaranteed more than 98% weed free. The best seed is plainly labeled "Less than one-half of one per cent weed seed." Why plant weeds? The best is cheapest.

KIND OF SEED: It is not good judgment to sow only Blue Grass seed each year; nor is the person who buys a general mixture for renewal seeding each season laying the foundation of a green lawn all summer. As explained on pages 43 and 44 Blue Grass is brown and dormant in midsummer while Red Top goes dormant later after the Blue Grass revives. The one complements the other. Blue Grass is a perennial or permanent grass which takes two seasons to become established. Charts issued by Rutgers University show that Red Top becomes established at once but lasts only one season under lawn conditions. It is Red Top therefore, which dies out and needs the most frequent renewing each year. On new lawns we have recommended four parts Blue to one part Red Top. In well-established lawns this should be reversed to two parts Blue and three of Red Top. Vary to suit lawn condition. Rough-stalked Meadow Grass (Poa trivialis), which is the best sod forming shade grass, takes two seasons to become established.

LIME AND FERTILIZERS: Don't sprinkle your grass with lime because you have moss. Moss is a sign of poor, not sour soil. Lime has a tendency to encourage weeds. If your soil is hard and packed, apply a compost (see page 32) as early as possible and later use chemical lawn food. Wood ashes from the fireplace may be distributed thinly over the surface just as the grass starts growing. The ashes may also be mixed with the compost. A fertilizer spreader will distribute compost and various fertilizers economically. It will save its cost the first year, save your time and patience and probably mean the difference between a good lawn and a poor one.

WEEDS: Don't fail to get after weeds early. Dig out plantain and shallow rooted weeds but if you dig dandelions you will probably only cause them to multiply. (See pages 49–50.) Spray creeping weeds with sodium chlorate but be sure to (1) mix it outside, (2) wear old shoes and a rubber or sacking apron and leave all splattered clothing outside, (3) destroy all papers, sticks, etc., used in mixing and wash sprayer and mixing utensils thoroughly before bringing inside. Carefully used, it is safe and easy. Carelessly used, it is a fire hazard.

DRESSING: Don't fail to start some compost now for a summer dressing. Get a box or pit to compost soil and humus, peat or leafmold with bone meal. DON'T USE STABLE MANURE ON YOUR LAWN.

KNOW WHAT YOU ARE DOING: Read all of Chapter III. Regardless of whether parts of it apply to your lawn or not, read it all. You will find something pertinent in each paragraph.

FLOWERS

EQUIPMENT: At this time of the year a coldframe or forcing frame is almost a necessity. Plants may be started indoors by various means but many more can be started outdoors in a coldframe. Also the indoor plants must be hardened to the weather before being placed in permanent position. A coldframe is excellent to protect them from late frosts or cold, dank days. See page 276.

SEED SOWING: Most of the gardener's attention during the early spring is devoted to seeds and what to do about them. We may divide annuals into three general groups. (1) Those extremely hardy which may be planted outdoors. Some of these may be planted in the fall or even sow themselves. The names of such plants may be found in lists 23 and 24 on page 151. (2) Other plants

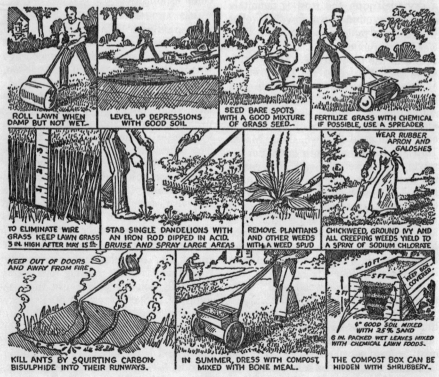

ROLL LAWN WHEN DAMP BUT NOT WET.

LEVEL UP DEPRESSIONS WITH GOOD SOIL

SEED BARE SPOTS WITH A GOOD MIXTURE OF GRASS SEED.

FERTILIZE GRASS WITH CHEMICAL IF POSSIBLE, USE A SPREADER

TO ELIMINATE WIRE GRASS KEEP LAWN GRASS 3 IN. HIGH AFTER MAY 15th.

STAB SINGLE DANDELIONS WITH AN IRON ROD DIPPED IN ACID. BRUISE AND SPRAY LARGE AREAS

REMOVE PLANTIANS AND OTHER WEEDS WITH A WEED SPUD

WEAR RUBBER APRON AND GALOSHES

CHICKWEED, GROUND IVY AND ALL CREEPING WEEDS YIELD TO A SPRAY OF SODIUM CHLORATE

KEEP OUT OF DOORS AND AWAY FROM FIRE

KILL ANTS BY SQUIRTING CARBON-BISULPHIDE INTO THEIR RUNWAYS.

IN SUMMER, DRESS WITH COMPOST MIXED WITH BONE MEAL.

10 FT
5 FT
2 FT
KEEP BOX COVERED
6" GOOD SOIL MIXED WITH 25% SAND
6 IN. PACKED WET LEAVES MIXED WITH CHEMICAL LAWN FOODS.

THE COMPOST BOX CAN BE HIDDEN WITH SHRUBBERY.

Some lawn work can be done in March to good advantage but much of the work is detrimental because it is started too early. Read lawn instructions given elsewhere in this Calendar.

are so tender that they should not be sown until all danger of frost is past. These are contained in list 20. (3) The last group requires a long time to mature and should be sown indoors in March or they will miss a lot of their best season. Some of these are contained in list 21.

Annuals are again divided into two general classes. Those which give a long period of bloom and those which require several sowings. The last mentioned are contained in list 25; many of them can be started indoors for early bloom followed by several sowings outdoors for later flowering. The perennials which bloom from seed the first year are usually planted in March. Some of these are contained in list 39, page 168.

SEEDS INDOORS: Many of us have become discouraged with seeds indoors, because we have not understood their needs. Instructions for planting will be found in the first part of Chapter XIX, page 282. The chief requirement is a high temperature (70–80) before germination followed by low temperature when growing. Light is not required until after the plants start to grow, so they should be well covered to keep them moist or placed next to the heating plant. After they germinate, they should be kept at a temperature of fifty degrees to make them stocky and healthy. High early growing temperatures make them shoot up too fast and they will acquire what is known as "legginess" which is top growth without sufficient roots to support them. This causes the plants to flop over and die.

The chief enemy of all seedlings indoors and out is a fungous disease known as damping-off. This is prevented by proper drainage, ventilation and, above all, the disinfecting of seeds and soil before a start is made. Small amounts of soil may be baked in an oven at a temperature over 212 degrees for two hours or the soil may be disinfected with preparations obtained at a seed store.

All receptacles must be thoroughly scrubbed. Seed flats can be scalded off with hot water or, better still, disinfected. New flower pots must be boiled to get the alkali out of them and soaked in water for several days. Old pots must be scoured inside and out. Enough seeds may be started in a five-inch pot to fill several trays when transplanted. Be sure you have enough room to transplant them properly and don't attempt too great a quantity or too many varieties.

Consult your germination chart on pages 296–97 for the length of time necessary to sprout each kind of plant. Plant the seeds which take the same time for germination so that they grow in the same receptacles. This will make the care much easier as you will thin them at the same time and avoid having large and small plants in the same tray. Sterilized soil germinates so many more plants from a packet of seeds that you may cut your seed order in half.

The seedlings may be kept in a little used bedroom, attic or hall to obtain the low temperatures necessary, but probably the best place to mature them is in a box made to hang outside a window so that it fits tightly to the frame and may be heated by raising the window and ventilated by manipulating the hinged sash top, which lets in the light to the plants.

Do not sow too thickly or you will lose many plants when thinning out. Also there is the danger of injuring the plants that you want to save because the roots become entangled. Thin them out early and then keep thinning them until you have the size you want.

Pinching off the stems while small helps plants such as Phlox, Petunia, Salpiglossis, Snapdragons, Chrysanthemums, Salvia, Scabiosa, Verbena, etc., to spread out into large bushy, strong-rooted plants.

Don't sow all of the seeds at once. Save some for further outdoor sowings and to guard against failure of the first batch.

PERENNIALS: Those perennials which need to be transplanted in the spring are mostly the ones which bloomed last fall. This is done as soon as the ground is dry enough to be readily handled. Never transplant when the soil is very wet. Chrysanthemums should be divided so that each sturdy shoot becomes a new plant. They benefit greatly from an entirely new location planted two or three feet apart. A new location often benefits many perennials. The hardy Sunflowers, the Phlox which was overlooked last fall, Sedums and other rank growing plants such as Daisies, Helenium, etc., should never be allowed to get out of bounds.

All perennials grow best from vigorous new plants. The process is explained in Chapter X. Do not divide Peonies or Gasplant without looking up the special instructions.

SWEET PEAS: The traditional time for planting Sweet Peas out of doors is March 17th. They require a rich deeply worked soil which contains clay but has excellent drainage. Extremely thin soils are not suitable as they dry out too quickly. Open sunny locations are best. The best plan is to prepare the trench deeply in autumn, mulch heavily to exclude frost and plant the seed in March. If this has not been done, however, dig trenches about two feet deep and the width of a spade. Fill the trench with good topsoil and manure well mixed and sow the seed about two inches below the surface. The young plants can be hilled up occasionally as they grow.

Seeds grown indoors in pots in an inch of sand on top of well drained soil, may be planted in this trench by moving the entire ball of earth without disturbing the roots. This may secure a blooming date three to six weeks prior

to the average. Outdoors, seeds may be sown one inch apart or even three inches apart, but they will have to be thinned to average not less than six inches apart when they begin to grow.

The flowers must be kept closely picked as the vine dies as soon as the seed pod forms. To facilitate the soaking of the soil which must be done at all times to the depth of eight to ten inches, a shallow trench should be allowed to remain. The plant is a deep rooter and will not thrive unless the trench is built as described. Feed every three and four weeks with plant food with a low nitrogen content, but high in phosphorus and potash. Seed may be treated in a 5% formaldehyde solution for five minutes to eradicate bacterial disease and dusting with a contact insecticide will take care of any aphids which appear.

ROCK GARDEN: Look it over often during the spring thaws to see that the tiny plants have not been heaved or washed out of the soil. When frost is past, see that they are firmly settled and well covered. Force some small stones about their crowns to hold them down.

BULBS AND ROOTS: Daffodils will soon be in bloom and it is not necessary to do very much about them, but the results from Tulips and Hyacinths will be endangered by freezing if they start too early. Loosen the mulch to keep them well covered and add some more mulch to those overvaliant shoots which insist on coming through. A cold night wind will dry them out and injure the bulb. The longer you hold them back with a loose airy mulch, the more sure you will be of the results later.

Cannas should be divided by cutting the eyes separately and rooting them in sharp sand or potting them in a light soil so that they may have an early start outdoors after all danger of frost is past.

Dahlia roots should be started into growth late in the month so that they may be easily divided or so that you may have cuttings made from them if you wish. Lay the roots upon a few inches of sand and water freely to start them into growth. Do not do this too early or give them too warm a temperature.

Be sure to burn over the Iris bed by following instructions in Chapter XII. Use care and judgment not to endanger the roots.

SANITATION: Look over the garden mulch when you remove it to see that it does not contain mildew or insect pests. Either dig it into the ground if it is fine enough, bury it in the compost heap or burn it. Be sure to spray Roses, Phlox and Delphinium with Bordeaux mixture before growth starts and dust thereafter at regular ten-day intervals, using Massey Dust (pages 258–59 or a similar formula. It is remarkable what this will do to eliminate mildew, black spot and many kindred diseases.

ROSES: In the Rose garden, the hardy Polyantha, Hybrid Perpetual and Rambler Roses can be pruned of dead and broken branches the latter part of the month, but the tender Hybrid Tea Roses should be left until later before being either pruned or uncovered. The best time to prune or uncover Roses is just before they start to bud out.

HOUSE PLANTS

STARTING PLANTS: The following is a list of plants which should be started in February or March for use indoors: Asparagus, Tuberous Begonia, Calceolaria, Cineraria, Dracaena, Fuchsia, Geranium, Gloxinia, Pot Primulus, Saintpaulia (African Violet), Smilax, Solanum (Cleveland Cherry). Special instructions will be found in various parts of the book for these. Also consult your seed catalogue.

CARE: The suggestions contained in February Calendar are still to be applied to the tired plants indoors at this time. More care is required now than at

any other time because they are greatly weakened by their long season under unnatural conditions.

FORCING: We discussed in Chapter XXVI the forcing of flowering branches which will work even better now, but at this season many of the spring blooming plants may be forced by bringing them indoors in clumps. Select a day when the ground is still frozen but not hard enough to prevent you from digging out clumps of Dwarf Iris, Violets, Crocus, Scillas and a few other bulbs to be planted in bowls or pots. Water them well, have good drainage and remember to keep them cool at first so that they may acclimate themselves to indoor conditions. The cooler you keep them, the longer they will last.

GREENHOUSE AND COLDFRAME

CONSTRUCTION AND USE: Details for constructions of coldframes are given on pages 276 to 281. The various types illustrated will give wonderful results from the temporary coldframe fitted over the cellar window to the more elaborate one heated by steam pipes. Electricity now comes to our rescue with some low price cables which, equipped with a thermostat, maintain an even temperature in all weather. Complete instructions are furnished by the manufacturers and it is well for you to consult your local electric company if you are interested. The types which are placed where some additional heat can be given, get a much earlier use but even the ones which are constructed in a sheltered place away from winds can be covered with mats at night and produce plants much sooner and with greater safety than can be obtained by sowing in the open with the consequent danger of frost. Their construction is simple and we recommend them both for starting seeds and hardening off those grown indoors.

The forcing of clumps of bulbs, Violets, etc., is very easily done in a frame.

If preparation is made in the fall you may have Pansies, Narcissus, Primulas, Wallflowers and all the early spring bulbs in bloom long before they appear in the open. You have only to bank the frame with manure and cover it with a mat to have them a month ahead of time even if winter still howls outside.

CUTTINGS: The list of uses to which a greenhouse or heated coldframe can be put is too long to enumerate here. Cuttings of all the various types of bedding plants should be started in sand early this month. Coleus, Geraniums, Lantana, Heliotrope, Ageratum, etc., are some of those which come under this general heading and are suitable for many situations. Chrysanthemums for next fall must be propagated at this time, if the space is available. It is good practice to put in a batch of cuttings every four weeks from now until early June so as to assure a long period of bloom that will extend well into the autumn.

SUMMER CARE: Better make the necessary arrangements now to use your greenhouse for some useful purpose this summer, instead of leaving it idle. Potted fruits, Chrysanthemums, Melons, English forcing Cucumbers, etc., are some of the many possible products which will be worth while.

SOIL: The soil in the greenhouse bed should be top-dressed with equal parts of turfy loam and sheep manure. This should be scratched into the upper soil with rake or claw and thoroughly watered.

DISBUDDING: Roses, Carnations and many other plants must be kept disbudded if you want high quality flowers and the maximum period of bloom. It is important that this be attended to when the buds are small, in order to conserve the strength of the plants and concentrate it on the production of blossoms.

VINES, TREES AND SHRUBS

PLANTING: Move or plant any shrubs as early as you can work the ground without trying to plant them with frozen clumps of soil. If you are transplanting budded stock, see that the buds are several inches under the ground to avoid suckers from the foster plant. Now is the last chance to safely and easily plant hedges, grapes, evergreens, dormant Roses, etc.

NEW PLANTS: If you are not ready to plant the new nursery stock as soon as it arrives, lay the plants slanting in a shallow trench and cover the roots deeply with soil. See page 56. Treated in this way both shrubs and trees may be kept in good condition for several weeks if absolutely necessary. Whether you are planting new stock or moving the old, see that roots are not dried out by wind or sun and that you do not plant any broken or bruised roots.

VINES: Look over the large permanent vines. Do your pruning and paint and repair the supports. If you are going to have your house painted this year, do something about your vines before their foliage develops. Either give them temporary support until your painting operation is over or arrange for a permanent support separate from the house.

COVERS: Do you remember the years when your flowering shrubs were killed by frost? Why not protect early flowering plants? Sew together some pieces of burlap sacking, or better still, some cheap unbleached muslin. Have this in pieces about 10 ft. long by 6 ft. wide. Throw them over the bushes on the nights that frost threatens and preserve the bloom for future enjoyment. Preserve the covers to use upon Chrysanthemums, Zinnias, Dahlias, Asters, etc., next fall.

PLANNING AND WORKING IN APRIL

A flower leaps to life—the quiet clod
  Has uttered music; noiselessly a tree
Flings forth green song; beauty whispers
    to the listening heart
And stars are vocal with tranquillity.
—*Adapted from a poem by* MARY HALLET.

The gardening fever is at its height by April, but there is still need for caution. Mulches should be removed with care and a little at a time. All beds should be carefully raked over, working the finer parts of the mulch into the ground and putting the balance in the bottom of the compost pile.

Get at the bottom of the compost pile and remove the oldest and most rotted parts to mix up for soil compost. This, forced through a screen, makes the best dressing for covering seeds. Early in the month begin to prepare the seed beds by digging them and letting them settle. Turn under the cover crops which you planted last year. Be careful to do all digging when the ground is fairly dry so that you will not destroy its structure. Break up all clumps so that they will not dry out and bake, causing you trouble later. See the illustration on page 391, and read Chapters II and XIX before doing your planting.

PESTS

Get a supply of spray materials on hand for the bugs and diseases which are sure to make their appearance even in the best of gardens. Supplies of Bordeaux mixture, arsenate of lead, nicotine sulphate, dusting sulphur and tobacco dust should be on hand. See that your sprays and dust guns are working.

As previously instructed, look over your trees and shrubs before they come out in leaf. Destroy any caterpillar egg masses before they hatch. If your cedars develop brown galls, destroy them at once as they produce spores that spread the disease to apple trees.

Wrap the trunks of newly planted trees (especially the smooth bark type) with burlap or kraft paper made for the purpose, to prevent sunscald. Fasten securely with twine at the top and bottom.

Spraying for various things now will save a lot of energy later. Spray Phlox, Delphinium, Larkspur, Aconites, Foxgloves, Hollyhocks and Roses with Bordeaux mixture before the foliage starts and then dust them with Massey Dust at least twice a month all summer, to prevent mildew. Get the bag worms this year by spraying the evergreens with arsenate of lead, during the latter part of the month. For red spider on Juniper and Arborvitae start dusting with Massey Dust, using a dust gun. Be sure to get the under-side of branches and repeat in about thirty days. If you have used miscible oil for a dormant spray as previously suggested, wait until about the first of May before using sulphur. For the blood louse on pines, spray with nicotine sulphate and some arsenate of lead mixed with mild soapsuds as a spreader. Oak and Elm trees should be sprayed early with arsenate of lead solution for canker and leaf rollers. Watch your Elms if the leaves were badly eaten last year. Another infestation this season may kill them.

LAWN

The care of the lawn was pretty well covered in the March Calendar but we show another picture on page 395. Read Chapter III on lawns and don't forget to read all of it, as many of the things which apply to lawn making also apply to the care of an established lawn. One of the best things to do for a lawn is to top dress it several times a year. If you have not been able to make a compost as previously recommended, purchase some good rich loam. Mix with this a liberal quantity of bone meal and scatter it evenly over the surface. Do this early so that it will wash down into the grass before mowing time and save wear and tear on your mower blades. Commercial humus is also a good dressing for the lawn, although hard to get in some localities. It will be worth your while to locate a supply of this at a reasonable price. Roll the surface of your lawn when it is fairly dry and springy to smooth it out.

HOUSE PLANTS

REPOTTING: Many of the house plants need repotting at this time. Place them out of doors during the day and help them recuperate from the hardships of the winter. Palms, Rubber Plants, Dracaenas and all other foliage plants usually need renewal, especially if they have outgrown their pots.

AFRICAN VIOLETS: Most plant lovers have trouble with African Violets. This plant has the advantage of tolerating ordinary room temperatures but is quite temperamental in other ways. It requires plenty of water but none of it must touch the hairy leaves or it will cause them to decay, so all watering must be done from below. It is bad practice to keep water in the saucers of most house plants but here it is an absolute necessity for healthy growth. Never let the water out of the saucer. They do best in a western window where there is plenty of fresh air and no drafts. Do not allow the foliage to come in contact with the glass or woodwork. They bloom continuously for about four months and then rest four months before flowering again. Do not attempt to stimulate them during their rest period. They require fairly rich soil. No attempt should be made to separate the roots. Transplant only when you are sure they are potbound. They suffer easily from root shock, and transplanting is quite a setback.

STARTING THE FLOWERS

PREPARATION: Prepare to dust all plants which are subject to disease. Be sure they are clean of old leaves, stalks and rubbish. Remove all dead foliage around them. Don't forget to spray at ten-day intervals with Massey Dust.

FERTILIZING: Bone meal is one of the best and safest all-round fertilizers. For quick growth use the finest grade, usually called "Bone Flour." When applying it, mix in some of the coarser raw bone which will support the plants later in the season. A little balanced plant food is good after the plants have attained some growth, but use it carefully. It is best applied in liquid form and two tablespoons to a gallon of water is sufficient. Although the plants need this in small quantities, while they are making leaves and stalks, they will need it more at blooming time. If you have liquid manure, use this at blooming time instead of chemical fertilizer. Wood ashes may be scattered on the lawn with real benefit. The potash that they contain is also beneficial to Roses, all bulbs and root plants. Scatter it thinly—don't overdo.

CULTIVATION: All borders or open spaces around plants should be kept loosened with a fork or cultivating hoe. It is extremely beneficial to the soil to admit the air and also to form a dust mulch which prevents rapid evaporation of moisture and nitrates. After July 1st the borders may be mulched with peat or other suitable material, if desired, but until then keep them open.

MARKING: One of the tedious jobs of the garden is to keep the plants marked. Permanent labels suggested in Chapter XXV will make this task lighter. Markers are inexpensive and a good gardener should know everything that grows in his garden.

SEEDS: See that the ground is well prepared and work in some well-rotted manure, if possible. If not obtainable, use leafmold, homemade compost or peat moss. See that beds are carefully prepared and disinfected before seeds are planted. Place the large ones by hand and sow the small ones mixed with sand. Soak Nasturtiums and others before planting. (See February Calendar.) Sow thinly in rows. Unless they are covered with burlap so that the seeds will not be disturbed, keep the soil constantly stirred between the rows, having first marked them with string. Be sure they are labeled with durable labels. If covered with burlap, destroy weeds between the rows as soon as the cloth is

removed. Thin the plants ruthlessly. A seedling cannot flourish when crowded. Protect such tender plants as Poppies from being trampled or blown down by some light brush placed over the beds as soon as they germinate.

TIME OF SOWING: Seedlings started indoors should be gradually accustomed to outdoor conditions to harden them off. Some seeds to be sown outdoors the first half of the month are Snapdragons, Asters, Alyssum, Calendula, Centaurea, Pansies, Violas, Scabiosa, Mignonette, Dianthus, Poppy, Cosmos, Gypsophila, Nasturtium, Annual Phlox, Verbena and

BEFORE SPADING COVER GROUND WITH SAND, PEAT OR LEAF MOULD

SPADE DEEPLY—THE ANGLE OF THE SPADE DETERMINES CULTIVATION

DON'T DO THIS! WORKING GROUND WHEN WET PUDDLES THE SOIL AND DESTROYS CRUMB STRUCTURE

START AT TOP OF A SLOPE AND CAST EARTH UPGRADE

ALL CLODS MUST BE PULVERIZED AS SPADING IS DONE

LEVEL CAREFULLY WITH A RAKE

TOP DRESS THE BED WITH COMPOST WHICH IS PRESSED THROUGH A SIEVE WITH A RUBBING BOARD

MARK ROWS WITH LATH—USE SEEDS SPARINGLY—PLACE LARGE SEEDS BY HAND.

PLANT SMALL SEEDS DIRECT FROM PACKAGE OR MIX VERY SMALL SEEDS WITH SAND.

COVER SMALL SEEDS LIGHTLY WITH SIFTED SOIL.

FIRM SOIL GENTLY WITH A BLOCK OF WOOD AND LABEL ALL ROWS.

COVER SOIL WITH WET BURLAP UNTIL SEEDS ARE UP—DO ALL WATERING THROUGH BURLAP

Soil conditioning, as explained in Chapter II, should be studied by everyone before attempting to prepare the seed bed out of doors. This is really April work but many try to do it in March. Don't be in too big a hurry or you will dig the ground when wet and run the chance of puddling the soil and ruining its structure. See page 29. Dig in the conditioning materials as deeply as possible and pulverize thoroughly. Use labels of celluloid on sticks as shown here or of zinc or wood. Paper never makes a good label. Remember seeds stop germinating when they dry out even for a day and may be attacked by a fungus which causes them to rot off at the soil surface unless the soil is well drained. Disinfect both seed and soil. See page 260, and consult your seed catalogue or seed store. It is marvelous what a difference this makes.

Ageratum. Be sure to protect the germinated plants from late frost. Marigolds should be planted late in the month and sowing of Sweet Alyssum should be made twice a month until July. Snapdragons, Annual Phlox, Verbenas and Ageratum do best if sown in the hotbed or coldframe. Much more information will be gained by a study of the plant lists starting with page 140. Don't overlook the value of portable forcing frames at this time of year. See page 280.

PERENNIALS: When you have uncovered the border see what new plants are needed. Dig under some good manure and give the bed a good dressing of raw crushed bone. Annuals should be planted between the younger clumps which are yet to fill out. You may now divide such plants as Delphinium, Helenium, Anemone japonica, Fall Asters, Ceratostigma and Shasta Daisy. Divide Chrysantheums as early as possible. Each small division will make a blooming plant by autumn if planted in good location and soil. Phlox and Michaelmas Daisies should be divided and only the live parts of the outer ring saved. When weather becomes settled, set out the plants which have been wintered in a coldframe: Pansies, Forget-me-not, Daisies, Canterbury Bells, Aquilegias, Foxgloves, etc. Rampant plants which try to overrun the gardens such as Achillea, Goldenglow, Boltonia, etc., should be thinned out so that those left will have room for new growth.

BULBS: Uncover the spring flowering bulbs carefully and get ready to plant the summer flowering varieties. Gladiolus may be planted about the middle of May for early flowering effect and continue plantings every ten days. Use methods advised on pages 192 and 193. Many summer flowering plants of easy culture are overlooked. Try some of them this year, planting them with a quantity of bone meal. Among the many to be recommended are Tuberoses, Galtonias, Summer-hyacinths, Montbretias, Hardy-amaryllis, Tigridia and Ismene calathina. Be sure to look up their culture before planting. Most of them need the same culture as Gladiolus. Plant the Gladiolus cormels, taken off when you cleaned the bulbs, in nursery rows in some secluded corner. They will become blooming plants next year.

DELPHINIUMS: Apply plenty of bone meal and humus after they start to grow. Any division of the plant may be made now. Three year old plants should be divided as soon as growth appears. Set out new plants in a loose, sandy loam, moderately limed—be sure it is well drained. Dust around the plant crowns with dry Bordeaux mixture. Remove all dead or weak shoots and water abundantly.

IRIS: Use bone meal and wood ashes on Iris but do not overdo. The bearded varieties profit from a dusting of lime. Do not use lime on the beardless or fibrous rooted varieties. Use leafmold or humus mixed with a little tankage.

HERBS: Small fragrant herbs used for flavoring, such as Thyme, Dill, Sage, Marjoram, etc., should be sown in open spots in the border.

ROSES: Wait until the buds are about to appear and then prune the Hybrid Tea Roses to three eyes but leave about four inches of wood on the Teas. Remember pruning of roses is largely to develop new wood and to make them grow so that there will be open air and sunlight in the center. Prune to buds which point towards the outside of the plants. The new wood will grow from these in the right direction. The weaker the Rose, the more it needs pruning. The first of April is about the best time in spring to plant dormant roses. Heap soil or peat moss around the newly planted bushes and keep it there for about two weeks. Remove it on a cloudy day. This prevents the bottom of the canes from drying out until the roots have a chance to take hold.

JAPANESE MORNING GLORY: Almost everyone wants to raise the beautiful Japanese Morning Glories, the most popular of which seems to be the "Heavenly Blue." They are best started indoors in pots, first having very lightly notched the seed (away from the scar) with a file and soaked it over night to soften the outer coating. Keep well-watered until four leaves are formed and then transplant into a large flower pot. Stake each plant and leave in a sunny window until it grows a foot and a half.

It must not be set out until all danger of frost is past. When this is done, crack the pot before placing it in the ground, but do not break it. The restriction of roots causes the plant to bloom better than if they are allowed to sprawl which seems to encourage leaves without flowers. The blooming type of plants will show round flower buds at the base of each leaf about the time you are ready to set them out. In the greenhouse they will probably be in bloom by that time. You can easily distinguish the flower buds from sprouting branches, as they appear. The flower buds are little balls, while the new side sprouts show pointed ends. The buds show singly at first, but later come in clusters.

The plants which show no round buds are the ones which usually run to leaves and often, in spite of best culture and restricted roots, will not bloom. It is best to plant enough seed so that these may be discarded, but if they are planted outdoors and do not bloom, you may be able to force them by cutting them back to a foot or so of the ground after they have achieved good growth.

In most localities the seed may be planted directly outside about the middle of May (earlier in the South) in soil dug to a depth of eighteen inches and made light with sand, fertilized with bone meal and cow manure. After they are up, set eight inches apart and fasten by soft string to the permanent support. About the first of July, cover the bed with several inches of peat moss and every day or two spray the vines until they are dripping wet. While they require a great deal of food and moisture, they do not like chemical fertilizer. Acid phosphate is sometimes used but other kinds seem to turn the leaves yellow and cause loss of the buds. Rich, well-drained soil and rotted manures are best. Nicotine sulphate will control aphis.

Planted indoors, they will probably bloom in June, otherwise they will be much later. Their color changes almost hourly in shades of blue with the various conditions which they meet. The blossoms unfold in the morning but if the sun strikes them when wet or if watered when hot, they disappear. New blossoms come each day in startling procession. Only good seeds give best results.

SOIL TESTING: Many plants have a decided perference as to the degree of acidity in the soil. Soil can be easily changed to suit the needs of the plants and their successful culture enhanced. All that is needed is the knowledge. This can be gained by the use of a soil-testing outfit for sale at seed stores. Its operation is non-technical and a kit, which can be had for about $2.00, usually contains a booklet of instruction.

TREES AND SHRUBS

EARLY PLANTING: Early planting is best for woody stock. Try to get all deciduous trees and shrubs planted before foliage starts. The exception is the Magnolia, which should be transplanted during May while it is in leaf. Evergreens should be set early so that there will be plenty of rain while they are establishing themselves. Stake and wire all newly planted trees to prevent them from swaying in high winds. Don't neglect new stock—liberal watering once a week in dry weather is essential and a heavy mulching of manure a little later is excellent. Do not remove stakes or guy wires until the plant is thoroughly established.

WHAT TO PLANT: Trees and shrubs that prefer spring planting are Birches, Magnolias, Tulip Trees, Sweet Gums, Japanese Maples, Large-flowering Dogwoods, Altheas, Flowering Almonds, Ornamental Cherries, Peaches, Buddleias, Hawthorns, Rhododendrons and Weigelas.

PRUNING: If you have not already done so, prune grape vines and orchard fruits at once. Box and Privet hedges should be trimmed before they start into growth. Young Dogwoods that have died back are fairly sure to send up new shoots, if cut back to the ground—prune and train them as shrubs. Evergreens in need of shaping and thickening may be sheared advantageously as the new growth gets under way. Prune back the Hydrangeas as directed in February Calendar and cut Spirea Anthony Waterer close to the ground to stimulate new growth. After the plants are out in leaf you may be able to find indications of weakness. Cut back the weak plants and fertilize well for a fresh start. Fertilize all trees and shrubs while they are coming out in leaf and see that they do not lack for water. If pruning of your early flowering shrubs is necessary, prepare to do it soon after they have bloomed. Forsythia is probably the earliest one. Rub water sprouts from fruit and other trees.

FERTILIZE: Roses and all other shrubs will benefit from a top dressing of bone meal applied now and scratched in lightly. Clean and pleasant to handle, bone meal may be called the safe fertilizer. Its effects will be apparent a month or more from now. If you had a tree or shrub which did not do so well last year, start feeding it now by one of the processes described in Chapter IV

and illustrated on page 63. Trees and shrubs put forth a tremendous effort when they manufacture such a large amount of foliage in so short a time. See that they have a plentiful supply of water and nitrates. For a sickly tree it may be well to dig a shallow trench in a ring under the outer spread of the branches and fill it with compost together with some chemical fertilizer or manure.

FRUITS: Begin to care early for your fruit plants. Watch the currant bushes and spray with arsenate of lead to kill the currant worms while they are small and first appear upon the leaves. It is almost impossible to raise currants without spraying. The roots of grape vines are close to the surface. Be careful not to damage them in cultivating at this time of year. Scratch in lightly some bone meal and mulch with cow manure.

PUSSY WILLOW: If you have sprays of Pussy Willows in the house, they will probably have made roots in the water. Later in the month plant them outdoors in a damp spot and they will eventually form bushes.

RHODODENDRONS: All broad-leaved evergreens may be fertilized or top-dressed with peat moss or rotted sawdust, but do not remove the windbreaks until strong spring winds are past. Prepare the mulch to be renewed in May. Composting in advance helps it. See pages 95–98.

GREENHOUSE AND COLDFRAME

REPAIR: Late April is a good time to start repairing. Broken glass should be replaced and loose glass reset. All wood framework should be painted now. Best results with painting are obtained during mild weather. After the sun becomes hot, painting on a warm surface dries out the oils too quickly and injures the protecting film. Have all surfaces thoroughly dry before applying paint. Spring and fall painting are always best.

HARDENING: Start hardening off the bedding plants in the greenhouse or frame. It is certain death to set out Coleus, Geraniums, etc., unless they have been gradually accustomed to the marked change in temperature. Give more and more cool, fresh air to them each pleasant day.

INDIVIDUAL POTS: Many flowering plants as well as vegetables are easily started indoors in individual paper pots or wooden bands sold for the purpose. These are made square to fit into trays so that they may be set outside without disturbing the roots by merely unfolding the bottom. Many of the home garden crops may be matured a month earlier by this process. Early Sweet Corn, Beans, Egg Plant, Okra, Pepper and Tomatoes work well this way. Fill the pots with rich compost, one-third old crumbly manure and two-thirds good soil and add a little sand if it is heavy. Plant twice as many seeds as you want and thin them as soon as they are well started. Water thoroughly a day in advance of planting and water sparingly before the plants are up. Plant Lima beans with the eye down. Withhold water (after soaking soil) until germination starts or they will rot. Do not set out any of these plants until the ground has warmed up. Stake them until they become firm in the soil.

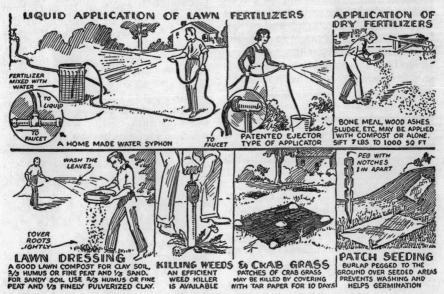

Fertilizers and lawn dressings are specially needed in April. They thicken the grass and exclude weeds as well as prepare for summer. Chemical fertilizers are easily measured and evenly applied in liquid form. Any dry applications to the lawn should be washed off the grass blades to avoid burning and injury to mower blades. Patches in the lawn may be seeded late in the season by covering with cheesecloth or burlap to preserve the necessary moisture. The notched peg permits a gradual exposure to air and sun after germination.

THE HOME GARDEN IN MAY

Happy the man, whose wish and care
A few parental acres bound,
Content to breathe his native air
In his own ground. . . .
—POPE'S ODE TO SOLITUDE.

GENERAL

We hope you have your tools ready and on hand to keep up the appearance of your garden during the summer. With the proper tools, the walks may be edged in a very few minutes, whereas a knife, hatchet or something of the sort will take half a day and not do such a good job. A one-wheel lawn mower is an excellent thing to use around the garden beds and close to the walls, while a grass whip swung like a golf club and cutting both ways allows us to get close to the fences and shrubbery without stooping. If you have a vegetable garden, investigate the wheel hoe—it is well worth while. Flowers which are staked early in the season are easy to train and also make disease more easily detected. Weed killers used on walks and drives, while the weeds are young, will prevent a great deal of damage and hard work later.

It is always well to have a supply of straw or other mulch handy as a guard against late killing frosts. Investigate the cloth covers which we mentioned in the March and April calendars. They come in handy almost all season.

Everything that is being transplanted, from tiny seedlings to young trees, must have its roots protected against drying while out of the ground. Unless this is done, these highly sensitive and vital parts will be severely injured if not killed. Transplant on cloudy days.

Have a supply of liquid manure readily accessible for use on weak plants and to increase the size of blooms. If you use a barrel, see that it is carefully covered with fine screen or it will be a breeding place for mosquitoes. Our illustration on page 193 shows the use of an ash can. The tight-fitting lid keeps away flies and mosquitoes and enables the can to do double duty all season. Get some dry manure from your seedsman if other supplies are not available.

PESTS

Don't wait for the leaf-eating insects to chew up your plants but start the poison spray (stomach poison) which will take care of them. Currant bushes, Gooseberries, Elms, Cherries, and, in fact, all trees and shrubbery should have at least one application of arsenate of lead, as soon as they are out in leaf. This does not involve great expense. With the exception of tall trees, a small pump sprayer with various nozzles and an extension rod will enable you to do the work single handed. Be sure to spray the underside of the leaves. In dry weather you may be troubled with the green fly and other plant lice—nicotine sulphate or tobacco solution is the remedy. Don't think these pests are harmless. They suck the juice of the plant and seriously weaken it. They are generally found working on the softest, most tender leaves or buds.

Keep up the use of Massey Dust on evergreens, Roses and perennials which are subject to mildew—Delphinium, Hollyhock, Phlox, Chinese Larkspur, etc. Should the mildew get out of hand, spray it every ten days with Bordeaux mixture, five teaspoons to one gallon of water, or use the dry powder on the leaves.

Mealy bugs are a scourge of house and greenhouse plants and many times become troublesome in the garden. These white cotton-like insects are often found on soft-stemmed plants such as

Coleus, Fuchsia, Begonia, Ferns, Gardenias and succulents. In the greenhouse they are controlled by fumigating but outside the remedy is a fine spray applied with as much force as possible. Control is by spraying with a nicotine-soap or pyrethrum-soap solution which is said to work best at 120° F. This temperature does not injure the plants but combined with the soap it helps to penetrate the wax coating which protects the bodies of the insects.

Glue is often used for red spider on evergreens and perennials. It is a good remedy if washed off with a hose in a day or so. Combine one pound of ordinary ground glue dissolved in ten gallons of water with one-half pound of wettable sulphur. Speaking of sulphur, ask your seedsman about the sulphur spray material which comes in tubes much as does tooth paste and shaving cream.

LAWNS

Good lawns are the result of liberal fertilization and frequent care. We have covered this subject thoroughly in the past two calendars but a good appearance will be kept up only by constant attention. Seed the bare spots as soon as they appear. In hot weather cover with a cloth as shown in the April calendar. Do not sprinkle the lawn. Wet it once in a while if it needs it. Frequent sprinklings cause much loss. Newly seeded lawns should be cut high until the grass begins to grow vigorously and thickens.

The eradication of crab grass should be started in the middle of the month. Shading is one successful method. (See pages 48 and 49.)

Fairly short mowing in the spring is beneficial to the grass. After May 15th it should be kept mowed at three inches high. It makes a better appearance, shades the crab grass seed and keeps it from germinating, retards the evaporation of moisture and nitrates by keeping the surface of the soil cool during hot

weather and crowds out weeds which flourish in hot soil.

HOUSE PLANTS

Read carefully the directions for re-potting, commencing with page 313. Examine your plants to see if they need attention before being set outdoors for summer recuperation. Also read summer care on page 315.

Tubbed plants of all kinds may be taken from their winter quarters and moved into place now that danger of real frost is past. They should be given liquid manure and, as growth becomes active, loosen the surface of the soil in their containers. Keep well watered. Bring out the Poinsettias to start them into growth (see January calendar) and dry out Callas so they can rest on their sides in the shade during the summer.

WITH THE FLOWERS

MARKING: The importance of proper labeling is felt very often in the spring. The areas in the perennial border in which the late maturing plants are placed are often dug up, ruining the plants. The Japanese Anemones, Japanese Bell-flowers (Platycodons), Hosta, (such a useful plant in shade) Bleeding-heart, Blue Mertensia and some of the tiny bulbs are easily killed by a little probing with the cultivating tool. The areas of such plants should be permanently marked to avoid this loss. While you are at it, start permanent markings for the other plants while they are in flower and easily identified. It adds much to the joy of the garden, as well as the satisfaction of your visitors.

PLANTING SEEDS: Plant only when the ground is workable. Read the March and April calendars. Consult plant lists on pages 139 to 168. There is still time to plant out many of the favorite annuals, but do not delay it—summer will soon be here. Prepare the ground thoroughly, although annuals do not need the deep cultivation which must be given for perennials. Continue to sow Sweet Alyssum and Candytuft for edging. Seeds of all the tender annuals may be sown now—Impatiens, Amaranth, Gomphrena, Celosia, Gaillardia, Browallia, Petunia, Portulaca, Torenia, Zinnia. These will replace the Pansies, English Daisies, Lobelias, and other very early annuals, now growing shabby. Thin and transplant those already set out and do not let them dry out or suffer from late frosts.

FLOWERING VINES: Plant vines to cover fences and garages: Coral Vine (Antigonon leptopus); Ipomea leari, the Heavenly Blue Morning-glory; the various Jasmines, white and yellow; Clematis paniculata, Solanum jasminoides, and the many annual climbers. Directions for some of these and many others will be found on page 114.

GOURDS: Sow the seeds of Gourds in late May or early June in the sun and in light loam, enriched with very old stable manure. Ten seeds to the hill, where they are to grow, for they do not transplant well. Provide some support as they grow ten feet high.

POTTED ANNUALS: To transplant seedlings from flat or pot into the open ground, loosen carefully the rootlets which have made tight little wads, so that they will be in condition to take up food and water. Dig a hole the full length of the plant's roots, place it in position, fill the hole half full of water, throw in soil to make soft mud about the roots, then fill the upper half of the hole with dry soil and water no more. By this method there will be no moisture on the surface of the ground for the sun to bake or steam. For a few days keep the plants covered with flower pots or strawberry baskets during the day to prevent evaporation from the leaves by sun or wind, removing the protection at night. To insure a stocky growth remove the central bud at the top of the plant when it is six inches tall. Calendulas, Ageratum, Snap-dragons, Stocks, Marigolds, Drummond Phlox, Alyssum and Petunias are types needing such treatment. Poppies, Asters and Nicotiana are best left alone.

PERENNIAL REPLACEMENT: You can now see what you need in the way of replacement. Secure hardy clumps and select a cool cloudy day for planting. Better to hold the plants for a day or so than to plant them in heat and wind. A newly set plant must develop its roots before it can support top growth. Keep the plants shaded if the weather is warm. Newspapers may be used but all shade should be removed at night. Do not overcrowd—plant firmly—press the soil around the edges of the plant, rather than the top of the plant itself—spread the roots naturally and fill the spaces between them. Each root must be surrounded with soil free from air pockets. Set the crowns as they were in the nursery. Cultivate often. Never walk on the soil or cultivate when it is wet. Newly planted perennials must be watered regularly, in early morning or just before sundown.

PEONIES: They require an abundance of water while the buds are being formed. A large flower pot or a piece of four-inch farm tile sunk about a foot away from each Peony plant and covered with a stone, enables you to get water down where it is most needed. The flowers may be removed while in the bud and opened in water. Remove some of the buds to give larger flowers. Peonies should be staked before the buds start to weigh down the stalks. An encircling support is better than stakes. Do not neglect the plants after they have bloomed. They are preparing for next year. Read pages 204 to 206.

DAHLIAS: They may be planted as soon as the weather is settled. Don't forget to stake them when you plant. Doing so when they are ready for support may injure the roots. Read instructions, pages 189 to 191 and study page 192.

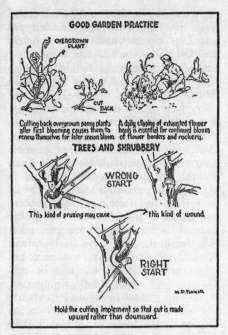

GOOD GARDEN PRACTICE

OVERGROWN PLANT

CUT BACK

Cutting back overgrown pansy plants after first blooming causes them to renew themselves for later season bloom.

A daily clipping of exhausted flower heads is essential for continued bloom of flower borders and rockery.

TREES AND SHRUBBERY

WRONG START

This kind of pruning may cause ——▶ this kind of wound.

RIGHT START

M.P.BAKER

Hold the cutting implement so that cut is made upward rather than downward.

GLADIOLUS: Start May 15th and plant every two weeks until July 10th to get bloom through to October. Study carefully instructions, pages 191 to 194.

MISCELLANEOUS BULBS: Get the summer flowering blubs into the ground before the end of the month. Hardy Gloxinias, Cannas, Begonias, Tuberoses, etc. are very satisfactory. Feed the Darwin Tulips with liquid manure when they are in bud. Daffodils do not need to be disturbed for several years, but when any bulb is naturalized in the lawn the grass should not be cut until their leaves begin to turn yellow. Unless you follow instructions contained in the illustration on page 182, do not dig any spring flowering bulbs until the leaves ripen.

ASTERS: Before planting Asters of any kind apply wood ashes to the soil. Contrary to popular belief they do not thrive well in poor soil. Manure it well, dig it deeply and give it a finely raked finish. Plant seed in the rows two inches apart with the rows ten inches. Planting half

an inch deep will give later flowers but better plants. Best results are secured with seeds which have been treated for disease. The best is bichloride of mercury—a 15-grain tablet to one quart of water. Soak seeds for thirty minutes in the solution warmed to 90° F. Dry on a cloth at room temperature—not in sun nor near heat. Get early and late blooming varieties and set them out about May 15th. Apply liquid manure to the wet ground before and during bloom. Watch the soil for aphids or other pests and control by liberal applications of tobacco dust well worked in. For other insect control see pages 265–68.

PLANT LILIES IN MAY: Fall planting is best for most Lilies but Regal Lily (regale), Goldband Lily of Japan (auratum) and any of the Show Lilies (speciosum) do very well with early spring planting. See page 199 for directions.

COLUMBINE: Aquilegia is one of the most popular plants in the garden but many of us become discouraged with it because it disappears after the second year. It is a wise gardener who keeps a supply coming along from seed sown in a propagating bed in spring or early summer. April and May seem the best months for sowing as it is easier to keep the seed bed moist. Columbines like a light rich soil which must be moist but have good drainage. A heavy wet soil will not suit them at all. They grow fairly well in full sunlight but benefit from shade for a few hours during the heat of the day. If given this shade, they will grow larger and bloom over a longer period. Space them nine and ten inches apart and set them in fall or very early spring. They require very little attention as they have few insect pests. If they suffer dry weather, red spider sometimes attacks them but it can easily be controlled by a strong force of water or spraying with nicotine sulphate in the spring.

LUPINES: So many gardeners have

tried to raise Lupines without success that the plant has a name for elusiveness that it does not deserve. For years these beautiful, candlelike blooms would grow readily and lustily in some locations, but refuse to repeat under similar treatment in others.

The answer was found to be bacterial inoculation. Lupines, like clovers, alfalfa, beans, peas or other legumes have collections of nitrogen-bacteria called "nodules" upon their roots. All of these plants actually improve the soil for other plants by adding nitrogen instead of extracting it.

For such plants the presence of special bacteria is necessary. Just as alfalfa bacteria will not do for clover, a special one is needed for Lupines. Your seedsman may be able to supply it or you can introduce it in soil from a bed where Lupines are thriving. The plants are sturdy growers with colors rivaling the rainbow. They make fine companions for Delphiniums.

The best medium is a soil on the alkaline side but not too strong in limestone. For this reason leafmold, peat moss, and manures are dug deeply into the bed to provide the necessary conditions. Perfect drainage is a necessity.

The first summer seems to be the test. Once established, they grow quite freely but do not like moving about. The long tap roots make moving difficult even with quite young plants. Annual Lupines make the easier plants to grow in the garden and excellent greenhouse plants.

ROSES: You may take the protection completely off of Roses by the last of the month. Remember extreme vigilance is the price of a good garden—keep them dusted. A last-minute Rose garden can be made even now if you buy pot-grown plants. They can be transferred without much harmful root disturbance. Be sure that the soil into which they go is well-drained and rich, and keep them regu-larly watered during dry weather. Cultivate the Rose beds daily to kill the rose-bug larvae which are just below the soil surface until June, when they emerge as beetles. In the larval stage they are easily killed by any disturbance of the soil. Cultivate in April, May and early June and also work in to the top-soil an insecticide, such as tobacco dust.

ROCK GARDEN: Fertilize your rock garden before the end of the month and see that it is well weeded. All replacements should be made before May 15th. Among these consider the Wild Cyclamen for August interest. See that there are plenty of stones around the crowns of the plants. Almost any creeping plant whether in the rock garden or elsewhere likes to run over stones or stone chips.

STAKING: Whenever we think of staking we think of the biblical quotation, "Train up a child in the way he should go, etc." A plant staked early in its growth is much easier to handle than when it becomes a tangled mass later on. Nearly all tall flowers will benefit by staking against the pressure of high winds and heavy rains. This is particularly true of Larkspur, Hollyhocks, Foxgloves, Garden Heliotrope, Dahlias and Gladioli. Use strong stakes and tie firmly with raffia or soft coarse cord in several places. Small flowers also deserve attention. Old coat hangers cut into sections make excellent small plant supports. Bend two to four inches over at right angles at the proper distance from the ground and form into a semi-circle or cork screw so that the plant may be loosely encircled to keep it from being broken off in the wind. Galvanized wire can be used for the same purpose.

CUTTING: All annuals will bloom longer if they are clipped. Snip them off and let them fall if you do not need them for cut flowers. The flowering stalks of the Iris can be cut freely without injury to the plants if care is taken to leave plenty of foliage for the promotion of subsequent growth. The same thing applies to May-flowering Tulips, Peonies and later on, the Gladiolus plantings. Cut blossoming shrubs as well as perennials and annuals freely to prolong the blooming season. The best way to prune Spirea, Philadelphus, Deutzia, Weigela, Abelia, Japanese Quince, and climbing Roses is to cut long sprays to give to friends, the church, and the sick. Plumbago, Perennial Phlox, and the other perennials: Hollyhocks, Columbines, and the other biennials: Daisies, Pinks, Gypsophila, and the other annuals, will all bloom longer if cut freely. Don't let seeds form.

WINDOW BOXES: Some of the more serviceable plants to grow in window boxes besides the common Geraniums are Petunias, Verbenas, Ageratums, Lobelias, Begonias, Fuchsias (for partial shade), Lantanas, Browallias and Alyssums. See page 310.

STIMULATING: Do not stimulate plants until they are well advanced in growth. When foliage production seems to lag, give them a little nitrate of soda or balanced plant food. Just before the flowering season begins, it is good practice to top-dress the beds with fine bone meal, well raked in. Liquid manure just before blooming time will cause larger and more blooms on plants. Do not expect results from stimulation unless you have conditioned the soil to hold enough moisture to supply it regularly.

THE PERFECT MONTH OF JUNE

There's a day in June before us,
  Lustrous green and blue,
Winds like heartbeats pulsing o'er us
  Quick with rapture new.
                    —H. A. BELLOWS.

GENERAL

Among the most important things in June is cultivation. It is often better than watering. It is a good preventive of insect troubles and contributes greatly to the fertility of the soil. Work the soil deeply and often and you will find it pays. Be careful not to injure plant roots. In the straight rows of the vegetable garden, use a wheel hoe.

Don't neglect mulching your acid loving plants. The wild garden should also have slightly acid soil and be permanently mulched with needles from beneath your evergreens and last year's oak leaves. This yearly mulching with new material early in the summer, helps get them ready for next year's bloom.

The sun dial should be chosen according to the degree of latitude in which the garden is located. That which fits the garden in a distant city will not do for yours. The time to set this clock is on June 15th and place it so that the shadow falls on 12:00 o'clock at exactly noon on this date.

PESTS

More and more we hear of the progress of preventive medicine. This is also applicable to the garden. Don't wait until disease has weakened your plants before attempting the cure. We know that Delphiniums, Hollyhocks, Phlox, Roses and many others are subject to fungous troubles and, therefore, we dust them several times each month. Aphis may seem inconsequential on your plants but they are sucking the juices and should be removed with a nicotine spray or dust.

Rose beds may harbor the grubs or larvae of a swarm of Rose bugs. Frequent cultivation until July 1st is the answer. A tablespoon of sulphate of iron scattered around each bush and worked into the soil will help. The same goes for Peonies and Magnolias. When once you have the brown beetles, which mutilate Rose and Magnolia blossoms, do not use poison sprays. Eradicate by knocking them into a can of kerosene.

Black spot on Roses and other leaf blights on perennials are difficult diseases to cure. Started off right and dusted, as previously instructed, your plants will not have them unless they come from new additions to your garden. Such infection is not incurable if plants are sprayed with Bordeaux and all foliage is kept off the ground where it might pick up infection. First dust the ground well with dry Bordeaux and treat with iron sulphate as previously prescribed. Water well and cover the entire bed with tar paper or, better still, mulch paper from your seed store. Fit tightly about each plant allowing sheets to overlap. Turn up the edges to form a saucer and each day carefully remove all fallen foliage. This is a chief cause of the spread of the disease. Continue to spray until cured but keep the paper on all season and continue to remove leaves. Holes with flaps for watering can be made near each plant and the paper can be turned up for an occasional ground cultivation or areation. Do not water at night.

Don't think that ants in your garden are harmless creatures. They harbor aphides which they use to produce food. Drive them away by cultivation, spreading poison or any of the other methods previously suggested.

Arsenate of lead is an effective remedy for leaf chewers. Mix it with mild soapsuds to make it spread. The leaves of all trees and shrubbery should have at least one application of it after they come out in full foliage. Use it on the evergreens to prevent bag worms, but do it as early as possible.

Moles disfigure our lawns and are blamed for eating bulbs and roots. The truth is that these little animals go through the ground searching for earth worms and bugs and in so doing, make run-ways which mice and other pests use to do the damage which is often attributed to the moles. Eradication is described on page 51. Use gloves to set traps and apply all poisons. Human scent scares them away. Tobacco dust or even stems scattered over the surface of the ground or, better still, worked into it, may drive away these pests as they cannot endure the smell.

Poison ivy at this season begins to become a great nuisance. We quote the following from the "House Beautiful" magazine. "No foliage is lovelier in its fresh green than poison ivy, springing up as it does in most unexpected places, but every inch is harmful to the average person. Small plants may be killed out in a few weeks by covering them closely with boards or heavy paper weighted down, a smothering process. Sodium chlorate applied like a weed killer, two pounds dissolved in a gallon of water and sprayed on the vines and poured around the roots will eradicate the menace, or dry powder may be sprinkled on the leaves when they are wet with dew in the morning. If anyone can be found to cut the vines down from tree or wall the destruction will be quicker, for the brush may be burned (keep out of the smoke!) and the roots killed by the chemical. Wear gloves at all times, and to protect the skin, bathe any exposed parts with a five per cent solution of ferric chloride added to a mixture of equal parts of water and glycerine, letting it dry on. A medical preventive, rhus tox, may be taken at poison ivy season. Sodium chlorate preparations can be had from seed houses under trade names, but as they are not particular about what life they kill, do not use them near any trees or other garden treasures. They also render the soil sterile for sometime." For current information send for bulletins of your State Agricultural Experiment Station and the U. S. Department of Agriculture.

WITH THE FLOWERS

THINNING AND STAKING: Thinning of all kinds of seedlings should be done when the plants are very small and before the roots interlock. Thinning of rampant growing plants to keep air in the center of the clumps, as well as around the outer edges, must be done all season. Do not confine your staking operations to Dahlias, Peonies and the plants which seem to cry for it. Attend to the little fellows also.

CLIPPING, MARKING AND BUDDING: Clip the blossoms of all flowers as they are about to fade. There may be some that will not benefit by this process but most of them will respond. It is essential if annuals are to continue blooming. All plants grow to produce seed. The longer you prevent seeding, the longer they will bloom. Many perennials will give a second blooming if the old stalks are removed. Removal of bloomed-out stalks is also necessary on Delphiniums and many others to keep them sending up new growth from the bottom. Remember that it pays big dividends for little labor.

We have already spoken of pinching off the tops of many plants to make them branch out. Cosmos are among the plants which need it this month but many others also benefit from it. Try pinching a few of all kinds of plants so that you may learn which will do best. An expert may do it with his fingernails but for beginners a knife or scissors is best.

Mark the areas occupied by such plants as Bleedingheart, Trillium, small bulbs, Mertensia, etc., which are going dormant now. You will need it next spring. Continue this process all summer. Mark all your plants with perma-nent labels. It is tedious business but pays.

PERENNIAL PROPAGATION: Sow seeds of perennials for next year's garden. The process is described on page 286. Sow the seed late in June and soak in warm water for a couple of hours. For soft-wood cuttings take the first shoots that appear when they are three inches high. Cut them with a heel and place them in sand as described on page 290.

MISCELLANEOUS: Watch the ROSES for suckers from the root stocks. Dress with liquid manure for larger blooms. Cultivate the areas until July 1st to destroy the Rose bugs. If infested, look over the plants each day and shake the bugs into a can of kerosene. If your Roses are healthy, you may save a lot of cultivation during the summer by mulching them with peat moss after July 1st. . . . Don't forget successive plantings of GLADIOLUS. Watch for thrips. If your plants are infested, soak the corms next spring as described on page 192 and spray every five days. . . . Train the DAHLIAS to one stalk and be sure they are staked firmly. We hope you have not overlooked the smaller varieties which grow in the flower borders. Fertilize when first buds form, unless growth is rank. . . . Water the DELPHINIUMS well. Cut down the stems as the bloom ends. A spray recommended for the Black Blight is one ounce of dry sulphate and one-half ounce of Blackleaf 40 in two gallons of water. If the blight persists take out the infested plants and burn them. . . . Watch the IRIS for the borer (soft and slimy leaves) and remove or burn affected plants. See page 196. You may extend the Iris season by using the Fibrous-rooted and Bulbous Iris described on pages 197 and 198. Plant CHRYSANTHEMUMS before the end of the month. . . . Early June is about the dead-line for sowing flower seeds for summer bloom.

LATE FLOWERS: The flowers which endure early frost should not be overlooked now. That beautiful late season is an interesting period in the garden if you provide it with bloom. Some of the perennials such as Delphiniums and Achillea should be cut back immediately after flowering in June or July, watered well and given an application of plant food. There will be a second flowering in September and October. Perennials for late bloom are: Anemone, Asters, Boltonia, Ceratostigma, Chrysanthemum, Cimicifuga, Coreopsis, Delphinium (second blooming), Lilies, Phlox. Annuals may be sown now including Salvia farinacea (Blue Bedder), Cynoglossum amabile, Asters, Ageratum, Calendula, California-poppy, Candytuft, Centaurea, Cornflower, Heliotrope, Marigold, Morning-glory Heavenly Blue, Petunia, Phlox drummondi, Salpiglossis, Salvia, Scabiosa, Snapdragon, Stock, Sweet Alyssum, Verbena, Zinnia. Also don't overlook the perennial Liatris (called Gay Feather or Blazing Star). Blooming in September, it is included in the list of perennials requiring acid treatment on page 101. See the two late blooming Clematis—virginiana and paniculata described on page 114. The Maximillian Sunflower (Helianthus maximillianus) sends out its graceful sprays of flowers for cutting during September and October.

A GARDEN BANK ACCOUNT: Over a long period of years this gardener was in the habit of entertaining some two hundred fifty people on his grounds each summer. Of course, he wanted the grounds to be at their best and invariably there was some failure of some particular fine bloom, whether the party be given in spring or fall. So came the idea of preparing a borrow garden, which is used much as a savings account for the proverbial rainy day. Every garden has annuals to throw away, when the beds are thinned. Some of these are placed in small pots and plunged in the corner of the vegetable garden or a space set aside for the purpose. Gladiolus were planted in the same manner. When the bare spots came and any part of the border showed lack of bloom, it was only the work of a minute to slip these out of the pots and into the places needed where they would be well watered and take hold at once. If height was needed they could be set upon the ground in pots and soil heaped about them.

When it becomes necessary to thin the plants in your border, pot some of them up and keep them shaded for a few days with plenty of water and some wise pruning. Bring them gradually in the full sun and then sink them in a sunny secluded spot where they will not be neglected. This is the garden bank account, ready to be drawn upon at any time. As you do not care what they look like until they are ready for use you need not hesitate to cut them back or deprive them of bloom until they are stocky and healthy. Petunias, Marigolds and faithful Geraniums fit beautifully into this idea. Every size and shape of handy receptacle has its use. Old butter tubs, nail kegs and soap boxes bound with wire may be painted green and filled with well composted soil, enriched with plenty of rotted manure. These will house about five plants apiece. Trailing Petunias which have been pinched back to form a number of leaders come in all shades and sizes. Aztec Marigolds, if planted now, will be a mass of pale yellow bloom four or five feet high in October. For a gay, quick vine plant Squash—three plants in a fourteen-inch wooden tub. Place them on the terrace or some place where you can give them attention. Then don't overlook the second or even third sowings of such plants as Alyssum, California and Shirley Poppies, Babysbreath, Mignonette.

The garden bank account is a great idea but like all bank accounts, there must be a deposit before there can be withdrawals.

TREES, VINES AND SHRUBS

CUTTING AND PRUNING: As soon as the spring flowering shrubs have finished blooming, cut out all unnecessary wood to the ground as illustrated on page 82. All hedge trimming should be done now; a second pruning may be needed in August. Frequent trimming of hedges makes a thick green surface growth and avoids unsightly open spots. Break or cut all seed pods from Azaleas and Lilacs but be careful with the Lilacs because next year's blooming buds are already being formed.

WATERING: Take care that newly planted materials receive a thorough soaking each week. Soak, do not sprinkle. Mulch them and wash the leaves. Read pages 64–66.

CLIMBING ROSES: They should be looked over carefully and any heavy growth should be firmly tied into the proper position. Prune them after blossoming according to illustrations on page 113 and instructions on page 116.

GARDENING IN JULY

*Give fools their gold and knaves their
     power,
   Let fortune's bubbles rise and fall;
Who sows a field or trains a flower,
   Or plants a tree is more than all.*
                              —WHITTIER

GENERAL

Watering time is again at hand and we must call your attention to the difference between watering and sprinkling. For the most part, sprinkling is harmful, especially upon lawns. See page 44. Watering means soaking—soak the soil to the bottom of the roots, then cultivate the topsoil to keep the moisture from evaporating and to kill the revived weeds. Do it thoroughly and less often. Investigate automatic watering devices. See our homemade irrigating system on page 22.

Now is the time to begin to sow cover crops between rows and in vacated beds. Sow clover, rye and vetch. These, dug under later, will return humus and nitrates to the soil. See "Green Manure," page 35.

LAWN

This month, we mow, water and weed. If our previous work has been wise we need not worry about our lawn. High mowing, deep waterings and weed watchfulness are still necessary. If fertilizing is done, use the hydraulic method shown in the April Calendar, and the weed treatments described on pages 48–49. Don't let the weed seeds form, and, above all, try to influence your neighbor to follow your example.

THE SUMMER FLOWERS

CULTIVATION AND MULCHING: Cultivation does not take the place of watering, but it does conserve the water in the soil. After July 1st much of this labor can be avoided by mulching, which, however, does more than that. It helps to keep available nitrates in the soil. These cannot be formed in the soil at a temperature of over 115 degrees—85 degrees is better. Under a summer sun the soil often goes over this maximum for long periods, thus starving the plants. Moisture is the great temperature regulator. The mulch acts as a parasol and an insulated seal. It keeps the soil cool and moist. It must be light to admit air but in turn its air spaces keep out excess heat.

First, cultivate, then water thoroughly, and cover with an inch, or better, two inches of peat moss, homemade humus, straw, leafmold or thoroughly rotted manure. It is well to give a ration of lime, thoroughly worked in, to all except the plants that prefer acidity. The mulch is slightly acid and, unless your soil is strongly alkaline, may retard some growth. You can rake it off in late fall and cultivate the ground, save it for the compost heap, or add to it for winter protection.

MISCELLANEOUS CULTURE: Cut back Viola cornuta, Forget-me-not and Nepeta to four inches and dress with sheep manure for August bloom. Phlox, Veronica and Hollyhock will bloom again if kept from seeding. Pinch back pink and white Boltonia and New England Aster to five inches, early in July, to keep them bushy. Make cuttings of Centaurea, Coleus, Alternanthera, Artemisia, Torenia, Impatiens, etc. Set out Coleus, Begonias, Geraniums, to enliven the borders.

Now is the time to sow vines along fences and near garages. Too late to plant any annuals, except Portulaca, Torenia, Balsam, Zinnias, Annual Lupines, Shirley Poppies and Mignonette. Cut back Chrysanthemums and Poinsettias, disbudding and removing surplus shoots. Order Colchicum (Autumn Crocus) for August planting. Sow perennial seed.

Spray Nasturtiums, Sweet Peas and Goldenglow with nicotine. Examine Aster roots for insects and dig in tobacco dust. Spray with nicotine for tarnished plant bugs which attack growing Aster tips, and spray Bordeaux mixture on the under side of leaves of young plants to act as a rust preventive. If the Sweet Peas are heavily mulched their roots will be kept cooler and their season prolonged. Use rough litter or grass clippings. If aphis appear, spray with nicotine. A little shade at midday will help to maintain the quality of the flowers and prolong the season.

ROCK GARDEN: A few good, late blooming rock plants are: The Campanula family lasts into July; Erigeron alpinus (dwarf purple Daisy, blooms all summer); Coronilla cappadocica (blue-green trailer racemes, in July); Dianthus knappi (dainty yellow-pink); Wahlenbergia tasmanica and W. dalmaticus (like dwarf Platycodons); Anemone narcissiflora (white flower heads); Allium thibeticum (waxy lilac flowers six inches high).

PROPAGATION: *House Beautiful* has said: "Some time this month when growth has stopped and vanished foliage indicates a dormant condition, dig up a good root each of Bleedingheart, Anchusa, Oriental Poppy. Cut these long roots into inch pieces and plant them where the soil has been made a mixture of sand and rich loam. Keep the area fairly moist and soon tiny leaves will shoot up. The new plants will be ready for permanent quarters in the spring."

In addition, don't overlook increasing plants by layering. See page 289. Verbenas, Pinks, Euonymus, Pachysandra, Ivy, Daphne cneorum, Climbing Roses, shrubs, in fact, all the things with reaching runners will probably take root if fastened down on soft earth with a wire and covered with some good soil.

DAHLIAS: The main stems of the Dahlias should be kept free of side shoots. In larger varieties, a single stalk is the best. Remove half the flower buds. Some sort of adequate support must be provided to prevent storm breakage. Water well and follow feeding directions.

IRIS: Bearded Iris should be divided if over three years old and if roots are crowding. See page 194. Replace the more common ones with some new specimens. Top dress the existing borders with bone meal—do not use manure. Water the Japanese Iris well before flowering and withhold water afterwards. Divide every three years after they have flowered, lifting and separating carefully with a sharp knife. Set much deeper than bearded kinds and water sparingly after transplanting.

PEONIES: They are now making ready for next year's bloom. Care for them. See page 204. Maybe they need division in September. Get them ready.

GLADIOLUS: Dig up and BURN every stunted yellow colored plant. They will not flower so you lose nothing and prevent infection spreading in your soil to other bulbs.

FLOWER BOXES: Soil in the porch boxes must be kept in a state of richness. A good stimulant is nitrate of soda, 1 lb.; phosphate, ½ lb.; sulphate of potash or wood ashes, ½ lb. One quarter of a teaspoonful in a quart of water every two days, being careful not to touch the leaves. Never depend on rains, but water daily. Plant tablets are convenient. See illustration, page 311.

HOW TO CUT AND CARE FOR FLOWERS

All plants reach their highest activity when distended by water. When the roots of growing plants fail to supply water faster than the leaves transpire it, the plants wilt. The problem of keeping cut flowers is to keep a supply of water coming up through their stems. All processes of cutting and care are to accomplish this end.

Cutting is done with a sharp flower shears or knife, taking care to avoid injury to the growing plant by having tools sharp. A special pair of cutting scissors may be bought which holds the cut-off stem, allowing the removal to be a one-handed operation. It is best to carry a bucket of water to the garden, rather than the familiar cutting basket.

After cutting, remove lower leaves and any excess foliage and recut under water if desired, leaving the flower in the same container. This will prevent air bubbles from entering the stem canals and obstructing the upward flow of water. Flowers wilted, can often be revived by this treatment or by placing them in fairly hot water for a few minutes. If this is done, the tops should be protected from any steam which would expand the stem cells, but shorten the life of the flowers.

PRESERVATIVES | GATHERING

ASPIRIN SALT

CHEMICALS

THESE THINGS ARE USELESS TO PROLONG THE BLOOM OF FLOWERS

SPECIAL SHEARS

CARRY IN BUCKET OF WATER INSTEAD OF BASKET

RECUT STEMS UNDER WATER

PLACE IN DEEP VASE OF COOL WATER FOR SEVERAL HOURS

SLIT WOODY STEMS AND PEEL BACK A LITTLE BARK

BURN ENDS OF PLANTS HAVING A STICKY OR MILKY SAP

SUPPLY FRESH WATER AND TRIM A THIN SLICE OF STEM, DAILY EXCEPT ON BURNED ENDS

KEEP ALL BOUQUETS OUT OF SUN AND DRAFT

THIS

NOT THIS

EBERTZ

CUT STRAW FLOWERS FOR DRYING HANG UPSIDE DOWN IN COOL SHADE UNTIL STEMS STIFFEN

A slanting cut will expose more absorbing surface and prevent the tubes being sealed by resting upon the bottom of the vase. Woody stems (shrubs, Peonies, etc.) should have the ends slit or a little bark peeled away. Chrysanthemum and stock stems do best when slightly battered but the stems of plants which exude a sticky or milky sap after cutting (Dahlias, Oriental Poppies, Heliotrope, Poinsettias) must be sealed by searing them with the flame of a match, or gas, or dipping the tips in boiling water. The tips of stems of Hollyhock may be dipped in a solution of one-tenth of one per cent nitric acid.

Another important step in making bouquets last is cutting at proper stage of development. Most flowers fade immediately after pollination. It is best to cut them just as they begin to mature and where possible remove the stamens to prevent pollination. This is quite easy on many flowers, such as Lilies, Amaryllis, etc. Cut Gladiolus as the first bud opens—Peonies as the outer petals develop—Roses in the soft bud—Dahlias in full bloom after the sun goes down—Poppies the night before and allow them to open in the water. A few drops of gelatine on the ends of the stems of Orientals help. Immediately upon cutting a Calla bloom, cover all leaves and stems for twenty-four hours with cool water. A bathtub or any large open receptacle will answer. Wilted arrangements may be revived in the same manner. Wild flowers except Buttercups, Daisies, and Goldenrod seldom keep as cut flowers. Iris, if going a distance, should be cut in the bud.

Plants are filled with sap in the morning. Therefore, cut at this time those which wilt easily.

Late afternoon, when the stems are empty is good for summer flowers with hollow stems such as Gladiolus and Zinnias. They will fill quickly when plunged deep in water and be in prime condition the next morning. Flowers can be too fresh; Calendulas, Chrysanthemums, Euphorbia, Mignonette, Roses, Stocks and Snapdragons need twenty-four hours to fill and harden off.

Flowers should never be crowded into a small-mouthed vase. Air should easily reach the water. Water must be clean, cool and pure.

In case of special arrangements which will not stand disturbing, three drops of formalin and a teaspoonful of charcoal to the quart of water will help keep it uncontaminated. Never allow leaves below the water, especially those of Chrysanthemums, Dahlias, Zinnias.

Drafts and sunshine cause rapid evaporation and place a hardship upon the flowers already burdened with the problem of trying to absorb moisture under unnatural conditions. Consequently, cut flowers do best in cool places. Gas present in the air in amount so small that it can only be detected by careful chemical tests, is often fatal to cut flowers.

THINGS TO DO IN AUGUST

GENERAL

Now is the time to locate some manure to compost and rot for use next spring.

The wise gardener who wants bulbs for fall planting orders them early. The stock of some varieties is usually limited and only the early comers can be served. Order alpine seed to plant late in autumn in an uncovered frame.

Every weed that ripens and spreads its seed means more trouble for you next year. Get weeds out of the ground before they mature. Surface cultivation two or three days after a rain or watering will kill innumerable seedling weeds in beds, vegetable garden and other tilled spaces.

Keep the bird bath filled, especially if a drought comes. The contents evaporate rapidly in such weather, to say nothing of what the birds themselves spatter about. It is a great convenience, to have the water piped direct from the regular house supply.

Remember water evaporates at this time of year. Water deeply and thoroughly. Use a mulch where it is specified and don't forget to water the compost heap.

WAGE WAR

Examine your plants for signs of distress and compare with diagnosis chart on pages 265–68. Dust roses weekly with Massey Dust and tobacco stem meal (see pages 258–59) or any prepared dust sold under a similar formula. Use this also on perennials. Aphis are accused of spreading various diseases. Let your war upon them be continuous and thorough.

THE LAWN

August is the time to go over your lawn, destroying insects and keeping weeds from seeding and weakening the stand of grass so that winter will do the rest. Look carefully after crab grass to keep it from seeding. Read chapter on "Lawns" and do your renovating now. Follow Nature's tip and do your seeding to the best advantage. If the lawn is in good shape, give it a dressing described on pages 44–45. A dressing of lawn food late in the month will be very beneficial if well watered down or applied with hose siphon. When sprinkling the lawn, do the job thoroughly so as to wet the ground several inches deep.

AMONG THE FLOWERS

CARE: Don't let your flower garden run down, as so many people tend to do at this season. Keep tall flowers well staked and cut out all your dead stalks. Keep edges trimmed and stir the soil on the surface as a weed preventive and to conserve moisture. Use a mulch to save labor and moisture. Use humus, peat, straw, or decayed leaves, at least two inches thick. Water well when water is needed.

GLADIOLUS: Taller growing varieties of Gladiolus should be staked to protect them from breakage by wind. For individuals and small clumps single stakes will suffice. For rows, use lines of twine on both sides of the row, stretched tight between stakes set ten feet or so apart, forming an alley. Apply manure water.

LILIES: Lilies like to have their roots fairly cool, especially during the hot weather. Unless foliage of some sort shades them and produces this result, mulch the ground with grass clippings or some kind of rough litter that is free from weed and grass seeds.

DAHLIAS: Feed and disbud the dahlias now. Keep the cut blooms away from windows and doors. They do not like drafts.

ORIENTAL POPPIES: *Do not* mulch oriental poppies. They prefer hot sun-baked ground when resting.

PEONIES: Feed and cultivate peonies now for next year's bloom; see illustration, page 204.

HELICHRYSUM: Cut Strawflowers intended for winter bouquets before the blossoms are fully open. Dry them in the shade, hanging head downward in small, uncrowded bunches. In handling, be especially careful not to crack the stems near the blossoms.

MANURE WATER: Use manure water on plants ready to bloom (especially Heliotrope) and to hasten the second blooming of delphinium, etc. See illustration, page 193.

WOOD ASHES: Use wood ashes around phlox, aster and cosmos. In using them, do not pile on too much at one time or the goodness will be leached away and wasted. Sprinkle them on the ground near the roots as thick as the sand on a sanded floor, allowing a little brown earth to show through.

PHLOX: Nothing will give as definite and as beautiful mass effects in the garden in August as hardy or perennial phlox provided it is well grown.

The secret of Phlox culture lies in these four essential conditions: full sun, deep preparation to make them grow tall, plenty of moisture at their roots especially during droughts, and preventing flowers from going to seed. Plants must be divided as soon as they get too thick, every three years or oftener. Never leave more than four or five stalks to a plant. Keep plants sprayed with Bordeaux or dusted every ten days from the time they appear above the ground, to prevent mildew. They should be grown in groups of no less than five plants. Phlox is used for masses of color rather than individual flower form effects. Cut the stems to the ground when they have finished blooming and feed the plants.

Much complaint comes from the so-called reverting of red and pink Phlox to lavender and magenta. This is caused by the parent stock dying of starvation or crowding and being replaced by seedlings which seldom come true to parent color and are usually poor bloomers. When transplanting be sure to label carefully both as to color and height, and when in full and early bloom and divide late in August (four or five stalks to the clump) using the outside pieces. Have soil thoroughly enriched, deeply dug and conditioned.

Phlox may also be successfully propagated from stem cuttings taken in late summer and rooted in a coldframe. (See page 289.) Protect over winter and set out in spring when six inches high. Propagation from root cuttings is done from clumps taken in the fall and protected in a coldframe until spring. These cuttings, two inches in length, are laid in flats of sandy loam and covered with one-half inch of soil. Transplant when from two to four inches high.

WINDOW BOXES: Use plant food tablets on porch boxes, and keep the soil well watered.

CUT FLOWERS: Pick exhibition blossoms the night before they are to be shown and keep them in a cool dark cellar in water up to their necks. It is well to keep on hand at least one ordinary florist vase in which to store flowers overnight or until they can be arranged.

ROSES: Avoid adding any quick-acting plant food to roses at this time. A light dusting of bone meal raked in is good just before a mulch is applied. Though this fertilizer does not necessarily improve the quality of the fall flowers it is sure to give the plant more vigor and will strengthen it in readiness for blossoming the following year. The mulch is best applied in July, but if you have not used it yet, do so now and save water and cultivation. Don't forget to add some tobacco dust to it.

HOUSE PLANTS, GREENHOUSE AND COLDFRAME

If you have a greenhouse make a compost heap of all discarded plants and vegetable refuse. Use topsoil with a sod growth, adding manure and bone meal for enrichment. The material will decompose and form the finest sort of soil for repotting or direct use in the greenhouse benches.

CUTTINGS: Cuttings should be taken of bedding plants such as Coleus, Geraniums, etc. If these are carried in a cool greenhouse through the winter they will make good stock for setting out next spring. Some of the modern varieties of Geranium are especially worth while.

ANNUALS: Sow annuals for winter

flowering indoors. It is only the old-fashioned gardener who limits himself to carnations, violets, and roses. Calendulas bloom well and keep long. Browallia, mignonette, sweet peas, lupine, ageratum, marigolds, stocks, snapdragons and many others are good subjects. One professional grower specialized in dandelions for table decorations and made them a success. Good keeping qualities, prolific and continuous bloom, are good reasons for giving a plant room in a greenhouse. Small plants may be purchased from growers who specialize in supplying such material.

BULBS: Bulbs intended for forcing in the greenhouse should be ordered at this time. Boxes, pans, soil and other materials needed for them should be made ready as some bulbs are available now. Successive plantings, of course, mean an extended period of bloom.

CHRYSANTHEMUMS: Buds will be forming on most of the greenhouse chrysanthemums by this time and strong feedings will be necessary if you want highest quality flowers. Unless you are experienced in their culture, it will pay you to get a good book on hothouse chrysanthemums.

REPAIR: It is well to go over all the coldframe sashes and greenhouse glazing, replacing broken glass, puttying and repainting. All should be finished ahead of time. Equipment which is taken care of in this way every year will last much longer and actually produce better results.

GARDEN PLANTS: If you are planning to take some garden plants indoors to provide for early fall bloom, use a sharp knife to root prune them now to a size a little smaller than the pot. Remove all buds and flowers and cut back the top growth severely. Water well until ready to lift.

HOUSE PLANTS: Look over the house plants which are summering out of doors to see that they are not suffering for want of water. Be careful not to disturb those now going through their rest periods.

COLDFRAME: If you do not have a coldframe, now is a good time to plan one.

VINES, TREES, SHRUBS

HEDGES: Hedges of all types, evergreens that have been confined to a form and plants that are clipped, should be gone over now as growth for the season is about to cease. One of the secrets of success with such plants is never to let them get unkempt and out of hand. Be careful *not* to fertilize to start new growth which will winterkill.

EVERGREENS: Evergreens, both broad-leaved and coniferous, should be planted from now to September 15. They need a great deal of water, so it is advisable, when resetting them, to saturate the soil. Where possible, too, let them be protected somewhat from the sweep of drying summer winds. Read carefully Chapters VI and VIII if you plan such work.

VINES: It is just as necessary to prune vines as other plants. All unproductive wood should be removed. This will give room for the more vigorous shoots and promote the general welfare of the plants. A fall top dressing of manure is advisable also, for best future results. See illustration, page 113.

TRANSPLANTING: Ornamental stock, woody as well as herbaceous, can be transplanted if it is well soaked several hours before lifting, reset quickly and firmly, and thoroughly watered. Where feasible, it is a good idea to provide shade and wind protection for a few days in very hot weather. If you plan to move them after freezing, root prune them now; see illustrations, pages 56 and 82.

SHRUBS: The Scholartree (Sophora japonica) is a tree found around temples and pagodas in Japan. It is a most beautiful flowering tree, useful especially because of its creamy white flowers in large panicles in August (when few trees are blooming). The flower is liked by the bees. It is a graceful tree, low branching where it has room. The foliage is similar to that of the locust and turns yellow in the fall and persists late.

The tree has a tremendous tap root. It is slow growing—slower than its relative, the yellow-wood—and does not flower when young. Old trees flower freely, especially in the hot season in August and September. It will stand drought. Use in well-drained sandy soil.

Our common summersweet bush (Clethra alnifolia) makes the hedgerows fragrant in August with its white flowers in upright panicles, and its crisp leaves. It likes a moist peaty or sandy soil, but will thrive in ordinary garden soil. There are several species of Clethra, but none so good as our common C. alnifolia. It is good in native and informal masses, especially, or used with cedar, azalea, blueberry and so forth in more refined spots, for August bloom. It averages four to six feet tall, and sometimes grows to ten feet.

The Arnold hawthorn (Crataegus arnoldiana) is one of the earliest among the hawthorns to fruit and is popular on that account. It flowers in May. It has a bright red fruit, about an inch in diameter, in August, and this also falls early. The tree grows to be twenty feet tall. It is easy to transplant if pruned severely, all over, at the time. It likes lime, in common with other hawthorns. Use sandy loam enriched with well-rotted manure.

PROPAGATING, SEEDING, AND PLANTING

IRIS: If you have not done so, divide iris now when it becomes crowded. Japanese iris which has grown in the same spot for three or four years should be divided at once. Use the yearly plan on the bearded iris for best bloom each season.

SEED SOWING: Pansies, Forget-me-not, English daisies, etc., are sturdier plants if sown this month. Parsley seed should be sown now for the green garden.

Biennials, such as Foxglove, can be started from seed now. It is inadvisable to set out any of the young plants in the border, for the winter would probably kill them. Be sure to shade the seedlings, see page 286. Get good seed. It pays.

SEEDLINGS: About this time of the year we will discover many self-sown seedlings of Hollyhocks, Larkspur, Columbine, Sweet William, etc. If the parent plant is worthy, these should be carefully guarded, for here is a way to stretch your garden budget. Tag these seedlings carefully for transplanting. Remember, phlox seldom comes true to color from seed.

WOODY PLANTS: Cuttings of various woody plants can be started in a shaded coldframe which can be covered with sash as cold weather comes. In most cases, use ripe, new wood with most of the foliage removed. Various combinations of sand, sand and soil or sand and peat moss are used. See page 289.

NARCISSUS: Transplant narcissus that have become crowded, using directions on page 187. Get some variety. There are now over six hundred varieties of daffodils.

MADONNA LILY: Transplant as soon as basal leaves wither. See page 202.

ORIENTAL POPPIES: Don't limit yourself to reds; get some of the fine ones in pinks and white. Now is the only time to buy and transplant. They require full sun and perfect drainage. They come easily from roots and will grow again if a small piece is left. To propagate, cut two-inch lengths as thick as a lead pencil. Cut straight across at top and slanting at bottom. Set straight up and down and cover one inch deep. Water well and cover with peat moss. Do not cover old established plants.

CLIPPING AND PRUNING

Clip off the dried heads of last spring's lilac blooms. Cut seed heads from all annuals if you want continuous bloom. Do not let them go to seed.

For the finest dahlias, disbudding should be continued to the end of the season. It results in larger flowers through concentration of the plants' energy on a smaller number. Generally speaking, the two side buds in every group of three are the ones to be removed. See page 190.

Watch chrysanthemums to keep them from bearing too many buds or growing too tall.

Deciduous trees that need only moderate pruning may receive it now. It is easier to gauge such work while the foliage is on than after it has fallen in the autumn. Large limbs, of course, should not be removed until the sap has stopped circulating through the branches in the autumn.

A PIECE OF SHEET METAL 12 *IN.* WIDE WILL KEEP CATS OUT OF TREES

DUST SULPHUR ON ARMS OR LEGS — OR SPRAY IT UPON THE GRASS TO PREVENT CHIGGER BITES

AFTER WORKING IN THE GARDEN, WASH HANDS AND ARMS WITH STRONG SOAP TO PREVENT POISON IVY

GIVE GOLD FISH A BATH IN EPSON SALTS WHILE POOL IS BEING CLEANED

CLOSE ALL TREE WOUNDS WITH TAR TO PREVENT THE ENTRANCE OF BORERS

STERILIZATION OF SEED BED HELPS THE YOUNG PLANTS

SPRAY AND DUST DELPHINIUM PHLOX AND PERENNIALS SUBJECT TO MILDEW

DUST ROSES EVERY WEEK DURING THE ENTIRE GROWING SEASON

PREVENTING TROUBLE

Sulphur is a good preventive of chiggers. Dust it on arms or legs from a sifting can and use a dust gun on the grass at picnics, etc. Ivy poisoning can be prevented by immediately washing with brown soap. Cats cannot disturb young birds in the nest if a twelve inch piece of sheet metal is fastened loosely around each tree, six feet from ground. Sick goldfish respond to a bath of table salt (one tablespoon to the gallon of water for five or ten minutes) and once a year a long tonic bath of two tablespoons of Epsom salts to a tub of water. To prevent fungous and bacterial troubles in propagating, sterilize the soil first. See page 260.

WHAT TO DO IN SEPTEMBER

Now that you have had the experience of the summer, were you satisfied with it? If not, get busy, plan for next year, order bulbs for planting soon; get after the evergreens, clean up the flower borders, order new roses and a host of other fall tasks. Schedule your tasks and get in every bit of work possible this fall. Try to remember how you fought the weather last spring and make these calm beautiful days count. Many things can be planted as well in the fall as in spring and some to a lot better advantage.

GENERAL

Even if you have occasional rains, remember that the soil dries out quickly now. See that propagating beds and newly planted or transplanted items are kept moist. They are making their first root growth now and need constant water supply. Don't forget to water the compost heap.

Do not neglect to sow down freely with Rye and Vetch the vacant patches of ground in the garden. When dug under next spring these cover crops will benefit the soil decidedly. Sowing can also be made between the rows of crops that are well spaced.

Before the leaves begin to fall, get your garden on paper. Plan the changes which you expect to make during the winter. See Chapter XXV.

Wire grass, Quack grass and other heavy growing grasses and weeds, if allowed to overrun your garden now, will be a serious factor to contend with next spring. Better haul them out roots and all, for they are persistent pests and seem to have at least nine lives when once well started.

THE LAWN

Keep on cutting the grass as long as it grows vigorously. Do not, however, cut as closely as in the spring, for now the roots need more surface protection than in the early season.

This is about the last chance for properly seeding down lawns; most weed growth is over and the grass will get sufficient start to carry it through the winter. You must be prepared, however, to water it abundantly in case the fall rains fail to put in an appearance.

AMONG THE FLOWERS

SANITATION: The flower garden should be given a final clean-up for the season; the walks properly edged, all weeds and old stalks removed and burned. Thus will you not only create a more pleasing setting for the fall flower display, but also prepare for next season's best results. Garden sanitation may seem like an affectation but its need is based on real facts. Disease germs and pests lurk in dead stalks and leaves left around even all winter. All dead matter which harbors them should be collected and completely destroyed by burning.

Do not stop using Massey Dust on the perennials. Delphinium is especially subject to fungous growth in September.

FROSTS: Watch for early frosts and cover tender plants with newspaper or muslin. A few strips of unbleached muslin sewed together and kept for this purpose is inexpensive and prolongs the blooming season.

BULBS: Get your bulb orders in now and carefully plan for the planting season. This means better results next spring. See Chapter XII. Don't let the Narcissi go into the winter in a crowded condition, get them in as early as possible. By all means, visit your bulb store and get a few Crocuses, Scillas and

Chionodoxas. Plant them either in the rock garden or at the edge of the foundation planting. It is not good practice to plant them in the lawn, for most gardeners start mowing before the leaves of these little flowers have completely ripened, thereby weakening the bulbs. Prepare beds now for bulbs to be planted later.

Field mice that roam through the burrows made by moles destroy thousands of Tulip bulbs annually. This can be prevented by planting in baskets made of ½" mesh wire. Sometimes they can be poisoned or gassed successfully by the same remedy recommended for moles on pages 51–52.

SEEDS AND ROOTS: You never know just what colors and forms you will get from flower seeds gathered from your own plants—that is what makes the experiment so interesting. Collect them when ripe and keep till spring in a dry, cool place. Both annual and perennial flowers are interesting subjects to try. However, do not limit your garden to home gathered seeds. It is always best to remember that new flower seeds each year come from selected flowers grown by experts under ideal conditions. You can hardly expect to approximate these conditions in your garden. Make newly purchased seeds a large part of your planting.

When the first bloom of the delphinium has withered, keep a few seeds of the choicest specimens on the stalk until ripe. Then plant them at once in a garden seed bed. They will grow into husky little plants that winter well where they are, ready to transplant into permanent quarters in the spring.

Hollyhocks respond in the same manner to the sowing of fresh ripe seed. If the color of the variety is one especially liked, protect the bloom with a glassine or cellophane bag, while the seed is forming, to keep off marauding bees.

Some time this month when growth has stopped and vanished foliage indicates a dormant condition, dig up a good root each of bleeding heart, anchusa, Oriental poppy. Cut these long roots into pieces and plant them where the soil has been made a mixture of sand and rich loam. Keep the area fairly moist. Soon tiny leaves will shoot up. They will be ready for permanent quarters in the spring.

If you want to have annuals early, try sowing some of the hardy varieties this fall. Some of these are larkspur, poppies, sweet alyssum, ageratum, calliopsis, cornflower, petunia and cosmos. If they come through you will gain considerable time; if not the seed lost will not amount to much.

LATE BLOOMING PLANTS: Chrysanthemums, fall perennials, second bloom of delphinium and other similar plants that are in bud should be fed freely with liquid manures of different kinds until the buds show definite signs of opening. It is important that all this material be kept well watered, lest it become dry and woody and flower poorly. If fresh manure is not obtainable, substitute the dried product which is sold by the garden supply stores. Spray Chrysanthemums for black aphis, using nicotine sulphate and if bothered by grasshoppers spray with arsenate of lead or dust with a combination dust.

HARDY ASTERS: Most of our garden asters are wild species brought in from the fields or improved descendants. Under good conditions of soil and culture these so-called Michaelmas daisies produce beautiful flowers long appreciated in England, but until lately rather neglected here.

Practically all asters need constant division in order not to deteriorate in the garden. Clumps should be divided every year leaving not over four or five stalks to a plant. All asters should be staked early in the season. Later on, when the larkspur is cut down, a few branches of aster staked to grow horizontally will help fill up the vacant spaces.

PHLOX: This is the last chance to tag phlox for division later. The flowers fade quickly toward the end of the month. Mark them for both height and color, so that you may plant for proper display in the border.

ROSES: It will not be necessary to feed the roses from now on, but they should be sprayed after each rain with a rose dust (Massey Dust) to prevent black spot. Also, keep them well watered or mulched. Late fall planting of hardy garden roses is becoming popular as its advantages are better understood. You will do well to prepare the bed now so it will have time to settle before actual planting time. In general, try to get the plants in just before hard freezing weather. Order the new plants now.

PEONIES: Try transplanting your peonies in rotation—a few each year. In this way you will not risk loss of bloom on all of them. Remember September 15th marks about the last safe opportunity for transplanting peonies. See page 204. Order roots at once and get ready for planting.

If your peonies are overgrown and

Much labor can be saved with proper tools. The dandelion rake easily takes off blossoms before they bloom without injuring grass roots. A lawn fertilizer spreader does hours of work in a few minutes. A grass whip, swung like a golf club, trims weeds, under fences and close to walls without stooping and with little effort. A floral spade or foot trowel, with 5 x 7 inch blade, can be used as a garden walking stick and is always handy for a multitude of garden tasks.

the entire bed needs transplanting, you may not have a bloom again for two years. A method which will avoid this is to dig a trench around one-half of a large clump, then separate one-half of the main plant for division, leaving just half of your established peony clump. The hole, if filled with rich soil, will supply new life to the old established peony and give you bloom until the new divisions are ready. If your clumps are extra large you may even remove three-fourths for division.

IRIS: Last chance to successfully divide iris this year. See page 195.

COSMOS: Transplant late cosmos to boxes on the porch to keep them blooming after frost. Securely stake exposed plants.

GAILLARDIA: Divide gaillardia clumps over two years old. They stop blooming after three years. They do not come well from seed, but can be propagated from cuttings even as late as this if they are grown inside for a few weeks and potted up for spring planting.

PANSIES: Pansies may be wintered outside if covered with straw or excelsior just before frost. If leaves are used be sure to have a poultry wire fence to hold them in place without letting them pack down. Transplant the August sown pansies and order more seed for earliest spring sowing.

LILIES: They may still be planted. Madonna lily should be in by September 15th.

SELECT NOW: Now while they are in bloom or have just finished is the time to make a list of fall blooming flowers to plant next spring. The following are a few to consider:

TORCH LILIES: Not so many years ago the "Tritoma uvaria grandiflora," a variety of the red hot poker plant, was a much admired hardy perennial which usually bloomed in the autumn. It was even in the older days a conspicuous plant of the border attaining a height of five or more feet. This plant still towers above its neighbors, but in many other ways it is quite different from its ancestors. We now have a type that will blossom profusely from July until November.

Tritoma pfitzerii (the everblooming flame flower) is one of the very best varieties for general culture. Its spikes of rich burnt orange seem like darting flames in the summer sunshine. It requires a moderately heavy loam; if grown in poor soil the flowers are likely to be imperfect reminding one of a poorly seeded ear of corn.

While the red hot poker plant is listed in some catalogues as hardy, this applies only to the southern half of the country. In northern sections, the bulbs must have some winter protection; perhaps the most satisfactory method of wintering the plants is to bury the roots in sand in a cool cellar.

SPIREA: The spirea is another herbaceous plant that should be in every border. This is one plant that cares little about soil, but usually does best in a soil composed of good loam, sand and manure, equal parts.

ANEMONE JAPONICA (Japanese Windflower): A hardy garden perennial that revels in sunshine but that will withstand moderate shade. Its colors range from pure white to deep pinks. This dainty flower begins to unfold its lovely buds in early August, when there is a dearth of bloom in the garden and continues its good work until late September.

FALL PLANTING OF PERENNIALS: When the results of fall planting are unsatisfactory it is generally either because the plants were put in too late in the fall or because they were plants of uncertain hardiness. Such plants should always be transplanted in the spring. Read Chapter X and especially pages 122–123 for transplanting instructions. Any planting done, in the fall should be early enough to let the plants get properly established roots before winter. Otherwise they are practically *ONLY HEELED IN* during this period and are more apt to be winterkilled.

HARVESTING TENDER BULBS: Harvest the Gladiolus as soon as the foliage turns brown. See pages 193–94. Lift and store Dahlias, Cannas and Caladiums as soon as the tops are blackened by frost. See pages 189, 191. Tuberous Begonias should be taken up before the first light frost. Retain a good sized clump of dirt and place in a frost proof but well ventilated cellar not too hot. Wait until the foliage wilts and then cut it loose from the clump. Dry out bulbs for a few days and store in dry sand at about 50 degrees.

Four-o'-clock roots can be lifted and stored in a dry cellar or packed in sand. The temperature should be low (a little above freezing is best), cut off and burn the dead tops but leave some soil on the roots to avoid breaking them. Planted in your garden, they will bloom several weeks earlier than those raised from seed.

BIENNIALS: Any left over hardy biennials may be gathered in a corner and easily protected with a loose mulch for planting next spring.

HOUSE PLANTS

HARDENING: Start bringing in your house plants while the windows may still be left open so that they will gradually become inured to the dry house air. Dwarf asters and other small plants of annuals may be taken from the garden and set in small pots to flower in the house.

STRAWFLOWERS: Do not forget to cut your strawflowers and seed pods for winter bouquets. It is surprising how many flowers can be used for this purpose. One old favorite, Globe Amaranth, is worthy of a place in any garden, provided a place can be found where its vivid coloring will not jar the harmony of color in your garden.

BULBS FOR BLOOM INDOORS: Those who want early bloom indoors should start Hyacinths, etc., now, following directions on pages 329–34.

GARDEN PLANTS INDOORS: Lift any plants, for indoor bloom, well before frost. See page 327 for details.

GREENHOUSE AND COLDFRAME

The greenhouse should be thoroughly overhauled before starting it into active operation for the cold season. Now is the time to do any necessary painting, glazing or repairing of its heating.

Soil for winter potting ought to be obtained and stored somewhere under cover. The best kind is light and modrately rich, containing plenty of humus and some sand. Chopped sod and garden loam, allowed to compost for several months, are ideal as a basis for the mixture.

Get cuttings of the outdoor bedding plants, such as Chrysanthemum, Coleus, etc., before they are destroyed by frost. These may be grown along and developed in the greenhouse or even on a glass enclosed and heated sun porch. Each variety should be marked and kept separate. See August Calendar.

Carnations that were planted out may now be put in the greenhouse for the indoor season, before the frost has a chance to catch them. The glass should be shaded slightly until the roots again become active, after which normal light is again allowed to enter the house.

Cold nights and hot days are productive of mildew in the greenhouse. To overcome this have the pipes painted with a paste of flowers of sulphur and water, and ventilate carefully, especially during the day. Try to maintain an even temperature through the twenty-four hours.

Keep the potting room clean and scour each pot and tray as soon as it is out of use. Be a good greenhouse keeper.

Take in hydrangeas.

Start freesias and set where they are to grow.

Buy shrubs for forcing.

Keep roses from developing buds as yet.

Plant Spanish iris in flats.

Transplant biennials, such as pansy and English daisy, in the frames for the winter to give early bloom.

Sow pansy seed in frames.

Propagate Japanese anemones by placing cuttings in the frames.

Sow annual lupine, snapdragon, sweet peas, schizanthus, annual larkspur, gypsophila, stock, calendula.

Plant violets and lilies.

Propagate by cutting geraniums, coleus, heliotrope, verbena, chrysanthemums, etc.

VINES, TREES, SHRUBS

DO NOT: Do not fertilize trees or shrubs at this time of year; it may start new growth which will winterkill. Do not prune your spring flowering shrubs now or you endanger next year's bloom by removing the flower buds.

EVERGREENS: This is really the season when evergreens are nearest dormant. Transplant now for best results. See August calendar. Pick off all bag worms and determine to spray at the proper time next year. Treat now for red spider. See Chapter VI.

PRUNING: Shape up trees and shrubs now while the foliage is on them and you can see what they will look like.

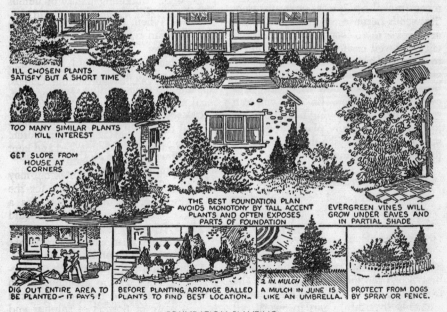

FOUNDATION PLANTING

Proper planting can help overcome many of the architectural shortcomings of a house, making it look wider and less top heavy. Choose the plants carefully so that they will not sprawl over your walks and hide your house after a year or two. Read Chapter VI.

Deadwood is easy to distinguish now. If you haven't completed your season's pruning do so now. See Chapter V for instructions.

TRANSPLANTING: As soon as the foliage turns on deciduous plants it is safe to transplant; the earlier the better, so that the roots will have a chance to take hold before cold weather. This turning of the foliage indicates that the sap has receded and the top growth is entering a dormant state. Read August calendar. Newly planted stock, especially if exposed to much wind, should be firmly staked for at least a year to hold it perpendicular. Be sure to protect from hot drying winds, and paint cuts immediately with special tree paint from the seed store or asphaltum paint. Magnolias, Dogwood, Birches and some others do better if spring planted.

COLLECTED STOCK: We do not recommend transplanting trees or shrubs from the woods because we think good nursery stock is more economical of time and effort as well as much more certain as to results. However, if you must, the chances of success in transplanting from the woods are best now when growth is over for the season. Be sure you can supply the right growing conditions before you take up any plants. Exposure, soil and drainage should approximate those of the original site.

WATERING: A great deal of our so-called winter losses, especially with evergreens, is the result of these plants being allowed to become bone dry at this season. They should always be well watered right up to the time the ground freezes hard, because they hold their leaves and evaporate water all during the winter. When unable to take it from the frozen ground they go through great hardship. Water them in fall, for health and, for safety, during the dry spells of winter.

FORETHOUGHT: A good way to stimulate the growth of trees next year is to cultivate beneath their branches now and sow winter cover crops to be turned under next spring. This is especially true of fruit trees and orchards. The trees benefit not only from the added humus and plant food but from the aeration and pulverizing of the soil.

PLANTING: Prepare the ground for planting new trees and shrubs in October or November.

VINES: When other vines begin to fade you can really appreciate the Virgin's Bower (Clematis paniculata) which remains green until November. Give some lime and a mulch of manure this fall and follow with a ration of bone meal next spring. It will repay you.

CLIMBING ROSES: Those who have not pruned the ramblers after they finished blooming should do so now. Now is the proper time to prune all the other kinds of climbing roses. See illustration page 113 and instructions on page 116.

WHAT TO DO IN OCTOBER

Too many people think that gardening is over when the leaves begin to turn brown or even after the first frost. The true flower lover continues his planting and his healthful garden work all through the season. Up to December the weather is usually favorable for out-door work a great part of the time. After that there are many things, which will be outlined later, that can be done for present and future enjoyment.

GENERAL

The time for raking leaves is at hand. It must be remembered that they are a source of humus and if you have space enough by all means start a compost pile as described on page 32. If you use a heap it may be held in place by piling strips of sod around the edges either to form a wall or as weights. Compost must be kept moist and in it you can empty the vacuum cleaner, soot or cleanings from the chimney or furnace and practically any vegetable matter or kitchen refuse which will decay. Add some manure or peat moss if you want to increase the supply. It usually takes two years to make a good compost so have two piles if there is room. If you already have a compost bed, fork it over and wet it down frequently.

See that all fallen leaves are raked out of the corners where they may smother the plants if they get too deep.

Do not allow weeds to seed. This will save much trouble next year. Burn the dead stalks of perennials to help control insects and disease.

Any changes in the borders should be made now. Be sure to fertilize well, referring to the proper chapter for each kind of plant.

Do not use quick acting fertilizers in preparing beds during the fall. They will be leached away before spring. Use the materials which act slowly and last a long time, such as coarse raw bone, etc. Where lime is needed, now is a good time to apply ground limestone for its sweetening effect.

This is also a good time to apply soil conditioners such as manures and forms of commercial humus. The manure does not need to be well rotted at this time if you are careful to keep it away from the plant roots. The freezing and thawing of winter will take a lot of the heat out of it before the spring growing season. Do not use manures on bulbs unless especially directed.

For general ground conditioning this writer prefers the domestic peat humus. Peat moss is also a good source of humus although it has no fertilizing value.

Toward the end of the month water should be drained from all sprinkling systems and the hose should be drained, taken indoors for the winter, and stored.

Small evergreens can be planted in the window boxes and if kept watered will do for replanting next spring or with proper care will last in the boxes all summer.

During any lull in garden work, from now on, repair any flats, frames, sash or tools for next year's use. Time is valuable in the spring and it is a great feeling to have everything in order.

PESTS

The falling of the leaves marks the beginning of the season for spraying to control scale insects. Lilacs, fruit trees, poplars and ash trees should be examined for scale and sprayed while they are dormant, using miscible oil, or commercial lime sulphur. This is also an excellent time to spray white pines and other evergreens with nicotine if they are subject to aphis. Read Chapter XVII. Watch the Chrysanthemums and other late flowering plants for aphis which flock to the tender new shoots and even devour the flowers. Spray with nicotine.

THE LAWN

Lawn mowing is to be kept up as long as new growth continues to be apparent. This policy not only keeps the turf looking well, but also improves its condition for next year. Long matted grass that has lain on the lawn all winter means trouble in the spring when mowing begins. Keep the lawn free of leaves and other litter during the winter. The grass smothers easily at this time.

AMONG THE FLOWERS

LILIES: Many lily bulbs get into the market late. If you intend to plant later on, prepare the beds and mulch the soil with manure to keep it from freezing. Don't forget to mulch the lilies already planted. Follow instructions on page 201.

FROSTS: Don't forget the hint contained in the September Calendar concerning muslin covers for late blooming flowers. You are protecting the beds not only for one day but so you can enjoy them for the many weeks of good weather ahead. If they are injured by frost you may be able to revive them by a very fine spray of cold water from the hose. But do this in the morning before the sun strikes them. A light wooden scaffold or some stakes help in applying protection. Do not put the cover in place until evening and be sure that you remove it when the sun is fairly up next morning. Chrysanthemum lovers, who have no greenhouses, may keep their plants in bloom far into the fall weather by using a few light frames, covered with cheesecloth, to form a little house. These may be made by any handy person from lath or lattice and easily fastened together with a few screen door hooks. A temporary stake or two will aid in keeping them upright.

Watch the thermometer on cold nights. A cold clear night when no wind is blowing usually means a destructive frost. Dampness or cloudiness are less injurious but any wind keeps the frost away. Better be prepared any way.

SPRING FLOWERING BULBS: Few gardeners are sufficiently impressed with the necessity of setting out fall planted bulbs at the proper time. Only Tulips should be held until after October 15th. The Narcissus, while much planted in October, should go in as early as possible as it takes three months of warm weather to properly develop their roots. Many of the smaller bulbs may or should be planted in September or early October, which also applies to Hyacinths. See Chapter XII. Some gardeners state that Hyacinths should go in when the maple leaves begin to color. However, a little earlier is better, and they will also do fairly well if planted a little later.

TENDER BULBS: Dig up and store all tender bulbous plants such as Gladiolus, Dahlias, etc. The Dahlias must be stored in sand or in boxes and kept in a cool, dark but not too dry cellar. One of the best packing materials for Dahlias is peat moss. Packing is not needed for Gladiolus corms. See Chapter XII.

TENDER PLANTS: Hydrangeas, Bay trees, Hibiscus, Oleander, Orange or Lemon, Crepe Myrtle, etc., which have been used to decorate the porch or terrace, must be brought into a cool fairly light cellar before freezing weather. Look over your garden for plants you wish to save or mature indoors: Cineraria, Geranium, Lobelia Erinus, Nasturtium, Petunia, Sweet Alyssum, Ageratum, etc.

ROCK GARDEN: Stone chips used as top dressing will not only minimize erosion in the rock garden, but also help to prevent soil heaving and resultant damage to roots. Work them up close around the crowns of the plants. Get them in place now and let them remain there permanently. Pine needles also make a good mulch. Where plants are grown which do not care for lime, use marble or granite chips which may be obtained from the manufacturer of monuments.

BORDERS: Any changes in the flower border should be made as early as possible. See Chapter X.

ROSES: The time for winter protection comes about the end of the month. Carefully study directions in Chapter XI, so that the plants do not suffer. The best time for fall planting of roses is just before freezing weather. Prepare the beds as early as possible and carefully follow directions.

If your climbing roses are in an exposed location, tie them up firmly with broad strips of rags so that the wind will not beat them against the trellis and bruise the bark. We hope you have observed the pruning rules so that there will not be a mass of useless branches to catch the wind. See illustration, page 113, and explanation, page 116.

FALL PLANTING: In many instances autumn planting of perennials is greatly to be preferred to spring planting. It is essential, however, that the transplanting be done early enough in the fall to allow the plants to become well established before the ground freezes for the winter. As a general rule perennials which bloom in early spring benefit by autumn planting, while perennials which bloom in late summer or autumn should be planted in the spring. Remember general rules are dangerous as Phlox and Oriental Poppy are best divided

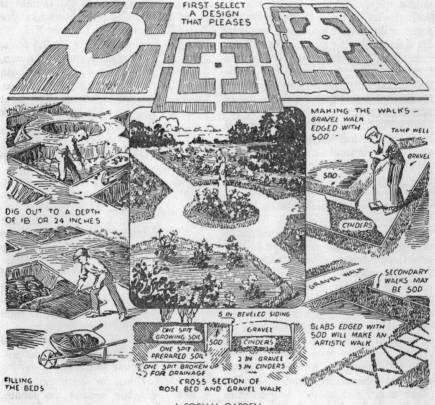

A FORMAL GARDEN

This is the time of year to construct a semi-formal garden, so that beds will settle for the rose planting just before freezing weather. Poor construction always leads to disappointment. Make the walks first and beds afterwards. Follow instructions in Chapters II and XI. Soak the five-inch beveled siding boards, used for walk edges with a hose and keep them wet for a few days so that they will bend nicely if firmly staked. Set them only one-half inch above soil level so that they do not interfere with mowing.

shortly after blooming, while Chrysanthemums, Lupines, Anemones, etc., must wait until the approach of warm weather. The only satisfactory way is to ascertain the needs of each plant.

In the autumn the soil and weather conditions are often more favorable for planting than in early spring and the plants will receive less check in being moved. If their root systems become well established before winter sets in they will be able to make rapid growth in the spring and will·receive no setback. In the autumn the average gardener will also have more time for planting than during the busy spring months.

In the fall the air becomes cooler than the soil which causes a cessation of the flow of sap to the leaves and all activity is centered in root growth. This is one of nature's wise provisions. Next spring the plant will suddenly be called to produce green leaves and blossoms before any great underground activity can take place. How necessary it is therefore that it have strong roots at this time. After any disturbance to the roots a plant should be allowed time to recover before top growth is demanded.

As long as the ground maintains a temperature of 40 degrees this root growth continues; long after early frosts have taken the tops and all apparent activity has ceased, the roots are completing their recovery. Then, too, the freezing and thawing of winter compact the soil loosely about them, eliminating all air pockets and setting them for spring activity.

In fall never use fertilizers rich in readily available nitrogen for fear the plants may be stimulated into late top growth which will winterkill.

In fall it is best to arrange the soil about the crown, so that the water flows away from it. The plant is likely to settle later and be injured if a pool forms about it during freezing weather. In spring it is best to plant level or even allow a little depression about the stem to catch the water. Be sure to mulch with hardwood leaves after the ground is frozen. This avoids heaving and root breaking.

Care should be taken that the plants are well watered during a period of autumn drought. Many annuals are best planted in the fall. See plant list 24, page 151.

WINTER PROTECTION: It soon will be time to apply winter protection to the perennial border. Study the details on pages 128–29 and plant list No. 1 and No. 2 on page 140.

SWEET PEAS: Insurance for good sweet peas next year is to dig the trench now (two to three feet) and mix the soil well with plenty of manure. Seeds are planted so early in the spring that there is hardly time to do it then.

RENOVATE THE FLOWER BED: Now is a good time to get ready for spring. Beds renovated or newly prepared now will be settled and ready for spring transplanting. See Chapter X.

HOUSE PLANTS

BULBS: It takes many weeks to get a bulb ready to bloom when forcing indoors. Read instructions from pages 329 to 339 and you may have indoor cheer all winter. Oxalis comes in yellow (Bermuda Buttercup) and pink (Grand Duchess). If planted now it will bloom in a few weeks and continue.

OTHER PLANTS: Those who expect to raise flowers indoors had best read the entire chapter on the subject, starting with page 313.

HERBS: A plant or two of parsley, taken up from the garden and reset in a pot of good soil, will do well all winter if kept watered and in a sunny window of the kitchen. This is one herb whose appearance, odor and flavor are all welcome through the cold weather. Chives, rose geranium, garden sage and thyme for seasoning can also be maintained in this manner.

CARE: The first few days in the house is the critical period for indoor plants. Use great care in watering and be sure to keep the foliage sprayed lest the plant dry up too quickly. There is a lot of difference between outdoor and indoor conditions, which must be considered.

GREENHOUSE AND COLDFRAMES

SEEDLINGS: When self-sown seedlings are found in the perennial border it is a simple matter to transplant them to deep flats and carry them through the winter in a coldframe. In many instances, of course, their blossom colors will vary somewhat from those of their parents.

Coldframes in which young perennial plants are being carried through the winter should be kept closed now except on warm days. When growth ceases, cover the sash with mats to exclude the sun and stabilize the temperature. Give them air during mild winter days.

BULBS: Don't neglect to get Hyacinths and other early flowering types of bulbous plants boxed up or planted in pots preparatory to forcing them in the greenhouse. When planning for this don't forget that many of the fine modern Daffodil varieties are good for forcing purposes.

CHRYSANTHEMUMS: Stop feeding the greenhouse Chrysanthemums just as soon as the buds show color. It is a good practice to shade the greenhouse slightly in order that development may be normal. Remember outdoor Chrysanthemums must be protected from frost on cold nights with cloth screens.

TREES AND SHRUBS

CONIFEROUS EVERGREENS: Don't forget to water the evergreens just before they go into the winter, if the weather is at all dry. All your evergreens will grow better if mulched with strawy manure after the ground freezes but especially don't neglect to mulch, with manure or at least with straw or some loose material, those evergreens that were transplanted during the current year. The results will well repay you. Before applying the mulch, soak the ground to a depth of two or three feet.

BROAD-LEAVED EVERGREENS: A final mulching with Pine needles or rotting Oak leaves should be given to the Rhododendrons and other broad-leaved evergreens. It will maintain soil acidity, conserve the soil moisture, and generally serve to protect the roots and create natural conditions favorable to growth. Where Rhododendrons are growing in places exposed to strong winds and winter sunlight it is a good idea to give them some protection with evergreen boughs.

FRUITS: Dwarf fruit trees, now available in excellent quality and variety, are highly desirable features for the home grounds, large or small. They can be planted successfully now. The espalier types can be grown against walls, trellises or fences.

TRANSPLANTING: The planting of new trees and shrubs may be attended to at this time. Fall plantings usually give better results than similar work done in spring, except with a few sorts which have soft fleshy roots—Rose of Sharon, Magnolias, Tulip trees, Birch, Dogwood, etc.

GRAPES: Grapevine cuttings can be taken when leaves fall. Let them be of the past season's growth, with two joints each. Bury them outdoors, butts up, for callousing. An often better plan is to cover them with sand in the cellar, watering lightly at long intervals until spring. See instructions for hardwood cuttings, page 293.

THE GARDEN IN NOVEMBER

A *haze on the far horizon,*
The infinite tender sky,
The ripe, rich tints of the cornfields,
And the wild geese sailing high;
And ever on upland and lowland,
The charm of the goldenrod—
Some of us call it Autumn,
And others call it God.
—W. H. CARRUTH

With the falling of the leaves and the coming of the frost, activity does not cease for the thrifty gardener. A garden properly put to sleep for its three-month dormant period, will show surprising results during the following nine months of its activity. In working out of doors at this time of year, gardeners should wear suitable clothes and avoid standing around when hot and sweaty.

GENERAL

First comes the problem of leaves. Hardwood leaves, such as Oak, Hickory and Beech, should be carefully put aside for winter mulching. They do not rot quickly nor pack down to smother the plants. Leaves of the quickly decaying sorts, such as Maple, become humus by spring if composted. The leaves which are not suitable for mulching should be composted for various purposes as shown on pages 46 and 280 and also described under "Humus" on page 32. Never pile new leaves on old heaps as it takes two years to make good compost and new leaves would spoil the already rotted ones. Keep them wet and shaded, if possible. Never burn them, for that is waste.

We must remember that root activity goes on until cold weather. Therefore, even after the top growth has ceased, stirring the soil surface between the larger plants is a distinct advantage. In most gardens this is neglected with resulting loss.

Ill-kept gardens breed disease and insects. Clean up all refuse and burn the stalks and other material likely to decay. Thoroughly sterilize the ground by consistent cultivation. Some gardeners use the stalks of garden flowers for winter mulching. This is extremely poor economy, as it offers disease an opportunity to take charge of your garden. The best preventive of disease is to remove all dead flower stalks. All peat which has been used for mulching during the summer should now be raked off and put aside to be used as ground conditioner, using new peat next season. This removes all dead and diseased plant leaves, allowing for a fresh clean start next spring.

Poison ivy, that gardener's bane, is relatively harmless at this season and by many can now be handled with impunity. The surest way to banish it at this time is to grub out every root from the soil. But be sure you are not susceptible before you handle it.

PESTS

Rabbits and field mice are a nuisance of the winter season. The depredations of field mice are to a large extent due to too early mulching, which causes them to seek a warm winter home in the mulch and to feed upon your plants or roots while snowed in. Field mice also inhabit drains if not prevented from entering them by gratings over the open end. The abandoned burrows of moles should also be destroyed and if evidence of the mice are found in them, they may be poisoned in the manner described for moles on pages 51 and 52.

Rabbits gnaw the bark of young trees. Protect them with a collar of tar paper or a fence of poultry wire or use one of the proprietary animal-repellent sprays obtainable at seed stores.

Lilacs, poplars, most smooth-barked trees and practically all fruit trees are subject to the attacks of San José scale and should be sprayed with one of the soluble oil mixtures. Sprays sufficiently strong to kill scale on shrubs and trees can be applied from now until March; at any other time they would injure buds or bark.

THE LAWN

Low spots in the lawn or irregularities in the surface may be top-dressed now. Use good soil, and when not more than two inches of it is applied, the grass has a chance to come through again.

If you have not done so, you may still apply a fall compost dressing as directed on page 45. Raw bone meal is especially good for grass if applied at this season. Be sure to keep all leaves and all other heavy matter off the grass as it smothers very easily during extremely cold weather.

AMONG THE FLOWERS

PERENNIALS: The early days of November bring the last call for the safe transplanting of herbaceous perennials. Firm the clumps well after watering them. Water which collects upon the surface of the garden during the winter

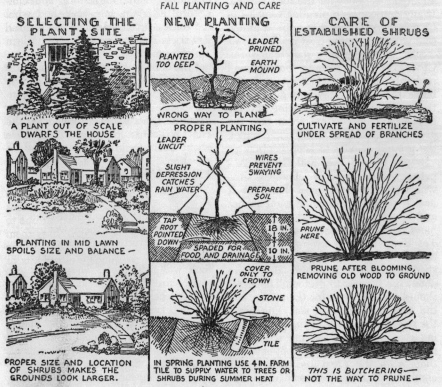

FALL PLANTING AND CARE

SELECTING THE PLANT SITE

A PLANT OUT OF SCALE DWARFS THE HOUSE

PLANTING IN MID LAWN SPOILS SIZE AND BALANCE —

PROPER SIZE AND LOCATION OF SHRUBS MAKES THE GROUNDS LOOK LARGER.

NEW PLANTING

PLANTED TOO DEEP
LEADER PRUNED
EARTH MOUND
WRONG WAY TO PLANT

PROPER PLANTING
LEADER UNCUT
SLIGHT DEPRESSION CATCHES RAIN WATER
WIRES PREVENT SWAYING
PREPARED SOIL
TAP ROOT POINTED DOWN
18 IN.
10 IN.
SPADED FOR FOOD AND DRAINAGE

COVER ONLY TO CROWN
STONE
TILE
IN SPRING PLANTING USE 4 IN. FARM TILE TO SUPPLY WATER TO TREES OR SHRUBS DURING SUMMER HEAT

CARE OF ESTABLISHED SHRUBS

CULTIVATE AND FERTILIZE UNDER SPREAD OF BRANCHES

PRUNE HERE
PRUNE AFTER BLOOMING, REMOVING OLD WOOD TO GROUND

THIS IS BUTCHERING — NOT THE WAY TO PRUNE —

Fall is the best time to plant trees and shrubbery. Be careful in your selection or you may injure rather than beautify your property. Installation of a piece of tile will facilitate watering next summer. Trim late flowering shrubs now but delay work on early flowering types until after they bloom next spring. Mulch with new straw-filled manure as soon as the ground is frozen solid.

will freeze and may damage perennials. Little ditches will carry this off. See that the beds drain well.

CHRYSANTHEMUMS: When they are through flowering remove the stalks at once within a few inches of the ground. This will help root development and make them send out vigorous sprouts in the spring. Some may be lifted and heeled into the coldframe. Plants for potting can be taken from the side sprouts which will develop next May.

BULBS AND ROOTS: This is a good time to work lime around the Iris. Tulips may be planted until December if the weather is mild. Ask your seedsman about the varieties for the rock garden. If any outdoor bulb planting remains to be done, do not forget to apply a mulch that will exclude the frost for five or six weeks, so that proper roots can form. Otherwise, next spring's flowers will probably be unsatisfactory and the bulbs themselves may suffer. Some of the hardy Lilies are late getting into the market. Be sure to get them into the ground as quickly as possible and mulch the ground heavily to keep it open.

ROSES: Hybrid Teas and Hybrid Perpetuals, shrubs, hardy climbers, etc., will winter well in most localities if heeled up with soil six or eight inches and covered, loosely, with leaves. The more tender varieties are more trouble. Tea Roses must be covered with straw and heeled up around the base to help shed the water. Standard Roses are about the hardest to protect. The stems should be laid down for the winter and the tops covered with soil. Dig away the soil from one side of the crown, taking care not to expose the roots, and then lay the canes in a trench, covering them with the excavated soil. Hardy climbers, of course, do not need this attention.

While the more severe pruning of Roses should be left until spring, shortening the branches will keep them from being blown about by the wind and make them easier to protect. Be sure to remove all leaves from the ground and burn them; also remove all summer mulch, as previously described. Do not be in too big a hurry to cover Roses as it is best to have a freeze first.

MULCHING: Late this month or in early December is the time to put on the perennial border mulch for the winter after the ground first freezes a couple of inches deep. Applying it earlier means the chance of harboring destructive field mice which are still on the lookout for comfortable winter quarters.

Heavy mulching of Peonies is not desirable. Winter protection is seldom needful after the first year, and when too thick a layer is applied the result is flowerless stalks. At most, apply a light mulch of manure over the root area, but not the crowns. Wait to do this until the leaves die. Do not use old stalks of your flowers as it may help to carry disease. Be especially sure to burn the stalks of Peonies, Delphinium, Hollyhocks, etc. Don't forget to apply a shovelful of ashes about each Delphinium and read instructions for winter protection on pages 128 and 129.

HOUSE PLANTS

CARE: Winter house plants need particular care to help them weather the generally adverse conditions. Feeding every month with concentrated plant food will help them. They benefit by moist air. To secure it indoors, try setting each pot in a tray of pebbles which is kept filled with water almost to the top level of the stones. Of course, the real remedy for too dry air lies in the use of one of the modern house humidifiers. Scrub the foliage with soap solution; scrub the green scum off the pots. Complete instructions will be found in Chapter XXII.

FORCING: If you are planning to have some Hyacinths indoors, November is the last chance to pot them. Read pages 329 to 339 and then ask your seedsman for some of the newer varieties of forcing bulbs. Hyacinths and many others respond especially well to various easy treatments and will bloom until April. Bring in bulbs the latter part of the month to bloom all winter.

GREENHOUSE AND COLDFRAME

VEGETABLES: Do not neglect to make successional sowings in the greenhouse of vegetable crops such as beans, beets, carrots, lettuce, etc. The secret of success is sowing in small quantities and frequently. Clumps of rhubarb can also be taken with a sharp spade, using care to get the whole clump. Plant them in deep boxes, kegs or other receptacles or in peat moss in the corner of the cellar and they will give excellent winter results.

FLOWER SEEDS: It is not too late to start seeds of some of the more rapid-growing annuals in the greenhouse for winter flowers. Of these may be mentioned Calliopsis, Candytuft and the ever-popular Mignonette.

PERENNIALS: There are a number of popular perennials which force well. Clumps of Coreopsis, Candytuft, Shasta Daisy, etc., may be lifted, potted and then plunged in a sheltered bed outside to ripen properly before forcing.

SWEET PEAS: Sweet Peas in the greenhouse should be fed freely with liquid manures. The first flowers to appear should be pinched off to conserve the plants' strength. Keep the atmosphere dry at night.

CHRISTMAS FLOWERS: Poinsettias, Primulas and other heat-loving crops intended for Christmas bloom must be forced evenly and not too rapidly. A temperature of 75 degrees or even 80 degrees when plenty of moisture is available, will be beneficial to them.

SHRUBS: At this time all hardwooded forcing plants such as Lilacs, Cherries,

Deutzia, Wisteria, etc., should be lifted from their places about the grounds and placed in tubs or boxes for winter forcing.

CARNATIONS: Carnation plants should be kept supported and properly disbudded. Never allow the benches to accumulate green mold. The surface of the ground should be kept stirred. Topdress with sheep manure.

TREES AND SHRUBS

PLANTING: Where circumstances are such as to necessitate very late planting of trees or shrubs, it is well to remember that heavy mulching will keep frost out of the ground. Thus the soil both around the stock and on the proposed site can be kept workable until December at least. Newly planted trees (even small ones) require some sort of steadying support against wind and storm. Stakes or guy wires are effective for this purpose, depending on the tree size. These should be securely placed at the time of planting and left for a year. Newly planted shade trees are often injured by the sun during the first winter. This is called "sun scald" and is prevented by wrapping the trunk with burlap or paper tree wrap. It is especially necessary on smooth bark trees. A collar about eighteen inches high fastened about the base of the tree will keep its bark from being injured by mice or rabbits.

Shrubs which have been transplanted from the wild will come up much more compactly if they are cut down to the ground and thereby forced to send up new growth. Before replanting, better trim off all broken roots, cutting them cleanly with a knife or pruning shears. Berry-bearing shrubs are most appreciated just now. Study the list on page 77 and 78, and order some for next season.

FRUITS: Dwarf fruit trees have a double purpose in furnishing flowers in the spring, as well as fruit in the fall.

They are particularly fitted to the small lot. Early in November is a good time to plant most of them, especially if a light mulch is applied to the roots. Apples and Pears are among the most satisfactory kinds. Cherries and Peaches are also available. Don't forget to protect them at the ground with a tar paper collar.

EVERGREENS: Late fall planting of evergreens is risky. This class of plant should always be given plenty of time to re-establish its roots before the advent of really cold weather stops underground growth. Don't forget to supply even well established evergreens with plenty of water before freezing weather.

RHODODENDRONS: Rhododendrons should have their roots protected by a heavy mulch of leaves or litter. Some branches of pines or other evergreen thrust into the ground between the plants will prevent sun scald. In districts where evergreen branches are not plentiful, a screen of painted wooden boards, cornstalks or palings (woven together by the method illustrated on page 18), or burlap stretched out on stakes to the east and south, will serve the purpose. See Chapter VII.

PRUNING: November and December is a good time to clean out the tangle of overgrown vines. Cutting out the old diseased wood will send the strength into the remaining branches. It is much better to prune the flowering vines now, than to risk disturbing the tender shoots after they start in the spring. Besides, there is the saving of valuable time then. See page 113, Chapter IX.

Most of the early spring flowering shrubs are pruned after blooming in the spring. See page 72, Chapter IV. The Peegee Hydrangea should be trimmed back to two to four buds on each shoot. Remove all flower heads and cut out the old branches of the blue and pink flowered variety, but remember that if you cut out the new shoots, you will lose your bloom next year. The dwarf pinkish Spirea (Anthony Waterer) should be cut back about two-thirds and deadwood removed. Summer flowering Tamarix should be brought into shape and old growth removed. Remove the suckers which spring up from the roots of the Lilac bushes and also the Snowberry. Cut out the oldest stems of the Mockorange (Philadelphus) to the ground—the blossoms, next year, will come on wood which grew this season. Shape up the Rose of Sharon. Take out the oldest parts of untrimmed Privet hedges and shape them up. Hill up soil around Butterfly Bush but do not cut off the tops until spring. They may live through.

WINTER PROTECTION

Mulches of leaves or other material applied to the plant before the ground is frozen often do irreparable damage. More plants are lost by smothering in this manner than by the severity of the weather. Any plant which is injured by the first light freeze of fall cannot be regarded as hardy and should be taken inside or at least wintered in a coldframe.

Many plants require cold weather and will not grow if they are not partially exposed all winter. Some alpines, for instance, are accustomed to mild summers and long severe winters. Therefore, they are rather difficult to handle in our more southerly states. Some of our hardy plants do not require any protection at all and the careless application of mulches about the garden will certainly bring havoc rather than the effect desired.

If we mulch with the kind of leaves which get soft and pack down quickly, they will soon form a heavy mass which will retain water and exclude air over long periods. In the spring, these leaves tend to ferment and generate heat, which coaxes the plants into activity too soon, exposing them to late frost. Hardwood leaves, such as Oak, Beech, and Hickory, do not absorb water so readily and remain loose all winter.

Most plants with evergreen leaves cannot stand complete covering. It is therefore well to place a row of stakes or a ring of poultry netting close about the plant so that the ground can be covered to prevent sudden thawing while the evergreen leaves are not. Let the mulch be somewhat funnel shaped inside the ring. Delphiniums require a shovel or two of coal ashes about their crowns, and some alpines or fuzzy-leaved plants need the cold but do not like water upon their leaves. For this reason we cover them with a piece of glass.

We illustrate some forms of windbreaks for evergreens of various kinds. For best results these should also be mulched after a thorough ground freeze, in the manner shown. Carefully grade the ground so that a basin is formed to hold the water. If this mulch is of manure it saturates the ground with its fertilizing value ready for the spring start. If growth is not desired, the mulch may be of leaves to prevent the evaporation of moisture from the ground. Deciduous trees also benefit from mulching. Smooth-bark trees are subject to sun scald, especially when newly planted, and a wrapping of burlap or heavy paper protects them against this as well as the entrance of borers in the spring.

Tender bedding roses must be protected with straw or cornstalks which will allow the entrance of air but prevent cold wind. Tender climbers must be taken from the trellis, covered with straw and buried in a trench so that

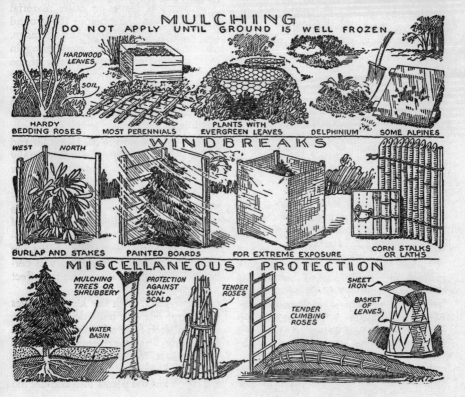

MULCHING
DO NOT APPLY UNTIL GROUND IS WELL FROZEN

HARDWOOD LEAVES
SOIL

HARDY BEDDING ROSES   MOST PERENNIALS   PLANTS WITH EVERGREEN LEAVES   DELPHINIUM   SOME ALPINES

WINDBREAKS

WEST   NORTH

BURLAP AND STAKES   PAINTED BOARDS   FOR EXTREME EXPOSURE   CORN STALKS OR LATHS

MISCELLANEOUS PROTECTION

MULCHING TREES OR SHRUBBERY
PROTECTION AGAINST SUN-SCALD
TENDER ROSES
WATER BASIN
TENDER CLIMBING ROSES
SHEET IRON
BASKET OF LEAVES

they have an inch or two of soil over them. This does not apply to ordinary bedding roses (see pages 174 to 176) or to hardy climbers and ramblers which only need to be pruned and securely tied to their supports so that the wind does not beat them about too much and bruise their bark.

Many exotic plants must be covered with baskets of leaves; in order to keep them from becoming damp, a piece of sheet iron is tacked over the basket to shed water.

With gardeners and investigators always on the lookout for new, effective methods and materials, interesting developments are occurring steadily. The invention, a few years ago, of glass wool, made of fine threads spun from molten glass, was the result of a search for insulating material. Actually, the cotton batting-like material, obtainable in rolls, makes a neat, good-looking, elastic mulch for plants that quickly resent being smothered. Also this material admits moisture and some light, does not mat down, and can be rolled up and stored between seasons, thus cutting down its cost. It should be handled with care (and gloves), since the tiny glass threads can break off and penetrate the skin.

Another new mulching material, excellent if it can be secured at a reasonable price, consists of cranberry tops and stems as cut from commercial bogs in New England, New Jersey and other cranberry regions. The matted stiff, wiry stems make a springy, not too heavy, durable protection that seems to be winning considerable popularity.

The real gardener takes care of his plants in the late fall so that they reach the winter season in a healthy condition to insure a good start for the coming year. Carefully read the instructions on page 128 and consider them in conjunction with these instructions.

GARDEN HINTS FOR DECEMBER

Under the snow of each December
Lie buds of next year's May, remember,
Under the snow lie next year's flow'rs,
And always ahead lie happy hours.
　　　　　　　　—Douglas Malloch

GENERAL

Now, until snow falls, is a good time to do any filling or grading about the grounds so that loose soil can settle during the coming cold months.

Unless fallen leaves, twigs and such rubbish are kept cleaned out of the drains the latter are likely to clog and freeze and sometimes result in destructive garden floods. A final cleaning out of such places had better be done just before freezing weather sets in.

Manure for next year's garden should be purchased now. It improves greatly with age and handling and it is usually possible to get manure in the fall, while next spring it is uncertain. Cover or protect it from excessive rainfall which will wash out valuable food elements.

Tools should be cleaned during the next ninety days until they look like new. Anyone who has adopted the policy of using only clean tools knows how much easier they work. Read the instructions on page 270 and get them in order for future use.

Before the winter really shuts down, give the compost heap a final turning over with a fork so as to mix in the latest additions and hasten their decomposition. A generous sprinkling of hydrated lime will help things along and correct any tendency to acidity.

All of the ashes from the open fires this winter ought to be saved for garden use in the spring. They are a fertile source of potash, an essential plant food. Store them in watertight containers over the winter and keep them dry as their strength easily leaches away. When applying them in the spring use them thinly, especially on lawns. They are said to help save Asters from blight and are sure to help loosen the soil if used consistently. Hardwood ashes can be bought by the bag, in case you haven't enough to meet your requirements.

Rhubarb may be forced in the cellar or attic of the dwelling by planting good-sized clumps in barrels or boxes and placing them beside the furnace or chimney. The soil should be kept moderately moist. Chicory is one of the best winter salad plants. It can be forced in any ordinary cellar by planting the roots in boxes and keeping them dark.

If you expect to secure any landscape service this year do it now as the man you select will have more time to give you now than later in the season, and while your grounds are bare he can get a better idea of your problems. Be sure that you have made the final clean-up of your grounds, removed all plant stalks, turned off the water and drained the hose. Be especially sure that any garden ornaments such as urns or jars are turned over to keep them from collecting water and being broken when it freezes.

CHRISTMAS FOR THE BIRDS

Why not a Christmas tree for the birds? Trim the branches with dried fruit, suet in pine cones, and as a special plum pudding tie on some packages of bird treat, so loved by the canaries.

Feeding the winter birds is an inter-

esting, useful and humane habit. Don't start it if you don't intend to keep it up, as they learn to depend upon it and are lost when you stop. Some of my apartment dwelling friends save their melon seeds all summer to attract the saucy fellows to their window sills in winter.

Be sure to keep water for them in pans that can be brought inside to be thawed out. This is one of their chief needs when everything is frozen. Grit or sand is another, so have a little fine poultry grit mixed with sand accessible for them.

A supply of sunflower, hemp and millet seed supplemented with table scraps will take care of the food matter very nicely. Suet wired to a branch is welcome to several species. A secluded fence corner facing south makes a good feeding station. A platform located in an open position in a hemlock, spruce or pine tree is also very good. Protect these stations from cats by a band of tin twelve inches wide, tacked around the post or tree, about six or eight feet from the ground to keep the cats from reaching the birds as they feed. This protection is illustrated in the August calendar.

Though it is nice to regale birds with bread crumbs and peanuts, natural foods served naturally are a more permanent satisfaction.

Seedheads of Sunflowers, Zinnias, Cosmos, Marigolds, and other common garden flowers are granaries quickly found and resorted to all winter by white-tailed juncos, goldfinches, chickadees, white-throated tree, song, and fox sparrows, and many others.

The junco is the most prevalent of our winter bird visitors. He comes about October 1 and stays until the last of May. The time to convince him he has reached a good stop is early in the fall before he is driven by hunger to seek other food. That is the time to teach him to feed from your window sill and insure his companionship throughout the winter. Juncos are absolutely fearless and radiate cheer in the garden. They come in tones of slate-gray and are often mistaken for English sparrows except when their outer tail feathers are conspicuously flashed in the light.

Who has not thrilled to see the cardinal fluttering about the low branches of shrubs in the spring? Yet the writer has observed this bird at all times of the winter. He makes no attempt at concealment but passes most of the time in the lower undergrowth, selecting a most conspicuous perch at a season when color is lacking, challenging the attention of the world. Next to the mocking bird he has the richest and mellowest voice and whistle of southern songsters. The female cardinal also sings but has less volume than her mate. The cardinal nests in bushes laying three or four brown speckled eggs in April.

The goldfinch, which goes by the common name of wild canary, wears a brown coat in the winter, but sheds it for his goldfinch costume in the spring, when he is ready for his song of "perchic-o-ree."

The chickadee is an active and ever welcome visitor to our lunch counters and often can be taught to perch on our hands. He can be identified by his clearly enunciated "chicadee" and its variations.

PESTS

Seeds which you have collected may be placed in dry paper packets and put in a tin box or glass jar so that they will not only be kept dry but be protected from mice. It is a little too much trouble to place each in a separate glass container but a great many paper packets may be put in one closed fruit jar. It is well to conduct a monthly examination of stored roots, bulbs and tubers to see if they are being injured by mice as well as to look for signs of shriveling from being too dry or of rotting from too much dampness. If they are sprouting remove them to a cooler place.

———

Tangled weed and grass patches make snug winter harbors from which field mice can forage. A word to the wise should suffice, but if you decide to burn out these refuges, choose a windless day to keep fire from spreading.

Do not scrape the bark on trees to destroy insect pests. It is impossible to get into the crevices where insects hibernate, and in many cases the tree is injured by removing the green outer bark. Use a stiff brush or broom to remove the cocoons of various sort found attached to the bark and in sheltered recesses of the tree. Close examination of Apple and Wild Cherry twigs may disclose small, dark, amber-colored collars or clusters of insect eggs from which will hatch husky colonies of tent caterpillars if not destroyed. They can be broken away from the bark or the twig can be cut off and burned.

Remember our previous suggestion that poison ivy can be best handled at this time. The oil which causes the skin irritation is most nearly absent now. If you are susceptible, be sure to wear gloves and wash your hands with brown soap after handling. Sulphuric acid or copper sulphate in strong solution poured upon the crowns will kill the roots. Loosen the soil slightly when it is not frozen and pour the poison upon it.

AMONG THE FLOWERS

BULBS AND ROOTS: By this time all the cultural work for the season seems over. All tender bulbs, roots and corms should be safely stored where they will neither mold nor dry out. A coat of manure should be sifted over the Lilies-of-the-valley and all spring flowering bulbs mulched with leaves after a thorough ground freeze.

PEONIES: Peonies seem to flower best after a heavy continual freezing during the winter. Do not mulch them or protect them unless newly divided and then only with a very light mulch.

ALPINES: It is good practice to sow alpine seed early in December in an outdoor coldframe. They will not germinate until spring, so the frame should be kept shaded and ventilated so that they may remain frozen until March. Seeds may also be sown in flats and placed in some convenient outdoor location where they will be shaded and well frozen. A good covering of snow seems to help.

ROSES: By the latter part of December there should have been sufficient ground freezes to permit placing manure between the hilled-up Roses. Do not cover the hills with new manure.

ROCK GARDEN: Some of the more tender rock plants may be protected with a thin (very thin) mulch of salt marsh hay, or better, evergreen boughs. These should be applied to act as windbreaks and the plants should be clearly visible through the mulch. Now is a good time to collect odd stones for extending the rock garden.

THE GARDEN INDOORS

GENERAL CARE: Much common failure of house plants is due to overwatering and poor drainage which is even more objectionable indoors than it is in the outdoor garden. They must have both food and drink, but wet soggy soil is not to their liking. A good soaking once a week is better than a little every day. Apply enough water so that it drips from the drainage hole in the bottom of the pot. Regular attention each day is more likely to insure success than an occasional thorough working over. The foliage must be kept free of insects. Sponging the leaves with a soap solution to which a good tobacco extract has been added will destroy white scale, red spider, mealy bug. Read carefully pages 313 to 320 and refresh your mind on this subject.

FERNS: Ferns, palms and other house plants should be treated occasionally to some of the concentrated plant foods sold for the purpose. Keep the surface of the soil loosened so that no green scum forms. They do best at a temperature of sixty to seventy degrees with a weekly spray from above, using a plant syringe.

HERBS FOR SEASONING: We want to again remind you of our suggestion in the October calendar that pots of parsley, chives, rose geranium, garden sage and thyme add life to the kitchen window and are a welcome addition for seasoning food.

BULBS: It is not too late to pot some bulbs in soil or to force them in water. It seems a long time to wait ten or twelve weeks for them to root but the time soon passes and properly handled they are easy and sure of bloom. Look over the instructions starting with page 329. Don't let the idea of plunging bulbs outside frighten you. It is quite easy and once tried will become a yearly habit.

INDOOR DECORATIONS: An outdoor flavor can be brought into our living rooms by the addition of branches kept in water. Small Laurel branches will last all winter and the common Japanese Barberry, with its attractive berries, Euonymus and other evergreens, all make an excellent bouquet. Try table decorations consisting of small boughs clipped from your evergreen trees.

CHRISTMAS DECORATIONS: It is surprising the amount of Christmas decorations that can be made in a few minutes with material from your own yard. Clippings from your evergreen trees and the broad-leaf evergreen plants such as Bittersweet, Myrtle, Mahonia, Holly, Laurel and berried shrubs lend themselves well to this purpose. For wreaths fasten the sprigs to wire coat hangers,

bent to the proper shape, with thread or short pieces of fine wire. Every gardener should have in his tool kit a bundle of tag wires, useful for many purposes, which can be purchased by the thousands from your stationer. Sprigs of White Pine, Hemlock and Pfitzer Juniper make nice soft wreaths, but the Hemlock can only be used outside because it drops quickly in the heat. Garnish these ornaments with sleighbells, red ribbon and silver tinsel. Other suitable material for wreaths includes: Pines (White, Red, Banksiana and Swiss Mountain); Spruces (Colorado, Blue, used sparingly), White, and Oriental; Arborvitae (this keeps well); Cypresses in varying shades of green.

For sprays use: Juniper with its colored berries, Red Cedar, mingled with one of the broad-leafed evergreens such as Rhododendron, Leucothoe, Galax, or a bit of Box.

For roping: Balsam Fir; Pine.

THE GREAT MAGICIAN TELLS HOW TO HAVE A MERRY CHRISTMAS AND HAPPY NEW YEAR.

FOR WINTER FOLIAGE: A welcome touch on a bleak winter day is the verdant vine of a common sweet potato growing in a jar of water. Hold it suspended in the water, using some toothpicks stuck into it if necessary. Kiln-dried potatoes are not so suitable for this purpose, and those that have been sulphured are useless. So get them direct from the grower if possible.

GREENHOUSE AND COLDFRAMES

EQUIPMENT CARE: As fast as seed flats are emptied to be stored for the winter they should be washed and boiling water should be poured over them. A good soil disinfectant (see soil sterilization, page 260) will serve the same purpose. Frames, tomato trellises, garden seats and other wooden garden material should be painted. Use good paint and where necessary apply two coats. This is considerably cheaper than constant renewals.

MATS FOR FRAMES: Frames in which semi-hardy plants are being wintered, or frames that are used as growing mediums should have some kind of covering. Loose hay may be used but the best covering is a jute mat. Home-made mats of old carpet or burlap stuffed with straw also serve the purpose. For real winter results, though, nothing can equal the installation of one of the electric heating systems.

MULCHING: Plants that are growing in benches, such as Carnations, Roses, Antirrhinum, etc., should be mulched with cow manure or soil made of equal parts of topsoil and well-rotted manure with a little bone meal added.

TREES AND SHRUBS

PLANTING: The planting of deciduous trees and shrubs may be continued just as long as the weather permits. Trees that are to be moved with a ball of frozen earth around their roots may now have trenches dug to encircle them and facilitate the final digging later on. To guard against the soil ball drying out, these trenches may be filled in with dead leaves or any rough litter.

NUT TREES: The fresh nuts of Hickory, Butternut and Black Walnut will often germinate quite readily if planted outdoors an inch or so deep and left there over the winter. The combined action of frost and moisture splits their hard shells and allows the root to emerge.

TRIMMING: Tree branches that have grown so much as to cast excess shade over the flower plantings should be cut off this winter when, in falling, they can do no damage to the bed. All deciduous tree and shrub trimming may be done now, but be careful in pruning shrubbery now not to do it too severely or you will destroy all the flowering branches for next spring. Tree surgery may be carried on at this time with the greatest safety. Be sure to follow instructions beginning on page 66 and coat all cuts of any size with a special wound dressing from your seed store, asphaltum paint or tar. Prune the fruit trees.

SNOW: The weight of wet snow upon evergreens will often bend and permanently distort or break them. Heavy sticky snow should always be removed as soon as possible so that the weak branches might be given the support of stakes or props.

GARDEN MAGIC MARCHES ON

A Supplementary Review of Recent Trends and Developments in Horticulture

By E. L. D. SEYMOUR

OVER-ALL PROGRESS IN HORTICULTURE

This appendix, like the book it supplements, deals with the simple, peaceful art and science of gardening. Yet in reviewing the trends and developments that have taken place since the book was written, it must recognize that the two outstanding events of the period have been neither simple nor peaceful. They were, of course, World War II and the discovery of the secret of nuclear fission followed by the fashioning of atom and hydrogen bombs. Each has had a marked, even if indirect, effect on gardening. Moreover, if the much hoped for application of the new atomic knowledge to peaceful uses becomes a reality, further effects are inevitable.

But before discussing ways in which gardening has been affected, it is well to recall that, in the last analysis, gardening is a timeless unchanging thing; part and parcel of Nature; controlled and governed by natural laws. Its elements are plants, the soil, animal life, climate, water, sunshine and all the natural manifestations of physical and chemical phenomena. So, whatever the results

of man's scientific research, inventive genius, mechanical ingenuity, and commercial enterprise, let us remember that the "magic" in the garden and in gardening remains unchanged, and marches on as it has since the dawn of time and will until the twilight of life on the earth.

World War II and Gardening

The first and most direct result of World War II was the Victory Garden Program, launched, after much urging by the Men's Garden Clubs of America and other citizen groups, in December, 1941, at a National Garden Conference called by the U. S. Department of Agriculture. The announced purpose was to plan "defense" measures aimed at increased food production, but the term "defense" was quickly discarded in favor of "Victory." Also, whereas the official idea at first was that more and larger farm gardens held the answer, it soon became clear that a vast potential source of vegetables and fruits existed in the small home plots of suburban and even urban areas, and in vacant lots that could be turned into community or neighborhood gardens. The Program thereupon raised its sights and for five years was active all over the country organizing, teaching, guiding, and stimulating citizens of all ages to more abundantly and efficiently grow, conserve, and use the garden crops so needed to insure an adequate, balanced diet. This resulted in some 20,000,000 home gardens and great benefit to those who grew and consumed (and shared) the huge tonnage of food produced. Additional results were lessened demands for transportation, containers, labor, and other factors involved in the commercial production and distribution of food crops, and the release of great quantities of cereals, meats, fats, and other staples urgently needed for our armed forces, the allied nations, and the starving peoples of liberated countries.

The Program, directed from the Extension Service of the Department of Agriculture, operated through State and County Extension agencies, wartime service organizations, garden clubs and centers, amateur and commercial horticultural organizations, botanical gardens, and thousands of volunteer local leaders working individually and in groups. Stimulated by a National Garden Institute, big industrial establishments urged and helped their employees to have gardens. A National Advisory Garden Committee was appointed to maintain contact between the government and the public, and annual Garden Conferences brought leaders in the horticultural field together to appraise results, consider recommendations, and formulate plans for still greater efforts.

All this brought a clearer understanding and greater appreciation of the importance of the home garden, not only as a part of the nation's wartime defenses, but also as one of its vital, permanent resources and one of the bulwarks of its security. As the Department of Agriculture's attitude broadened, increasing attention was given to the needs of nonfarm gardeners, and to plans for expanding Extension Service activities and facilities so as to give more horticultural help to homeowners in villages, cities and suburbs.

Meanwhile, five years of instruction and experience in growing food crops gave millions of people a new basic knowledge of plants and their culture, introduced them to the merits of freshly grown, high quality fruits and vegetables, and inoculated them with a new interest and enthusiasm—that of the gardener. As the wartime emergency lessened, many continued to make a small food garden a part of their home grounds because of the satisfaction and material rewards it gave them. An even larger number, having experienced the pleasure of working in the soil, shifted their attention more and more to ornamental plants—flowers, shrubs, vines, trees, etc., with which to enhance the beauty of their home surroundings. Reflecting that trend, the National Garden Conference of 1946 took up, as one of two major subjects, "a permanent garden program as a feature of the national policy, as a means to a richer, fuller life." After vigorous discussion on broad, far-reaching lines, a resolution was adopted urging the President to create "a permanent advisory commission to secure the necessary leadership . . . for the effective furtherance of progress in the planning and improvement of the home, its grounds, and its community."

Although that particular objective has not yet been attained, a liaison Garden Committee has continued to function, and one result of its efforts was, in June, 1955, Publication PA 262 of the Department of Agriculture entitled "Home and Community Improvement through Gardening and Landscaping."

Another related development was the organization of The National Council for Community Improvement, "a national clearinghouse of information and ideas to help communities help themselves," with headquarters in St. Louis, Mo.

Within the Government there has come slowly but surely realization of the importance of the nursery industry, accompanied by the listing of its organizations in the U. S. D. A. Directory of Horticultural Groups, and the recognition by its Research Branch of horticultural crops on a level with other farm crops. Increasing attention has been given by the Census Bureau to horticultural crop and industry statistics and several special reports compiled by Mr. M. Truman Fossum, agricultural economist, have been issued. Similar examples of the growing stature of horticulture can be seen on regional and state levels, as in New York where a revision of the State Seed Law, effective January, 1956, makes its protective labeling requirements applicable, for the first time, to flower seeds as well as the agricultural and vegetable seeds which were formerly affected.

Post-war Growth of Garden Interest

The postwar years have brought, not only expansion in manufacturing, business and, especially, the building of homes for veterans and for a steadily increasing population, but also a marked proportional increase in the number of individual homes and lots. Add to this larger incomes, more leisure, increasing auto-traffic congestion, greater mechanization of home and garden equipment, and a tremendous upsurge of activity in hobby and do-it-yourself pursuits, and the result has been an unprecedented multiplication of home gardens and home gardeners. In August, 1953, an article in *The Saturday Evening Post* entitled "Thirty Million Gardeners" said, in part: "More individual homes and more free time inevitably mean more gardens and gardeners. But there is also a special compulsion about growing things that helps greatly to place the hobby ahead of all others. Amateur gardeners cannot often take gardening or leave it alone. They are driven by a man-earth attachment that wells up every spring."

In 1955, the American Association of Nurserymen, somewhat more conservatively, estimated the nation's home gardens at 28,500,000. About that time the annual volume of sales of seeds, plants, tools, and other materials needed for those gardens was put at $4 billion, with some $50,000,000 being spent for rose plants alone!

Along with that rising tide of in-

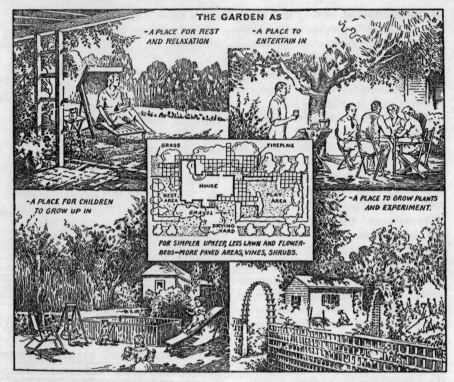

THE GARDEN AS

-A PLACE FOR REST AND RELAXATION

-A PLACE TO ENTERTAIN IN

-A PLACE FOR CHILDREN TO GROW UP IN

-A PLACE TO GROW PLANTS AND EXPERIMENT.

GRASS · FIREPLACE · HOUSE · REST AREA · GRAVEL · PLAY AREA · DRYING YARD

FOR SIMPLER UPKEEP, LESS LAWN AND FLOWER-BEDS—MORE PAVED AREAS, VINES, SHRUBS.

dividual activity, there has come a steady growth of organized activity in the horticultural field. The National Council of State Garden Clubs in 1955 (its 26th year) was composed of 44 state organizations, 10,530 local clubs, and 347,655 members. The Men's Garden Clubs of America had increased in ten years from 50 clubs to more than 150, distributed from coast to coast and from border to border. The American Rose Society, one of the largest of the special-flower organizations, numbers more than 10,000 members, and the African Violet Society, many years its junior, is approaching, if it has not passed, that figure. Garden centers are increasing in number, usefulness, and interest; flower shows break attendance records, and competition for medals and other awards for outstanding new flowers steadily gains impetus and new participants.

Nor is the good these organizations do limited to making more and better gardens. With energy and force that are increasing their prestige, they are starting, carrying forward, and supporting many projects whose benefits spread far. Among these are the memorial Blue Star Highways, the promotion of junior gardening, the testing of new plants, roadside improvement and protection, soil and wildlife conservation, "Plant America," "Keep

America Beautiful," and "Anti-Litterbug" campaigns, the development of gardens for the blind, and the extension of the immensely important garden therapy into more hospitals, especially those for psychiatric patients.

Back of all these endeavors is a determination to co-ordinate them for greater efficiency and economy, as exemplified by the American Horticultural Council. Incorporated in 1945 "to foster understanding and mutual benefit among the organizations and individuals representing the art and science of horticulture —scientific, professional, commercial, and amateur," this organization emerged out of many years of thought and planning that visioned a "United Horticulture—for a more adequate representation of horticulture in national affairs, a more general appreciation of the value of plants to humanity, and a more beautiful America." By 1956, the Council will have sponsored ten National Horticultural Congresses, awarded a number of citations for outstanding horticultural achievement, published a "Directory of American Horticulture" and a "Flower Color Detector," and investigated, through special commissions, problems of plant nomenclature and registration, a plant hardiness zone map, and standards and ethics in horticultural advertising.

Credit for significant progress in the last mentioned field (which, of course, affects the public both as consumers and as gardeners) belongs not only to organized amateurs, but also to the American Association of Nurserymen, the commercial bulb interests, the National Better Business Bureau and its local affiliates and, in the government, the Federal Trade Commission and the Post Office Department. With the aid of the F. T. C., Codes of Trade Practice have been adopted for the gladiolus industry and the chemical soil conditioner industry, and one for the nursery industry is scheduled for a hearing, probably in 1956. Like the laws of the land, these codes and other efforts may not completely prevent misrepresentation and business malpractice, but they are convincing evidence of a growing, widespread desire to clean house when necessary, and to keep it clean.

Gardening in the Atomic Age

Less can be said about the effects on gardening of work in the nuclear fission field—largely because the surface has barely been scratched. At the Brookhaven Laboratories on Long Island and in other places the effects of radioactivity on the performance of plants, the development of new genetic forms, etc., are being studied, but no results have reached the practical, garden utilization stage. However, science is making increasing use of radioactive isotopes or "tracing particles" in exploring the mysteries of plant as well as animal physiology. Just as a dose of bismuth can be traced by X ray on its passage through a human subject, so a substance made radioactive, be it a food element, a pesticide, or a normal component of a plant, can be followed in its course from the soil into and through the system of a plant. To what this may lead is anybody's guess, but it is, at all events, the utilization of new knowledge along paths of peace and, be it hoped, the welfare of mankind.

MODERN THOUGHT AND GARDEN PLANNING

Recent trends in connection with the principles and practices discussed in Chapter I of "Garden Magic" can be summed up by saying that "garden design is becoming more and more an expression of philosophy and a mode of life than a matter of theory, rule, and style." That is, more thought is being given to the purpose and usableness of a garden plan than to its attractive appearance on paper, as an example of artistic design. Says one landscape authority: "Trends in garden design are freer, more casual in effect, more in sympathy with our fast-moving world." Some indications of this, and guideposts for you to use in your own planning, are included in these noticeable trends:

1. Arrangement of garden space for maximum usefulness and enjoyment.

2. The retaining of as much of the character and individuality of the site as possible.

3. A close relationship between the rooms of a house and the garden areas outside them, thus making the outdoors, in effect, an extension or expansion of the indoor living space.

4. Maximum provision for privacy and solitude, especially for those who seek rest and change from the turmoil and strain of city or business life.

5. Provision for outdoor living—cooking, eating, entertaining, relaxation, and fun—in addition to (perhaps even more than) intensive horticultural activity.

6. The inclusion of food plants (many of which are definitely ornamental) among the flowering kinds, or of a vegetable plot as an intrinsic part of the garden.

7. The appreciation and use of vistas and other attractive features outside the confines of the garden as part of the over-all garden picture.

8. The intelligent use of more native plant materials, because they "belong" in a locality and, being adapted to it, can be grown successfully with less effort.

9. The choice of plants on the basis of the appeal of all their characteristics throughout the year—form, habit, color of bark, foliage color and texture, etc., as well as the usually emphasized flower and fruit qualities.

There are, of course, divergent views as to what a garden should be. Says Clement Gray Bowers, "Today's garden must be easy of maintenance . . . no garden should impose unwelcome burdens of upkeep upon its owner. . . . A few superb plants or flowers, strategically placed, can be more imposing than a whole acre of blooms in a hodgepodge. Backgrounds can be much more important than loud features." Thus we often see fences or walls recommended instead of hedges; paved or graveled terraces and patios at the expense of lawn; raised plant boxes rather than more extensive beds, and other measures designed to cut down maintenance requirements.

Another school, typified by Chester P. Holway, denounces the tendency of "certain builders and interior decorators . . . to present to us a home yard 'turfed' with concrete and accented with a few plants stuck in pots and boxes, and herald it as 'The American Garden.'" According to this viewpoint, "The essential delight in having a garden is in the continual act of gardening. Since this new alfresco decorative scheme banishes that act, except for perfunctory housekeeping, whatever it may be— it cannot be a garden."

Obviously, then, there is no one kind of garden or garden design to fit all places, conditions, needs, and

desires. Or, as F. W. G. Peck, an experienced landscape architect, has said, "There never can be stock plans for home grounds." This emphasizes the importance of planning home grounds *in advance*, and of including some provision for their development in the homemaking budget from the very inception of the idea of possessing a home. Most families, even though inexperienced in homemaking, give some thought to purchase or construction costs, perhaps an architect's fee, taxes, essential furnishings and decorating, and frequently unessential luxuries such as radio, television, etc. But all too often, not until they are actually

A LOG PAVED TERRACE IS DIFFERENT
—
TO MAKE ONE FOLLOW STEPS AS DIRECTED IN CAPTION —

2- SPREAD, RAKE AND TAMP GRAVEL, THEN SAND.

1- DIG OUT TOP SOIL, ROUGHLY LEVEL BOTTOM.

5" LOG SECTIONS

3- ON SAND BED LAY LOG SECTIONS AND LEVEL THEM.

5"
SAND 2"
GRAVEL 4" TO 8"
SUBSOIL

4- TAMP ROUNDS FIRM, SPREAD SAND AND SWEEP TO FILL SPACES

established in their "lovely new home," do they sense the need of "doing something" to make the surroundings as attractive, convenient, and livable as the interior. By that time, in many cases, they have exhausted their funds and are unable to pay either for professional advice and services to make up for their lack of knowledge as to what to do and how and when to do it, or for the plant materials they will need.

Fortunately, there is an increasing tendency to seek (or develop) even a simple basic "master plan" as described in Chapter I, to serve as a guide for systematic, step-by-step garden making over the years as rapidly as circumstances permit. Expert advice at this stage is a sound investment and besides facilitating the work will often prevent mistakes which are always costly to correct. Sometimes a start can be made with the grading, the installation of a drive and other permanent features, and the planting of some slow-growing trees even before the house itself is begun; but in this case building operations must be closely supervised so they will not damage established trees, shrubs, etc.

The picture on page 442 illustrates the planning of a property to provide for a variety of family needs, tastes, and ways of living—probably more than could or would be included on a single small plot. If the prime need is for a place for children to grow up in, plantings of fancy flowers, thorny bushes, aquatic plants in pools and other horticultural specialties may have to be sacrificed for play space and the children's safety. If much entertaining is to be done, shaded terraces and picnic or cooking areas will be wanted. For elderly people, invalids, or those with little time for garden work, the plan should include mainly trees, shrubs and perennials to provide pleasure with a minimum of care. Whereas, if the family includes ardent gardeners, there will be needed ample space for cultivation, a coldframe or hotbed, perhaps a small greenhouse, and certainly a toolshed.

There is much discussion of "modern" gardens to fit modern developments in home architecture, but relatively little agreement as to just what the term means. Builders have at their disposal many new materials such as plywood, plastics, glass products, wallboards and so on with which they can achieve distinctive effects; and architects are devising new models along one-story, split-level, and other lines to meet consumer tastes. But the garden maker works with the same general line of plant materials as always. They can be modified to some extent, at least in form, by pruning, training, espaliering, etc.; they can be arranged in different ways with relation to the house and various garden structures; and there are constantly becoming available new flower colors and patterns as new varieties are introduced. But in the last analysis, the "modernity" of a garden design will probably depend more upon the attitude and outlook of the individual who plans it and of those for whom it is planned, than upon details of the plants used and their placement. Probably the best and most satisfying results will continue to come from the exercise of good taste and restraint in fitting the garden to the home of which it is a part—meaning by "home" the geographical location, the environment, the site, the climate, and the members of the household and their activities, as well as the house itself.

Speaking of climate, considerable attention has been given of late to the possibility of controlling, or at least modifying, the temperature, humidity, and wind conditions in and around a home by the proper selection and arrangement of trees, hedges, windbreaks, etc. Factors involved are orientation and exposure, sun and shade at different times of the day and different seasons of the year, the direction of prevailing winds, local topography, and artificial modifiers of all these. Progressive landscape architects and nurserymen can offer valuable suggestions along these lines covering the kinds of plants needed, and their distribution and after care.

A novel and interesting method of working out a garden plan is the so-called "spatial planning" technique illustrated on page 15, as described and taught at Cornell University by Thomas J. Baird. It consists of working out a plan in three dimensions (instead of one plane with lines drawn on paper) by using little blocks to represent buildings, and twigs, bits of sponge, pebbles and so on to represent plants, boulders, etc. Choose objects of proper size in relation to the dimensions of a rough plan drawn on cardboard or plywood in the same way the actual objects would relate to the size of the plot; then, by placing and replacing them try to work out a composition that will have pleasing forms and proportions as well as practicability. While this is much simpler than building a scale topographic model of a property, it will provide a helpful miniature reproduction of the actual conditions sought and worked out far more realistically than a flat ground plan, elevation, or cross section which gives no composite idea of height and bulk. It is surprising, says Mr. Baird, how, almost unconsciously, the average person tends to develop satisfying designs by employing this method.

Another way to present in advance a three-dimensional picture of a garden has been perfected by Extension Horticulturist R. P. Korbobo of New Jersey who also uses it to show the effects of good (and bad) planning as the plants grow to mature size. He employs cutouts of felt or flak paper to represent the garden elements as well as a perspective replica of the house, placing these against a green felt background spread over an easel. The pieces stick to the background, but can be pulled off and replaced as often as, and wherever, desired; or others can be substituted for contrast. The preparation of the material calls for considerable artistic skill and ingenuity, but the result is a most convincing demonstration of landscaping possibilities and principles. This is a good example of the vast and varied amount of information and help available from many sources for the homeowner who, inspired and guided by Mr. Biles' advice, seeks to go further in the rewarding field of home garden planning.

PROGRESS IN SOIL CONSERVATION AND MANAGEMENT

A continuing national problem is that of soil conservation. Great progress has been made in the last quarter century through the efforts and leadership of the U. S. Soil Conservation Service; farmers and other landowners have formed hundreds of Districts through which to learn about and apply improved practices; fine educational work is being done by public spirited organizations such as the Friends of the Land. Yet the country is still losing each year hundreds of thousands of acres of much needed and irreplaceable topsoil as a result of erosion by wind and water caused in large measure by man's ignorance, carelessness, and indifference. To that must be added the tragic loss of crops and crop land in the path of spectacular flash floods caused sometimes—but not always—by hurricanes that have been more numerous in recent years than over all the nation's past history.

Don't think for a minute that these matters don't concern *you*, as a home gardener. They do, first because you with all other Americans must bear any loss of the country's natural resources, whatever the cause; secondly, because even if you don't witness or feel the effects of

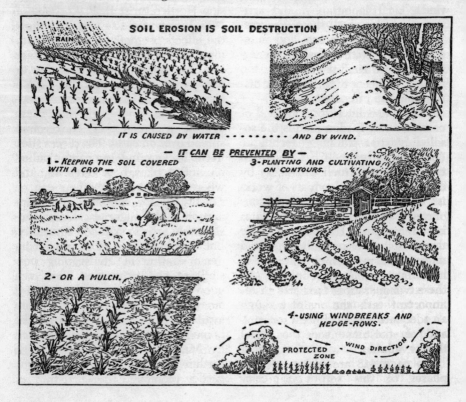

SOIL EROSION IS SOIL DESTRUCTION

IT IS CAUSED BY WATER · · · · · · · · AND BY WIND.

— IT CAN BE PREVENTED BY —

1 - KEEPING THE SOIL COVERED WITH A CROP —

2 - OR A MULCH.

3 - PLANTING AND CULTIVATING ON CONTOURS.

4 - USING WINDBREAKS AND HEDGE-ROWS.

PROTECTED ZONE · WIND DIRECTION

such devastation, you *can* see erosion forces at work on a small scale almost anywhere, even in backyard gardens. Wherever the land slopes, wherever the soil lies bare of vegetation and is allowed to bake and become impervious to rainfall, wherever steps are not taken to prevent it, the soil is likely to be blown or washed away, perhaps into streets, gutters, and ultimately the sewer, perhaps onto a neighbor's property where it may do damage or, at the least, become a nuisance. In either case, it and its fertility are lost to the person who hoped and planned to cultivate it.

The basic principles of good land use (which is what soil conservation is) are the same whether on farm, ranch, or plantation, in orchard, flower garden, or vegetable patch. They consist of: first, keeping the soil covered with either growing vegetation or some kind of mulch, so as to prevent its being dislodged by falling raindrops and carried away by wind or water, usually aided by the force of gravity; and, second, keeping the soil supplied with absorbent humus (organic matter) which retains moisture for plants to use and permits any excess to seep in slowly and replenish the underground supply instead of running off over the surface. (Also, as it decomposes, this humus adds to the soil's store of nutrients and feeds microorganisms which turn fertilizers into usable plant food.) Thus these two operations facilitate a third important task—the maintaining of an adequate supply of plant nutrients and of moisture needed to make them available.

On page 448 are pictured a few phases of this soil management struggle and things every gardener can do to help himself and his fellows. Note that planting and cultivation of a crop up and down a slope induces erosion; that planting on contours—that is, around the face of a slope—tends to check it and enable rain and melting snow to sink into the ground. Note how soil is "anchored" by growing crops (trees, pasture grass, grains, or, in home gardens, a cover crop of rye, clover, etc.), and how it can be protected by a mulch of straw, leaves, litter, or even closely laid stones or strips of building paper, newspaper, or aluminum foil spread between the rows or around the plants. Applied on freshly cultivated soil between rows, hills, or individual plants, a thick, loose mulch keeps the ground cool, friable, and absorbent; checks loss of moisture by evaporation; prevents soil spattering and the dissemination of plant disease spores that may inhabit it, and provides a clean surface for plant foliage and such fruits as strawberries, tomatoes, squash and the like to rest on. These benefits are increased if the soil is light and sandy and when the weather is hot and dry.

The vigorous controversy that followed the publication, some years ago, of a book called "Plowman's Folly" gradually died down as it became evident that the book was not a blanket indictment of moldboard plowing and all deep tillage, but rather an endorsement of shallow tillage under certain circumstances, a criticism of plowing that inverts an unbroken layer of sod (which would usually be called "poor plowing"), and a recommendation that thin soil

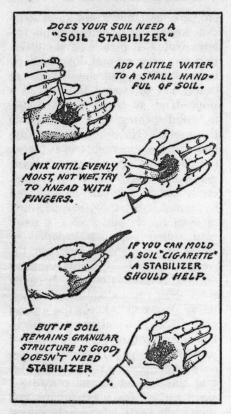

DOES YOUR SOIL NEED A "SOIL STABILIZER"

ADD A LITTLE WATER TO A SMALL HAND-FUL OF SOIL.

MIX UNTIL EVENLY MOIST, NOT WET, TRY TO KNEAD WITH FINGERS.

IF YOU CAN MOLD A SOIL "CIGARETTE" A STABILIZER SHOULD HELP.

BUT IF SOIL REMAINS GRANULAR, STRUCTURE IS GOOD; DOESN'T NEED STABILIZER

A simple test will show whether a soil stabilizer will help your soil. See text, page 451.

be improved *from the top down.* (This is, of course, logical where there is no strong subsoil to work on and incorporation of manure and other soil modifiers is out of the question.) As a matter of fact, all these practices are actually used and endorsed by many soil conservationists who often advise the disking or scratching of a field of stubble as preferable to plowing it.

This brings us to a brief consideration of a type of farming and gardening called "Organic," "Bio-Dynamic," "Natural" and by other names indicating that it emphasizes following natural methods. It includes the returning to the soil of all that is possible of what is taken from it; the use of carefully prepared compost rather than fresh manure or green cover crops; the use of only "organic" or untreated mineral fertilizers (such as ground limestone and other rocks), bone meal, tankage, etc.; the maintenance of soil conditions congenial to earthworms, and, as a corollary, the use and fostering of earthworms for soil improvement. Organic gardeners also disapprove of the use of chemical pesticides, claiming that properly grown crops are less subject or more resistant to attack by insects and diseases, and, if untouched by poisons, are more healthful and nutritious for those who consume them, either as vegetables or when transformed into meat, milk, eggs, honey, or other animal products.

While most scientists (and, naturally, fertilizer manufacturers) show little sympathy for the claims of organic gardening, proponents of the system are certainly increasing in number and enthusiasm. Also, of late years, advocates of the use of chemical fertilizers have retreated from a position of denouncing organic manures to one of conceding that they, as well as the commercial plant foods, are needed for best results. As often happens when any proposal or philosophy goes counter to long-accepted and well-entrenched theories, arguments on both sides of this controversy have at times included some extravagant-sounding and perhaps hard-to-prove statements and claims. But the fact remains that the history of organic plant growing methods is a much older one than that of the use of man-made chemical fertilizers. Also there is much justification for measures aimed at preserving soil and plants as links in a natural chain of life phenomena. Finally, whatever the merits of particular details of such arguments, great good is accomplished by bringing these subjects to the attention of more people and stimulating thought and constructive action regarding the vital problems of land use, soil management, the relation of soil and crops to human health, and all other aspects of the conservation of natural and national resources.

Meanwhile, interesting things have happened that we will merely mention so "Garden Magic" readers can look into them, get the current facts about them and, if they wish, make their own tests of their usefulness. Much publicity was given for a time to newly developed "soil conditioners" which, later, were more accurately called "soil stabilizers." These were synthetic chemical compounds which, applied in dry or liquid form to fine-grained clay or silt soil, caused its particles to come together and form granular aggregates, thus making the soil structure more open and porous. The fact that gypsum has long been used for this purpose was generally ignored or lost sight of in the promotion (sometimes more colorful than accurate) of these materials as "miracle workers" that would turn sterile soils into fertile loams, do away with digging and cultivating, and make the gardener's life one of ease and relaxation. As a matter of fact, the structure of some soils can be improved (or, rather, an improved structure can be stabilized) if one of these substances is thoroughly mixed with them as deeply as the effect is desired; and a simple test, as shown on page 450, will show whether the treatment is warranted. However, the excitement over this development, like the Vitamin B-1 flurry of some years before, gradually simmered down to a recognition of the real facts—which did not include a gardening millennium.

Somewhat similar claims were made for another material, long known to technologists as a "soil surfactant," whose effect is to reduce the surface tension of water to which it is added, making it, in effect, "more slippery," so it will drain away into a stiff soil more freely and provide a more satisfactory supply of moisture for plants. With lawns suffering from an extended drought, this product was offered to gardeners (one is tempted to add the adjective "gullible") as a solution to one of their main problems (adequate moisture), and as another labor saver.

Less dramatically introduced, but perhaps with sounder claims for recognition, were materials called chelates, or chelated fertilizers, which chemically change, or release from unavailable form, iron and other plant food elements so that plants can take them up and correct certain nutritional deficiencies. Still another material designed to supplement standard fertilizers has appeared with the name "fritted trace elements." It provides, in a slowly available, lasting form, a supply of certain minor elements—manganese, iron, zinc, copper, boron, and molybdenum—which are essential to balanced plant growth but sometimes deficient in certain soils or regions.

Of a different character are the highly concentrated, quickly available plant foods which have been offered in numerous proprietary forms—one garden magazine article listed two score of them—for quick and easy application to lawns, plants, trees, etc., by means of various automatic sprinkler-feeders. Some retain the cartridge or tablet form that has been on the market for years; others are potent liquids which are properly diluted when introduced into a hose line. Their increased use has resulted in part from the successful results of experiments with foliar feeding, that is, the application of plant foods in liquid form to the leaves and other above-ground parts of plants. Here is a technique that has really proved its usefulness and convenience and that will doubtless continue as a permanent feature of good gardening. It offers a further advantage in that certain insecticides and fungicides can be combined with the plant foods so as to accomplish several tasks at the same time.

Before leaving the subject of soil fertility, remember that, in addition to simple tests for acidity (described on pages 99 and 100), there are also tests and kits whereby home gardeners can ascertain a soil's content of various plant food elements. (See illustration, page 453.) This do-it-yourself sort of testing, while less revealing than complicated laboratory procedure, can give interesting, often helpful results.

The excellent catalogue and "Soil Handbook" of one maker of such devices, is accompanied by a compact "Soil Reaction Slide Rule," which enables the user to quickly ascertain the lime requirements of different types of soil on the basis of soil-acidity tests much as a mathematician can solve arithmetical problems with a comparable appliance.

However, just as accurate weather forecasting calls for more than the reading of barometer and thermometer, so accurate determination of the fertilizer needs of a particular soil requires more than test-tube study of a soil solution. Also conditions change, often rapidly. The nitrogen content of even a good soil may vary from season to season, according to bacterial action, moisture conditions, crop growth, the use of mulches, etc. So supplement any soil tests you make with constant observation of soil and plant conditions throughout your garden.

MODERN LAWNS AND THEIR CARE

The lawn is often and deservedly called the most important single feature of the home grounds. Certainly a good one is something to be proud of, as both carpet and background for the outdoor living room and its furnishings. It is as important viewed from within the property, as from adjoining properties or the highway. But there is no such thing as a self-maintaining lawn (except perhaps the sometimes advocated green-painted concrete slab!), so it is necessary to work out a system of keeping it in good condition with minimum care.

Preliminary preparation of a deep,

well-drained seedbed (well covered by Mr. Biles in Chapter III) is of fundamental importance. So is the selection (and proper sowing) of the right grass seed mixture for each locality, soil type, exposure, density of shade, etc. Many state experiment stations will recommend on request proven mixtures; and the better lawn seed firms will supply abundant advice as well as mixtures best suited for particular conditions. Don't give in to the temptation to "save money" by buying cheap grass seed in the

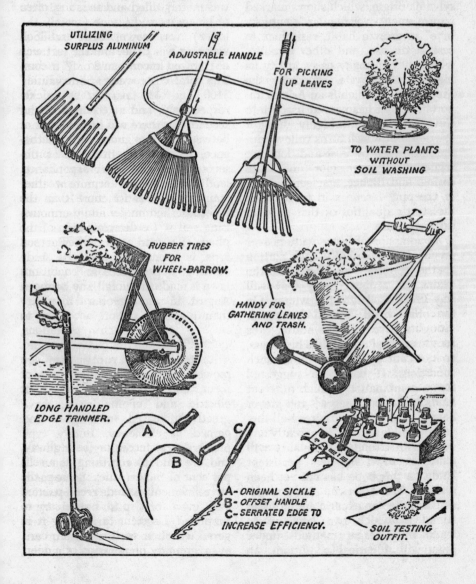

UTILIZING SURPLUS ALUMINUM

ADJUSTABLE HANDLE

FOR PICKING UP LEAVES

TO WATER PLANTS WITHOUT SOIL WASHING

RUBBER TIRES FOR WHEEL-BARROW.

HANDY FOR GATHERING LEAVES AND TRASH.

LONG HANDLED EDGE TRIMMER.

A
B
C

A- ORIGINAL SICKLE
B- OFFSET HANDLE
C- SERRATED EDGE TO INCREASE EFFICIENCY.

SOIL TESTING OUTFIT.

hope that *this time* you are really getting a bargain, or that by sowing cheap seed extra thick you will make up for lack of quality.

Among recent introductions that have attracted special attention are: Merion bluegrass, a strain of Pennsylvania origin, which shows marked improvement over regular "Kentucky blue" in growth habit, resistance to certain disease, and other qualities which may in many cases justify its higher cost; Zoysia, especially the Meyer strain, which is an Asiatic importation that has proved hardy into New England and highly drought tolerant, but which turns yellow with the first touch of frost and does not regain its green color until late spring; and Illahee, a selected strain of creeping fescue said to have all the sturdy qualities of that grass in extra measure.

A succession of warm winters over much of the normally cold portion of the country has intensified the desire for a lawn grass that will stay green well into the winter. On the other hand, extended summer droughts have brought added calls for grasses that do not, like bluegrass, go dormant and brown under such conditions. It has been suggested that a combination of such different kinds as Merion bluegrass and Meyer Zoysia might give a green-all-the-year-round lawn; but apparently any grass with strong individuality will tend to crowd out less persistent kinds, so this hope has not yet been realized. *The American Home* magazine reported an experiment on Long Island in which two lawns were made by different methods under practically identical conditions. In one case considerable topsoil, generous high test fertilizer, and an expensive mixture of bent and other specialty grasses were used, a sprinkler system was installed and the turf was consistently mowed about an inch high. In the other case, the soil was merely tilled and fed, a mixture of bluegrass and fescue (mainly the latter) was sown, little artificial watering was done, and the turf was not mowed lower than 2 or 2½ inches. The total costs were approximately $100 and $10 per 1,000 sq. ft. respectively; and at the end of the second year there was little to choose between the two lawns with the balance, if anything, in favor of the second. This and other experiments lend force to the argument that, many times, a satisfactory lawn can be established on definitely unpromising soil if (1) ample food is supplied, (2) good seed of a vigorous type is used, (3) relatively high mowing is practiced, and (4) the lawn is made in the fall, say between August 15 and October 15, rather than in spring.

Lawn Maintenance Advances

As to mowing, rubber tires on mowers are now standard equipment, and power machines, both electric and engine-driven, have greatly increased in number and gained in efficiency. Rotary type mowers are increasingly available and are said to represent some 50 per cent of mower sales. Some modern refinements include recoil starters and even one push-button type; simplified height adjustment; staggered wheels to facilitate use on uneven ground; demountable handles for easy storing; attachments for "weed-topping" and leaf-grinding; silent mufflers, and headlights for night operation. One recent model that is almost in the multi-purpose tractor field, includes a power unit and handle that can be used interchangeably on a reel- or a rotary-type base, an edge-trimming device, and a snowplow!

There are, of course, champions of the different type mowers, but it seems obvious that, in general, the reel type is best adapted for maintaining an immaculate, short turf of quality grasses where labor is not a major problem, whereas the rotary type, while suitable for many a lawn of that sort, is especially suited to one of average quality where frequent attention cannot be assured, and where there is often need to cut tall weeds and other coarse growth.

The importance of aerating the soil, especially of lawns, playgrounds, athletic fields, etc., has led to the development of tools to do it, ranging from simple hand operated "spikers" to self-propelled machines whose wheels are set with knives, spikes, or sharp-edged tubes that lift out small cores leaving holes into which water and plant food, as well as air, can enter freely.

As emphasized in Chapter III, lawn watering, when necessary, should be done generously; brief superficial sprinklings at daily or other definite intervals do more harm than good. The dense building-up of suburban areas is creating an increasing water supply problem in many places, but where water is available, there are innumerable devices for applying it (and also, as mentioned,

food and pesticides at the same time). Fixed and movable sprinklers, including the self-propelled type shown on page 456, can be had in many forms, and the introduction of plastic piping and fixtures has led to a boom in permanent, underground sprinkling systems, many of which can be easily installed by the handyman homeowner. These can be manually operated or, for the mechanically minded, there are instruments that can be set to turn the water on and off at stated intervals or even as directed by solenoid valves, controlled by sensitive elements that react to moisture conditions just as thermostats react to temperature changes. Or, the gardener can install a kind of "moisture-meter" to show the amount of water in the soil and thus supplement his interpretation of the appearance of soil and plants.

The porous or soil-soaking hose continues popular as a convenient and economical way to water lawns and flower beds, and there are now flexible plastic tubes, single or in pairs, perforated at intervals so as to distribute moisture over any desired pattern. Actually these are a simpler, less expensive, portable form of the underground pipe and sprinkler-head systems.

As noted farther on, many new chemicals are being offered for the control of lawn pests, including insects, like Japanese beetles and chinch bugs, various fungous diseases, and, of course, weeds. Their use is so fully discussed in experiment station bulletins, garden magazines, and other current literature that it is unnecessary, even if it were possible, to treat them here. With regard to weed control, even crab-grass and chickweed have become less menacing in the face of specific herbicides, and the more recently developed pre-emergence sprays and dusts which, applied to the soil some weeks before seeding time, kill weed seeds already there and give the grass seeds, when sown, a clear field for maximum germination and growth. It remains true, however, that the best way to have a weed-free lawn is to make the soil conditions so favorable, and to establish such a fine, thick stand of suitable grass grown from high-class seed, that weeds can never get a foothold. High mowing (from 2 to 3 inches) also helps, both by shading out the weed seedlings while they are small, and by leaving more leaf area with which the grass can make more food and attain thicker, stronger growth.

The use of weed-killers is becoming so widespread that it is well to recall that while some of them are, to a certain extent, selective (killing certain kinds of vegetation without harming other kinds), this is not generally the case. So whether you are using 2,4-D or some other chemical

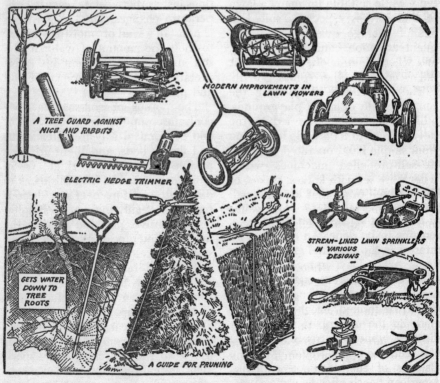

Some recently developed aids for gardeners in connection with the care of trees, shrubs, and lawns. See pages 453 and 475 for other modern labor savers.

on a patch of weeds in the lawn, or on poison ivy behind a shrub border, or along a path or drive, watch out that it does not carry over, or be blown, onto plants that you definitely don't want to kill. Even the old-fashioned, relatively safe weed-killers like salt brine, borax, calcium chloride and certain crude acids, if applied carelessly along a drive or sidewalk can spread underground and kill turf, flowers, shrubs and even trees growing alongside.

An interesting development in lawn care has been the utilization by firms in different parts of the country of tank trucks (as used to deliver fuel oil) and spray equipment for applying liquid plant food (and sometimes weed-killers) to lawns on a contract basis—so many treatments per season, etc. Offering the companies an attractive way to keep equipment busy when otherwise it might be idle, such a program could indeed relieve the homeowner of another chore. Its practical value will probably depend on the thoroughness with which oil tanks can be cleaned, and the expertness and intelligence with which a treatment schedule is planned and carried out.

Also to be noted are new promotional and research organizations for the dissemination of information and advice about lawns and grasses. The Turf Research Foundation, with headquarters in Chicago, is the outgrowth of a group especially interested in Merion bluegrass. The Better Lawn and Turf Institute, with headquarters in Kansas City, Mo., evolved from a former organization of bluegrass seed growers and a subsequent Bluegrass Research Institute. Here again are evidences of industry's desire to maintain standards of service and business practice.

TREES AND PLANTS, PLANTING AND CARE

It seems logical to discuss together some developments in the related fields covered in Chapters IV to XII.

As with the conservation of soil, much attention is being given to the preservation and increased planting of trees, but at the same time much remains to be done. An evidence of interest is the proposal that one national Arbor Day, instead of, or in addition to, different state days, be named, and that an Arbor Day Association be formed. Progress is being made in the control of some plant diseases, while new troubles like the oak wilt, the plane tree canker and diseases of the dogwood and the American beech offer new problems. Chemotherapy, the injection of cura-

tive materials into the sap of trees through trunk or limbs, is receiving increasing attention as is the introduction of pesticides via the soil solution. Foliar feeding, already mentioned, provides a means of quickly supplying needed nutrients for growth or recovery after injury or shock. Work on blight-resistant hybrid chestnut trees has progressed to a point where varieties with mixed American, European and Asiatic parentage are being recommended as orchard and game-cover trees, even if not as forest or timber material.

The appraisal of shade trees for street, park and home grounds is supplying valuable suggestions for homeowners. The New Jersey Association of Nurserymen seeking "The Ten Top Trees of Tomorrow" prepared the following list:

Major trees (50 ft. and up)—Honey Locust, Pin Oak, Norway Maple, Oriental Plane, Sugar Maple, Red Oak, Japanese Pagoda-tree, Scarlet Oak, and Littleleaf Linden.

Minor trees (20 to 50 ft.)—Columnar Norway Maple, Hedge Maple, Kwanzan Japanese Flowering Cherry, European Mountain-ash, American Hophornbeam, White Birch, Golden-rain-tree, Hopa Crab, and Kobus Magnolia.

Another selection recommended by a leading tree expert company included:

Tall trees (over 50 ft.)—American Elm, White, Red and Scarlet Oaks, Sugar Maple, Horsechestnut, Cucumber Magnolia, and Tulip-tree.

Medium trees (30 to 50 ft.)—Red Maple, Sweet and Sour Gums, American Hornbeam, Yellow-wood, Ginkgo, White Ash, London Plane, Native Sycamore, Pin Oak, Linden, Thornless Honey Locust and European Beech.

Small trees (to 30 ft.)—Flowering Dogwood, Magnolia, Washington Thorn, Japanese Maple, Flowering Crabapple, Sorrel-tree, Native Birches, and European White Birch.

Continuing experience with hurricanes along the Atlantic coast has given rise to useful advice for homeowners as to tree planting. Many overturned trees have been found to have broad but shallow root systems —pancakelike, as it were. These are the result of shallow soil preparation and planting where a topsoil only a foot or so thick is underlain by loose, infertile sand and gravel into which

the roots do not penetrate. The obvious moral is that any tree, even a small one, should be planted in a good, big, deep hole filled with soil rich in plant food and humus. As it grows it will send its roots downward as well as laterally in search of food and moisture and thus develop a deep anchorage and greater stability. Results of hurricane damage to limbs strongly endorse the advice given elsewhere in this book to make clean pruning cuts and not leave stubs into which decay organisms can enter to weaken the rest of the tree.

The increase in home building and accompanying tree planting has made new opportunities for irresponsible "tree quacks" to victimize uninformed gardeners. Responsible arborists and nurserymen and their organizations have therefore increased their efforts to check or prevent these operations, through publicity, education and co-operation with Better Business Bureaus. Also there has been progress in the certification of tree expert firms on the basis of examinations and evidences of "honesty, diagnostic ability, quality of workmanship and worthiness of ethics." In New Jersey, as of 1955, 84 applications for such certificates had been approved.

Shade tree values: Speaking of trees and thinking back to earlier comments on planning and planting the home grounds, it is interesting to note how much value is attributed to the landscaping of a property. In Massachusetts, the Forest and Park Association took a canvass of expert opinion in a residential section where land value averaged 15 cents per square foot and where a house and bare lot were worth $8,000. The difference in the estimated value of two homes, one on bare land and the other artistically planted, ranged from 1.2 per cent to 26.5 per cent, with an average of 9 per cent. It was also estimated that, on a scale of 100, 12.5 points could be credited to landscape beauty. Other real estate surveys have shown that money spent on landscaping brings, over a ten-year period, considerably better returns than if it were invested at 8 per cent interest.

Various methods have been proposed for appraising the value of an individual shade tree, either for income tax deduction or other purposes. One of these uses $10 per inch of trunk diameter for trees up to 5 in., then a gradually increasing rate ranging from $12.50 per inch for 6 to 7 in. trees, up to $50 an inch for specimens 56 to 60 in. across. Another method sometimes used multiplies the trunk diameter in inches by the value per front foot of the property on which the tree is growing. Thus a 10 in. tree on land valued at $20 per front foot, would be $200. A more complicated plan, based on one proposed by the late Dr. E. Porter Felt, sets a basic figure of at least $2 per square inch of the tree trunk at breast height, then increases or diminishes this by specified units according to various factors, such as the species of tree, its location and condition, and the residential value of the property involved. As an example, leaving out species, location and condition, this would give a tree 30 in. in diameter a basic value of $1,414, which, if the property were worth $10,000 an acre, would be increased by $180, making a total of $1,594.

Of course, all such estimates have to take into consideration the health, typical form and accessibility of the tree. If on a front lawn and in perfect condition, it is naturally worth more than if located at the far end of a property, and picturesque mainly because of gnarled or broken limbs. Nevertheless, enough has been said to emphasize the value of every tree you have on your place, and the wisdom of giving all of them the care and attention they need to continue beautiful and fruitful.

In connection with Planting, Transplanting and Pruning (Chapter V), there has probably been more progress in commercial methods than in those of the home gardener whose careful handwork does not have to be charged up at prevailing prices for labor. But many of these trade practices can be used to advantage in garden operations. Among these are the wrapping of root balls in polyethylene film, as illustrated on page 460; the use of plastic bags and aluminum foil for wrapping bare root plants (such as roses) for shipment; the wrapping of dahlia tubers in aluminum foil for storage; the use of wilt-preventing spray preparations on evergreens to reduce loss of foliage in transplanting; the use of certain hormones to hasten defoliation and dormancy, if, for example, you want to dig and move roses or shrubs in advance of the normal fall season.

The use of "starter solutions" (of highly soluble, high analysis fertilizers) or of root-inducing hormones will often insure the life and vigorous recovery of a transplanted tree or shrub; and the commercial practice of growing plants in wire baskets, tin cans, and heavy paper containers so they can be moved more easily from temporary to permanent locations are other useful tricks first used by commercial growers.

With space in modern homes often more limited than in the past (and more taken up with television sets, etc.), the old-fashioned big Christmas trees have given way to smaller ones which, to an increasing extent seem to be live plants, balled and burlapped or in tubs so they can be planted in the garden after the holidays. Also there has been increased planting of Christmas trees (and also of holly) as a crop. State certification of cut trees has helped as a conserva-

FLEXIBLE PLASTIC— A NEW AID TO GARDENERS

HOUSE PLANTS WRAPPED IN PLASTIC WILL GO A WEEK OR MORE WITHOUT WATERING.

DIG PLANT WITH A GOOD FIRM SOIL BALL

WRAP BALL IN SHEET OF PLASTIC TIED AROUND BASE OF PLANT.

NOW YOU CAN MOVE IT OR KEEP IT OUT OF SOIL AS LONG AS IT IS IN BLOOM—THEN REPLANT.

CUTTINGS ROOT IN MOIST SPHAGNUM MOSS WRAPPED IN PLASTIC SHEET TIED AROUND STEM WITH RUBBER BAND—

—OR A LOT OF CUTTINGS CAN BE ROOTED (AND SHIPPED) IN A PACKAGE LIKE THIS.

AIR LAYERING BY THE PLASTIC METHOD

1-REMOVE ½" RING OF BARK FROM BRANCH AND DUST WITH ROOTING HORMONE.
2-WRAP TREATED AREA IN HANDFUL OF SPHAGNUM MOSS SOAKED AND SQUEEZED DRY.
3-4- WRAP MOSS IN SQUARE OF PLASTIC AND TIE EACH END WITH RUBBER BAND.
5-WHEN ROOTS FILL MOSS CUT FREE FROM BRANCH UNWRAP AND PLANT.

tion measure by checking the uncontrolled cutting of wild trees, and the organization of Christmas tree producers should be a further stabilizing influence of benefit to consumers and growers alike.

We have already noted a tendency to use fences and walls as boundaries for small properties instead of hedges, which usually take an increasing amount of space and need considerable care. One hedge plant, however, has received unusual attention of late, namely the introduced species rose, *Rosa multiflora*, once much used as a stock for budding. Hailed as the "living fence" and justifiably praised for its hardiness, vigor, and attractiveness of flower, foliage, and fruit, it was at first advocated for farm boundary planting. Then, with rather unrestrained enthusiasm, it was urged upon small homeowners as a lovely, impenetrable, colorful barrier. So it can be, if pruned severely and often, and if there is space for it; otherwise its 8-ft. or greater spread may make it more of a garden problem than a solution. It has also been recommended for planting along highways and between parkway traffic lanes, for it has been shown that automobiles driven into a multiflora thicket (both by accident and design) have been brought to a stop quickly, smoothly and with only the paint scratched instead of the usual wreckage and driver injury.

In the Flower Garden

Coming now to flower gardens and flowers, we note some influences that are giving gardeners better materials than formerly obtainable, and with less of a gamble as to their worthiness. Plant breeders and growers in all lines continue, of course, to produce novelties with various claims for recognition, such as greater beauty, size, productivity, hardiness, resistance to enemies, etc. There has also been considerable organized effort to test and prove such claims in advance and save the ultimate consumer (that is, the grower) unnecessary disappointment.

25 Years of Plant Patents: In 1930, an amendment to the Patent Act provided for the patenting of "any distinct and new variety of plant other than a tuber-propagated plant." Its purpose was to protect the originator and enable him to control the propagation and sale of his novelty just as the basic act serves inventors of devices and methods. When, in 1955, the 25th anniversary of plant patents was celebrated, nearly 1,400 had been issued, the majority for roses (the first was for the everblooming climber, New Dawn), with other flowering plants and fruit- and nut-bearing plants making up most of the remainder. For the consumer, that is, the gardener, a plant patent is evidence of the faith of the originator in his product. His willingness to spend some $200 and go to considerable trouble to protect it; the willingness of other growers to pay a royalty for the right to handle it, and the use of extensive publicity to promote it indicate a degree of merit that justifies a higher than average price and hopes for better than average results. Patented plants are identified by special tags and special descriptions in catalogues and advertising.

All-America Selections: In 1933, leaders in the seed industry, in an attempt to reduce the number of new (and often not very different) varieties of annual flowers and vegetables featured each year in the catalogues, started a program of co-ordinated testing and promotion of a few selected new sorts, giving it the title "All-America Selections." Entries for each year's trials are grown in a score of test grounds in different parts of the country where they are examined at intervals and scored by a jury of experts. Those considered most promising are awarded medals or citations and given the benefit of special advertising and distribution. Of course, they do not include all the good varieties brought out that year; and occasionally the judgment of the judges is challenged when an All-America winner does not continue among the "best sellers." Nevertheless, the system has called attention to some outstanding things, ended much former confusion by reducing the flood of mediocre offerings and the unwarranted claims that used to be an accepted but undesirable part of the seed business, and helped to give prominence to gardening and horticulture generally. In the twenty-odd years of All-America Selections, the leading flower winners have been the following in approximately this order: Petunias, marigolds, asters, snapdragons, verbenas, zinnias, nasturtiums, phlox, and scabiosas, with some 30 others having received a scattering of votes.

Adapting the same ideas, and for similar reasons, a group of large rose-growing nursery firms, in 1939, started the "All-America Rose Selections." Up to and including 1956 (each year's selections are put on the market the previous fall), the All-America Roses have been the following:

NAME	COLOR	VARIETY
	1940	
Dicksons Red	Scarlet Red	Hybrid Tea
Flash	Oriental Red	Climber (Pillar)
The Chief	Salmon Red	Hybrid Tea
World's Fair	Deep Red	Floribunda
	1941	
Apricot Queen	Apricot	Hybrid Tea
California	Golden Yellow	Hybrid Tea
Charlotte Armstrong	Cerise Red	Hybrid Tea
	1942	
Heart's Desire	Deep Rose Red	Hybrid Tea
	1943	
Grande Duchesse Charlotte	Wine Red	Hybrid Tea
Mary Margaret McBride	Rose Pink	Hybrid Tea

NAME	COLOR	VARIETY
	1944	
Fred Edmunds*	Apricot	Hybrid Tea
Katharine T. Marshall	Deep Pink	Hybrid Tea
Lowell Thomas	Butter Yellow	Hybrid Tea
Mme. Chiang Kai-shek	Light Yellow	Hybrid Tea
Mme. Marie Curie	Golden Yellow	Hybrid Tea
	1945	
Floradora	Salmon Rose	Floribunda
Horace McFarland	Buff Pink	Hybrid Tea
Miranda	Crimson Red	Hybrid Tea
	1946	
Peace	Blend (Pale Gold)	Hybrid Tea
	1947	
Rubaiyat	Cerise Red	Hybrid Tea
	1948	
Diamond Jubilee	Buff	Hybrid Tea
High Noon*	Yellow	Climber (Pillar)
Nocturne	Dark Red	Hybrid Tea
Pinkie	Light Rose Pink	Polyantha
San Fernando	Currant Red	Hybrid Tea
Taffeta	Two-tone Pink Yellow	Hybrid Tea
	1949	
Forty-niner	Bicolor (Red, Yellow)	Hybrid Tea
Tallyho	Two-tone Pink	Hybrid Tea
	1950	
Fashion	Coral Pink	Floribunda
Mission Bells	Salmon	Hybrid Tea
Capistrano	Pink	Hybrid Tea
Sutter's Gold	Golden Yellow	Hybrid Tea
	1952	
Fred Howard	Yellow, Penciled Pink	Hybrid Tea
Vogue	Cherry Coral	Floribunda
Helen Traubel	Apricot Pink	Hybrid Tea
	1953	
Chrysler Imperial	Crimson Red	Hybrid Tea
Ma Perkins	Coral-shell Pink	Floribunda

(*Denotes sectional, not country-wide, recommendation)

NAME	COLOR	VARIETY
	1954	
Lilibet	Clear Pink	Floribunda
Mojave	Apricot-orange	Hybrid Tea
	1955	
Tiffany	Bicolor (Yellow, Pink)	Hybrid Tea
Jiminy Cricket	Coral-orange	Floribunda
Queen Elizabeth	Delicate Pink	Grandiflora
	1956	
Circus	Multicolor (Yellow, Pink, Red)	Floribunda

Note that in 1955 one of the Selections, Queen Elizabeth, is listed as a Grandiflora, the first time that class name appears. This class was created and named to take care of certain hybrids of Hybrid Tea and Floribunda varieties which resemble both parent types in certain respects but are identical with neither. Examples of the new class, of which only a handful had been recognized up to 1956, are characterized by: 1. Plants of relatively tall growth; 2. Plants free flowering, often with individual stems long enough for cutting; 3. Flower size not necessarily as large as Hybrid Teas but larger than the average Floribunda; 4. Hybrid Tea standard for bud and flower form.

With this addition, the recognized main classes of roses are: Hybrid Tea, Floribunda, Grandiflora, Climbing, Trailing, Species (or Shrub), and Miniature. Of course, there can still be found in some gardens and catalogues varieties of older classes such as Hybrid Perpetuals, Teas, Ramblers, and Polyanthas or Baby Ramblers.

Following the lead of seedsmen and commercial rose growers, Camellia growers in 1952 and Gladiolus specialists in 1953 set up All-America Selection machinery, information about which can be had from the secretaries at 13531 Fenton Ave., San Fernando, Calif., and 5027 North 35th St., Arlington, Va., respectively. During the first year of gladiolus trials 29 varieties were tested in 25 trial grounds and one, Royal Stewart, was given an All-America award. However, its identity was kept secret until 1955 to allow two years of propagation of sufficient stock to permit general announcement and listing by dealers.

Bulb Standards: Mention has already been made of a proposed Code of Trade Practice for the nursery industry. It might be noted here that in the last (1951) revision of the American Standards for Nursery Stock, there were added specifications and descriptions covering bulbs. Much confusion has occurred in the past because of lack of catalogue and advertisement uniformity in giving bulb sizes. In some cases they referred to diameter, in other cases to circumference; for some bulbs they were given in inches, for others, in centimeters. The new standards, in which such details are clearly designated, will be the basis for Trade Practice Code provisions if and when promulgated.

Garden Pool Pointers: Though the lily and goldfish pool is but a minor factor in gardening, yet it, too, has been touched by the wand of "garden magic." While principles and practices of its planting and care have not changed, and while some people will still prefer to make their own of concrete or even puddled clay, there are convenient modern materials available for those who

want to use them. Plastics are playing an important part here, as in the larger swimming pool field, and the illustration on this page shows one small, useful, inexpensive type together with a miniature pump that simplifies the making of waterfalls and brooks and economizes by circulating the same water until evaporation calls for replenishing. Similar pools in various sizes can be had in non-rusting steel, which is even more lasting and more attractive if painted. A shallow depression lined with sheets of some of the new flexible plastics would no doubt provide a satisfactory temporary water feature, and sheet lead has proved an excellent material since it can be shaped to conform to any excavation and made watertight by simple folded and hammered seams. In color it blends well into natural surroundings, and, being practically indestructible, it is not necessarily as expensive in the long run as its first cost might suggest.

With increased interest in garden pools and in automatic lawn sprinkling systems, a health safety problem has arisen that should be noted. Under certain conditions, a water line connected with a house supply in which the pressure varies may sometimes set up a siphon action and draw water from pool, sprinkler line, or other, perhaps contaminated, source back into circulation where it will be used. This is easily prevented by using proper connections and trap valves, and leaving a certain minimum height between inlet and outlet levels. If there seems any chance of such a condition developing, consult the nearest water supply de-

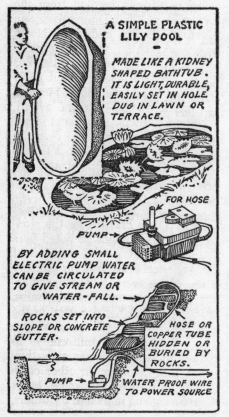

A SIMPLE PLASTIC LILY POOL

MADE LIKE A KIDNEY SHAPED BATHTUB. IT IS LIGHT, DURABLE, EASILY SET IN HOLE DUG IN LAWN OR TERRACE.

FOR HOSE

PUMP→

BY ADDING SMALL ELECTRIC PUMP WATER CAN BE CIRCULATED TO GIVE STREAM OR WATER-FALL.

ROCKS SET INTO SLOPE OR CONCRETE GUTTER.

HOSE OR COPPER TUBE HIDDEN OR BURIED BY ROCKS.

PUMP→ WATER PROOF WIRE TO POWER SOURCE

partment or company; sometimes dealers in sprinkler systems and other garden irrigation equipment are prepared to explain what should be done and how best to do it.

Food-crop Gardening: Progress in vegetable and fruit gardening is largely reflected in current seed and nursery catalogues that list new and presumably improved varieties. Carefully controlled hybrids, first developed in corn where they now represent the greater part of the kinds planted, are becoming more numerous in tomatoes, cucumbers and other vegetables as well.

New varieties of fruits are constantly being tested and put on the market as their merits are proved. Watermelon popularity has been enhanced by the appearance of better quality "midget" and extra hardy sorts; there has even been introduced from Japan a truly seedless watermelon for which a bright future may be expected if it lives up to claims made as to its quality and if the supply of seed becomes sufficient to bring the price to a reasonable level.

According to a "Garden Facts" bulletin of the U. S. D. A. Extension Service issued in August, 1955, "The outlook for the homeowner who wants to raise some tree fruits has greatly improved. Effective general purpose spray mixtures are a reality." Then, quoting from the July, 1955, issue of "Farm Research," a bulletin of the New York State Agricultural Experiment Station, it continues: "In recent years a number of safe and effective materials have been developed. Efforts were made to combine these so as to provide all-round effectiveness . . . The composition of a mixture which has proved effective in tests throughout the northeast, and quantities required separately or in combination are to be found in the table below.

"Malathion and methoxychlor are effective against insects, while Captan is included for control of plant diseases. Mixtures of this general type are being marketed under various trade names. Those having essentially this composition should prove satisfactory. Their identity can be verified by checking the label on the package which by law is required to state the ingredients. Safety precautions in the use of pesticides are also printed on the label and these should be carefully observed." (Note, in this connection, safety precautions in regard to the use of all such materials given on pages 473, 474.—EDITOR.)

COMPOSITION OF SPRAY FOR TREE FRUITS

Material	Per cent of mixture	Quantities required to make	
		1 gallon	25 gallons
Malathion (25% wettable powder)	30	2 tbsp.	½ pound
Methoxychlor (50% wettable powder)	35	3 tbsp.	¾ pound
Captan (50% wettable powder)	35	3 tbsp.	¾ pound
Complete mixture	100	8 tbsp.	2 pounds

The best planting dates for vegetables should be easier to determine as a result of experiments carried on by the California Agricultural Extension Service. It found the soil temperatures listed in the table below were optimum (best) and minimum (lowest possible) for the germination of the vegetable seeds listed.

While freezing has apparently taken the place of many older methods of storing and preserving fruits and vegetables, canning, drying, brining, pickling, and even natural pit storage still have their good points for those who favor them. Farmer's Bulletin 1939, a 1955 revision of an earlier publication on "Home Storing of Vegetables and Fruits," is one of the many valuable leaflets obtainable free from the U. S. Department of Agriculture while the supply lasts. It can also be had for 10 cents (coin) from the Superintendent of Documents, Government Printing Office, also at Washington 25, D. C.

Before leaving the vegetable garden, we might mention again the importance of mulching, not only to protect plants and their root systems, keep their fruits clean, and conserve moisture in the soil, but also as "an easy and more lasting way than any other to prevent weeds" as a Cornell University publication puts it. Among the materials it lists as used by gardeners are: wild grass or lawn cuttings; straw; old hay; ground corn cobs, stalks, and other waste products; peat moss; sawdust, shavings, wood chips, shredded bark and other woodworking by-products; newspapers; corrugated and building papers, and aluminum foil. Any of these must, of course, be used at such times and in such ways as produce, rather than prevent, the desired effects. On a heavy soil and in wet, cold weather a mulch may cause rotting, may foster slugs and other pests, and may retard growth, whereas on a sandy soil and in dry hot weather no such bad effects would be seen.

Former criticism of sawdust and wood chips (sometimes obtainable for nothing from tree-pruning and

SOIL TEMPERATURES FOR SEED GERMINATION

Kind	Soil temperature—Degrees F.	
	Optimum	Minimum
Cucumber, muskmelon, okra, pumpkin, squash, watermelon	95	60
Snap bean, eggplant, pepper	85	60
Sweet corn, tomato	85	50
Beet, broccoli, cabbage, radish, Swiss chard, turnip	85	40
Lima bean	80	60
Carrot, cauliflower, parsley	80	40
Onion	80	32
Asparagus	75	50
Pea	75	40
Endive, lettuce	75	32
Celery	70	40
Parsnip, spinach	70	32

line-clearing firms) is no longer valid according to experiment station reports. But it must be remembered that any coarse vegetable or cellulose material coming in contact with the soil is quickly attacked by soil organisms; that these organisms feed on nitrogen; that by taking it from the soil they deplete the supply available for plants and may actually starve them. Hence, with the regular use of mulches there should be supplementary feeding with a high-nitrogen plant food. Usually a half pound of nitrate of soda or 1½ to 2 lbs. of a 5-10-5 fertilizer per bushel of coarse mulch, sprinkled evenly on top of it will meet this requirement.

HORMONES, PESTICIDES AND OTHER CHEMICALS

At one time plant breeding meant merely the crossbreeding of individuals or species (that is, hybridizing) and the selection of the best of the progeny with, perhaps, now and then a lucky break in the discovery of a desirable "sport" or natural mutation. Today, an important phase of plant breeding is the deliberate, planned stimulation or inducement of variations in the hope that they will show desired improvement. This leads into deep and intricate mazes of scientific research that need not be discussed here. However, experimentally-minded gardeners may want to explore some phases of the subject, and it is of general interest to know how some of our new plants have come into being. For this sort of information consult the many articles, bulletins and other publications available in libraries, especially those of horticultural societies and schools. One of the older but popular and relatively simple books is James P. Haworth's "Plant Magic" published in 1946. In it are discussed these methods of inducing mutations: (1) Chemical, including the use of hormones and hormone-like acids, bacteria, and two plant substances, namely colchicine and sanguinarine; (2) Temperature changes; (3) Me-

chanical means, such as pressure, irritation, shock, vibration; (4) Radiation, including cosmic rays, radium, neutrons, X rays, and ultraviolet rays (no doubt much could now be added here as a result of nuclear fission research). There is also discussed a laboratory technique that few amateurs may have attempted but which has proved important in scientific work. It consists of removing embryos from seeds and growing them on carefully prepared cultures to supply needed nutrients and carry the plantlings over difficulties that seeds germinated in the ordinary way might not survive.

The use of colchicine can be tried by gardeners with materials provided in a commercial kit. This material, obtained from the autumn crocus (*Colchicum autumnale*), is exceedingly poisonous and should be handled with great care. When extracts made from it are applied to plants, physiological changes result involving the number of chromosomes or microscopic bodies within living cells through which the mysterious forces of heredity function. A multiplication of their usual number turns the plant subject into quite a different thing, for example, from a normal "diploid" as the geneticist calls it, into a "tetraploid," "octaploid," or some other kind of polyploid.

Seed catalogues now list varieties that have resulted from such operations; doubtless there will be more of them in future. What proportion will represent important, permanent improvement, probably no one can say. But men are working along these lines and others trying to understand what it all means and implies, and to turn their increasing knowledge and skill to the advantage of you gardeners and the rest of mankind.

The so-called hormones or auxins do many other things than change plant characteristics. A recent book, "Plant Growth Substances" by L. J. Audus of England, calls them "Initiators of new organs" as in the rooting of cuttings; "Stimulants of cambial activity," in wound healing and grafting; "Initiators and stimulators of fruit development;" and "Growth inhibitors," citing bud-growth and induced dormancy and general toxicity, as in weed-killers. A discussion of the same subjects published in this country in 1947 is "Growth Regulators" by J. W. Mitchell and Paul C. Marth of the U. S. D. A. Bureau of Plant Industry. Either work will make for a much clearer understanding of much of the contemporary writing—and advertising—in horticultural and general publications.

For example, much was made, for a time, of a chemical—maleic hydrazide—which was promoted as a long sought solution of the problems of keeping lawn grass the right length without mowing, keeping a hedge in shape without clipping, etc.

The material is indeed a growth inhibitor, and sprayed along a highway, it will check growth of roadside grass and weeds and lessen the number of mowings necessary in a season —thus cutting maintenance costs. But in due course it was demonstrated and acknowledged, that on mixed vegetation, as in the average lawn, its effect was uneven, variable, and potentially harmful. Hence, while it might be of use in keeping edges or narrow strips of grass from becoming untidy, it is not likely to do away with lawn mowers and hedge shears. Turf agronomists in Rhode Island recommend it "*only* for limited and careful use on areas that are hard to get at with a mower and where turf discoloration and possible injury are not important."

Protecting Plants from Pests: On this subject, whole books have been, and will continue to be, written. But, in the words of a leading plant pathologist, "any book, no matter how recent, is out of date on chemicals." As evidence of this, Dr. Cynthia Westcott, in her "Gardener's Bug Book," published only about a decade ago, gave 20 pages to describing some 70 kinds of materials available for fighting garden pests. A little later, the Colorado Experiment Station's 172-page bulletin on "Diseases of Ornamental Plants," described 14 types of fungicides alone. And in 1955, Frear's "Pesticide Handbook" named 6,204 products, which is less than one-fifth of the 30,000 odd insecticides, fungicides, herbicides, and rodenticides registered with the Department of Agriculture and offered for sale.

Obviously, only an incomplete outline of the more important developments and trends can be given here. Obviously, too, the average home gardener cannot hope to keep abreast of all the new facts discovered, the new methods devised, and the new materials put on the market. Despite the optimistic claims often made, he cannot assume that any method or material now available is that hoped for "all-purpose cure-all." He cannot and should not expect ever to be able to have a successful garden without working for it, season by season. Nevertheless, by keeping in touch with his county agent (and the state and federal services that he represents); by reading articles, bulletins, and books by recognized authorities; by buying only sprays, dusts, and other products recommended by such authorities and manufactured by reliable firms that have reputations to protect and maintain; and, especially, by studying and *following exactly* the directions supplied by those firms for the use of their products, he can go a long way toward getting maximum garden results with minimum disappointment.

In general, a gardener can follow either, or a combination of, two courses in protecting his plants. One employs chemical preparations, as just referred to, to repel plant enemies, destroy them, or keep them in subjection. The other aims primarily at the growing of immune or resistant plants, and the use of cultural methods that promote vigorous plant growth and tend to discourage attack by insects and diseases.

The idea of a successful combination of the two programs was well presented in the wartime Circular 155 of the Connecticut Experiment Station entitled "Controlling Pests of War Gardens." It assumed that the average garden is normally visited by some insects and diseases and that the gardener's objective is maximum production of usable crops in spite of them. It then outlined two possible courses of action. One, which it called the "armchair method" is based on thoughtful planning and selection of crops and cultural precautions designed to outwit the enemy. This would include (1) growing crops least subject to attack; (2) adjustment of planting dates so crops would escape periods of greatest insect or disease activity; (3) adjustment of soil acidity to control certain diseases (as potato scab and cabbageclub root); (4) rotation of crops; (5) keeping away from plants when they are wet and most susceptible to infection; (6) use of resistant and disease-free seed (or seed that has been treated to immunize it from certain troubles) or the home treatment of seed when practicable; and (7) soil sterilization.

The second alternative is the more familiar and generally followed "up and at 'em" method of fighting the pests with sprays and dusts designed to prevent or cure disease and to destroy or repel invaders, and in other ways. The latter include the more old fashioned practices of (1) hand picking of large pests when not too numerous and (2) destruction of weeds on which insects feed and overwinter.

Still another type of protection is "biological control," which means fostering the parasites and other natural enemies of the harmful organisms. We do this when we harbor insect-eating birds, toads and snakes in the garden, and spare the lady bird beetles, praying mantids, and other beneficial insects. The government helps in this direction by introducing foreign species known to destroy certain pests (and not likely themselves to become troublesome), and by making available such agents as the spores of the "milky disease" that kills Japanese beetles.

In view of the countless and steadily increasing proprietary materials mentioned above and so vigorously advocated in publications of all kinds, over radio and television, etc., it might seem that this book, written by Mr. Biles before many present-day products were even thought of, was necessarily and hopelessly out-of-date. But this editor does not think so. For the most part, the materials and techniques he recommends are still known to be effective within their recognized limits, practical, and considerably safer to use than many of the newer and more potent chemicals. So the person who does not object to being called old-fashioned or to doing things a little more slowly and with a little more effort, can still follow Mr. Biles' suggestions with an excellent chance of having a good garden. What has happened is that certain practices have become outmoded as people have sought short cuts and quicker results with less bother, less "elbow grease," more mechanization. It is perhaps worthwhile to stop and wonder which way lies the greatest satisfaction.

It is true, of course, that insects and diseases cause immense losses of farm crops. But those crops are being grown in greater volume, more intensively, under more "forced draught" than ever before. Breeding for the development of certain characters may have resulted, in some cases, in lessened resistance and stamina. And it is always possible that the upsetting of a natural balance by the destruction of certain organisms may lead to unexpected results in the way of increased numbers and activity of other kinds that in time present entirely new problems.

For all those reasons we will simply note some of the types of plant protecting materials now available without making recommendations. They can be used in various ways—in the new aerosol bombs for both indoor and outdoor use, in which a gas under pressure takes the place of pumped-up air; as sprays, in solution or emulsion form; as extra-fine mists; as dusts, and as gases for fumigation. And they can be used separately or in combination within limits prescribed by their compatibility which is usually noted in their descriptions and also in charts and tables available from dealers and other sources.

As to the kinds of material, the following are named in a paper read by R. B. Neiswander, entomologist of the Ohio Experiment Station at a short course for arborists in 1955. The names used are the comparatively simple trade designations; the technical or scientific names are long, complex, and, in many cases, as unpronounceable as they are meaningless to the average layman.

Lime-sulphur is an old-time standard insecticide and fungicide; also a most useful acaricide or mite-killer.

Sulphur in its natural state is used for the same purposes, usually with a wetting agent added. It is not compatible with oils or dinitro compounds (mentioned below).

Oil sprays, formerly much used on dormant plants, are now available also in more refined summer forms less likely to injure plant tissues.

Dinitro compounds, for dormant use (usually alone) against aphis and mite eggs, scale, etc.

Lead arsenate, another old-time stomach poison, is still widely used; it has the advantage of not killing certain natural enemies of certain mites and pests against which it is not effective.

Chlorinated hydrocarbons are organic compounds developed during and since World War II in many forms including DDT, BHC (benzene hexachloride), and chlordane, to name only a few. They are contact insecticides, compatible with most fungicides and other insecticides (except, perhaps, oils) and in the presence of lime. They are in varying degrees poisonous to the higher animals, including man, and should be kept on hand and used with the utmost caution at all times.

Organic phosphates form another group of post-war, highly poisonous (to humans) insecticides, such as HETP (hexaethyl tetraphosphate) or TEPP, parathion, malathion, demeton, etc.

Other organic materials include the familiar nicotine, available both in extract form and as tobacco stems and dust; rotenone, originally used by savages to poison fish and a good, relatively safe-to-use, contact insec-

ticide; and pyrethrum, made from dried flower heads and the basis of old-time insect powders.

Fungicides include sulphur, already mentioned; fixed copper compounds; organic mercury preparations offered under various trade names and all so poisonous as to call for very careful handling; dithiocarbamates, such as dithane, ferbam, ziram and others with equally strange names; and miscellaneous commercial organic materials such as Captan, Phygon, etc., some of which are applied in various forms to growing plants, while others are used to treat seed.

Not included among the active poisons are various "wetting agents" which are added to different chemicals or mixtures to make them spread and adhere better to certain kinds of foliage.

Some of the modern antibiotics that are accomplishing so much in the treatment and prevention of human and other animal ills are being investigated by scientists with a view to finding out what they may be able to do, if anything, to control plant diseases. As yet nothing of this sort has been made available for the use of the average gardener, but this is a field in which (as is said of Ebbets Field in Brooklyn) "anything can happen." We may yet be advised to use penicillin, streptomycin or other such materials in our garden practice.

Weed-killers: Some of these and their uses have been discussed under lawn care. They are of various types and varying degrees of effectiveness on different kinds of nuisance plants, including crabgrass, chickweed, and poison ivy. Some are used for spot-killing of large weeds; some for over-all lawn or roadside spraying to kill broad-leaved plants without destroying desirable grasses; some are to be applied to the soil in advance of seeding to kill weed seeds. One of the latter is a highly nitrogenous calcium cyanamid which, when first applied, kills the seeds or plants it touches but later becomes, not only harmless, but a valuable source of nitrogen for later-sown grass to feed on.

In this connection, a simple and effective way to protect seedlings from the common damping-off fungus is the use of a layer of pulverized sphagnum moss on the surface of the soil of flats and other seed beds as clearly explained in this illustration.

Poisons and Safety Precautions: The development of modern chemical plant protectors that involve real risk to the unwary user has raised serious problems for everyone. Congress has changed the Federal Insecticide, Fungicide, and Rodenticide Act so as to require proper labeling, in addition to registration of all pesticides by manufacturers or distributors before they can be shipped interstate; and also the meeting of strict tolerance limits for residues of these materials on food products offered for sale. State control legislation similarly aims to protect the public from injury resulting from misrepresentation, carelessness, or the marketing of insecticides and fungicides that have not been exhaustively tested. All this is desirable and necessary, but it does not render any less necessary great care on the part of users of these materials, both

commercial, large-scale growers and home gardeners. The following rules prepared by the National Agricultural Chemicals Association, should be carefully followed by any family by which any of the modern pesticides are used:

Read everything on the label of a package of any chemical to be used against insects, rodents or plant diseases before you even open it, let alone use it.

Keep the pesticide out of reach of children, pets, and irresponsible persons. In case of accidental poisoning by any material marked "poisonous,"

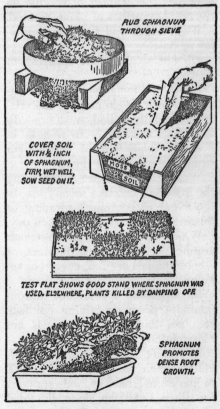

RUB SPHAGNUM THROUGH SIEVE

COVER SOIL WITH ½ INCH OF SPHAGNUM, FIRM, WET WELL, SOW SEED ON IT.

MOSS
SOIL

TEST FLAT SHOWS GOOD STAND WHERE SPHAGNUM WAS USED. ELSEWHERE, PLANTS KILLED BY DAMPING OFF.

SPHAGNUM PROMOTES DENSE ROOT GROWTH.

How sphagnum moss helps seedlings.

call a physician or get the patient to a hospital at once.

Keep the material in the original container, tightly closed, and properly and legibly labeled.

Never give a neighbor or anyone a portion of a pesticide chemical in an unlabeled container.

Store all such materials in a safe, separate room, or locked cabinet, or closet, or on a high shelf, where they will not be exposed to excessive sunlight, heat, or cold.

Do not store where food or feed materials are stored or handled.

Observe special precautions to minimize the chances of residue on the edible portions of plants treated.

Wash hands and face after spraying or dusting.

Do not smoke while spraying or dusting.

Avoid spilling insecticidal chemicals on skin or clothing. If material is accidentally spilled, wash immediately and thoroughly to remove it.

Avoid inhalation of sprays (or vapor from them) or dusts.

Wash clothing worn when using the materials before a second use; in the event of continued spraying or dusting operations, wash it each day.

When using pesticide chemicals around pet or livestock quarters, or where animals are fed, cover (or remove) food, and wash containers.

Be especially careful not to contaminate pools containing goldfish, etc.; see that dust or spray is not blown into or across them.

In using hormone-type weedkillers (such as 2,4-D and 2,4,5-T preparations), have separate sprayers for the use of them alone. Removal of residues from such implements is very difficult, if not impossible; even minute amounts carried onto valuable plants in subsequent sprayings with harmless materials may kill or seriously injure them.

Dispose of empty pesticide containers so that they present no hazard to human beings, animals, or valuable plants.

If in doubt about any of the above cautions or any other detail in connection with the use of pesticide chemicals, consult your Agricultural County Agent, or your State Agricultural Experiment Station.

There still remain various questions that only time, research, and experience can answer, such as the accumulative effect of chemicals on plants, on the soil, on the surroundings, and on people. It has been suggested that "if DDT is used continuously for insect control on crops it might become a soil problem much as lead arsenate did years ago in the Pacific Northwest's apple and pear orchards." The long distance effect of various sprays on the quality and flavor of vegetables and fruits produced by treated plants is under investigation. Claims and counterclaims are expressed as to the possible effect of spray practices on the health of animals and people consuming the crops grown as a result of them.

Apparently there is much yet to learn here, just as in the realms of atomic bomb use, supersonic speed travel, and all fields of modern scientific discovery. Meanwhile, as we have suggested from time to time, gardening is a pursuit closely allied with nature and still amenable to natural principles and practices. So

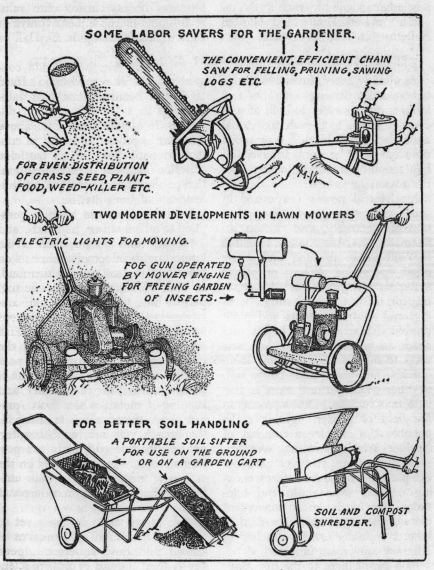

SOME LABOR SAVERS FOR THE GARDENER.

THE CONVENIENT, EFFICIENT CHAIN SAW FOR FELLING, PRUNING, SAWING LOGS ETC.

FOR EVEN DISTRIBUTION OF GRASS SEED, PLANT-FOOD, WEED-KILLER ETC.

TWO MODERN DEVELOPMENTS IN LAWN MOWERS

ELECTRIC LIGHTS FOR MOWING.

FOG GUN OPERATED BY MOWER ENGINE FOR FREEING GARDEN OF INSECTS. →

FOR BETTER SOIL HANDLING

A PORTABLE SOIL SIFTER FOR USE ON THE GROUND OR ON A GARDEN CART

SOIL AND COMPOST SHREDDER.

See other labor-saving devices illustrated on pages 453 and 456.

use judgment in making use of the best advice available, such as the recently revised Home and Garden Bulletin No. 16, "Vegetable Gar-

dener's Handbook of Insects and Diseases" obtainable from the Office of Information, U. S. Department of Agriculture, Washington 25, D. C.

PROGRESS IN GARDEN EQUIPMENT AND PLANT PROPAGATION

As already noted, inventive genius is constantly turning out time- and labor-savers in every branch of gardening. Here, too, each individual must decide for himself how much time and effort he wants to save, and how much he is willing to spend for the advantage gained.

Mechanical power (expressed in small, compact engines, the application of electricity, and various refinements) has been made available for soil-tilling, pruning and many other operations. A host of plastic materials now provide aids for growing, protecting, propagating, packing, and shipping plants and plant products. Study of the habits and needs of plants has revealed new ways to induce them to grow more quickly, bear more abundantly and, in other ways, perform more in line with man's wishes. Developments in the field of garden lighting make possible the simple installation of outdoor wiring systems, weatherproof outlets, etc., so that a gardener can plug in tools, light fixtures, cooking devices, even radio and television sets in the most convenient places, just as, in many gardens, a hose or sprinkler can be attached to different convenient faucets.

As a supplement to the directions for simple methods of plant propagation given in Chapter XIX, there can be mentioned here the helpful little circular of the West Virginia Agricultural Experiment Station (Mor-

gantown, W. Va.) published in June, 1955 and entitled "Rooting Holly Cuttings in a Window Box." It describes in detail both the simple structure needed and the simple methods employed. While free distribution of State Experiment Station publications is usually limited to residents of the state, libraries, etc., individual copies can often be supplied to others at very nominal cost.

Plastics and Propagation: Two interesting developments have taken place in the plant propagation field, in both of which the new flexible plastics have played a part. One is a modernized version of the ancient art of Chinese- or pot-layering. This originally consisted of binding the two halves of a flower pot around a shallow cut made in a tree or shrub branch, filling the pot with soil, and keeping it moist. When roots from just above the wound filled the soil, the branch was severed below the pot and the free end, with its newly formed roots, was planted and grown as a new individual. The main differences between that procedure and the new one are that now a square of flexible plastic can take the place of the pot; a handful of sphagnum moss soaked and then squeezed almost dry is used instead of soil; and, instead of making a cut in the stem, the operator removes a band of bark about as wide as the branch is thick, as in the old trick of "ringing" a grape cane to stimulate fruit production. This method of air-layering seems to have been devised by a Florida nurseryman and simultaneously, or later, at a middle western experiment station. At first colorless polyethlene plastic was used, then a firm started by the Florida originator developed a way to imprint green stripes on the film with ink containing small amounts of root-stimulating substance and soluble plant food.

A further development involved the rooting of cuttings and the starting of seeds in handfuls of moist moss wrapped in plastic squares gathered up and fastened at the top with rubber bands (somewhat as in the plastic wrap in the "Air-wrap" layering technique). Then it was

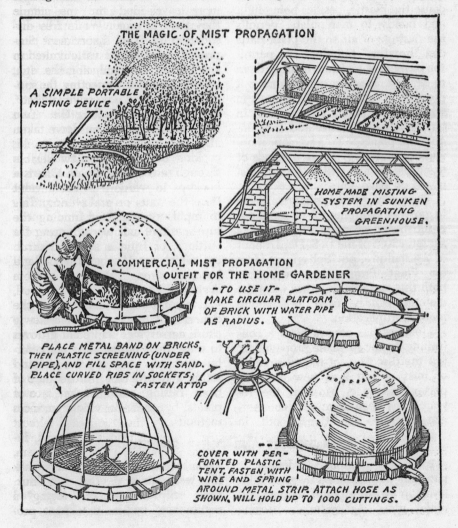

THE MAGIC OF MIST PROPAGATION

A SIMPLE PORTABLE MISTING DEVICE

HOME MADE MISTING SYSTEM IN SUNKEN PROPAGATING GREENHOUSE.

A COMMERCIAL MIST PROPAGATION OUTFIT FOR THE HOME GARDENER

-TO USE IT- MAKE CIRCULAR PLATFORM OF BRICK WITH WATER PIPE AS RADIUS.

PLACE METAL BAND ON BRICKS, THEN PLASTIC SCREENING (UNDER PIPE), AND FILL SPACE WITH SAND. PLACE CURVED RIBS IN SOCKETS; FASTEN AT TOP

COVER WITH PERFORATED PLASTIC TENT, FASTEN WITH WIRE AND SPRING AROUND METAL STRIP. ATTACH HOSE AS SHOWN. WILL HOLD UP TO 1000 CUTTINGS.

found that by placing a long band of moss in a folded strip of plastic, and laying a number of cuttings in it before rolling it into a bundle, rooting could be done with considerable saving of time and space, and the bundles of rooted cuttings could be shipped to buyers with a minimum of disturbance or injury to the new roots. These results are possible because the plastic, besides being light and handy to manipulate, permits the passage of air so the plant parts can "breathe," but does not permit the passage of moisture causing them to dry out. This last quality makes it possible to wrap soil balls, or pots in which house plants are growing, in large pieces of plastic and thus enable the plants to go a week or more without watering. These methods of using plastic film will be found illustrated on page 459.

The use of ground sphagnum moss to prevent damping-off of seedlings is illustrated on page 473; Farmer's Bulletin 2085 of the U. S. Department of Agriculture, on "Sphagnum Moss for Plant . Propagation," describes both this and various other ways the material can be used to facilitate plant multiplication.

Moisture has always been a controlling factor in plant propagation, but the discovery of the advantages of mist or fog is a new and important advance. Most of the research has been done with commercial nursery conditions, both in greenhouses and in outdoor frames or propagating beds, in mind; but a few devices intended for the home garden have appeared, and two of them are illustrated on page 477. Briefly, the idea is that cuttings bathed in a fog or mist cannot lose moisture, will not wilt or dry out even if exposed to bright sunlight, and can therefore be taken with more leaves intact; in consequence, they tend to root more rapidly and successfully. The theory has been proved correct, and various devices can be had for producing the right sort of mist, for protecting the cuttings from wind, excessive sunlight, etc., and for controlling the water flow. The latter can be done manually; by means of clockwork (as cooking operations are timed); or through rather complicated electrical hookups in which a solenoid valve turns the water on and off according to impulses transmitted from a moisture-sensitive unit placed among the cuttings, or from a sort of electric eye which reacts when the sunlight becomes strong enough to exert a drying effect.

It is not expected that enough gardeners will use these inventions to cause nurserymen and plant growers to cease their propagating activities; but certainly there is a lot of interesting and profitable fun to be had from raising some of one's own plants by these ingenious modern methods.

GREENHOUSES AND OTHER STRUCTURES

Increased outdoor gardening is naturally accompanied by greater interest in growing plants indoors and under glass. As materials became available and manufacturing activities were resumed after their wartime eclipse, new and improved equipment began to appear in greater volume and more varied forms. Some types are suggested in the drawings on page 480. More lumber permitted the construction of lath houses which are especially useful in regions of high temperatures and intense sunlight. Ferns, various begonias including the delightful tuberous kinds, fuchsias, and many of the more delicate bulbous subjects can be successfully handled when the sunlight and the wind's force are broken. A delightfully cool and inviting garden house or grotto can be made in such a structure by hanging pots of ferns, vines and mosses along the sides and by building rock gardens or raised beds along their base.

Among the small home greenhouses now obtainable, a good type to start with is a sectional model which is delivered with all the members cut and fitted, even to the panes of glass. It can be made as long as desired, and may be set up as an independent building with two glazed ends; with a housed-in section for boiler room and work shed, or attached to a dwelling, garage or other structure from which heat can be piped.

If space is wanted primarily to start seedlings in spring and perhaps carry over half hardy plants in pots, an unheated greenhouse, partly sunk in the ground and glazed only on one side, may be entirely satisfactory. All the excavation needed here is enough to take the walls (of concrete, stone or cinder brick), and provide for the center walk, with space on either side of it for 6 in. deep beds of soil. Under the soil may be sand, in which a lead electrical heat-

ing element can be laid, or a foot or so of stable manure if the springtime heating is to be done in the old-fashioned hotbed manner. The affair, of course, should be located so the glass expanse is to the south. A small window in the north or board side is not essential, but it is an advantage when the weather becomes warm enough to make ventilation desirable. The basement window hotbed shown at the left of the illustration on page 480 is a sort of miniature version of the greenhouse just described. It receives heat from the cellar where the gardener stands in caring for his flats or pots of plants. On extra cold nights some old rugs or burlap mats can be spread over it to give the plants additional protection.

The structure shown at the right and below it is an enclosed propagating bench devised by the U. S. Department of Agriculture in which seedlings can be started or cuttings rooted in a basement or storeroom. Ordinarily 30- or 40-watt fluorescent lamps provide all the light necessary, and if the room is not sufficiently warm, a simple heating unit equipped with a hotbed or chicken brooder thermostat can be installed in the space below the 4- to 6-in. tray of soil or sand in which the seeds are sown or the cuttings are rooted. Above the latter is sufficient room for the source of light and a reflector far enough from the top to be safe. A hinged cover or door of the same material as the rest of the box (plywood, waterproof composition board or even lighter material if built on a solid wooden frame) prevents loss of heat and moisture and maintains uniform conditions. A case six feet long, can be heated by two 40-watt lamps; if it is a foot less in height and width, one lamp is sufficient. Ordinary light potting soil, sphagnum moss as previously described, vermiculite, or (for propagating only) sharp sand can be used in such a case. Desirable stocky growth is promoted by lowering the temperature after germination or rooting occurs; if conditions make it necessary to keep the plants in the case for some time, they should have plenty of ventilation and receive some plant food in solution. Details of construction and operation can be obtained from the U. S. Bureau of Plant Industry, Soils and Engineering, Beltsville, Md.

Gardening Indoors: This may mean in greenhouses, in hotbeds and other simple structures, or in the home. Here, too, plastics offer light, tough, durable coverings for all kinds of structures. Plastic pots in many styles, sizes, and colors are convenient for growing plants and also for shipping them. Aluminum foil and different kinds of waterproofed paper offer satisfactory liners for window and indoor plant boxes. The latter, by the way, are being increasingly used as built-in features of homes in order to economize space, to serve as room separators, and to beautify halls, enclosed porches, etc. Fluorescent lighting fixtures, which give off much less heat than the ordinary incandescent type, are proving

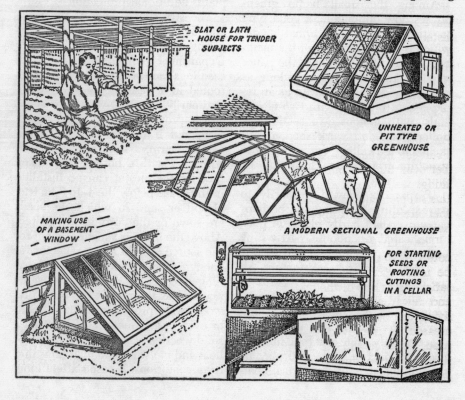

SLAT OR LATH HOUSE FOR TENDER SUBJECTS

UNHEATED OR PIT TYPE GREENHOUSE

MAKING USE OF A BASEMENT WINDOW

A MODERN SECTIONAL GREENHOUSE

FOR STARTING SEEDS OR ROOTING CUTTINGS IN A CELLAR

excellent sources of light to supplement and even, in some cases, to take the place of daylight for house plants.

Mechanization of greenhouse operation is a logical trend and even the small greenhouse owner can probably look forward to increased automatic control of ventilators, lights, shade, heat, moisture, etc. From Texas come reports of research into ways to cool greenhouses during the summer—a parallel to the air-conditioning of houses that makes the old-fashioned term "hot house" even more old-fashioned. And small greenhouses are being advertised as "winter living room and playroom" additions even where not needed or wanted primarily for horticultural activities. These two functions can be combined to excellent effect.

AND IN CONCLUSION—

This is perhaps a logical place to end this brief review of what has happened to gardening over a score of years. How varied the developments have been is indicated by the following ways in which gardeners have been assisted by science as listed in an article in the magazine *Popular Gardening*, May, 1955. The 12 headings are: New plant foods—Soil conditioners—New pesticides—Crabgrass controls—New weed-killers—Soil fumigants—Rooting hormones—Air layering—Growth retardants—Antidessicants (non-wilt materials)—Fruit-set hormones—Aerosol sprays. Yet even that list omits some of the things we have called attention to in this supplement, and probably others that are still just appearing on the horizon.

The main objective of this book, of course, is to show how gardening can be made more enjoyable and more satisfying as one of the major factors and rewards of home life. Outdoor living can be fun, and the fun is increased as improved equipment is used. On page 482, for example, are illustrated two simple types of outdoor fireplace, grill or barbecue.

They are but suggestions, for the size, style, and materials used are usually decided on according to the situation, the amount to be spent and the skill of the builder. Essential features are a solid foundation of stone or concrete; a firebox (or fireplace) lined with firebrick for durability; some means for insuring satisfactory draft (unless the grill is of the simple U-shaped type shown at the top of the drawing); a grill or griddle with, if possible, a removable cover of metal; a chimney sufficiently high to carry the smoke out of the eyes of chef and guests and equipped with a slanting smoke shelf and, preferably, a damper. If an oven can be included, it will increase the usefulness of the outfit, as will shelves on one or both sides where kettles and utensils can be placed. Sometimes one or more openings with doors are provided around the base of the fireplace in which to keep firewood and the culinary equipment between feasts. In still more elaborate designs, walls and benches are carried off at each side to provide more seating space and partially enclose the picnic area.

Describing his method of making the grill pictured (as originally shown and described in *The American Home* magazine) Mr. S. Minneci said: "I began by digging up a couple of small stumps; then the excavation for the foundation was made of four 12 in. boards into which the concrete was poured as mixed in a steel wheelbarrow. When the concrete had set, the ash pit was built up using common brick. (Having never laid brick, I was amazed to find how thirsty dry bricks are and how much it helps to wet them.) The iron grate was put in place as shown and the firebox and chamber leading to the chimney were lined with firebrick, common brick being used for the chimney itself. Then the whole structure was faced with stones set in concrete to give a pleasing, informal effect.

"The selection and fitting of the stones was a large part of the job. After experiencing several 'slides,' I found that I could get better results by laying a tier of stones all the way around, filling the space between the stones and bricks with a mixture of broken stone and mortar, and allowing it to set before proceeding with the next tier. The smaller, upper steel plate is used for toasting rolls or warming dishes while the regular cooking surface is in use. A removable plate with an insulated handle is placed in front of the firebox to control the draft and effect a more uniform distribution of heat over the cooking plate. The materials used, exclusive of the stones and brick (which were salvaged), cost exactly $8.25, and although I had never slung any plaster or concrete before I

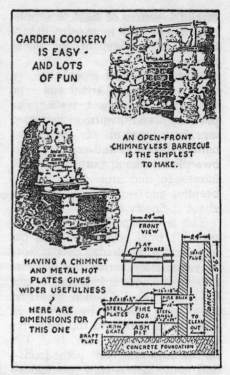

GARDEN COOKERY IS EASY - AND LOTS OF FUN

AN OPEN-FRONT CHIMNEYLESS BARBECUE IS THE SIMPLEST TO MAKE.

HAVING A CHIMNEY AND METAL HOT PLATES GIVES WIDER USEFULNESS

HERE ARE DIMENSIONS FOR THIS ONE

FRONT VIEW

FLAT STONES

CONCRETE FOUNDATION

started building our fireplace, I completed it single-handed in approximately 60 hours of work, done mostly in the evening over a period of not more than three weeks."

In the words of another self-taught builder, "An outdoor fireplace does surprising things to family habits—and appetites. One friend tells me that for three solid months after he finished his fireplace in the spring, not a single meal was cooked indoors, so enthusiastically did his family take to the primitive. . . . The design may be entirely a matter of individual preference. The main consideration is to have things comfortable and permanent."

There is a good note on which to close—the idea of gardening so as to make the setting of the home "more comfortable and more permanent." People are moving in increasing number from crowded cities out to the less crowded suburbs or the open countryside in order to enjoy the wider spaces, more independence, pleasanter and healthier surroundings. In order to do this they should not only develop and care for their own plots of land, but also take an interest in, and protect, the natural beauties and resources of the land about them—its soil, its wild plants and the birds and friendly animals that live among them, its streams, its woodlands, its fields and its roadsides. These are the things that comprise the larger or environmental "garden" that all of the people are entitled to enjoy. So give a thought to, not only the garden within, but also the garden beyond, your property boundaries. And may the reward of great fulfillment come to you from the wise employment and the intelligent enjoyment of all that is meant by "garden magic."

INDEX

M